Natural Resources Management and Biological Sciences

Edited by Edward R. Rhodes and Humood Naser

Published in London, United Kingdom

IntechOpen

Supporting open minds since 2005

Natural Resources Management and Biological Sciences
http://dx.doi.org/10.5772/intechopen.82948
Edited by Edward R. Rhodes and Humood Naser

Scinetific contributors
Mohd Nazip Suratman, Sumit Chakravarty and Gopal Shukla

Contributors
Daniel George Neary, Jackson Leonard, Hussein El-Naggar, Julius Kotir, Kossi Adjonou, Kokou Kouami, Ouinsavi Christine, Rabiou Habou, Komla Elikplim Abotsi, Johnson Benziwa Nathalie, Alaba Pyoabalo, Quashie Épouse Mensah Attoh Akossiwoa Marie-Luce, Kokutse Adzo Dzifa, Segla Kossi Novinyo, Stephen Mattia, Sampha Sesay, Sebua Semenya, Matjutla Mokgoebo, Jafari R. Kideghesho, Sekar Veera, R. Rajasekaran, Srinivasan Balakrishnan, Michel Soto Chalhoub, Fiona Campbell, Fabio Pieri, Reinaldo Martins Cunha-Junior, Pamela Buenos Aires Domingues, Rafael De Oliveira Ambrósio, Caio Augusto Freitas Martins, Jéssica Genoveva Boline Passarelli Capaz Pinto Da Silva, Neji Mahmoudi, Mosbah Mahdhi, Mohamed Mars, Bienvenu Magloire Takem Mbi, Aloysious Aloy Kohtem Lebga, Marlenne Gomez-Ramirez, Sergio A Tenorio-Sánchez, Oddvar Skre, Emmanuel Torres Quezada, Bielinski Santos, Isabel Torres Quezada, Rodrigue Constant Sandjong Sani, Mama Ntoupka, Toua Vroumsia, N Tchobsala, Adamou Ibrahima, Olumuyiwa Idowu Ojo, Masengo Francois Ilunga, Prasanna Pal, Snigdha Chatterjee, Satarupa Ghosh

First published in London, United Kingdom, 2021 by IntechOpen
IntechOpen is the global imprint of INTECHOPEN LIMITED, registered in England and Wales, registration number: 11086078, 5 Princes Gate Court, London, SW7 2QJ, United Kingdom
Printed in Croatia

British Library Cataloguing-in-Publication Data
A catalogue record for this book is available from the British Library

Additional hard and PDF copies can be obtained from orders@intechopen.com

Natural Resources Management and Biological Sciences
Edited by Edward R. Rhodes and Humood Naser
p. cm.
Print ISBN 978-1-83880-464-0
Online ISBN 978-1-83880-465-7
eBook (PDF) ISBN 978-1-83968-600-9

For EU product safety concerns:
IN TECH d.o.o., Prolaz Marije Krucifikse Kozulić 3, 51000 Rijeka, Croatia, info@intechopen.com or visit our website at intechopen.com.

Meet the editors

Edward Ronald Rhodes has a BSc in Agriculture from the University of Sierra Leone and a Ph.D. in Soil Science from Aberdeen University, United Kingdom. He is a Professor Emeritus of Soil Science in the Department of Soil Science, Njala University, Sierra Leone. He has about 30 years' experience in teaching and conducting and supervising research at Njala University. He was a Fulbright-Hays Research Scholar at Colorado State University, USA. He was a staff member (Senior Scientist) of IFDC, in Togo and of the FAO (Component Advisor) in Malawi. He is a member of the College of Research Associates United Nations University Institute for Natural Resources in Africa. Professor Rhodes was President of the University of Sierra Leone Research Council and, more recently, the Prochancellor of Njala University.

Dr. Humood Naser is an Associate Professor of Environmental Biology at the Department of Biology, College of Science, University of Bahrain. Naser holds a Ph.D. in Environmental Biology from Newcastle University, and an M.Sc. in Integrated Environmental Studies from the University of Southampton, UK. He is the author of four books, five chapters, and several articles published in reputed journals. His general research interests include environmental and ecological impact assessment, conservation biology, effects of environmental pollutants on species and ecosystems, environmental quality monitoring, and sustainable development.

Contents

Preface XIII

Section 1
Classification and Inventory of Natural Resources 1

Chapter 1 3
Taxonomical Keys for Morphological Identification of Coral-Associated Polychaetes from Great Nicobar Islands
by Veeramuthu Sekar, Ramadoss Rajasekaran, Srinivasan Balakrishnan and Ramamoorthy Raguraman

Chapter 2 37
Ground Forest Inventory and Assessment of Carbon Stocks in Sierra Leone, West Africa
by Stephen Brima Mattia and Sampha Sesay

Section 2
Impacts of Environmental Factors and Human Activities on Natural Resources 57

Chapter 3 59
Physical Vulnerabilities from Wildfires: Flames, Floods, and Debris Flows
by Daniel G. Neary and Jackson M. Leonard

Chapter 4 77
Succession after Fire in a Coastal Pine Forest in Norway
by Oddvar Skre

Chapter 5 91
Human Impacts on Coral Reef Ecosystem
by Hussein A. El-Naggar

Chapter 6 109
Human Factors: The Impact on Industry and the Environment
by Fiona J. Campbell

Section 3
Soil, Water and Waste Management 123

Chapter 7 125
Soil Carbon Restoration through Conservation Agriculture
by Snigdha Chatterjee, Satarupa Ghosh and Prasanna Pal

Chapter 8 149
Effects of Arbuscular Mycorrhizal Fungi on Plant Adaptation to Arid Ecosystem of Bou-Hedma National Park in Tunisia
by Mahmoudi Neji, Mahdhi Mosbah and Mars Mohamed

Chapter 9 165
Use of Geoinformatics Techniques for the Assessment and Mapping of Soil Salinity: Concepts and Applications
by Olumuyiwa Idowu Ojo and Masengo Francois Ilunga

Chapter 10 183
Water Management Strategies and Cultural Practices for Strawberry Establishment in Florida
by Emmanuel Torres-Quezada, Isabel Torres-Quezada and Bielinski Marcelo Santos

Chapter 11 197
Managing and Sustaining the Coupled Water-Land-Food Systems in the Context of Global Change: How Qualitative System Dynamic Modelling Can Assist in Understanding and Designing High-Leverage Interventions
by Julius H. Kotir

Chapter 12 219
Need for a Collaborative Natural Resource Management Strategy for the Marine Environment—The Case of Plastics in the Mediterranean
by Michel Soto Chalhoub

Chapter 13 237
Treatment of Solid Waste Containing Metals by Biological Methods
by Marlenne Gómez-Ramírez and Sergio A. Tenorio-Sánchez

Section 4
Exploitation and Conservation of Forest, Wild Plant and Wildlife Resources 251

Chapter 14 253
Protected Areas in Cameroon at the Mercy of the 2035 Emergent Project
by Bienvenu Magloire Takem Mbi and Aloysious Kohtem Lebga

Chapter 15 267
Sustainable Management of Tropical Dry Forests: An Overview from Cameroonian Context and the Special Case of Mozogo-Gokoro National Park
by Rodrigue Constant Sandjong Sani, Mama Ntoupka, Toua Vroumsia, Tchobsala and Adamou Ibrahima

Chapter 16 289
Challenges of Conservation and Sustainable Management of African Rosewood (*Pterocarpus erinaceus*) in West Africa
by Adjonou Kossi, Houetchegnon Towanou, Rabiou Habou, Segla Kossi Novinyo, Abotsi Komla Elikplim, Johnson Benziwa Nathalie, Alaba Pyoabalo, Ouinsavi Christine A.I. Nougbodé, Quashie Akossiwoa Marie-Luce, Kokutse Adzo Dzifa, Mahamane Ali and Kokou Kouami

Chapter 17 317
The Utilization and Conservation of Indigenous Wild Plant Resources in the Limpopo Province, South Africa
by Sebua S. Semenya and Matjutla J. Mokgoebo

Chapter 18 339
Brazilian Amazon Plants: An Overview of Chemical Composition and Biological Activity
by Reinaldo Martins Cunha Junior, Pâmella Buenos Aires Domingues, Rafael de Oliveira Ambrósio, Caio Augusto Freitas Martins, Jéssica Genoveva Boline Passarelli Capaz Pinto da Silva and Fabio Alessandro Pieri

Chapter 19 355
The Contribution of Research in Combating Wildlife Poaching in Tanzania: Review of Existing Literature
by Jafari R. Kideghesho

Preface

The air, land, soils, water, plants, and animals make up the natural resources without which life on earth, as we know it, would not be possible. These resources are highly complex and dynamic with each made up of various components and reacting differently in various environments.

Knowledge of their status and changes is critical for sustainable management that takes into consideration the wellbeing of future generations. However, there are gaps in the knowledge and understanding of the characteristics of these resources and processes they are subject to. Hence the need for further studies and synthesis of findings. Climate change amplifies these challenges because of increased risks of bushfires, rises in sea levels leading to flooding of agricultural lands with salty water, dry spells, changes to the habitats of plants and wildlife, et cetera.

Sound management of natural resources should be based on the application of the principles of the basic sciences. The links with biological sciences are most evident in this book. This book aims to present reviews and research reports on classification and inventorying, impacts of environmental factors and man-made activities, and exploitation and management of key natural resources in a number of countries in various parts of the world. It contains 19 chapters in 4 sections.

Section 1 (chapters 1-2) deals with the classification of polychaetes on coral reefs and forest inventorying, which are initial steps in natural resource management. Section 2 (chapters 3-6) presents the negative impacts of environmental factors and human activities on natural resources, with examples on the hazards of wildfire, on the water quality of a special nature reserve, and on threats to coral reef ecosystems. One chapter looks at the effect of humans on the environment as a result of rapidly changing technology. Section 3 (chapters 7-13) covers a wide range of topics on the management of natural resources: soil organic carbon improvement through conservation agriculture; soil and plant beneficial fungi facilitating adaptation to climate change; mapping soil salinity as a component of soil fertility management in irrigated agriculture; management of irrigation water in commercial fruit production; sustaining the water-land-agricultural production nexus in a river basin; treatment of solid wastes by biological methods and a regional strategy to control pollution of the Mediterranean ocean. Section 4 (chapters 14-19) focuses mainly on the exploitation and/or conservation of forest, wild plant, and wildlife resources and biodiversity with some chapters dealing with protected areas including a national park.

It is hoped that lessons will be learned by scientists, practitioners, and policy makers working in the field of natural resource management, from the various experiences reported across the world, in terms of the design and implementation of studies and development projects. We acknowledge the contributions of Dr. Mohd Nazip Suratman, Universiti Teknologi, MARA, Malaysia, and Dr. Sumit Chakravarty and Dr. Gopal Shukla both of North Bengal Agricultural University, India in the review of selected chapters. We also thank the staff of IntechOpen for copyediting and proofreading all the chapters.

Emeritus Edward R. Rhodes
Professor,
Department of Soil Science,
Njala University,
Freetown, Sierra Leone

Dr. Humood A. Nasser
Associate Professor of Environmental Biology,
Department of Biology,
University of Bahrain,
Zallaq, Bahrain

Section 1

Classification and Inventory of Natural Resources

Chapter 1

Taxonomical Keys for Morphological Identification of Coral-Associated Polychaetes from Great Nicobar Islands

Veeramuthu Sekar, Ramadoss Rajasekaran, Srinivasan Balakrishnan and Ramamoorthy Raguraman

Abstract

The present study illustrates the insufficient taxonomy records and highlights the use of microscopic diagnostic tool in polychaete taxonomy. It leads to a better understanding of coral-associated polychaete taxonomy in Great Nicobar Islands, India. A total of 24 species under 14 genera, 7 orders, and 11 families were identified, in spite of 3 species of Phyllocidae, 8 species of Nereidae, 5 species of Eunicidae, 2 species of Spionidae, and 1 species of Opheliidae, Sabellariidae, Terebellidae, Polynoidae, Amphinomidae, and Sabellidae. The current status of taxonomic information varies greatly among taxa and among geographic areas within taxa. The problems encountered included nomenclature, diagnoses, and determination of taxonomic relationships. We provide examples of a variety of these problems. Each species has distinct features of the particular families, and taxonomic section to assist the polychaete identification that is necessary to assess the biodiversity and taxonomy at any level. This chapter considers the importance of monitoring biological diversity, current morphological taxonomy of polychaetes and describes the approach developed for protected areas in Great Nicobar Islands.

Keywords: polychaetes, taxonomy, Great Nicobar, identification, coral reef

1. Introduction

Generally, taxonomy is essential for basic identification keys for the animal kingdom to learn about the global biodiversity, and gain the knowl-edge and understanding of bio-resources and its wise use. Correct identification of organisms is necessary to analyze and assess the biological diversity of an ecosystem at all levels, namely, diversity among ecosystems, phyletic diversity or diversity of species, and their genetic diversity among species [1, 2]. Polychaetes are a large group of segmented worms that display a wide range of morphological diversity [3]. Identifying organisms precisely at spe-cies level is fundamental to any ecological research and environmental monitoring. Generally, identification of polychaetes at species rank is quite difficult without illustrated monographs which may have been hampered by their morphological similarity to their fully marine counterparts [4]. Polychaetes vary widely from generalized pattern and can display a range of different body forms. The most gen-eralized polychaetes are those that crawl along the bottom, but others have adapted many different ecological niches including burrowing, pelagic life, tube dwelling or boring, and commensalism and parasitism, requiring various modifications to their body structure.

In polychaete taxonomy, parapodia are the important organs for identification particularly segment of origin, shape, and structural composition in body regions. Special features of branchiae or occurrences of multiple cirri are also important. A key morphological feature of seta construction, notopodia for the superfamilial and ordinal levels, and development of each ramus with the various parapodial lobes and cirri are very important at the generic and species levels. The presence of branchiae may not even be considered a specific character [5]. A number of pioneering conventional taxonomic studies on polychaetes were made by Fauvel [6, 7], Day [8] and Fauchald [9]. There is yet a lag in making taxonomic information available in many ecological programs and databases for polychaetes. In early studies, all the characteristics were mainly featured by diagrammatic figures. The importance of accurate examination of the setae is still underestimated by most taxonomists; the precise observations require close microscopic analysis to make proper identification, which should be followed for all taxonomic studies as a routine [9]. Thus, the present study was focused on analysis of the taxonomical features of Great Nicobar Island polychaetes through advance magnification techniques to improve the quality and precision of identification through key characteristic features.

2. Materials and methods

2.1 Study area

Great Nicobar Islands, the southernmost land piece of India, has the greatest length of about 55 km between North Murray Point and South Indira Point. It has a width of about 30 km in the north but narrows down to about 3 km at the southern tip (**Figure 1**). In the present study, samples were collected from 11 different stations in the intertidal region of the Great Nicobar Islands (**Tables 1** and **2**).

2.2 Sample collection

Samples were collected from the intertidal areas, and the dead coral material were bro-ken down into smaller fragments with the help of hammer and chisel. Polychaetes picked with the help of forceps were transferred to plastic containers, before fixation, into strong alcohol to have their pharynx everted, which will aide in the identification of the group. Samples were fixed with 10% formalin diluted with seawater and were later transferred to 70% ethanol the purpose of staining with Rose Bengal.

2.3 Examination of specimens

Stained specimens were placed in petri dishes containing tap water to dissect the morphological features of parapodia and proboscis of the jaws and other features of all the family which were made into thin sections with a surgical blade (No. 2). They were then mounted on slides and examined under a compound binocular microscope (Olympus CX41). Specimens were sorted up to genus level, and later detailed exami-nation staining of specimens with Rose Bengal provided a useful diagnostic tool.

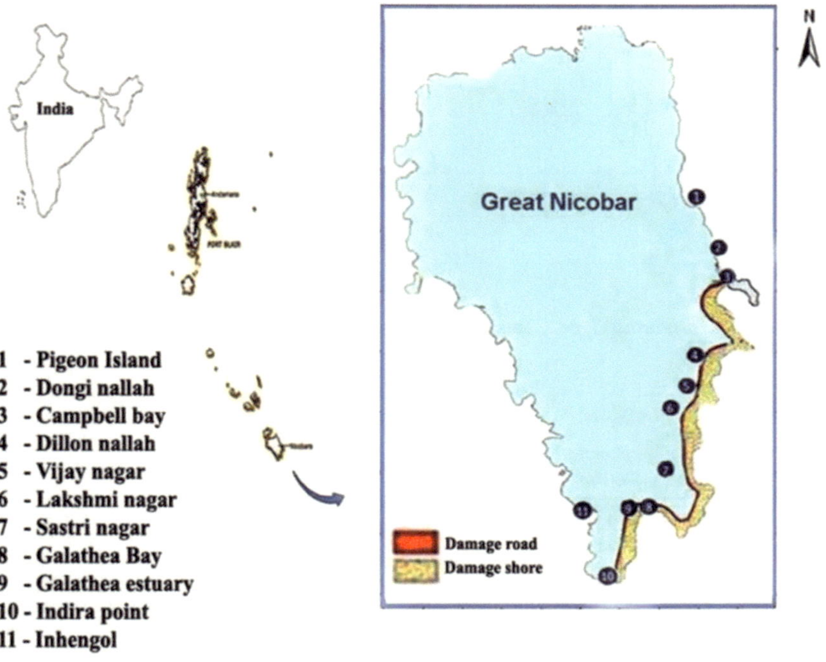

Figure 1.
The map showing the sampling point along the Great Nicobar Islands.

Station no.	Station name	Latitude	Longitude	Coast	Substrate type
1.	Pigeon Island	07°05.823′ N	93°53.010′ E	East	Small pebbles on the western side and huge rocks on the eastern side
2.	Dongi nallah	07°01.700′ N	93°53.933′ E	East	On the northern side of the nallah, the coast is rocky
3.	Campbell Bay	06°55.962′ N	93°55.896′ E	East	Vast dead coral patches are found on the northern side between the "B" quarry and breakwaters
4.	Dillon nallah	06°55.962′ N	93°54.770′ E	East	The coast is sandy on the southern side, while vast stretches of coral rubbles are on the northern side of the seashore
5.	Vijaynagar	06°54.606′ N	93°55.770′ E	East	Up to 3 km seawards during low-tide periods, vast stretches of dead corals and rocks extend both northwards and southwards being exposed
6.	Lakshmi Nagar	06°52.993′ N	93°55.990′ E	East	At this station, dead coral patches observed on the landward side
7.	Sastri Nagar	06°48.163′ N	93°53.304′ E	East	Rocky shore and vast stretches of coral reefs. These rocks and dead corals are exposed up to a distance of 2 km
8.	Galathea Bay	06°49.166′ N	93°51.544′ E	East	This bay has a sandy coast for about 2 km along with rocky shore
9.	Galathea estuary	06°48.974′ N	93°51.810′ E	East	Collection sites were mangroves surrounding the estuarine region about 1.5 km upstream

Station no.	Station name	Latitude	Longitude	Coast	Substrate type
10.	Indira Point	06°45.293′ N	93°49.648′ E	South	The Great Channel (international sea route) lies at a distance of 60 km south from this point in the Indian Ocean. Vast stretches of dead corals and sand substratum
11.	Inhengloi	06°48.185′ N	93°47.871′ E	West	The dead coral patches are found at the northern end which are exposed to about 2.5 km during low tides

Table 1.
Sampling stations and substrate type of the Great Nicobar Islands.

Sl. no.	Scientific name	Habitat	Collected station
1.	*Eurythoe complanata* (Pallas, 1766)	Rocks and dead corals	St. 2, 3, 5, 6, 7, 8, and 10
2.	*Iphione muricata* (Savigny, 1818)	Dead corals, cervices and surface of live corals	St. 1–8, 10. and 11
3.	*Phyllodoce quadraticeps* (Grube, 1878)	Dead corals crevices and beach rocks	St. 3, 4, 5, 7, 8, 10, 11. and 13
4.	*Phyllodoce fristedti* (Bergstrom, 1914)	Crevices of dead corals and beach rocks	St.1 and 4
5.	*Phyllodoce castanea* (Marenzeller, 1879)	Crevices of dead corals and beach rocks	St. 2–7 and 8
6.	*Ceratonereis mirabilis* (Kinberg, 1866)	Silty sand substratum under coral rubbles and surface of dead corals	St. 1–10
7.	*Perinereis nigro-punctata* (Horst, 1889)	Found among oysters and dead coral crevices of low tide	All station except St. 9
8.	*Perinereis nuntia brevicirrus* (Grube, 1876)	Found among barnacles and oysters and in dead coral crevices at low tide	St. 2, 3, 5, 6,7. and 11
9.	*Perinereis nuntia caeruleis* (Hoagland, 1920)	Boring into dead corals to live on cavity	St. 2, 3, 6, 7, 8, 10. and 11
10.	*Perinereis vancaurica* (Ehlers, 1868)	Occurs in intertidal areas of oyster- and barnacle-encrusted coral rocks	St. 1, 2, 3, 5, 7. and 11
11.	*Perinereis cultrifera* (Grube, 1840)	Boring in dead corals and living in coral cavity	All the 11 stations
12.	*Perinereis cultrifera typica* (Grube, 1840)	Boring in dead corals and living under rocks	All the stations except St. 6
13.	*Pseudonereis variegata* (Grube, 1857)	Burrowing on rocks and dead and live corals	All the 11 stations
14.	*Eunice antennata* (Savigny 1820)	Boring into dead corals and beach rocks	St. 1–8 and 11
15.	*Eunice vittata* (Delle Chiaje, 1825)	Boring into dead corals and living on cavity of dead corals and rocks	St. 1, 3, 5. and 9
16.	*Eunice afra punctata* (Peters, 1854)	Boring into beach rocks and dead corals	St. 2–8 and 10
17.	*Lysidice collaris* (Grube, 1870)	Boring in dead corals and living on cervices of dead corals	St. 1–8, 10, and 11
18.	*Lysidice ninetta* (Audouin & Milne Edwards, 1833)	Boring in dead corals and living on cavity of corals	St. 2–8 and 10

Sl. no.	Scientific name	Habitat	Collected station
19.	*Malacocers indicus* (Fauvel, 1928)	Occurring in silty coral line sediments with sandy shore regions	St. 3
20.	*Scolelepis squamata* (Muller, 1806)	Silty sediments in sandy shore areas	St. 1, 2, 3, 9, and 11
21.	*Aramandia leptocirrus* (Grube, 1878)	Silty sediments in littoral region of sandy shore	St.1–7, 9–11
22.	*Idanthyrsus pennatus* (Peters, 1985)	Hard tube formed with sand particles on corals and rocks	St. 2–7 and 10
23.	*Terebella ehrenbergi* (Grube, 1870)	Soft tube forming on dead and live corals at 1 m water depth	St. 2, 4, 5, 7, 8, and 11
24.	*Megalomma quadrioculatum* (Willey, 1905)	Tube forming (boring) on corals at 1 m water depth, living inside of the tubes	St. 3 and 7

Table 2.
Systematic account and species habitat along the Great Nicobar Islands.

The diagnostic tool in some families had good refractive qualities even at high magnification, and thickness of the mount was easily controlled. A thicker mount was necessary when viewing larger structures such as parapodia, cross sections, and the whole animal as such. The specimen was mounted in lactophenol and then heated carefully to avoid air bubbling. This procedure clears the tissue immediately making chitinized internal structures such as jaws and acicula more visible. Compound microscope was used to elucidate the small structures of setae and the permanent mounts of the parapodia and setae with polyvinyl lactophenol. All the characteristic features of the polychaetes focused in the light microscope and labeled image were done by correct pathway. All the species were identified with the help of the standard illustrated manuals of Fauvel [7] and Day [8].

3. Results

At all stations, polychaetes were found to be the dominant group with 24 species belonging to 2 major classes, 14 genera, and 7 orders with 11 different families selected for the morphological studies. Among these Polynoidae, Amphinomidae, Sabellariidae, Terebellidae, Sabellidae, and Opheliidae accounted for 1 species in their group, and the rest comprised of 3 Phyllocidae, 8 Nereidae, 5 Eunicidae, and 2 Spionidae. Each species has distinct features, and the taxonomic section serves as a key to genera, generic diagnoses, and species identification with their physiological characteristics. Each species description comprised several sections.

3.1 Systematic account

3.1.1 Species description

Eurythoe complanata **(Pallas, 1766)**
Aphrodita complanata [10]: 109.
Eurythoe alcyonaria [11]: 248, pl. 9 figs. 140–143, pl. 10 figs. 144–146, text-figs. 257–268.

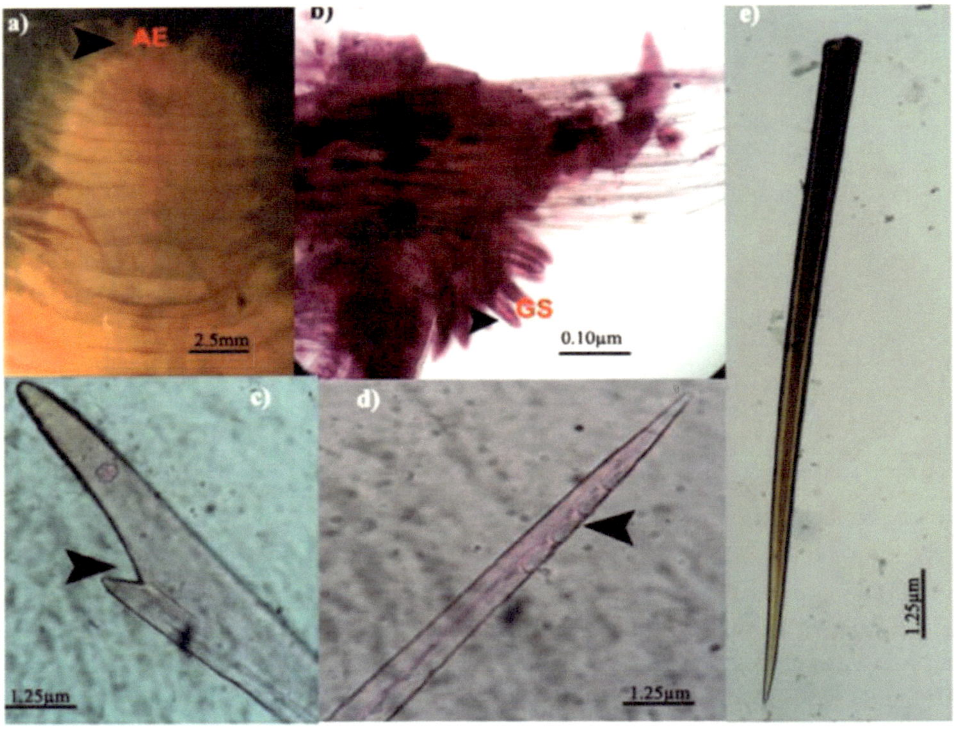

Figure 2.
Eurythoe complanata (a) anterior end, (b) anterior foot, (c) stout neurosetae, (d) Harpoon setae, and (e) smooth notopodial spine.

Eurythoe complanata [7]: 83, fig. 38b-m; [8]: 128–129, fig. 3.2i-l; [12]: 734; [13]: 200; [14]: 74; [15]: 95.

Habitat: Living in crevices of rocks and dead corals.

Description: Body elongated, 10–15 mm wide, and dorsoventrally flattened; prostomium with pair of eyes having three antennae (**Figure 2a**). One pair of palps is color pale red with light brown branchiae and white setae. The caruncle terminates on the anterior part of the fourth setiger. Its lateral lobes are not very clear since they are hidden. Gills begin on the second setiger and extend to the end of the body (**Figure 2b**). The notosetae vary greatly and are long and white with a slender, elongated tip and a few serrations along the cutting edge together with a spur below the serrations; large, straight, and harpoon-shaped setae with recurved fangs (**Figure 2d**). The neurosetae are short forked with unequal prongs (**Figure 2c**), and slender setae have a small spur (**Figure 2e**).

Remarks: On irritation, the worms erect their setae which break off easily releasing the poisonous contents.

Distribution: Tropical waters of Pacific, Indian, and Atlantic Oceans, Mergui, Ceylon, Great Barrier Reef, Florida, West Indies, Australia, Zanzibar, Maldives, and Madagascar. India: Lakshadweep, Gulf of Mannar, Andaman and Nicobar Islands, and Gujarat and Orissa coast.

***Iphione muricata* (Savigny, 1818)**

Polynone muricata [16]: 308, pl. 3 fig. 1.

Iphione muricata [11]: 226, pl. 9 figs. 129-135; [7]: 32; fig. 13a–e; [8]: 43 fig. 1.3a–f; [13]: 197; [17]: 55; [18]: 140.

Habitat: Dead corals and cervices and surface of live corals.

Description: Body oval, much flattened, 20–22 mm long (**Figure 3a**). Prostomium is square deeply bilobed with two tentacles and four eyes (**Figure 3b**).

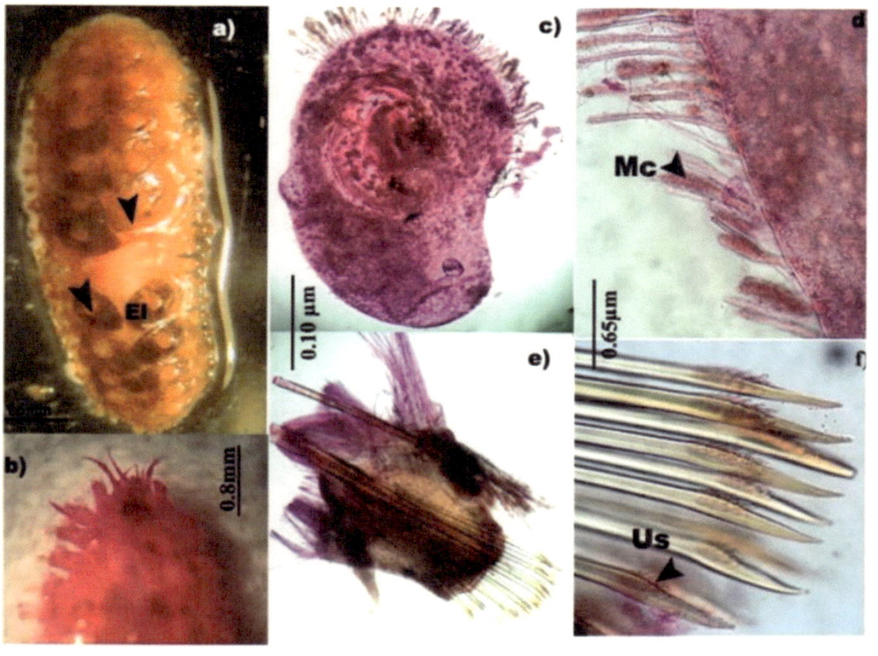

Figure 3.
Iphione muricata (a) entire worm, (b) anterior end, (c) elytra, (d) marginal capillaries, (e) setae, and (f) enlarged view of setae.

Lateral antenna terminal with large ceratophores is fused to the facial tubercle. Median antennae are represented by a small papilla posterodorsal in position and usually hidden under the nuchal fold dorsally covered by 13 pairs of tough imbricating elytra (**Figure 3c**) which are large and reniform; they are divided into punctate polygonal areas with one to two rows of stout chitinous projection and long adhesive papillae near the posterior margin (**Figure 3d**). Ventral cirri are papillose, and notopodium has very fine numerous short setae (**Figure 3e**). Neurosetae are stout with smoothly curved apical portion (**Figure 3f**). Neuropodium is large and truncate with numerous stout unidentate setae ornamented with transverse striations.

Remarks: The present material agrees well with the earlier descriptions.

Distribution: Mozambique, South Africa, Madagascar, Maldives, Sri Lanka, Mergui, Philippines, Japan, and Solomon Islands. India: Lakshadweep, Andaman and Nicobar Islands, and Gulf of Mannar.

***Phyllodoce quadraticeps* (Grube, 1878)**

Phyllodoce quadraticeps [19]: 98; [20]: 198, pl. 10 figs. 22-24, text-figs. 56-60; [8]: 145, fig. 5.2h–j; [13]: 201.

Habitat: Crevices of dead corals and beach rocks of intertidal zone.

Description: Body elongated, 400–460 mm long with numerous segments. Each segment is slender and yellowish with a dark crossbar on. Prostomium is oval or square with an occipital papilla in the posterior notch (**Fig. 4a**). Antennae are ovoid dorsally; first tentacular segments are not visible, but the second and third are distinct and separate. Tentacular cirri are cylindrical; others are tapered having long cirrophores and short swollen cirrostyles. Tentacular segments without setae. Dorsal cirri are reddish, oval, broader, and long (**Figure 4b**). Setigerous lobes are long and faintly bilobed. Ventral cirri are oval and uniramous, and parapodia have compound seta spinigers (**Figure 4c** and **d**).

Remarks: The present material agrees well with the descriptions of Day [8].

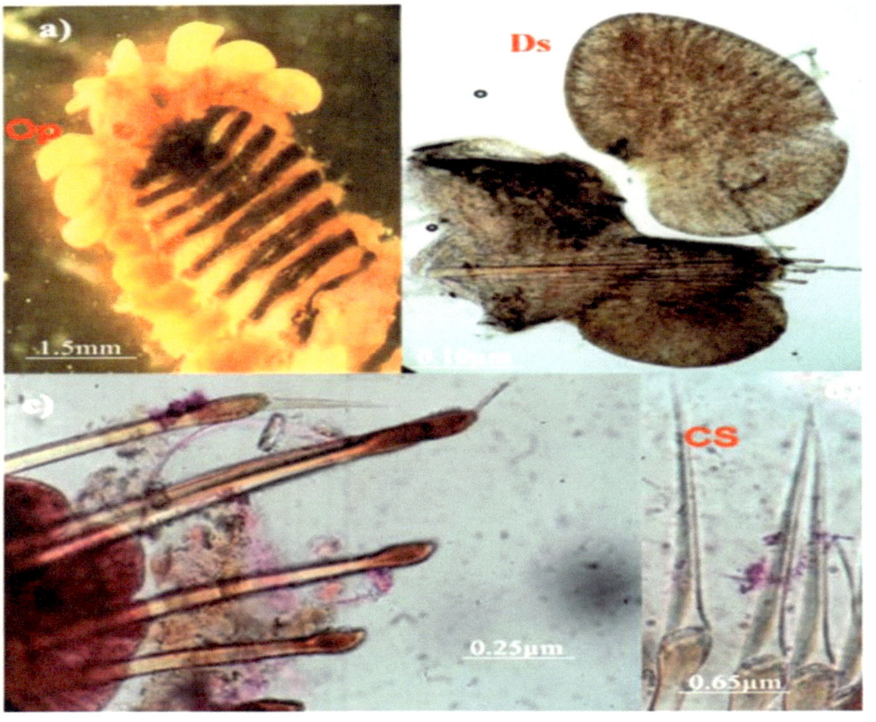

Figure 4.
Phyllodoce quadraticeps (a) anterior end, (b) anterior foot, (c) setae, and (d) spinigers.

Distribution: Pacific Ocean, Korea, New Caledonia, Philippines, Indian Ocean, and Red Sea. India: Andaman and Nicobar Islands.

***Phyllodoce fristedti* (Bergstrom, 1914)**

Phyllodoce fristedti [21]: 152, pl. 3 fig. 1, text-fig. 49; [7] :118, fig. 58a–b; [22]: 636, 1967: 147, fig. 5.2k–m; [23]: 104.

Habitat: Crevices of dead corals and beach rocks in intertidal zone.

Description: Body long, slender with numerous segments. Prostomium is heart shaped with a pair of prominent black eyes (**Figure 5a**). Posterior margin of prostomium is notched and a small occipital tentacle is present. Four short subulate tentacles. The longest tentacular cirri reach back to the seventh setiger. Numerous irregular rows of short papillae at the base of the long proboscis. Feet are uniramous (**Figure 5b**). Dorsal and ventral cirri are foliaceous, lanceolate, nearly twice as long, and broad. Ventral cirri are small and broad (**Figure 5c**). Compound setae are minutely serrated (**Figure 5d**).

Remarks: The present material agrees well with the descriptions of Day [8].

Distribution: Indian Ocean and Ceylon. India: Andaman and Nicobar Islands.

***Phyllodoce castanea* (Marenzeller, 1879)**

Carobia castanea [24]: 127; [25]: 199, pl. 21 fig. 3.

Genetyllis castanea [26]: 158, fig. 53, pl. 3 fig. 3; [7]: 115, fig. 56a–c.

Phyllodoce castanea [8]: 149, fig. 5.3d–f.

Habitat: Crevices of dead corals and beach rocks of intertidal zone.

Description: Body is short with some red pigmentation; prostomium is bluntly triangular with four antennae (**Figure 6a**); no occipital tentacles. Tentacular segments are separated from the prostomium, but the first is often fused to the second, and only the third is separated dorsally and distinct. Proboscis is slender with covered small irregular arranged papillae. All tentacular cirri are short and spindle

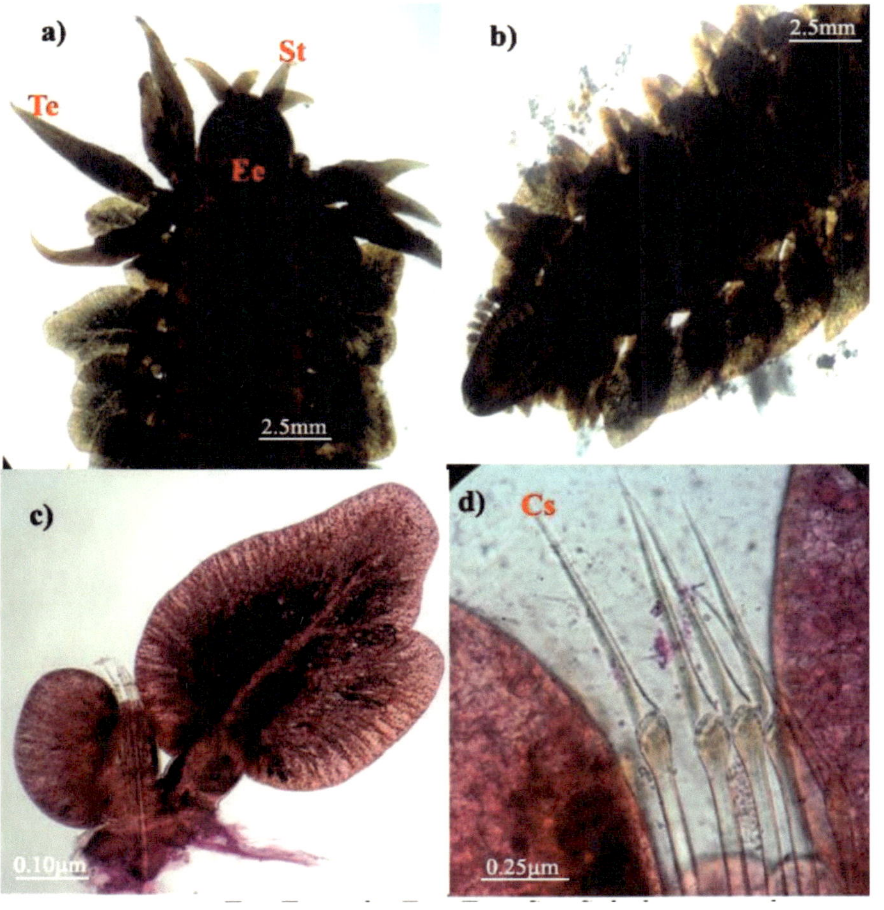

Figure 5.
Phyllodoce fristedti (a) anterior end, (b) anterior foot, (c) posterior foot and (d) setae.

shaped. The second and third tentacular segments with setae. Dorsal cirri are cordate and reddish, and setigerous lobes are bluntly rounded apically (**Figure 6b**). Ventral cirri are oval. Setae are few, with long shafts ending in truncate and strongly striated shaft heads. Blades are short and dagger-like (**Figure 6c**).

Remarks: In earlier description this species is the first record in Andaman and Nicobar waters.

Distribution: Australia, Japan, New Zealand, Ceylon, Read Sea, California, Tuticorin pearl bank, and India.

***Ceratonereis mirabilis* (Kinberg, 1866)**

Ceratonereis mirabilis [27]: 170; [11]: 172, pl. 11, fig. 42; [7]: 200, fig. 103a–e; [8]: 324, fig. 14.10a–f; [18]: 145.

Habitat: Silty sand substratum under coral rubbles and surface of dead corals.

Description: The prostomium is broad, more than twice as wide as long and has a deep cleft between the antennae. The basalia of palps is quite long, and terminalia is button shaped (**Figure 7a**). Two pairs of eyes in rectangular arrangement. The longest peristomialcirus extends back to the 17th setiger. Prostomium and dorsum of palps are light green, and dorsum of segment has distinct light green or green-brown band, which becomes lighter toward posterior. The other parts of the body are white. Paragnaths are present only on maxillary ring of the proboscis: I = 0; II = 10–13 cones in 2 oblique clusters; III = 7–9 cones in 1 cluster; and IV = 10–14 cones.

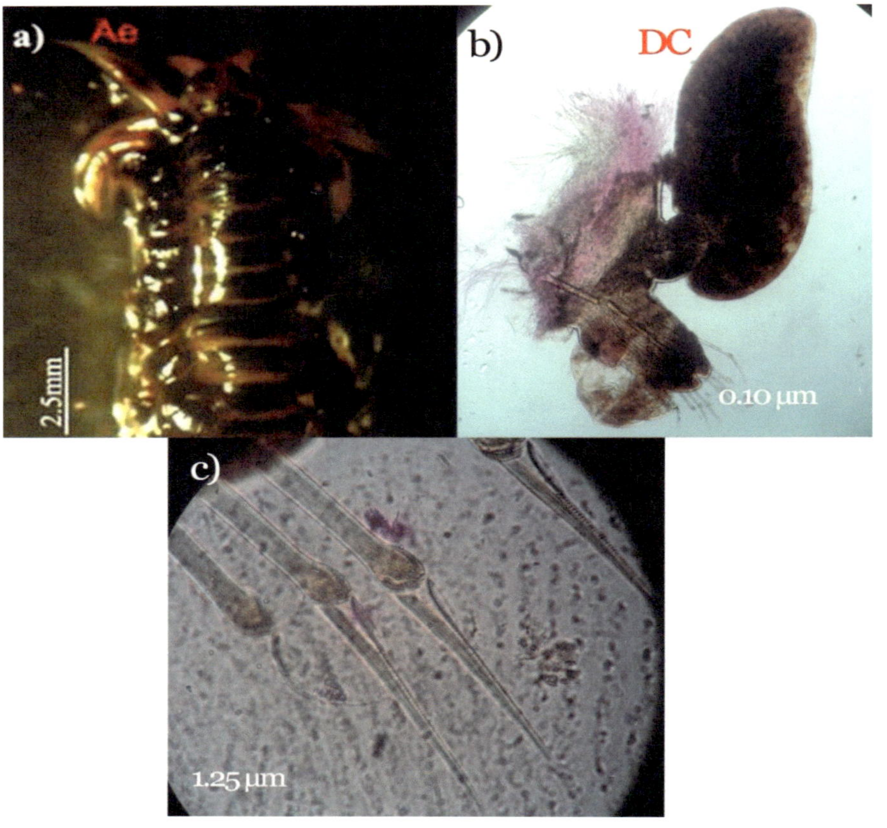

Figure 6.
Phyllodoce castanea (a) anterior end, (b) anterior foot and (c) setae.

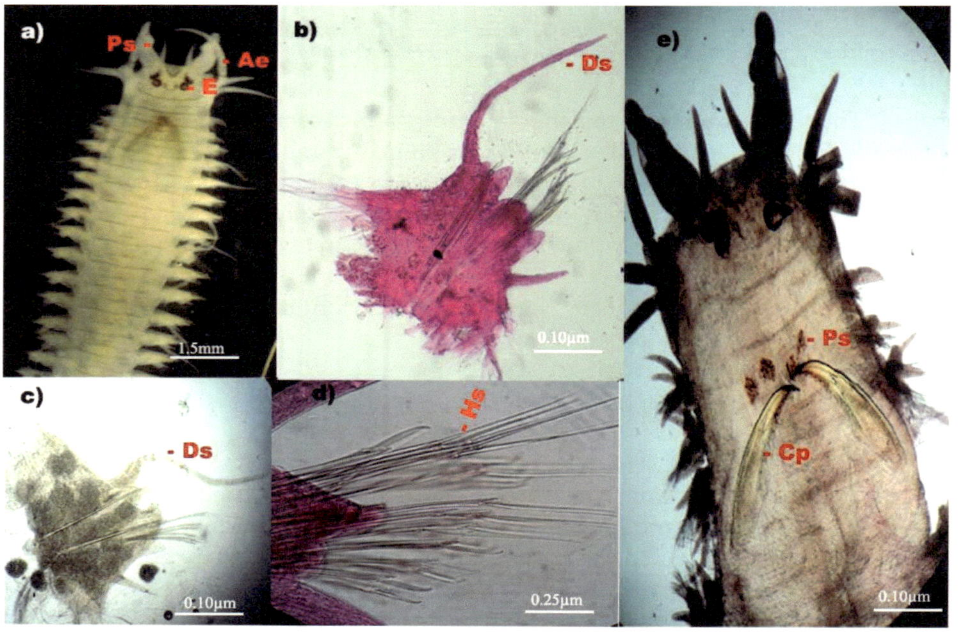

Figure 7.
Ceratonereis mirabilis (a) anterior end, (b) anterior foot, (c) posterior foot, (d) setae, and (e) dorsal view of proboscis.

Lateral teeth of the jaw are indistinct (**Figure 7e**). The first two pairs of parapodia are uniramous, the rest biramous. The dorsal cirrus is very long, three times as long as notoligule. Neuroligule is slightly shorter but thicker (**Figure 7b** and **c**). The dorsal and ventral cirri are digitate; acicular lobes are very small, only as a projection, shorter than ventral cirrus. The dorsal cirrus of anterior parapodia is five times long as notoligule, and notoligules digitate, while supra-notoligules are thicker.

The acicular lobes of neuropodium are short and distally obtuse; neuroligule is short but slightly longer than neuro-acicular lobe. The dorsal segments of middle and posterior cirrus are rather long. Anterior notoseate are homogomph spinigers. Indistinct heterogomph falcigers appear from the middle parapodium, and the end of terminal piece is beaked. Some posterior setigers bear homogomph falcigers in which the end of terminal piece is bifid. Notopodial falcigers are homogomph; neuropodial falcigers are homogomph (**Figure 7d**).

Remarks: The species is characterized by its cleft prostomium and the presence of notopodial falcigers on posterior setigers.

Distribution: Red Sea, Persian Gulf, Indian and Atlantic Oceans, Japan, New Caledonia, New Zealand, Honolulu, Australia, Brazil, and West Indies. India: Lakshadweep, Andaman and Nicobar Islands, Krusadai Island, Pamban, Kilakarai, Maharashtra, and Goa Coast.

***Perinereis nigro-punctata* (Horst, 1889)**

Nereis nigro-punctata [28]: 171.

Perinereis marjorii [29]: 595.

Perinereis nigro-punctata [30]: 107; [7]: 210; [8]: 337, fig. 14.13r-v; [12]: 741; [14]: 77; [31]: 325; [32]: 202.

Habitat: Found among oysters and dead coral crevices of low tide.

Description: Body 50–60 mm long with three rows of brown marks, and prostomium is "V"-shape trapezoidal with deep median furrow anteriorly; tentacular cirri are short. Palps with robust, short palpophores, and globular palpostyles. Antennae two short, triangular longest tentacular cirri usually extend to third setiger. Peristomium is relatively long (**Figure 8a**). Anterior notopodia, subtriangular; notopodial ligules, conical; median ligules with small superior lobes (**Figure 8b**). Dorsal cirrus is as long as dorsal notopodial lobes on anterior setigers and slightly longer posteriorly (**Figure 8c**). Neuropodia with digit firm superior lobe; low, rounded inferior lobe; shorter post-setal lobe with straight border.

Ventral ligule elongates digitiform longer than remaining notopodial ligules, and ventral cirrus is approximately half as long as ventral ligule. Dorsal notopodial ligule increases in length and expands in posterior setigers with dorsal cirrus distally inserted. Notosetae homogomph spinigers only, with 1–3 robust heterogomph falcigers (**Figure 8d**). Anal cirri are narrow and elongated.

Remarks: The present materials agree well with the earlier descriptions.

Distribution: Malay Archipelago and Great Barrier Reef. India: Andaman and Nicobar Islands, Chilika Lake, Orissa, Gujarat coast, Tuticorin, Cape Comorin, Ganges Delta, Madras Coast, and Bombay Coast.

***Perinereis nuntia brevicirrus* (Grube, 1876)**

Nereilepas brevicirrus [33]: 19.

Perinereis mictodonta var. *mictodontoides* [34]: 117.

Perinereis nuntia var. *brevicirrus* [30]: 110; [7]: 214; [12]: 742.

Habitat: Found among barnacles and oysters and in dead coral crevices at low tide.

Description: Maximum length of specimen is 100 mm long and 6 mm wide. Prostomium is pyriform, with pairs of eyes in trapezoidal arrangement situated on the posterior part of prostomium (**Figure 9a**). Tentacles are short and small and distally slender; the palps are large, and the basalia is expanded; the terminalia is

Figure 8.
Perinereis nigro-punctata (a) anterior and posterior end, (b) anterior foot, (c) posterior foot, and (d) setae.

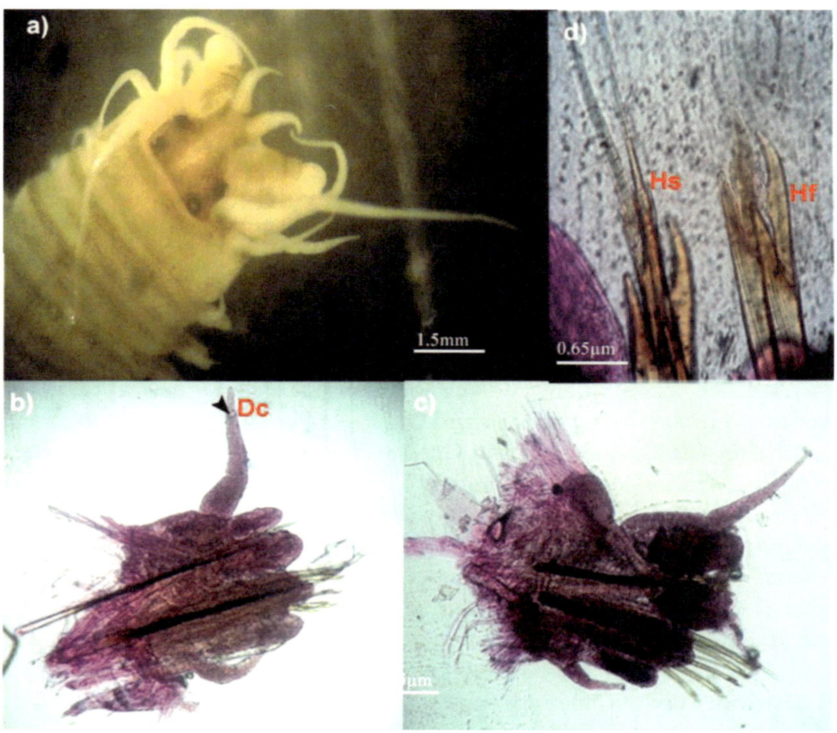

Figure 9.
Perinereis nuntia brevicirrus (a) anterior end, (b) anterior foot, (c) posterior foot, and (d) setae structure.

very small and button shaped. The longest peristomial cirrus extends back to the seventh setiger.

The paragnaths on proboscis have the following arrangement: I = 3 cones, II = 12–15 cones in 3 oblique rows; III = 13 cones in 3 longitudinal rows; IV = a dense triangular group; V = 3 cones in a triangle; VI = a transverse row of 5–8 flattened broad paragnaths; and VII and VIII = 30–40 cones in 3 irregular rows.

Typical parapodia have all ligules conical with the dorsal longest ones (**Figure 9b**). Dorsal cirri are slender and extend distally somewhat beyond the tips of dorsal ligules (**Figure 9c**). The anterior setigers, more than 10 in a live specimen, are blue-black or green-black; the posterior region is pale-brown. Notosetae with homogomph spinigers and neurosetae with heterogomph falcigers (**Figure 9d**).

Remarks: The present materials agree well with the description of Fauvel [7].

Distribution: Japan, Australia, New Zealand, New Caledonia, Malay Archipelago, Indian Ocean, Saint Paul Island, and Red Sea. **India**: Gulf of Mannar, Tuticorin, Cape Comorin, Andaman and Nicobar Islands, Maharashtra, and Goa Coast.

***Perinereis nuntia caeruleis* (Hoagland, 1920)**

Nereis (Heteronereis) caeruleis [35]: 608–610, pl. 47 fig. 13–16, pl. 48 fig. 1–4.

Perinereis nuntia caeruleis [36]: 261–262.

Habitat: Boring into dead corals to live on cavity.

Description: Body 120–125 mm long, eyes black in color. A prominent, circular depression present in anterior prostomium between the antennae. Antennae are one third long as prostomium. Tentacular cirri extend back to 2–4 setigers (**Figure 10a** and **b**). Jaws are dark brown with no teeth. Paragnaths I = 0; II = 0; and III = 60–90 in central group; IV = 80–100 cones, bars absent; V = 1 large cones plus 10–15 small cones; VI = 8–12 bars; VII–VIII = about 100–150 very small cones, plus 3–4 large

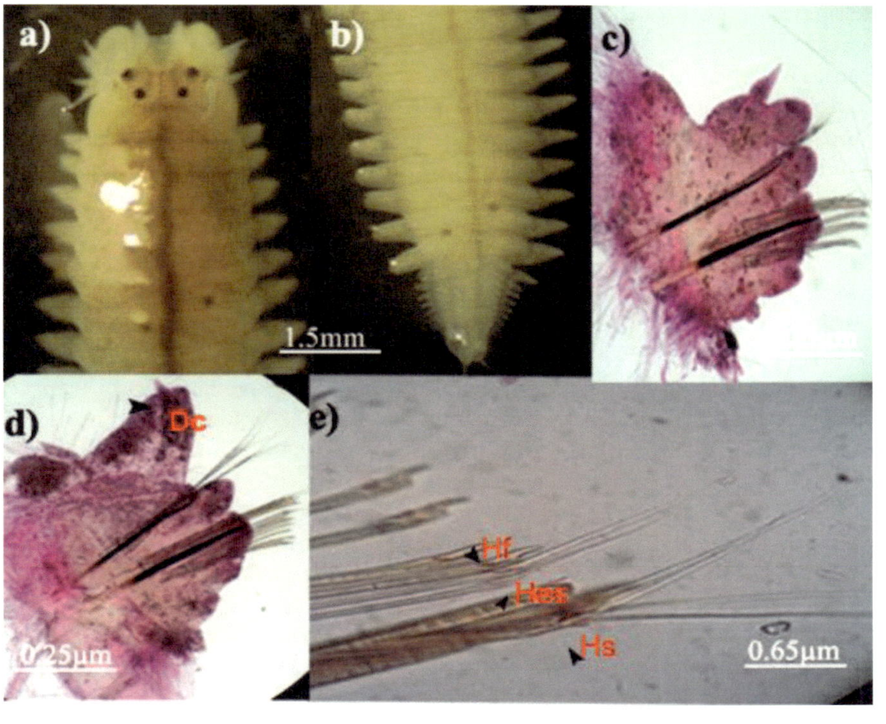

Figure 10.
Perinereis nuntia caeruleis (a) anterior end, (b) posterior end, (c) anterior foot, (d) posterior foot, and (e) seta structure.

cones on each side close to area VI. Parapodia of first and second setigers are anteriorly directed. Anterior notopodia with two equal lobes (**Figure 10c**) and basal lobe becoming expanded from median setigers up to twice as long as ventral lobe with distally attached dorsal cirri. All notosetae are homogomph spinigers. Neurosetae are heterogomph spinigers and heterogomph falcigers in both supra-acicular and infra-acicular positions. Neuropodial heterogomph spinigers are absent from anterior-most 24th–35th setigers. Anal cirri are as long as posterior-most fourth setigers (**Figure 10d**).

Remarks: The present material agrees well with the description of Wilson and Glasby [36]. In earlier collections as a new distribution record species in Andaman and Nicobar Islands [37].

Distribution: Australia and Philippines.

***Perinereis vancaurica* (Ehlers, 1868)**

Nereis vancaurica [38]: p. xx.

Perinereis horsti [11]: 182, pl. 11, fig. 47, text-figs. 182-4.

Perinereis vancaurica [30]: 103; [7]: 205, fig. 105f–g; [8]: 334, fig. 14.12, k–o; [12]: 740; [15]: 96; [14]: 77; [18]: 146.

Habitat: Occurs in intertidal areas of oyster- and barnacle-encrusted coral rocks.

Description: Paragnaths are arranged as follows: I = 1, II = 16–20 in triangle, III = 32–40, IV = 25–45 cones, V = 3 cones in a triangle, VI = 2 long flattened bars, and VII–VIII = 58–80 in 3 irregular rows. Paragnaths in VII–VIII in 2 bands. The band closest to the oral end of the pharynx consists of large cone in two irregular rows. Anterior notopodia with conical notopodial ligule (**Figure 11b**). Dorsal cirrus is slightly longer than dorsal ligule (**Figure 11c**). Neuropodia with superior lobe are poorly developed and inferior lobe is dome-shaped. Posterior notopodia with dorsal ligule triangular are broad. Dorsal cirri are becoming distally inserted on notopodial ligule on posterior setigers. Other parapodial lobes are posteriorly similar to anterior setigers. All notosetae are homogomph spinigers. Neurosetae are heterogomph falcigers in both supra-acicular and infra-acicular positions (**Figure 11d**).

Remarks: The present material agrees well with the earlier description.

Distribution: Philippines, Indochina, Great Barrier Reef, New Zealand, Singapore, Mergui, Red Sea, Atlantic Ocean, and French Guiana. **India**: Andaman and Nicobar Islands, Lakshadweep, Maharashtra, Goa Coast and Gujarat.

***Perinereis cultrifera* (Grube, 1840)**

Nereis cultrifera [39]: 74.

Perinereis cultrifera [40]: 352, fig. 137, 11953, p. 206, fig. a–l; [8]: 337, 14.13, fig. o–q; [41]: 71, [18]: 146.

Habitat: Boring in dead corals and living in coral cavity.

Description: Body 85–90 mm long. Prostomium is broadly triangular; palps are large; tentacular cirri are rather long and slender (**Figure 12a**). Faint transverse pigmented bands on several anterior setigers, otherwise lacking pigmentation patterns. Eyes are black, antennae one-third as long as prostomium, longest tentacular cirri extend back to fifth setiger. Jaws about five distinct teeth. Paragnaths: I = 1–2; II = 5–9; III = 9–11; IV = 9–12 cones; V = 3 cones in triangle; VI = 1; VII–VIII = 26–30 cones in 2 regular rows. Notopodia with 2 equal lobe anteriorly. Dorsal cirrus as long as dorsal notopodial ligule anteriorly (**Figure 12b** and **c**). Heterogomph spinigers present in ventral neuropodial fascicles from the first setiger. Anal cirri extend back to about seven setigers (**Figure 12d**).

Remarks: The present material agrees well with the earlier descriptions.

Distribution: Cosmopolitan; Indian, Pacific, and Atlantic Oceans; Mediterranean Sea; Israel; Japan; and Burma and Diamond Island. India: Lakshadweep, Maharashtra coast, Travancore, Cape Comorin, Tuticorin, Gulf of Mannar, Orissa coast, and Andaman and Nicobar Islands.

DOI: http://dx.doi.org/10.5772/intechopen.88668

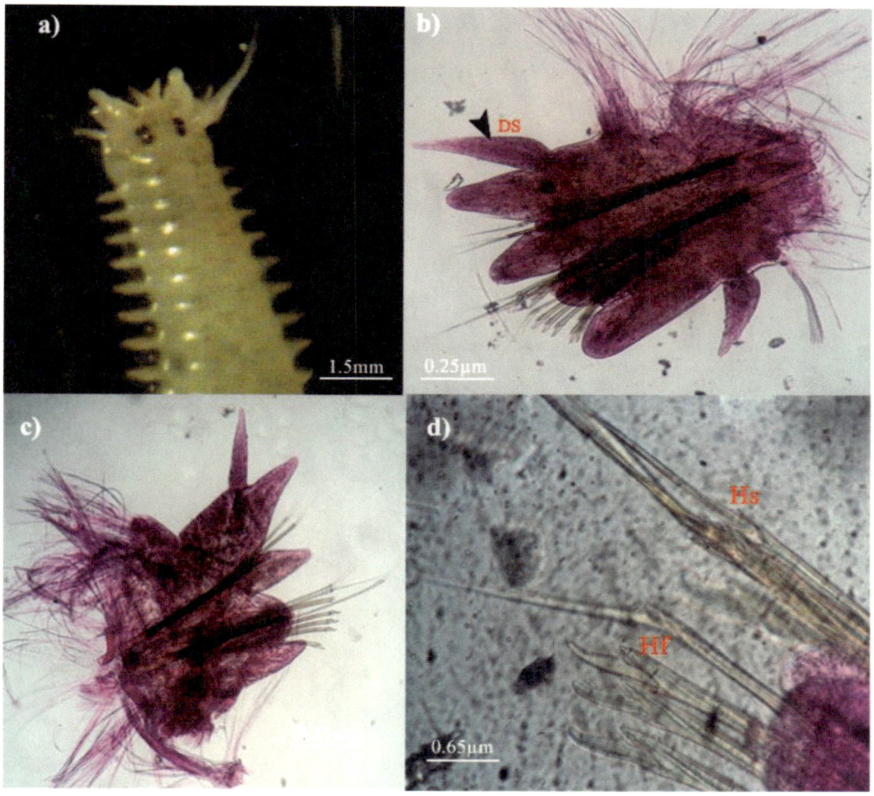

Figure 11.
Perinereis vancaurica (a) anterior end, (b) anterior foot, (c) posterior foot and (d) seta structure.

***Perinereis cultrifera typica* Grube, 1840**
Perinereis cultrifera typica [39]: 74; [40]: 352, fig. 137; [7]: 208; [12]: 740.
Habitat: Boring in dead corals and living under rocks.

Description: Specimen is 80–90 mm long. Prostomium is pyriform and bears two short, small digitate tentacles. Palps are large (**Figure 13a**). Two pairs of black eyes in rectangular arrangement. The longest peristomial cirrus extends backward to 5–6 setigers (**Figure 13b**). Proboscis has paragnaths on both rings: I = 2 cones; II = 12–18 cones in 3 oblique rows; III = 14–20 cones in 3–4 transverse rows; IV = 10–20 cones in 3 oblique rows; V = 3 cones in a triangle; VI = a single flat triangular cone; VIII and VIII = 20–30 cones in 2 rows. And the jaws have 4–5 lateral teeth. Anterior parapodium is enlarged about two times as large as the uniramous one, and dorsal cirri are located at the dorsum of notoligule (**Figure 13c**). The dorsal cirrus is slightly longer than notoligule, and ventral cirrus is shorter than neuroligule. Ventral cirri with pointed end. Posterior parapodium is smaller, but supra-notoligules are very distinct, large, long, terminate, slender, and pointed carrying the dorsal cirrus on top. The ventral cirrus is short, digitate, and distally slender. Notoselae are homogomph spinigers throughout, and neurosetae are homogomph spinigers and heterogomph falcigers in supra-acicular position. Heterogomph spinigers and heterogomph falcigers in infra-acicular position (**Figure 13d**).

Remarks: The present material agrees well with the original description.

Distribution: Red Sea, Persian Gulf, and Indian Ocean. India: Tuticorin, Pamban backwaters, Chandipore, Andaman and Nicobar Islands, Maharashtra, and Goa Coast.

Figure 12.
Perinereis cultrifera (a) anterior end, (b) anterior foot, (c) posterior foot and (d) seta structure.

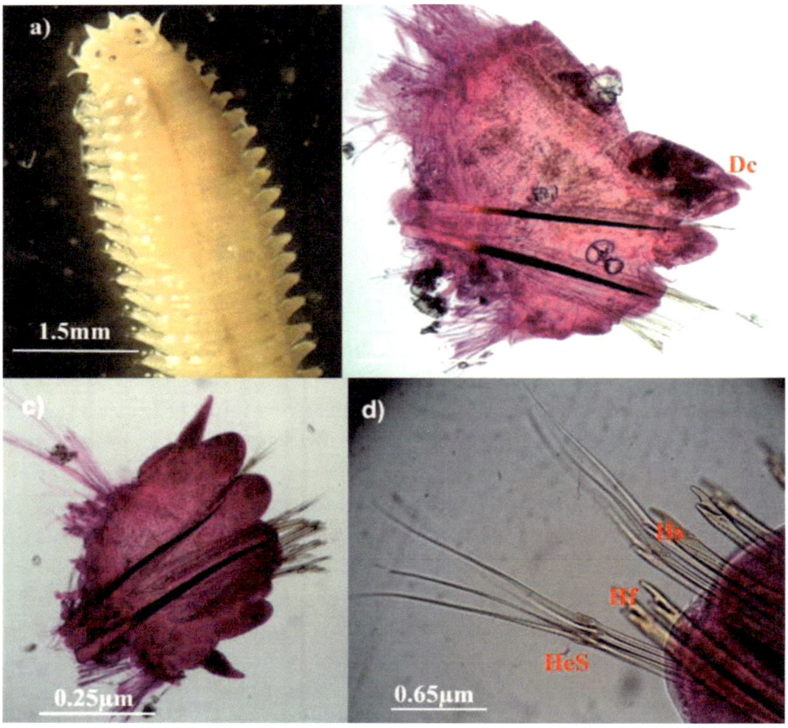

Figure 13.
Perinereis cultrifera typica (a) anterior end, (b) anterior foot, (c) posterior foot, and (d) setae.

Pseudonereis variegata **(Grube, 1857)**
Nereilepas variegata [42]: 164.
Nereis (Mastigonereis) variegata [43]: 37, pl. 1 figs. 6–10, pl. 2 figs. 11, 12.
Pseudonereis gallapagensis [27]: 174; [7]: 215, fig. 110a–e.
Pseudonereis variegata [8]: 331, fig. 14-12.a–f; [44]: 74; [15]: 961 [14]: 77.
Habitat: Burrowing on rocks and dead and live corals.

Description: Body up to 90 mm long, prostomium somewhat pyriform. Two pairs of eyes in trapezoidal arrangement, tentacles are small, and palps are large with bulbous tip. The longest peristomial cirrus reaches backward to five setigers (**Figure 14a**). Proboscis is large, paragnaths are present on both rings; I = 1 cone; II = 16–20 points in a regular triangular cluster; III =12–18 points in 3 triangular rows; IV = 17–22 points; V = 1 cone; VI a single transverse bar; VII and VIII have 30–40 cones in 3–4 irregular rows.

Anterior parapodia bear rounded supra- and infra-ligules (**Figure 14b**). Both dorsal and ventral cirri are digitate, and middle parapodia have almost the same size as notoligule; but the end of the supra-notoligule is slender. The dorsal cirri are longer than notopodial lobes slenderized toward the end. The ventral cirrus is very short, situated at the base of infra-neuroligule (**Figure 14c**). Beyond the 50th setiger, supra-notoligule expands toward the posterior end in rectangular shape; it is carrying the dorsal cirrus at the end; ventral cirrus is very short. The upper margin or supra-notoligule in posterior parapodia bears a gland. Notosetae are

Figure 14.
Pseudonereis variegata (a) anterior end, (b) posterior end, (c) anterior foot, (d) posterior foot, and (e) setae.

homogomph spinigers throughout, and neurosetae in anterior and middle parapodia are homogomph spinigers and heterogomph falcigers. Posterior neurosetal lobes with heterogomph spinigers and falcigers (**Figure 14d**).

Remarks: The present material agrees well with the description of Day [8].

Distribution: Pacific Ocean, Galapagos, Peru, Chile, Strait of Magellan, Indochina, Indian Ocean, Madagascar, and Brazil. **India**: Orissa coast, Gulf of Mannar, Andaman and Nicobar Islands, Goa, and Gujarat.

***Eunice antennata* (Savigny 1820)**

Leodice antennata [45]: 50.

Eunice antennata [46]: 312; [47]: 17; [7]: 138 & 240; [8]: 384, fig. 17.2 k–q; [12]: 743; [13]: 204; [18]: 148.

Habitat: Boring into dead corals and beach rocks.

Description: Body 30–155 mm long, prostomium is bilobed with five prostomial tentacles, pair of tentacular cirri on the second apodous segment, and the dorsal cirri and anal cirri are moniliform. The first apodous segment is about three and a half times as long as the second apodous segment (**Figure 15a**). The setae of the first foot are arranged in two bundles. A bundle of simple capillaries at the base of the dorsal cirrus (**Figure 15b**). Branchiae first start on the 6th setigerous segment well developed between the 10th and 25th segments, where they have 6th or 7th filaments, and decrease to two or three in median region; thereafter, the number increases again in posterior segments (**Figure 15c**). The anal segment bears two long anal cirri. Acicular setae are first present in the 19th setigerous segment; they are yellow, tridentate, and distally hooded. Other setae include slender capillary, bidentate compound falcigers with rounded hood, and pectinate setae with lateral, asymmetrical extensions (**Figure 15d**).

Remarks: Present material agrees well with the earlier descriptions.

Distribution: Red Sea, Persian Gulf, Indian Ocean, Philippines, Pacific Ocean, Indochina, and Ceylon. **India**: Lakshadweep; Gulf of Mannar; Andaman and Nicobar Islands; Pamban, Krusadai, and Shingle Island; and Tuticorin and Maharashtra Coast.

***Eunice vittata* (Delle Chiaje, 1825)**

Nereis vitta [48]: 195.

Eunice vitta [40]: 404, fig. 158 h–n; [8]: 385, fig. 17.3a–e.

Habitat: Boring into dead corals and living on cavity of dead corals and rocks.

Description: Body 30–35 mm long, anterior segments with red bars which fade in alcohol, antennae and cirri are smooth without annulations, the longest or median one extends back to the sixth segment (**Figure 16a**). A pair of circular eyes at the outer bases of the median antenna, tentacular cirri are smooth and extend forward not quite to the front of the prostomium. Branchiae are first present from the third parapodium (**Figure 16b** and **c**) and continue back to 45th segment; they have 10–18 filaments. Acicula is yellow with blunt tips, slightly curved. Acicular setae are yellow and tridentate with small apical tooth. Compound setae are falcigerous and are distally bifid and covered with a pointed hood (**Figure 16d**).

Remarks: In earlier findings of Rajasekaran [37], this species is the first record from Indian waters.

Distribution: Australia.

***Eunice afra punctata* Peters, 1854**

Eunice punctata [49]: 611.

Eunice afra var. *punctata* [50]: 89; [8]: 393; [13]: 204; [17]: 59; [18]: 150.

Habitat: Boring into beach rocks and dead corals.

Description: Body 130–140 mm long, brown in color with dotted tiny white punctations on the anterior portion. Prostomial antennae are smooth, and peristomial cirri are long as the peristomial segment (**Figure 17a**). From the first segment,

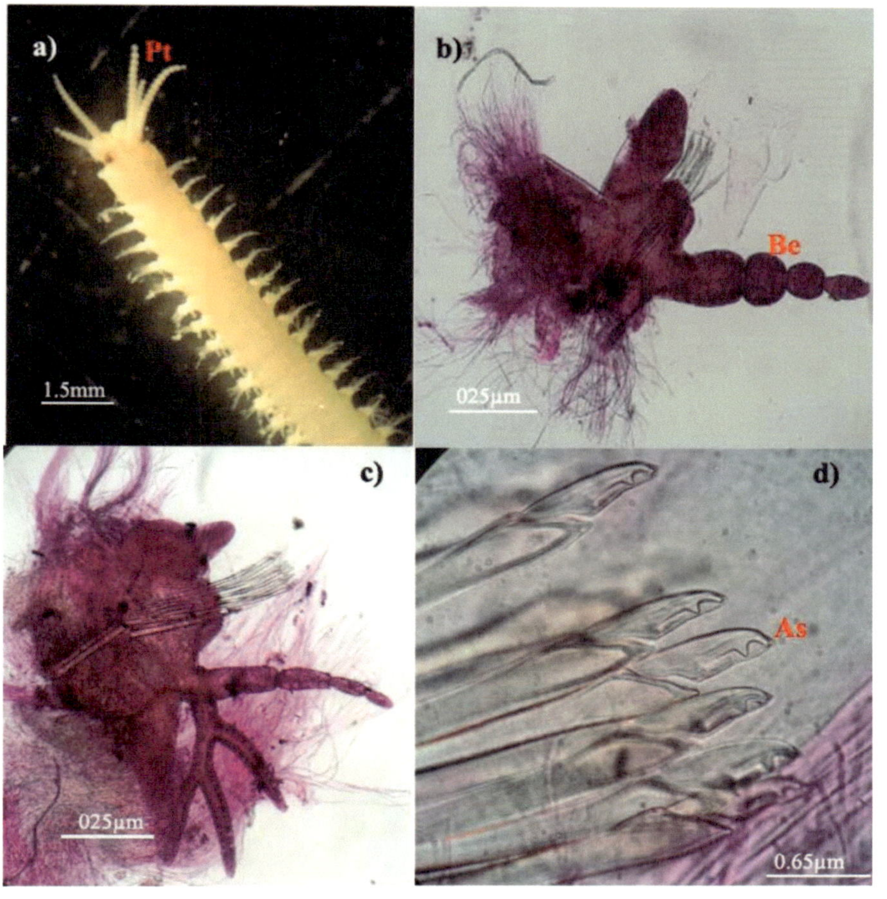

Figure 15.
Eunice antennata (a) anterior end, (b) anterior foot, (c) posterior foot and (d) setae.

branchiae are absent (**Figure 17b**) Branchiae are starting from about 16th segment, with 2–4 filaments; they are pectinately divided and attain a maximum of 8 filaments at the 30th setiger; the last 10 segments lack them (**Figure 17c**). There are 2 acicula each of the first 28–30 parapodia and only 1 in others. Acicular hooks are first present in 30th segment; they are distally bidentate and subdistal tooth is directed laterally. Other setae are of three kinds: slender capillary (**Figure 17d**), pectinate (**Figure 17f**), and bidentate compound falcigers in which the hood is distally rounded (**Figure 17e**).

Remarks: Present material agrees well with the original descriptions.

Distribution: South Africa. **India**: Lakshadweep, Gulf of Mannar, and Andaman and Nicobar Islands.

***Lysidice collaris* Grube, 1870**

Lysidice collaris [51]: 495; [20]: 272, pl. 14 figs. 93–95, text-figs. 144–147; [8]: 402-403, fig. 17.8.a–f; [7]: 248, fig. 124a–g; [13]: 205; [14]: 78.

Habitat: Boring in dead corals and living on cervices of dead corals.

Description: Prostomium is distinctly bilobed in front and has two reniform eyes located near the outer base of the paired antennae (**Figure 18a**). The three prostomial antennae are slender, and the second dental plate has three heavy teeth. In anterior segments the dorsal cirri are slenderer than ventral ones (**Figure 18b** and **c**). In posterior segments the dorsal cirri become shorter. Setae include capillary setae (**Figure 18d**), bidentate composite falcigers, and comb setae, and bidentate

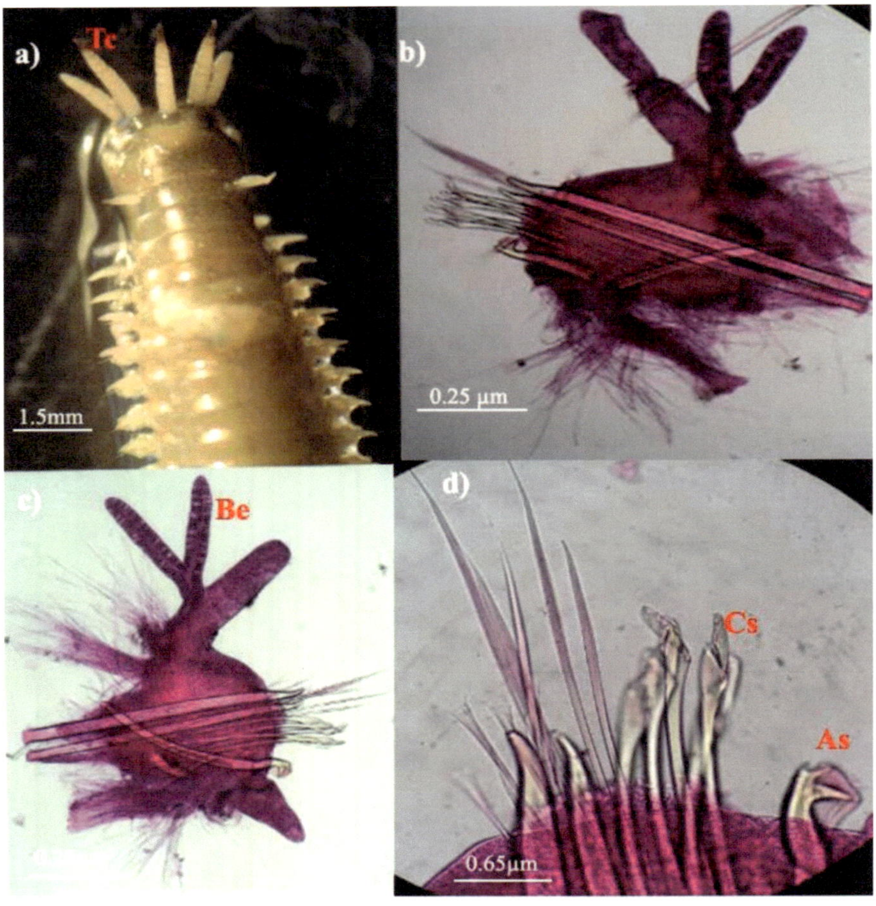

Figure 16.
Eunice vittata (a) anterior end, (b) anterior foot, (c) posterior foot and (d) setae.

sub-acicular hooks are first present at the 21st setiger and continue posteriorly (**Figure 18e**).

Remarks: Present materials agree well with the descriptions of Day [8].

Distribution: Indian Ocean, Pacific Ocean, Persian Gulf, and Red Sea. **India:** Andaman and Nicobar Islands, Kilakarai, Pamban, Gujarat coast, and Gulf of Mannar.

***Lysidice ninetta* (Audouin & Milne Edwards, 1833)**

Lysidice ninetta [52]: 235; [40]: 411, fig. 162a–f; [8]: 403, fig. 17.8g-I; [18]: 150.

Habitat: Boring in dead corals and living on cavity of corals.

Description: Body 75–100 mm long, reddish with white spots and white bar on the second and fifth setiger (**Figure 19a**). Prostomial antennae are short and three in number, and peristomial appendages and gills are absent. Each parapodium with bluntly conical dorsal cirrus, rounded ventral cirrus, and a broad setigerous lobe (**Figure 19b**). Setae include capillaries with pectinate setae, composite falcigers, and bidentate acicular hooks (**Figure 19c**). Acicula black with blunt tips. Bidentate sub-acicular hooks from the 22nd–25th setigers onwards.

Remarks: Present material agrees well with the descriptions of Day [8].

Distribution: Red Sea, West Indo-Pacific, north Atlantic Ocean, North Carolina, Mediterranean Sea, and Angola. **India**: Lakshadweep, Kilakarai, Pamban, and Andaman and Nicobar Islands.

Figure 17.
Eunice afra punctata (a) anterior end, (b) anterior foot, (c) posterior foot, (d) simple capillary seta, (e) heterogomph falciger, and (f) comb setae.

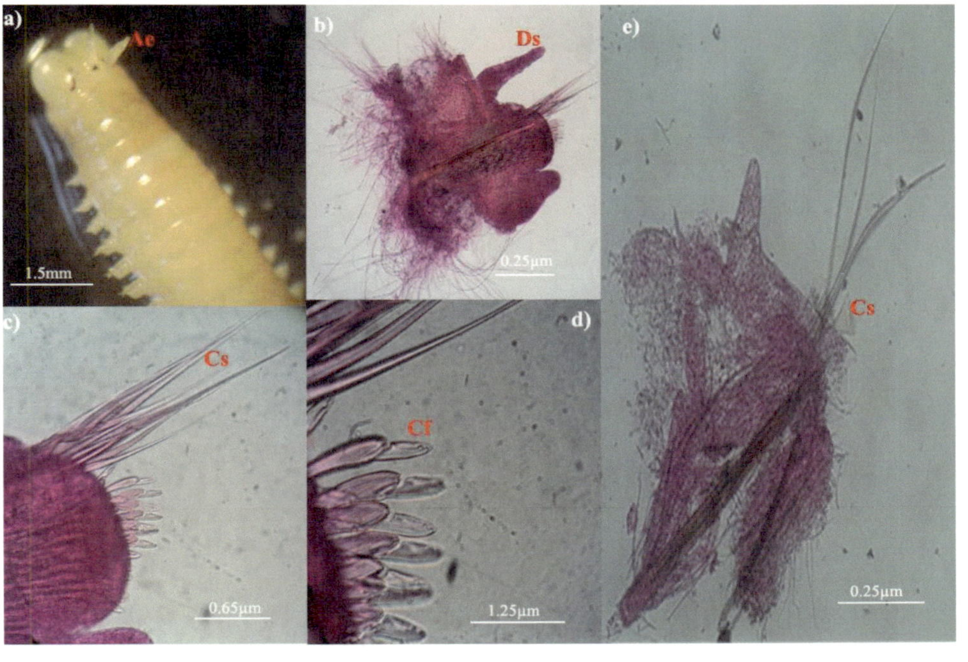

Figure 18.
Lysidice collaris (a) anterior end, (b) anterior foot, (c) posterior foot, (d) limbate capillary, and (e) falciger and comb setae.

***Malacocers indicus* (Fauvel, 1928)**
Scolelepis indica [53]: 93–94, fig. 2g–n; [6]: 35, **fig. 7g–n;**, [18]: 153.
Malacoceros indicus [54]: 219; [55]: 6–7, figs. 2a–g, 3a–j; [8]: 447, fig. 18.5p-u.
Malacoceros indicus [56]: 50–53; [44]: 74.

Description: Body 45–55 mm long, yellowish tan in alcohol, prostomium with lateral peaks tapering with posteriorly and blunt caruncle extending to posterior edge of the first setiger, with irregular clusters of small 6–8 eyespots (**Figure 20a**). Branchiae are present from the first setiger continuing to the end of the body. Notopodial lamellae are slender and triangular, with tapered end attached only at the base of the branchiae (**Figure 20b**). Neuropodial lamellae are rounded anteriorly with a nipple-like projection posteriorly (**Figure 20c**). Notosetae capillaries through the body (**Figure 20d**); neurosetae capillaries in anterior setigers and hooded hooks in posterior setigers (**Figure 20e**).

Remarks: In earlier findings 9 specimens are collected from station 2 and 10 and the first record of the genus is from Andaman and Nicobar Islands.

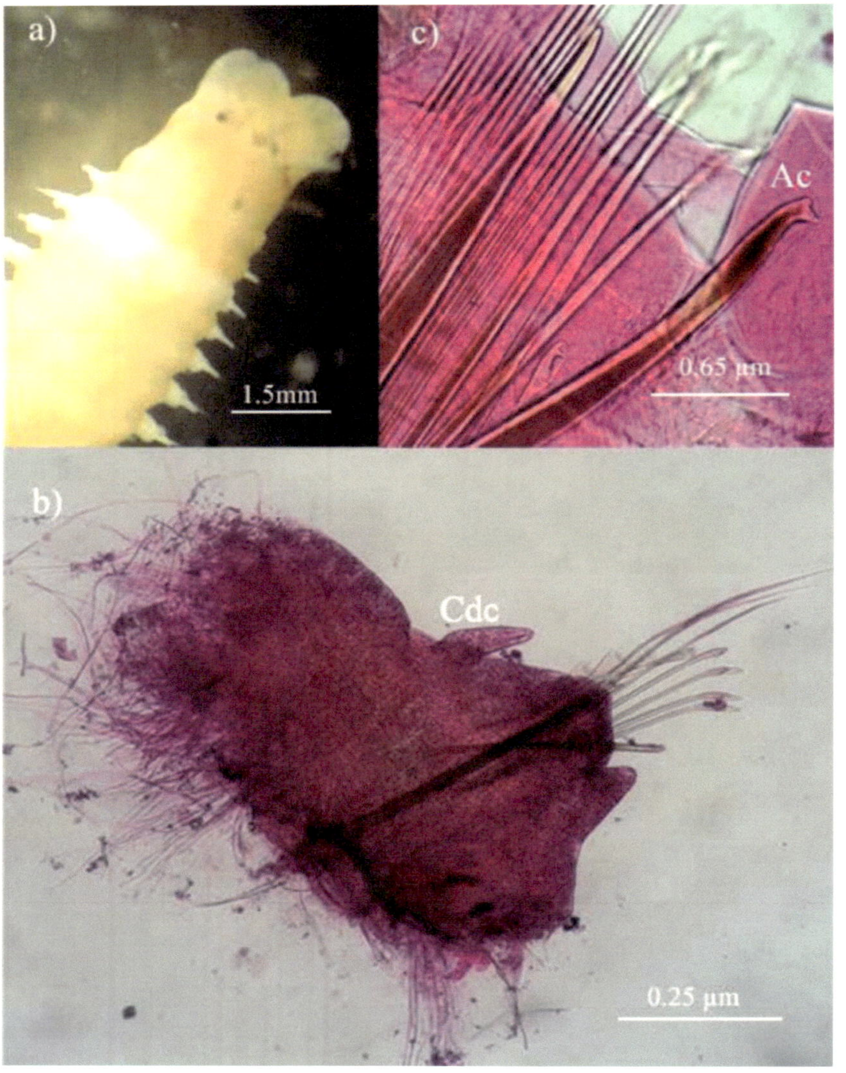

Figure 19.
Lysidice ninetta (a) anterior end, (b) middle foot and (c) acicular seta.

Distribution: Caribbean, New Caledonia, Chile, Japan, and Australia. **India**: Lakshadweep, Gulf of Mannar, Orissa, and Visakhapatnam.

***Scolelepis squamata* (Muller, 1806)**

Lumbricus squamatus [57]: 39.

Lumbricus cirratulus [48]: 196.

Nerine cirratulus [58]: 36, fig. 11g–n; [59]: 412, fig. l–j; [60]: 26.

Scolelepis squamata [8]: 483, fig. 18.7c–h, [18]: 153.

Habitat: Silty sediments in sandy shore areas.

Description: Body 55–60 mm long, prostomium is pointed anteriorly with 4–5 pairs of eyes in a row and a well-marked occipital keel reaching the second setiger (**Figure 21a**). A pair of long and stout coiled palps; branchiae start from the second setiger and continue to the posterior end and attached to the dorsal lamellae (**Figure 21b**). Only capillary setae are present in the first few segments (**Figure 21c** and **d**). Bidentate hooded hooks in the neuropodia from the 30th–35th setigers onwards and in the notopodia from the 60th setiger (**Figure 21e**). A maximum of 12 neuropodial hooks, pygidial cushion is small, broader, and long.

Remarks: This is the first record of the genus from Andaman and Nicobar Islands [37].

Distribution: Mozambique, Madagascar, Atlantic Ocean, and Mediterranean Sea. **India:** Orissa coast, Rushikulya estuary, Visakhapatnam coast, Pulicat Lake, Vellar estuary, and Godavari estuary.

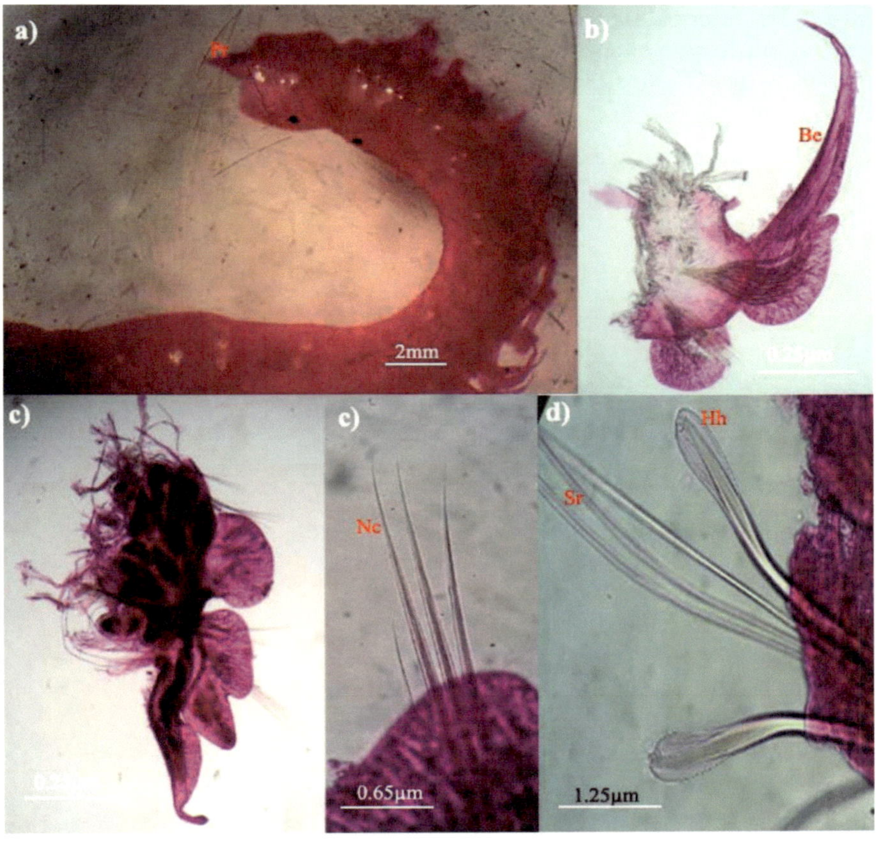

Figure 20.
Malacocers indicus (a) anterior end, (b) anterior foot, (c) posterior foot, (d) notopodial capillary, and (e) saber setae and hooded hook.

Aramandia leptocirrus **(Grube, 1878)**

Aramandia leptocirrus [19]: 194; [61]: 435; [62]: 50; [8]: 577; fig. 25.2h; [18]: 157.

Habitat: Silty sediments in littoral region of sandy shore.

Description: Body elongated, 20–30 mm. long, pointed anteriorly, and not divided into two regions (**Figure 22a**). The gills arise from the second setiger to the last setiger. Eyes are lateral—spots on the 7th setiger to around the 18th setiger. The parapodia arise from the dorsal margin of the ventrolateral folds. Parapodia with short presetal lobe, short ventral cirrus (**Figure 22b**), and two bundles of capillary setae (**Figure 22c**). Anal funnel is long and obliquely truncate so that the anus opens upward. It has long ventral cirrus and 12 fine dorsal papillae.

Remarks: *Aramandia leptocirrus* is extremely specialized, being highly adapted to life within sandy sediments. The branchiae are directed backwards and are present from the anterior end of the ventral groove.

Distribution: Red Sea, Mozambique, South Africa, Persian Gulf, Philippines, Indochina, and New Caledonia. **India**: Lakshadweep, Gulf of Mannar, and Andaman and Nicobar Islands.

Idanthyrsus pennatus **(Peters, 1985)**

Sabellaria (*Pallasia*) *pennata* [63]: 613.

Idanthyrsus pennatus [64]: 88; [23]: 117; [8]: 675, fig. 2j–n; [13]: 207.

Habitat: Hard tube formed with sand particles on corals and rocks.

Description: Body 30–60 mm long, prostomium covered by two large opercular stalks bearing modified setae in two rows, paleae of the opercular peduncle with a number of 19–32 pairs in the outer row and 15–18 pairs in the inner one (**Figure 23a**). Outer paleae with strongly curved shaft and slender denticles giving the general impression of a feather or a palm leaf (**Figure 23c**). Inner paleae smooth with tapering tips (**Figure 23b**). The middorsal line of the opercular peduncle has a

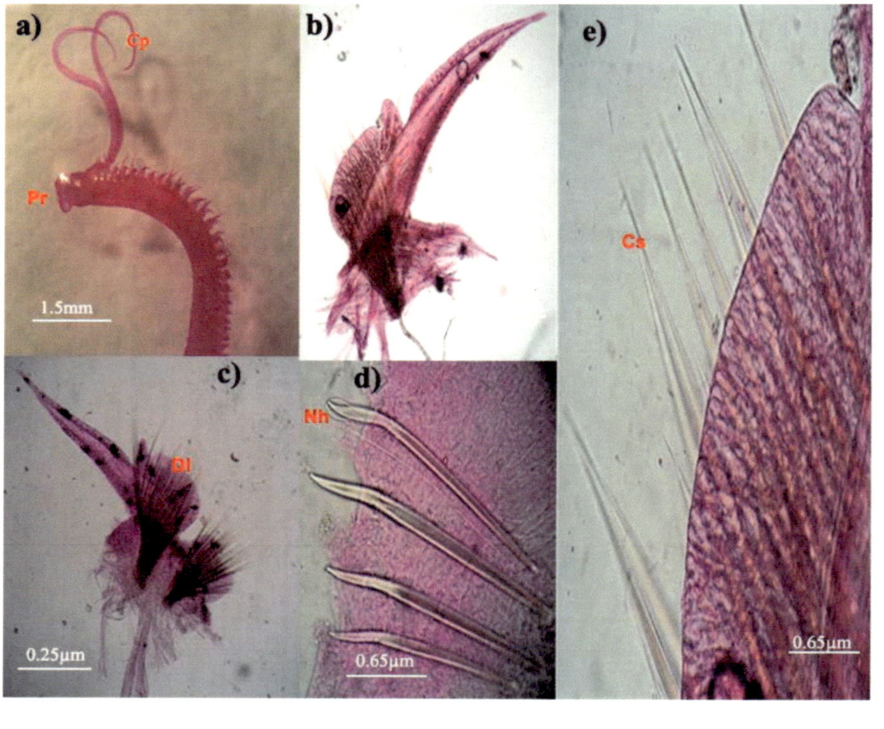

Figure 21.
Scolelepis squamata (a) anterior end, (b) anterior foot, (c) posterior foot, (d) hooded hook, and (e) notosetae.

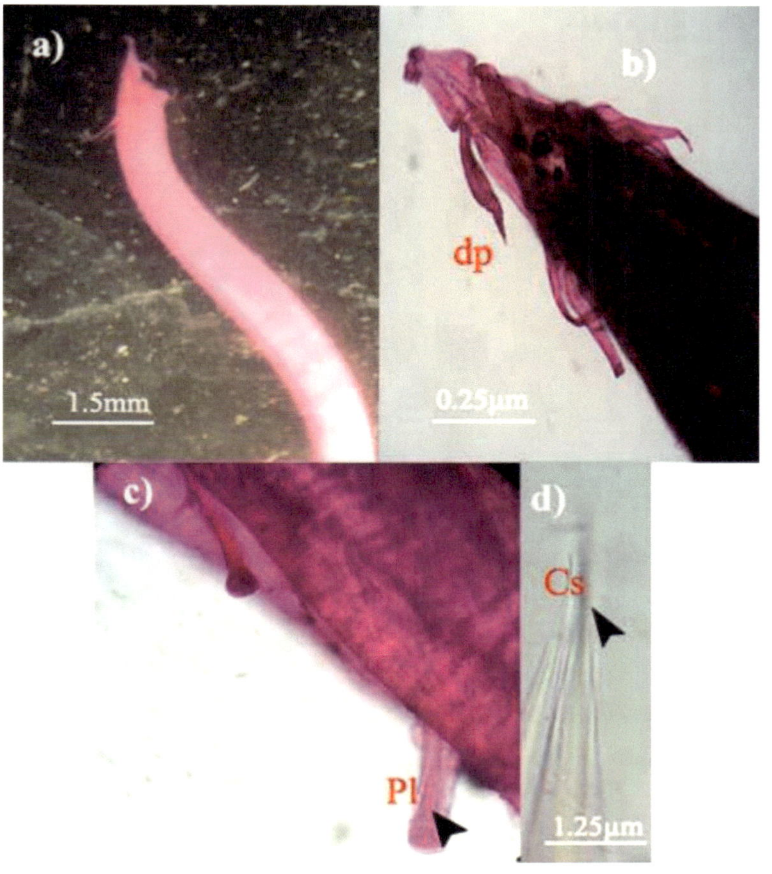

Figure 22.
Aramandia leptocirrus (a) posterior end, (b) middle foot, and (c) simple capillary.

pair of nuchal hooks (**Figure 23e**) and a pair of long papillae. The second segment has a pair of branchiae. The three parathoracic segments are biramous. Thoracic uncini have eight teeth (**Figure 23d**). Caudal region is achaetous and apodous. Segments are numerous and indistinguishable.

Remarks: The present material agrees well with the description of Day [8].

Distribution: Atlantic Ocean, Indian Ocean, and Pacific Ocean. **India:** Andaman and Nicobar Islands.

***Terebella ehrenbergi* (Grube, 1870)**

Terebella ehrenbergi [51]: 511; [65]: 213, pl. 4 figs. 224–225; [66]: 188; [8]: 748, fig. 36.10g–i; [14]: 81; [32]: 207.

Habitat: Soft tube forming on dead and live corals at 1 meter water depth.

Description: Body 35–40 mm in length with long and coiled tentacles; tentacles are filamentous, numerous, and slender. Three pairs of arborescent gills are present on segments 2, 3, and 4 (**Figure 24a**). Lateral lobes are lacking. The peristomium has eye spots. Notosetae are first present from the fourth segment and continue posteriorly but are absent from the last 40 segments. Setae are very slender and distally serrated (**Figure 24b**). Uncini are in single rows on segments 5–10 and the last segment and in double rows on other segments. Each uncinus has 3–5 large teeth (**Figure 24c**).

Remarks: The present material agrees well with the original description.

Distribution: Japan, China Sea, Burma, and Red Sea. **India:** Gulf of Mannar, Andaman and Nicobar Islands, Mahanadi River Estuary, and Gujarat.

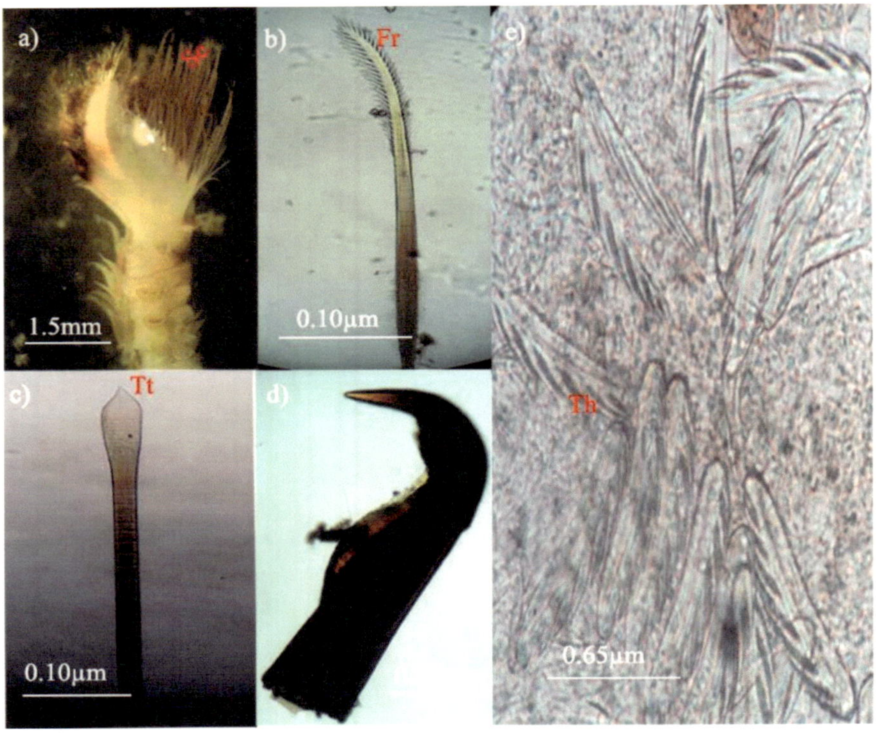

Figure 23.
Idanthyrsus pennatus (a) anterior end, (b) inner palea, (c) outer palea, (d) uncinus, and (e) opercular hook.

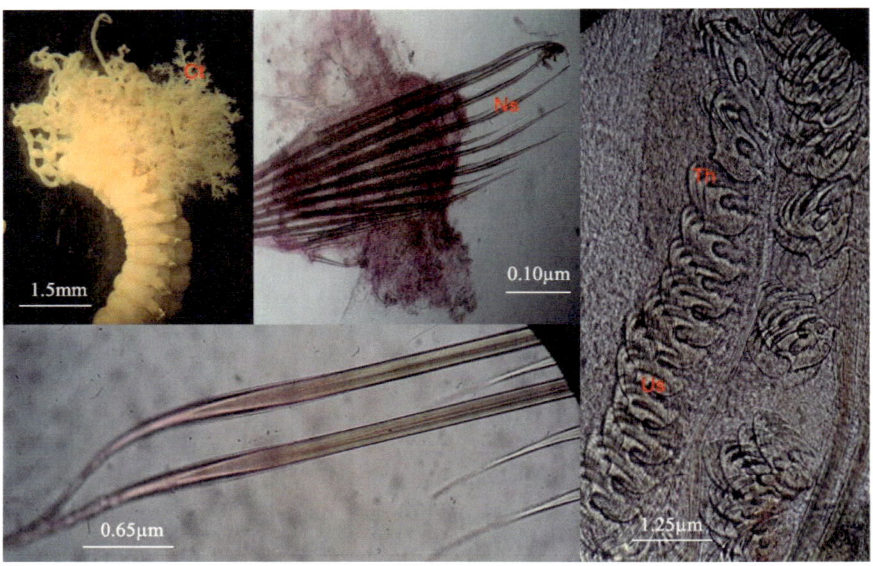

Figure 24.
Terebella ehrenbergi (a) anterior end, (b) notopodial seta, and (c) Thoracic uncinus.

Megalomma quadrioculatum **(Willey, 1905)**
Branchiomma quadrioculatum [67]: 307.
Branchiomma mushaensis [68]: 94, pl.7 fig. 267–270, fig. 447–453.
Megalomma quadrioculatum [8]: 758, fig. 371h–o.

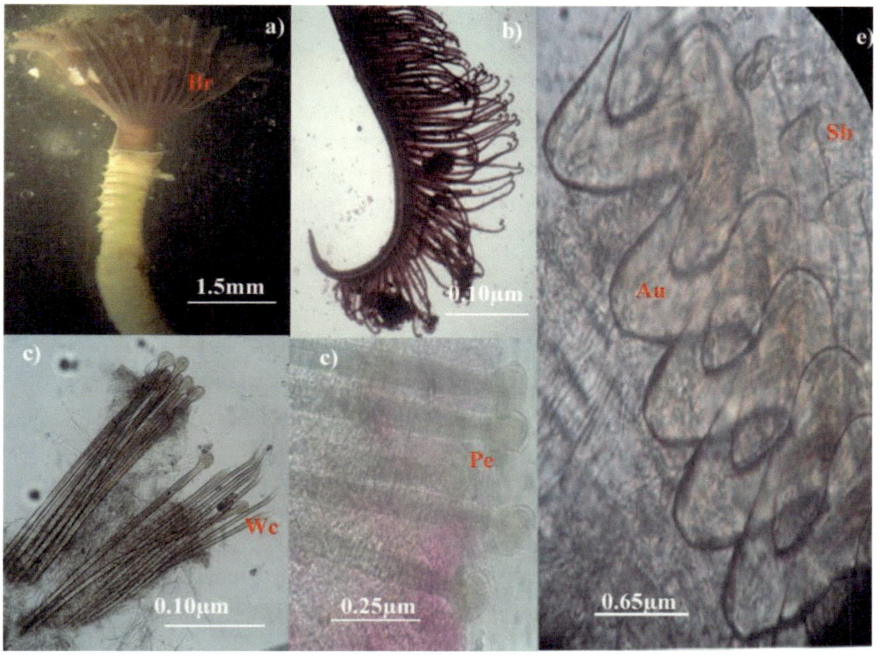

Figure 25.
Megalomma quadrioculatum (a) entire worm, (b) radioles with subterminal eye, (c) paleae with slender tip, (d) thoracic winged capillary, and (e) pick ax setae and Avicular uncinus.

Habitat: Tube forming (boring) on corals at 1 m water depth and lives on inside of the tubes.

Description: Body 35–40 mm long (**Figure 25a**). About 20–30 branchial radioles (**Figure 25b**) with the tips coiled inwards each bearing large subterminal eye. Collar is notched back dorsally to form two small and large lateral lobes, and palps are short. Thoracic notosetae of the 2nd–8th setigers include two types of setae: long slender winged capillaries (**Figure 25c** and **d**) and paleae with pointed tips (**Figure 25e**). Thoracic neurosetae include avicular uncini with long tails and striated crests, plus two rows of pick ax setae with symmetrical blades and tapering tips (**Figure 25f**).

Remarks: This is the first record of the species from Indian waters.

Distribution: Red Sea, Madagascar, and Sri Lanka.

4. Discussion

The present study is an attempt to understand the basic polychaete taxonomical tools, diversity, and morphological identification of the common coral-reef-associated polychaetes of Great Nicobar Islands. Over 5400 species of polychaetes have been described so far worldwide. Many polychaete worms are beautiful and strikingly colored red, green, or pink or with a combination of different colors, and some are iridescent. The most common and visible polychaetes found on coral reefs are feather dust and Christmas tree worms. Hence, in the present survey, a total of 24 species belonging to 14 genera, 7 orders, and 11 families were identified Three species of Phyllocidae, 8 species of Nereidae, 5 species of Eunicidae, 2 species of Spionidae, 1 species of Opheliidae, Sabellariidae, Terebellidae, Polynoidae, Amphinomidae, and Sabellidae of coral-reef associate polychaetes are so far reported from Great Nicobar Island coastal waters. Fauvel [7] gave about

450 species from the waters in and around India and rightly stated that this was probably half of the total number occurring in these waters. A total of 30 species of polychaetes belong to 8 families and 23 genera. Each species has specific features for the representative family, and all species were recorded for the first time from the Andaman and Nicobar Islands, of which 15 species are new to Indian waters. Prior to the study periods in Great Nicobar Islands, very little polychaete taxonomical study has been reported; the present study clearly highlights the polychaete taxonomical tools of Great Nicobar Island.

5. Conclusion

This chapter concludes the taxonomy status and identification tools of polychaete diversity in Great Nicobar Islands. Polychaeates are one of the best indicator species in marine environment. Coral associated polychaete identification is very difficult to carry out. The study of polychaete taxonomy is a better tool for understanding the conventional taxonomy. In recent trends various molecular tools have been used for identification purpose. In spite of molecular techniques, conventional taxonomy is one of the basic important tools. Taxonomic identification is very dif-ficult in the coral-reef region. This could be solved by re-establishing species names at present regarded as subordinate synonyms; formerly the type or topotype resources were analyzed. Our hope is that the present list may prove useful for such a major reconsideration of this distinctive fauna and that it may encourage regional colleagues to expand our worldwide understanding of the polychaete diversity in Great Nicbar region, This region may very well be the Island ecosytem of the uppermost polychaete diversity in India. The results highlight the importance of the taxonomical keys and evaluate the species information in around Great Nicobar Islands. In many of the previous literature only line drawings were used, but the present study describes the clear illustration of digital snapshots of animal parts.

Acknowledgements

The authors are thankful to the director of CAS in Marine Biology, Faculty of Marine Sciences, Annamalai University, for providing the necessary facilities. The first author (V. S.) thanks to the Ministry of Environment, Forest and Climate Change, New Delhi, for financial support.

Author details

Veeramuthu Sekar[1*], Ramadoss Rajasekaran[2], Srinivasan Balakrishnan[3] and Ramamoorthy Raguraman[4]

1 OMCAR Palk Bay Environmental Education and Research Centre, Tamil Nadu, India

2 Centre of Advanced in Marine Biology, Faculty of Marine Sciences, Annamalai University, Tamil Nadu, India

3 Marine Aquarium and Regional Centre, Zoological Survey of India, Ministry of Environment, Forest and Climate Change, Government of India, Digha, West Bengal

4 National Centre for Sustainable Coastal Management (NCSCM), Ministry of Environment, Forest and Climate Change, Government of India, Chennai, Tamil Nadu, India

*Address all correspondence to: sekarveera15@gmail.com

References

[1] Vecchione C. The central role of systematics in marine biodiversity issues. Oceanography. 1996;**9**(1):44-49

[2] Vecchione M, Mickevich MF, Fauchald K, Collette BB, Williams AB, Munroe TA, et al. Importance of assessing taxonomic adequacy in determining fishing effects on communities. ICES Journal of Marine Science. 2000;**57**:677-681

[3] Eklof J. Taxonomy and Phylogeny of Polychaetes. Intellecta Infolog, Goteborg, Sweden: University of Gothenburg, Department of Zoology; 2010. ISBN: 978-91-628-8092-7

[4] Bilton DT, Paula J, Bishop JDD. Dispersal, genetic differentiation and speciation in estuarine organisms. Estuarine Coastal Shelf Sciences. 2002;**55**:937-952

[5] Fauchald K. Polychaetous annelids of the families Eunicidae, Lumbrineridae, Iphitimidae, Arabellidae, Lysaretidae and Dorvilleidae from western Mexico. Allan Hancock Monograph Marine Biology. 1970;**5**:1-335

[6] Fauvel P. The littoral fauna of Krusadai Island in the Gulf of Mannar. Bulletin of the Madras Government Museum. New Series Natural History Section. 1930;**I**(2):1-72

[7] Fauvel P. Annelida Polychaeta. The Fauna of India Including Pakistan, Ceylon, Burma and Malaya. Allahabad: The Indian Press Ltd; 1953. 507 pp

[8] Day JH. A monograph on the Polychaeta of Southern Africa. Pts. I and II. British Museum Natural History. 1967;**656**:1-878

[9] Fauchald K. The polychaete worms. definition and keys to the orders, families and genera. Natural History Museum Angeles Science Series. 1977;**28**:1-188

[10] Pallas PS. Miscellanea zoological, etc., pp. 72-145. Hagae Comitum. 1766;**VII**:224 pp

[11] Gravier C. Contribution to the study of polychaete annilides Red Sea. Archives du Muséum d'Histoire Naturelle, Paris. 1901;**4**(3):147-268

[12] Parulekar AH. Polychaete from Maharashtra and Goa. Journal of Bombay Natural History Society. 1971;**68**(3):726-749

[13] Soota TD, Rao CAN. On some polychaetes from Andaman and Nicobar islands. Records of Zoological Survey of India. 1977;**73**(1-4):197-210

[14] Rao CAN, Soota TD. On some polychaetes from Gujarat coast. Records of Zoological Survey of India. 1981;**79**(1&2):73-82

[15] Soota TD, Misra A, Chakraborty RK. Polychaete fauna of Gujarat coast. Records of Zoological Survey of India. 1981;**79**(1&2):93-104

[16] Savigny JC. Annelides. In: Lamarck JB, editor. Histoire Naturelle des Animaux Sans Vertebras. 1818. 612 pp

[17] Soota TD, Misra A, Chakraborty RK. Polychaete fauna of Andaman and Nicobar Islands. Records of Zoological Survey of India. 1980;**77**:55-69

[18] Misra A, Chakraborty RK. Polychaetes from Lakshadweep. Fauna of Lakshadweep. State Fauna series. Zoological Survey of India. 1991;**2**:137-165

[19] Grube AE. Annulata Semperiana. Beitrage zur Kenntniss der Anneliden-fauna der Philippinen nach den von

Herrn Prof. Semper mitgebrachten Sammlungen. Mémoires de l'Académie Impériale des Sciences de St. Pétersbourg. 1878;**25**:1-300

[20] Gravier C. Contribution to the study of polychaete annelids. I partie. Archives du Muséum d'Histoire Naturelle. 1900;**3**:137-282

[21] Bergstrom E. Zur Systematik der Polychaeten Familie der Phyllodociden. Zoologiska Bidrag Fran Uppsala. 1914;**3**:37-324

[22] Day JH. Polychaeta from several localities in the Western Indian Ocean. Proceedinds of Zoological Society Londan. 1962;**139**(4):627-656

[23] Tampi PRS, Rangarajan K. Some polychaetous annelids from the andaman waters. Journal of Marine Biological Association of India. 1964;**6**(1):98-123

[24] Marenzeller EV. Sudjapanische annelids. I. Denkschriften der Mathematisch-naturwissenschaftlichen classe der Kaiserliche Akademie der Wissenschaften, Wien. 1879;**41**(2):109-152

[25] Izuka A. The errantiate polychaeta of Japan. Journal of the College of Science, Imperial University, Tokyo. 1912;**30**

[26] Kinberg JGH. Annulata nova. Öfversigt af Königlich Vetenskapsakademiens förhandlingar. 1866;**22**:167-169

[27] Horst R. Contributions towards the knowledge of the Annelida Polychaeta. Notes from the Leyden Museum. 1889;**11**:38-45, 161-186

[28] Southern R. Polychaeta of the Chilka Lake and also of fresh and brackish waters in other parts of the India. Memoirs of the Indian Museum. 1921;**5**(8):563-659

[29] Fauvel P. Polychaeta of Indian Museum, Calcutta. Memory of Indian Museum. 1932;**12**:1-262

[30] Rao CAN. Annelida: Polychaeta. In: Ghosh AK, editor. Fauna of Chilka Lake. Calcutta: Zoological Survey of India; 1995. pp. 319-336

[31] Rao CAN. Polychaete fauna of Mahanadi Estuary, Orissa. Zoological Survey of India, Esturine Ecosystem Series. 1998;**3**:199-209

[32] Grube AE. Bemerkungen uber die Familie der Aphroditeen, (Gruppe Polynoina, Acoeta, Polylepidea). Jahresbericht der Schlesischen Gesellschaft für Vaterländische Kultur. 1876;**53**:46-72

[33] Augener H. Polychaeta. I. Errantia. Die fauna Südwest-Australiens. 1913;**IV**:63-304

[34] Hoagland RA. Polychaetous annelides collected by United States fisheries steamer "albatros" during the Philippines expedition of 1907-1909. Bulletin of the United States National Museum. 1920;**100**(1):603-634

[35] Wilson RS, Glasby CJ. A revision of the *Perinereis nuntia* species group (Polychaeta: Nereididae). Records of the Australian Museum. 1993;**45**(3):253-277

[36] Rajasekaran R. Studies on coral and seagrass associated polychaete of India [Ph.D. thesis]. India: Annamalai University; 2005. 1-65 pp

[37] Ehlers E. Die Borstenwiirmer nach systematischen und anatomischen Untersuchungen dargestellt. Leipzig. 748 pp (pp. 1-268 published in 1864; 1868; pp. 269-748)

[38] Grube AE. Actinien Echinodermen und Wiirmen des Adriatischen und Mittlelmeeres. Konigsberg. 1840. 88 pp

[39] Fauvel P. Polychetes errants. Fauna France. 1923;**5**:1-488

[40] Misra A, Chakraborty RK. Further records of polychaetes from Gujarat coast. Records of Zoological Survey of India. 1983;**81**(1&2):69-75

[41] Grube AE. Annulata Oerstediana. Videnskabelige Meddelelser Dansk Naturhistorisk Forening, Kobenhavn Pt. II., 1857. 158-166 pp

[42] McIntosh WC. Marine Annelids (Polychaeta) of South Africa. Pt. 1 & 2. Marine Investment South Africa. 1904;**3**:17-56, 57-92

[43] Misra A, Chakraborty RK, Soota TD. Fauna of Orissa: Polychaeta. Zoological Survey of India. 1987;**1**:69-89

[44] Savigny JC. Systeme des annelids, principalement de celles des cotes de l'Egypte et la Syrie, etc. Paris. 1820. 128 pp

[45] Crossland C. On the marine fauna of Zanzibar and British East Africa from collection made by Cyril Crossland in the years 1901 and 1902. Polychaeta. Pt. III. Proceedinds of Zoological Society Londan. 1903;**73**(1):169-176

[46] Gravely FH. The littoral fauna of Krusadai Island in the Gulf of Mannar. Chaetopoda. Bulletin of Madras Government Museum (N.S). Natural History Section. 1927;**I**(I):55-86

[47] Delle CS. Memorie sulla storia e notomia degli animali senza vertebre del regno di Napoli. Naples. 1825;**3**:1-232

[48] Peters WC. Uber die Gattung Bdella Savigny, (Limnatus, Moquin-Tandon) und die in Mossambique beobachteten Anneliden. Monatsberichte der Königlichen Preussische Akademie des Wissenschaften zu Berlin. 1854;**1854**:610-614

[49] Day JH. The polychaete fauna of South Africa. Part 4: New species from Natal and Mozambique. Annals of the Natal Museum. 1957;**14**:59-129

[50] Grube AE. Beschreibung neuer oder wenig beakannten von Heron Ehrenberg gesammalter Anneliden aus den Rothen Meeres. Monatsberichte der Königlichen Preussische Akademie des Wissenschaften zu Berlin. 1870;**1870**:484-521

[51] Audouin JV, Milne-Edwards H. Classification des Annelides et descriptions de celles qui habitent les cotes de la France. Annales des Sciences Naturelles. 1833;**27**:187-247

[52] Fauvel P. Polychaeta new Morocco. Bulletin Zoological Society France. 1928;**53**:9-13

[53] Blake JA, Kudenov JD. The Spionidae from South-Eastern Australia and adjacent areas with a revision of the genera. Memoirs of the National Museum of Victoria. 1978;**39**:171-280

[54] Imajima M. Spionidae (Annelida: Polychaeta) from Japan VI. The genera *Malacoceros* and *Rhynchospio*. Bulletin of the National Science Museum, Tokyo, Series A. 1991;**17**(1):5-17

[55] Foster NM. Spionidae of the Gulf of Mexico and the Caribbean Sea. Studies of Fauna Curaçao Caribbean Island. 1971;**36**:1-183

[56] Muller OF. Zoologia Danica Seu Animalium Daniae et Norvegiae rariorum ac minus notorum descriptiones et Historia. Havniae; 1806. 160 pp

[57] Fauvel P. Polychetes sendentaries. Addenda aux Errantes, Archiannelida, Myzoztomaires. Fauna France. 1927;**16**:1-494

[58] Day JH. The Polychaeta of South Africa. Part 3: Sedentary species from cape shores and estuaries. Journal of the Linnean Society of London, Zoology. 1955;**42**:407-452

[59] Rao CAN. Polychaete fauna of the godavari estuary. Zoological Survey of India, Esturine Ecosystem Series. 2001;**4**:21-32

[60] Fauvel P. Annelides Polychaetes de Madagascar, de Djibouti et du Golfe Persique. Archives Zoological Experimental General. 1919;**58**:315-473

[61] Day JH. The polychaete fauna of South Africa. Part I: The intertidal and estuarine Polychaeta of Natal and Mosambique. Annals of the Natal Museum. 1951;**12**(1):1-67

[62] Peters WC. Scientific trip to Mozambique ausgefürt in 1842-1848. Akademie Knowledge Berlin. 1854;**1854**:610-614

[63] Johansson KE. Beitrage zur Kenntniss der Polychaeten-Familien Hermellidae, Sabellidae und Serpulidae. Zoologiska Bidrag Fran Uppsala. 1927;**11**:1-184

[64] Gravier C. Sur les annilides polychetes de la Mer Rouge (Cirratuliens (suite), Mald'aniens, Amphictenians, Terebelliens). Bulletin Museum History Natural, Paris. 1905;**11**:319-326

[65] Hessle C. Zur Kenntniss der terebellomorphen Polychaeten. Zoologiska Bidrag Fran Uppsala. 1917;**5**:39-258

[66] Willey A. Report on the Polychaeta collected by Prof. Herdmann, at Ceylon in 1902. Ceylon Pearl Oyster Fisheries Supplementary Reports. 1905;**4**(30):243-324

[67] Gravier C. Contribution a l'etude des annelids polychetes de la Mer Rouge (suite). Nouvelles Archives du Muséum d'Histoire Naturelle. Paris. 1908;**4**(10):67-168

[68] Rajasekaran R, Fernando OJ. Polychaetes of Andaman and Nicobar Islands. In: Venkataraman K, Raghunathan C, Sivaperuman C. editors. Ecology of Faunal Communities on the Andaman and Nicobar Islands. Berlin, Heidelberg, Germany: Springer; 2012:1-22. DOI: 10.1007/978-3-642-28335-2_1.2012

Chapter 2

Ground Forest Inventory and Assessment of Carbon Stocks in Sierra Leone, West Africa

Stephen Brima Mattia and Sampha Sesay

Abstract

Forest and woodland are renewable natural resources providing basic human necessities. They have the ability to sequester carbon and mitigate climate change. Sustainable forest management is guided by forest mensuration and inventory which include measuring and calculating growth and changes in trees and forests. The objective of the study was to estimate timber resources and carbon stock using simple hand tools in Kasewe and Singamba forests in the southern part of Sierra Leone. All trees with diameter at breast height (DBH) ≥ 10 cm were measured in every plot for DBH, and three trees were measured for height. The correlation between mean wood volume and carbon stock was highly significant. For Kasewe plantation forest, mean wood volume and carbon stock were 151 $m^3\ ha^{-1}$ and 44 t C ha^{-1}, respectively, and for the Singamba natural forest, they were 181 $m^3\ ha^{-1}$ and 82 t C ha^{-1}, respectively. The linear correlation between basal area and volume, DBH and volume and basal area and total biomass was significant for the plantation species tested. Realistic national forest inventory and community forestry are inevitable for sustainable forest management in Sierra Leone.

Keywords: biomass, community forestry, carbon stock, forest mensuration and inventory, sustainable forest management

1. Introduction

Forest and woodland (tree and shrub savannah, parklands and bush fallows [1]) are renewable natural resources providing basic human necessities [2, 3]. Although both ecosystems are wooded habitats where trees predominate [3], the former consists of closed canopy [4, 5] which permits very little sunlight to penetrate to the ground below, while the later has a more open canopy [5] and its sparse woody mid-storey allows more sunlight to reach the ground [4]. They have the ability to sequester carbon and mitigate climate change [6]. Forest ecosystems are mostly viable carbon sinks [6, 7] globally due to net growth in planted trees [7] with the majority of sequestered carbon held in woody biomass [8] but can also be a carbon source when degraded [7]. The rainforest of West Africa, a hotspot of biodiversity, has approximately 9000 species of vascular plant, including 1800 endemic species [8, 9] and an estimated area of 621,705 km^2. This forest area declines every year through anthropogenic activities [1] and natural disasters such as landslides, earthquakes and flooding [10].

Forest resource assessment in relation to timber volume [11–13] and carbon stocks [14, 15] provides information about the status of the productivity of the forest. This assessment is traditionally done through ground forest inventory. Forest assessment is very important for decision-making and policy formulation [11] and establishment of sustainable management plans at both national and international levels.

The objective of the study was to estimate timber resources and carbon stock using simple hand tools in Kasewe and Singamba forests in the southern part of Sierra Leone.

2. Materials and methods

2.1 Sampling design

2.1.1 Method of sampling in Kasewe plantation forest

A systematic sampling design was established for conducting timber inventory in this plantation forest at the age of 14 years. A trunk road (Bo-Freetown highway at Moyamba Junction) passing through the forest served as the baseline.

In the *Gmelina arborea* stand, three transects, 40 m apart and at right angle to the baseline—the Bo-Freetown Highway—were established; and every transect was 75 m long. Two square plots, 30 × 30 m, were demarcated along each transect at an interval of 5 m, making sure that each plot was bisected by its corresponding transect and the first plot was located 5 m away from the baseline. The plots were considered to be representative of the stand [15]. For the purpose of this research, a total of six plots were laid out covering a sampling area of 0.54 ha (**Figure 1**) in the *Gmelina* stand.

This method was replicated in the adjacent *Tectona grandis* stand about 100 m away from the *Gmelina* stand, giving a total of 12 plots. The above sampling design is demonstrated in the forest as shown in **Figure 2**.

2.1.2 Sampling design in Singamba natural forest

Within the Singamba mixed forest, two vegetation communities or ecology types, namely, secondary forest (aged over 5 years after its last farming disturbance) and forest regrowth (resulting from shifting cultivation farming about 2-- 5 years ago), adjacent to each other, were identified for data collection. Systematic sampling was employed for this study area. Circular plots of radius of 10 m were adopted for data collection. These have the advantage of reducing the edge effect in the sample. Using an existing footpath as a baseline, two quadrants, 100 m by 80 m and 100 m by 60 m, respectively, were demarcated; a total of 20 plots, 12 and 8 plots in the respective quadrants, was laid out systematically on transects that were 25 m apart (**Figure 3**) in each ecology type.

2.2 Data collection

2.2.1 Data collection in Kasewe plantation forest

All trees within each plot were measured for diameter at breast height (DBH) at 1.3 m above the ground, and three dominant trees were measured for total height. A minimum of 10 cm DBH [16, 17] was considered for a tree to be enumerated, targeting commercial stems. Tree height was measured using a Suunto hypsometer,

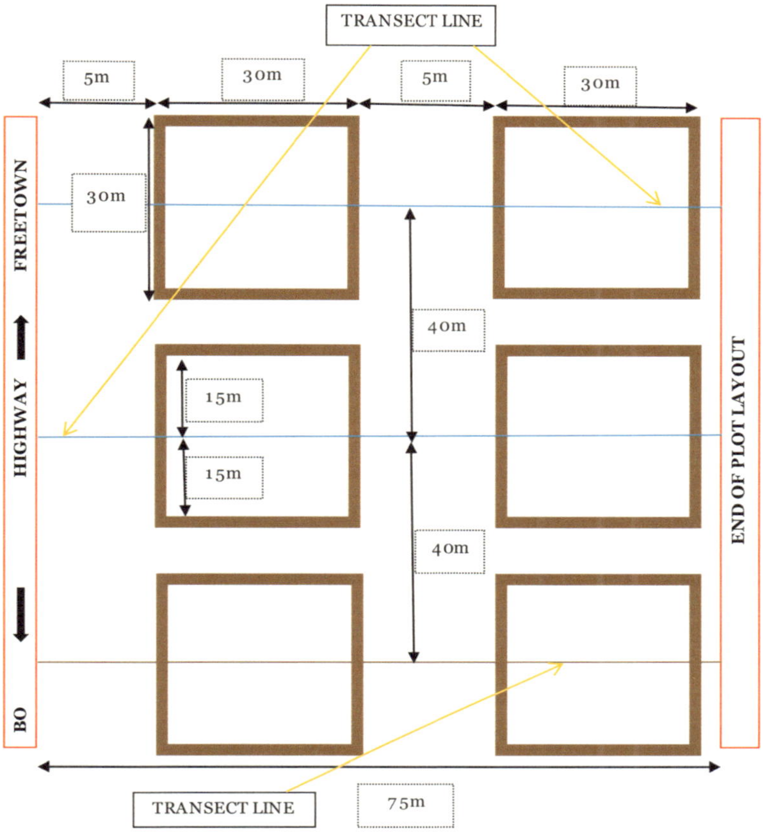

Figure 1.
Plot layout and dimensions in systematic sampling design.

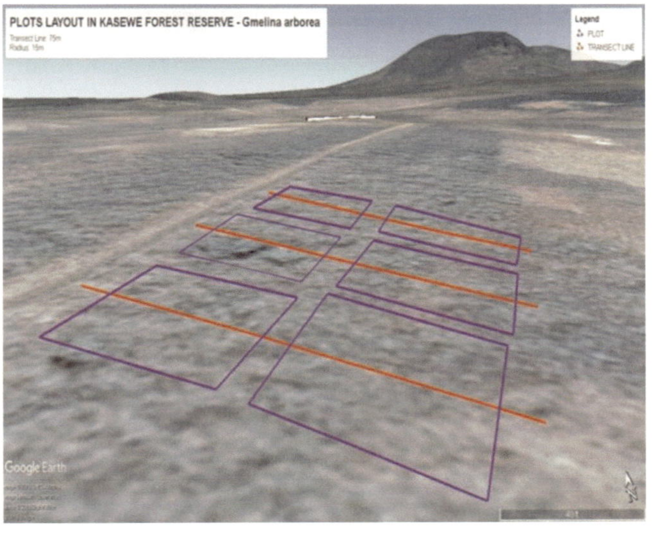

Figure 2.
Photograph of plot layout in Kasewe plantation forest.

and DBH was measured using a diameter tape. A linear function of DBH and height (**Figure 4**) was developed from the data for dominant trees for estimating the height of the remaining trees not measured in the field.

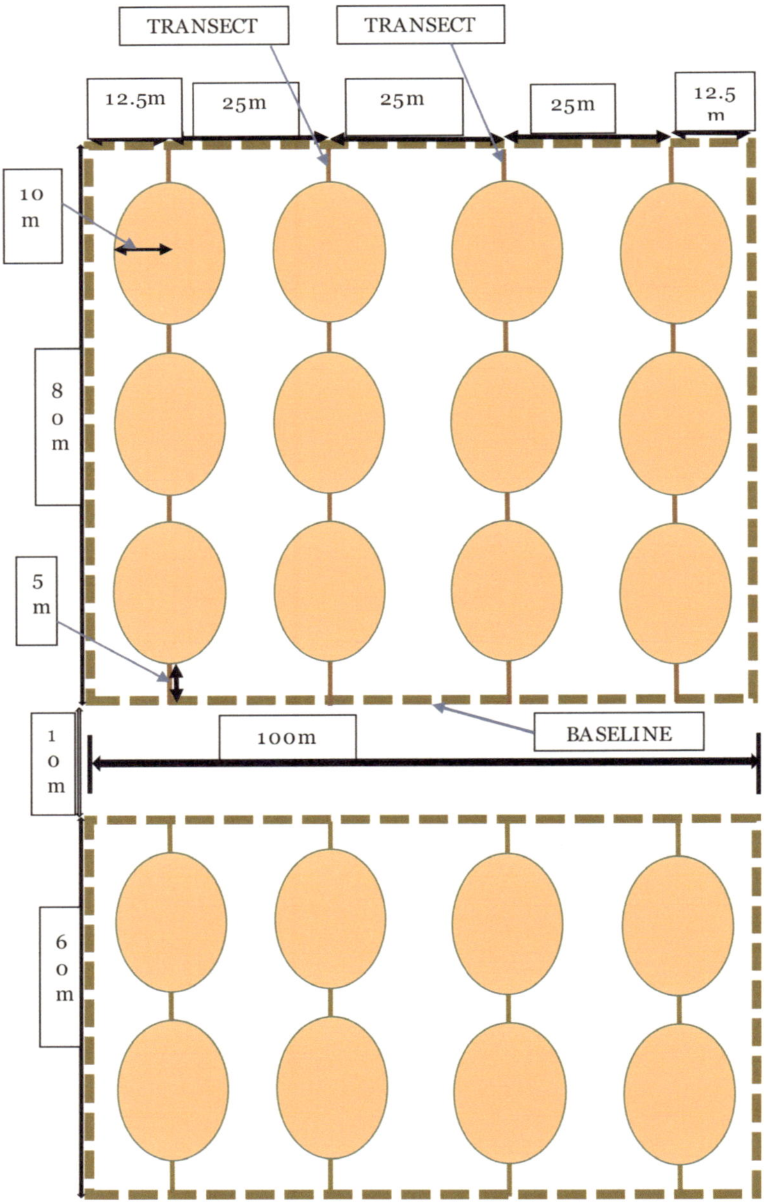

Figure 3.
Plot layout in Singamba natural forest.

Bark thickness of all sample trees in every plot was measured in both the *Gmelina* and *Tectona* stands. In the absence of a Swedish bark gauge, a knife and a ruler were used to measure the bark thickness of the trees in the sample plots. The knife was used to cut a small square portion of the bark at the point of measurement for DBH. This was done carefully, and the bark removed was measured in millimetres using a ruler.

2.2.2 Data collection in Singamba natural forest

In each circular plot located in both secondary forest and forest regrowth (within the natural forest), tree or shrub species of a minimum DBH of 10 cm was

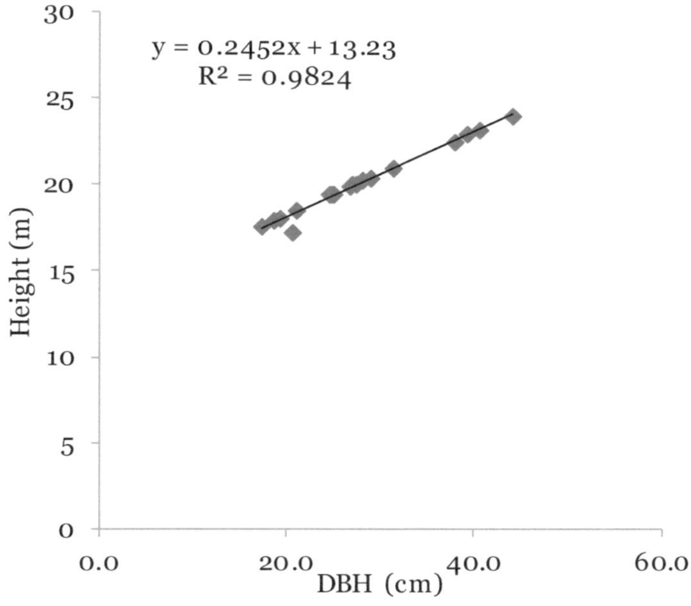

Figure 4.
Linear function for estimating tree height of Gmelina at Kesewe plantation forest. Note: y → tree height (m), x → DBH (cm).

identified by a local tree spotter in the Mende language; this was recorded and later translated to botanical name using Trees of Sierra Leone [18] and further verified from [19]. Diameter measurement was taken for all trees 10 cm and above at 1.3 m above ground level in each plot. The total height of three dominant trees was also measured in every plot.

2.3 Data analysis

2.3.1 Kasewe plantation forest

For the estimation of tree yield (stem count, basal area and volume), biomass and carbon non-harvest techniques [4] were adopted for the following parameters:

- Basal area
- Volume over bark
- Standing biomass
- Carbon stock in standing trees

2.3.1.1 Yield parameters

A linear function was first developed (from the dominant trees) for estimating the height of all the trees not measured for height in the field.

2.3.1.1.1 Stem count

The DBH tally was used to determine stand density for the standing trees [20–22]:

$$N = (1/n)\sum (x_i/a_i) \tag{1}$$

where N is number of stems per ha, n is number of plots, x_i is number of stems in plot and a_i is area of plot i in ha.

2.3.1.1.2 Basal area calculation

The basal area (m^2) of all trees in the sample plots in both the *G. arborea* and *T. grandis* stands were calculated using the formula [23, 24]:

$$G = \sum \left(\sum \pi d_i^2/40{,}000\right)/A \tag{2}$$

where G is basal area per hectare and A and d_i are the total sampling area (ha) and DBH (cm) of stem i, respectively.

2.3.1.1.3 Volume estimation of trees per hectare

The volume (m^3) of all trees in the sample plots in both the *T. grandis* and *G. arborea* stands was estimated using separate predetermined allometric equations, initially in m^3 per tree and then converted to m^3 ha^{-1}. For *G. arborea*, the volume over bark (ob) was estimated by the following volume equation according to Mattia and Dugba [25]:

$$\text{Volume (ob)} : V = 0.24950005 + 0.000018027\left(DBH^2 ht\right) \tag{3}$$

(Note: Eq. (1) is applied best to trees with DBH ≥ 10 cm)
Volume under bark (ob) was estimated from DBH under bark.
For *T. grandis* the volume (ob) was estimated according to [26]:

$$V = 0.0012DBH^{1.9912} \tag{4}$$

where V = total volume over bark in m^3, DBH = tree diameter at breast height, 1.3 m aboveground level in cm and ht = total height in m.

2.3.1.2 Estimation of live tree biomass and carbon stock for Gmelina arborea *stand*

For the purpose of this study, biomass carbon has been considered and studied for only trees of minimum DBH of 10 cm in both natural and plantation forests. The accumulated biomass and carbon contained in the standing trees of *G. arborea* were estimated by individual trees and by plots.

2.3.1.2.1 Aboveground biomass

To estimate the aboveground biomass (AGB), the equation according to Arias [27] was adopted for *Gmelina*, initially in kg per tree:

$$AGB = 0.075 * DBH^{2.4167} \tag{5}$$

Then, it was converted to tonne ha^{-1} (t ha^{-1}) after multiplying by a scaling up factor (SF) [28]: SF = 10,000/NA; NA is the area of single plot in m^2.

$$SF = 10,000/NA = 10,000/900$$

2.3.1.2.2 Belowground biomass

The belowground biomass (BGB) was estimated according to the recommendation of the Intergovernmental Panel for Climate Change (IPCC) [28]:

$$\text{BGB} = \text{AGB} * 0.235, \text{ i.e.}23.5\% \text{ of AGB}. \tag{6}$$

$$\text{Total biomass} = \text{AGB} + \text{BGB in t ha}^{-1} \tag{7}$$

2.3.1.2.3 Carbon stock for Gmelina arborea

Carbon (C) stock was derived from aboveground biomass by assuming that nearly 50% of the biomass is made up by carbon [28–30].

$$\text{C} = \text{Biomass}\left(\text{t ha}^{-1}\right) * 0.47. \tag{8}$$

CO_2 was calculated as follows:

$$\text{CO}_2 = \text{Carbon}\left(\text{t Cha}^{-1}\right) * 44/12. \tag{9}$$

2.3.1.3 Estimation of live tree biomass and carbon for Tectona grandis

The AGB for teak was estimated using a method similar to that for *Gmelina* but adopting the following equation for initial estimate [26]:

$$\text{AGB} = 0.5043 * \text{DBH}^{2.0636} \tag{10}$$

The BGB, total biomass, carbon stock and CO_2 for teak were calculated according to Eqs. (6)–(9), respectively.

2.3.2 Data analysis for Singamba forest

2.3.2.1 Wood production parameters

The quantitative metric data was used to estimate three parameters for wood production: the number of stems ha^{-1} (N), basal area ha^{-1} (G) and wood volume ha^{-1} (V).

2.3.2.1.1 Number of stems ha^{-1}

This was estimated using Eq. (1) (Section 2.3.1.1)

2.3.2.1.2 Basal area ha^{-1}

The formula used was Eq. (2) (Section 2.3.1.1).

2.3.2.1.3 Wood volume ha^{-1}

This was estimated using the formulae according to Eqs. (12) and (13) [23]; a form factor of 0.562 from Mattia and Dugba [25] for natural mangrove forest (comprised of seven mangrove species) in Tanzania was employed:

$$\text{V} = \left\{\sum\left(\sum \text{v}_{\text{ij}}\right)\right\}/\text{na} \tag{11}$$

$$\text{v}_{\text{ij}} = \text{g}_{\text{i}}\ \text{h}_{\text{i}}\ \text{f} \tag{12}$$

where V = average volume ha^{-1} in m^3 estimated from n sample plots, v_{ij} = volume (m^3) of individual standing tree measured on the ith plot, g_i = basal area (m^2) of jth stem in the ith plot, n = number of sample plots, a = area of a single plot in ha, h_i = total height (m) of jth stem and f is form factor, i.e. the coefficient employed to reduce the volume of a cylinder.

2.3.2.2 Estimation of live tree biomass and carbon stock for Singamba rainforest

The following equation was adopted for estimating biomass of the natural forest [31]:

$$\text{AGB} = 0.0547 * \text{DBH}^{2.2148} * \text{Ht}^{0.6131} \tag{13}$$

And the scaling factor applied was 10,000/(314.16).

The calculation of BGB, AGC, BGC, total biomass and total carbon followed the same method as that for Kasewe plantation forest (Section 2.3.1.2; definitions of all terms remain the same as before).

2.3.3 Statistical analysis

The above tree parameters were calculated using Excel software. Means, standard deviations, variances, standard errors and confidence intervals [32, 33] for various wood production parameters were computed. Relationships between basal area and wood volume, between basal area and total biomass and between total biomass and carbon stock, were determined using regression analysis.

3. Results

3.1 Kasewe plantation forest

3.1.1 Wood volume

The mean DBH and height are shown in **Table 1**. The overall mean wood volume of Kasewe plantation forest was 151.06 m^3 ha^{-1}; the mean volumes over bark for *G. arborea* and *T. grandis* were 157.88 and 144.23 m^3 ha^{-1}, respectively (**Table 1**).

The volume of wood for *Gmelina* was recorded by plots (**Figure 5**).

The percentage of volume (ob) of *Tectona* generated by plots is given in **Figure 6**.

Species	Mean DBH (cm)	Mean height (m)	M. BA (m^2 ha^{-1})	Wood volume ob (m^3 ha^{-1})	M. D. DBH (cm)	M. D. ht (m)	Stem count (stem ha^{-1})
G. arborea	29.01	20.34	18.73 (±1.28)	157.88 (±10.42)	43.97	24.01	264
T. grandis	21.56	15.81	9.71 (±0.79)	144.23 (±11.67)	35.4	20.44	240
Plantation	25.38	18.13	14.22	151.06	39.7	22.23	253

Values in the table are means ± CI = confidence interval at 95%. M. BA is mean basal area; M. D. DBH is mean dominant diameter at breast height; M. D. ht is mean dominant height; ob is over bark; ub is under bark.

Table 1.
Wood production parameters for Kasewe plantation forest.

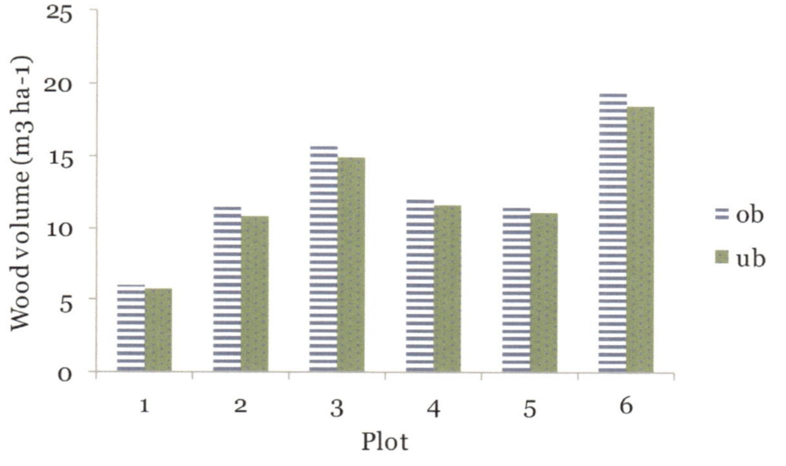

Figure 5.
Volume of Gmelina by plots at Kasewe plantation forest.

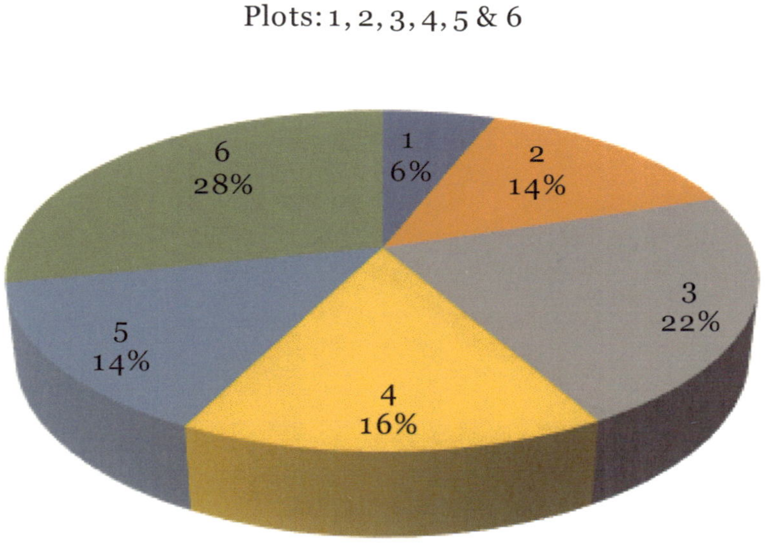

Figure 6.
Percentage volume (ob) of Tectona by plots at Kasewe plantation forest.

3.1.2 Stem count and basal area

The stem density of the plantation forest at Kasewe was 253 stems per ha; 264 and 240 stems per ha were recorded for *Gmelina* and *Tectona* stands, respectively (**Table 1**).

The mean basal area of the Kasewe plantation forest was 14.22 m^2 ha^{-1} (**Table 1**).

3.1.3 Relationship among different growth parameters

The number of *Gmelina* stems enumerated was 143, with a minimum DBH of 13.80 cm and maximum of 52.90 cm; and the tree height ranged from 16.61 to 26.20 m. A positive and linear correlation was found between the wood volume of *G. arborea* and the basal area (**Figure 7**), which implies that the basal area is a good

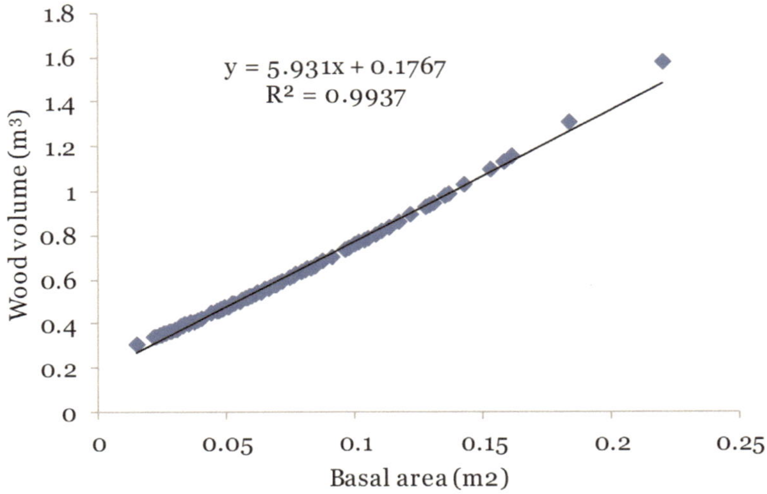

Figure 7.
Linear correlation between basal area and volume of G. arborea standing trees of Kasewe plantation forest.

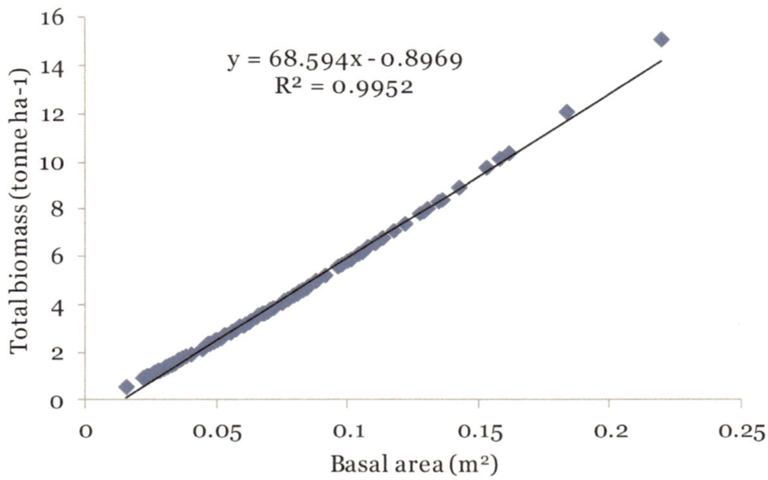

Figure 8.
Linear correlation between basal area and biomass of G. arborea trees at Kasewe plantation forest.

predictor of volume (R^2 = 0.9937). The basal area explains 99% of the variation in volume.

Similar to the volume, the total biomass of trees varied positively and linearly with variation in its basal area (**Figure 8**). The basal area explains slightly higher proportion (i.e. 99.5%) of variation recorded in total biomass than the volume.

The carbon stock of trees of *G. arborea* varied positively and linearly with variation in its total biomass (**Figure 9**). The biomass explains the highest proportion (i.e. 100%) of variation recorded in total carbon stock, denoting perfect and positive correlation.

3.1.4 Accumulated biomass and carbon in Gmelina *trees*

The estimated net biomass of the stems and roots (total biomass) ranges from 51 to 136 tonne ha^{-1} with a mean of 94.26 tonne ha^{-1}; the carbon stock ranges from

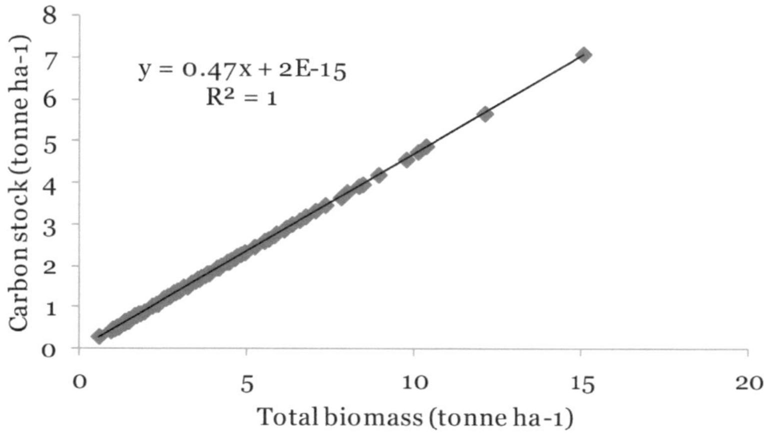

Figure 9.
Perfect and positive linear correlation between total biomass and carbon stock of G. arborea trees at Kasewe plantation forest.

Plots	DBH (cm)	Height (m)	AGB (t ha^{-1})	BGB (t ha^{-1})	Total biomass (t ha^{-1})	Carbon stock (t ha^{-1})	CO_2 (t ha^{-1})
1	26.33	19.69	30.75	7.23	37.97	17.85	52.98
2	29.70	20.51	65.42	15.37	80.80	37.97	112.75
3	32.98	21.32	104.94	24.66	129.60	60.91	180.84
4	30.00	20.59	73.38	17.24	90.62	42.59	126.45
5	26.26	19.67	61.39	14.43	75.82	35.63	105.79
6	28.14	20.13	122.08	28.69	150.77	70.86	210.39
Total	173.41	121.91	457.95	107.60	565.57	265.82	789.21
Mean	**29.0**	**20.34**	**76.33 ±34.30**	**17.94 ±8.06**	**94.26 ±42.36**	**44.30 ±19.91**	**131.53 ±59.11**

Values in the table are mean ± CI = confidence interval at 95%; AGB = aboveground biomass; BGB = belowground biomass; Av = average per plot.

Table 2.
Biomass and carbon stock in standing trees of Gmelina arborea of Kasewe plantation forest.

24 to 64 tonne ha^{-1} with a mean of 19 tonne ha^{-1}; and the CO_2 sequestered ranges from 72 to 190 tonne ha^{-1} with a mean of 131.21 tonne ha^{-1} (**Table 2**).

3.1.5 Accumulated biomass and carbon in teak trees at Kasewe plantation forest

As in the case of *G. arborea*, the accumulated biomass and carbon contained in the standing trees of teak were estimated by individual trees and by plots. The estimated total biomass ranges from 47 to 141 tonne ha^{-1} with a mean of 94 tonne ha^{-1}; the carbon stock ranges from 22 to 66 tonne ha^{-1} with a mean of 44 tonne ha^{-1}; and the CO_2 sequestered ranges from 66 to 197 tonne ha^{-1} with a mean of 131 tonne ha^{-1} (**Table 3**).

3.1.6 Estimation of wood volume, biomass and carbon stock in standing trees of teak of Kasewe plantation forest

Estimation of volume, biomass and carbon stock using DBH and height was highly significant ($p = 0.000 < 0.0001$) according to ANOVA of the regression,

Plot	DBH (cm)	Height (m)	AGB (t ha^{-1})	BGB (t ha^{-1})	Total biomass (t ha^{-1})	Carbon stock (t ha^{-1})	CO_2 (t ha^{-1})
1	19.16	14.86	26.17	6.15	32.31	15.19	45.09
2	21.90	15.95	64.39	15.13	79.52	37.37	110.96
3	24.32	16.90	101.56	23.87	125.43	58.95	175.02
4	22.54	16.20	70.91	16.66	87.58	41.16	122.20
5	19.15	14.86	64.91	15.25	80.17	37.68	111.87
6	21.36	15.73	131.62	30.93	162.55	76.40	226.82
Total	128.43	94.50	459.56	108.0	567.55	266.75	791.97
Mean	**21.41**	**15.75**	**76.59 ±37.87**	**18.00 ±8.90**	**94.59 ±46.77**	**44.46 ±21.98**	**131.99 ±65.27**

Values in the table are mean ± CI = confidence interval at 95%; AGB = aboveground biomass; BGB = belowground biomass; Av = average per plot.

Table 3.
Biomass and carbon stock in standing trees of teak of Kasewe plantation forest.

Vegetation type	Av. DBH (cm)	Av. height (m)	Av. basal area (m^2 ha^{-1})	Av. stocking (stems ha^{-1})	Av. wood volume (m^3 ha^{-1})
Forest regrowth	15.85	12.40	6.33 ±0.07	283	54.94 ±0.72
Secondary forest	21.87	18.45	26.65 ±0.40	637	308.55 ±4.99
Whole forest	20.02	16.59	16.49 ±0.13	920	181.75 ±1.58

Values in the table are mean ± CI = confidence interval at 95%, Av = average per forest ecology.

Table 4.
Wood volume, basal area and stocking for Singamba natural forest.

which implies that variability in volume or biomass was regulated by the independent variables of DBH and height. From the model summary table, R^2 is 0.998 meaning that 99.8% of the variability in carbon stock was accounted for.

3.2 Results for Singamba natural forest

3.2.1 Diameter and height

The overall mean diameter for all the trees enumerated in the whole forest was 20.02 cm; the mean diameter for the secondary forest ecology was 21.87 cm, and the forest regrowth ecology was 15.85 cm. The overall mean height for the entire forest was 16.59 m, 18.45 m for the secondary forest and 12.40 m for the forest regrowth.

3.2.2 Wood volume, basal area and stocking of Singamba natural forest

The mean wood volume is summarized in **Table 4**. The overall wood volume and basal area for the entire forest were 181 and 16 m^2 ha^{-1}, respectively, and the stocking was 920 stems ha^{-1}.

Ecology	Mean DBH (cm)	AGB (t ha^{-1})	BGB (t ha^{-1})	Total biomass (t ha^{-1})	Carbon stock (t ha^{-1})	CO_2 (t ha^{-1})
Forest regrowth	15.85	44.72 (±11.33)	10.51 (±2.66)	55.22 (±13.99)	25.95 (±6.57)	77.06 (±19.52)
Secondary forest	21.87	240.01 (±77.98)	56.42 (±18.32)	296.41 (±96.31)	139.31 (±45.26)	413.62 (±134.39)
Whole forest	20.02	142.36 (±49.12)	38.45 (±11.54)	175.82 (±60.66)	82.63 (±28.51)	245.34 (±84.65)

Values in the table are mean ± CI = confidence interval at 95%; AGB = above ground biomass; BGB = belowground biomass.

Table 5.
Biomass and carbon stock of Singamba natural forest.

Wood production parameters	Plot count	Mean (value ha^{-1})	Variance	Standard error
Basal area (m^2/ha)	40	16.50	0.159	0.063
Volume (m^3/ha)	40	181.75	24.454	0.782
AGB (t/ha)	40	142.31	23590.442	24.285
AGC (t C/ha)	40	66.91	5211.129	11.414
CO_2 (t/ha)	40	245.34	70060.732	41.841
BGB (t/ha)	40	33.43	1302.782	5.707
BGC (t C/ha)	40	15.72	287.785	2.682
Total biomass (t/ha)	40	175.82	35980.733	29.992
Total carbon (t C/ha)	40	82.63	7948.144	14.096

Table 6.
Means and variances for selected wood production parameters in Singamba natural forest.

3.2.3 Accumulated biomass and carbon sequestration in Singamba natural forest

The biomass and carbon stock of the natural forest are presented in **Table 5**. For the whole forest, the estimated biomass ranges from 115 to 236 tonne ha^{-1} with a mean of 60.66 tonne ha^{-1}; the carbon stock ranges from 54 to 111 tonne ha^{-1} with a mean of 28.51 tonne ha^{-1}; and the CO_2 sequestered ranges from 160 to 330 tonne ha^{-1} with a mean of 84.65 tonne ha^{-1}.

3.2.4 Estimation of wood volume, biomass or carbon stock for the entire Singamba forest

ANOVA of the regression showed that estimation of wood volume, biomass or carbon stock using DBH, height or basal area was significant ($p < 0.05$), denoting that variation in volume or biomass was regulated by the independent variables of DBH and height. Statistic is shown in **Table 6**.

4. Discussion

4.1 Stand yield of plantation species

4.1.1 Stand volume

In the present study, it was found that volume and biomass and subsequently the carbon stock increased with growth of DBH and height of the stems of all the plantation species. Various allometric equations for volume and biomass (developed by different researchers) were used to estimate these parameters. Of the two species in Kasewe, *Gmelina arborea* proved better in terms of vertical and horizontal growth with mean DBH and height of 29.0 cm and 20.34 m, respectively, compared to *Tectona grandis* with mean DBH and height of 21.57 cm and 15.81 m, respectively. The results were in agreement with the findings of [12, 13] in Nigeria and [14] in India.

The results showed that the *G. arborea* stand produced a higher yield than the *T. grandis* in Kasewe plantation forest, both species being of the same age. This may be as a result of *Gmelina* being a fast growing species [32] of *Verbenaceae* family. It is a medium to large deciduous tree that attains a height of 35 m or more, with a DBH of over 120 cm in natural stands in tropical and subtropical regions of Asia [30, 31]. In Oyinmo forest (Nigeria), the estimated volume for both *Gmelina* and teak stands ranges from 347.92 to 508.33 $m^3 ha^{-1}$ and from 21.25 to 259.06 $m^3 ha^{-1}$, respectively [13]; similarly, in Oluwa State [12] report a volume of 422.8 $m^3 ha^{-1}$ (10 years) and 1023.4 $m^3 ha^{-1}$ (25 years) for *G. arborea* and 445.8 $m^3 ha^{-1}$ (10 years) and 978.3 $m^3 ha^{-1}$ (25 years) in Omo State in Nigeria for the same species. This high productivity in Nigeria is attributed to the management practices leading to fast growth rate and high stand density [11]. The increase in the yield in their result could be attributed to the proper management of their plantation sites as there were intensive silvicultural treatments adopted, whereas the management of Kasewe plantation forest (14 years) is poor; thinning and clearing are most times not done which have led to the development of undergrowth, thus competing with trees for nutrients, space and water. As reported, plantations receiving various silvicultural treatments such as pruning, irrigation, fertilization and inter-cultivation have better growth and timber productivity than sole trees or poorly managed plantations [33].

4.1.2 Basal area

Basal area is known to be an indication of site potential [23] which gives support to the growth rate of trees in the forest. The result of this research for Kasewe is in agreement with those of other researchers, for example, in Nigeria. A basal area of 17.5–20.0 $m^2 ha^{-1}$ was recorded for *Gmelina* and 9.0–10.0 $m^2 ha^{-1}$ for teak; similar result was also obtained by Adekunle et al. [13] in Nigeria's rainforest ecosystem, and they reported the basal area in *G. arborea* stand to be 46.41 $m^2 ha^{-1}$, while the basal area per hectare ranged between 9.50 and 27.81 $m^2 ha^{-1}$ in the *T. grandis* stand. Onyekwelu et al. [12] obtained mean basal area of 45.6 $m^2 ha^{-1}$ (10 years) and 80.7 $m^2 ha^{-1}$ (25 years) in the *Gmelina* stands at Oluwa, while 44.4 $m^2 ha^{-1}$ (10 years) and 77.8 $m^2 ha^{-1}$ (25 years) were obtained at Omo State, respectively, in Nigeria. The basal areas reported by [2, 13] are larger than those for Kasewe forest which can be as a result of better site quality in those forest stands in Nigeria. If age and management are similar, good sites are capable of supporting more species of trees, higher densities of trees and larger, faster growing trees as compared to poor sites [13].

4.1.3 Stocking

The estimated stem density for Kasewe plantation forest was 253 stems per ha; *Gmelina* (with mean DBH and height of 29.01 cm and 20.34 m, respectively) contributed 52%, while *T. grandis* (with mean DBH and height of 21.56 cm and 15.81 m, respectively) contributed 48%. The former was more better stocked than the latter, not only for its higher proportion of stems, but this could be attributed to

Gmelina stand having larger-sized stems than the teak stand. This resulted to higher volume yield of wood for *Gmelina* stand than that of teak. In other words forest yield depends mainly on the size and age of the stand [23, 31]. By comparing growth variables, *Gmelina* grows faster than *T. grandis* [12–14].

4.1.4 Biomass and carbon stock of plantation stands

As already stated, volume and biomass and subsequently the carbon stock increased with the increase in growth of DBH and height of the stems of all the plantation species. The range of coefficient of determination was found to be 98 and 99% for *Tectona grandis* and *Gmelina arborea*, respectively. This could be explained by the fact that volume and aboveground components of trees were highly dependent upon DBH and height [14].

The means of carbon stock of living trees (stems DBH $\geq$ 10 cm and roots), in the present study, from all plots were 94.26 and 94.59 t ha^{-1} for *Gmelina* and teak, respectively. The carbon stock appears to be the same for the two species since the initial estimation of biomass differed in allometric equations applied. They are, however, efficient in storing carbon. These results are comparable to those obtained by [14] in India—185 and 139 for 10-year-old plantation of *Gmelina* and teak, respectively.

4.2 Natural stands

4.2.1 Forest productivity

The estimated wood volume was 245.24 m^3 ha^{-1}. Within Singamba forest the secondary forest ecology was found to be more productive than the forest regrowth, meaning the former has more usable trees than that of the latter. The basal area was 21.87 m^2 ha^{-1} for Singamba forest. This parameter estimate seems to be relatively high for Singamba forest and can be compared with other tropical areas [31], generally serving as an indication for good site potential for wood production. As suggested before, deforestation was actively reducing the potential wood production of Kasewe plantation forest as a result of intensive sawmill and farming activities, and farming was also evident in Singamba natural forest.

The wood volume and basal area of Singamba forest are in close agreement with that for Gola rainforest [17]. This could be attributed to these two being natural forests which have higher soil nutrient for tree growth from litter fall, decomposition and high rate of microbial activities. Also, they could be less undisturbed than the forests of National Agricultural Training Centre (NATC), Njala University [32] and Kasewe plantation forest in Sierra Leone and are of high stand density and species diversity [32] which can help in increasing growth variables such as height and diameter at breast height which are responsible for the volume and basal area measurement.

The quantitative estimates of current and future wood volume and biomass of timber and other forest products are essential for forest management practices. Thus the information (e.g. mean height, DBH, volume and stem density) derived from the natural stands could be used by forest managers, researchers and policy makers at national and local levels.

4.2.2 Biomass and carbon stocks of the natural stand

The present study has attempted to provide the first estimate of tree biomass and carbon stock in Singamba based on representative field sampling. This has demonstrated how carbon density can vary across a disturbed forest ecosystem [17] with respect to human activities. Patterns of biomass [17] largely reflected past farming history in Singamba forest, demonstrating impact of disturbance on forest biomass, as had been noted for logging impact on Gola forest [17]. Despite human disturbance in the forest in the recent past (forest regrowth), there is clearly an indication (secondary forest) that the Singamba forest still retains substantial carbon stocks and can accumulate further if left undisturbed.

The estimates of C stock for the entire Singamba forest (from all 40 plots) were found to be 82 t C ha^{-1} (**Table 5**), and this included all above- and belowground biomass of living trees over 10 cm DBH but excluded standing dead wood, woody debris and leaf litter [17]. There was variation in C biomass for the plots and ecology, but the higher biomass was found in the secondary forest which seems relatively stable.

The overall C stock for Gola forest was 160 t C ha^{-1} [17], but the overall carbon stock for Singamba was far lower than that of Gola in the present study. Although values of Singamba did not accord well with those for Gola, if disturbance by the forest edge communities is minimized, especially the slash and burn farming; this could improve the carbon stock for Singamba.

5. Conclusion

Timber inventory using simple hand tools is an efficient measure to manage these resources especially for land owners. One hundred percent enumeration of trees in a discrete forest is tedious, time-consuming and not economical. Hence forest sampling is professionally accepted.

Management of forest carbon is a concern across the globe for mitigation of global warming. The two plantation species being studied at Kasewe, *Gmelina arborea* and *Tectona grandis* have high yield of volume and biomass and exhibited significant carbon sequestration.

This chapter enhances foresters and related technicians to be able to estimate and give account of carbon stocks in the forests of West Africa which are undergoing rapid deforestation, degradation and even encroachment [17]. In Sierra Leone, community-based forestry and forest inventory at national level are recommended for sustainable exploitation and conservation of forests.

Author details

Stephen Brima Mattia[1*] and Sampha Sesay[2]

1 Department of Forestry, School of Natural Resources Management, Njala University, Freetown, Sierra Leone

2 Miro Forestry Company, Sierra Leone

*Address all correspondence to: sbmattia@njala.edu.sl

References

[1] West Africa: Forest cover. Available from: http://www.fao.org/3/Y1997E/y1997e0k.htm#TopOfPage. [Accessed: 2015/09/11]

[2] Fore TA. State of the World Forest. Issue Paper. DP 501/87/0101. Rome, Italy: FAO; 2003. 214 p

[3] Laar A, Akça A. Forest Mensuration: Managing Forest Ecosystems. Dordrecht, Netherlands: Springer; 2007. 384 p

[4] What are the differences between forest and woodland? Available from: http://www.quora.com/What-are-the-difference-between-forest-and-woodland/answer/Melody-Burke-3. [Accessed: 2015/9/11]

[5] Global Forest Resources Assessment 2015. Country Report Sierra Leone. Rome: FAO; 2014. 76 p. Available from: http://www.fao.org [Accessed: 2015/9/11]

[6] Karki S, Joshi NR, Udas E, Adhikari MD, Sherpa S, Kotru R, et al. Assessment of forest carbon stock and carbon sequestration rates at the ICIMOD knowledge park in Godavari, Nepal. In: ICIMOD Working Paper 2016/6. Kathmandu: ICIMOD; 2016. p. 52

[7] IPCC Climate Change. Synthesis report. In: Contribution of Working Groups I, II and III to the Fourth Assessment Report of the Intergovernmental Panel on Climate Change (IPCC). Geneva, Switzerland. 2007. 104 p.

[8] Mittermeier RA, Robles GP, Hoffmann M, Pilgrim J, Brooks T, Goettsch Mittermeier C, et al. Hotspots Revisited: Earth's Biologically Richest and Most Endangered Terrestrial Ecoregions. Mexico City, Mexico: University of Chicago Press; 2004

[9] Penner J, Wegmann M, Hillers A, Schmidt M, Rodel MO. A hotspot revisited—A biogeographical analysis of West African amphibians. Diversity and Distributions. 2011;**17**:1077-1088. DOI: 10.1111/j.1472-4642.2011.00801.x

[10] United States Agency for International Development. West Africa Environmental threats and opportunities assessment. In: Final Report. 2013. 119 p

[11] Mercker D, Henning J. Alabama's Treasured Forests. 2011. Available from: http://www.forestry.alabama.gov [Accessed 2015/9/11]

[12] Onyekwelu JC, Mosandl R, Stimm B. Productivity, site evaluation and state of nutrition of *Gmelina arborea* plantations in Oluwa and Omo forest reserves, Nigeria. Forest Ecology and Management. 2013;**229**:214-227

[13] Adekunle VAJ, Alo AA, Adekayode FO. Yields and nutrient pools in soils cultivated with *Tectona grandis* and *Gmelina arborea* in Nigerian rainforest ecosystem. Journal of the Saudi Society of Agricultural Sciences. 2011;**10**: 127-135. Available from: http://www.ksu.edu.sa and www.sciencedirection.com [Accessed: 2014/11/4]

[14] Bohre P, Chaubey OP, Singhal PK. Biomass accumulation and carbon squestration in *Tectona grandis* Linn. f. and *Gmelina arborea* Roxb. International Journal of Bio-Science and Bio-Technology. 2013;**5**(3):153-174

[15] Daouda BO, Aliou S, Léonard AE, Yasmine AJF, Vincent EA, Irénikatché APB, et al. Assessment of organic carbon stock in cashew plantations (*Anacardium occidentale* L.) in Benin (West Africa). International Journal of Agriculture and Environmental Research. 2017;**03**(4): 3601-3625. Available from: http://www.ijaer.in [Accessed: 2019/5/25]

[16] Beets PN, Kimberley MO, Oliver GR, Pearce SH, Graham JD, Brandon A.

Allometric equations for estimating carbon stocks in natural forest in New Zealand. Forest Ecology and Management. 2012;**3**:818-839. DOI: 10.3390/f30308818

[17] Lindsell JA, Klop E. Spatial and temporal variation of carbon stocks in a lowland tropical forest in West Africa. Forest Ecology and Management. 2013; **289**:10-17. Available from: https://www.journals.elsevier.com/forest-ecology-and-management/ [Accessed: 2017/12/4]

[18] Savill PS, Fox JED. Trees of Sierra Leone. 1967. 316 p. Available from: http://www.bodley.ox.ac.uk/users/millsr/isbes/ODLF/TSL.pdf [Accessed: 2019/05/25]

[19] Hawthorne W, Jongkind C. Woody Plants of Western African Forests: A Guide to the Forest Trees, Shrubs and Lianes from Senegal to Ghana. Kew, UK: Royal Botanic Gardens; 2006. 1023 p.

[20] Mattia SB. Species and structural composition of natural mangrove forest case study of Rufiji delta [thesis]. Morogoro, Tanzania: Sokoine University of Agriculture; 1997

[21] Mattia SB, Kargbo S. Species richness and structure of natural Gola Forest, Eastern Province, Sierra Leone. Njala Journal of Agriculture, Science and Technology. 2013;**2**(1):74-84

[22] Mattia SB, Omiyale O, Sesay S. Productivity and tree species richness in mixed forest of National Agricultural Training Centre (NATC), Njala University. Journal of Sustainable Environmental Management. 2015;**7**: 93-104

[23] Philip MS. Measuring Trees and Forests. 2nd ed. Wallingford, UK: CAB International; 1994. 310 p.

[24] Hamilton GJ. Forest Mensuration Handbook. Forestry Commission Booklet No. 39. London, UK: Forestry Commission, Her Majesty's Stationery Office; 1988. 274 p.

[25] Mattia SB, Dugba SA. Allometric equations for volume estimation of *Gmelina arborea* Roxb wood at Singamba forest reserve in Njama, Sierra Leone. Journal of Sustainable Environmental Management. 2015;**7**:1-10

[26] Mwangi JR. Volume and biomass estimation models for *Tectona grandis* grown at Longuza forest plantation [thesis]. Morogoro, Tanzania: Sokoine University of Agriculture; 2015

[27] Arias D, Calvo-Alvarado J, Richter DD, Dohrenbusch A. Productivity, aboveground biomass, nutrient uptake and carbon content in fast-growing tree plantations of native and introduced species in the southern region of Costa Rica. Biomass Bioenergy. 2011;**35**: 1779-1788. Available from: http://www.sciencedirect.com [Accessed: 2015/09/11]

[28] IPCC Guidelines for National Greenhouse Gas Inventories: Agriculture, Forestry, and other Land Use. 2006. Available from: http://www.ipcc-nggip.iges.or.jp [Accessed: 2015/09/12]

[29] Basuki TM, van Laake PE, Skidmore AK, Hussin YA. Allometric equations for estimating the above-ground biomass in tropical lowland Dipterocarp forests. Forest Ecology and Management. 2009;**257**:1684-1694

[30] Hung ND, Giang LT, Tu DN, Hung PT, Lam PT, Khanh NT, et al. Tree allometric equations in evergreen broadleaf and bamboo forests in the North East region, Vietnam. Canadian Journal of Forestry Research. 2012;**16**: 390-394. Available from: www.GlobAllomeTree [Accessed: 2016/05/01]

[31] Hossain MK. *Gmelina arborea*: A popular plantation species in the tropics. Quick guide multipurpose trees from

around the world. In: FACT 99-05. Arkansas, USA: Forest, Farm and Community Tree Network; 1999

[32] Dvorak WS. World View of *Gmelina arborea*: Opporunities and Challenges. Recent Advances with *Gmelina arborea*. Raleigh, USA: CAMCORE, North Carolina State University; 2003. CD-ROM

[33] Dhanda RS, Verma RK. Timber volume and weight tables of farm grown poplar (*Populus deltoides* Bartr. Ex Marsh.) in Punjab (India). Indian Journal of Foresry. 2001;**127**:115-130

Section 2

Impacts of Environmental Factors and Human Activities on Natural Resources

Chapter 3

Physical Vulnerabilities from Wildfires: Flames, Floods, and Debris Flows

Daniel G. Neary and Jackson M. Leonard

Abstract

Humans live in or adjacent to wildland ecosystems that burn periodically and are part of nearly all ecosystems that are in the pyrosphere. There are many hazards posed by wildfire and certain consequences of living in these ecosystems. Most are associated with wildfire, but the increased use of prescribed fire is an issue because of associated risks with human attempts to manage ecological goals. The hazards posed by wildfire involve cultural and economic loss, social disruption, infrastructure damage, human injury and mortality, damage to natural resources, and deterioration in air quality. The economic and human health and safety costs are on the rise due to increasing wildland-urban interface problems and extreme wildfire behavior brought on by climate change. In the past, urban fires have been the greatest threat to human health and safety killing over 100,000 people. World ecosystems have been modified extensively by fire. We live on a "fire planet." With larger human populations and a changing, drying climate, the impact of fire on humans and the hazards faced by our natural and developed world will continue to increase. The increase in wildfire hazards in the twenty-first century will require higher levels of training, increased investments in wildfire personnel and infrastructure, greater wildfire awareness, and improved planning to reduce fire impacts.

Keywords: wildfires, floods, debris flows, hydrologic impacts

1. Introduction

Fire is a dynamic process, predictable but uncertain, that varies over time and landscape space. It has shaped plant communities for as long as vegetation and lightning have existed on earth [1, 2]. Wildland fire covers a spectrum from low-severity, localized prescribed fires, to landscape-level high-severity wildfires. Earth is a fire planet whose terrestrial ecosystems have been modified and impacted by fire since the Carboniferous Period, some 300–350 million years before the present time. In the Holocene Epoch of the past 10,000 years, humans have played a major role in fire spread across the planet. In the present Anthropocene Epoch (11,700 years before the present to the current date) of the twenty-first century, climate change, as well as the burgeoning human population, is now poised to increase the ecosystem hazards of wildland, rangeland, and cropland fire [3, 4].

Fire plays an important function in ecosystem processes [5]. Recycling of carbon (C) and nutrients depends on biological decomposition and fire.

IntechOpen

Figure 1.
High-severity wildfire, Mt. Carmel Fire, Haifa, Israel, 2017 (photo courtesy of Naama Tessler, University of Haifa).

In regions where decay is constrained either by dry or cold climates or by saturated soil conditions, fire has a dominant role in recycling organic matter and maintaining some vegetation types [3]. In warmer, moist climates, decay plays the dominant role in organic matter recycling [6], except in soils that are predominantly water saturated such as hydric soils. Periodic wildfire has an important function in wildland ecosystems. However, the wildfire trend in the past several decades has raised the risk of short- and long-term damage to natural resources, infrastructure, and human health and safety.

The worldwide threat to humans and natural resources from catastrophic wildfire is greater now than at any other time in human history (**Figure 1**). Changes brought on by global warming, land management, and population expansion have resulted in much larger, more destructive wildfire events [7]. This has given rise to greater loss of life and property as well as the occurrence of postfire hazards including flooding, erosion, desertification, and environmental degradation [5, 8]. This chapter will look at the physical hazards and effects of wildfire both during and after conflagrations in wildland ecosystems.

2. Wildfire hazards

The hazards produced by wildfires affect both the biotic and abiotic components of ecosystems. They occur during active fire as well as afterwards. While the destruction produced by combustion is spectacular, the effects after burning has ceased can be subtle or dramatic and often long lasting [3, 5]. Hazards and deleterious effects produced by wildfires during the active combustion phase include vegetation combustion, loss of human and animal life, air quality deterioration, human health deterioration, destruction of personal property, loss of commercial property, and infrastructure damage and destruction. After a wildfire is extinguished, hazards and risks arise from potential flooding, erosion, debris flows, and infrastructure damage. Water supplies and infrastructure, if not damaged during the active fire period, can be at risk during subsequent postfire flood events. Economic losses accrue from declines in tourism, loss of timber and wood fiber resources, and declines in property values. Ecological impacts not assessed by traditional economic valuations include vegetation type conversion, aquatic species loss, decreased water quality, increased stream temperatures, and reduced soil quality. All of these changes are hazards in that they reduce the values and services of ecosystems or threaten human health and safety.

3. Hazards during active fire

3.1 Fire trends

The trend of a growing occurrence of fire around the world brings with it many of the consequences both direct and indirect [9]. This analysis indicated that the future for potential wildfire increases significantly in fire-prone regions of North America, South America, central Asia, southern Europe, southern Africa, and Australia [9]. Fire potential is projected to increase in these regions, from currently low to future moderate potential or from moderate to high potential. The increased fire risk is driven by climate warming in North and South America and Australia, and by the combination of temperature increases and desertification in the other regions. The analysis in Ref. [9] indicates that future increases in wildfire trends will require substantial investment of financial resources and management actions for wildfire disaster prevention and recovery.

In a discussion to the contrary [10], the argument is made that there is evidence of reduced fire worldwide today than centuries ago. Regarding fire severity, limited data are available. They indicate evidence of little change in the western USA and declines in the area of high-severity fire compared to eighteenth and nineteenth century conditions. The authors argue that direct fatalities from fire and economic losses also show no clear trends over the past 30 years [10]. Trends in indirect impacts are insufficiently quantified to be examined in any significant degree.

On the other hand, an analysis of large wildfire trends in the western USA reported a significant increase in fire numbers and area burned [11]. This was particularly true in southern mountain regions with drought. The reported increase of wildland fires in these areas has amounted to 355 km^2 $yr.^{-1}$. An analysis of wildfire in Russia demonstrated an acceleration of wildfire in the twenty-first century as a result of climate change [12]. Trends in wildfire on US Forest Service lands from 1970 to 2002 were examined in a 2005 paper in the Journal of Forestry [13]. Authors reported that the number of large fires has more than doubled over this period and the area burned has increased fourfold. The number of fires and area burned by wildfires in eastern Spain from 1941 to 1994 documented increasing fire activity in southern Europe [14]. They reported that even during this time period the areas and numbers of fires were increasing significantly and were associated with high fire hazard indices.

Wildfire appears to be on the increase globally but not uniformly. Drought and elevated temperatures are major factors contributing to wildfires and the hazards they pose to natural ecosystems and humans. Wildfire sizes and severity thus have the potential to present significant hazards to human health and safety and infrastructure in the twenty-first century [5].

3.2 Vegetation impacts

3.2.1 Hazard

The immediate and most obvious hazard of wildfire is the effect on vegetation. Impacts of wildfire on vegetation vary greatly, not only by vegetation type but also by the severity of the fire. Grassland vegetation in general is thought to be fire resilient, burning often and regrowing quickly after a fire event [15]. Some mixed conifer stands on the other hand have historically burned very infrequently and can take centuries to return to a climax state after a severe wildfire event [3]. The overall trend however is that areas that have been prone to burn in the past are now burning more frequently and at higher severity due to climate change [16]. Areas thought to rarely burn such as tropical systems or be incapable of burning such as permafrost are now undergoing changes that result in more frequent occurrences of fire [17, 18].

3.2.2 Fire regime

The general character of fire that occurs within a particular vegetation type or ecosystem across long successional time frames, typically centuries, is defined as the characteristic fire regime [3]. The fire regime describes the typical fire severity that occurs and the hazard it presents to humans and wildlife. But it is recognized that, on occasion, fires of greater or lesser severity also occur within a vegetation type. For example, a stand-replacing crown fire is usually seen in long fire-return-interval forests (**Figure 2**). The fire regime concept is useful for comparing the relative role of fire between ecosystems, describing the degree of departure from historical conditions, and assessing the relative hazards of wildfires [19]. The development of fire regime classifications has been based on fire characteristics, effects, and combinations of factors including fire frequency, periodicity, intensity, size, pattern, season, depth of burn, and severity [15, 20]. There are four main fire regimes: understory, stand replacement, mixed, and nonfire. The understory and nonfire regimes are normally not important for understanding fire hazard.

The stand replacement regime fires are lethal to most of the dominant aboveground vegetation. Approximately 80% or more of the aboveground dominant vegetation is either consumed or dies as a result of fire, substantially changing the aboveground vegetative structure and creating substantial hazards. This regime applies to fire-susceptible forests and woodlands, shrublands, and grasslands.

The mixed regime severity of fires varies between nonlethal understory and lethal stand replacement fires with the variation occurring in space or time. First, spatial variability occurs when fire severity varies, producing a spectrum from understory burning to stand replacement within an individual fire. This results from small-scale changes in the fire environment (fuels, terrain, or weather) and random changes in plume dynamics. Within a single fire, stand replacement can occur with the peak intensity at the head of the fire, while a nonlethal fire occurs on the flanks. These changes create gaps in the canopy and small- to medium-sized

Figure 2.
Stand replacement wildfire, 2002 Rodeo-Chediski Fire, Apache-Sitgreaves National Forest, USA (photo courtesy of Dr. Peter Ffolliott, University of Arizona).

openings. The result is a fine pattern of young, older, and multiple-aged vegetation patches. This type of fire regime commonly occurs in some ecosystems because of fluctuations in the fire environment [3, 21]. For example, complex terrain favors mixed-severity fires because fuel moisture and wind vary on small spatial scales. Secondly, temporal variation in fire severity occurs when individual fires alternate over time between low-intensity surface fires and high-severity stand replacement fires, resulting in a variable fire regime [15, 21]. Temporal variability also occurs when periodic cool-moist climate cycles are followed by warm-dry periods leading to cyclic (in other words, multiple decade-level) changes in the role of fire in ecosystem dynamics and human hazards. For example, in an upland forest, reduced fire occurrence during the cool-moist cycle leads to increased stand density and fuel buildup. Fires that occur during the transition between cool-moist and warm-dry periods can be expected to be more severe and have long-lasting effects on vegetation dynamics [22].

3.2.3 Fire severity

The commonly accepted term for describing the ecological, hydrological, and geological effects of a specific fire is fire severity. This term describes the magnitude of the disturbance and, therefore, reflects the degree of change in ecosystem components. Fire affects both the aboveground and belowground components of ecosystems due to energy pulses aboveground and heat pulse transferred downward into the soil. It reflects the amount of energy (heat) that is released by a fire that ultimately affects natural resources and their functions, and human infrastructure. It reflects the amount of energy (heat) that is released by a fire that ultimately affects resource responses. Fire severity is largely dependent upon the nature of the fuels available for burning, and the characteristics of combustion that occur when these fuels are burned [3, 7].

3.2.4 Fire intensity versus fire severity

Although the literature historically contains confusion between the terms fire intensity and fire severity, a fairly consistent distinction between the two terms has been emerging in recent years. Fire managers trained in fire behavior prediction systems use the term fire intensity in a strict thermodynamic sense to describe the rate of energy released [23]. Fire intensity is concerned mainly with the rate of aboveground fuel consumption and, therefore, the energy release rate [24]. The faster a given quantity of fuel burns, the greater the intensity, the higher the severity, the greater the energy release, and the shorter the duration [25]. Fire intensity is not necessarily related to the total amount of energy produced during the burning process. Most energy released by flaming combustion of aboveground fuels is not transmitted downward. For example, Ref. [26] found that only about 5% of the heat released by a surface fire was transmitted into the ground during Australian bushfires. Therefore, fire intensity is not necessarily a good measure of the amount of energy transmitted downward into the soil, or the associated changes that occur in physical, chemical, and biological properties of the soil. For example, it is possible that a high-intensity and fast-moving crown fire will consume little of the surface litter because only a small amount of the energy released during the combustion of fuels is transferred downward to the litter surface [27]. In this case, the surface litter is blackened (charred) but not consumed. In the extreme, examples have been reported in Australia, Alaska, and North Carolina where fast-spreading crown fires did not even scorch all of the surface fuels [7]. However, if the fire also consumes substantial surface and ground fuels, the residence time on a site is greater, and more energy is transmitted into the soil. In such cases, a "white ash" or "red ash" layer is often the only postfire material left on the soil surface [27] (**Figure 3**). Because one can rarely measure the actual energy release of a fire, the term fire intensity can have limited practical application when evaluating ecosystem responses to fire. Increasingly, the term fire severity is used to describe the effects of fire on the different ecosystem components and human resources [3].

3.3 Loss of life

Fires have been major hazards for humans for many centuries. With the development of large cities, fire became a significant risk to infrastructure and human life. The lack of organized and trained fire-fighting resources was a big factor in some of the more notorious urban fires. Rome burned in A.D. 64 during windy conditions from a fire that escaped from the Circus Maximus [28]. Of the city's 14 districts, only 4 escaped fire damage. Deaths numbered in the thousands. An urban fire in Tokyo in 1657 destroyed 70% of the city and killed 100,000 inhabitants. Moscow burned during the French invasion in 1812 killing 55,000.

Wildfire in forests became a hazard factor in urban fires in the nineteenth century. The Miramichi Fire in Canada in 1825 burned 2 million ha of land and resulted in the death of 160–300 people. It was fueled by drought and spread at a rate of 1.6 km min^{-1}. The real toll was unknown and could be much higher (3000) due to inaccurate accounts of persons in the rural area [29]. Seven towns were severely damaged or destroyed. The Peshtigo Fire of 1871 burned over 250,000 ha of Wisconsin and Michigan [28]. Sixteen communities were destroyed with a loss of 1150 lives.

Although human mortality rates associated with wildfires have declined in the twentieth century, wildfires continue to exact a toll on human lives because of the increase in area burned and the numbers of large fires [13]. Wildfire fatalities from 1910 to 2017 resulted in a cumulative toll of 1128 deaths for the USA [30]. Most fire years had human losses of less than 10 per year (**Table 1**). Of the yearly fatalities over 20 per year, 67% have occurred since 1990. Most wildfire-related deaths are caused by vehicle accidents, airplane crashes, and medical incidents. The exceptions involved fatalities in fire crews (1910, 1933, 1994, 2003, and 2013). Risks and incidents from wildfires that have spread into urban areas have been on the increase in

Figure 3.
Red and white ash deposits on high-severity burn areas after the 2006 Brins Fire, Coconino National Forest, Arizona (photo by Daniel G. Neary, Rocky Mountain Research Station, USDA Forest Service).

Fatality grouping	Number per grouping	Percentage
0	3	1.3
1–4	13	16.7
5–9	18	23.1
10–14	20	25.7
15–19	11	14.1
20–24	7	11.5
>25	6	7.6

Table 1.
USA wildfire-related fatalities per year 1929–2017 by grouping (National Interagency Fire Center 2019).

the twenty-first century due to population expansion into wildland-urban interface areas, increased wildfire area coverage, greater numbers and size of wildfires, and higher fire severity [5]. Consequently, urban fatalities from wildfire incursions into urban areas have increased since 2017.

Australia suffered high human fatalities from the Black Saturday Kilmore East Fire in Victoria in 2009 [31]. Over 450,000 ha of forest and native bush burned in February of 2009 due to drought conditions and gale force winds. Speeds of 46–68 km $hr.^{-1}$ with gusts to 91 km $hr.^{-1}$ from hot air originating in the deserts of central Australia drove fire spreads of 68–153 m min^{-1}. Spot fires developed 5–33 km ahead of the main fire front. The 173 human fatalities occurred mainly among the local rural population due to the rapid fire spread and insufficient time to evacuate the wildfire-threatened areas. At one point, the fires consumed 100,000 ha in <12 hours. Wildfires of this size and severity are extremely hazardous and almost impossible to comprehend.

In 2017, Portugal experienced its most deadly fire season on record losing at least 66 people to catastrophic summer wildfires. The following year, wildfires in Greece damaged over 2000 homes and killed at least 100 people. Although nationally deaths due to wildfires are on the decline, record-breaking wildfires in northern California in 2017–2018 produced substantial increases in deaths, mostly civilians [32]. A total of 8527 fires burned an area of 766,439 ha and resulted in 102 fire-fighter and civilian deaths.

3.4 Economic losses

In the summer of 2018, the Camp Fire in Northern California burned 62,053 ha and destroyed 18,804 structures including the entire town of Paradise, California. In total, the fire caused $16.5 billion in damages with over a quarter of those damages uninsured [33]. It was the costliest single natural disaster in the world to that point and caused the bankruptcy of a major utility provider, the Pacific Gas and Electric Company, which was held responsible for starting the fire due to faulty equipment.

Unfortunately, it is part of a trend in California, driven mostly by climate change, of increasing destruction and cost of seasonal wildfires. Just the previous year (2017), in December, the Thomas Fire destroyed at least 1063 structures at a cost of $2.2 billion in damages [34] and was preceded by only a couple of months by a complex of fires in the northern part of the state, which destroyed at least 8900 structures and cost in excess of $14.5 billion in damages [35].

Similar trends are being seen around the world. In 2017, Portugal experienced its most deadly and expensive fire season on record due to catastrophic summer wildfires. The 2018 wildfires in Greece suffered through what was considered to be one of the worst fire events in Europe in over a century. Canada set successive records in area burned with 1,216,053 ha 2017 and 1,298,450 ha 2018, losing at least 305 and 50 structures in those respective years [36].

Common factors in these events include months of below-average precipitation followed by untimely ignitions, both natural and anthropogenic and wind events that caused fires to spread in a dramatic fashion. The speed and ferocity with which these fires burned were commonly described as "unheard of" in the past and in many cases completely uncontrollable. The only choice of fire managers at the time was to stand-down and wait for conditions to improve. Unfortunately, this predicament appears to be a hazard becoming more common worldwide.

Fire events, particularly in California, USA, where dense population areas border highly fire-prone wildland areas have seen staggering losses as described above. A study conducted by the U.S. Department of the Interior in 2016 estimated that total "costs," which includes preparedness, mitigation, and suppression, as well as "losses," which includes both direct (e.g., deaths, structure loss, timber loss, etc.) and indirect (e.g., property devaluation, supply chain disruption, evacuation costs, etc.) of wildfire within the USA range from $71.1 to $347.8 billion annually [32]. Estimates like these continue the long debate of who should pay for natural disaster losses in an era of global warming as they become more expensive and what should the future costs be to insure assets in fire-prone areas? These are difficult and complex questions to answer and are made even more urgent in an era where losses seem to be compounded every year.

3.5 Air quality

Another immediate effect of fire is the release of gases and particulate pollutants by the combustion of biomass and soil organic matter. Air quality in large-scale airsheds can be degraded during and following fires [37]. Among the pollutants emitted, the release of fine particulate matter and ozone (O_3) can have particularly deleterious effects on human health, which can be exacerbated when smoke from wildfires affect large population centers. Unfortunately, our understanding of the hazard that large-scale wildfires have on air quality is lacking and current estimates of emissions and impacts may be significantly underestimated [38].

Wildfires can cause both short- and long-term air quality impacts that are usually viewed as negative effects on environmental quality (**Figure 4**). Scientific information about air pollution from wildfires is motivated by government policies to restore the role of fire in ecosystems, to improve air quality, to protect human health, and to minimize emissions of greenhouse gases that are driving climate change [37]. Managing both fire and air quality to the standards set by national and regional governments requires sophisticated scientific knowledge of fire-related air pollution, a delicate management balancing act, and comprehensive educational outreach to both the public and government officials. The three main components of wildland fire and air quality are air resource, scale of impact, and fire management. Air resource includes such factors as smoke source, ambient air quality, and effects on receptors. Scales at which air quality is affected by wildland fires range from site and event to regional and global. Since wildland fire is a pervasive global, regional, and local phenomenon (**Figure 5**), air quality issues and interactions are inter-regional, transnational, and global. Fire management factors that are involved in air quality include planning, operations, and monitoring [39].

National and international air quality standards are set by legislative acts or agency regulations to protect the human population of negative health effects of fire-derived air pollutants [40, 41]. For most of the twentieth century, smoke emissions from prescribed fires were treated as human-caused, while wildfires

Figure 4.
Smoke plume from the Schultz fire, June 2002, Coconino National Forest, Arizona (photo courtesy of USDA Forest Service, Peaks Ranger District, Coconino National Forest).

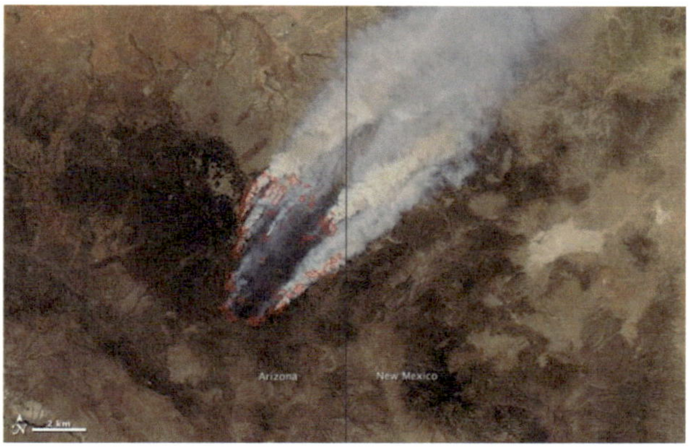

Figure 5.
Regional air quality impacts from smoke generated by the Wallow Fire, 2011, Arizona, USA (image courtesy of MODIS web, U.S. National Aeronautics and Space Administration).

were considered to be natural [37]. Policy debates have blurred the distinct separation between the two types of fires since some lightening starts are managed as prescribed natural fires for ecosystem restoration and fuel reduction purposes, and some wildfires have human ignition sources and burn in fuel loads made unnaturally high by human activity or the lack of management.

Some of the key pollutants targeted in air quality regulations include PM10 (particulate matter <10 μm in diameter), PM2.5 (particulate matter <2.5 μm in diameter) total suspended particulates, sulfur dioxide (SO_2), nitrogen dioxide (NO_2), carbon monoxide (CO), ozone (O_3), and lead and other heavy metals. The amounts and types of pollutants released by fires are affected by area burned, fuel characteristics prior to combustions, fire behavior, combustion stages, level of fuel consumption, and source strength [37]. Wildfires occur as episodic events that can threaten public health, cause smoke damage to buildings, and disrupt public activities [42]. Particulate concentrations rarely affect large city's air quality, but they can rise to harmful levels (e.g., 600 $\mu g\ m^{-3}$) in smaller communities located in forested regions. In some regions, wildfire smoke is the main cause of visibility reductions.

Although the public can be exposed to and become affected by wildland smoke and its constituents, the main concern is for firefighters and fire managers. Anyone who has been involved in wildfire suppression or prescribed fire management understands this. Unlike structural firefighters who utilize PBAs (personal breathing apparatus), wildland fire fighters at best have dust masks that reduce exposure to dust and large particulates but not small particulates and gases. Many data gaps exist in the understanding of human health hazards of wildland fire suppression and management [43].

The individuals whose health is most at risk include those with cardiopulmonary diseases and the elderly. However, normally healthy individuals, such as firefighters, are at increased risk of developing cardiopulmonary disease over the long term. Effects of PM10 and PM2.5 particulates, dust-borne silica, aldehydes, carbon monoxide, polyaromatic hydrocarbons, ozone, and heavy metals are poorly understood. The temporary nature of wildland fire personnel assignments make compilation of long-term health data difficult or impossible to achieve. Permanent fire personnel can be adequately assessed and monitored, but the bulk of wildland fire personnel cannot be properly evaluated.

4. Postfire hazards

4.1 Flooding and debris flows

In many cases, the greatest hazard posed by wildfires occurs in the postfire period when flooding events, made worse by the loss of vegetation, create debris flows (**Figure 6**). These catastrophic events often result in property and infrastructure destruction and in some cases loss of life [3, 7]. Debris flows typically occur in areas with steep topography after being subjected to wetting rains, which mobilize soil, rock, and other debris into a concrete-like torrent that moves downslope toward low-lying areas. These flows tend to have immense force due to the speed in which they move and can cause total destruction of objects in their path and contribute to human mortality. For example, it has been estimated based on insurance claims following the Thomas Fire southern California in 2017 that postfire damage assessments were mostly related to massive debris flows that originated in the burned area. The economic cost of these debris flows exceeded $1.8 billion [34].

While these events can be highly destructive and very costly, they can also be somewhat mitigated through prefire planning and zoning regulations as well as adequate infrastructure. The problem is that often the size of flooding events

Figure 6.
Flood flows in an urbanized area below the 2010 Schultz Fire in Arizona, USA (photo by Daniel G. Neary, Rocky Mountain Research Station, USDA Forest Service).

following wildfire can fall into a once in a century or even a millennia event making the cost justification for accommodating such an event beforehand challenging. However, as these events begin to become more common and costs begin to escalate, the argument for increased preparation must be considered.

Take for example the Schultz Fire, which occurred just outside of Flagstaff, Arizona, USA, in 2010. The fire burned on steep slopes within the Coconino National Forest immediately adjacent to subdivisions located in the valley below. Summer rainfall events following the fire initiated massive flooding and debris flows into the area. Fortunately, there was only one flood-related mortality. While estimates of the costs related directly to the fire suppression were around $9,460,909, the cost of the response to the flood was nearly twice that at $16,470,682. However, both these costs were outdone by the nearly $33,172,803 that was invested in infrastructure over the following 4 years needed to mitigate future flood risk. The financial analysis published on this event [44] in 2013 also pointed out that the cost estimates were only for official expenditures by government agencies and local utilities. The loss in property devaluation, infrastructure damage, increased insurance premiums, and other associated costs totaled more than $60 million in additional losses, making the argument for increased spending on hazard mitigation valid. The economic hazards of the fire were 10 times the funds expended to suppress the Schultz Fire. And this accounting did not include the value of lost or damaged natural resources.

4.2 Water quality

Landscape scale fire events can have profound influence on elements of water quality including increasing turbidity, temperature, and contaminants sometimes for many years following the fire [45–49]. One study near Denver, Colorado, found that average spring and summer water temperatures increased by 5–6°C and that nitrate concentrations increased over 100 times greater than typical stream concentrations following the Hayman Fire in 2002. In addition, summer storms continued to mobilize sediment and create surface runoff corresponding to spikes in nutrient concentration and turbidity for years following the fire event [50].

Ecologically, flooding events following a wildfire can be catastrophic on aquatic communities. This is due primarily to the depletion of oxygen and the increase in turbidity in ash-laden debris flows (**Figure 7**). The two biggest factors affecting long-term recovery and health of aquatic habitats impacted by fire are physical channel stability and water temperature [51]. Loss of streamside vegetation due to fire and instability or changes in physical habitat due to flooding can diminish aquatic habitats for decades. The timing and severity of flooding events are directly related to preceding fire incident. Typically, low order or headwater streams are more susceptible to vegetation changes and flooding than higher order streams; however, depending on the magnitude of input, even larger rivers and reservoirs can be subjected to diminished water quality and loss of aquatic species due to ash-laden flow inputs.

4.3 Ecological changes

The increase in scope and scale of wildfire worldwide tends to have a more intrinsic effect on ecosystem function, affecting qualities that are not always measureable in economic terms. Degradation of soil [8] and water resources [3, 5] along with landscape scale changes in vegetation [51] has the ability to shape ecosystems for decades if not centuries [52]. These cascading effects are becoming selective for plant and animal species, which are pioneer species at first and later are disturbance oriented as these

Figure 7.
Post-fire runoff with high concentrations of sediment, ash, and charcoal, Rodeo-Chediski Fire, Apache-Sitgreaves National Forest, Arizona, 2002 (photo by Daniel G. Neary, Rocky Mountain Research Station, USDA Forest Service).

systems begin the slow process of recovery, often punctuated by reoccurring disturbance events such as flooding or even subsequent fire events. At relatively small scales, the input of fire, even high-severity fire, can introduce heterogeneity into a landscape that can be beneficial to the ecosystem as a whole, creating niches and freeing up resources for new species to establish in an area. However, there is a size threshold that once crossed starts to become an impediment to recovery and results in long-term loss of habitat suitability for specific species. For example, the loss of seed sources both in the soil bank and from mature plants for obligate seed species can have a limiting effect on the recolonization and distribution of many long-lived conifer species [53]. Similarly, the impact from flooding events on fragmented streams due to anthropogenic or natural barriers may make the recolonization of some aquatic species impossible and result in permanent extirpation [54]. In these cases, wildfire begins to act on a genetic level to influence the long-term stability and ecosystem function of an area. This poses a serious environmental hazard due to the permanent loss of important species in an ecosystem and increasing the risk of desertification [8].

5. Summary and conclusions

Humans live in or adjacent to wildland ecosystems that burn periodically and are part of nearly all ecosystems that are in the pyrosphere. There are many hazards posed by wildfire and certain consequences of living in these ecosystems. Most are associated with wildfire but the increased use of prescribed fire is an issue because of associated risks with human attempts to manage ecological goals. The economic and social consequences of wildfire have been discussed by a number of authors [3, 5, 7, 42]. These consequences involve cultural and economic loss, social disruption, infrastructure damage, human injury and mortality, damage to natural resources, and deterioration in air quality. The economic and human health and safety costs are on the rise due to increasing wildland-urban interface problems and extreme wildfire behavior brought on by climate change. In the past, urban fires have been the greatest threat to human health and safety killing over 100,000 people.

With modern fire control organizations in cities, the greatest hazard has shifted to wildlands. The Miramichi Fire in Canada's eastern woodlands in 1825 may have killed 3000. In the USA, the most devastating wildland wildfire known was the

Peshtigo Fire of 1871 that killed over 1150 people. Recent wildfires in Australia in 2009 and California in 2017 and 2018 claimed up to 270 lives in a single fire event in each country. The increasing development of the wildland-urban interface in the USA and other countries is raising the risks that a similar fatal event could occur in the future. Large fatalities due to wildfire hazards may be a thing of the past, but frequent deaths such as those in Australia in 2009 may tally up to greater numbers. In addition, the economic hazards of wildfires are growing. The large amounts of funds needed to suppress large wildfires are a small fraction of the total economic damage. Nationally, in the USA, fire suppression, collateral infrastructure damage, urban destruction, and other wildfire mitigation efforts exceed the total management budgets of the state and federal agencies.

World ecosystems have been modified extensively by fire. We live on a "fire planet" [1, 2, 42]. With larger human populations and a changing, drying climate, the impact of fire on humans and the hazards faced by our natural and developed world will continue to increase. The increase in wildfire hazards in the twenty-first century will require higher levels of training, increased investments in wildfire personnel and infrastructure, greater wildfire awareness, and improved planning to reduce fire impacts.

Acknowledgements

The authors would like to thank the Rocky Mountain Research Station, Air-Water-Aquatic Environments Research Program, and the Program Manager, Frank McCormick, for support of this effort.

Conflict of interest

There are no "Conflicts of Interest" associated with this paper. It was produced by US Forest Service employees during normal work hours and on appropriated funding.

Author details

Daniel G. Neary* and Jackson M. Leonard
USDA Forest Service, Rocky Mountain Research Station, Air, Water, Aquatic Environments Program, Flagstaff, Arizona, USA

*Address all correspondence to: dan.neary@usda.gov

References

[1] Pyne SJ, Andrews PL, Laven RD. Introduction to Wildland Fire. New York: John Wiley & Sons; 1996. 769 p

[2] Scott AC. The pre-quaternary history of fire. Palaeogeography, Palaeoclimatology, Palaeoecology. 2000;**164**:281-329

[3] DeBano LF, Neary DG, Ffolliott PF. Fire's Effects on Ecosystems. New York: John Wiley & Sons; 1998. 333 p

[4] Monastersky R. The human age. Nature. 2015;**519**:144-147

[5] Neary DG, Leonard JM. In: Bento A, Vieira A, editors. Multiple Ecosystem Impacts of Wildfire, Wildland Fires—A Worldwide Reality. Hauppauge, New York: Nova Science Publishers; 2015. pp. 1-79

[6] Harvey AE. Integrated roles for insects, diseases and decomposers in fire dominated forests of the inland Western United States: Past, present and future forest health. Journal of Sustainable Forestry. 1994;**2**:211-220

[7] Neary DG, Ryan KC, DeBano LF, editors. Fire effects on soil and water. USDA Forest Service General Technical Report RMRS-GTR-42. Vol. 4. Fort Collins, CO: Rocky Mountain Research Station; 2005. 250 p

[8] Neary DG. Wildfire contribution to desertification at local, regional, and global scales. In: Squires VR, Ariapour A, editors. Desertification. Hauppage, New York: Nova Science Publishers; 2018. pp. 199-222. ISBN-978-1-53614-212-9

[9] Liu Y, Stanturf J, Goodrick S. Trends in global wildfire potential in a changing climate. Forest Ecology and Management. 2018;**259**:685-697

[10] Doerr SH, Santin C. Global trends in wildfire and its impacts: Perceptions versus realities in a changing world. Philosophical Transactions of the Royal Society B. 2016;**371**:1471-2970

[11] Dennison PE, Brower SC, Arnold JD, Moritz MA. Large wildfire trends in the western USA 1984-2011. Geophysical Research Letters. 2014;**41**:2928-2933

[12] Shvidenko AZ, Shchepashchenko DG. Impact of wildfire in Russia between 1998-2010 on ecosystems and the global carbon budget. Doklady Earth Sciences. 2011;**441**:1678-1682

[13] Calkin DE, Gebort KM, Jones JG, Neilson RP. Forest service large fire area burned and suppression expenditure trends 1970-2002. Journal of Forestry. 2005;**103**:179-2002

[14] Piñol J, Terradas J, Lloret F. Climate warming, wildfire hazard, and wildfire occurrence in coastal eastern Spain. Climatic Change. 1998;**38**:345-357

[15] Brown JK, Smith JK. Wildland Fire in Ecosystems: Effects of Fire on Floral. General Technical Report RMRS-GTR-42. Vol. 2. Fort Collins, CO: U.S. Department of Agriculture, Forest Service, Rocky Mountain Research Station; 1998. 257 p

[16] Flannigan MD, Krawchuk MA, de Groot WJ, Wotton BM, Gowman LM. Implications of changing climate for global wildland fire. International Journal of Wildland Fire. 2009;**18**:483-507

[17] Sanford RL, Saldarriga J, Clark K, Uhl C, Herra R. Amazon rain forest fires. Science. 1985;**227**:53-55

[18] Uhl C. Perspectives on wildfire in the humid tropics. Conservation Biology. 2008;**12**:942-943

[19] Hardy CC, Schmidt KM, Menakis JP, Sampson RN. Spatial data for national

fire planning and fuel management. International Journal of Wildland Fire. 2001;**10**:353-372

[20] Frost CC. Presettlement fire frequency regimes of the United States: A first approximation. In: Pruden TL, Brennan L, editors. Fire in Ecosystem Management: Shifting Paradigm from Suppression to Prescription. Proceedings; Tall Timbers Fire Ecology Conference; 1996 May 7-10. Vol. 20. Tallahassee, FL: Tall Timbers Research Station; 1998. pp. 70-81

[21] Ryan KC. Dynamic interactions between forest structure and fire behavior in boreal ecosystems. Silva Fennica. 2002;**36**:13-39

[22] Kauffman JB, Steele MD, Cummings D, Jaramillo VJ. Biomass dynamics associated with deforestation, fire, and conversion to cattle pasture in a Mexican tropical dry forest. Forest Ecology and Management. 2003;**176**:1-12

[23] Stocks BJ. The extent and impact of forest fires in northern circumpolar countries. In: Levine JS, editor. Global Biomass Burning: Atmospheric Climate and Biosphere Implications. Cambridge: Massachusetts Institute of Technology Press; 1991. pp. 197-202

[24] Albini FA, Reinhardt ED. Modeling ignition and burning rate of large woody natural fuels. International Journal of Wildland Fire. 1995;**5**:81-91

[25] McArthur AG, Cheney NP. The characterization of fires in relation to ecological studies. Australian Forest Research. 1966;**2**:36-45

[26] Packham D, Pompe A. The radiation temperatures of forest fires. Australian Forest Research. 1971;**5**:1-8

[27] van Wagner CE. Fire behavior in northern conifer forests and shrublands. In: Wein RW, MacLean DA, editors. The Role of Fire in Northern Circumpolar Ecosystems. Scope 18. New York: John Wiley & Sons, Inc.; 1983. pp. 65-80

[28] Withington J. A Disastrous History of the World. London: Piatkus Books; 2008. 391 p

[29] Wein RW, Moore JM. Fire history and rotations in the New Brunswick Acadian forest. Canadian Journal of Forest Research. 1977;**7**:285-294

[30] National Interagency Fire Center. 2019. Available from: https://www.nifc.gov/safety/safety_documents/Fatalities-by-Year.pdf

[31] Cruz MG, Sullivan AL, Gould JS, Sims NC, Bannister AJ, Hollis JJ, et al. Anatomy of a catastrophic wildfire: The black Saturday Kilmore East fire in Victoria, Australia. Forest Ecology and Management. 2012;**284**:269-285

[32] Evarts B. Fire Loss in the United States During 2017. Quincy, MA: National Fire Protection Association; 2018. 18 p

[33] Reyes-Velarde A. California's camp fire was the costliest global disaster last year, insurance report show. Los Angeles Times. 2019;**11**. Available from: www.latimes.com [Accessed: February 22, 2019]

[34] Ding A. Charting the Financial Damage of the Thomas Fire. 2018. The Bottom Line. Accessed: [February 22, 2019]

[35] Benfield A. California Wildfire Industry Losses Put at $13.2bn. Artemis. 2018. Available from: www.artemis.bm [Accessed: February 22, 2019]

[36] British Columbia Fire Information. Available from: http://bcfireinfo.for.gov.bc.ca/hprScripts/WildfireNews/Statistics.asp. [Accessed: February 22, 2019]

[37] Sandberg DV, Ottmar RD, Peterson JL, Core J. Wildland Fire on Ecosystems:

Effects of Fire on Air. General Technical Report RMRS-GTR-42. Vol. 5. Ogden, UT: U.S. Department of Agriculture, Forest Service, Rocky Mountain Research Station; 2002. 79 p

[38] Liu X, Huey LG, Yokelson RJ, Selimovic V, Simpson IJ, Müller M, et al. Airborne measurements of western US wildfire emissions: Comparison with prescribed burning and air quality implications. Journal of Geophysical Research-Atmospheres. 2017;**122**:6108-6129

[39] Sandberg DV, Hardy CC, Ottmar RD, Snell JA, Kendall JA, Acheson A, et al. National Strategic Plan: Modeling and Data Systems for Wildland Fire and Air Quality. U.S. Department of Agriculture, Forest Service, Portland, Oregon: Pacific Northwest Research Station; 1999. 60 p

[40] World Health Organization. Air Quality Guidelines for Europe. WHO Regional Publications, European Series, No. 91; 2000. 251 p

[41] Ministry for the Environment. Revised National Environmental Standards for Air Quality—Evaluation under Section 32 of the Resource Management Act. Publication No. ME-1041, Ministry of the Environment, Wellington, New Zealand. 2011; 39 p

[42] Pyne SJ. Fire: Nature and Culture. Chicago, Illinois: University of Chicago Press; 2012. 207 p

[43] Booze TF, Reinhardt TE. A screening-level assessment of the health risks of chronic smoke exposure for wildland firefighters. Journal of Occupational and Environmental Hygiene. 2004;**1**:296-305

[44] Combrink T, Cothran C, Fox W. Issues in Forest Restoration: Full Cost Accounting of the 2010 Schultz Fire. Ecological Restoration Institute White Paper, Northern Arizona University, Flagstaff, Arizona; 2013

[45] Brass JA, Ambrosia VG, Riggan PJ, Sebesta PD. Consequences of fire on aquatic nitrate and phosphate dynamics in Yellowstone National Park. In: Proceedings of the Second Biennial Conference on the Greater Yellowstone Ecosystem. 1996. pp. 53-57

[46] Gerla P, Galloway J. Water quality of two streams near Yellowstone Park, Wyoming following the 1988 clover-mist wildfire. Environmental Geology. 1998;**36**(1):127-136

[47] Hauer F, Spencer C. Phosphorus and nitrogen dynamics in streams associated with wildfire: A study of immediate and longterm effects. International Journal of Wildland Fire. 1998;**8**(4):183-198

[48] Bladon KD, Silins U, Wagner MJ, Stone M, Emelko MB, Mendoza CA, et al. Wildfire impacts on nitrogen concentration and production from headwater streams in southern Alberta's Rocky mountains. Canadian Journal of Forest Research. 2008;**38**:2359-2371

[49] Mahlum SK, Eby LA, Young MK, Clancy CG, Jakober M. Effects of wildfire on stream temperatures in the Bitterroot River basin, Montana. International Journal of Wildland Fire. 2011;**20**:240-247

[50] Rhoades CC, Entwistle D, Butler D. The influence of wildfire extent and severity on streamwater chemistry, sediment and temperature following the Hayman fire, Colorado. International Journal of Wildland Fire. 2011;**20**:430-442

[51] Leonard JM, Magana HA, Bangert RK, Neary DG, Montgomery WL. Fire and floods: The recovery of headwater stream systems following high-severity wildfire. Fire Ecology. 2017;**13**:62-84

[52] Rugenski AT, Minshall GW. Climate-moderated responses to wildfire by macroinvertebrates and basal food resources in montane wilderness streams. Ecosphere. 2014;**5**(3):25

[53] Gray AG, Jenkins MJ. Climate warming alters fuels across elevational gradients in Great Basin bristlecone pine-dominated sky island forest. Forest Ecology and Management. 2017;**392**:125-136

[54] Rinne J. Short-term effects of wildfire on fishes and aquatic macroinvertebrates in the southwestern United States. North American Journal of Fisheries Management. 1996;**16**:653-658

Chapter 4

Succession after Fire in a Coastal Pine Forest in Norway

Oddvar Skre

Abstract

Biomass and chemical composition in six dominant field and bottom layer species have been recorded for 5 years after a wildfire in a coastal pine forest in Sveio, West Norway, in June 1992. As a follow-up of this study, the percentage coverage of field and bottom layer species and the regeneration of main tree species (*Pinus sylvestris*, *Betula pubescens,* and *Salix* spp.) were recorded in 1997, 2001, and 2008. Preliminary results indicate that the three dominant field layer species, *Calluna vulgaris, Molinia caerulea,* and *Pteridium aquilinum*, had expanded at the expense of other species, in particular *Vaccinium myrtillus, V. vitis-idaea*, *Deschampsia flexuosa,* and pioneer moss species, for example, *Polytrichum* spp. Seedlings of pine and saplings of birch and other deciduous species had established in the burned areas, and the succession of these species was followed and compared with nearby control plots. The strong growth of *Calluna vulgaris* after the fire indicates that periodic controlled burning may be an alternative management method of balancing carbon uptake rates in coastal areas of western Norway.

Keywords: succession, fire, coastal pine, coverage, regeneration

1. Introduction

Forest fires have become more common recently as a result of climatic change resulting in warmer and drier summers. However, their effects are not only negative. The reason is that a forest fire makes nutrients more available, by increasing decomposition rates in the forest floor, removing trees and makes light more accessible for plants in the field and bottom layer [1, 2]. Many plant and insect species are dependent on periodic fires in order to survive, and in Norway, as many as 40 red-listed species are related to forest fires [3]. Forest fires may also remove competition from some species, thereby favoring others [4]. Finally, some species like the heather (*Calluna vulgaris*) and the herb *Geranium bohemicum* have seeds that are activated by fire [5, 6]. Most pine species like the coastal *Pinus sylvestris* growing in Fennoscandia are adapted to fire in the sense that they reproduce by seeds, which germinate more easily after a fire.

In an earlier study [7], biomass and chemical composition in six dominant field and bottom layer species was recorded for 5 years after a wildfire in a coastal pine forest in Sveio, West Norway, in 1992, as compared with a control site outside of the burned area. As a follow-up of this study, the percentage coverage of field and bottom layer species and the regeneration of main tree species (*Pinus sylvestris, Betula pubescens,* and *Salix* spp.) were recorded in 1997, 2001, and 2008. The

IntechOpen

present study was carried out as part of an integrated study on the rate of succession after fire in coastal pine and heath vegetation types. Although the total amounts of nutrients in soil may decrease as a result of the fire [8], their availability may be temporarily increased by conversion from organic to inorganic forms [9], leading to increased availability of nutrients during several years due to leaching [10]. According to Moe [11], a number of pine trees in the study site survived the fire and produced the seeds that were able to regenerate due to improved light and soil conditions (cf. [12, 13]). Because of the improved light and nutrient conditions, increased productivity was expected on short term in the burned areas. Experiments with pine [14] have shown that controlled burning may be a more successful method of regeneration of *Pinus sylvestris* than, for example, clear cutting.

The reproduction and establishment of vascular plants after a forest fire may take place in three ways, for example, (1) by the transport and spreading of seeds from surviving mother trees, (2) by germination from a seed bank, and (3) by vegetative reproduction from surviving roots, rhizomes, and stumps. In the present study, the further growth and succession rates of the most common trees and field layer species were followed up by comparing results from 1998, 2001, and 2008 with the results from the initial 5 years of succession after the fire in 1992 [7].

Based on the abovementioned relationships, the objectives of the present study may be formulated as follows:

- How has the growth of the main tree and field layer species changed in terms of percentage cover and biomass?
- Will the total plant biomass and productivity change permanently as a result of the fire?
- What are the implications of the present study for the long-term carbon balance?

2. Materials and methods

The forest fire took place in June 1992 south and west of Hopsfjellet in Sveio, western Norway after an extremely warm and dry period. The burned site covered an area of about 300 ha and is located at 59°30′ N, 5°20′ E (see **Figure 1**). Mean temperatures (1961–1990) vary from 2°C in February to 14°C in August, with annual precipitation about 2000 mm [8]. Different parts of the area burned with different intensities [11], depending on soil depth and humidity. *Calluna* heaths dominated in the dry parts of the burned site, while *Vaccinium myrtillus* was more common on moist sites with deeper soil system. The topography is rather variable, and the thickness of the humus layer varied from <2 cm in the most dry and nutrient-poor areas to >20 cm where peat accumulation had taken place. In some cases, the mineral soil was almost absent, and the dry humus layer was burned off, leaving the underlying rock exposed. The fire intensity reached its maximum in these areas, while areas with high water level in soil were relatively little damaged by surface fire [13]. Six representative plots of 10 by 10 m size were established in 1993, covering the whole range of fire intensities.

Growth estimation. Instead of destructive biomass sampling of field layer species, the growth was estimated by measuring the percentage coverage and the corresponding shoot density in pure stands of the same species in 1997 and 2001. From these two parameters and estimates of biomass per shoot (**Table 3**), the total biomass per area was estimated (cf. [15]). The percentage coverage of regenerating

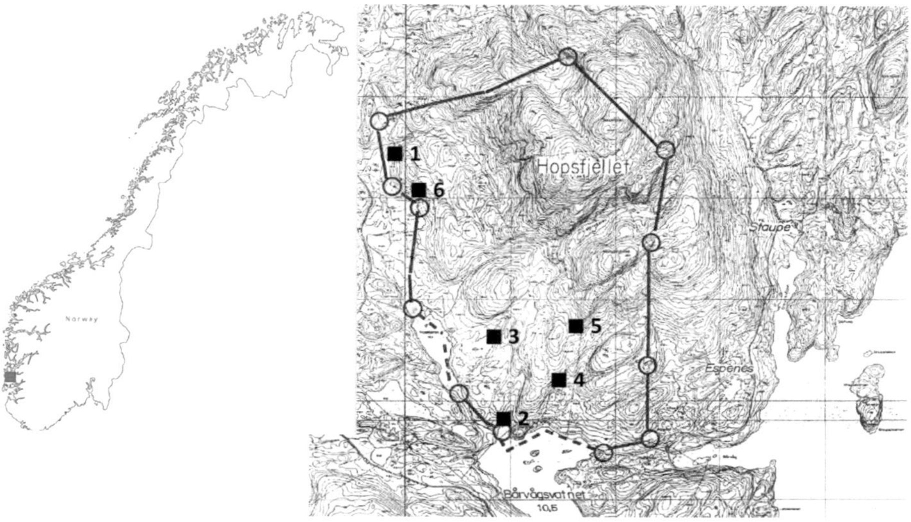

Figure 1.
Map of Norway showing the location of the study area (left). The six study sites are classified on the small-scale (1:15,000) map over the burned study area (right), as follows: low fire intensity (1–2), medium fire intensity (3–4), and high fire intensity (5–6). The control site was located about 500 m outside and west of the burned area.

seedlings of *Pinus sylvestris, Betula pubescens*, and *Salix* spp. was recorded in 1995, 2001, and 2008, as well as tree density on 10 by 10 m plots and the stem base diameter (mm), age, and total height (cm). The following field layer species were recorded: *Calluna vulgaris, Vaccinium myrtillus, V. vitis-idaea, Pteridium aquilinum, Deschampsia flexuosa, Molinia caerulea*, and the mosses *Polytrichum commune* and *P. juniperinum*. The number of shoots per m^2 in pure stands were extrapolated from sampling squares of 10 by 10 cm (*Calluna, Deschampsia, Polytrichum*), 20 by 20 cm (*Vaccinium*), or 1 by 1 m (*Pteridium*). The overall biomass per unit area was then estimated by multiplying the calculated biomass in pure stands with the corresponding percentage cover of each species (cf. [7]). The method was tested out by harvesting random samples of each species by ordinary sampling method using a core with known surface area [15]. In the present study, the results are given as mean values (n = 5) from each of the six study sites.

In earlier studies, the biomass per shoot or leaf (*Pteridium*) in most cases was not found to be significantly different from the control plot and was therefore used to estimate the overall biomass of field layer species (cf. [7]). In this study, the shoot density, height, and diameter growth was tested by ordinary statistical methods by using variance analysis [16] in order to find significant differences.

3. Results and discussion

The observations of the sample plots in 1997, 2001, and 2008 confirmed the results from the short-term study [7]. The overall biomass of main field layer species was therefore estimated using the mentioned indirect method [15] where the biomass per shoot was multiplied with the shoot density and the coverage of the same species. The shoot density in pure stands is shown in **Table 1**, where the numbers in the table are referring to the size of the sample plots in cm^2 (10 by 10 cm vs. 20 by 20 cm or 100 by 100 cm). **Table 1** shows a strong increase in shoot density of *Calluna vulgaris* and a moderate increase in *V. myrtillus* during the period of 1997–2001. In the other species, the shoot density was decreasing, and in *Deschampsia flexuosa* partly missing (see **Table 1**).

Biomass estimates. There was a significant increase from 1993 to 1995 (cf. [7]) in biomass per shoot in green and nongreen *Pteridium*, and in nongreen *Calluna vulgaris* tissue, and a corresponding decrease in green tissue of *Calluna* and *Deschampsia*, and nongreen *V. myrtillus* and *V. vitis-idaea*. During the following period, from 1995 to 2001, however, there were no significant changes in biomass per shoot in any of the investigated species (**Table 2**). The mean values of this parameter were therefore used to estimate the overall biomass of green and non-green tissue in each species in 1995, 1997, and 2001.

The mean estimated biomass in g/m^2 of each of the investigated species was shown in **Figure 2**. From this figure, it may be concluded:

- There was a strong increase in green and nongreen *Calluna* tissue during the period from 1993 to 2001 to a top level that is 3–7 times as high as in the control plots, and the highest level was found in the green tissue.

- In the remaining six investigated species (*Vaccinium myrtillus*, *V. vitis-idaea*, *Pteridium aquilinum*, *Molinia caerulea,* and the moss *Polytrichum* spp.), the biomass in green and nongreen tissue increased from 1993 to 1997 and then decreased – but still at a higher level than in the control plots, except from *Vaccinium vitis-idaea* (see **Figure 2**).

The *Calluna* biomass increased strongly during the whole period, due to a combined effect of increased shoot density and increased coverage. The green biomass in the *Calluna* regrowth after the fire was still very high in 2001, with a shoot/root ratio of 3.7, while the corresponding value was 0.5 at the control plot. The *Calluna vulgaris* has probably been enhanced by a high number of seeds that were present in the soil already before the fire (e.g., [17, 18]) and activated by the fire and better light and nutrient conditions [8]. This result was also confirmed by Måren [19] and Måren and Vandvik [6], who studied the succession after a controlled fire in a coastal heathland and found that seed germination in *Calluna* could be stimulated by smoke and ash from the fire. They also found that the seed bank in the soil was acting as a refuge and was not influenced by the management with prescribed burning (cf. [20]).

Coverage of main species. The coverage (%) of the main field layer species in 2001 and 2008 (**Table 3**) was recorded and compared with earlier measurements from 1995 [7]. There was a strong increase in the coverage of *Calluna vulgaris* and in the two *Vaccinium* species (*V. myrtillus* and *V, vitis-idaea*) as well as in the bracken (*Pteridium aquilinum*) during the period from 1995 to 2001 and a moderate increase in the coverage of the grass species *Molinia caerulea*. During the following period from 2001 to 2008, there was a further moderate increase in the coverage of these species, but in *Deschampsia flexuosa* and *Polytrichum* spp., the coverage was decreasing during the whole period. The coverage of *Pinus sylvestris* and *Betula pubescens* seedlings increased during the same period, from 22 to 28%. The total coverage increased strongly from 83 to 152% during the period of 1995–2001, but during the following period up to 2008, there was only a slight increase, from 152 to 157%. Strong variations were found in 2001 between sample plots, from a total of 109% on the nutrient-poor plot 5 to 223% on the mesotrophic plot 4 in accordance with soil conditions [21].

The coverage of *Calluna* was more than 50% already in 2001, and strong competition between the well-adapted *Calluna* and more slow-growing plants seemed

Species/plot	1995	2001							2008							Ctr
		1	**2**	**3**	**4**	**5**	**6**	**Mean**	**1**	**2**	**3**	**4**	**5**	**6**	**Mean**	
Calluna	30	48	64	56	58	48	60	**54**	51	60	71	55	32	78	**58**	20
V. myr	4	4	3	5	0	26	10	**9**	3	13	2	10	30	19	**13**	40
V. v-i	2	11	13	14	6	3	14	**11**	11	10	17	14	7	3	**10**	10
Pteridium	15	46	22	22	19	6	10	**21**	36	30	24	26	1	20	**23**	8
D. flex	6	2	10	2	2	3	3	**4**	0	4	3	0	0	0	**1**	4
Molinia	7	20	12	6	13	11	0	**10**	13	7	3	20	11	9	**11**	12
Polytrichum	19	13	70	16	5	2	13	**20**	12	23	2	5	16	2	**10**	2
Pinus	14	15	5	16	6	5	**12**	18	14	11	8	7	12	**14**		45
Betula	7	14	4	16	4	4	**10**	13	20	9	11	8	11	**14**		20
Total	**83**	**165**	**223**	**130**	**135**	**109**	**119**	152	157	**186**	**156**	**149**	**98**	**165**	157	**161**

Table 1.
Percentage coverage in field layer species, including pine and birch seedlings, at each of the six study sites during 1995–2008 (n = 5) with mean values, as compared with the control site (Ctr).

Species	cm²/plot	1997							2001						
		1	2	3	4	5	6	**Mean**	1	2	3	4	5	6	**Mean**
Calluna	100	97	118	98	84	117	79	**99**	155	143	122	156	168	151	**149**
V. myr	400	142	121	76	135	85	126	**114**	98	166	92	166	107	127	**126**
V. v-i	400	65	43	49	35	54	53	**50**	39	57	40	45	56	39	**46**
Pteridium	10000	12	12	14	14	13	10	**13**	15	12	11	10	10	6	**11**
D. flex	100	84	147	180	182	130	76	**150**	116						
Molinia	100	39	40	36	41	42	34	**39**	31	26	29	26	28	**28**	
Polytrichum	100	113	98	70	139	128	73	**120**	72	104	127	112	114	63	**99**

Table 2.
The density in pure stands of the investigated species at each of the six study sites in 1997 and 2001 (n = 5), as related to the size of the sample plots in cm² and the mean density per species.

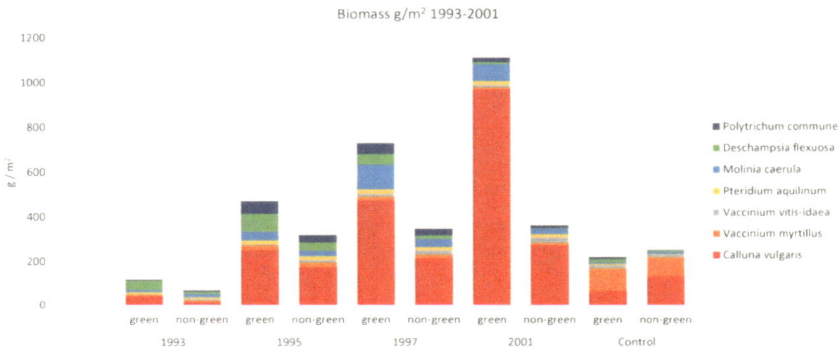

Figure 2.
Mean estimated overall biomass (g/m²) in green and nongreen tissue of the investigated field layer species during the period from 1993 to 2001 as compared with control plants from an unburned area outside the fire.

to have caused a slight decrease in light-dependent species like *Vaccinium myrtillus* and *Deschampsia flexuosa* after an initial rapid period of establishment after the fire. Unlike *Calluna*, the regeneration of the two *Vaccinium* species takes place mainly from surviving rhizomes, and a comparison with the control plots shows that the green biomass had been strongly reduced by the fire (e.g., [22]).

In addition to *Calluna vulgaris*, two other species seemed to have taken advantage of the fire, for example, the bracken *Pteridium aquilinum* and the light-sensitive grass *Deschampsia flexuosa*. Both of these species are reproducing vegetatively, the *Pteridium* by putting out a very deep rhizome network that can survive medium and low intensity fires [23] and producing large leaves that are able to compete successfully on light and nutrients. *Deschampsia* are surviving as resting buds in the upper soil layer [18, 24] that take advantage of improved light and nutrient conditions after the fire [8]. However, the long-term study indicates that increased competition after 2001 may have caused a strong reduction in growth and survival rates of *Deschampsia* (cf. [7]).

The coastal and oligotrophic grass species *Molinia caerulea* also survived the fire because of its deep root system and humid soil conditions. It was not shown in the samplings from the short-term study, but then its coverage increased strongly from 1995 to 2001 and then stayed constant (see **Table 3**). Like *Deschampsia, Pteridium,* and *Calluna*, the *Molinia* tussocks seem to be favored by improved light conditions and are reported to inhibit pine reproduction by removing access to the mineral soil layer [25].

In the two moss species *Polytrichum commune* and *P. juniperinum,* there was also a strong increase in biomass after the fire. The pioneer mosses *Polytrichum juniperinum* and *Ceratodon purpureus* [8] are dominating at the nutrient-poor sites 5 and 6 (see map on **Figure 1**), and in agreement with earlier reports [18] seem to culminate 2–3 years after the fire (**Table 3**).

The present results agree well with the results from a short-term study on the succession in a pine forest in Mykland, southern Norway after a forest fire in 2008 [25]. They found strong *Pinus* regeneration already 4 years after the fire (cf. **Table 4**), and the corresponding mean height of pine seedlings was then 10–50 cm, while the mean height of pine seedlings in the present study 9 years after the fire (2001) was 190 cm. The four most common pioneer species after the fire were the same as in the present study, but in a different order. In the present study, *Calluna vulgaris* was the dominant species with about 30% coverage already 3 years after the fire (**Table 3**), while in the Mykland study, *Molinia caerulea* was the most abundant (5–15%), with *Calluna* only covering 2–4% 4 years after the fire [25]. In both studies, the *Polytrichum* moss species were very common during the first year after the fire.

Long-term successions. Due to a strong increase in the total plant cover during the three first years after the fire, and to a certain degree in the shoot density, there was a strong increase in the overall biomass (cf. **Figure 2**), in particular in *Calluna* and *Molinia caerulea*, but also to a certain degree in *Deschampsia, Polytrichum,* and *Pteridium*. This increase continued in 1997, but then it culminated in all the investigated species except *Calluna*, which was totally dominating in 2001, probably due to the improved light and nutrient conditions. As a result, a gradual increase took place also in the total plant cover in the field layer and reached 90% by 1995 and

	Species	**mg/shoot**
	Green	**Non-green**
Calluna vulgaris	118	40
Vaccinium myrtillus	86	88
Vaccinium vitis-idaea	160	96
Pteridium aquilinum	7290	5500
Desdhampsia flexuosa	90	30
Molinia caerula	270	90
Polytrichum spp.	20	12

Table 3.
Mean biomass in mg per shoot of green and non-green tissue of the investigated species, measured in 2001 (n = 30).

	2001							2008						
Species/plot	**1**	**2**	**3**	**4**	**5**	**6**	**Sum**	**1**	**2**	**3**	**4**	**5**	**6**	**Sum**
Pinus	1.4	5.6	3.6	2.4	1.2	0.8	**2.5**	3.4	6.2	4.6	2.0	2.0	1.6	**3.3**
Betula	0.8	2.4	1.8	3.0	0.6	1.4	**1.7**	2.2	6.4	1.6	4.0	1.6	1.4	**2.9**
Salix	0.2	0.9	1.0	0.6	0.2	0.2	**0.6**	0	0.3	0	0	0	0.2	**0.1**

Table 4.
Mean tree density (n = 5) of Pinus sylvestris, Betula pubescens *and* Salix *spp. on 10 m^2 study sites at the six investigated study sites, measured in 2001 and 2008.*

150% by 1997 and then stayed constant (**Table 3**). The improved light and nutrient conditions may partly also be a result of the accumulation of dead organic matter after the fire, as reported by Vestmoen [26] and Nygaard and Brean [25], on a much higher scale, and by similar studies in Sweden [27, 28]. The total biomass of the investigated species in 2001 was much higher than the corresponding biomass at the control plot, mainly because of the strong growth of *Calluna*. However, with increasing competition for light, water, and nutrients, a decrease is expected in the production rates of the field layer. **Tables 4** and **5** indicate that in the future there will be more competition also from *Pinus* and *Betula* seedlings that are expected to gradually replace the more light-dependent species in the field layer (see **Figure 3**).

The regrowth and density of trees in 2001 and 2008, that is, 9 and 16 years after the fire, are shown in **Tables 4** and **5**. Seedlings of *Pinus sylvestris* and saplings of surviving *Betula pubescens* seemed to have established at all plots in 2001, and there was a further increase in density, to maximum of 3.3 and 2.9 trees per 10 m^2 in 2008. In *Salix*, the regrowth was small and insignificant (**Table 4**).

	2001							2008						
Species/plot	**1**	**2**	**3**	**4**	**5**	**6**	**Sum**	**1**	**2**	**3**	**4**	**5**	**6**	**Sum**
Diameter (mm)														
Pinus	3.1	1.8	2.8	4.0	3.2	3.4	**3.1**	7.7	3.4	4.1	3.7	5.2	4.2	**4.7**
Betula	2.8	1.6	3.4	3.7	3.1	3.1	**3.1**	5.4	4.3	2.9	4.0	3.5	2.4	**3.8**
Height (m)														
Pinus	2.3	1.7	2.0	2.1	1.4	2.1	**1.9**	4.0	2.5	2.6	2.7	1.8	2.1	**2.6**
Betula	2.7	1.7	2.7	2.8	2.3	2.6	**2.5**	4.0	5.0	2.6	3.2	2.3	1.7	**3.1**
Age (yrs)														
Pinus	9.3	8.8	8.3	9.0	8.9	10.7	**9.2**	13.0	11.0	11.2	11.5	12.3	11.0	**11.7**
Betula	10.0	7.3	9.1	10.3	10.4	10.7	**9.6**	14.2	16.6	9.9	12.2	11.8	12.7	**12.9**

Table 5.
Diameter and height (n = 5) of Pinus sylvestris *and* Betula pubescens *seedlings at the six investigated study sites, with mean values, measured in 2001 and 2008.*

Figure 3.
View of the low-intensity burned site 2 from 2008 with pine regeneration competing with Calluna *and* Pteridium *in the field layer.*

Further information on tree growth and development is shown in **Table 5**. The established seedlings and saplings showed a strong (50%) height and diameter growth during the period from 2001 to 2008 in both species. Finally, it is interesting to note that the recorded age (years) of the two tree species corresponded well with the observed age in 2001 but was considerably lower in 2008, indicating a certain seed regeneration from surviving mother trees also after the fire, in accordance with the results from a similar study by Nygaard and Brean [25].

Carbon-binding capacity. One of the implications of **Figure 2** is that on short term, the CO_2-binding capacity of the forest is severely damaged as a result of the fire, but on longer terms (10–15 years), the reduction in CO_2 uptake is partly compensated by the strong growth in aboveground green *Calluna* tissue. This conclusion is partly supported by results from coastal heathland studies (e.g., [19]) but not by Kjønaas et al. [29] in long-term successional studies on a spruce plantation in southeastern Norway as influenced by clear cutting. They found that the CO_2 uptake in understorey biomass and litter during the first 10–15 years after a clear cut was of the same order as the corresponding annual CO_2 output in the living tree biomass during the following succession, up to the mature stage of 130 years. **Table 3** indicates that the percentage coverage of *Calluna* 10–15 years after the fire is of the same order or higher than the combined coverage of the two dominating tree species (*Pinus sylvestris* and *Betula pubescens*) at the control plot. The much higher shoot/root ratio in young *Calluna* relative to old plants at the control plot (3.7 vs. 0.5) also indicates that regularly controlled burning at intervals, for example, 5 or 10 years as described by Måren [19] and Kaland [30], may be as efficient as, for example, spruce plantation in the carbon uptake process as climatic regulators. These results have also been supported by other studies from northern boreal forests, for example, by Ivanova et al. [31], Kukavskaya et al. [32], and Tarasov et al. [33] on succession after fire in Siberian pine forests. Also, other studies emphasize the function of forest fires in the process of recycling nutrients and speeding up regeneration, photosynthesis, and growth, including the CO_2-binding capacity (e.g., [34, 35]; see also [36]).

4. Conclusion

In line with the three objectives of the study, some species may have taken advantage of improved light and nutrient conditions after the fire. This refers particularly to the heather (*Calluna vulgaris*), which seems to be particularly well adapted to fire. In fact, the coastal heaths with pine forests in Norway have been regularly burned for more than 2000 years in order to enhance the growth of green *Calluna* tissue as food for animals [30] and to facilitate seed regeneration in pine [14]. However, the fire also favors other light-dependent species like *Pteridium aquilinum* and *Molinia caerulea*. According to, for example, Måren et al. [37], *Pteridium* is competing with *Calluna* on burned areas of coastal heathlands, but repeated cutting of *Pteridium* will help favoring *Calluna* growth. Furthermore, because seed regeneration of pine is favored by exposed mineral, the fire will increase pine regrowth and juvenilization. On the other hand, plants dependent on vegetative reproduction like *Vaccinium myrtillus* may be permanently suppressed [38].

In some parts of the study site (plots 4 and 5), the humus layer and soil were almost burned off, and the regrowth may have been permanently restricted by lack of nutrients and water (**Figure 4**). In these areas, the succession process may take place over a very long time, after a new soil layer has been formed by mosses and other pioneer plants. But, on the remaining part of the study site, where water and

Figure 4.
View of the high-intensity burned site 5 from 2008 with missing or sparse soil cover and dead fallen pine trees. In the background Hopsfjellet and Mardalsfjellet.

nutrients are not limiting factors, increasing pine and birch growth is expected to shadow out light-dependent plants such as *Deschampsia flexuosa*, *Molinia caerulea*, *Pteridium aquilinum,* and *Calluna vulgaris*, and after a period of time that may take 100 years or more [8], the ecosystem may have reached its climax stage again and be back to the starting point (cf. **Figure 3**).

The study also indicates that periodic burning of old-growth *Calluna* heath (cf. [19]) may be as efficient in the CO_2 uptake process in short terms (10–15 years) as climate regulators as spruce plantations in coastal districts of Norway.

Author details

Oddvar Skre
Norwegian Forest Research Institute, Skre Nature and Environment, Norway

*Address all correspondence to: oddvar@nmvskre.no

References

[1] Rolstad J, Blanck Y-L, Storaunet KO. Fire history in a western Fennoscandian boreal forest as influenced by human landuse and climate. Ecological Monographs. 2017. DOI: 10.1002/ecm.1244

[2] Storaunet KO, Rolstad J, Toeneiet M, Blanck Y-L. Strong anthropogenic signal in historic forest fire regime; A detailed spatio-temporal case study from south-central Norway. Canadian Journal of Forest Research. 2013;**43**(9):836-845

[3] Storaunet KO, Gjerde I. Skog. In: Nybø S, editor. Naturindeks for Norge 2010. 2010

[4] Solbraa K. Brannflatedynamikk i skog. Sammendrag fra et seminar 13–14. Januar 1997 i Norges Forskningsråd, Oslo. Rapport Skogforsk 2/97. 1997

[5] Fægri K, Danielsen A. Maps of Distribution of Norwegian Vascular Plants III. The Southeastern Element. Fagbokforlaget; 1996

[6] Måren IE, Vandvik V. Fire and regeneration; the role of seed banks in the dynamics of northern heathlands. Journal of Vegetation Science. 2009; **20**(5):871-888

[7] Skre O, Wielgolaski FE, Moe B. Biomass and chemical composition of common forest plants in response to fire in western Norway. Journal of Vegetation Science. 1998;**9**:501-510

[8] Klingsheim JM. Post-fire succession in two southern boreal coniferous forests in Norway, Hopsfjellet in Sveio and Turtermarka in Maridalen [MSc thesis]. University of Oslo; 1996

[9] Chandler C, Cheney P, Thomas P, Trabaud L, Williams D. Fire in Forestry. Vol. 1–2. N.Y.: Wiley; 1983

[10] Kimmins JP. Forest Ecology; A Foundation for Sustainable Management. 2nd ed. NJ: Prentice Hall; 1997

[11] Moe B. Botaniske undersøkelser etter skogbrannen i Sveio; suksesjoner, skogstruktur og brannkart. Fylkemannen i Hordaland, Miljøvernavd. rapport 6/94. Bergen. 1994

[12] Yli-Vakkuri P. Emergence and initial development of tree seedlings on burnt-over forest land. Acta Forestalia Fennica. 1962;**74**:1-51

[13] Moe B. Suksesjonsstudier etter skogbrann. In: Solbraa K, editor. Brannflatedynamikk i skog, Aktuelt fra Skogforskning. Vol. 2. 1997. pp. 25-26

[14] Øyen BH. Punktbrenning–et aktuelt hjelpetiltak ved foryngelse av. kystfuruskog? In: Solbraa K, editor. Brannflatedynamikk i skog. Aktuelt fra Skogforsk. Vol. 2. 1997. pp. 16-17

[15] Skre O. Measuring changes in biomass and shoot density in some dominant field layer species after a forest fire in western Norway. In: Woxholtt S, editor. Proceedings from the Ninth IBFRA Conference in Oslo, September 21–23, 1998. 1999. pp. 72-78. Aktuelt fra. Skogforsk 4/99: 1–83

[16] Goodnight JH. The new general linear modes procedure. In: Proceedings of the First International SAS Users Conference. Cary, NC: SAS Institute Inc.; 1976

[17] Granstrom A. Seed banks in five boreal forest stands originating between 1810 and 1963. Canadian Journal of Forest Research. 1987;**60**:1815-1821

[18] Schimmel J. On fire; fire behaviour, fuel succession and vegetation response to fire in Swedish boreal forests [PhD thesis]. Umeå: Swedish University of Agricultural Sciences; 1993

[19] Måren IE. Effects of management on heathland vegetation in Western Norway [PhD thesis]. University of Bergen; 2009

[20] Velle LG, Nilsen LS, Norderhaug A, Vandvik V. Does prescribed burning result in biotic homogenization of coastal heathlands? Global Change Biology. 2013;**20**(5):1429-1440

[21] Klingsheim JM. Revegetering og jordsmonnsutvikling de første årene etter skogbrann på Hopsfjellet i Sveio og Turteråsen i Maridalen. In: Vitensk. Mus. Rapp. Bot. Ser. 1995–1. Trondheim: Universitet i Trondheim; 1995

[22] Schimmel J, Granstrom A. Skogsbranderna och vegetationen. SkogForsk. 1991;**4**(91):39-46

[23] Whelan RJ. The ecology of fire. In: Cambridge Studies in Ecology. Cambridge, UK: Cambridge University Press; 1995

[24] Viro PJ. Effects of forest fire on soil. In: Kozlowski TT, Ahlgren CE, editors. Fire and Ecosystems. 1974. pp. 7-95

[25] Nygaard PH, Brean R. Dokumentasjon og erfaringer etter skogbrannen i Mykland 2008. In: Rapport Skog og Landskap 02/2014. 2014. pp. 33

[26] Vestmoen SM. Effects of forest fire on production of down woody debris in Aust-Agder County in Norway [MSc thesis]. Ås, Norway: UMB; 2011

[27] Zackrisson O, Nilsson M-C, Wardle D. Key ecological function of charcoal from wildfire in the boreal forest. Oikos. 1996;**77**:10-19

[28] Østlund L, Zackrisson O, Axelsson A-L. The history and transformation of a Scandinavian boreal forest landscape since the 19th century. Canadian Journal of Forest Research. 1997;**27**:1198-1206

[29] Kjønaas OJ, Skre O, Tau Strand L, Børja I, Clarke N, de Wit HA, et al. Understorey vegetation makes a difference: Above- and belowground carbon and nitrogen pools in a Norwegian Norway spruce chronosequence. Plant and Soil. 2010;**334**

[30] Kaland PE. The origin and management of Norwegian coastal heaths as reflected by pollen analysis. In: Behre KE, editor. Anthropogenic Indicators in Pollen Diagrams. Boston: A.A. Balkema; 1986. pp. 19-36

[31] Ivanova GA, Ivanov VA, Kovaleva NM, Conard SG, Zhila SV, Tarasov PA. Succession of vegetation after a high-intensity fire in a pine forest with lichens. Contemporary Problems of Ecology. 2017;**10**:52-61

[32] Kukavskaya EA, Ivanova GA, Conard SG, McRae DJ, Ivanov VA. Biomass dynamics of central Siberian Scots pine forests following surface fires of varying severity. International Journal of Wildland Fire. 2014;**23**(6): 872-876

[33] Tarasov PA, Ivanov VA, Gaidukova AF. Analysis of growth dynamics and development of self-sowing Scots pine on post-fire sites. Khoinye Boreal'noi Zony. 2012;**30**(3–4): 284-290

[34] Brockway DG, Gatewood RG, Paris RB. Restoring fire as an ecological process in hortgrass prairie ecosystems; initial effects of prescribed burning during the dormant and growing seasons. Journal of Environmental Management. 2002;**65**(2):135-152

[35] Brown JK, Smith JK. Wildland fire in ecosystems; effects of fire on flora. In: Gen. Tech Rep. RMRS-GTR-42-vol. 2. Dept of Agriculture, Forest Service, Rocky Mountain Research Station; 2000

[36] Ivanova GA, Conard SG, Kukavskaya EA, McRae DJ. Fire impact

on carbon storage in light conifer forests of the Lower Angara region, Siberia. Environmental Research Letters. 2011;**6**

[37] Måren IE, Vandvik V, Ekelund A. Restoration of bracken-induced *Calluna vulgaris* heathlands; effects on vegetation dynamics and non-target species. Biological Conservation. 2008; **141**:1032-1041

[38] Engelmark O. Fire history correlations to forest type and topography in northern Sweden. Annales Botanici Fennici. 1987;**24**: 317-324. Proceedings of the First International SAS Users Conference. SAS Institute Inc.

Chapter 5

Human Impacts on Coral Reef Ecosystem

Hussein A. El-Naggar

Abstract

Healthy, Coral reefs are the most spectacular, diverse and economically valuable marine ecosystems on the planet, Complex and productive, coral reefs are extremely important for biodiversity, providing a home to 35,000–60,000 species of plants and animals (over 25% of all marine life), many of which are not described by science. They are also vital for people and business. They provide nurseries for many species of commercially important fish, protection of coastal areas from storm waves. They are providing hundreds of billions of dollars in food, jobs and significant attraction for the tourism industry. Yet coral reef ecosystems have undergone phase shifts to alternate, degraded assemblages because of the combined human activates of unsustainable overfishing, intensive tourism, urbanization, sedimentation, declining water quality, pollution and primarily from the direct and indirect impacts of climate change. Most coral ecologists confirm that coral reef degradation has increased dramatically during the last three decades due to enhanced anthropogenic disturbances and their interaction with natural stressors. So, it is necessary to recognize the threats facing coral reefs from anthropogenic activities and try to minimize and mitigate these impacts.

Keywords: coral reef ecosystem, anthropogenic activities, natural threats, climate change, coral protection, proposed solutions

1. Introduction

Coral reefs are extraordinary living geological diverse underwater ecosystems held together by calcium carbonate structures secreted by corals. They represent the most conspicuous and magnificent community in the tropical and subtropical regions. Coral reefs are built by colonies of tiny living animals found in shallow subtidal marine waters that contain few nutrients. Most coral reefs are built from stony corals, which in turn consist of polyps that live together in groups. The polyps belong to a group of animals known as Cnidaria, which also includes sea anemones and jellyfish. The polyps secrete a hard carbonate exoskeleton which support and protect their bodies. Most reefs grow best in warm, shallow, clear, sunny and agitated waters. The oldest coral reefs on the earth occurred about 500 million years ago, as well as the first relatives of recent corals developed in the south of Europe from about 230 million years ago. Most corals get their color from the symbiotic single-celled algae called zooxanthellae. Millions of these single-celled algae are living as symbionts within polyp tissues, intercellular in the gastrodermis layer. Zooxanthellae produce organic nutrients and oxygen through photosynthesis thus helping the coral in the growth and the process of producing limestone or calcium carbonate. Corals grow

IntechOpen

much faster with the help of the zooxanthellae. Corals get up 90% of their nutrients from their zooxanthellae. Zooxanthellae produce pigments visible through the clear body of the polyp and give the coral its beautiful color [1, 2].

Coral reefs provide a home for at least 25% of marine origin fauna, including fishes, echinoderms, crustaceans, mollusks, sponges, tunicates, and other cnidarians and so on. Coral reefs ecosystem (CRE) provides many services to tourism, fisheries in addition to coastline protection from wave action. The global economic value of coral reefs ecosystem is estimated between US $29.8 and 375 billion per year. However, coral reef is a fragile ecosystem, because it is very sensitive to elevations of water temperature. Coral reef ecosystems are exposed to many threats most of them resulting from humans such as global warming, oceanic acidification, climate change, water pollution, Irrational tourism, blast fishing, overfishing, illegal fishing for aquarium fish, overuse of reef resources, harmful land-use practices including urbanization and agricultural runoff which may be harmful for reefs by enhancing algal overgrowth [3, 4].

Coral reef ecosystem degradation has increased dramatically during the last three decades due to enhanced anthropogenic disturbances and their interaction with natural stressors [5]. These stressors are thought to cause coral diseases and bleaching leading to a loss of coral cover. Unfortunately, very little is currently known about the prevalence, distribution and pathology of coral diseases in the Red Sea [1, 6].

The annihilation of the reef ecosystem will lead to the disappearance of 25% of marine habitats, and a quarter of marine life that needs to productive and diversified this three-dimensional building to stay alive. Graham et al. [7] found a serious decline in coral reef fish populations as a result of climate change. Coral reefs provide food and are a source of income for hundreds of millions of people scattered in many countries. The loss of this ecosystem will lead to unexpected effects with serious damages already beginning to appear. It has been estimated that the volume of services and natural resources offered by the coral reefs to humanity from 10 years ago to be about US $30 billion per year, through benefits such as fisheries, tourism and shore protection; it is perhaps greatly increased now [8]. The mass coral bleaching and death of CRE is one of the most obvious effects of climate changes which warn the world that we should take global warming seriously. The loss of the oceans to most if not all effective CREs could lead to unexpected disasters. We are on the verge of these disasters, but they can be avoided if the necessary international efforts are combined for adverse impact mitigation [9].

2. The main components of the coral reef ecosystem

Coral reefs form some of the world's most productive ecosystems, providing complex and varied marine habitats that support a wide range of other organisms. The coral reef ecosystem is a collection of diversified communities which interact together and with the environment. The primary source of energy for any ecosystem including coral reef is the sun. Phytoplankton, algae, and other plants use the sun light for photosynthesis. During photosynthesis, the light energy from the sun in the presence of water and nutrients is converted into chemical energy. The chemical energy that is made by photosynthesis is passed from plants to animals then other animals then to simple nutrients by bacteria through the food chain. Although, the corals are the main organisms that form the basic structure of reef ecosystem, members of all other animal phyla and classes may be found on coral reefs, in addition to the significant role for certain species of algae in reef formation. The following is a short summary of the more important and abundant groups that make up coral reef composition [9, 10].

1. **Algae:** Coral reefs are chronically at risk of algal encroachment. Overfishing and excess nutrient supply from onshore can enable algae to outcompete and kill the coral. There are three groups of algae, these are:

    a. **The coralline algae:** These groups are very important in constructing and maintaining reef. They belong to the red algae, and can precipitate calcium carbonate as do corals, but tend to be encrusting and spreading out in thin layers over the reefs, cementing the various pieces of calcium carbonate together. These algae form what is called "the algal ridge" on reef which is the most rapidly calcifying zone on reef.

    b. **Calcareous green algae:** These algae include certain species of green algae, such as Halimeda, which grow erect and secrete calcium carbonate, giving much of reef sand by breaking up.

    c. **Other free living algae:** They include the free living algae that exist just below the surface layers of calcium carbonate in the coral colonies themselves but are inconspicuous on the reef.

2. **Members of phylum Cnidaria**

    a. **The stony corals:** These groups belong to the Order Scleractinia (Madreporaria) and form the major structure of reefs.

    b. **Order Gorgonacea:** Its members are commonly called sea fan and sea whip, which have an internal skeleton of spicules. They are abundant in Atlantic Ocean.

    c. **Order Alcyonacea:** This order comprises the soft corals, which may be abundant in some Indo-Pacific regions than the stony corals, but very rare in Atlantic. Several species of soft corals have internal spicules of calcium carbonates.

    d. **Order Hydrocorallina:** It includes the hydrocorals, which belong to the class hydrozoa, and called "Fire corals," for their powerful nematocysts. The hydrocorals are conspicuous in the Atlantic Ocean.

3. **Mollusca:** Mollusks have significant role in reef formation due to the ability of their species for calcium carbonate deposition. The most important of mollusk are the giant clam, *Tridacna* spp. and *Hippopus* spp. which may be up to 2200 individuals per square meter. Also there is a prominent role of other gastropods and bivalves in deposition of $CaCO_2$ at the coral reefs.

4. **Echinodermata:** Some species of echinoderms have adverse effects on coral reef, particularly the sea star, *Acanthaster planci*, which predates the coral polyp and cause coral bleaching. However, other species of sea urchin, sea cucumbers, starfish and feather stars are found but their role in reef ecosystem is understood.

5. **Crustaceans and Polychaetes:** Members of these groups are very abundant on coral reefs but there is little information about their role in reef formation.

6. **Sponges:** They are essential for the functioning of the coral reefs ecosystem. Algae and corals produce organic material. This is filtered through sponges

which convert this organic material into small particles which in turn are absorbed by algae and corals. It was recorded that, some species of Siliceous sponges (class: Demospongiae) may be important in holding coral and rubble together, and prevent loss from reef until it can be fused together by coralline algae. Other sponges have symbiotic blue green algae responsible for net primary productivity.

7. **Coral reef fishes**: Fishes are very conspicuous and abundant and many of them may have an adverse effect on coral structure due to their feeding regime.

8. **Bacteria:** The role of these organisms is very important in reefs structures. This group is very abundant and is responsible for the decomposition and quick cycling of organic matter.

9. **Other communities:** Sea eels and snakes as well as marine birds; such as boobies, pelicans, gannets and herons, all feed on fish and other coral reef components'. Land-based reptiles such as monitor lizards, marine crocodile and semiaquatic snakes such as *Laticauda colubrina* can be intermittently associated with reefs and feed on some of their components. Sea turtles, such as hawksbill sea turtles, feed on sponges between reefs.

3. The importance of the coral reef ecosystem

Coral reef ecosystems are one of the most diverse and beautiful natural environments on earth. Coral reefs have an important role in the marine and coastal environments. They provide valuable habitat (food and shelter) for a great diversity of plants and animals, including important breeding and nursery grounds for many marine organisms [10].

Coral reefs also provide protection from coastal erosion by acting as natural breakwaters for big waves and storms. Also, the breakdown of corals and other organisms living in the reef habitat creates beaches, which are an important resource for the survival of many coastal organisms, including endangered sea turtles and monk seals. Coral reefs are an important environmental and economic resource for people. In addition to shoreline protection, reefs provide food, recreational and employment opportunities, and are a potential source for new medicines [11, 12]. Coral reefs also provide economic benefits to coastal communities from tourism. The major benefits from coral reef ecosystem will be described as follows:

3.1 Reef as a source of income

The diversity of marine life and coasts protected and supported by coral reefs supply attractive conditions and ambience for visitors, reef lovers, divers and snorkelers. Actually, there are more than 8.5 million certified divers in the USA who spend money on diving during each year. The coral reef destruction generates a considerable loss of tourism employment, marine recreation industries and fishing activities. These can have huge impacts on inhabitants of coral reef areas that essentially rely on income from tourism [13, 14].

The coral reefs ecosystem provides a significant protein source for millions of people, and is considered as part of their lives. The people inhabiting coral reef areas madly love it, because the coral reef is considered a part of their lives, providing them with the major part of their food through fishing and tourism services. Coral reefs are also strongly linked with cultural, spiritual and traditional values of many people who live in areas nearest to reefs [10].

3.2 Coral reefs act as protector from storm and wave action

Another benefit to people from coral reefs is that they act as the guards of our coast. They serve as a buffer and protection for the shore areas from the pounding of ocean waves. In the absence of coral reefs, many of beaches and coastal cities would become vulnerable to storm damage and wave action. In the Maldives, when the coral reef and sand were mined away along the coast, it cost $10 million American dollars for each kilometer to construct a wall for coastline protection. In Indonesia, the value of this protective service of coral reefs is estimated at 314 million American dollars [15].

3.3 Coral reefs save our lives

Just as in the rain forest, plant and animal life in reef ecosystem contain promising medicinal components, several of which are just being detected. Already, many important drugs have been developed from chemicals extracted from coral reef organisms. AZT is the most famous of these drugs, it is a treatment for HIV infections, which relies on chemicals extracted from sponge inhabiting Caribbean reef [16].

Several unique compounds extracted from coral reefs have also produced the treatments for skin cancer, leukemia, ulcers and cardiovascular diseases. In addition, the unique skeletal structures produced from reef have been used to produce the advanced forms of bone grafting materials. Surprisingly, more than half of all new research related cancer drug discovery focuses on marine organisms. The fragile and beautiful organisms of coral reefs have the potent to make even huge contributions to our lives through providing new treatments for diseases that are threats to our lives [11, 12].

3.4 Coral reefs serve as a home for fishes

Over the last 350 million years, coral reefs have developed to become one of the most and largest complex ecosystems on the earth planet. Coral reefs provide shelter for about 25% of all known marine species. They serve as a home to 4000 fish species, 700 corals species and thousands of other forms of flora and fauna. Ecologists estimate that more than one million of biota species are associated with the coral reef ecosystem [15, 17].

4. Global threats facing reef ecosystems

Coral Reef ecosystems are facing many natural and anthropogenic threats. Many human impacts are resulting in the destruction and degradation of coral reefs ecosystem to cause loss in biodiversity, fundamental supplies for food and reef economic revenue. Combined with threats from nature in the form of diseases, earthquakes, climate change, typhoons and storms, coral reefs are struggling to survive. Natural stressors are made worse by human disturbances. For example, the diseases may be present at a higher level in corals stressed by human influences such as pollution and mechanical damage [18].

A majority of the problems threatening coral reefs are the direct (and indirect) result of human activities on land, and in the marine environment. Marine debris, water pollution, sedimentation, overfishing, careless recreation, and global warming are some examples of human-caused threats to the coral reef habitat. Each of these threats has a significant impact on the health of coral reefs. Coral reefs grow very slowly and can take hundreds of years to form. If damage to coral reefs continues at the current rate, over half of all reefs in the world could disappear in our lifetimes. Currently, millions of acres of reef have already been severely damaged or destroyed. Through education, awareness, and action, people can help to preserve and protect coral reefs [15]. The threats facing coral reef ecosystems can be summarized as below:

4.1 Natural Impacts

4.1.1 Earthquakes and storms

Disasters such as earthquakes and storms occur periodically and naturally and devastate massive areas of coral reefs. These natural events can be more severe if the communities of coral reef are already weakened by other influences and recovery is inhibited by algal overgrowth due to the lack of grazing organisms, removed by fishing.

4.1.2 Climate change and acidification

Climate change impacts have been identified as one of the greatest global threats to coral reef ecosystems. If the temperatures of sea water stay higher than the usual for some weeks, the symbiotic algae "zooxanthellae" that corals rely on for their food leave the coral tissue. Actually, without zooxanthellae the corals turn to white color, because it gives corals their color. Unhealthy white corals are called bleached. Bleached corals are weak and lose their ability to combat diseases and then die [18]. As climate change continues, bleaching will become more common, and the overall health of coral reefs will decline [19, 20].

Since the late nineteenth century, the global temperature of oceans has risen by 1.3°F (0.74°C), causing more frequent and severe corals bleaching around the world. At the recent increasing emissions rate of greenhouse gases, the global temperature could rise up to 7.3°F (4.1°C). These changes in global temperature already have harmful effects on coral reef ecosystems and will continue to impact on coral reef ecosystems over the world during the next century. The decline and loss of coral reef ecosystems have significant social, cultural, economic, and ecological bad impacts on people and communities around the world [21].

As water temperature rises, infectious diseases and huge bleaching may likely become more frequent. In addition, carbon dioxide absorbed into the sea water from the atmosphere has begun to reduce the calcification rates in reef-building corals and organisms associated with coral throughout change of water chemistry by decreases in pH (ocean acidification). In the long term, the failure in addressing carbon emissions and the impacts of rising water temperatures and ocean acidification could make the several efforts to coral reef ecosystems managements futile. In summary, climate change and ocean acidification have been identified as the most important threats to CRE on a global basis [22].

In the last decades, 33–50% of corals were significantly degraded, because of the negative impacts that accompanied climate change [10]. Recently, some areas have lost about half or more of their living coral and more deterioration can occur over the next two decades due to continued temperature rise. Because of the destruction of the CRE, 25% of marine species would be in danger while the economic losses will showcase hundreds of millions of people to the lack of food security and increasing poverty [23]. Wilkinson [10] recorded bleaching and death of about 16% of the global reefs communities together with high average of surface temperature in 1998. Since then, the bleaching and death of coral occur on a large scale, with increasing severity of these effects over the successive decades [24].

Other reasons for coral bleaching are the extreme lowering in tides levels, increased UV radiation and changes in salinity and nutrient levels. Coral reefs may recover but this extreme incident is generally presumed to weakened it. The death may be occurring largely due to starvation, although it is thought that some autolysis (tissue destruction) occurs. The physiological mechanisms involved with bleaching are not fully understood and are currently a source of investigation.

4.1.3 Crown-of-Thorns

Historically, tropical cyclones and poor water quality that cause outbreaks of crown of thorns starfish have been the major causes of coral loss. Current increases in the Crown-of-Thorns starfish populations that eat corals are considered as another natural threat to reefs. When present in huge numbers, these stars are able to destroy massive areas of coral reef. Recovery of the coral reef from the outbreaks of Crown-of-Thorns may take up to 20–40 years, where the damage is not severe. However, coral recovery in some world areas may never occur when the coral is being taken over by sponge, algal cover and other coral species. *Acanthaster planci* can produce many million babies during 1 year. People have contributed to their population increase through increase of the nutrients from sewage and over harvesting of their natural predator Triton Trumpet and so on. Crown-of-Thorns babies gave more plant food (seaweed) to survive and become devastating adults for coral [25].

4.1.4 Coral diseases

Coral reefs when are under stress, suffer many bacterial infections as a result of growing production of protective mucus. The coral production for excessive mucus due to natural and man-made influences (e.g., global warming, toxic chemicals, increased sedimentation and so on) can also promote the growth of many blue green algae; this algae is thought to be responsible for black band disease (Intense black band of filaments across coral colonies). This disease kills the Coral polyps and the black band advances then leaving the reef as a white limestone behind it [16].

Although this disease is rare, the pathogenic bacteria and parasites resulting from fecal contamination may cause some diseases in coral reefs, particularly if corals are stressed by unfavorable environmental conditions. Naturally, the diseases occur for corals in healthy ecosystems, but the pathogen-containing pollution inputs could exacerbate the intensity and frequency of disease outbreaks [16].

A change of environmental conditions such as higher temperatures or a change in salinity but also disease can cause the polyps to expel the zooxanthellae algae. The coral becomes totally white (= coral bleaching). If the coral regains some algae it might survive, but bleaching can be irreversible and then the coral dies. Coral bleaching is the loss of intracellular endosymbionts (zooxanthellae) from coral tissue, when corals are stressed by changes in conditions such as temperature, light, or nutrients, they expel the symbiotic algae living in their tissues, causing them to turn completely white [2].

4.1.5 Invasive alien species

Invasive alien species are non-native (exotic) species that may cause huge environmental damages and can have effects on fisheries stock, economy and even on human health. They should not be confused with introduced spe-cies which are also non-native and have been deliberately introduced for a benefit or purpose within the limits imposed on them. It is estimated that of the several of the introduced species to different habitats and different climes have threats to native ecosystems. These invasive alien species have the ability to rapidly grow, vigorously compete with the native species. These species in the absence of their natural preda-tors can lead to the pushing out native species and finally to ecological havoc. They can be able to change and threaten native biodiversity and contribute to economic hardship and social instability, placing constraints on environmental conservation, economic growth and sustainable development [26]. Actually, the threat to global biodiversity from Invasive Alien Species is the second after habitat destruction. Ballast water is the major channel of spreading Invasive Alien Species in marine habitats. Ships discharge their cargo of ballast water at ports; with this discharge, they also release organisms that were taken in accidentally with the ballast water from other ports [27].

4.2 Anthropogenic impacts

4.2.1 Use the coral reefs in construction and curio trade

Coral reefs are used as a construction tool for many purposes. They may be used for the construction of house foundations, canals, streets, embankment of fish ponds and lime kilns. Large businesses also are keen on collecting coral reefs for selling them as souvenirs or in the aquarium trade.

4.2.2 Chemical pollution

Coastal waters suffer from huge amounts of a variety of agricultural and industrial chemicals that are released into them. Fertilizers and pesticides used in agricultural development projects are discharged into the sea and might lead to coral reef destruction. Pesticides pollution may destroy or harm to reef communities. They lead to further deterioration through accumulating in tissues and may affect physiological processes of animals. Herbicides may impact the basic food chain; they can destroy and damage symbionts zooxanthellae algae in coral reef, other algal, sea grass and even free living phytoplankton communities.

The chemical spillage from oil tankers, harbors and pipelines have heavy impacts on feeding, growth rate, reproduction, defensive responses and even on cell structure in coral reefs. Industrial activities such as dredging, mining and refining produce heavy metals and hydrocarbon pollutants that are released into coastal waters. Many coral species are more sensitive to these pollutants, which can damage the ecosystem of coral [28]. Herbicides and pesticides can affect coral reproduction, growth, and other physiological processes, in particular, can affect the symbiotic algae (plants). This can damage their partnership with coral and result in bleaching.

4.2.3 Nutrients loading/sewage

The discharge of aquacultural and agricultural inputs such as fertilizers, herbicides, pesticides, feed waste and other materials can result in more nutrients loading into coastal areas. These organic compounds lead to increases of eutrophi-cation status of coastal areas and subsequent oxygen depletion. When the nutrient loading into coastal areas and eutrophication occur, the community becomes dominated by algae and seaweed, to the limit transcend grazing organisms' capacity to control. These can leads to light reduction, oxygen depletion and perhaps death of the communities living there. When coral reef ecosystems are subjected to huge quantities of nutrients, they are easily taken over by algae and may be severely damaged, if not killed.

4.2.4 Fishing and overfishing

Illegal fishing such as blast "dynamite," cyanide or poison (duva) fishing and hunting by gum boots, are all destructive of any ecosystem. Other injurious practices of fishing include reef structure disintegration in order to remove hiding places, weight traps and herd fish into nets by beating coral surfaces. Accidental grounding of boats and anchor damage may be significant threat to coral reef ecosystem. Such practices lead to annihilation and degradation of habitat of coral reef ecosystem. For instance, 3150 km^2 of coral reef were destroyed when one cruise ship anchored on one occasion [29].

Overfishing may alter food-webs structure of coral reef ecosystem and cause cascading impacts, such as decrease of the grazer fish numbers that remove algal overgrowth and keep corals clean. Blast fishing (kill fish by explosives) may create physical damage to coral reefs [30].

The vast majority of the world's reefs are affected by over exploitation of resources. This may lead to decrease of average size of the fish and reduction of target predatory fish. Removal of main predator and herbivores species may result in change of large scale reef ecosystem. When grazers are removed from reef ecosystem, the algae quickly take over and dominate, particularly if the ecosystem is also suffering from organic pollution [31].

4.2.5 Construction and sedimentation

Sedimentation is an extremely important cause of destruction of coral reef ecosystem. Predominating, coastal development and construction can lead to heavy amounts of sediment. There are other effects caused by inadequate land management and deforestation, where sediment run off from farms and land and settling on the reefs. In this context, Watersheds that are cleared of their vegetation cover are vulnerable to flooding and erosion and can lead to increase of sedimentation levels reaching coral reefs. Agriculture chemicals also make their way reaching coral reefs through run off from land, streams and rivers [32].

Dredging has several serious impacts on coral reefs ecosystem. The most spectacular effects are produced by sedimentation, turbidity, silt suspension, reduction of oxygen and release of bacteria and toxic substances. Great quantities of either fine or coarse particles can cover corals, which are unable to withstand cover for more than 1 or 2 days [33].

The corals secrete protective mucus in a bid to rid themselves of the sedi-mentation. This process requires high energy levels, which have to be diverted away from essential processes. If this problem is exacerbate by other stresses, for example, temperature change, then the reefs become extra stressed and may die. The mucus secretion for sediment clearing makes the reefs more susceptible to infection by bacteria and therefore more probable to suffer from diseases [15]. The higher level of sedimentation that exceeds the clearing capacity of mucus secretion of coral reefs can reduce light breakthrough and may change the vertical distribu-tion of plants and animals on coral reefs [34].

4.2.6 Cutting of mangroves

Mangroves destruction by obvious cutting or pollution has resounding consequences on reef ecosystem. Mangroves destruction leads to the removal of the main source of leaf litter, a food resource for the set of reef animals. Also, mangroves provide the nutrient rich feeding grounds for several marine species. Moreover, mangroves protect the shoreline against storms and cyclones and give it stability against land loss by erosion.

4.2.7 Rubbish/litter

Trash such as discarded fishing gear, bottles and plastic bags that get to the coast may settle on reefs and prevent the sunlight required for photosyn-thesis or decomposition and kill reef organisms and damage or break corals. Degraded plastics and small pieces of plastic can be ingested by coral, turtles, fish and other reef animals, which can block their digestive tracts and kill them.

Litter and rubbish are one of the groups of largest problems facing any ecosystem. The decomposition of this artificial rubbish takes a very long time. Plastic bottles decomposed in 150 years, plastic bags 50 years, batteries in 200 years, paper in 1 year and cigarette in 75 years. A turtle facing a plastic bag similar to jellyfish may swallow it and can choke it. Batteries leak poisons as they breakdown and can con-taminate the fish we eat, as well as kill corals and other marine life. Rubbish should be disposed of properly, by recycling or taking it back to the mainland dump. If rubbish is left lying around, it can easily get blown into the sea.

4.2.8 Tourism

Tourism has a large potential to contribute to sustainable socio-economic development and environmental conservation. It can support the protection of natural resources, as local residents realize the value of their assets and try to preserve it. Tourism can also provide another form of land use (other than agriculture) which supports land conversion. It can also contribute to maintaining livelihoods and preserving cultural practices. Opportunities arise for education and awareness-raising to understand and respect cultural diversity along with biodiversity. All these benefits can be derived from the tourism if optimally used and controlled in the required form to preserve the environment, biological diversity and natural habitats. The uncontrol and misuse of tourism can lead to the degradation and collapse of ecosystems and biodiversity that are essentially the real attraction of tourism [4, 14, 35].

Tourism and biodiversity are closely linked both in terms of impacts and dependency. Many types of tourism rely directly on ecosystem services and biodiversity (ecotourism, agritourism, wellness tourism, adventure tourism, etc.). Tourism uses recreational services and supply services provided by ecosystems. Tourists are looking for cultural and environmental authenticity, contact with local communities and learning about flora, fauna, ecosystems and their conservation. On the other hand, too many tourists can also have a negative, degrading effect on biodiversity and ecosystems. Therefore, the tourism sector has both a strong influence on biodiversity loss and a role to play in its conservation [36]. Regrettably, the tourism-environment relationship is unbalanced; tourism is depending on an environment that is vulnerable to the tourism impacts [37]. Yet it's not easy to achieve sustainable development in many developing countries that heavily rely on tourism income, particularly in ecologically sensitive areas. Other influences come from the tourists services area such as domestic wastes, garbage and many bad practices from site visitors. The main harmful human activities that can destroy the biodiversity stock in any area result from uncontrolled tourism and fishing activity [1].

4.2.9 Coral harvesting for the aquarium trade

Coral harvesting for the aquarium trade, jewelry, and curios can lead to over-harvesting of specific species, destruction of reef habitat, and reduced biodiversity. The practice of keeping marine aquaria as a hobby has increased in the last decade. It is reported that, globally, between 1.5 and 2 million people keep saltwater aquaria [38, 39]. Murray et al. [40] confirmed that the areas of southern California rocky shores which have been used by humans intensely for recreational activities such as fishing, exploration, walking, enjoyment of the out-of-doors, and educational field trips had suffered from reduction of species abundance and diversity due to visitors collection of intertidal organisms for consumption, fish bait, home aquariums and other purposes. The most direct effects of intensive collection are decreased abundances of exploited species and because humans preferentially collect larger individuals, altered population size structures. El-Naggar et al. [4] attributed the reduction of certain gastropod shells (Cypraeidae) from Aqaba Gulf to their intensive collection by visitors because they have beautiful shells.

4.2.10 Fish-feeding

The feeding behavior of reef fishes, eels, sharks and even rays has come to a "selling point" through commercial fish feeding dive tours and "interactive diving." However, many do not realize the harmful effects this activity has on these animals. Studies done around the world have indicated that fish feeding significantly alters behavioral patterns by "training" these wild creatures with human food handouts. In addition, fish feeding causes health problems for the fed animals and disrupts the natural processes within the marine community. Here in the Mamanucas, particularly at sites where fish feeding occurs, there has been an increase in aggressive behavior within schools of surgeonfish, fighting amongst themselves and causing injury, even to the point of destroying their own reef habitat by breaking hard corals. Triggerfish have also been observed biting and destroying the reef structure. Sergeant Damselfish swarm around snorkelers or divers expecting to be fed. The fish that are fed often "peck' at the snorkelers or divers entering the water, taking away the pleasure of observing the reef and its inhabitants in a calm and inoffensive manner. By feeding the algae eaters that control algae growth, they become handout feeders that soon neglect their important role of eating algae, which in turn can overgrow corals. Major conservation organizations, including UNEP, DAN, WWF and Environmental Defense, encourage passive interaction with marine life and avoiding feeding and petting, which may lead to accidental injury.

5. Proposed solutions to mitigation of the coral reef threats (methods for conserve the coral reef)

The aggregate effects of these stressors can decrease resilience of the reef overall and increase susceptibility to disease and invasive species. The anthropogenic stressors on coral reef ecosystem are suggested potential factors respon-sible for the degradation and instability of any ecosystem. Any bad practices from human; directly and indirectly can have effects on coral reef ecosystem. So, it is necessary to create new strategies to protect coral reef ecosystems. Given that 20% of the coral reefs in the world have already been destroyed much has to be done in the future for the preserve of coral reef ecosystem.

5.1 Establishment of marine protected areas

One of the key techniques of conserving coral reef ecosystem is the establishment of Marine Protected Areas (MPAs). Marine Protected Areas (MPAs) are important tools for marine conservation and management. Although there are many types of MPAs, in all them, there are areas set aside for unlimited human activities. When the MPAs restriction is highest, they are considered as "no-take" areas, where the deal-ing with all forms of marine life is prevented; even recreation, research and educa-tion are restricted. Many of MAPs were constructed specifically for management of a special purpose (for instance, for biodiversity preservation, as a refuge of a certain species to breed, for conservation of a historical site or even for recreation). Multiple use management protected areas are zones to permit for complete limitation on dealing in some areas and managed use in others [41]. However, a main problem in MPAs is that they fail to achieved their management objectives and become parks on paper only [42]. Even though MPAs may be gazetted legally, enforcement of relevant laws (zoning, prohibiting certain activities) is often poor.

5.2 Prevention of over-harvesting through legislation

Many species are protected under general species protection laws across the region. Most of this protection is afforded to marine vertebrates, but some countries–such as India and Sri Lanka–have laws protecting several species of coral, mollusks and echinoderms. In India, all Stony corals, all Black corals, all Fire corals, and all Sea fans are protected by law [43]. In Sri Lanka, all Stony corals are protected by law [44].

5.3 Monitoring

Coral reefs monitoring is a substantial process for developing efficacious strategies of management. Only through monitoring only, is it possible to assess patterns and trends of coral reefs health and use. There are many worldwide organizations specializing in monitoring of coral reefs status. The Global Coral Reef Monitoring Network (GCRMN) devote their efforts and coordinates in order to improve coral reefs management in the whole world, this through capacity building and knowledge sharing and works closely with Reef Base (Global database about coral reef related information) and Reef Check. After the coral bleaching event in 1998 and with the continuous threat of coral degradation as a result of other anthropogenic activities, Coastal Ocean Research and Development in the Indian Ocean (CORDIO) commenced in 1999. CORDIO supports and funds the scientists and organizations in the Indian Ocean Region, for assurance of monitoring of coral reefs status in the region with focus on both socio-economic and ecological impacts of coral reef degradation. Monitoring plays a critical role in managing Marine Protected Areas. The importance of monitoring and research is in guiding management of the fisheries and biodiversity resources. It is necessary to develop a long term monitoring plan for management of abundance and diversity of biota coupled with an assessment of fishing and habitats quality including coral reef [1].

5.4 Building awareness

Building awareness about coral reef ecosystems, their biodiversity, services they provide and their business are highly supportive of mitigation of the threats that are facing these fragile ecosystem of coral reefs. Awareness at the community levels is extreme efficient as it may help to encourage coral reefs users to change their behavior to sustainable use of these ecosystems. On the other hand, the awareness at national level through conservation education by the media and other means is necessary to guarantee that decision makers integrate coral reef preser-vation into all development stages. It is also important to ensure that some envi-ronmental issues, such as poorly planned or unplanned inland development and pollution, are prevented in order to protect coastal ecosystems such as coral reefs. Worldwide, 1997 was designated as International Year of the Coral Reef Because of growing threats to coral reefs in the whole world. Also, 2008 was designated as International Year of the Coral Reef.

5.5 Support of sustainable livelihoods and participation in reef dependent communities

The relationship between reef ecosystems and poverty is very significant, whereas 67% of all countries having reef areas are developing countries and about 25% of these countries are least developed countries [45].

Coral reef ecosystems contribute to the national economies and provide significant resources for poor people. The current direction of growing threats to coral resources is projected to impact poor communities dependent on reef ecosystem. To make matters worse, the predominating objectives of reef ecosystem management for preservation restrict community access to their resources thus reducing livelihood options for these communities. Oftentimes, these restrictions are not followed by communities which may have weak understanding or low participation in the process of reef management.

It is now well recognized that these communities need to be offered alternates for livelihoods in order to assure that reefs are not further damaged, as well as to mitigate poverty for these communities. Therefore, managers of coastal areas are highly switching toward more integrated as well contributory approaches for coral reefs conservation and management. These approaches include identifying and supporting alternate livelihoods for reducing reliance on reef components, in addition to promoting the activities of current livelihood to make them more cost and resource use effective . Rather than comprehensive restrictions on reefs resources use, recently, limited and controlled uses of these resources are advocated in certain circumstances. The reef access rights, resolution of struggles over resource uses, local community involvement and cooperative reef management are now being integrated in to reefs resources management [46].

5.6 New management initiatives

It is now understood that the standard approaches of management of coastal zones have not been successful in realizing sustainable development and reef preservation aims and there is need for change in approaches [16].

The shifting from small and isolated efforts of management to large-scale networks using cooperative management is a new trend. Increasing reefs area under high conservation is a main propulsion for this shifting, thus now 33% of Great Barrier Reef has been declared as a highly protected areas or as no-take zones, where no activity is permitted except in the narrowest limits. The cooperation for creating greater network of Marine Protected Areas is another meth - od that has been favored by main Non-governmental organizations (NGOs) such as Conservation International, the Nature Conservancy and the World Wildlife Fund who are developing training modules to identify and develop a network of Marine Protected Areas in Asia depending on zones of highest biodiversity. Another shift is in the effort to focus research on real-life problems that resource managers face [16].

Author details

Hussein A. El-Naggar
Zoology Department, Faculty of Science, Al-Azhar University, Cairo, Egypt

*Address all correspondence to: hu_gar2000@yahoo.com

References

[1] Mona MH, El-Naggar HA, El-Gayar EE, Masood MF, Mohamed ENE. Effect of human activities on biodiversity in Nabq Protected Area, South Sinai, Egypt. Egyptian Journal of Aquatic Research. 2019;**45**:33-43

[2] El-Naggar HA. Student Lectures, Faculty of Science, Al-Azhar University; 2019

[3] Wilkinson C, Brodie J. Catchment Management and Coral Reef Conservation: A Practical Guide for Coastal Resource Managers to Reduce Damage from Catchment Areas Based on Best Practice Case Studies. Townsville, Australia: Global Coral Reef Monitoring Network and Reef and Rainforest Research Centre; 2011

[4] El-Naggar HA, El-Gayar EE, Mohamed ENE, Mona MH. Intertidal Macro-benthos diversity and their relation with tourism activities at Blue Hole Diving Site, Dahab, South Sinai, Egypt. SYLWAN. 2017;**161**(11):227-251

[5] Ali AAM, Hamed MA, Abd El-Azim H. Heavy metals distribution in the coral reef ecosystems of the Northern Red Sea. Helgoland Marine Research. 2011;**65**:67-80

[6] Al-Moghrabi SM. Unusual black band disease (BBD) outbreak in the northern tip of the Gulf of Aqaba (Jordan). Coral Reefs. 2001;**19**:330-331

[7] Graham NAJ, Jennings S, Macneil MA, Mouillot D, Wilson SK. Predicting climate-driven regime shifts versus rebound potential in coral reefs. Nature. 2015;**5181**:94-97

[8] de Groot R, Brander L, Van Der Ploeg S, Costanza R, Bernard F, Braat L. Global estimates of the value of ecosystems and their services in monetary units. Ecosystem Services. 2012;**1**:50-61

[9] ISRS "International Society for Reef Studies". ISRS Consensus Statement on Climate Change and Coral Bleaching. Prepared for the 21st Session of the Conference of the Parties to the United Nations Framework Convention on Climate Change, Paris, December 2015. Available from: http://coralreefs.org/wp-content/uploads/2014/03/ISRS

[10] Wilkinson C. Status of Coral Reefs of the World: 2008. Townsville, Australia: Global Coral Reef Monitoring Network and Reef and Rainforest Research Centre; 2008. 296 p

[11] Hasaballah AI, El-Naggar HA. Antimicrobial activities of some marine sponges, and its biological, repellent effects against *Culex pipiens* (Diptera: Culicidae). Annual Research & Review in Biology. 2017;**12**(3):1-14

[12] El-Naggar HA, Hasaballah AI. Acute larvicidal toxicity and repellency effect of *Octopus cyanea* crude extract against the filariasis vector, *Culex pippiens*. Journal of the Egyptian Society of Parasitology. 2018;**48**(3):721-728

[13] Mathieu L, Langford IH, Kenyon W. Valuing marine parks in a developing country: A case study of the Seychelles. CSERGE Working Paper GEC. 2000;**27**

[14] Emerton L. Seychelles Biodiversity: Economic Assessment. Paper prepared for National Biodiversity Strategy and Action Plan, Conservation and National Parks Section, Division of Environment, Victoria; 1997

[15] Burke L, Selig L, Spalding M. Reefs at Risk in Southeast Asia. Washington, DC: World Resources Institute; 2002. 72 p

[16] Wilkinson C. Status of the Coral Reefs of the World. Vol. 1 + 2. Townsville, Australia: Global Coral Reef Monitoring Network and Australian Institute of Marine Science; 2004. 557p

[17] Hughes TP, Baird AH, Card M, Connolly SR, Folke C, Grosberg R, et al. Climate change, human impacts, and the resilience of coral reefs. Science. 2003;**301**:929-933

[18] Dalton SJ, Smith DA. Coral disease dynamics at a subtropical location, Solitary Islands Marine Park, Eastern Australia. Coral Reefs. 2006;**25**:37-45

[19] Beeden R, Willis BL, Raymundo LJ, Page CA, Weil E. Underwater Cards for Assessing Coral Health on Indo-Pacific Reefs. Coral Reef Targeted Research and Capacity Building for Management Program. Melbourne: Currie Communications; 2008 22pp

[20] Kleypas JA, Yates KK. Coral reefs and ocean acidification. Oceanography. 2009;**22**(4):108-117

[21] NOAA "National Oceanic and Atmospheric Administration". NOAA declares third ever global coral bleaching event. 2015. Available from: http://www.noaanews.noaa.gov/stories2015/100815-noaa-declares-third-coral-bleaching-event.html

[22] IPCC "International Panel on Climate Change". The Physical Science Basis. Contribution of Working Group I to the Fifth Assessment Report of the Intergovernmental Panel on Climate Change (Stocker TF, et al., ed.). Cambridge, United Kingdom and New York, NY, USA: Cambridge University Press; 2013. 1535 p

[23] Jackson JBC, Donovan MK, Cramer KL, Lam VV. Status and Trends of Caribbean Coral Reefs: 1970-2012. Gland, Switzerland: Global Coral Reef Monitoring Network, IUCN; 2014. 304 pp

[24] Hoegh-Guldberg O, Cai R, Poloczanska ES, Brewer PG, Sundby S, Hilmi K, et al. The ocean. In: Climate Change 2014: Impacts, Adaptation, and Vulnerability. Part B: Regional Aspects. Contribution of Working Group II to the Fifth Assessment Report of the Intergovernmental Panel on Climate Change. Cambridge University Press, Cambridge, United Kingdom and New York, NY, USA; 2014. pp. 1655-1731

[25] Forbes E. Coral Reefs and the Crown-of-Thorns Starfi sh. 2006. Available from: http://jrscience.wcp.muohio.edu/fieldcourses06/PapersMarineEcologyArticles/CoralReefsandtheCrown-of-.html

[26] IUCN. Guidelines for the Prevention of Biodiversity Loss Caused by Alien Invasive Species. Gland: Switzerland: IUCN; 2000. p. 21

[27] ten Hallers-Tjabbes C. Marine Biodiversity threatened by ballast water transported by ships; curbing the threat. In subtheme, Coping with Aliens. In: Proceedings of Biodiversity loss and species extinctions, managing risk in a changing world. A global synthesis workshop convened at the IUCN World Conservation Forum 18-20 November 2004. Bangkok, Thailand; 2004

[28] Available from: http://www.iucn.org/themes/wcpa/newsbulletins/webstories/guimarassep2006htm.htm

[29] Jackson JB et al. Historical over-fishing and the recent collapse of coastal ecosystems. Science. 2001;**293**(5530):629-637

[30] Donaldson TJ, Graham TR, McGilvray GJ, Phillips MJ, Rimmer MA, Sadovy YJ, et al. While Stocks Last: The Live Reef Food Fish Trade. Asian Development Bank. Available from: http://www.adb.org/Documents/Books/Live_Reef_Food_Fish_Trade/62289_summary.pdf; 2003

[31] Baillie J, Groombridge B (Compilers and Editors). IUCN Red List of Threatened Animals. IUCN: Gland, Switzerland and Cambridge, UK. 2007.

[32] Brown BE, Dunne RP, Scofi TP. Coral rock extraction in the Maldives, central Indian Ocean–limiting the damage. Coral Reefs. 1995;**2007**(14):236

[33] Rajasuriya A, Zahri H, Venkataraman K, Islam Z Tamelander J. Status of coral reefs in South Asia: Bangladesh, Chagos, India, Maldives and Sri Lanka. In: Souter D, Linden O, editors. Coral reef degradation in the Indian Ocean Status Report. Sweden: CORDIO; 2004. pp. 213-233

[34] Nybakken JW. Marine Biology: An Ecological Approach. 3rd ed. New York: Harper Collins; 1993. 579 pp

[35] Hilmi N, Safa A, Reynaud S, Allemand D. Coral reefs and tourism in Egypt's Red Sea. Topics in Middle Eastern and African Economies. 2012;**1**:416-434

[36] EUBBP (European Union Business and Biodiversity Platform). Tourism Sector and Biodiversity Conservation, Best Practice Benchmarking. Outcome of a workshop by the European Union Business and Biodiversity Platform; 2010. 25 p

[37] Wong PP, editor. Tourism vs. Environment: The Case for Coastal Areas. Dordrecht: Kluwer Academic Publishers; 1993

[38] Wabnitz C, Taylor M, Green E, Razak T. From Ocean to Aquarium. Cambridge, UK: UNEP-WCMC; 2003

[39] Sadovy YJ, Donaldson TJ, Graham TR, McGilvray F, Muldoon GJ, Phillips MJ, et al. While Stocks Last: The Live Reef Food Fish Trade. Manila, Philippines: ADB S; 2003

[40] Murray SN, Teri GD, Janine SK, Jayson RS. Human visitation and the frequency and potential effects of collecting on rocky intertidal population in Southern California Marine Reserves. CalCOFl Reports. 1999;**40**

[41] Agardy MT. Advances in marine conservation: the role of marine protected areas. Trends in Ecology and Evolution. 1994;**9**:267-270

[42] Jameson SC, Tupper MH, Ridley JM. The three screen doors: Can marine "protected" areas be effective? Marine Pollution Bulletin. 2002;**44**:1177-1183

[43] Wlidlife Protection Act India. 1972. Available from: http://envfor.nic.in/legis/wildlife/wildlife1.html

[44] Fauna & Flora Protection Ordinance No. 2 of 1937 as amended 1993. Sri Lanka: Government of Sri Lanka Press

[45] UNDP. Human Development Report 2002. United Nations Development Programme. 2002. Available from: http://hdr.undp.org/en/reports/global/hdr2002/

[46] Whittingham E, Campbell J, Townsley PP. Poverty and reefs. DFID–IMM–IOC/UNESCO; 2003. 260 pp

Chapter 6

Human Factors: The Impact on Industry and the Environment

Fiona J. Campbell

Abstract

New technology is evolving rapidly, creating new environmental and industrial challenges that must be considered. Technology continues to focus on the demands of industry to increase efficiency and production output. At the same time, industry must quickly adapt to new technologies in order to compete and grow and also face the increased awareness for the need to evaluate and mitigate environmental impact. Recent studies indicate that the use of automation in the workplace will nearly double in the next few years. If we look at the control room as being the core of the industrial environment, the focus was previously on the physical and automated components. Little focus has been on the humans that control this rapidly evolving technology, and there is still not enough focus on the most critical component that can not only impact production and output but also create a negative impact on the environment as a result of human error that could have been avoided. It is time to take a step back and look at what impact the humans are having on the environment as a result of the rapidly changing technology.

Keywords: human factors, human error, control room environment, control room design, control room operator

1. Introduction

If we look at the generally accepted definition of the word environment as the natural world, and industry as the processing of raw materials from this natural world, then the link between the human impact on industry and the environment can be easily understood. Industry is a man-made function developed specifically to maximize the value of raw materials. The next logical step is to examine how human error can be directly related to negative environmental impact and how this could be mitigated, if not prevented. If we look back in history at the evolution of industry, we can see a pattern emerge as industry began and continues to be more driven by technology. With Industry 4.0 focusing on the latest and greatest technology, the concern is that the human involved in developing, implementing and monitoring this technology will be overshadowed by technology itself. No matter how quickly technology advances, industry will always ultimately be controlled by humans. The risk of human error must be mitigated—one mistake can result in huge and in some cases irreversible environmental damage. The increasing need for a focus on the psycho-social work environment must be considered. How has this critical element been downplayed to a point that it is almost non-existent when it comes to evaluating environmental risk? The purpose of this chapter is to take a step back and identify some key considerations that should be a baseline when analyzing the impact of industry on the environment.

2. Industry 4.0—how did we get here?

Industry is driven by technology which can be traced back to the beginning of the first industrial revolution in the eighteenth century. This is commonly understood as the transformation from an agrarian economy to one that was transformed by industry and machine manufacturing. The technological changes involved the use of iron and steel, new energy sources including fuel and coal, and the invention of new machines to process these sources to increase production which then led to the development of factories to house the machines [1].

This was followed by the second industrial revolution, which led to the development of automated factories, and an expansion into the use of additional resources such as different metals, as well as the start of production of other products (plastics and chemicals for example) that required the further development of automation and factories as well as the start of mass production. The third industrial revolution, brought semiconductors, computing and later on the internet—this is known as the Digital Revolution [2]. Now it is generally accepted that we are now into the fourth industrial revolution, or Industry 4.0 which can be defined as "a new era that builds and extends the impact of digitalization in new and unanticipated ways" [3]. The result is even further and quicker development of technologies, automation and factories that are developing more rapidly than we thought possible.

If we look at the advancement of industry through each of these periods, there are two key elements that need to be considered as critical, especially as they relate to human factors and the potential impact on the environment. First, as factories became more automated, the processes also became more streamlined—over time it became possible to control multiple actions within an industrial setting from one centralized area: the control room. Second, as automated and advanced these processes became (and continue to become), the human was, and today still is, involved. No matter how advanced the technology, there is always a human either watching the process or controlling the process and, in many cases, it is both. As much as technology facilitates industrial automation, it also creates new challenges. Smart and intuitive technology and the resulting requirement for increased employee expertise will have a major impact on how these new technologies are both implemented and at the same time controlled.

The control room is the core of all industrial production facilities—this is where technology is monitored, analyzed and where all processes that are taking place as part of production are operated. The humans that work in a control room are commonly referred to as operators, and for the purposes of this discussion, the term "operator" unless otherwise specified, will refer to the human who is working in the control room. Operators today are overloaded, and unless we consider all aspects to mitigate the stress of the environment in the control room, it will affect not only production but also safety and has the potential to lead to both positive and negative impact on the environment as a whole.

3. Major industrial disasters reported to be caused by human error

If we look at a few well-known major disasters that had major impact on the environment, we can see where and how human error was identified as the cause.

Take for example Union Carbide in Bhopal, India in 1984. The analysis of that accident determined two out of three safety systems in place were shut down or broken—operators were so used to hearing alarms go off, for other reasons, they did not pay attention to the one that was critical resulting in 40 tons of toxic gas and chemicals released into the environment [4]. Which raises the question of how could this have been avoided? Why was there no system in place to prevent this? It would suggest that had the safety systems been updated, repaired or at the very least maintained, this might have been avoided.

A few years later there was Chernobyl in 1986. In that case, control room operators ran the plant at very low power, without adequate safety precautions and without properly coordinating or communicating the proper procedures with other personnel, the end result being the meltdown of one of the nuclear reactors [5]. It led to the mass release of radiation that is estimated to have traveled across nearly 8000 square miles (over 20,000 square km) of Europe [6]. With both of these disasters, there is still no definitive estimate of the resulting impact on the environment; however, it is undoubtably substantial and ongoing. Many studies of both examples have been done, and many questions asked about technology and physical and mechanical failure. Yet ultimately, both were traced back to the control room and the operator—human error.

In 1989, there was the Exxon Valdez disaster, which arguably was one of the largest environmental disasters, and was seen as the worst oil spill in US history: "The impact on local wildlife was devastating: An estimated 250,000 sea birds died in the months after the spill, and 14 members of the 36 local Prince William Sound killer whale pod had disappeared by 1990. The so-called carcass count also tallied, among other creatures, 1000 dead sea otters as well as 151 dead bald eagles..." [7]. There have been many articles and analyses of this very well-known disaster, but the common underlying theme in these studies ultimately also points back to the key cause of this disaster: human error. The inquiry that followed the disaster identified "... drinking, exhaustion of depleted crews, unqualified pilots on the bridge, violations of basic sailing rules, lax Coast Guard monitoring and a blind reliance on new technology all figured in the grounding on March 24 of the Exxon Valdez" [8]. In this case, it was multiple events all leading back to the human that resulted in the disaster. Could this have been avoided?

With the explosion on the Deepwater Horizon offshore oil rig in 2010, the analysis of the cause was multifaceted. It was a combination of years of cutting corners while moving forward with technology and advances, not one careless mistake that was to blame—however, one key point in this case was that despite all the experience of the crew on the rig, combined with the technology, the operators did not see the sign of trouble until it was too late, and did not act quickly enough to contain it, in fact did not know how to [9]. Environmental impact in this case was substantial: the oil was toxic to a wide range of organisms, including fish, birds, and sea mammals such as dolphins and sea turtles, not to mention corals as well as other ecosystems [10]. The final report on the Deepwater explosion concluded that it was not mechanical failure, but human error that was the root cause of the explosion [11]. It was also stated that "... regulators, however, failed to keep pace with the industrial expansion and new technology" [11]. Not only was the actual disaster caused by an error from the operator controlling the technology, we can see that it was human error on multiple levels which led to the disaster—regulators, management focusing on cutting costs with the expectation to increase financial results, all the way down the chain to the operator who failed to react correctly in a critical situation.

In 2011, there was the Fukushima Daiichi nuclear explosion in Japan. Where the initial thought was that the blame for this incident could be directly related to an earthquake and the tsunami that followed, reality is that this disaster was also the result of human error. An independent panel that was commissioned by the government of Japan to analyze the disaster determined that the meltdowns of reactors at the Fukushima Daiichi nuclear plant had "...less to do with the earthquake and tsunami that hit Japan ... and more to do with the plant owners' and government's failure to anticipate and prepare for emergencies on such an epic scale" [12]. Furthermore, the report to the Japanese government was that it was human error: "The crisis at the Fukushima nuclear plant was "a profoundly man-made disaster" [13]. Once again, a major disaster with ongoing effect on the environment that is still having an impact today. And once again, a multifaceted case of human error on more than one level.

A more recent example was the Columbia Gas explosions in Massachusetts in 2018. According to US Federal investigators preliminary report, customers received gas from a low-pressure distribution network, which in turn was fed from high pressure main pipeline. At the time, workers were replacing some of the piping but due to faulty procedures, faulty work orders and lack of proper communication, full pressure from the main pipeline fed into the local distribution network, which then lead to a chain reaction resulting in multiple explosions [14]. Once again, a large-scale disaster caused directly by human error. Some of the dangers of natural gas are obvious such as pollution, and the resulting impact on public health, and some are not so obvious, including but not limited to the impact on mental health as a result of major incidents such as the one in noted above as well as the fear of potential similar incidents occurring in the future. Considering that there are thousands of miles of outdated infrastructure, and no real way of predicting when the next explosion might occur [15], the concerns are very real. The outdated infrastructure not only applies to the gas industry, but undoubtably in every major industry worldwide. This not only is a concern due to the potential loss of life caused by these accidents, but also the resulting potential effects on the environment as a whole.

The above-mentioned cases further serve to highlight the fact that the human is often forgotten when major environmental disasters occur. In 1998 it was noted that "So much attention is devoted to the cost of industrial disasters in financial terms and to the technologies that fail at times, that it is possible to lose sight of the fact that disasters involve people, individually and in societal groups. Although awareness and concern about the human factor in industrial disaster has grown considerably over the last 15–20 years, many continue to see human error in a very narrow perspective" [16]. It is important to note that it is now 2019, and the risk of human error is still viewed as an afterthought. A key point to consider is that as we are now in the midst of the fourth industrial revolution, the focus is arguably even more on increasing production, combined with continuing to advance technology to aid in this goal. Yet the role of the human as an integral part of this is still being underestimated, not the least of which is the lack of focus of the direct effect of the human on the environment, and conversely, the effect of the industrial control room environment on the human.

4. Focus on the environment

As environmental impact is becoming more of a worldwide concern on a large scale, the actual physical environment where the human is monitoring and effectively tasked with preventing a major incident must also become a priority. With the ongoing and increasing demand for governments to react to increasing concerns of the effect of industry on the environment and climate change, the pressure is increasing even more on industry to actively focus on ways to contribute to the solution. The Paris Accord of 2015 states that the "... central aim is to strengthen the global response to the threat of climate change by keeping a global temperature rise this century well below 2°C above pre-industrial levels and to pursue efforts to limit the temperature increase even further to 1.5°C" [17]. So what does this mean for industry?

With the push on efficiency leading to the development of even more advanced technology, the impact of this on the human as well as the role of the operator seems to be falling to the wayside. It is not simply a question of updating dated infrastructure and adding extra screens for the operator in the control room to monitor. No matter how advanced technology becomes, it will always be designed and operated by the human. The key factor being that it is the humans who are the one who will ultimately push or not push the button to prevent a future large-scale disaster. As we can see all frequently, major industrial disasters are still taking place. At what point will industry take a step back and realize that the operational environment can have a direct impact on the natural environment? As technology and automation continue to rapidly evolve, the focus of industry must now shift from not only increasing production, maximizing efficiency, and reducing environmental impact through cutting emissions among other key factors, but also analyzing the humans who are controlling the technology to achieve this, and specifically, the environment in which this technology is centered.

5. The control room environment: design is critical

As stated previously, the control room is the centralized location where all technology is monitored. It has been argued that the control room environment is effectively the heart of a production facility—it is viewed as the core of the operations, where technology is centered and the intent is to be able to operate 24 hours a day, 365 days a year [18]. The main goal of an effective control room is to ensure production is continual, uninterrupted and efficient, with as minimal downtime as possible. Creating a control room that considers the human element is one of the most challenging yet also arguably the most critical factor when contemplating not only how to optimize production, but also how to prevent serious environmental impact. The technology needs to be effective, but the human machine interface (HMI) must also be a key focus. What has been neglected previously must now be considered—the control room needs to factor in as many points as technology does when it advances. The psycho-social aspect of the control room environment and the human involvement can no longer be ignored. With up to 90% of accidents that can be attributable to human error [19], and with accidents still continuing to occur, it is apparent that changes need to be made.

There have been many papers written about specific elements of a control room, more often than not looking at ways to increase efficiency, production, and updating technology; however, the focus on the operator in this environment is still a secondary element that is not often considered when evaluating industrial advancement. There is so much technology out there today we are still learning what it does—the amount of information that is instantly available at the touch of a button is unprecedented. Another key point is that 1 week's worth of information in the news today provides more information than an average person in the seventeenth century encountered in their lifetime [20]. If you consider this within the environment of an industrial control room, the amount of information that is monitoring every aspect of production (and subsequently immediately provided to the operator) can be overwhelming to the average person. The operators are having to process massive amounts of information quickly, accurately, and safely. Unfortunately, this is not easy, and there are many challenges which are continuing to grow as fast as the advances.

There are many challenges industry is facing when considering the control room environment. When speaking to companies across various industrial environments today, there are multiple concerns that surface almost immediately. When speaking in depth with operations management, the initial conversations usually start with "management wants us to increase our production output, so we need to look at upgrading our technology". As the discussion continues, often we find out that in actual fact, the technology is causing more problems than previously thought. Referring back to the Union Carbide disaster, it was noted that there were so many alarms going off in the control room that the operators chose to ignore the one that was truly critical. What is concerning is that this is still occurring today.

Recent discussions with an oil company led to the operation manager stating that the operators in the control room were dealing with 86,000 alarms a day, which meant each operator was dealing with approximately 60 alarms per minute, or one alarm going off every second. It simply is not humanly possible for an operator to be able to process and react to that kind of situation. In this case, the alarms simply become white noise, or background noise, and are ignored as way for the operator to be able to cope with the constant barrage of notifications.

A similar situation was noted in an amino acid producing company, where the operations supervisor stated that the operators had been experiencing so many alarms, that they had simply decided to turn them all off to try to reduce the operator stress. When asked how they were monitoring to ensure there were no major indicators of serious problems, the response was they were watching the screens. When asked how many screens they had, it was determined they had more than a dozen monitors requiring constant observation. Once again, how is it possible for the operator to be able to observe and react to the critical situations when there is a massive amount of information that constantly needs to be processed?

These are only two examples of existing situations relating specifically to alarms—there are many more. However, the key underlying point in both these cases is how will it be possible for the operator to react to an actual alarm? In the first case, there are so many alarms that the operator simply cannot be capable of quickly determining which one is critical. In the second case, with no audible alarms, the operator is expected to react based on visual monitoring, requiring constant focus. And if they need to walk away from a screen, what happens if that is the moment when a critical situation occurs?

These conversations usually lead to the identification of yet another recurring theme: the ability to attract and retain operators in a control room environment. Notable comments include: "we are finding it hard to fill operator positions, I'm not sure when we will be able to find the staffing to keep up with the demands for increased production", as well as "our experienced operators are starting to retire, and taking their experience with them, how do we transfer the knowledge if we can't even fill the positions?". Add to this common comments from operators themselves: "I haven't had the time to really be trained on the new system, so I'm just doing what I can to maintain production as best as I can", along with "I have brought up concerns several times but nothing ever changes, so its getting more stressful every shift". Another common comment "I'm trying to get management to let us have a coffee machine in the control room, but so far they won't agree. I can't take the risk to go down the hall to get a coffee in case I miss something on the screen, and with the long shifts, I really need the coffee to help me stay alert." All these comments are red flags that are unfortunately too common.

The human challenge in today's industrial control room, is not only with finding more technologically advanced operators, but is also in creating workplaces that retain those skilled employees. This in and of itself presents its own challenges. How will industry attract and keep the operators required to keep up with the fast paced, technology-driven new operational environment? Difficulties in retaining good employees needs to also be factored into industrial planning. Understanding the challenges and being aware of the obstacles from the employee/employer standpoint is of paramount importance for the workforces of the future. This increasing need for a focus on the psycho-social work environment is critical—unfortunately, this has not been the focus to date. There are solutions that are not immediately apparent, that can be applied to all industry sectors, but a start must be made to address the human factors that can affect industry and as a result, the environment.

6. Human factors in the control room

Industry is now at a point where it must consider the control room as the starting point in terms of preventing industrial disasters and the resulting environmental impact. Updating technology is only one component of that. In the examples listed previously with regards to alarms, there are solutions to reduce alarms to a manageable and acceptable level which can then help reduce the stress of the operator. It must be noted that the example of alarms is, however, only one concern. We have briefly touched on alarms, however there is also the topic of cybersecurity and the risks that can be found as a result of improper system design, and again can be directly related to the control room operator. Cybersecurity itself is a topic that can be discussed in great depth as it relates to the control room and needs to be considered.

A quick example of how critical this is can be observed when looking at the attack on the power grid in the Ukraine in December 2015. In that case, hackers were able to get into the control system being used and take the power system offline and all the operator could do was watch it happen: "The operator grabbed his mouse and tried desperately to seize control of the cursor, but it was unresponsive. Then as the cursor moved in the direction of another breaker, the machine suddenly logged him out of the control panel. Although he tried frantically to log back in, the attackers had changed his password preventing him from gaining re-entry. All he could do was stare helplessly at his screen while the ghosts in the machine clicked open one breaker after another, eventually taking about 30 substations offline. The attackers didn't stop there, however. They also struck two other power distribution centers at the same time, nearly doubling the number of substations taken offline and leaving more than 230,000 residents in the dark." [21]. What would happen if this had been a chemical company? Or oil company? Or nuclear reactor? The possibilities are frightening in terms of what could have happened. Although this specific example did not lead to an environmental disaster, it is an important point to consider as part of the human factor discussion, especially as it relates to control rooms. Another factor which will not be touched on in this discussion is the potential effect of a disgruntled employee. Yet another topic that can have a direct impact on the environment, and at the same time can be the result of the industrial environment. The increased pressure for production, cost cutting, government pressure on industry in order to be able to meet environmental obligations can all take a toll. Unfortunately, this is not something that is considered.

There are other key factors that need to be analyzed as well, such as lighting, air quality, communication, workflow analysis, traffic patterns, operator health all of which can contribute to operator fatigue and stress if not properly considered. Each one of these are topics that have been analyzed in depth and offer solid research that can directly relate to the control room. Which is why proper design of the control room must be completely evaluated. The benefits of a well-designed control room environment include increased operator awareness, alertness and quicker reaction times in a critical situation. It can increase safety and establish more efficient operations, create a sense of unity and teamwork, and can improve data integrity and data availability by making sure the correct data is being provided as required. It also allows for the ability to expand more easily in the future. Most importantly? It can create a relaxed, safe environment where employees want to work.

If we look a little more closely at the operator which is the key focus for the purposes of this chapter, more automated systems require less but more highly educated operators that are more analytical and have the ability to quickly react when needed. This in itself requires industry to fully understand the new generation that is coming into the workforce. The new generation has a completely different set of requirements and demands that are a direct result of being brought up in the digital age. There are many surveys and statistics available that help pinpoint the requirements and demands of this new generation as well all of which need to be referred to when considering the control room environment. The start point is the human. The environment of the control room can have a major impact on how the operator is able to react in a critical situation. Keeping in mind that these rooms run 24 hours a day, and are staffed during this time, operator fatigue is a yet another concern. A recent study notes that: "All kinds of industries are finding a link between fatigue and work-related injuries: the risk of errors, accidents and injuries—especially in high-risk, safety-critical environments—jumps when workers are tired and cannot function at their peak level" [22]. So what does this mean? As noted previously, industry is finding it harder to attract operators to the control room environment. Staffing is becoming an issue, and as a result, existing operators in some cases are being required to work longer shifts.

If we examine the issues identified above, the effect of the control room environment on the human can be linked to operator error. And as a result, operator error, identified as being the cause of major industrial disasters, can then be directly related to human impact on the environment. The increase in the demand for production leads to operators having to work more efficiently and in some cases with longer hours to meet demand. Coupled with advancing technology, the operator is now facing new challenges as part of their day to day operations, as they are expected to learn these new technologies and apply them. If this technology is applied on top of existing systems, we can see that it is not necessarily making it easier for the operator to monitor (think of the alarm example), and in fact is increasing their stress. For more experienced operators, it can be a challenge to learn the technology; for the new generation, the technology itself might easier to learn, however the environment of the control room is not always suited to their expectations. With a world that is being driven by technology, what is the attraction to work in a 24/7 environment, especially the night shift, if an opportunity can be found in another market segment for similar pay? Let us take for example a large industrial production company that is based in a small town. When meeting with them to discuss their control room concerns, they mentioned several of these issues yet they could not understand why they were having so many problems attracting operators. Their experienced operators were retiring and they were concerned about how they would replace them. They were finding that they were able to hire, but within a few weeks of working in the control room, the new hires were leaving, citing the control room environment as being an unappealing work environment.

A similar situation was echoed by another large production facility—in their case, they were located in an even smaller town with access to a smaller pool of technologically qualified operators who would be able to operate the system that they had recently upgraded. To counter this, they decided the best course of action was to hire operators and train them. What they found out is that it was taking them 6–12 months to train the new operators—but often before the end of the training, the operators were taking other positions in different market segments, citing the lack of desire to work in a very high stress environment. The remaining operators were tasked with taking on extra shifts to ensure the production output goals set by management were met. The operations manager in that example was exhausted, and had no idea how to deal with the situation or even where to start. The comment from the manager was "our system needs to be updated, the training time on the technology is limited, its so advanced that we are barely touching the surface, operators are leaving, we can't find replacements and yet we must continue to meet the production output and learn new ways to reduce our emissions as mandated by upper management—where do we start?"

If we add in the pressure to reduce environmental impact, this is leading industry to find ways of cutting corners in order to meet the requirements. The additional pressure is flowing down directly into the control room, to those who are the ones who control production. So now not only is there the pressure that was experienced previously, there are additional elements added to the list and the demand on the human is increasing even further. As noted previously, the major industrial disasters that have occurred in the past were caused by human error. As much as technology develops, the risk of another major disaster is not necessarily going to diminish unless industry is able to realize that the human will always be involved. It must become a priority.

The importance of human factors cannot be underestimated. "It has been found, after countless accidents and incidents, some including fatalities, that it is the actions (or sometimes the lack of action) of the system users who more often than not are the actual pre-cursors to the events actually occurring... As such the "Human Factor" element is an extremely important aspect..." [23]. Unfortunately, this does not seem to be the focus in many industrial environments. Although it is often discussed, it is more often ignored or relegated to a lower level on a priority list.

7. Human factors: we need to focus on the human

It would appear that there has been no real consistently implemented plan developed to ensure that the human is considered as part of the rapid developments in industry. Despite the fact there are repeated common occurrences across all different types of industry, it would seem that the combined impact of the human on the environment and the impact of the environment on the human have still not become the focus. There are however, some arguments that can be put forth that can perhaps help with the creation of a more human focused approach. If we accept that it is the human who is creating the technology that is driving the changes in industry, then we must also accept the fact that these changes in technology are also impacting the human. Yet not all of these changes are necessarily positive. As we have noted, as much as production is increasing, and information is becoming available at lightning speed, this is also leading to increased stress, fatigue, and at times lack of communication that can then lead to the potential for even more risk of human error.

If we are able to take a step back and look at the processes that require technology, the best start point would perhaps be to look at the human who is controlling the technology. Even as industry becomes more automated and artificial intelligence is becoming more prevalent in this process, ultimately the human will always be involved. Many of the processes have become easier, allowing the human to take a step back and let technology take over. But there is a risk in assuming that all new technology will run itself with no human involvement and will be free from error. As we noted in recent conversations with control room operators, there are other elements that are not being considered. The best information will always come from the human. Considering that technology is developed based on production needs that are identified and for problems that need to be solved, a good start point would be to begin with the human.

When looking specifically at the control room as it relates to upgrades that are required, the best start always involves operator input. Why? Because as much as management identifies production goals that must be met, and engineering can identify and provide solutions for technical challenges, and information technology is able to create programming solutions to tie all the technology together, the operator can provide the best feedback on what is working, what is not working and what needs to change in the control room. Where the operator feedback at times can have the appearance of being unimportant, in actual fact it can help identify issues that can potentially lead to serious consequences if not properly addressed. This does not necessarily need to be an obvious technical requirement.

Take for example the comment noted earlier from an operator requesting a coffee maker be in closer proximity. That seems like a fairly innocuous request that has no direct impact on production. Or does it? Why would they ask for this? First of all, the operator currently has to walk out of the control room and down a hall to get a coffee. This means they are walking away from the screens and the alarms and should something come up that would need a quick reaction, they might not be able to respond quickly enough. Second, if the operator is specifically requesting coffee that would indicate that perhaps they need the caffeine to stay awake and fight off fatigue. Delving a bit deeper, it turns out that these two points were indeed the reasons for the request. The operator was not comfortable with leaving the system to run without being constantly monitored, even for a few minutes. At the same time, having to monitor every aspect of the technology running the production very closely was causing the operator to become fatigued. However, it also identified a few other points that were not immediately apparent—the technology was dated and was not running optimally, there was too much information coming in that required constant monitoring, and the operator was becoming even more stressed and fatigued as a result. All factors that as we have noted previously, have the potential to increase the risk of human error, and a major disaster.

This example is only one of many that can come from taking the time to speak with all involved in the production process, and specifically the humans who are tasked not only with creating the technology but also with operating it. It helps to fully understand every aspect that goes into running an efficient and smooth process with the aim of minimizing potential risks that could lead to a major disaster. With the rapid advances today outpacing our ability to keep up, this is becoming even more critical. Taking a step back, gathering the information, and coming up with a plan is the best start point. Unfortunately there are many situations where this is seen as wasting time because it is assumed that technology will be able to handle everything. Or will it?

When industry is able to realize the importance of putting the human back into the equation, they find that many issues can be identified and solved early on. Not only can it solve production challenges, but it can also help with other challenges that can directly impact both output and bottom line. When presented in terms of impact on financials, management has a clearer view of the priorities as well as the requirements to maximize efficiency. This then becomes a win-win situation from the human factor standpoint as well because the operator environment is improved, production and safety are improved and there is the chance that major impact on the environment can be mitigated as a direct result of proper planning. Technology may be able to solve some of the challenges, but no matter how quickly it develops, it will never be able to fully consider the human aspects that are as impactful on the environment as the technology itself.

DOI: http://dx.doi.org/10.5772/intechopen.90419

8. Conclusion

In looking at the major disasters that have occurred in the past, all of which have had a direct impact on the environment, it is evident that there are recurring elements that are still of concern today. Fatigue, lack of communication, stress, outdated infrastructure, cost cutting measures, lack of training, underestimated understanding of technology all can be related directly back to the impact on operators in industrial environment. Coupled with increased pressure to produce more which is leading to cutting corners to maximize output and income in an attempt to stay ahead of technology or at least maintain the ability to keep up. At the same time, to produce more, technology needs to become more advanced. Advanced technology then leads to the inability to keep up with the changes. The result? Both human factors and human error can be directly related to environmental impact. It is time to take a step back and put the human back into focus. Humans are the ones who are creating the technology that is driving us to a more automated industrial process. The reality is that in many control room situations the number of alarms and the speed with which they occur is such that no human operator can keep up. In such circumstances artificial intelligence (AI) can potentially help especially with key factors. Here intelligent design can potentially help the human operator with the challenges that rapid technological change brings. However, in order to do so, the human must be consulted. But at the same time, what is being lost in the rapid changes we are facing in this newest phase of the industrial revolution, is the impact of the environment on the human and the resulting impact of the human on the environment. It is time to make a change in the way we currently think before another major disaster occurs that might change the world as we know it.

Author details

Fiona J. Campbell
Control Room Design and Human Factors, ABB AB, London, Ontario, Canada

*Address all correspondence to: fiona.campbell@sympatico.ca; fionapersonal@gmail.com

References

[1] Encylopedia Brittanica: Industrial Revolution [Internet]. 2019. Available from: https://www.britannica.com/event/Industrial-Revolution [Accessed: September 23, 2019]

[2] Meet the Three Industrial Revolutions [Internet]. 2019. Available from: https://trailhead.salesforce.com/en/content/learn/modules/learn-about-the-fourth-industrial-revolution/meet-the-three-industrial-revolutions [Accessed: September 23, 2019]

[3] Davis N. What is the Fourth Industrial Revolution [Internet] 2016. Available from: https://www.weforum.org/agenda/2016/01/what-is-the-fourth-industrial-revolution/ [Accessed: September 27, 2019]

[4] Mandavilli A The World's Worst Industrial Disaster is Still Unfolding [Internet]. 2016. Available from: https://www.theatlantic.com/science/archive/2018/07/the-worlds-worst-industrial-disaster-is-still-unfolding/560726/ [Accessed: September 28, 2019]

[5] Chernobyl Accident and Its Consequences [Internet] 2019. Available from: https://www.nei.org/resources/fact-sheets/chernobyl-accident-and-its-consequences [Accessed: September 29, 2019]

[6] Hopps K. Chernobyl Radiation Map: How Far Did Radiation from Chernobyl Travel—Did it Affect UK? [Internet] 2019. Available from: https://www.express.co.uk/news/world/1144581/chernobyl-radiation-map-how-far-radiation-travel-did-Chernobyl-affect-Britain [Accessed: September 30, 2019]

[7] Hadhazy A. 20 Years After the Exxon Valdez: Preventing—and Preparing for—the Next Oil Spill Disaster [Internet] 2009. Available from: https://www.scientificamerican.com/article/exxon-valdez-20-years-later-oil-spill-prevention/[Accessed: September 30, 2019]

[8] Egan T. Elements of Tanker Disaster: Drinking, Fatigue, Complacency [Internet] 1989. Available from: https://www.nytimes.com/1989/05/22/us/elements-of-tanker-disaster-drinking-fatique-complacency.html [Accessed: September 30, 2019]

[9] Miegs, J. Blame BP for Deepwater Horizon. But Direct Your Outrage to the Actual Mistake [Internet]. 2016. Available from: https://slate.com/technology/2016/09/bp-is-to-blame-for-deepwater-horizon-but-its-mistake-was-actually-years-of-small-mistakes.html [Accessed: September 30, 2019]

[10] Environmental Effects of the Deepwater Horizon Oil Spill: A Review [Internet] 2017. Available from: https://www.niva.no/en/publications/environmental-effects-of-the-deepwater-horizon-oil-spill [Accessed: September 30, 2019]

[11] Deep Water: The Gulf Oil Disaster and the Future of Offshore Drilling. Report to the President [Internet]. 2011. Available from: https://www.iadc.org/archived-2014-osc-report/documents/DEEPWATER_ReporttothePresident_FINAL.pdf [Accessed: September 30, 2019]

[12] Human Error Blamed for Fukushima Meltdown [Internet]. 2012. Available from: https://www.newscientist.com/article/mg21528753-800-human-error-blamed-for-fukushima-meltdown/#ixzz63OkDWqfQ [Accessed: October 01, 2019]

[13] Japan Panel; Fukushima Nuclear Disaster 'Man-Made' [Internet] 2012. Available from: https://www.bbc.com/

news/world-asia-18718057 [Accessed: October 01, 2019]

[14] Preliminary Report Pipeline: Over-pressure of a Columba Gas of Massachusetts Low-pressure Natural Gas Distribution System [Internet] 2019. Available from: https://www.ntsb.gov/investigations/AccidentReports/Pages/PLD18MR003-preliminary-report.aspx [Accessed: October 01, 2019]

[15] Raymond-Read A. Merrimack Gas Explosions: A Tragic Byproduct of Natural Gas [Internet]. 2019. Available from: https://www.clf.org/blog/merrimack-explosions-natural-gas/ [Accessed: October 01, 2019]

[16] Granot H. The Human Factor in Industrial Disaster [Internet]. 1998. Available from: https://www.emerald.com/insight/content/doi/10.1108/09653569810216315/full/html [Accessed: October 01, 2019]

[17] Reducing Risks Through Emissions Mitigation [Internet]. 2018. Available from: https://nca2018.globalchange.gov/chapter/29/ [Accessed: October 05, 2019]

[18] Campbell F. A modern control room—Human factors and their impact on plant safety and optimization. In: Proceedings of the XXVIII International Mineral Processing Congress (IMPC 2016); 11-15 September 2016. Quebec City: Canadian Institute of Mining, Metallurgy and Petroleum; 2016. ISBN: 978-1-926872-29-2

[19] Brindley F. Human Factors in Accident Investigation [Internet]. 2009. Available from: http://www.hse.gov.uk/chemicals/workshop/human-factors-09/accident-investigation-lessons.pdf [Accessed: October 07, 2019]

[20] Schuessler J. Too Much Information About 'Information' [Internet] 2011. Available from: https://artsbeat.blogs.nytimes.com/2011/03/23/too-much-information-about-information/ [Accessed: October 10, 2019]

[21] Zetter K Inside the Cunning, Unprecedented Hack of Ukraine's Power Grid. 2016. Available from: https://www.wired.com/2016/03/inside-cunning-unprecedented-hack-ukraines-power-grid/ [Accessed: October 22, 2019]

[22] Fatigue is the New 'F' Word [Internet] 2018. Available from: http://www.energysafetycanada.com/blog/fatigue-is-the-new-f-word/ [Accessed: October 22, 2019]

[23] Hollender M. Smart Ergonomic Control Room Workplaces Engage Generation "G"—Part 1 [Internet] 2014. Available from: http://www.processautomationinsights.com/martin-hollender/operator-effectiveness/2014/06/30/smart-ergonomic-control-room-workplaces-engage-generation-g---part-1 [Accessed: October 23, 2019]

Section 3

Soil, Water and Waste Management

Chapter 7

Soil Carbon Restoration through Conservation Agriculture

Snigdha Chatterjee, Satarupa Ghosh and Prasanna Pal

Abstract

Poor soil fertility and soil degradation induced by persistent conventional farming with repeated tillage and removal or in situ burning of crop residue are major limitations to food security and environmental sustainability. However, degraded agricultural lands with depleted soil organic carbon (SOC) stocks are capable of soil carbon restoration through improved management practices like aggregation, humification and deep placement of C that can increase SOC sequestration. According to FAO, conservation agriculture (CA) is arrived at as a solution to restore SOC with three pillars of minimum soil disturbance, permanent organic soil cover and diversified crop rotations. A significant increase in SOC levels under zero tillage (ZT) over conventional tillage (CT) was found; returning more crop residues to the soil is associated with an increase in SOC concentration that is further increased by crop diversification. Additionally, the incorporation of high-value trees with CA is treated as a working model for C storage. Thus, conservation agriculture is an operational approach to restore SOC that aggrades soil, reduces environmental footprints and makes agricultural systems more resilient to climate change.

Keywords: conservation agriculture, crop residues, soil carbon restoration, zero tillage

1. Introduction

The increasing global population with a high demand for food is putting pressure on agricultural sector forces to replace traditional agricultural practices with advanced technologies. As a result, the sustainability of crop production systems based on soil quality gets affected by the nature of the farming system being implemented like prolonged cultivation of agricultural lands including tillage and inversion combined with the removal of crop residues accelerate the decomposition of soil organic matter and causes 20–67% soil C loss [1] and leads to soil degradation and diminished physical, chemical and biological properties of the soil [2]. Consequently, the depletion of carbon from soil elevates the atmospheric concentration of carbon dioxide (CO_2) from 316 to 400 ppm and global temperature by 0.12°C per decade [3]. A loss of soil organic carbon (SOC) of 42 and 59% due to changes in land-use pattern from forest to crop and from pasture to crop respectively has been found [4]. In general, agricultural activities directly produce about 10–12% of the atmospheric greenhouse gases (GHGs), such as CO_2, methane (CH_4), and nitrous oxide (N_2O) [5]. Soils of the world constitute the third-largest carbon (C) pool after oceanic and geologic pools. Thus, the twin crisis of food insecurity and climate change can be addressed through the restoration of the soil carbon achieved through the implementation of recommended management practices on agricultural soils [6]. Understanding the dynamics of SOC in relation to land use and management strategies is of foremost importance to identify pathways of C sequestration in soils. It is necessary to build up soil carbon contents by increasing carbon inputs or decreasing decomposition of organic matter in the soil for sustainable agricultural productivity and a stable environment. Several management practices are recognized to improve soil organic carbon (SOC) contents in croplands, such as organic amendments, cover crops, diversified crop rotations, biochar, agroforestry, or conservation agriculture (CA) to address sequestration of carbon (C) in agroecosystems, especially in agricultural soils [7, 8]. Among them, CA is increasingly promoted as an alternative to tackle soil degradation resulting from agricultural practices that deplete soil fertility, aiming at higher crop productivity as short term benefit [9]. In practice, CA includes three basic principles of minimal soil disturbance, permanent soil cover through mulch or crop residues, and crop rotations. Rehabilitation of degraded soils to restore biomass productivity, in order to secure the various functions of CA, depends on above and belowground plant biomass. This may sometimes be aided by the adoption of agroforestry as a management practice of forest plantations with the agricultural crop to enhance SOC stock through C sequestration [10]. Presently CA is being practiced in about 180 million hectares (Mha) all over the world [11] of which 1.5 Mh area covered under CA in India [12] mainly in Indo-Gangetic plains (IGP) with rice-wheat (RW) cropping system. This chapter reviews studies on SOC forms and explores new initiatives taken for restoring C content in soil to mitigate climate change, improve soil health and maintain sustainable productivities with the help of CA practices.

2. Soil organic matter (SOM) in relation to SOC

Soil organic matter is the complex organic substances consisting of organic residues, humic substances, microbial bodies that undergo decomposition at various stages. It influences plant growth and yield by improving soil structure and acts as a reservoir of plant nutrients containing 2.5 Eg carbon (1Eg = 10^{18} g) (**Table 1**). The formation of the clay-humus complex increases the buffering capacity of the soil and forms stable complexes with some metals to make them available for plant uptake. Soil carbon is mainly present as organic matter or humus and varies from 1% (coarse-textured soil) to 3.5% (grassland). But Indian soils are deficient in SOC due to prevalence of the tropical, sub-tropical, arid and semi-arid climatic condition, persistent tillage practice, non-judicious use of agrochemicals, removal of crop residue from land etc. SOM can be divided into different pools based on the time needed for full decomposition and the derived turnover time of the products in the soil:

1. Active pools: turnover in months or a few years,

2. Passive pools: turnover in up to thousands of years.

SOM contains about 58% of soil carbon which can be classified according to its physical and chemical stability as:

1. **Fast pool** (labile or active pool): After the addition of fresh organic carbon to the soil, faster decomposition in a few days with a turnover in 1–2 years.

	Reservoir	Estimates of the C pool (10^{18}g)
1.	Sedimentary rocks	60,000
2.	Oceans	38
3.	Fossil fuels	5
4.	Terrestrial biosphere	0.6
5.	Soils (1 m)	2.5
6.	Atmosphere	0.8

Source: [13, 14].

Table 1.
Estimates of global carbon reservoirs.

2. **Intermediate pool:** Comprises organic carbon that is partially stabilized on mineral surfaces and/or protected within aggregates, with turnover times in the range 10–100 years.

3. **Slow pool** (stable): Highly stabilized SOC, enters a period of very slow turnover of 100 to >1000 years.

3. Global carbon cycle

Soil carbon stocks consist of soil organic carbon (SOC), soil inorganic carbon (SIC) and total carbon (TC). Soils contain carbon in both organic and inorganic forms, i.e., oxidized carbon and non-oxidized carbon. The sum of the two forms of carbon is referred to as total carbon.

The global soil carbon, estimated to be 2500 Pg (1 Pg = 10^{15} g) which is nearly 3.3 times the atmospheric pool and 4.5 times the biotic pool size (760 Pg) [15] whereas, the total amount of SOC and SIC stored worldwide are estimated to be 1550 Pg C 950 Pg in the top 1 m of soils in a dynamic equilibrium of gains and losses (**Figure 1**). Pools of C in rocks are inert and changes over the millions of years of time while pools of C in the terrestrial biosphere, atmosphere, oceans constitute active pools

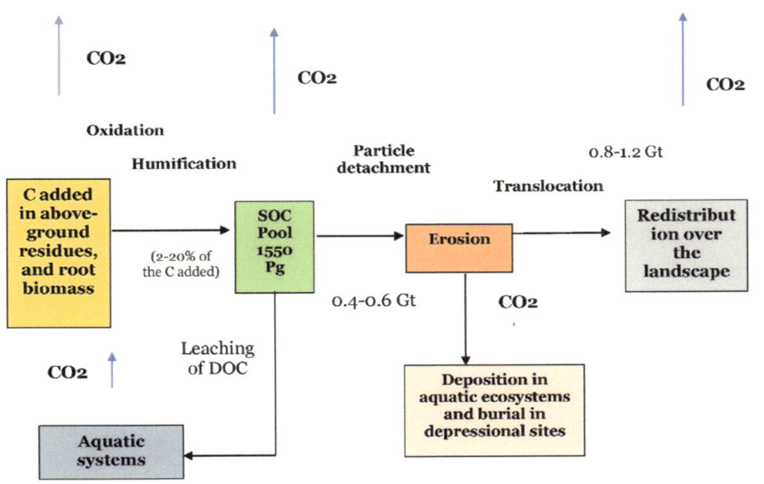

Figure 1.
Soil organic carbon dynamic equilibrium [6].

that are vulnerable to anthropogenic activities. Exchange of C among these pools over a short and long period of time is known as the Global Carbon Cycle (GCC). The Global Carbon Cycle has been changing due to the increase in atmospheric C pool and decrease in biosphere and soil C pool consequently resulting in global warming. Conversion of natural to agricultural ecosystems causes 60% depletion of the SOC pool of temperate regions and 75% or more in cultivated soils of the tropics, and further creates severe soil degradation when the output of C exceeds the input.

4. Salient causes of carbon loss from soil

Loss of C from the SOC pool occurs in the form of CO_2 and CH_4 while SIC fraction produces only CO_2. There are certain processes like mineralization; erosion and leaching responsible for the loss of C pool in disturbed soil [16]. Environmental factors like an increase in soil temperature mainly stimulate the rate of mineralization of the SOC pool while calciferous materials are subjected to certain climatic factors leading to the dissolution of carbonates and bicarbonates releases of CO_2 to the atmosphere. There are certain anthropogenic activities that instigate the Soil C losses are discussed below:

1. Deforestation
2. Soil erosion
3. Excessive plowing
4. Burning of crop residues
5. Summer fallow
6. Bare soil during the winter season
7. Monocropping
8. Weak recycling of elements
9. Nutrient depletion
10. Water deficiency
11. Low input subsistence farming and soil fertility mining
12. Intensive cropping and cultivating marginal soil

The depletion of the SOC leads to land degradation which decreases biomass productivity and reduces the quantity of biomass returned to the soil. Among factors responsible for soil degradation, accelerated soil erosion has the most severe impact on the SOC pool depletion. Moreover, soil degradation comprises of:

1. **Physical degradation:** reduction in aggregation, a decline in soil structure, crusting, compaction, reduction in water infiltration capacity and erosion.
2. **Chemical degradation:** nutrient depletion, a decline in pH and acidification, a build-up of salts in the root zone, imbalance and disruption in elemental cycles and

3. **Biological degradation:** reduction in activity and species diversity of soil fauna, a decline in biomass C and depletion of SOC pool.

However, the depleted SOC pool can be restored through conversion to appropriate land use, and adoption of recommended management practices (RMPs) e.g., mulch farming, reduced tillage, crop rotation, conservation agriculture (CA), integrated nutrient management (INM), integrated pest management (IPM), precision farming [17].

- **Aggregation:** Increase in stable micro-aggregates to protect against microbial activities through the formation of organo-mineral complexes encapsulates C.

- **Humification:** Formation of chemically recalcitrant humic compounds that improve the relative proportion of passive fraction of SOC by the presence of a higher proportion of high activity clays (HACs).

- **Translocation into the sub-soil:** Accumulation of SOC into the sub-soil through deep root placement discouraging the loss of C from a zone of disturbance by tillage and intercultural operations, and minimizing the risks of erosion.

- **Formation of secondary carbonates:** Soil inorganic carbon (SIC) sequestration mainly prevalent in arid and semi-arid land-use systems through the formation of secondary carbonates [18] and leaching of carbonates into the groundwater in irrigated soils [19].

5. Soil carbon sequestration

The Paris Agreement at the 21st Conference of Parties (COP21) of the United Nations Framework Convention on Climate Change (UNFCCC), set an agenda for reducing global warming below 2°C and limiting the temperature increase to 1.5°C by lowering GHG emissions to encourage climate resilience through diverse pathways without compromising food production. But, under the current scenario, GHG emissions by anthropogenic activities could increase 55 Gt CO_2 equivalents in 2030 [20] and to achieve the objective of COP21, anthropogenic emissions need to hit the highest point within the next 10 years and subsequently decline in trends towards net GHG removal by the end of the century. The "4 per 1000" initiative was launched as a part of the Lima-Paris Action Agenda promotes SOC sequestration to improve food security and mitigate climate change. According to this initiative, anthropogenic GHG emissions should be counter-balanced by a yearly increase of global soil carbon stocks in the top 40 cm of soils by 0.4% considerably. Moreover, agricultural activities and land-use change may enhance GHGs emissions like 25% of the CO_2, 50% of the CH_4, and 70% of the N_2O that perhaps compensate by SOC sequestration [21]. To achieve this target, improved management practices should be adopted for C sequestration in agricultural, forest and wetland land along with rehabilitation of degraded soils. Various institutions in more than 170 countries initiated a highly ambitious goal with the collaboration between scientists, educator and farmers, policymakers to implement suitable practices for increasing SOC stocks. In addition to that, 103 countries have set mitigation and adaptation targets related to agricultural practices, and about 129 countries developed goals related to forests and degraded land [22]. This initiative creates a global enthusiastic target to increase 0.4% SOC stock per year in all land uses, including forests. Generally, an optimistic point of view was reported from 20 countries in a survey on SOC stock estimates with their feasibility to achieve the 4 per 1000 target [23]. Water resources are appreciably important in SOC sequestration to adapt and mitigate climate change to fulfill SDGs as a demand for water increased by the intensification of agroecosystems [24] which becomes more successful with proper nutrient management strategies, especially N, along with soil and water [25]. Soil C sequestration is the process of transfer of atmospheric CO_2 into SOM as C held in recalcitrant forms is less susceptible to losses by decomposition. SOC sequestration involves three basic steps:

1. Removal of CO_2 from the atmosphere via plant photosynthesis;

2. Transfer of carbon from CO_2 to plant biomass; and

3. Transfer of carbon from plant biomass (crop residues) to the soil where it is stored in the form of SOC, i.e., labile pool with highest turnover rate.

Thus, SOC sequestration should be done in such a way that captured atmospheric CO_2 can retain C in the slow SOC pool. But, it is a fact that the stable pool has little potential for carbon sequestration due to its resistance to change by management practices [26]. In the short term, it is important to manage the easily decomposable SOM by enhancing the cropping intensity that has the major impact on microorganisms, humic complex production, which ultimately sequesters C. For the medium and long term, C sequestration can be achieved through the placing of recalcitrant C to the deeper layer which is resistant to rapid mineralization. It can be done by creating a positive C budget as the rate of SOC sequestration varies from 100 to 1000 kg C ha^{-1} $year^{-1}$. However, the rate of SOC change is greater in the tropics, thus leading to a shorter time for SOC equilibrium to be attained in tropical regions. The SOC sequestration is affected by many factors including C input, crop rotation, tillage management, climate condition, fertilization, and soil texture (**Figure 2**). Carbon sequestration in soil can be done by following four major processes:

1. Decreasing the level of soil disturbance to enhance the physical protection of soil carbon in aggregates.

2. Increasing the agricultural inputs (e.g., organics) to soils.

3. Improving soil microbial diversity and abundance.

4. Maintaining continuous living plant cover on soils year-round.

Successful carbon sequestration is achieved when C storage through soil conservation practices exceeds their losses [28] by transforming atmospheric CO_2 into biomass through photosynthesis, and incorporation of biomass into the soil to enrich humus. Carbon sequestration is possible through a range of processes, occurring naturally in plants and soils but soil contains approximately three times more C than the amount stored in living plants [29]. However, the C inputs from various sources like trees, shrubs, and vegetation in the form of litterfall, roots, and rhizodeposition contribute towards enhancing SOC stocks, mostly within woody components. Thus, SOC stocks can be increased by practicing agroforestry adjacent to the cultivation of agricultural lands [7]. Agroforestry with two main segments of agroforestry systems: belowground and aboveground is potent enough in increasing

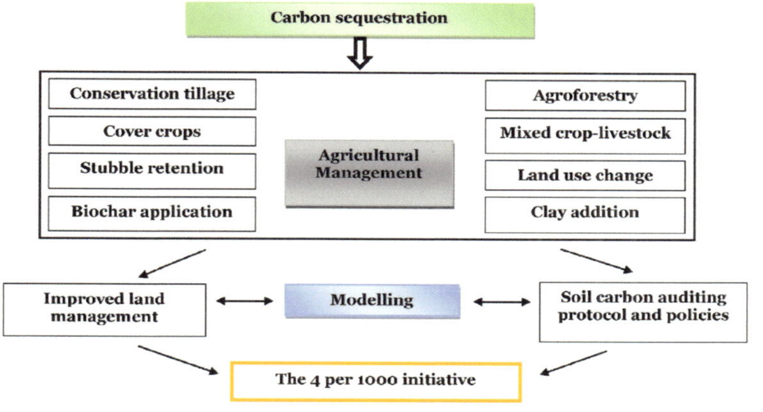

Figure 2.
Impact of improved management practices on SOC dynamics [27].

Sources	Mi C year^{-1}
Water land restoration	20
Restoration of degraded land	50
Agroforestry	600
Forest management	250
Grazing management	375
Rice management	20
Cropland management	150

Source: [30].

Table 2.
Potential of carbon sequestration by 2040.

sequestration of carbon in agricultural lands where the aboveground component is described as stem and leaves of herbaceous plants and trees while the below-ground component contains roots and microorganisms associated with roots [30]. Although, in the belowground segments carbon is more stabilized due to interactions between soil particles with root biomass [31] and slow decomposition rate is observed over above-ground biomass [32]. **Table 2** indicates that agroforestry has the greatest capability for carbon sequestration among various other sources.

6. Mechanism of carbon sequestration through carbon stabilization

The carbon stabilization process of C sequestration starts with the formation of unstable macroaggregates, subsequently stabilization and the contemporary formation of microaggregates within macroaggregates, and finally concludes with the breakdown of macroaggregates with the liberation of the microaggregates. Young macroaggregates offer physical protection to C and N from microbial enzymes but need to be further stabilized. Microaggregates within macroaggregates are occluded intra- aggregate particulate organic carbon (iPOM C) in soil microag-gregates which may responsible for long-term soil C sequestration in agricultural soils as these are relatively stable and secluded habitats for microorganisms.

Carbon sequestration depends on turnover time and physical and chemical protec-tion against microorganisms which is further influenced by the quality and physical location of SOC fractions in the soil system (**Table 3**). In most soils, young and unstable macroaggregates are formed with the help of biological factors like growing roots, fungal, bacterial and faunal activity by mixing fresh organic matter with exudates and soil particles. When partially decomposed intra-macroaggregate organic matter encapsulated with clay minerals and microbial products, microaggregates are formed, which lead to long-term carbon stabiliza-tion in macroaggregates by protection from mineralization. With time, the macroaggregates lose labile binding agents and release minerals; highly recalcitrant SOM and microaggregates released may again be occluded within new macroaggregates. It is evident that physical disturbances like tillage disrupt macroaggregates exposing coarse iPOM C to microbial attack and preventing its incorporation into microaggregates as fine iPOM C. The slower turnover rate of microaggregates within macroaggregates in zero tillage allows greater protection of coarse POM. The organic C in the soil is mainly stabilized through the following mechanisms:

6.1 Physical protection

Carbon sequestration in soils through physical protection is mainly done by aggregation [33] formed by clumps of soil particles adhered by clay, fine roots, and glue-like substances generated by microbes decomposing organic matter, such as glomalin produced by arbuscular mycorrhizal fungi [34, 35]. As these aggregates form, small particles of C, like partially decayed plant residues, are captured in the center of the aggregates which are physically protected from microbial attack as they cannot penetrate the center of these stable aggregates where oxygen and water are low, thereby discouraging microbial metabolism [36]. Roots, fungal hyphae and less degraded organic materials stabilize macroaggregates and their oxidation of C is dependent on management practices [37]. On the other hand, highly decomposed organic components stabilize more C in microaggregates, facilitated by its high surface area and polyvalent cation bridging, as the oxidation of C in these aggregates is least [38]. It is evident that the turnover time of C is higher in microaggregates (412 years) than C in macroaggregates (140 years) [39] due to the higher level of physical protection of organic matter across the aggregate-size classes, depending upon the amount and type of clay in soil [40]. These stable aggregate can protect SOC for very long but can be degraded by tillage exposing soil carbon to microbial attack [41].

Types of organic matter	Location	Turnover time, Year	Category
Microbial biomass	Pores, particle/aggregate surface	0.1–0.5	Libile
Litter	Soil surface, pores	1–5	Rapid
Light fraction	Voids, aggregate surface	5–15	Moderate
Particulate	Voids, bio pores	5–20	Moderate
Humus	Inter-microaggregate	20–50	Slow
Humus	Adsorbed on intra-microaggregate	50–3000	Passive

Source: [42].

Table 3.
Turnover time of soil organic carbon depending on the quality and physical location within the soil.

6.2 Chemical stabilization

Apart from the physical protection of SOC through aggregate formation, C compounds can be chemically protected from decomposition. Chemical stabilization of SOM is controlled by the quantity and type of clay minerals, amorphous minerals, exchangeable cations, and the chemical composition of SOM. The surfaces of clay particles are strongly negatively charged. Soil microbial community produces some by-products having strong positive charges forming strong bonds with negatively charged clay particles, effectively protecting the molecules from microbial attack [33]. The protection of soil organic matter is enhanced by silt and clay content [43] due to the sorptive capacity provided by the larger surface area of minerals [44] which further depends on clay mineralogy [40]. Several studies show that 2:1 clay minerals generally have a greater ability to stabilize SOM than 1:1 clays [45] of which vermiculite and smectite are probably more efficient for the sorption of SOM due to higher specific surface areas compared to illite [45, 46]. However, amorphous iron (Fe) and aluminum (Al) oxides present in acid soils have higher potential to stabilize SOM than clay minerals [47]. Carbon stabilization in saline soils is done through a higher concentration of exchangeable Ca which increases the bridging of organic ions with clay minerals [48].

6.3 Biochemical stabilization

Biochemical stabilization of SOM is the function of structural bond strengths, the regular degree of occurrence of structural units and the degree of aromaticity [49] which are related to the inherent chemical composition of residues [33]. Non-hydrolyzable forms of C are considered as chemically stable structures, such as lipids, waxes, insoluble polyesters, and microbial-synthesized macromolecules because of their high aliphatic nature whereas, lignin being an aromatic compound is more resistant to decomposition [50]. So, aliphatic and aromatic C compounds present in soil constitute stable or passive pools [51].

7. Conservation agriculture to restore soil carbon

Conservation agriculture was introduced as a concept of the resource-efficient agricultural crop production system based on integrated management of agro-ecosystems combined with input use efficiency [52]. Conservation agriculture is a broader concept than conservation tillage, where more than 30% of the soil surface cover with crop residues is practiced. As per FAO definition, CA aims to achieve acceptable profits, high and sustained production levels and conserve the environment based on three basic principles: (1) minimum or no mechanical soil disturbance; (2) permanent soil cover (consisting of a growing crop or a dead mulch of crop residues); and (3) diversified crop rotations. Recently, a 4th basic principle was proposed by [53] i.e., improving soil fertility by integrated nutrient management (INM) to transform biomass carbon into soil organic matter for healthy crop management. Development of cereal straw retention or incorporation technique significantly reduced the problem of crop residue burning in South Asia which is a major contributor to environmental pollution [54]. Presently CA is being practiced in about 180 million hectares (Mha) all over the world in which tropical and temperate regions cover 85.3 Mha and 95.12 Mha areas respectively (**Table 4**). These CA principles are applicable to a wide range of crop production systems from low-yielding, dry, rain-fed conditions to high-yielding, irrigated conditions following site-specific management practices to deal with various crop

Climate	Region	The area under CA (Mha)	% of the world
Tropics/Sub-tropics	South America	69.9	38.7
	Asia	13.9	7.7
	Africa	1.51	0.8
	Sub-total	85.3	47.2
Temperate	North America	63.2	35.0
	Russia/Ukraine	5.70	3.2
	Europe	3.56	2.0
	Australia/New Zealand	22.70	12.6
	Sub-total	95.16	52.8
	Grand Total	180.46	100.0

Source: [11].

Table 4.
Global cropland area under conservation agriculture in 2015–2016.

development factors such as pest and weed control tactics, nutrient management strategies, rotation crops, etc. Laser land leveling is one of the few mechanical prerequisites in intensively cultivated irrigated agriculture and improves the input use efficiencies.

1. **Minimal soil disturbance:** The first objective is the application of zero tillage or reduced tillage seeding systems without disturbing more than 20–25% of the soil surface. It maintains optimum proportions of gaseous exchange in the rooting-zone, reduces C losses as atmospheric CO2, moderates organic matter oxidation, improves porosity for water movement and limits the germination of weed seeds.

2. **Permanent soil cover:** The second objective is the retention of sufficient residue on the soil surface to protect the soil from erosive agents, water run-off and evaporation to improve water productivity and to enhance soil physical, chemical and biological properties associated with long term sustainable productivity by augmenting biomass C.

3. **Diversified crop rotations**: The objective is to employ economically viable, diversified crop rotations (preferentially leguminous plants) to help deep placement of SOC through the root network of different crops. It also moderates the outbreak of weed, disease, and pest problems; enhances soil biodiversity and takes advantage of biological nitrogen fixation (BNF). Apart from these soil enhanc-ing properties, crop diversification reduces labour requirement and provides farmers with new economic opportunities that can reduce risks in crop cultivation (**Table 5**).

Proper CA can create a positive ecosystem carbon budget and improves agronomic productivity. Bulk density and tillage practices are the two main factors governing TC content when comparing SOC under different management scenarios [55].

	Conventional agriculture	Conservation agriculture
1.	Cultivating the land, using science and technology to dominate nature	Least interference with natural processes
2.	Excessive mechanical tillage and soil erosion	No-till or drastically reduced tillage
3.	Residue burning or removal (bare surface)	Permanent surface retention of residues
4.	Free-wheeling of farm machinery increased soil compaction	Controlled traffic, compaction in a tramline, no compaction in crop area
5.	Mono cropping, less efficient rotations	Diversified and more efficient rotations
6.	Poor adaptation to stresses, yield losses greater under stress conditions	More resilience to stresses, yield losses are less under stress conditions
7.	Heavy reliance on manual labour, the uncertainty of operations	Mechanized operations, ensure timeliness of operations
8.	Productivity gains in long-run are in declining order	Productivity gains in long-run are in incremental order
9.	Water infiltration is low	Water movement is high

Source: [56].

Table 5.
Some distinguishing features of conventional and conservation agriculture systems.

1. **Bulk density**: With the adoption of zero tillage (ZT), bulk density may be increased than conventional tillage (CT). The apparent mass of SOC in ZT could increase as more mass of soil should be taken from ZT soil over conventionally tilled soil if surface soil samples are taken at the same depth.

2. **Tillage practices**: Carbon content of surface soils have higher under ZT than CT while a higher SOC content in the deeper layers of CT plots where the residue is incorporated through tillage.

8. Influence of tillage practice on soil organic carbon

It has already been pointed out that soil disturbance stimulates the rate of decomposition of SOC and loss of C from soil to the atmosphere. Classic studies show that the disruption of soil aggregates in surface layers and decreases in the amount of total SOC, mainly in macroaggregates, occurs under conventionally tilled soil (**Figure 3**). Hence, by minimizing the disturbance through the adoption of reduced tillage (RT) practices, it is expected that such CO_2 emission from soil to the atmosphere can be reduced and thereby combat global climate change. Hence, RT is known to enhance SOC in the surface soil horizons over the CT mainly in tropi-cal and sub-tropical regions compared to temperate regions due to various reasons among which alterations of soil temperature and moisture regimes and erosion control are important. From a global database, a significant increase in SOC levels under ZT over CT was found whereas there was no statistically significant difference between conven - tional and RT. The average SOC sequestration rate (up to 30 cm depth) under ZT was 0.57 ± 0.13 Mg C ha^{-1} $year^{-1}$ [57]. However, the adoption of ZT practices enhances the physical protection of SOC where soil bulk density is relatively high because the volume of small macro-pores (15–150 μm) gets reduced which is important for microbial activity. Management practices are sensitive to climatic conditions as the largest change in SOC is observed under tropical moist environment followed by tropical dry, temperate moist and temperate dry [58]. Moreover, soil erosion and redistribution over a prolonged period is associated with better storage of SOC under ZT practices that shifted from conventional tillage [59].

Some distinguished factors affecting SOC content in soil are discussed here:

1. **Baseline C content:** Old weathered soils with less carbon content have more potential to sequester C compared to young C rich soils. So, eroded soils with less SOC have a higher potential to gain SOC when converted from CT to ZT.

2. **Porosity**: Smaller pore sizes can physically protect C within them to form microaggregates that are less susceptible to microbial decomposition.

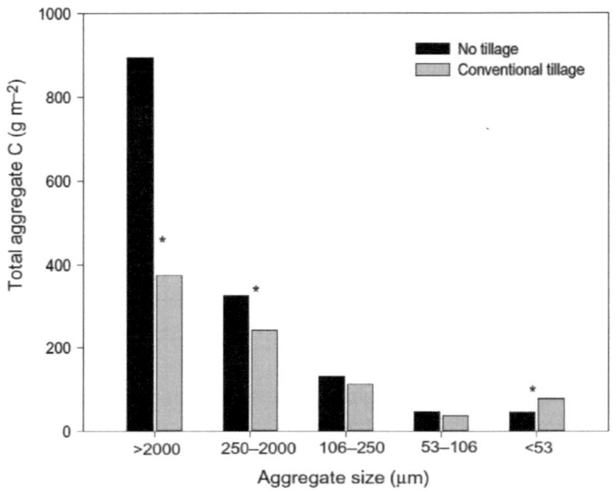

Figure 3.
Distribution of total aggregate C in no tillage and conventional tillage soils at 0–5 cm depth (indicates significant differences at P = 0.05 level) [60].*

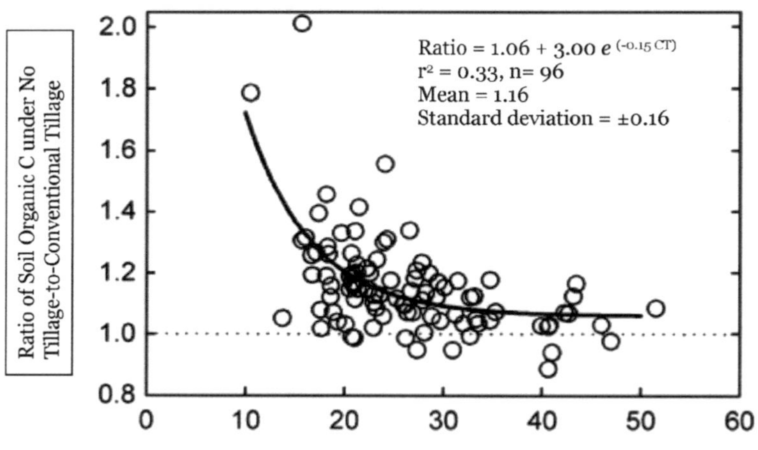

Figure 4.
The ratio of soil organic C under conservation tillage-to-conventional tillage as related to the initial soil organic C content under conventional tillage [61].

3. **Climate:** Changes in SOC under different management practices are sensitive to the climate in the order of tropical moist > tropical dry > temperate moist > temperate dry.

4. **Landscape position:** Landscape positions that had a low SOC stock in the past due to past erosion generally show gains in SOC.

The impact of ZT on soil organic C sequestration may be greater in degraded soils than in fertile soils which can be observed in **Figure 4** where the ratio of soil organic C with conservation tillage-to-conventional tillage was logarithmically greater in soils with lower SOC than in soils with higher SOC.

9. Influence of residue application on soil organic carbon

Crop residues retention in fields is a well-known management practice deals with several positive effects like improving better soil structure, water retention, and reducing erosion loss [62]. They have potential enough to improve the nutrient content of soils [63] and help in SOC accumulation in soils due to increased crop rhizodeposition [64]. Nevertheless, returning straw up to 50 cm depth approximately increases SOC concentration by 13% in bulk soil as found from a global meta-analysis of 176 fields where labile pools contribute about 27–57% increase in SOC content in soils. A study suggested that crop residue removal is not recommended in SOC-poor tropical and temperate soils, while partial residue removal is commendable in organic C-rich temperate soils. The degree of SOC dynamics on residue application depends on many factors such as rate of addition, climate, soil texture, and quality of the substrate [65]. The SOC content is further influenced by the quality of crop residues [66] which is partly determined by its C:N ratio as crop straw with a low C:N ratio decomposes more rapidly [62]. For example, maize residues with higher C input and C:N ratio decompose slower than soybean residues contributing higher SOC content in the soil. Nowadays, burning of straw is commonly practiced, to manage stubble loads which continuously enhances nutrient loss, air pollution and reduces soil health. Moreover, it also causes a loss of SOC as evident by a field trial over a period of 19 years in south-eastern Australia where a loss of 1.75 Mg C ha^{-1} (0–10 cm layer) was reported [67]. But, residue retention increases SOC content in soil mainly during the first two decades than in the longer term [68]. By considering all the fluxes, straw incorporation can lead to improving C sink in upland soils and decreases in fluxes of GHGs like CH_4 as a decrease in CH_4 emissions following maize straw incorporation [44]. Apart from that several studies showed that application of supplementary nutrients (inorganic N, P, and S) enhanced SOC storage by minimizing positive priming of SOC mineralization during incorporation of C-rich crop residues into the soil [69]. Management of crop residues (retention or incorporation) improves organic matter levels in soils. Returning more crop residues to the soil is associated with an increase in SOC concentration [70]. The rate of decomposition of crop residues depends not only on the amount retained but also on the composition of the residues and soil types. As lignin is resistant to rapid microbial decomposition, it can promote the formation of a complex structure, which often encrusts the cellulose-hemicellulose matrix and thus slows down the decomposition while the soluble fraction is decomposable in nature and helps in the decomposition of hemicellulose [71]. The SOC content was increased from 0.45% to 0.55% and from 0.29% to 0.35% with the residue mulch treatments at 0–15 cm and 15–30 cm, respectively [72]. A higher amount of SOC was observed

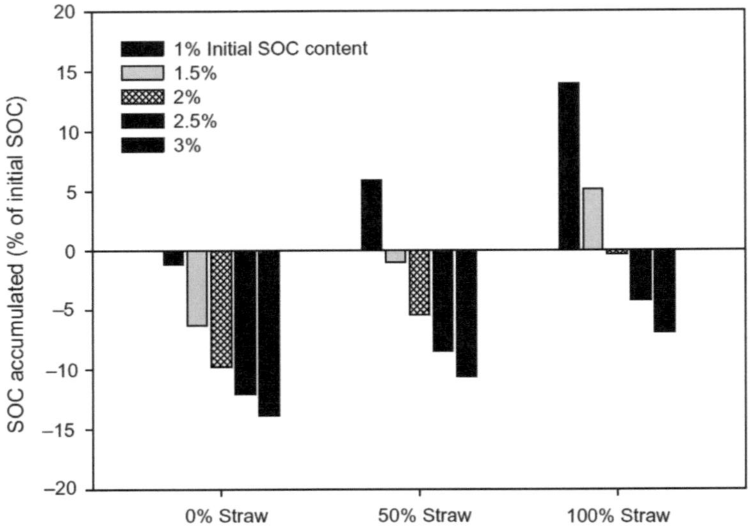

Figure 5.
Impact of residue incorporation on SOC storage at 0–3 m after 100 years continuous wheat cropping [74].

in surface soil than subsurface soil due to surface retention of crop residue under CA over CT [73]. A 100-year simulation study that demonstrates the loss or gain of SOC stocks at various straw incorporations in wheat cropping in sandy loam soils is depicted in **Figure 5**.

10. Influence of crop rotation on soil organic carbon

Conservation agriculture can increase the possibility of crop intensification due to faster turnaround time between harvest and planting. Diversified crop rotation provides an opportunity to produce huge biomass C that influences SOC by changing the quantity and the quality of organic matter input more than under monocropping. Conservation of moisture as practiced under CA can result in growing an extra cover crop right after harvest of the main crop that leads to higher SOC contents by increasing the input of plant residues and providing a vegetal cover during critical periods. In many annual cropping systems, the field is left free after crop harvest, thus lowers annual biomass production as C inputs to the soil, which is unable to compensate the soil C losses throughout the year. On the contrary, the introduction of cover crops or periodic green fallows increases average annual biomass production and leads to a net gain of carbon rather than a loss [75]. Crop diversification with legume crops can increase the complexity and diversity of C as they contain carbon compounds resistant to microbial metabolism, thus increasing C stabilization [76]. These strategies greatly increase the total amount of aboveground as well as belowground biomass entering agricultural systems by increasing the roots proliferation compared to annual cropping systems (mainly cereal crops) with a shallow rooting network. However, the increase in SOC concentration can be negated when the crop cover is incorporated in the soil. In general, it has been observed that enhancing the rotation complexity results in an increase in SOC but the magnitude is lower than that observed when shifting from conventional to zero tillage. It is still more effective in retaining C and N in soil than a monoculture. The effect of crop rotation on SOC contents can be due to increased biomass input, because of the greater total production, or due to the changed quality of the residue

Treatment	Soil organic carbon ($g\ kg^{-1}$)		Total soil organic C stock ($t\ ha^{-1}$)		Change in total SOC stock ($t\ ha^{-1}$)
	0–15 cm	15–30 cm	0–15 cm	15–30 cm	0–30 cm
ZT	6.23	5.23	14.8	13.4	7.72
CT	4.73	4.33	11.2	10.7	0.88

Source: [73].

Table 6.
Effect of long-term tillage on total soil organic carbon in the 0–15 cm and 15–30 cm layers in the maize-based cropping system.

input. For instance, legume-based systems contain greater amounts of aromatic C content maintaining ideal C:N ratios, and thus productivity is increased. The SOC was increased by 72% with a CA-based maize-wheat-mungbean system and 83% with the rice-wheat-mungbean system compared to conventional RW system [77]. Conservation agriculture significantly increased SOC content in both 0–15 cm and 15–30 cm depth compared with CT in the maize-based cropping system [73] (**Table 6**).

11. Conservation agriculture with trees

It is the strategy of inclusion of trees in order to combine the best of CA leading to a working model under different social, economic, biophysical, institutional and policy conditions. This practice is aimed at improving the uptake of CA through the provision of fodder, fuel, construction materials, agricultural implements, biomass, nutrients, fencing, fruits, among other products and services. Agroforestry is a widely practiced system of agricultural production around the world. It can be grouped under silvoarable systems (alley crop-ping, parklands), silvopastoral systems (e.g., Dehesas, Montados), protective systems (windbreaks, shelterbelts, riparian buffers), multistorey systems (e.g., home-gardens), rotational woodlots, and shifting cultivation [78]. Besides providing agricultural crops, fodder, and firewood/timber, these systems sustain a number of environmental benefits and ecosystem services such as erosion control, water availability, increased diversity of species, improved esthetics of agricultural landscapes improved soil fertility by SOC sequestration, and by C fixa-tion in tree biomass as well as deposition of C -containing materials in topsoils and subsoils, lower decomposition of recalcitrant litter, reduced soil disturbance, and improved physical protection of organic matter by aggregates [79]. Incorporation of nitrogen-fixing and high-value trees is an important objective besides the three basic principles of CA since a complex interaction between C and N is found in soils. Nitrogen- fixing trees (especially Gliricida) together with maize increased yield by 42% over non-fertilized fields and similar to fields receiving 92 kg N ha^{-1} in a field study conducted in Malawi and Zambia [80]. A worldwide meta-analysis found that 0.3–7.4 Mg ha^{-1} per year C is being sequestered under different systems [78] in which rates of sequestration are higher in tropical agroforestry systems than in temperate environments as this mechanism largely varies depending on the climate conditions, soil conditions, tree species and management practices [79]. So, land-use extensification is a hopeful strategy for SOC sequestration [17] as 0.3–1.9 Mg ha^{-1} of C gets sequestered per year due to conversion of arable land to forest/grassland [81] and the build-up of SOC stocks is primarily because of shifting from stable to labile SOC [82]. Moreover, the age of the system is also an important factor in improving the total soil C as it is evident that total C stock under 27-year-old pine oak stand (117 Mg ha-1) is much lower than 69-year-old oak beech stand (227 Mg ha^{-1}) [83]. Establishment of bioenergy plantation crops can enhance SOC stock and offset fossil fuel combustion; besides, woody crops sequestered considerable organic C belowground primarily as large roots (79%) and to a lesser extent as fine roots (21%) [84]. Agroforestry land-use systems can also be managed by increasing the SOC reservoir in the soil by avoiding burning and minimizing soil disturbance/tillage practices and by erosion control.

12. Conclusion

Conservation agriculture minimizes C loss from the soil and helps in C restoration to manage agroecology with sustained productivity. Conservation agriculture is a holistic approach related to the cropping system that characterized the maximization of crop production on short term basis as well as potential long-term sustainability. Conservation tillage in association with suitable management practices, depending upon climatic conditions, enhances SOC content efficiently under tropical environments compared to temperate ones. Diversified crop rotation provides an opportunity to produce huge biomass C that influences SOC more than under monocropping. Moreover, straw incorporation can lead to improving C sink in upland soils and decreases fluxes of GHGs like CH_4. Crop diversification with legume crops can increase the complexity and diversity of C as they contain carbon compounds resistant to microbial metabolism, thus increasing C stabilization. Future studies need to cover the site-specific component of CA. Development of CA-based best resource management, efficient inputs with stress tolerance characters should be taken into consideration to mitigate the adverse effect of climate change. Thus, the key to enhancing soil quality and achieving food security lies in managing agricultural ecosystems using ecological principles which lead to the enhancement of SOC pool and sustainable management of soil and water resources. The increasing evidence points to the validity of conservation agriculture as a carbon storage practice and justifies further efforts in research and development. Concerning the potential of CA as a strategy for C sequestration, important research still needs to be done. To promote CA, appropriate policy, institutional support, advanced technologies, suitable economic incentives should be given to the farmers.

Author details

Snigdha Chatterjee[1], Satarupa Ghosh[2] and Prasanna Pal[3]*

1 Department of Agricultural Chemistry and Soil Science, Bidhan Chandra Krishi Viswavidyalaya, Mohanpur, Nadia, West Bengal, India

2 Department of Aquatic Environment Management, West Bengal University of Animal and Fishery Sciences, Kolkata, West Bengal, India

3 Animal Physiology Division, ICAR-National Dairy Research Institute, Karnal, Haryana, India

*Address all correspondence to: drpalprasanna@gmail.com

References

[1] Yang Y, Tilman D, Furey G, Lehman C. Soil carbon sequestration acceleration by the restoration of grassland biodiversity. Natural Communications. 2019;**10**(1):1-7

[2] Lal R. Societal value of soil carbon. Journal of Soil and Water Conservation. 2014;**69**(6):186A-192A

[3] IPCC. Climate Change 2013: Executive Summary. Geneva, Switzerland: Intergovernmental Panel on Climate Change; 2014

[4] Guo LB, Gifford RM. Soil carbon stocks and land-use change: A metaanalysis. Global Change Biology. 2002;**8**(4):345-360

[5] Smith P, Martino D, Cai Z, Gwary D, Janzen H, Kumar P, et al. Agriculture. In: Metz B, Davidson OR, Bosch PR, Dave R, Meyer LA, editors. Climate Change 2007: Mitigation. Contribution of Working Group III to the Fourth Assessment Report of the Intergovernmental Panel on Climate Change. Cambridge, United Kingdom and New York, NY, USA: Cambridge University Press; 2007

[6] Lal R. Soil carbon sequestration impacts on global climate change and food security. Science. 2004;**304**:1623-1627

[7] Lorenz K, Lal R. Soil organic carbon sequestration in agroforestry systems. A review. Agronomy for Sustainable Development. 2014;**34**:443-454

[8] Paustian K, Lehmann J, Ogle S, Reay D, Robertson GP, Smith P. Climate smart soils. Nature. 2016;**532**:49-57

[9] Kassam A, Friedrich T, Shaxson F, Pretty J. The spread of conservation agri-culture: Justification, sustainability and uptake. International Journal of Agricultural Sustainability. 2009;**7**:292-320

[10] Lal R. Forest soils and carbon sequestration. Forest Ecology and Management. 2005;**220**(1-3):242-258

[11] Kassam A, Friedrich T, Derpsch R. Global spread of conservation agriculture: Interim update 2015-2016. In: 7th World Congress of Conservation Agriculture; Rosario, Argentina; 1-4 August, 2017

[12] Jat ML, Malik RK, Saharawat YS, Gupta R, Bhag M, Paroda R. et al. Regional dialogue on conservation agriculture in South Asia. In: Proceedings of Regional Dialogue on Conservation Agricultural in South Asia; New Delhi, India: APAARI, CIMMYT, ICAR; 2012. p. 32

[13] Falkowski P, Scholes RJ, Boyle E, Canadell J, Canfield D. The global C cycle: The test of our knowledge of earth as a system. Science. 2000;**289**:270-277

[14] Lal R. Sequestration of atmospheric CO_2 in global C pools. Energy and Environmental Science. 2008;**1**:86-100

[15] Lal R. Managing soils and ecosystems for mitigating anthropogenic carbon emissions and advancing global food security. BioScience. 2010;**60**:708-721

[16] Izaurralde RC, Rosenberg NJ, Lal R. Mitigation of climate change by soil carbon sequestration: Issues of science, monitoring, and degraded lands. Advances in Agronomy. 2000;**70**:1-75

[17] Lal R. Agricultural activities and the global carbon cycle. Nutrient Cycling in Agroecosystems. 2004;**70**:103-116

[18] Monger HC, Gallegos RA. Biotic and abiotic processes and rates of pedogenic

carbonate accumulation in the southwestern United States-Relationship to atmospheric CO_2 sequestration. In: Global Climate Change and Pedogenic Carbonates. 2000. pp. 273-289

[19] Nordt LC, Wilding LP, Drees LR. Pedogenic carbonate transformations in leaching soil systems; implications for the global carbon cycle. In: Global Climate Change and Pedogenic Carbonates. 2000. pp. 43-64

[20] Fawcett AA, Iyer GC, Clarke LE, Edmonds JA, Hultman NE, McJeon HC, et al. Can Paris pledges avert severe climate change? Science. 2015;**350**:1168-1169

[21] Hutchinson JJ, Campbell CA, Desjardins RL. Some perspectives on carbon sequestration in agriculture. Agricultural and Forest Meteorology. 2007;**142**:288-302

[22] Richards M, Bruun TB, Campbell BM, Le G, Huyer S, Kuntze V, Stn M, Oldvig MB, Vasileiou I. How countries plan to address agricultural adaptation and mitigation: An analysis of intended nationally determined contributions. CCAFS dataset. 2016

[23] Minasny B, Malone BP, McBratney AB, Angers DA, Arrouays D, Chambers A, et al. Soil carbon 4 per mille. Geoderma. 2017;**292**:59-86

[24] Lal R, Mohtar RH, Assi AT, Ray R, Baybil H, Jahn M. Soil as a basic nexus tool: Soils at the center of the food-energy-water nexus. Current Sustainable/Renewable Energy Reports. 2017;**4**:1-13

[25] Kadyampakeni D. Soil, water, and nutrient management options for climate change adaptation in southern Africa. Agronomy Journal. 2014;**106**(1):100-110

[26] Kane D, Solutions LLC. Carbon Sequestration Potential on Agricultural Lands: A Review of Current Science and Available Practices. National Sustainable Agriculture Coalition Breakthrough Strategies and Solutions LLC; 2015

[27] Singh BP, Setia R, Wiesmeier M, Kunhikrishnan A. Agricultural management practices and soil organic carbon storage. In: Soil Carbon Storage. Academic Press; 2018. pp. 207-244

[28] Smith P, Bustamante M, Ahmmad H, Clack H, Dong H, Elsidding EA, et al. Agriculture, forestry and other land use (AFOLU). In: Climate Change 2014: Mitigation of Climate Change. Contribution of Working Group III to the Fifth Assessment Report of the Intergovernmental Panel on Climate Change. Cambridge, United Kingdom/ New York, NY, USA: Cambridge University Press; 2014

[29] Lal R. Crop residues as soil amendments and feedstock for bioethanol production. Waste Management. 2008;**28**:747-758

[30] IPCC. Land Use, Land Use Change and Forestry. Special Report. Cambridge, UK: Cambridge University Press; 2000. pp. 127-180

[31] Rasse DP, Rumpel C, Dignac MF. Is soil carbon mostly root carbon? Mechanisms for a specific stabilization. Plant and Soil. 2005;**269**:341-356

[32] Cusack DF, Chou WW, Yang WH, Harmon ME, Silver WL. Controls on long-term root and leaf litter decomposition in neotropical forests. Global Change Biology. 2009;**15**:1339-1355

[33] Six J, Conant RT, Paul EA, Paustian K. Stabilization mechanisms of soil organic matter: Implications for C-saturation of soils: A review. Plant and Soil. 2002;**241**:155-176

[34] Six J, Bossuyt H, Degryze S, Denef K. A history of research on the link between (micro) aggregates, soil biota, and soil organic matter dynamics. Soil and Tillage Research. 2004;**79**:7-31

[35] Wilson GWT, Rice CW, Rillig MC, Springer A, Hartnett DC. Soil aggregation and carbon sequestration are tightly correlated with the abundance of arbuscular mycorrhizal fungi: Results from long-term field experiments. Ecology Letters. 2009;**12**(5):452-461

[36] Six J, Elliott ET, Paustian K. Soil macroaggregate turnover and microaggregate formation: A mechanism for C sequestration under no-tillage agriculture. Soil Biology and Biochemistry. 2000;**32**(14):2099-2103

[37] Tisdall JM, Oades JM. Organic matter and water-stable aggregates in soils. Journal of Soil Science. 1982;**33**:141-163

[38] Balesdent J, Chenu C, Balabane M. Relationship of soil organic matter dynamics to physical protection and tillage. Soil and Tillage Research. 2000;**53**:215-230

[39] Jastrow J, Miller R, Boutton T. Carbon dynamics of aggregate-associated organic matter estimated by carbon-13 natural abundance. Soil Science Society of America Journal. 1996;**60**:801-807

[40] Hassink J. The capacity of soils to preserve organic C and N by their association with clay and silt particles. Plant and Soil. 1997;**191**:77-87

[41] Grandy AS, Robertson GP, Thelen KD. Do productivity and environmental trade-offs justify periodically cultivating no-till cropping systems? Agronomy Journal. 2006;**98**:1377-1383

[42] Lal R. Residue management, conservation tillageband soil restoration for mitigating greenhouse effect by CO_2-enrichment. Soil and Tillage Research. 1997;**43**(1-2):81-107

[43] Chantigny MH, Angers DA, Pr'evost D, V'ezina LP, Chalifour FP. Soil aggregation and fungal and bacterial biomass under annual and perennial cropping systems. Soil Science Society of America Journal. 1997;**61**:262-267

[44] Nguyen TT, Marschner P. Retention and loss of water extractable carbon in soils: Effect of clay properties. Science of the Total Environment. 2014;**470**:400-406

[45] Barre P, Fernandez-Ugalde O, Virto I, Velde B, Chenu C. Impact of phyllosilicate mineralogy on organic carbon stabilization in soils: Incomplete knowledge and exciting prospects. Geoderma. 2014;**235**:382-395

[46] Steffens M. Soils of a semiarid shortgrass steppe in inner Mongolia: Organic matter composition and distribution as affected by sheep grazing [Doctoral dissertation]. Munich, Germany: Technische Universtat Munchen; 2009

[47] Wiseman CLS, Puttmann W. Soil organic carbon and its sorptive preservation in Central Germany. European Journal of Soil Science. 2005;**56**:65-76

[48] Setia R, Rengasamy P, Marschner P. Effect of exchangeable cation concentration on sorption and desorption of dissolved organic carbon in saline soils. Science of the Total Environment. 2013;**465**:226-232

[49] Krull E, Baldock J, Skjemstad J. Soil texture effects on decomposition and soil carbon storage. In: Net Ecosystem Exchange CRC Workshop Proceedings; 2001. pp. 103-110

[50] Krull ES, Baldock JA, Skjemstad JO. Importance of mechanisms and

processes of the stabilisation of soil organic matter for modelling carbon turnover. Functional Plant Biology. 2003;**30**:207-222

[51] Coleman K, Jenkinson D, Crocker G, Grace P, Klir J, Korschens M, et al. Simulating trends in soil organic carbon in long-term experiments using RothC-26.3. Geoderma. 1997;**81**:29-44

[52] FAO. Investing in sustainable crop intensification: the case for improving soil health. In: International Technical Workshop. Rome: FAO; July 22-24, 2008

[53] Lal R. Sequestering carbon and increasing productivity by conservation agriculture. Journal of Soil and Water Conservation. 2015;**70**(3):55A-62A

[54] NAAS. Innovative viable solution to rice residue burning in rice-wheat cropping system through concurrent use of super straw management system-fitted combines and turbo happy seeder. In: Singh Y, Jat ML, Sidhu HS, Singh P, Verma A, editors. Policy Brief No. 2. New Delhi: National Academy of Agricultural Sciences; 2017. p. 16

[55] Govaerts B, Verhulst N, Castellanos-Navarrete A, Sayre KD, Dixon J, Dendooven L. Conservation agriculture and soil carbon sequestration: Between myth and farmer reality. Critical Reviews in Plant Sciences. 2009;**28**(3):97-122

[56] Bhan S, Behera UK. Conservation agriculture in India—Problems, prospects and policy issues. International Soil and Water Conservation Research. 2014;**2**(4):1-12

[57] West TO, Post WM. Soil organic carbon sequestration rates by tillage and crop rotation: A global data analysis. Soil Science Society of America Journal. 2002;**66**:1930-1946

[58] Ogle SM, Breidt FJ, Paustian K. Agricultural management impacts on soil organic carbon storage undermoist and dry climatic conditions of temperate and tropical regions. Biogeochemistry. 2005;**72**:87-121

[59] VandenBygaart AJ, Yang XM, Kay BD, Aspinall D. Variability in carbon sequestration potential in no-till soil landscapes of southern Ontario. Soil and Tillage Research. 2002;**65**:231-234

[60] Beare M, Hendrix P, Coleman D. Water-stable aggregates and organic matter fractions in conventional-and no-tillage soils. Soil Science Society of America Journal. 1994;**58**:777-786

[61] Franzluebbers AJ. Soil organic carbon sequestration and agricultural greenhouse gas emissions in the southeastern USA. Soil and Tillage Research. 2005;**83**:120-147

[62] Blanco-Canqui H, Lal R. No-tillage and soil-profile carbon sequestration: An on-farm assessment. Soil Science Society of America Journal. 2008;**72**:693-701

[63] Kuzyakov Y, Schneckenberger K. Review of estimation of plant rhizodeposition and their contribution to soil organic matter formation. Archives of Agronomy and Soil Science. 2004;**50**:115-132

[64] Liu C, Lu M, Cui J, Li B, Fang C. Effects of straw carbon input on carbon dynamics in agricultural soils: A meta-analysis. Global Change Biology. 2014;**20**:1366-1381

[65] Chivenge PP, Murwira HK, Giller KE, Mapfumo P, Six J. Long-term impact of reduced tillage and residue management on soil carbon stabilization: Implications for conservation agriculture on contrasting soils. Soil and Tillage Research. 2007;**94**:328-337

[66] Chan KY, Heenan DP. The effects of stubble burning and tillage

on soil carbon sequestration and crop productivity in southeastern Australia. Soil Use and Management. 2005;**21**:427-431

[67] Poeplau C, Katterer T, Bolinder MA, Borjesson G, Berti A, Lugato E. Low stabilization of aboveground crop residue carbon in sandy soils of Swedish long-term experiments. Geoderma. 2015;**237**:246-255

[68] Kirkby CA, Richardson AE, Wade LJ, Conyers M, Kirkegaard JA. Inorganic nutrients increasehumification efficiency and C-sequestration in an annually cropped soil. PLoS One. 2016;**11**:e0153698

[69] Dolan MS, Clapp CE, Allmaras RR, Baker JM, Molina JAE. Soil organic carbon and nitrogen in a Minnesota soil as related to tillage, residue and nitrogen management. Soil and Tillage Research. 2006;**89**:221-231

[70] Sanger LJ, Whelan MJ, Cox P, Anderson JM. Measurement and modelling of soil organic matter decomposition using biochemical indicators. In: Van Cleemput O, Hofman G, Vermoese A, editors. Progress in Nitrogen Cycling Studies. Dordrecht: Springer; 1996. pp. 445-450

[71] Vanlauwe B, Dendooven L, Merckx R. Residue fractionation and decomposition—The significance of the active fraction. Plant and Soil. 1994;**158**:263-274

[72] Singh VK, Dwivedi BS, Singh SK, Majumdar K, Jat ML, Mishra RP, et al. Soil physical properties, yield trends and economics after five years of conservation agriculture based rice-maize system in North-Western India. Soil and Tillage Research. 2016;**155**:133-148

[73] Parihar CM, Prihar MD, Sapkota TB, Nanwal RK, Singh AK, Jat SL, et al. Long-term impact of conservation agriculture and diversified maize nitrogen fractions and nitrous oxide fluxes in inceptisol of India. Science of the Total Environment. 2018;**640**:1382-1392

[74] Peltre C, Nielsen M, Christensen BT, Hansen EM, Thomsen IK, Bruun S. Straw export in continuous winter wheat and the ability of oil radish catch crops and early sowing of wheat to offset soil C and N losses: A simulation study. Agricultural Systems. 2016;**143**:195-202

[75] Tiemann LK, Grandy AS, Atkinson EE, Marin-Spiotta E, McDaniel MD. Crop rotational diversity enhances belowground communities and functions in an agroecosystem. Ecology Letters. 2015;**18**:761-771

[76] Wickings K, Grandy AS, Reed SC, Cleveland CC. The origin of litter chemical complexity during decomposition. Ecology Letters. 2012;**15**(10):1180-1188

[77] Powlson DS, Stirling CM, Thierfelder C. Does conservation agriculture deliver climate change mitigation through soil carbon sequestration in tropical agroecosystems? Agriculture, Ecosystems and Environment. 2016;**220**:164-174

[78] Kim DG, Kirschbaum MUF, Beedy TL. Carbon sequestration and net emissions of CH_4 and N_2O under agroforestry: Synthesizing available data and suggestions for future studies. Agriculture, Ecosystems and Environment. 2016;**226**:65-78

[79] Stavi I, Lal R. Agroforestry and biochar to offset climate change: A review. Agronomy for Sustainable Development. 2013;**33**:81-96

[80] Sileshi GW, Debusho LK, Akinnifesi FK. Can integration of

legume trees increase yield stability in rainfed maize cropping systems in southern Africa? Agronomy Journal. 2012;**104**:1392-1398

[81] Post WM, Kwon KC. Soil carbon sequestration and land-use change: Processes and potential. Global Change Biology. 2000;**6**:317-327

[82] Poeplau C, Don A. Sensitivity of soil organic carbon stocks and fractions to different land-use changes across Europe. Geoderma. 2013;**192**:189-201

[83] Schauvlieghe M, Lust N. Carbon accumulation and allocation after afforestation of a pasture with pin oak (*Quercus palustris*) and ash (*Fraxinus excelsior*). Silva Gandavensis. 1999;**64**:72-81

[84] Tolbert VR, Thornton FC, Joslin JD, Bock BR, Bandaranayake W, Houston AE, et al. Increasing below ground carbon sequestration with conversion of agricultural lands to production of bioenergy crops. New Zealand Journal of Forest Science. 2000;**30**:138-149

Chapter 8

Effects of Arbuscular Mycorrhizal Fungi on Plant Adaptation to Arid Ecosystem of Bou-Hedma National Park in Tunisia

Mahmoudi Neji, Mahdhi Mosbah and Mars Mohamed

Abstract

Plants interact with beneficial microbes living in their rhizosphere, promoting their growth and development. In arid ecosystems, specific plant-associated microbes grant plants access to nutrients that would otherwise be inaccessible. Arbuscular mycorrhizal fungi (AMF) are probably one of the better known below-ground functional networks with plants. AMF plays a crucial role in plant performance and consequently in ecosystem functioning. AMF activities also determine the bio-availability of nutrients and therefore soil fertility. The main objective of the present study was to evaluate the plant-AMF interactions on soil functions under arid ecosystem in Tunisia. AMF colonization was evaluated by visual observation of AMF in fine roots of *Astragalus corrugatus* and *Lotus creticus* on Bou-Hedma National Park in Tunisia. Mycorrhizal colonization varied between plants, and the spore number was significantly different across rhizosphere soils. Statistical analysis showed a clearly positive correlation between the number of spores and plant-mycorrhizal intensity. For microbiological proprieties, our results showed that mycorrhizal plants improved significantly the different microbiological parameters. The results of the present study specified the association plant-AMF and highlight AMF importance as a tailored mechanism of plant adaptation to arid ecosystems.

Keywords: beneficial microbes, arid ecosystems, arbuscular mycorrhizal fungi (AMF), mycorrhizal colonization, microbiological proprieties

1. Introduction

Most arid and semiarid regions of Tunisia are frequently exposed to high temperatures and prolonged droughts, which reduce natural vegetation biodiversity and increase soil erosion and sand dune advance [1–3]. Under arid conditions, plant adaptation and survival depend obligatory on the plants' strategies to overcome drought and deficiencies on nutrients [4]. Low soil fertility in these types of ecosystems makes plants highly dependent on symbiotic association as plant's strategies. The developed symbioses, especially "mycorrhizal symbioses," have been noted for their importance in the stability of the ecosystem subject to degradation and desertification. The symbiotic association with mycorrhizal fungi plays a

IntechOpen

significant role in the vegetative cover durability, especially in degraded soil of arid ecosystems [5].

Arbuscular mycorrhizal fungi (AMF) is a widespread group of soil fungi in natural ecosystems, forming a symbiotic association with roots of most of the terrestrial plants [6]. AMF play a significant role in the dynamic of ecosystem and growth and adaptation of plants to their environments [7]. AMF improve the ability of the plant to absorb water and nutrients from the soil, thus increasing their growth and development under unfavorable conditions [8]. AMF protect also their host plants against divers' biotic and abiotic stresses because of their beneficial roles in improving growth and drought tolerance [9].

AMF formed a symbiotic association between plant roots and the surrounding soils. Root systems play a crucial function in the acquisition of nutrients by exploiting a good volume of soil absorption [4]. When colonizing the roots of plant species, AMF developed two important structures: intra- and extra-radical mycelium. The intra-radical hyphae penetrate the root cells and develop some structures (developed vesicles and arbuscules) to improve the exchanges between the fungi and the plant host [10]. The extra-radical hyphae developed beyond the root surface and colonized the surrounding substratum. AMF significantly increased in the area of root absorption of plants colonized by the increase in the volume of soil explored [11]. So, AMF formation was exactly an adaptive strategy that provides the plant with an increased ability for nutrients in soils with low nutrient availability, particularly in arid and semiarid ecosystems [12].

AMF created an advantaged space for microbial development and activities. They play a crucial role in terrestrial ecosystems' functioning, especially in arid ecosystem, where root exudates are the major carbon source supporting soil microbial activities [13]. Apart from the nutritional benefits of the host plant, AMF increased the tolerance to drought [14], salt stress [15], and protection from root pathogens. As an important ecological function, AMF enhances soil structure and stability through the formation of hydro-stable aggregates [16, 17].

Generally, the symbiotic association AMF-plant communities are strongly dependent on the local environmental factors [18]. Soil physical, chemical, and biological properties are key factors to determine the AMF community and activity [19]. It has been reported that edaphic and climatic characteristics affect the diversity and composition of the AMF communities [20]. Some studies established a strong relationship between AMF colonization and environmental conditions such as temperature, rainfall, and physicochemical properties of soils [21, 22].

Therefore, in order to understand the effects of mycorrhization on plant development and their impact in the ecology of plant communities, it is important to assess the activities of the AMF community. Due to the relevant and important role these fungi play in the stability of the ecosystem, in this study we investigated the plant-AMF interactions on soil functions under arid ecosystem in Bou-Hedma National Park in Tunisia.

2. Materials and methods

2.1 Study site

The study site is the Bou-Hedma National Park (34°39′N and 94°8′E). This area is located in the Governorate of Sidi Bouzid, in central and southern Tunisia (**Figure 1**). The park was established in 1980 and covers an area of 16,488 hectares of which 6000 are under full protection. The mean annual rainfall varies between 150 and 250 mm. The mean annual temperature is about 17.2°C, while the minimal

Figure 1.
Location of the studied site: Bou-Hedma national park.

and maximal monthly temperature means are, respectively, 3.8°C (January) and 36.2°C (August).

2.2 Roots and soil samples

Fine roots of *Astragalus corrugatus* and *Lotus creticus* were collected at 25 cm depth. Four replicate samples were collected at each plant. Roots were washed with distilled water to remove attached soil for root colonization assessment.

Separate soil samples were collected from underneath each plant species. Control soil was recovered in an area which does not contain any vegetation. The soil samples were sieved to 2 mm to remove plant debris, gravel, and earthworms. They were then stored at 4°C for further analysis.

2.3 Assessment of root colonization by AMF

Root mycorrhizal colonization was checked for 90 root pieces per plant. Root segments of 1–2 cm were cleaned in 10% (w/v) potassium hydroxide (KOH) at 90° C for 1 h and acidified with 1% (w/v) hydrochloric acid (HCl) for 5 min. Then, the root segments were stained for 90 min at 60°C in 0.05% trypan blue (Phillips and Hayman, 1970). AMF colonization percentage was evaluated according to the grid interception of Giovannetti and Mosse [23]. Mycorrhizal frequency and intensity were calculated as described by Trouvelot et al. [24].

The parameters evaluated are:

- The mycorrhizal frequency (F %), which reflects the importance of the host plant root system infection by mycorrhizal fungi:

$$F\% = 100 \text{ X } (N - N0)/N \tag{1}$$

where N, number of the observed fragments; N0, number of non-mycorrhizal fragments

- The mycorrhizal intensity (M %), which is defined as the proportion of the root invaded by endomycorrhizal:

$$M\% = (95n5 + 70n4 + 30n3 + 5n2 + n1)/N. \tag{2}$$

where n = number of fragments assigned with the index 0, 1, 2, 3, 4, or 5.

2.4 Extraction and enumeration of AMF spores from soil samples

AMF spores were extracted from 100 g of each soil sample using the wet sieving method in sucrose gradient as described by Gerdemann and Nicolson [25]. 100 g of each studied soil sample were submerged in 1 L of tap water. After 1 min of stirring and 30 s of settling, the supernatant was sieved through three nested sieves with mashes of 1000, 100, and 32 μm. The filtrate was collected and sieved again (each soil suspension was sieved twice). Deposition in the sieves of 32 μm was recovered in centrifuge tubes of 25 ml. A viscosity gradient was created by adding 25 ml of aqueous sucrose solution at 60%. After 2 min of centrifugation at 2000 at 3000 rpm/min, the supernatant was poured onto the sieve of 32 μm; the fraction retained was rinsed with distilled water to remove sucrose. After extraction, spores were counted under a stereomicroscope (40X magnification), and the average number was calculated per 100 g of dry soil.

2.5 Soil analysis

For chemical analyses, soil pH and electrical conductivity (Ec) were determined by the saturated paw method in water by pH meter and conductivity meter, respectively. Total nitrogen (TN) was determined by the Kjeldahl method, and soil organic carbon (Corg) was determined by the Walkley and Black method. All soil analyses were performed in triplicate.

2.6 Soil microbial biomass

Microbial biomass carbon (Cmic) present in the different soil samples was determined by the method of "fumigation–extraction" as described by "Amato and Ladd [26]". This method is based on the use of ninhydrin-N reactive compounds extracted from soils with potassium chloride (KCl) after an incubation period (around a 10-day fumigation period). All soil analyses were performed in triplicate.

2.7 Biochemical properties

For enzyme activities, phosphatase and β-glucosidase activities were determined as described by Caravaca et al. [27]. The p-nitrophenol (PNP) formed in phosphatase activity and the p-nitrophenol glucopyranoside in β-glucosidase were determined in a spectrophotometer at 398 nm. The dehydrogenase activity was determined according to Garcia et al. [28]. The iodonitrotetrazolium formazan (INTF) formed was measured using a spectrophotometer at 490 nm. All soil analyses were performed in triplicate.

2.8 Statistical analyses

All the statistical analyses were performed by using the SAS statistical package. The effects of AMF on soil proprieties were subjected to ANOVA for repeated measures. The least significant difference values at 5% level of significance ($P \leq 0.05$) were calculated to assess differences between parameters.

3. Results

3.1 Physical and chemical proprieties of the studied site

The different physical and chemical proprieties of studied soil are shown in **Table 1**. Data showed that the pH was basic (pH > 7) and the electrical conductivity

Granulometry	Available phosphorus (ppm)	Available nitrogen (ppm)	pH	Electrical conductivity (s m^{-1})	Organic carbon %	Water content %
Sandy loam	6.0 ± 0.2	110 ± 10	7.8 ± 0.1	2.0 ± 0.1	1.2 ± 0.1	3.2 ± 0.2

Table 1.
Physical and chemical properties of the studied site.

was 2 sm $^{-1}$. The present studied the soil studied was of sandy loam texture. A low values of water content and available P were registered. The mean soil organic carbon and total available nitrogen (TN) were around 1.2% and 110 ppm, respectively.

3.2 AMF colonization of roots

Microscopic examinations of root fragments (**Figure 2**) demonstrated the development of different endogenous structures characterizing mycorrhizal fungi (intracellular hyphae, vesicles of varying shapes and arbuscules) in the root cells of the two studied plants.

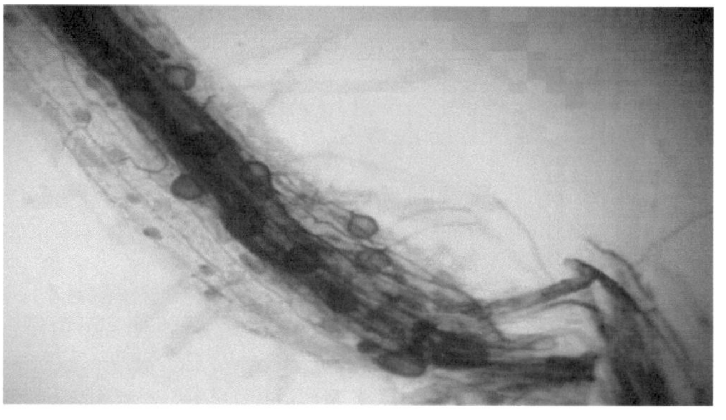

Figure 2.
Endogenous structures of AMF colonization (intraradical hyphae, and spores) within a root of A. corrugatus.

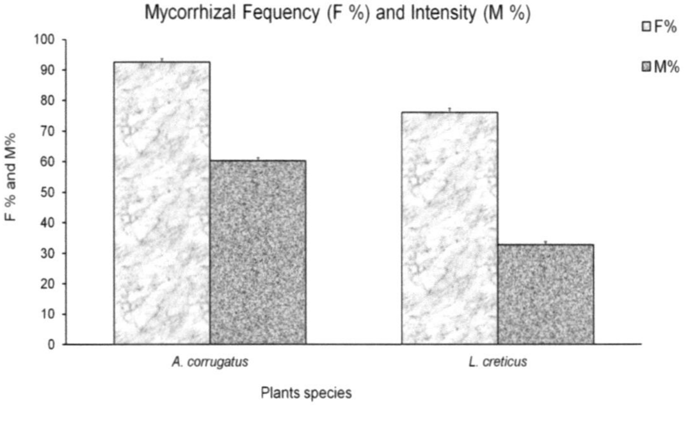

Figure 3.
Data from AMF colonization (mycorrhizal frequency and mycorrhizal intensity) of plant roots: A. corrugatus *And* L. creticus. *Error lines correspond to the standard deviation (n = 3). The significant differences calculated at P < 0.05.*

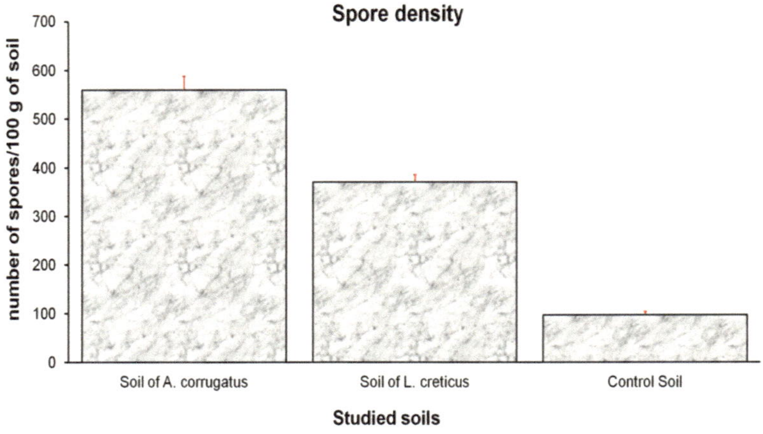

Figure 4.
Data from spores' density (number of spores) of studied soils. Error lines correspond to the standard deviation (n = 3). The significant differences calculated at P < 0.05.

Mycorrhizal frequency in the roots varied between the two studied Fabaceae plants, reaching 76.2% (*L. creticus*) and 92.6% (*A. corrugatus*) (**Figure 3**).

The mycorrhizal power that corresponds to the percentage of the mycorrhizal intensity of root cortex showed a significant difference (**Figure 3**). The roots of *A. corrugatus* have the highest mycorrhizal intensity (60.4%), while the roots of *L. creticus* have the lowest values (32.9%).

3.3 Abundance of spores' densities

AMF spores were detected in all studied soil samples (**Figure 4**). The majority number of AMF spores isolated from the rhizosphere varied significantly ($P < 0.05$) among the three studied soils; the average numbers ranged from 560 spores to 96 spores per 100 g dry soil. The highest value was recorded in the rhizosphere of *A. corrugatus* and the lowest in the control soil devoid of any plant cover (**Figure 4**).

Static analyses registered significant differences in the values of spore density (**Figure 4**) across the different studied samples, with an increasing trend in

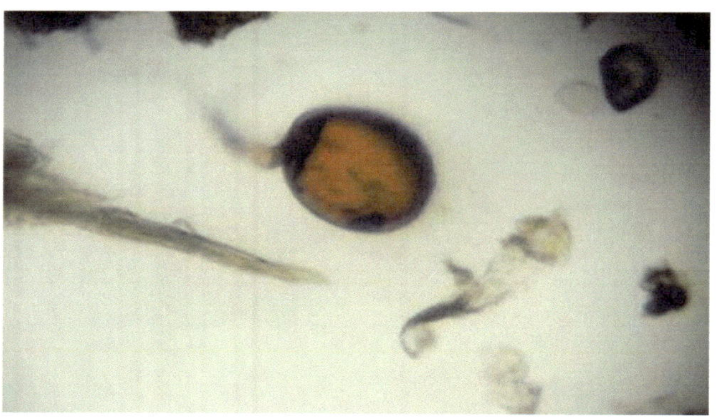

Figure 5.
Morphological appearance of some spores in a soil suspension of rhizospheric of A. corrugatus *(magnification: 100X).*

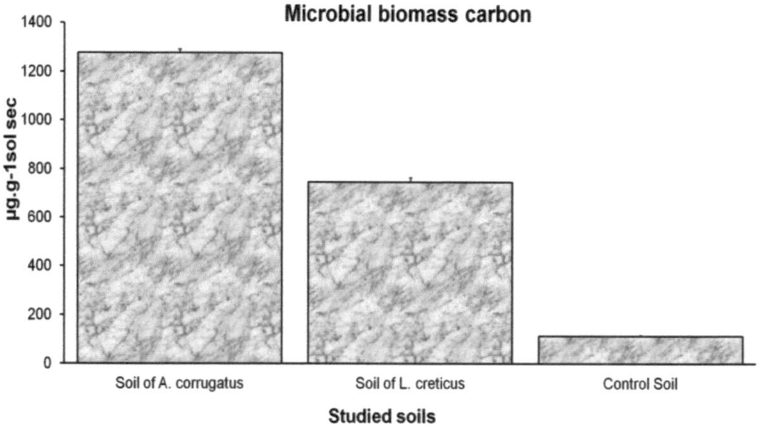

Figure 6.
Data from microbiological parameters (microbial biomass) of studied soils. Error lines correspond to the standard deviation (n = 3). The significant differences calculated at P < 0.05.

sporulation and with the increasing percentage of mycorrhizal colonization shown in the root samples of plant species.

A high variability in spore size, color, and shape was observed. The majorities of the spores were yellow-colored and did not exceed 70 µm in size (**Figure 5**).

3.4 Microbiological properties: microbial biomass

Microbial biomass varied significantly between the three studied soils (**Figure 6**). Rhizospheric soil of *A. corrugatus* presents the highest values (1277.22 µg C/g soil) compared with the control soil (112.31 µg C/g soil). The results showed a very significant effect of the mycorrhizal plant. However, across the different soil samples, **Figure 6** showed significant differences in the values of microbial biomass,

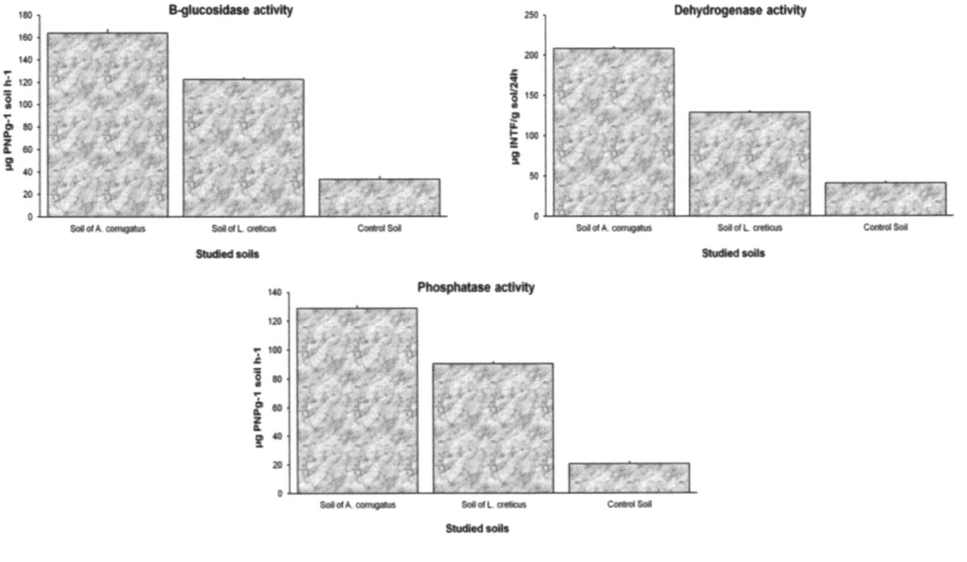

Figure 7.
Data from biochemical parameters (dehydrogenase, β-glucosidase and phosphatase activity) of studied soils. Error lines correspond to the standard deviation (n = 3). The significant differences calculated at P < 0.05.

with an increasing trend of microbial communities and with the increasing percentage of mycorrhizal colonization.

3.5 Biochemical properties: enzymatic activities

Across the different studied soils, static analyses indicated significant differences in the values of dehydrogenase activity (**Figure** 7), with an increasing trend in enzyme activity and with the increasing percentage of mycorrhizal colonization. Phosphatase and β-glucosidase activities showed the same trends as dehydrogenase activity, values were higher in the high mycorrhizal intensity, and they decreased along with soil devoid of any vegetation types (**Figure** 7).

4. Discussion

Arbuscular mycorrhizal fungi as symbiotic microorganisms were a major microbial component in the soil that is registered in all different climates and ecosystems [11]. AMF plays crucial roles in the restoration and retention of soil fertility, improving significantly the development of the host plant in degraded soils in the arid and semiarid region [5].

In general, the predominant mycorrhizal associations in natural ecosystems (such as our study area: Bou-Hedma National Park (**Figure 1**)) are arbuscular and vesicular mycorrhizal fungi [29]. The presence of different AMF structures such as vesicles and arbuscules (**Figure 2**) in the root cortex of the two studied plants indicates that these species had a higher mycotrophic status and the mycorrhizal activity can improve their successful growth in arid regions. Our result is consistent with the finding that more than 80% of terrestrial plants are mycotrophic plants [30]. The percentage of mycorrhizal colonization (**Figures 2** and **3**) varies between studied plants. However, many plant species have very different levels of dependence to AM fungi to satisfy their nutritional needs [31, 32]. All these can explain the results obtained in our study since *Astragalus corrugatus* showed the highest dependence on mycorrhizal fungi.

Our study revealed considerable variability in spore number. The spore densities detected in the different studied soil ranged from 96 to 560 spores per 100 g dry soil. The abundance of AMF spores in the different prospected soils suggests the high AMF diversity that can characterize our arid studied ecosystem.

Mycorrhizal plant species promote the development of different fungal propagules (spores) in their rhizospheric soil [33]. For this reason, as shown in **Figure 4**, the spore number registered in the rhizospheric soil of the two studied plants was higher than in the open areas (control soil).

As shown in the microscopic observation of spore suspensions (**Figure 5**), a high variability in spore size, color, and shape was observed, and the majority of the spores did not exceed 70 μm in size (a dominance of small spores). Thus, in general, the predominance of this type may be a strategy of selective adaptation to the major abiotic stress process and especially the drought stress [34].

We observed as indicated in **Figure 4** that spore densities in the plant rhizospheres are correlated significantly with the intensity colonization registered on their corresponding mycorrhizal root systems [35]. However, the highest mycorrhizal plant (*A. corrugatus*) registered the highest spore's number in their rhizospheric soil.

The plant-AMF symbiotic association is dependent on multiple factors: soil nutrient availability [nitrogen (N) and phosphorus (P)], environmental variables (temperatures), and soil properties (water, pH, salinity, and organic matter) [36].

In general, AMF play important roles for nutrient acquisition to the host plant [11]. Thus, the levels of mycorrhizal colonization are reduced by high value of P and N [20]. However, it is not the case in our area of study which is characterized by low soil nutrient availability (**Table 1**). Temperature, pH, and water availability also seem to affect the percentage of root AMF colonization. Thus, it has been reported that an important value of water content inhibits spore germination by increasing AMF mycelium growth [34]. As indicated in **Table 1**, our result showed that all environmental factors (low values) influence significantly AMF development on these types of ecosystems which explain the high level of AMF colonization and spore densities registered in the park.

It is well established that the rhizosphere is a very dynamic biological environment clearly distinct from the bulk soil (control soil), where microbial diversity and activity are characteristic. Various microbiological communities in the rhizospheric soil are essential for the occurrence of fundamental processes (biochemical cycling) that improve the formation and fertility of the soil and consequently the maintenance and sustainability of arid ecosystems [37]. The measurement of the status and activities of specific microbial communities contributing to the soil fundamental processes has the potential to provide particularly rapid and sensitive means of characterizing changes in soil quality and fertility [3].

Microbiological soil parameters are well known to be used as an important indicator of soil quality and dynamics. Biological parameters used are those engaged to characterize the size, structure, and dynamic of the microbial communities in the soil [38]. As a first biological indicator, soil microbial biomass carbon (Cmic) has been increasingly considered an environmental marker [39]. Our results (**Figure 6**) agree with those reports, which also showed the positive effect of the rhizospheric soil of mycorrhizal plant on Cmic compared to control soil devoid of vegetation. The important value of microbial density, estimated by the microbial carbon, was significantly registered in the soil recovered from two studied plants. The control soil (opened area) devoid of any vegetation has the lowest Cmic. This finding is in consistence with the reports, indicating at first that a soil-containing plant maintains a higher microbial biomass than soil devoid of vegetation cover [40] and also that plant species promote the development, the abundance, and the diversity of the microbial communities in their rhizosphere, which improve soil fertility and levels of organic matter in the soil [41, 42]. In general, plants can influence the microbial community by the secretion of different root exudates [43]. Our analyses showed that the high mycorrhizal plant registered the high densities on microbial communities.

However, similarly to roots, AMF are leaky and lose nutrients into the mycosphere, which will selectively promote the development of different microorganisms. In this context, it is to be expected that AMF play a crucial role in the biological characteristics of the rhizosphere [27, 44]. In this particular respect, the importance of the AMF in promoting the development of the microbial community is confirmed by the low levels of microbial carbon observed in the soil without plant cover (control).

It is notable that rhizosphere activity improves significantly plant fitness and soil quality because the microbial activity (as biochemical cycling) can help the host plant to better adapt to stress conditions concerning water and mineral deficit [45]. Soil enzymes take part in organic matter decomposition and the major nutrient cycling. They are important components for biochemical functioning of soils [3].

Soil enzyme activities have been used as good indicators of microbial activity. With regard to enzymes present in the different studied soils, dehydrogenase, phosphatase, and β-glucosidase are considered as a microbiological activity index of soil quality in semiarid and arid soils. The potential activities of the three studied enzymes

(**Figure 7**) were higher in the rhizosphere of the high mycorrhizal plants than in that of the bulk soil (soil devoid of vegetation cover). However, AMF increase the diversity of the carbon sources available to the microorganisms in the rhizosphere [46], which in part is due to their nutritional mode and excretion of catabolic enzymes to the surrounding medium. The importance of the soil microbial activity in association with enzyme activity was highlighted by the similarity in the activity patterns of the three studied enzymes, an indicator of microbial activity [47].

Furthermore, the major biological activity of soil was a highly sensitive indicator to biotic and abiotic environmental factors. It is a useful microbiological parameter of the soil improvement or degradation [48].

At this point it is clear that the impact of AMF on plant community composition and functioning was a key factor for ecosystem functioning and stability [49].

5. Conclusion

In conclusion, this study is among the firsts report on AMF communities associated with some herbaceous plant species in arid Tunisia and especially in protected ecosystem "Bou-Hedma National Park." Little is currently known about the AMF composition and activity and their impact on the stability of arid regions on Tunisia. *A. corrugatus* have the highest mycorrhizal colonization registered in their roots, and consequently they registered the highest spore density in their rhizospheric soil. Our study also reported that the soil microbial activity was improved with the high levels of AMF. Therefore, the influence of AMF on soil biochemical properties (enzymatic activities) and their dynamics is significant. The findings of the present study should be considered on appropriate soil management and the preservation of the protected ecosystem, especially in the arid region.

Acknowledgements

This work was supported by the Tunisian Ministry of High Education and Research Development. We are grateful to Bou-Hedma National Park for making the experimental site available.

Conflict of interest

We declare we do not have any conflict of interest.

Author details

Mahmoudi Neji[1,2]*, Mahdhi Mosbah[1,3] and Mars Mohamed[1]

1 Faculté des Sciences de Gabès, Unité de Recherche: Biodiversité et Valorisation des Bio-ressources en Zones Arides (BVBZA), Erriadh Zrig, Tunisie

2 Faculté des Sciences de Tunis, Université Tunis Al Manar, Tunisie

3 Center for Environmental Research and Studies, Jazan University, Kingdom of Saudi Arabia

*Address all correspondence to: neji.2012@yahoo.com

References

[1] Mahmoudi N, Cruz C, Mahdhi M, Mars M, Caeiro MF. Arbuscular mycorrhizal fungi in soil, roots and rhizosphere of Medicago truncatula: Diversity and heterogeneity under semi-arid conditions. PeerJ. 2019;7:e6401. DOI: 10.7717/peerj.6401

[2] Mosbah M, Philippe DL, Mohamed M. Molecular identification of arbuscular mycorrhizal fungal spores associated to the rhizosphere of Retama raetam in Tunisia. Soil Science & Plant Nutrition. 2018;**64**:335-341. DOI: 10.1080/ 00380768.2018.1431012

[3] Fterich A, Mahdhi M, Mars M. Impact of grazing on soil microbial communities along a chronosequence of Acacia tortilis subsp, raddiana in arid soils in Tunisia. European Journal of Soil Biology. 2012;**50**:56-63. DOI: 10.1016/j.ejsobi.2011.12.002

[4] Yao Q, Wang LR, Zhu HH, Chen JZ. Effect of arbuscular mycorrhizal fungal inoculation on root system architecture of trifoliate orange (*Poncirus trifoliata* L. Raf.) seedlings. Scientia Horticculturae. 2009;**121**:458-461. DOI: 10.1016/j.scienta.2009.03.013

[5] Duponnois R, Plenchette C, Prin Y, Ducosso M, Kisa M, Ba AM, et al. Use of mycorrhizal inoculation to improve reafforestation process with Australian Acacia in Saheliane cozones. Ecological Engineering. 2007;**29**:105-112. DOI: 10.1016/j.ecoleng.2006.09.008

[6] Gianinazzi S, Gollotte A, Binet MN, van Tuinen D, Redecker D, Wipf D. Agroecology: The key role of arbuscular mycorrhizas in ecosystem services. Mycorrhiza. 2010;**20**:519-530. DOI: 10.1007/s00572-010-0333-3

[7] Brundrett M. Mycorrhizal associations and other means of nutrition of vascular plants: Understanding the global diversity of host plants by resolving conflicting information and developing reliable means of diagnosis. Plant and Soil. 2009;**320**:37-77. DOI: 10.1007/s11104-008-9877-9

[8] Requena N, Perez-Solis E, Azcon-Aguilar C, Jeffries P, Barea JM. Management of indigenous plant microbe symbioses aids restoration of desertified ecosystems. Applied and Environmental Microbiology. 2001;**67**:495-498. DOI: 10.1128/aem.67.2.495-498.2001

[9] Yang HS, Zhang Q, Dai YJ, Liu Q, Tang JJ, Bian XM, et al. Effects of arbuscular mycorrhizal fungi on plant growth depend on root system: A meta-analysis. Plant and Soil. 2015;**389**:361-374. DOI: 10.1007/s11104-014-2370-8

[10] Van Aarle IM, Cavagnaro TR, Smith SE, Smith FA, Dickson S. Metabolic activity of *Glomus intraradices* in Arumand Paris-type arbuscular mycorrhizal colonization. The New Phytologist. 2005;**166**:611-618. DOI: 10.1111/j.1469-8137.2005.01340.x

[11] Smith SE, Read DJ. Mycorrhizal Symbiosis. San Diego: Academic Press; 2008. p. 787

[12] Allen MF. Mycorrhizal fungi: Highways for water and nutrients in arid soils. Vadose Zone Journal. 2007;**6**:291-297. DOI: 10.2136/vzj2006.0068

[13] Bago B, Vierheilig H, Piché Y, Ázcon-Aguilar C. Nitrate depletion and pH changes induced by the extraradical mycelium of the arbuscular mycorrhizal fungus Glomus intraradices grown in monoxenic culture. The New Phytologist. 1996;**133**:273-280. DOI: 10.1111/j.1469-8137.1996.tb01894.x

[14] Auge RM. Water relations, drought and vesiculararbuscular mycorrhizal symbiosis. Mycorrhiza. 2000;**11**:3-42. DOI: 10.1007/s005720100097

[15] Garg N, Chandel S. Effect of mycorrhizal inoculation on growth, nitrogen fixation, and nutrient uptake in *Cicer arietinum* (L.) under salt stress. Turkish Journal of Agriculture and Forestry. 2011;**35**:205-214. DOI: 10.3906/tar-0908-12

[16] Daynes CN, Field DJ, Saleeba JA, Cole MA, McGee PA. Development and stabilization of soil structure via interactions between organic matter, arbuscular mycorrhizal fungi and plant roots. Soil Biology and Biochemistry. 2013;**57**:683-694. DOI: 10.1016/j.soilbio.2012.09.020

[17] Peng S, Guo T, Liu G. The effects of arbuscular mycorrhizal hyphal networks on soil aggregations of purple soil in Southwest China. Soil Biology and Biochemistry. 2013;**57**:411-417. DOI: 10.1016/j.soilbio.2012.10.026

[18] Velázquez M, Stürmer SL, Bruzone C, Fontenla S, Barrera M, Cabello M. Occurrence of arbuscular mycorrhizal fungi in high altitude sites of the Patagonian Altoandina region in Nahuel Huapi National Park (Argentina). Acta Botânica Brasílica. 2016;**30**:521-531. DOI: 10.1590/0102-33062016abb0223

[19] Oehl F, Laczko E, Bogenrieder A, Karl Stahr K, Bösch R, Vander Heijden M, et al. Soil type and land use intensity determine the composition of arbuscular mycorrhizal fungal communities. Soil Biology and Biochemistry. 2010;**42**:724-738. DOI: 10.1016/j.soilbio.2010.01.006

[20] Johnson NC. Resource stoichiometry elucidates the structure and function of arbuscular mycorrhizas across scales. The New Phytologist. 2010;**185**:631-647. DOI: 10.1111/j.1469-8137.2009.03110.x

[21] Xu X, Chen C, Zhang Z, Sun Z. The influence of environmental factors on communities of arbuscular mycorrhizal fungi associated with *Chenopodium ambrosioides* revealed by MiSeq sequencing investigation. Scientific Reports. 2017;**7**:45134. DOI: 10.1038/srep45134

[22] Frater PN, Borer ET, Fay PA, Jin V. Nutrients and environment influence arbuscular mycorrhizal colonization both independently and interactively in *Schizachyrium scoparium*. Plant and Soil. 2018;**425**:493-506. DOI: 10.1007/s11104-018-3597-6

[23] Giovannetti M, Mosse B. An evaluation of techniques for measuring vesicular-arbuscular mycorrhizal infection in roots. The New Phytologist. 1980;**84**:489-500. DOI: 10.1111/j.1469-8137.1980.tb04556.x

[24] Trouvelot A, Kough JL, Gianinazzi-Pearson V. Evaluation of VA infection levels in root systems. Research for estimation methods having a functional significance. In: Gianinazzi-Pearson V, Gianinazzi S, editors. Physiological and Genetical Aspect of Mycorrhiza. Paris: INRA Press; 1986. p. 1986

[25] Gerdemann W, Nicolson TH. Spores of mycorrhizal endogone species extracted by wet sieving and decanting. Transactions of the British Mycological Society. 1963;**46**:235-244. DOI: 10.1016/s0007-1536(63)80079-0

[26] Amato M, Ladd JN. Assay for microbial biomass based on ninhydrinreactive nitrogen in extracts of fumigated soils. Soil Biology and Biochemistry. 1988;**20**:107e114. DOI: 10.1016/0038-0717(88)90134-4

[27] Caravaca F, Alguacil MM, Torres P, Roldán A. Plant type mediates rhizospheric microbial activities and soil aggregation in a semiarid Mediterranean salt marsh. Geoderma. 2005;**12**:375e382. DOI: 10.1016/j.geoderma.2004.05.010

[28] Garcia C, Hernandez T, Costa F. Potential use of dehydrogenase activity

as an index of microbial activity in degraded soils. Communications in Soil Science and Plant Analysis. 1997;**28**: 123e134. DOI: 10.1080/0010362 9709369777

[29] Neree AO. Diversity and Dynamics of Mycorrhizal Associations in Tropical Rain Forests with Different Disturbance Regimes in South Cameroon. Vol. 2000. Netherlands: Wageningen University; 2000. p. 167

[30] Wang B, Qiu YL. Phylogenetic distribution and evolution of mycorrhizas in land plants. Mycorrhiza. 2006;**16**:299-363. DOI: 10.1007/ s00572-005-0033-6

[31] Bagayoko M, Buerker A, Lung G, Bationo A, Romheld V. Cereal/legume rotation effects on cereal growth in Soudano-Sahelian West Africa: Soil mineral nitrogen, mycorrhizae and nematodes. Plant and Soil. 2000; **218**:103-116. DOI: 10.1023/a: 1014957605852

[32] Barea JM, El-Atrach F, Azcon R. The role of VA mycorrhizas in improving plant N acquisition from soil as assessed with 15N. In: Flitton C, editor. The Use of Stable Isotopes in Plant Nutrition, Soil Fertility and Environmental Studies. Vienna: Joint IAEA, FAO, Division; 1991. pp. 677-808

[33] Lovelock CE, Andersen K, Morton JB. 2003: Arbuscular mycorrhizal communities in tropical forests are affected by host tree species and environment. Oecologia. 2003;**135**: 268-297. DOI: 10.1007/s00442-002-1166-3

[34] Boddington C, Dodd J. The effect of agricultural practices on the development of indigenous arbuscular mycorrhizal fungi. I. Field studies in an Indonesian ultisol. Plant and Soil. 2000; **218**:137-144. DOI: 10.1023/a:1014 966801446

[35] Houngnandan P, Yemadje RG, Kane A, Boeckx P, Van Cleemput O. Les glomales indigènes de la forêt claire à Isoberliniadoka (Craib et Stapf) à Wari-Maro au centre du Bénin. Tropicultura. 2009;**27**(2):83-87

[36] Liu Y, Shi G, Mao L, Cheng G, Jiang S. Direct and indirect influences of 8 yr of nitrogen and phosphorus fertilization on Glomeromycota in an alpine meadow ecosystem. The New Phytologist. 2012;**194**:523-535. DOI: 10.1111/j.1469-8137.2012.04050

[37] Barea JM, Pozo MJ, Azcón R, Azcón-Aguilar C. Microbial co-operation in the rhizosphere. Journal of Experimental Botany. 2005;**56**:1761-1778

[38] Schloter M, Dilly O, Munch JC. Indicators for evaluating soil quality. Agriculture, Ecosystems and Environment. 2003;**98**:255-262. DOI: 10.1016/s0167-8809(03)00085-9

[39] Franco I, Contin M, Bragato G, De Nobili M. Microbiological resilience of soils contaminated with crude oil. Geoderma. 2004;**121**:17-30. DOI: 10.1016/j.geoderma.2003.10.002

[40] Bastida F, Moreno JL, Hernandez T, Garcia C. Microbiological degradation index of soils in a semiarid climate. Soil Biology and Biochemistry. 2006;**38**: 3463-3473. DOI: 10.1016/j.soilbio.2006. 06.001

[41] Cao CY, Jiang DM, Teng XH, Jiang Y, Liang WJ, Cui B. Soil chemical and microbiological properties along a chronosequence of Caraganamicrophylla lam. Plantations in the Horqin sandy land of Northeast China. Applied Soil Ecology. 2008;**40**:78-85. DOI: 10.1016/j. apsoil.2008.03.008

[42] Sileshi G, Akinnifesi FK, Ajayi OC, Place F. Meta-analysis of maize yield response to planted fallow and green manure legumes in sub-Saharan

African. Plant and Soil. 2008;**307**:1-19. DOI: 10.1007/s11104-008-9547

[43] Dennis PG, Miller AJ, Hirsch PR. Are root exudates more important than other sources of rhizodeposits in structuring rhizosphere bacterial communities? Microbial Ecology. 2010; **72**:313-327. DOI: 10.1111/ j.1574-6941.2010.00860.x

[44] Cruz RE, Garcia MU. Nitrogen fixation and mycorrhizae in acacias on degraded grasslands. In: Kamiset A, Taylor DA, editors. Tropical Acacias in East Asia and the Pacific. Bangkok: Winrock Intenational Institute for Agriculture Research; 1992. pp. 59-71

[45] Barea JM, Azcon R, Azcon-Aguilar C. Mycorrhizosphere interactions to improve plant fitness and soil quality. Antonie van Leeuwenhoek International Journal of General and Molecular Microbiology. 2002;**81**(1–4):343-351. DOI: 10.1023/a:1020588701325

[46] Rillig MC. Arbuscular mycorrhizae and terrestrial ecosystem processes. Ecology Letters. 2004;**7**:740-754. DOI: 10.1111/j.1461-0248.2004.00620.x

[47] Nannipieri P, Kandeler E, Ruggiero P. Enzyme activities and microbiological and biochemical processes in soil. In: Burns RG, Dick RP, editors. Enzymes in the Environment. Activity, Ecology and Applications. New York: Marcel Dekker; 2002. pp. 1-33

[48] Gil-Sotres F, Trasar-Cepeda C, Leiros MC, Seoane S. Different approaches to evaluating soil quality using biochemical properties. Soil Biology and Biochemistry. 2005;**37**: 877-887. DOI: 10.1016/j.soilbio.2004. 10.003

[49] Martínez-García L, Miranda J, Pugnaire FI. 2011. Impacts of changing rainfall patterns on mycorrhizal status of a shrub from arid environments. European Journal of Soil Biology. 2011; **50**:64-67. DOI: 10.1016/j.ejsobi.2011. 12.005

Chapter 9

Use of Geoinformatics Techniques for the Assessment and Mapping of Soil Salinity: Concepts and Applications

Olumuyiwa Idowu Ojo and Masengo Francois Ilunga

Abstract

Irrigated agriculture has a major impact on the environment, especially soil degradation. Soil salinity is a critical environmental problem, which has great impact on soil fertility and overall agricultural productivity. Since, soil salinity processes are highly dynamic, the methods of detecting soil salinity hazards should also be dynamic. Remote sensing data are modern tools that provide information on variation over time essential for environmental monitoring and change detection, as they also help in the reduction of conventional time-consuming and expensive field sampling methods, which is the traditional method of monitoring and assessment. This chapter thus reviewed the concepts and applications of remote sensing, GIS-assisted spatial analysis and modelling of the salinity issue in irrigation fields. Generally, compared to the labour, time and money invested in field work devoted to collecting soil salinity data and analysis, the availability and ease of acquiring satellite imagery data and analysis made this concept very attractive and efficient.

Keywords: soil salinity, empirical model, salinity model

1. Introduction

Since civilization, irrigation has enabled societies to produce sufficient food, as irrigated agriculture has contributed immensely to increased food production and improved quality of life for millions over the past years [1]. According to Thomas [2], irrigation represents an alteration of the natural conditions of the landscape by extracting water from an available source, adding water to fields where there was hitherto little or none, and introducing man-made structures and features to extract, transfer and dispose water, while achieving the main objective of providing plants with sufficient moisture. All methods of irrigation are prone to affect the environment negatively if not properly managed. Surface irrigation methods could lead to waterlogging, which degrades the plant root environment and thus leads to increase in soil salinity and erosion [3]. In addition, the sprinkler method may lead to soil structure destruction due to impacts of water drops and crust formation on the soil [4]. The realisation of the adverse effects, the need to avoid them and to ensure long-term benefits of projects led to the concept of sustainability. Thus this chapter critically reviewed the concepts and applications of geoinformatics techniques for the assessment and mapping of soil salinity.

IntechOpen

2. Irrigation and agricultural soils

Irrigation development and practices have been observed to have adverse impacts on the physical and chemical properties of soil and the environment in general. According to Amdihun [5] some of the adverse impacts of irrigation schemes on soils include salinisation, alkalization, waterlogging, soil pollution and soil acidification. These have adverse effects on sustainable soil productivity, especially if not regularly monitored and assessed. Soil salinity is a major environmental factor limiting productivity of agricultural lands and has been observed as a major adverse effect of irrigation. It has been known to cause destruction of many agricultural projects [6]. The application of irrigation water even when considered to be of excellent quality is a major source of soluble salts and leads to input of salts onto the soil. According to Sharma and Rao [7], these accumulated soluble salts content in the soil is called soil salinity and they cause land degradation and affect food production resulting into toxicity to sensitive crops at high concentration. This problem does not only reduce agricultural productivity but also has a consequential effect on the livelihood strategies of small farmers [8]. Although salinisation is a natural process, which accompanies irrigation practice, proper irrigation management can prevent salt accumulation by providing adequate drainage to leach soluble salts from the soil and constantly lower the water table. Tsutsi's [9] study reported that about 2.1 million ha of irrigated land in Central Asia is affected by salinisation and nearly 1.0 million ha of land has been abandoned to prevent further soil degradation. A study by Stockle [1] indicated that about one-third of the irrigated land in the major irrigation countries of the world is already badly affected by salinity. The estimates showed that 13% of the irrigated lands in Israel, 20% from Australia, 15% from China, 50% from Iraq and 30% from Egypt have been affected by salinity. In India alone, Singh [10] reported that 3.4691 million ha of land has been seriously affected by salt. The effect of salinity on irrigated lands was documented by Surujmia [11] as shown in **Table 1** for top five irrigation countries in the world in the mid-1980s.

2.1 Soil salinity

The United States Department of Agriculture (USDA) according to Richards [13]defined electrical conductivity of the saturation extract of soil (ECe), pH of the saturated soil paste (pH) and exchangeable sodium percentage of the soil (ESP) of saline soils as ECe more than 4 dS/mat 25°C, pH less than 8.2 and ESP less than 15.

Country	Area damaged Million ha	Share of irrigated land damaged %
India	20.0	36
China	7.0	15
United States	5.2	27
Pakistan	3.2	20
Soviet Union	2.5	12
Total	37.9	24
World	60.2	24

Source: Surujmia [11] (adapted from Postel [12]).

Table 1.
Irrigation land damaged by salinity in the mid-1980s.

He also defined sodic soils having pH more than 8.2 and ESP of 15 or more. Based on USDA classification, ECe may be high for salts capable of alkali hydrolysis, while saline-sodic soils have pH greater than 8.2 at 25°C, ECe greater than 4 dS/m and the ESP greater than 15. These soils are often formed due to a combined process of salinisation and sodification. Thomas [14] classified salt-affected soils according to EC (electrical conductivity), SAR (Sodium Adsorption Ratio) and pH of the soil extract (**Table 2**).

2.2 Soil salinity assessment

Saline fields can be simply identified by the presence of spotty white patches of precipitated salts. Such precipitates usually occur in elevated or non-vegetated areas, where water evaporates and leaves salt behind.

2.2.1 Field measurement

Soil salinity is measured on the field by its electrical conductivity (EC). The SI unit of EC is dS/m and is measured with hand-held conductivity meter. Soil salinity on a large scale is mapped with an electromagnetic (EM) conductivity meter [15]. **Table 3** gives the criteria for soil salinity and sodicity measurement.

2.2.2 Geoinformatics techniques

Salinity is a dynamic process and to assess the extent of salinity, modelling is often required. Geoinformatics approach is a modern technique, which involves the combinations of global positioning system (GPS), satellite remote sensing data (SRS) and geographical information system (GIS) modelling tools. Geoinformatics involves the acquisition, processing, analysis and management of geographic or spatial information. Spatial information is concerned with knowing what (object) is where (space) and when (time). Data are usually collected using techniques such as GPS, remote sensing, orthography, total station and the use of the more traditional surveying equipment such as theodolite, level. Among these techniques, the newer and more prominent of them are the GPS and remote sensing [16].

	EC (mmhos/cm)	pH	SAR
Saline soil	>4	<8.5	<13
Sodic soil	<4	8.5–10	>13
Saline-sodic soil	>4	<8.5	>13
Source: Thomas [14].			

Table 2.
Classification of salt-affected soils.

Key to degree of salinity/sodicity	Salinity ECe (dS/m)	Sodicity pH	ESP
Slight	4–8	8.2–9.0	<15
Moderate	8.25	9.0–9.8	15–40
Strong	>25	>9.8	>40
Source: Adapted from Ojo [15].			

Table 3.
The criteria for soil salinity and sodicity.

2.2.2.1 Global positioning system (GPS)

GPS is a satellite positioning and navigating system technology that continues to gain wide usage and applications worldwide. Input of data directly on the field this way, saves time and greatly facilitates subsequent processing. The GPS data logger permits direct interfacing with GIS, the data base management system (DBMS) for spatial analysis [17].

2.2.2.2 Geographical information system

A computer system for the input, editing, storage, maintenance, management, retrieval, analysis, synthesis and output of geographically referenced or spatial information is defined as a GIS [18]. Ojo [15] stated that GIS is a tool used to analyse and interpret the remotely sensed data. It can also be used for the analysis and interpretation of physically collected data as well. A model is a representation of reality; models can help understand, describe or predict how things work in the real world. According to ESRI [18], there are two types of models, namely those that represent the objects in the landscape (representation models) and those that attempt to simulate processes in the landscape (process models). Representation models describe the objects in the landscape, such as buildings, streams or forest, while process models describe the interaction of the objects that are modelled in the representation model. Process models include suitability modelling, distance modelling and hydrological modelling [15].

2.2.2.3 Satellite remote sensing (SRS) concepts

Monitoring environmental changes is quite difficult with the traditional method of surveying. In recent years, satellite remote sensing techniques have been developed, which have proved to be of immense value for preparing accurate land use/land cover maps and monitoring changes at regular intervals of time [19]. This technique, in cases of inaccessible region, is the only method of obtaining the required data on a cost- and time-effective basis. In this technique, a remote sensing device records reflective response, which is based on many characteristics of the land surface, including natural and artificial cover. In addition, an interpreter uses the element of tone, texture, pattern, shape, size, shadow, site and association to derive information about land cover. It is often believed that no single classification could be used with all types of imagery and all scales as information about change is necessary for updating land cover maps and the management of natural resources and such information may be obtained by visiting sites on the ground and or extracting it from remotely sensed data [20]. Change detection is defined by Singh and Dwivedi [21] as the process of identifying differences in the state of an object or phenomenon by observing it at different times. Monitoring and managing natural resources and urban development is an important change detection process because it provides quantitative analysis of the spatial distribution. Detecting the changes that have occurred in the process involved identifying the nature of the change, measuring the area extent of the change and assessing the spatial pattern of the change [22].

3. SRS application for mapping of salt-affected soils

Application of satellite remote sensing for surveying and mapping of salt-affected areas began with the use of photography (black and white). The relatively bright appearance provides the information about salinity due to the efflorescence of salt crust [21]. The aerial photographs have been used to delineate units based on the combination of geomorphologic differences and differences in greytones. Attempts were also made to relate the differences in the greytones with the salt content [23]. In addition, indirect features like landscape may help to identify the problems of soil salinity. Relative elevation is one of the most evident landscape features in relation to salinity and moisture provided by saline and shallow groundwater table. Satellite remote sensing (SRS) data are modern tools that provide information on variation over time essential for environmental monitoring and change detection in mining areas [24–26]. SRS also helps in the reduction of conventional, time-consuming and expensive field sampling methods, which are the traditional methods of monitoring change detection [27–29]. Dehaan and Taylor [30] used field-derived spectra of salinized soils and vegetation as indicator of irrigation-induced soil salinisation for identification of saline soil regions. In a study using spectral un-mixing method in snow cover estimation, NOAA-AVHRR data was used to examine the ability of real times now cover estimation at sub-pixel level [15]. Also, Okin and Roberts [31] showed the used of multiple end member spectral mixture analysis (MESMA) in retrieving information about soil. He showed that MESMA is capable of mapping soil surface types even when vegetation type cannot be reasonably retrieved. McGwire et al. [32]compared linear mixture model based on calibrated atmospherically corrected hyper spectral imagery to show its relative ability to measure small differences in per cent green vegetation cover for the areas of sparse vegetation in arid environments. Metternicht and Zink [33] reported that multi-temporal optical and microwave remote sensing can significantly contribute to detecting temporal changes of salt-related surface features. Bastiaanssen [34] reported the IWMI review of different RS applications for water resources management. According to him, bands in the near- and middle-infrared spectral bands give information on soil moisture and salinity [35, 36]. A salinity index based on greenness and brightness indicating leaf moisture influenced by salinity, with classical false colour composites of separated bands or with a computer-assisted land-surface classification can be used to identiy salinized and cropped areas [37–40]. In order to detect soil salinity anomalies, some studies used the brightness index appearing at high levels of salinity with TM bands 5 and 7 as the best in showing the physiological conditions of a crop while, TM bands 3 and 4 are better suited to describing overall crop development [40–43]. Most of these studies were based on multispectral scanner (MSS) and thematic mapper (TM) data because the Satellite Probatoire d'Observation de la Terre (SPOT) and Indian *Remote Sensing* Satellite (IRS)'s sensors used have no bands greater than 1.7 mm. In another study by Joshi and Sahai [44], they discovered that TM with an accuracy of 90% for soil salinity mapping was better than MSS, which has 74% accurate. Thus, comparing the accuracy of TM, MSS, and SPOT, TM was found to be the best multispectral radiometer for soil-salinity mapping and thus TM was better in application [45].

3.1 SRS applications in different countries

Johnston and Barson [46] found that the application of SRS in Australia for the identification of saline areas was most successful during peak vegetation growth and also in other periods but salinized areas with low fractional vegetation cover could not be distinguished from areas that were bare because of overgrazing, erosion or ploughing. However, Siderius [47] concluded the opposite, that is, salinity is best seen at the end of irrigation or the rainy season when the plots are bare. In another study by Johnston and Barson [46] on SRS applications in Australia, they found that discrimination of saline areas was most successful during peak vegetation growth. It was also discovered that salinity was best expressed at the end of the irrigation or rainy season with bare plots. In a study in Punjab, India by Venkataratnam [48] using MSS images of pre-monsoon, post-monsoon and harvest seasons to map soil salinity, he concluded that the spectral curves of highly and moderately saline soils change considerably during the annual cycle, which significantly complicates the time-compositing procedure. In another study by Vincent et al. [40] in Pakistan, which was based on a classification-tree procedure, the first treatment was to mask vegetation from non-vegetation using normalised difference vegetation index (NDVI). Thereafter, the brightness index was calculated to detect moisture and salinity on fallow land and abandoned fields. His approach was suitable for locating blocks that had malfunctioning drainage networks and that were based on these two classes; the levels of soil salinity could be mapped with an accuracy of 70%. Areas of high salinity were 66% accurate and non-saline areas were 80% accurate. Goossens and Ranst [49] as reported in Salman [50] analysed the beginning, middle and end of the growing season in the western Nile Delta and concluded that single image may be suitable for detecting severely salinized soils, but more gradations can be determined using temporal images.

Different studies by researchers on direct observations on bare soils and indirectly by vegetation cover as reported by IDNP [51] showed that for the visible part of the spectrum, the soil reflectance of salt cover areas was found to be prominent. The bands in the middle infrared gave information of moisture content, because they are often associated with salt content differences. The report depicted that lack of vegetation or scattered vegetation and highly salt-affected soil surfaces make it possible to directly detect salt on the surface. The main factors affecting the reflectance are the quantity and mineralogy of salt, moisture, colour and roughness as indicated by ground observations and radiometric measurements as the evaluation of soil surface remains under the influence of external factors such as ground water quality, variation of depth, wetting/drying cycles and wind. Metternicht and Zinck [52] through their study stated that the main factors affecting the reflectance are the quantity and mineralogy of salts together with soil moisture, soil colour and terrain roughness, which in turn are controlled by different combinations of salts and type of soil surface, texture and organic matter content as measured with ground observation and radiometric measurement in the visible and near infrared wavelengths.

The SPOT spectral data, soil morphological, physical and chemical properties when analysed showed that many surface and some subsurface soil properties were significantly correlated. The ratio of the values in red and infrared band seems to be a better technique to employ when subsurface soil properties are of interest using brightness index, which has proved to be a more useful spectral parameter if surface soil properties are to be extracted from satellite data. The near and middle infrared bands give reasonable information on soil moisture and salinity [36]. The spectral behaviour of salt-affected soils when compared to normal cultivated soils showed relatively high spectral response in visible and near infrared regions as the new ratio is immune to colour variations and provides an indication of leaf water potential. Because the vegetation cover modifies the overall spectral response pattern of salt-affected soils especially in the green and red spectral bands, strongly saline-sodic soils were found to have higher spectral response as compared to moderately saline-sodic soils.

Spatial resolution has significant effect on enhancing the identification of salt-affected soils and crops. Steven et al. [53] stated that based on some past research in comparing the accuracy of TM, MSS and SPOT, they found TM to be the superior multispectral radiometer for soil salinity mapping and that digital classification techniques can also help in improving the identification and mapping of salt-affected soils or crops. According to Salman [50], excess soil moisture can cause a change in soil colour and a change in soil reflectance properties being detected by remote sensing and accumulation of organic matter; soil colour is generally darker in poorly drained areas than well-drained soils. The visible bands in Landsat-MSS data can be used to identify this colour. Baber [54], as cited in IDNP [51], pointed out that colour infrared photography could indicate drainage problems by soil moisture saturation or plant stress. Shallow water tables exhibit an increase in surface moisture, which can be detected from visible reflectance and microwave emissivity.

3.2 SRS Landsat and other sensors

With the launching of the Landsat Satellite 1972, researchers began to use satellite data for monitoring mining activities in different parts of the world [23]. The applicability of Landsat imagery for monitoring soil-salinity trends was tested in two areas of Punjab and Sindh, India using black-and-white mosaics of Landsat MSS band 5 at a of scale 1: 250,000 during the months of March, April and December, thereafter were visually interpreted and compared with surface salinity maps of the same scale. As reported by WAPDA [55]. Sahin et al. [56] used three Landsat geo cover datasets from 1970 to 2000 to detect temporal changes in the Zonguldak coal test field. Landsat MSS was discovered for the identification of broad land cover changes of the Western part of Horqin steppe, Inner Mongolia Autonomous Region [57]. Landsat images were used for studying land use dynamics and soil degradation in Tamduong district of Vietnam by van Trinh et al. [58]. Landsat data from 1976 to 2002 were used to detect changes in land cover in the Yazd-Ardakan basin, Iran [59]. The analysis of land cover change of the Oil Sands Mining Development in Athabasca, Canada was carried out by Latifovic et al. [60] using information extraction method applied to two Landsat scenes. Vegetation and brightness indices derived from SPOT XS were used to classify salinity for vegetative and non-vegetative areas by Vidal et al. [61] and Tabet [62]; the results were used to identify highly saline and non-saline areas. Cialella et al. [63] used the combined GIS/RS approach for predicting soil drainage classes that does not focus on soil salinity, but can be modified for salinity detection using airborne NDVI data, digital elevation data and soil types. The problem of spectral similarity where the dull-white tones of salt-affected and sandy soils have been difficult to distinguish was studied by Verma et al. [64] by combining the TM false colour composite (FCC) bands 2, 3 and 4 with thermal data at 10.4–12.5 mm to solve it. Salt-affected soils in Etah, Aligarh, Mainpuri and Mathura districts were classified into S1: <10% of the salt-affected area, S2: 10–30%, S3: 30–50%, S4: 50–75% and S5: >75%, using the integrated approach to image interpretation. It was discovered that data between March and first week of April were significantly better because of maximum contrast. The standard deviation and correlation coefficient values of TM data were used to compute a statistical parameter called the optimum index factor (OIF) in order to identify the most appropriate three-band combination of Landsat TM reflective-band data for identifying salt-affected soils [65]. Three bands combination of 1, 3, and 5 was found to be the best in terms of information content. The validation of results revealed a mixed relationship between rankings obtained from OIF values and estimated accuracy. The potential of image transformations such as principal-component analysis (PCA), rationing and image differencing to detect changes in extent and distribution of salt-affected soils using Landsat MSS data for 1975 and 1992 to study the alluvial plains of Uttar Pradesh was demonstrated by Dwivedi and Sreenivas [66]. Results indicated that the third principal component, image differencing and rationing of the first two bands provided substantial information about behaviour of salt-affected soils over time in the two periods. A synergistic approach to map salt-affected surfaces, combining digital image classification with field observation of soil-degradation features and laboratory determinations was carried out by Metternicht and Zinck [33]. In order to obtain the highest separability between salt- and sodium-affected soils, Landsat TM bands 1, 2, 4, 5, 6 and 7 were combined to result in an overall accuracy of 64% while for some soils 100% accuracy was obtained. To compare differences in salt-affected and waterlogged lands before and after implementation of the SCARP-1 programme, Chouchri et al. [67] used aerial photographs from 1953 to 1954 and 1976. Their study concluded that the waterlogged areas had decreased in extent but had often become saline and that large areas with salt-affected soils were still out of cultivation leaving only small patches of slightly saline soils under cultivation. Dean et al. [68] used processed satellite images for change detection in order to monitor expansion of mining activity and its progressive reclamation and to support environmental management, monitoring and sustainable development reporting of the Shell Canada and Albian Sands mine operations in northern Alberta, Canada. Therefore, data collected by the MSS and TM will continue to be used as a historical global database [69], but updated and newer sensors with greater spectral/temporal resolution will allow even more precise land cover classification.

3.2.1 Radiometric correction

Many studies have shown the wide application of Landsat images being used for land cover mapping and the creation of vegetation inventories at different spatial scale information on the earth's surface characteristics [70, 71], despite the existence of limitations in the use of Landsat data for multi-temporal studies because of problems in obtaining homogeneous time series. Efforts have been made in the past to reduce non-surface noise in Landsat images and to calibrate the sensor to correct radiometric trends [72] and reduce the influence of topography [73, 74]. According to Schroeder et al. [75], other studies have shown that the application of accurate sensor calibrations and complex atmospheric corrections does not guarantee the multi-temporal homogeneity of Landsat datasets because complete atmospheric properties are difficult to quantify, and simplifications are commonly assumed. There are many protocols proposed in pre-processing multi-temporal Landsat datasets [76]; these protocols are geometric correction, calibration of the satellite signal to obtain top of the atmosphere radiance, atmospheric correction to estimate surface reflectance, topographic correction and relative radiometric normalisation between images obtained on different dates. Prior to geometric processing, radiometric processing is recommended to be done, since this re-sampling step generally *smoothens* the dataset [77]. Some studies have analysed the role of complete radiometric correction protocols in processing multi-temporal Landsat data when a number of different vegetation processes are of interest. Their results found out that land classification and forest succession serve as a function of the radiometric correction applied [75, 78]. Radiometric correction and geometric correction processes are required to obtain accurate time series of Landsat imagery.

3.3 Soil salinity digital analysis and modelling

The process of delineation of salt-affected soils under bare condition and cropped condition using remote sensing investigation has enabled the soil salinity analysis, mapping and modelling. A brightness index is meant to detect high levels of brightness appearing at high levels of salinity; thus salinity index based on greenness and brightness that describes leaf moisture as influenced by salinity salinized and cropped areas can be identified with classical false colour composites of separated bands, or with a computer-assisted land surface classification [39, 40]. The unique patterns of geomorphologic shapes are thought to be helpful in discriminating the salinisation process from a physiographic perspective. A review by

Salman [50] stated that the application of remote sensing in contextual classifier for soil salinity mapping with a built GIS to link the location of the irrigation feeders and drainage master canals in the western Nile Delta with digital elevation data and satellite classifications is possible. He stated that the distance of field from the main irrigation canals, as well as to the field elevation difference with the main irrigation canals are considered proportional to soil salinity risks. In order to classify three different stages of waterlogging according to simple supervised procedure, TM bands 2, 3, 4, 5, 6 and 7 were used. Salinity can be detected through its impact on the vegetation and vegetation index is a common spectral index that identifies the presence of chlorophyll. A few vegetation indices have been proposed. In the study by Richardson et al. [79], an inverse relationship was observed between reflectance and salinity, as salt content induces less plant cover (decreasing of density, LAI and height) and sometimes slight salt deposition on surface associated with vegetation has similar reflectance as that of normal cropped area. Salt-tolerant plants are good references of salinity level on salt marshes but require good calibration. Contrasted associations of vegetation and bare soils can be more useful for salinity detection than individual surface types. RS information can be improved and modelled when it is integrated with other tools or platforms, for which a GIS is an appropriate tool.

3.3.1 Multi-criteria decision evaluation

Decision theory is concerned with the logic by which one arrives at a choice between alternatives [80]. The recommended alternatives vary from problem to problem. They might be alternative actions, alternative hypotheses about a phenomenon, alternative objects to include in a set and so on. Resource allocation decisions are also prime candidates for analysis with a GIS. Indeed, land evaluation and allocation are the most fundamental activities of resource development [81]. To meet a specific objective, several criteria are to be evaluated. Such a procedure is called Multi-criteria evaluation [82, 83]. One of two procedures most commonly achieves multi-criteria evaluation (MCE). A pair-wise comparison method has been used for the development of weights of the factors in the salt-affected soil analysis. The technique described and implemented in IDRISI is that of pair-wise comparisons developed by Saaty (1997) in the context of a decision-making process known as the Analytical Hierarchy Process (AHP). The first introduction of this technique to a GIS application was that of R*ao* et al. [84]; the procedure was developed outside the GIS software using a variety of analytical resources. In Saaty's technique, weights of this nature can be derived by taking the principal eigenvector of a square reciprocal matrix of pair-wise comparisons between the criteria. Purevdorj et al. (1998) listed the current available methods to assess and model land vegetation cover and biomass from remotely sensed data into three basic methods: spectral mixture models, calibrated cover-radiance relationships and vegetation indices approaches.

3.3.2 Spectral mixture modelling

Linear and non-linear are the two types of mixture modelling. Linear mixture modelling assumes that each field within a ground pixel contributes an amount characteristic of the cover type in that field to the signal received at the satellite sensor and is proportional to the area of the cover type. The use of linear mixture method for modelling soil salinity is difficult because the location of pure end member for the green cover component. Non-linear mixing modelling occurs when radiation transmission occurs through one material and second reflectance occurs from other materials, or there are multiple reflections within or between materials;

thus a non-linear mixing model is needed to be generated to deal with this situation. According to Kimes and Nelson [85], non-linear models are more accurate in some circumstances, but certain non-linear curves or forms should be learned before application.

3.3.3 Cover-radiance relationships

To investigate the relationship between field collected canopy cover data and radiance data, cover-radiance relationship approach is required. Sensor data, such as Landsat TM, MSS and SPOT, are best suited to medium spatial resolution satellite since they require accurate measurement of vegetation cover on the ground covering the same area. This approach has been used in many earlier studies [86–89]. Problems with comparing satellite data and ground measurement include the accuracy of estimating a large area and the efficiency of the model for describing the canopy condition.

3.3.4 Vegetation indices

A vegetation index is a common spectral index that identifies the presence of chlorophyll. Various crop indices have been derived using the fact that chlorophyll strongly absorbs the light energy in the red part and highly reflects in the near infrared part. Research for specific analyses proposed number of vegetation indices [79]. As salt content induces less plant cover, an inverse relationship is observed between reflectance and salinity [79]. Salt-tolerant plants are good references of salinity level on salt marshes but require good calibration. Contrasted associations of vegetation and bare soils can be more useful for salinity detection than individual surface types. Although the soil profile cannot be evaluated on remotely sensed imagery, spectral characteristics of the earth surface features that are indicative of subsurface conditions can be analysed. Because satellite multispectral data denote changes that aid in locating mapping units, they hold great promise for soil surveys and land use planning. Some relationships have been established between soil properties and spectral data; while most of these properties have been from the surface soil, subsurface properties that influence some surface characteristics were considered. Both subsurface and surface conditions are regarded as plant canopy parameters while soil conditions are affected by genetic factors though satellite sensors observe only the ground surface. Therefore, when satellite imagery depicts a pattern based on a different spectral response, it is not unreasonable to attempt some inferences about subsurface soil patterns as limited attempts have been made in the past to identify the waterlogging and soil salinity problems using remote sensing techniques. Therefore, several studies were attempted to develop a methodology for diagnosis of waterlogging and soil and green vegetation have different modes of reflectance characteristics. The mixture of soil, green vegetation and shade in the pixels makes remote sensing of land cover a challenge but red and near infrared have been found to be good at detecting green vegetation [88]. Therefore, most vegetation indices make use of the red and near infrared portions of spectral reflectance. The selection and suitability of a vegetation index is generally determined by its sensitivity to the characteristics of interest [87, 90]. Frequently used vegetation indices include simple ratio (SR), normalised difference salinity index (NDSI), normalised difference vegetation index (NDVI), soil-adjusted vegetation index (SAVI), enhanced vegetation index (EVI), green vegetation index (GVI) and transformed soil adjusted vegetation index (TSAVI) [71, 91]. These indices are not complete without the support of field-collected information.

3.4 Hybrid method: SRS data, field data and GIS tool

The identification and mapping of saline soil is a combination of visual interpretation of photographs, digital analysis of false colour composite (FCC) and digital analysis of surface radiation and vegetation index methods. Ground truth information for calibration and validation is used to consolidate the methods. The combined use of field and spectral data termed hybrid method is highly encouraged as studies have shown that there are high correlations between variation of field-collected variables of vegetation canopy and spectral variation [92–94].

4. Conclusion

This work depicted the concepts and applications in the use of geoinformation techniques for the assessment, mapping and modelling of soil salinity as it relates to irrigated agriculture. It has been shown that the application of RS and GIS combined with field data can be used for mapping and modelling of soil surface salinity in order to generate simple models that can be interpreted in physically meaningful maps in accordance with the subject paradigms. The studies of the use of Landsat TM and ETM+ to map and model soil surface salinity confirmed by the findings of Dimyati [95], Lewis [96] and Goossens et al. [45] that there are close relationships between field data and spectral data and that TM and ETM+ have high detection accuracy compared with MSS and SPOT. The process of mapping and modelling of salinity is necessary for updating land cover maps and the management of natural resources as suggested by Xiaomei and Ronqing [20] since irrigation-induced salinity results in environmental, social and economic impacts of greater damage than benefit to the area [97]. Therefore, maps and models development on salinity are of great importance to planners in monitoring the consequences of land use change and in predicting future changes. Conclusively, a hybrid approach with the combination of supervised classification based on field visits to adjust the parameters is being considered at field salinity levels. Also, since Landsat sensor detects only the salinity on the surface of the soil and gives no detailed idea about the conditions below the surface, the use of overlaying salinity methods using advanced sensors like SPOT, hand-held hyper or aircraft-mounted spectrometer should be applied to increase the accuracy of detection.

Author details

Olumuyiwa Idowu Ojo* and Masengo Francois Ilunga
Department of Civil and Chemical Engineering, University of South Africa, South Africa

*Address all correspondence to: olumuyiwaojo@gmail.com

References

[1] Stockle CO. Environmental Impact of Irrigation. State of Washington Water Research Center. USA: Washington State University; 2001. Available from: http://134.121.74.103/newsletter/irrimpact2.pdf [Accessed: July 20, 2019]

[2] Thomas WL. Surface irrigation system. 2003. Available from: http://www.fao.org/3/T0231E/t0231e04.htm [Accessed: July 26, 2019]

[3] Sharma RK, Sharma TK. Irrigation Engineering. 3rd ed. New Delhi, India: S Chand and Company Limited; 2007

[4] Getahun M, Adgo E, Atalay A. Impacts of Irrigation on Soil Characteristics of Selected Irrigation Schemes in Upper Blue Nile Basin, June 16-19, 2008. Ethiopia: Addis Ababa; 2008

[5] Amdihun A. GIS and Remote Sensing Integrated Environmental Impact Assessment of Irrigation Project in Finchaa Valley Area, Catchment and Lake Research. Ethiopia: Addis Ababa University; 2007. pp. 118-128

[6] Sanda AO, Ayo SB. Impact of Irrigation Projects on Nigeria Environment, Chapter 4. Nigeria: Fact Finders International Ibadan; 1994. pp. 62-80

[7] Sharma DP, Rao KVGK. Strategy for long term use of saline drainage water for irrigation in semi-arid regions. Soil and Tillage Research. 1998;**48**:287-295

[8] Tanwir FA, Nwa NU. Soil salinity and the livelihood strategies of small farmers: A case study in Faisalabad District, Punjab, Pakistan. International Journal of Agriculture and Biological Sciences. 2003;**5**:440-441

[9] Tsutsi H. Soil salinization and water Management in Arid Region of Aral Sea basin. In: AgEng Warwick 2000: Agricultural Engineering into the Third Millennium. 2000. pp. 1-40

[10] Singh NT. Irrigation and Soil Salinity in Indian Sub-Continent. USA: Lehigh University Press; 2005

[11] Surujmia MD. Identification of salt sensitive stages of wheat [thesis MSc. Agricultural Engineering Department], Bangladesh Agricultural University2011. pp. 1-59

[12] Postel L. The mesozooplankton response to coastal upwelling off West Africa with particular regard to biomass. Marine Science Reports. 1990;**1**:1-127

[13] Richards LA. Diagnosis and improvement of saline and alkali soils. USDA Agricultural Handbook 60. 2010. Available from: http://www.ars.usda.gov/Services/docs.htm?docid=10158&page = 2 [Accessed: March 22, 2019]

[14] Thomas GW. Exchangeable cations. In: Page AL et al., editors. Methods of Soil Analysis. Part 2. 2nd ed. Madison, WI: ASA and SSSA; 1996. pp. 159-165

[15] Ojo OI. Mapping and modeling of irrigation induced salinity in Vaal Harts Irrigation scheme, South Africa [DTech thesis] Submitted to the Department of Civil Engineering. South Africa: Tshwane University of Technology; 2013

[16] Ochieng GM, Ojo OI, Otieno FAO, Mwaka B. Use of remote sensing and geographical information system (GIS) for salinity assessment of Vaal-harts irrigation scheme, South Africa. Environmental Systems Research. 2013;**2**:4

[17] Adeleke OO, Aremu AG. Application of GPS for mapping of Nigerian roads. Nigerian Journal of Technological Development. 2002;**2**(1):62-68

[18] ESRI. Introduction to ARC View GIS. USA: Environmental System Research Institute, Inc.; 1998

[19] Olorunfemi JF. Monitoring urban land—Use in developed countries—An aerial photographic approach. Environmental International. 1983;**9**:27-32

[20] Xiaomei Y, Ronqing LQY. Change Detection Based on Remote Sensing Information Model and its Application to Coastal Line of Yellow River Delta – Earth Observation Center. China: NASDA; 1999

[21] Singh AN, Dwivedi RS. Delineation of salt-affected soils through digital analysis of Landsat MSS data. International Journal of Remote Sensing. 1989;**10**:83-92

[22] Macleod S, Congalton K. A quantitative comparison of change detection algorithms for monitoring eelgrass from remotely sensed data. Photogrammetric Engineering and Remote Sensing. 1998;**64**(3):207-216

[23] Coker AE. The application of remote sensing technology to assess the effects of and monitor change in coal mining in Eastern Tennessee. In: Proceedings of the First Annual William Symposium, Falls Church. 1997. pp. 95-105

[24] Manu A, Twumasi YA, Coleman TL. Application of remote sensing and GIS technologies to assess the impact of surface mining at Tarkwa, Ghana. Proceedings of IGARSS'2004 Symposium, Honolulu, Hawaii, July 24-28. 2004

[25] Schmidt H, Glaesser C. Multi-temporal analysis of satellite data and their use in the monitoring of the environmental impacts of open cast lignite mining areas in Eastern Germany. International Journal of Remote Sensing. 1998;**24**(16):3311-3340

[26] Serra P, Pons X, Sauri D. Post-classification change detection with data from different sensors: Some accuracy considerations. International Journal of Remote Sensing. 2003;**19**:2245-2260

[27] Haboudane D, Bonn F, Royer A, Sommer S, Mehl W. Land degradation and erosion risk mapping by fusion of spectrally based information and digital geomorphometric attributes. International Journal of Remote Sensing. 2002;**23**:3795-3820

[28] Limpitlaw D, Woldai T. Land use change detection as an initial stage in environmental impact assessment on the Zambian Copperbelt. In: Proceedings: 28th ISRSE: Information for Sustainable Development, Cape Town, 27-31 March, 2000. 2000

[29] Rathore CS, Wright R. Monitoring environmental impacts of surface coal mining. International Journal of Remote Sensing. 1993;**14**:1021-1042

[30] Dehaan RL, Taylor GR. Field-derived spectra of salinized soils and vegetation as indicators of irrigation-induced soil salinization. Remote Sensing of Environment. 2002;**80**:406. DOI: 10.1016/S0034-4257(01)00321-2

[31] Okin GS, Roberts DA. Practical limits on hyperspectral vegetation discrimination in arid and semi arid environments. Remote Sensing of Environment. 2001;**77**(2):212-225

[32] McGwire KC, Friedl MA, McIver DK. An overview of uncertainty in optical remotely sensed data for ecological applications. In: Hunsaker CT, Goodchild MF, Friedl MA, Case TJ, editors. Spatial Uncertainty in Ecology. New York, NY: Springer; 2000

[33] Metternicht G, Zinck JA. Spatial discrimination of salt and sodium-affected soil surfaces. JRS International. 1997;**18**(12):2571-2586

[34] Bastiaanssen WGM. Remote Sensing in Water Resources Management: The State of the Art. Colombo: IWMI; 1998

[35] Agbu PA, Fehrenbacher DI, Jansen IJ. Soil-property relationships with SPOT satellite digital data in east Central Illinois. Soil Science Society of America Journal. 1990;**54**:807-812

[36] Mulders MA. Remote sensing in soil science. In: Developments in Soil Science. Vol. 15. Amsterdam: Elsevier Publication; 1987

[37] Hardisk MA, Klemas V, Daiber FC. Remote sensing saltmarsh biomass and stress detection. Advances in Space Research. 1983;**2**:219-229

[38] Kauth RY, Thomas GS. Thetasselledcap-A graphic description of the spectral-temporal development of agricultural crops as seen by Landsat. In: Proceeding of the Symposium on Machine Processing of Remotely Sensed Data. Indiana: Purdue University of West Lafayette; 1976. pp. 41-49

[39] Steven FG, Zagrafos C, Oglethorpe D. Multi-criteria analysis in soil salinity: using goal programming to explore solutions. Current Issues in Soil Conservation. Available from: http://www.multilingualmatters.net/cit/007/0020/cit05200350.pdf. 1992 [Accessed: March 13, 2009]

[40] Vincent B, Vidal A, Tabbet AB, Kuper M. Useofsatellite remote sensing for the assessment of water logging or salinity. In: Vincent B, editor. Evaluation of Performance of Subsurface Drainage Systems: 16th Congress on Irrigation and Drainage, Cairo, Egypt, 15-22 September 1996. New Delhi: International Commission on Irrigation and Drainage; 1996. pp. 203-216

[41] Menenti M, Lorkeers A, Vissers M. An application of thematic mapper data in Tunisia. ITC Journal. 1986;**1**:35-42

[42] Mulders MA, Epema GF. The thematic mapper: A new tool for soil mapping in arid areas. ITC Journal. 1986;**1**:24-29

[43] Zuluaga JM. Remote sensing applications in irrigation management in Mendoza, Argentina. In: Menenti M, ed. Remote Sensing in Evaluation and Management of Irrigation. 1990. Mendoza, Argentina: Instituto Nacional de Ciencia y Tecnic; pp. 37-58

[44] Joshi MD, Sahai B. Mapping of salt-aff ected land in Saurashtra coast using Landsat satellite data. International Journal of Remote Sensing. 1993;**14**:1919-1929

[45] Goossens REA, El Badawi M, Ghabour TK, de Dapper M. A simulation model to monitor the soil salinity in irrigated arable based upon remote sensing and GIS. EARSeL Advances in Remote Sensing. 1993;**2**(3):165-171

[46] Johnston RM, Barson MM. Remote sensing of Australian wetlands. An evaluation of Landsat TM data for inventory and classification. Australian Journal of Marineand Freshwater Research. 1993;**44**:235-242

[47] Siderius W. The use of remote sensing for irrigation management with emphasis on IIMI research concerning salinity, water logging and cropping patterns. In: Mission Report. Enschede, Netherlands: International Institute for Aerospace Survey and Earth Sciences; 1991. 97 p

[48] Venkataratnam L. Monitoring of soil salinity in the Indo-Gangetic plain of NW India using multidate Landsat data. In: Proceedings of the 17th International Symposium on Remote Sensing of the Environment. Vol. 1. Ann Arbor, Michigan, USA: Environmental Research Institute of Michigan; 1983. pp. 369-377

[49] Goosens R, Joshi DC, Ranst EV. The use of remote sensing to map gypsiferous soils in the Ismailia soil (Egypt). Geoderma. 1998;**87**:47-56

[50] Salman A. Using the State-of-the-Art Remote Sensing and GIS for Monitoring Water Logging and Salinity. Lahore, Pakistan: International Water-Management Institute; 2000

[51] Indo-Dutch Network Project (IDNP). A Methodology for Identification of Water Logging and Soil Salinity Conditions Using Remote Sensing. Kamal and Alterra-ILRI, Wageningen: CSSRI; 2002. p. 78

[52] Metternicht G, Zink JA. Spatial discrimination of salt and sodium affected soil surfaces. International Journal of Remote Sensing. 1996;**18**:2571-2576

[53] Steven MD, Malthus TJ, Jaggard FM, Andrieu B. Monitoring responses of vegetation to stress. In: Cracknell AP, Vaughan RA, editors. Remote Sensing from Research to Operation: Proceedings of the 18th Annual Conference of the Remote Sensing Society. Nottingham, UK; 1992. pp. 369-377

[54] Baber JJ. Detection of crop conditions with low-altitude aerial photography. Remote Sensing for Resource Management. 1982:407-412

[55] WAPDA. Applicability of Landsat Imagery for Monitoring Soil Salinity Trends, Publ. 529. Lahore, Pakistan: Directorate of Reclamation and Investigation Organization; 1984

[56] Sahin H, Oruc M, Buyuksalih G. Temporal analysis of multi epoch Landsat geocover images in Zonguldak test field. Proceedings of ISPRS Ankara Workshop, 7th session 16 February 2006. 2006

[57] Brogaard S, Prieler S. Land cover in the Horqin grasslands, North China. Detecting changes between 1975 and 1990 by means of remote sensing. Interim report IR-98-044/July on work of the International Institute for Applied System Analysis. 1998

[58] Van Trinh M, Duong ND, Van Keulen H. Using Landsat images for studying land use dynamics and soil degradation: Case study in Tamduong District, Vinhphuc Province, Vietnam. In: International Symposium on Geoinformatics for Spatial Infrastructure Development in Earth and Allied Sciences. 2004

[59] Ernani MZ, Gabriels D. Detection of land cover changes using Landsat MSS, TM, ETM+ sensors in YHazd-Ardakan Basin, Iran. In: Proceedings of Agro Environ 2006. 2006. pp. 513-519

[60] Latifovic R, Fytas K, Chen J, Paraszczak J. Assessing land cover change resulting from large surface mining development. International Journal of Applied Earth Observation and Geoinformation. 2005;**7**:29-48

[61] Vidal V, Tabet D, Ahmad MD, Asif S, Zimmer D, Strosser P. Salinity Assessment in Irrigation Systems Using Remote Sensing and Geographical Information Systems—Application to Christian Subdivision, Pakistan. Report R-47. Lahore, Pakistan: IIMI; 1998

[62] Tabet D. Intérêtd'uneapprochespatiale pour suivi de la salinité des sols dans les systèmesirrigués: cas de la subdivision de Chistian dans le Punjab, Pakistan [PhD thesis]. Montpellier, France, Ecole Nationale du Génie rural, des Eaux et Forêts. 1999

[63] Cialella AT, Dubayah R, Lawrence W, Levine E. Predicting soil-drainage class using remotely sensed and digital elevation data.

Photogrammetric Engineering and Remote Sensing. 1997;**63**(2):171-178

[64] Verma KS, Saxena RK, Barthwal AK, Deshmukh SN. Remote-sensing technique for mapping salt affected soils. International Journal of Remote Sensing. 1994;**15**(9):1901-1914

[65] Dwivedi RS. Monitoring of salt-affected soils of the indo-Gangetic alluvial plains using principal component analysis. International Journal of Remote Sensing. 1996;**17**(10):1907-1914

[66] Dwivedi RS, Sreenivas K. Image transforms as a tool for the study of soil salinity and alkalinity dynamics. International Journal of Remote Sensing. 1998;**19**(4):605-619

[67] Choudhri MB, Mian MA, Rafiq M. The nature and magnitude of salinity and drainage problems in relation to agricultural evelopment in Pakistan. In: Pakistan Soils Bulletin. Vol. 8. Pakistan: Lahore; 1978

[68] Dean A, Hughes S, Gibbons W, Syed A, Renou C, Dow D, et al. Monitoring sustainable development in the oil sands region of Alberta, Canada, using SPOT-5 and ENVISAT ASAR and MERIS imagery. 2007. Available from: http://www.eomd.esa.int/files/docs/131-176-149-30-2007101113598.pdf [Accessed: December 5, 2019]

[69] Stefanov WL, Ramsey MS, Christensen PR. Monitoring urban land cover change: An expert system approach to land covers classification of semiarid to arid urban centres. Remote Sensing of Environment. 2001;**77**:173-185

[70] Bossard M, Feranec J, Otahel J. CORINE Land Cover. Copenhagen (EEA). 2000. Available from: http://terrestrial.eionet.eu.int . Technical Guide-Addendum 2000. Technical Report No. 40.

[71] Cohen WB, Spies TA, Alig RJ, Oetter DR, Maiersperger TK, Fiorella M. Characterizing 23 years (1972-95) of stand replacement disturbance in Western Oregon forests with Landsat imagery. Ecosystems. 2002;**5**:122-137

[72] Teillet PM, Helder DL, Ruggles TA, Landry R, Ahern FJ, Higgs NJ, et al. A definitive calibration record for the Landsat-5 thematic mapper anchored to the landsat-7 radiometric scale. Canadian Journal of Remote Sensing. 2004;**30**:631-643

[73] Gu D, Gillespie A. Topographic normalization of Landsat TM images of forest based on subpixel Sun-canopy-sensor geometry. Remote Sensing of Environment. 1998;**64**:166-175

[74] Pons X, Solé-Sugrañes L. A simple radiometric correction model to improve automatic mapping of vegetation from multispectral satellite data. Remote Sensing of Environment. 1994;**48**:191-204

[75] Schroeder TA, Cohen WB, Song C, Canty MJ, Yang Z. Radiometric correction of multi-temporal Landsat data for characterization of early successional forest patterns in western Oregon. Remote Sensing of Environment. 2006;**103**:16-26

[76] Han G, Zhou G, Xu Z. Biotic and abiotic factors control-ling the spatial and temporal variation of soil respiration in an agri-cultural ecosystem. Soil Biology and Biochemistry. 2007;**39**:418-425

[77] Paolini L, Grings F, Sobrino JA, Jiménez Muñoz JC, Karsebaum H. Radiometric correction effects in Landsat multi-date/multi-sensor change detection studies. International Journal of Remote Sensing. 2006;**27**:685-704

[78] Norjamäki I, Tokola T. Comparison of atmospheric correction methods

in mapping timber volume with multitemporal Landsat images in Kainuu, Finland. Photogrammetric Engineering and Remote Sensing. 2007;**73**:155-163

[79] Richardson AJ, Gerbermann AH, Gausmann HW, Cuellar JA. Detection of saline soils with skylab multi-spectral scanner data. Photogrammetric Engineering and Remote Sensing. 1976;**42**:679-684

[80] Saaty TL. A scaling method for priorities in hierarchical structures. Journal of Mathematical Psychology. 1977;**15**:234-241

[81] FAO. A Framework for Land Evaluation, Soils Bulletin 32. Rome: Food and Agricultural Organization; 1976

[82] Carver SJ. Integrating multi-criteria evaluation with geographical information systems. International Journal of Geographical Information Systems. 1991;**5**:321-329

[83] Voogd H. Multi-Criteria Evaluation for Urban and Regional Planning. London: Pion, Ltd.; 1983

[84] Rao M, Sastry SVC, Yadar PD, Kharod K, Pathan SK, Dhinwa PS, et al. A Weighted Index Model for Urban Suitability Assessment-A GIS Approach. Bombay, India: Bombay Metropolitan Regional Development Authority; 1997

[85] Kimes DC, Nelson RF. Attributes of neural networks for extracting continuous vegetation. International Journal of Remote Sensing. 1998;**19**(14):2639-2663

[86] Ferro V. Evaluating overland flow sediment transport capacity. Hydrological Processes. 1998;**12**:1895-1910

[87] Schmidt H, Karnieli A. Remote sensing of the seasonal variability of vegetation in a semi-arid environment. Journal of Arid Environments. 2002;**45**(1):43-60

[88] Todd SW, Hoffer RM, Milchunas DG. Biomass estimation on grazed and ungrazed rangelands using spectral indices. International Journal of Remote Sensing. 1998;**19**(3):427-438. DOI: 10.1080/014311698216071

[89] Wang N, Dong J. Chinese energy and water balance monitoring system based on remote sensing technique. Remote Sensing Information. 2002;**6**:7-10

[90] Gao Y, Zhang XB, He R, Wang YL, Zhu XZ, Tian B, et al. Application of spatial distribution model to predict the impact of 1998's flood on snail distribution in marshland of Yang Zhou. Chinese Journal of Schistosomiasis Control. 2000;**2001**(13):285-288

[91] Chen HM, Arora MK, Varshney PK. Mutual information-based image registration for remote sensing data. International Journal of Remote Sensing. 2003;**24**:3701-3706

[92] Gould W. Remote sensing of vegetation, plant species richness, and regional biodiversity hotspots. Ecological Applications. 2000;**10**(6):1861-1870

[93] Lauver C. Mapping species diversity patterns in the Kansas shortgrass region by integrating remote sensing and vegetation analysis. Journal of Vegetation Science. 1997;**8**:387-394

[94] Zhang C, Guo X, Wilmshurst J, Sissons R. Application of radars atimagery on grassland heterogeneity assessment. Canadian Journal of Remote Sensing. 2006;**32**(4):1-7

[95] Dimyati E. An analysis of land use/land cover change using the combination of MSS Landsat and land

use map—A case study of Yogyakarta, Indonesia. International Journal of Remote Sensing. 1995;**17**(5):931-944

[96] Lewis M. Species composition related to spectral classification in an Australian spinifex hummock grassland. International Journal of Remote Sensing. 1994;**15**:3223-3239

[97] Moshen A. Environmental Land Use Change Detection and Assessment Using with Multi—Temporal Satellite Imagery. Iran: Zanjan University; 1999

Chapter 10

Water Management Strategies and Cultural Practices for Strawberry Establishment in Florida

Emmanuel Torres-Quezada, Isabel Torres-Quezada and Bielinski Marcelo Santos

Abstract

Florida's strawberry (*Fragaria × ananassa* Duch) production system is mainly dependent on short-day cultivars produced as bare-root (BR) transplants, which are high-yielding and low-cost options for Florida growers. The strawberry industry in Florida is greatly dependent on early yield (mid-November, early December). Therefore, Florida growers must secure rapid establishment of the BR transplants and for that reason, high volumes of irrigation water are applied to reduce air temperature around plant crowns and mitigate desiccation. This practice accounts for nearly 14.7 million m^3 of irrigation water between mid-September and early October. Several alternatives are available to growers to reduce irrigation water for establishment. One of those alternatives suggests replacing BR transplants for actively growing strawberry plugs (SPs). However, the higher price of SP transplants seems to be the main limitation for their implementation. Alternately, growers could explore the possibility of introducing intermittent irrigation or low-volume sprinklers into their system to establish BR transplants. An inexpensive option, based on a large body of research, would be the application of crop protectants against excessive sun radiation, which could reduce irrigation water for establishment by up to 30%. Despite the suggested alternatives, there is still a great deal of work needed to increase grower's confidence in these technologies.

Keywords: crop protectants, kaolin clay, strawberry plugs, bare-root, intermittent irrigation, low-volume sprinklers

1. Introduction

Florida is the second largest strawberry producer in the U.S. with 3799 ha planted in 2017 [1]. The strawberry season in Florida goes from mid-September to April, depending on the production system and location in the state. The highest strawberry prices are obtained early in the season, between late November and the first few weeks of December, before strawberry imports flood the market. Mexico and California are the biggest competitors to the Florida strawberry. Imported strawberry from Mexico competes directly with Florida during the winter months. Mexican strawberry usually enters the U.S. market during the third week of December, making Florida strawberry growers greatly dependent on early yield to secure profitability in their individual production systems.

In order to secure their first harvest between November and early December, Florida growers rely on BR transplants, which are shipped to Florida from northern-latitude states in the U.S., Canada, or high-altitude nurseries. During nursery stage, BR transplants are grown under inductive conditions for flowering, which translate to early flowering after transplanted in Florida. In addition, their low acquisition cost make BR transplants an attractive option for Florida growers. Days before the beginning of the strawberry season, BR transplants are dug out from the ground, cleaned up, packed, and shipped to southern states in the U.S. for the winter season. Handling of the transplants usually leads to reduced number of functional leaves and roots, creating sites for pathogen infection and increases variability in transplant size and flowering patterns. Moreover, for growers to secure rapid establishment of BR transplants in Florida in September and October, high volumes of irrigation water are used to reduce air temperature around plant crowns as well as to decrease leaf desiccation. This practice represents an underground water depletion of nearly 14.7 million m^3 between mid-September and early October. Controversy surrounds this establishment practice; as in combination with water consumption for freeze protection, it has been related to an increasing occurrence of sinkholes in urban areas near the production sites.

Strawberry yield is strongly influenced by environmental conditions, plant physiology, and the grower's management practice. Furthermore, grower profitability will be partially determined by the time of entry in the market and transplant quality. Given the interaction among several factors that affect profitability in strawberry production, this chapter touches on the physiological characteristics of strawberry transplants, followed by the application of the traditional establishment practices and potential alternatives to this method with aims to reduce irrigation water consumption during strawberry establishment in Florida, USA.

2. Strawberry response to high temperatures

The commercial strawberry is a perennial hybrid commonly described as herbaceous, though it is a true woody plant, given the presence of secondary xylem in roots and crowns [2]. The stem (also called crown) consists of a compressed central core surrounded by a vascular ring [3]. The crown gives origin to leaves, runners, lateral crowns, roots, and flowers. The modern strawberry originated from the hybridization of two wild octoploid species [4, 5], *F. virginiana* and *F. chiloensis* [6]. Darrow [7] extensively reviewed the history of this hybrid. The plant is commonly propagated by stolon or crown division [8], and while the crop can be successfully cultivated in a broad range of climates, the most common production areas are limited to temperate and Mediterranean climates between latitudes 27 and 60 [9]. The strawberry root system originates from the base of the crown in plant clones. Adventitious roots emerge from the pericycle and depending on soil conditions, roots might develop into a fibrous mass, with about 70% concentrated in the upper 15 cm of soil. The plant produces leaves arranged spirally in short intervals, roots in the base, and a flower meristem at the terminal position, terminating in a primary blossom, followed by two lateral secondary flowers, four tertiaries, and sometimes eight quaternary flowers [10]. The strawberry plant is composed of multiple meristems regulated by plant age, water and nutrient availability, temperature, and photoperiod [3, 9, 11].

Heat stress can be defined as a rise in temperature above a particular threshold level long enough to cause irreparable damage to plant growth and development [12]. Strawberry roots, leaves, and crowns are particularly susceptible to high temperatures. Soil temperatures above 25°C reduced crown dry weight by 22%

compared to 17°C, while soil temperatures above 17°C reduced root dry weight by 15% compared to 10°C, culminating in root death at 32°C in 'Aliso' strawberry [13]. Authors suggested an increase in oxygen and carbohydrate consumption due to increasing tissue temperatures [13]. Electrolyte leakage, protein denaturalization, and inhibition of protein synthesis are common on leaf tissues following high temperature exposure [14]. Although crop response differs when exposed to gradual heat stress and shock heat stress [15, 16]. Gradual heat stress (5°C increased every 48 h until 45°C) triggered heat acclimation in strawberry with reduced electrolyte leakage. On the contrary, shock heat stress (45°C; common in newly transplanted BR) increased electrolyte leakage from leaves and decreased total protein content, leading to protein denaturalization and reduction of protein synthesis [15, 16].

Multiple authors reported that growth analyses are usually dependent on genotype, cultivation systems, and seasonal changes in the environment [10, 16]. Kesici et al. [12], evaluated 15 strawberry cultivars under high temperature conditions (5°C increased every 24 h until 50°C). The authors identified differences in the leaf relative water and chlorophyll contents and heat stress tolerance among cultivars. 'Elsanta', 'R. Hope', and 'Camarosa' were reported as relatively heat tolerant, while 'Whitney', 'Fern', and 'Festival' were relatively heat-sensitive [12]. Additionally, water stress can aggravate the effects of heat stress, decreasing fruit weight and total yield. Ikeda et al. reported a decrease of 37% in fruit weight of 'Sachinoka' when grown on 30/15°C under water stress compared to plants with adequate water. Besides induced differences, the annual strawberry cropping system also plays a major role in the plant response to high temperatures and water stress [17].

3. The Florida production system

Florida strawberry production is specifically designed based on its soils and weather patterns. Commercial strawberry production in Florida started in 1878, at Plant City (28° N latitude) becoming the largest production area of the state. Strawberries are grown in an annual hill culture system [18, 19] with planting dates ranging from mid-September to mid-October. Transplants are set in double rows (30–35 cm apart) with plants 30–40 cm apart (avg. plant density 47,500 plants/ha), in a fumigated bed seeking to reduce nematodes, diseases, and weed pressures [20]. Beds are covered with a black polyethylene mulch and a single drip line in the middle. Nitrogen (N) requirements are 170 kg/ha for a 200 days season [21], although recommendations can change depending on the cultivar selected. Most of the N fertilizer is injected through the irrigation system, as preplant applications do not necessarily improve yield [22]. Although some growers tend to incorporate part of the phosphorus and potassium requirements as preplant applications. Most irrigation schedules are based on grower's experience. However, statewide recommendations suggest that irrigation amounts should be scheduled to meet monthly evapotranspiration, ranging from 7570 L/ha in October to 28,387 L/ha in April [22]. Strawberry growers strongly rely on early yield (mid-November to mid-December) to secure profitability of the system, before Mexican strawberry imports diminish market prices [18, 23, 24]. Average commercial yield ranges from 26,363 kg/ha to 30,000 kg/ha, depending on cultivar selection, season, and variations in production system.

3.1 Bare-root transplants

Florida production system is mainly dependent on short-day cultivars produced as BR transplants. BR is a high yielding, low-cost option for Florida growers, with prices ranging from $0.13–0.14 per transplant [24]. However, growers need to meet several conditions to overcome the challenges that accompany the use of BR in Florida. Strawberries are commonly classified into short-day (June bearing), long-day (ever bearing), or day-neutral cultivars, according to their photoperiodic requirements for flower induction [2]. However, this classification system is deceiving of the physiological responses of the plant, as flower induction is influenced by air temperature, plant development, CO_2 concentration, and photoperiod [2, 7, 25]. In general, short-day cultivars will initiate flowering under photoperiods of 14 h, while long-day cultivars will require photoperiods longer than 13 h, as long as air temperature is permissive. Additionally, the plant needs a minimum of inductive cycles, ranging from 7 to 24 depending on cultivar and air temperature [25]. Increments in air temperature will generally increase the number of inductive cycles required by short-day plants to flower. High air temperatures (28°C) tend to inhibit flower induction, while temperatures ranging between 10°C and 15°C will promote flowering in short day plants.

BR transplants are generally produced in northern latitudes of the U.S., Canada, or at high altitude, to take advantage of the low air temperatures to pre-induce flowering in short-day cultivars. During nursery stage, BR transplants are exposed to the photoperiod and air temperature at the nursery site. Plants are commonly planted in April and grown throughout the summer, before being shipped to the different planting areas in Florida and other southern states.

Maximum air temperatures at the nursery site in June and July are comparable to the early months of the Florida strawberry season (**Figure 1**). However, minimum air temperatures from June to August at the nursery site allow fully-grown transplants to accumulate chilling induction cycles before being shipped, despite photoperiod being longer than 14 h (depending on nursery latitude) (**Figure 2**). In early September, transplants are dug out from the ground, cleaned, and shipped to southern planting areas.

Under Florida conditions, at the beginning of the season, photoperiod in the Plant City area is around 12 h, dropping to 11 h in December and January. Minimum temperatures range from 19.6°C to 2.8°C from September to December, allowing flower induction conditioning after mid-October (**Figure 1**). Average air temperature in September is 26.1°C, dropping to 23.4°C in October and 19.5°C in December

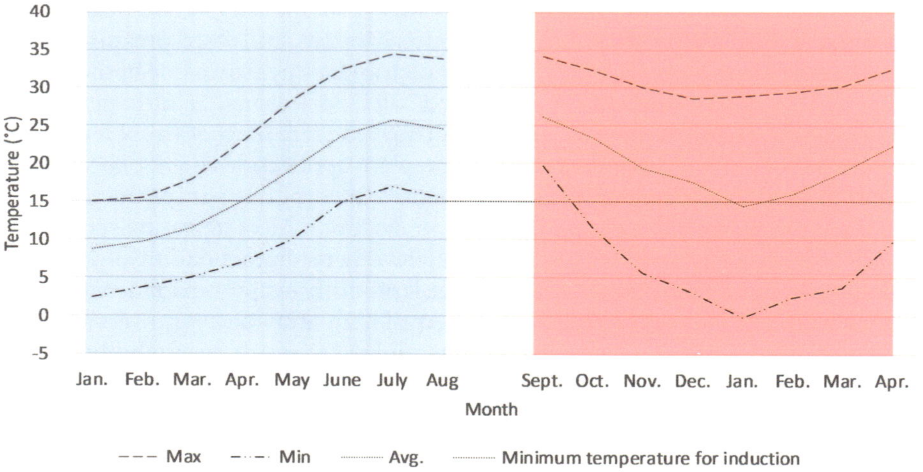

Figure 1.
Ten-year summary of maximum, minimum, and average air temperature at MacDoel, California, USA during strawberry nursery stage (blue) and at Balm, Florida, USA during the strawberry growing season (red).

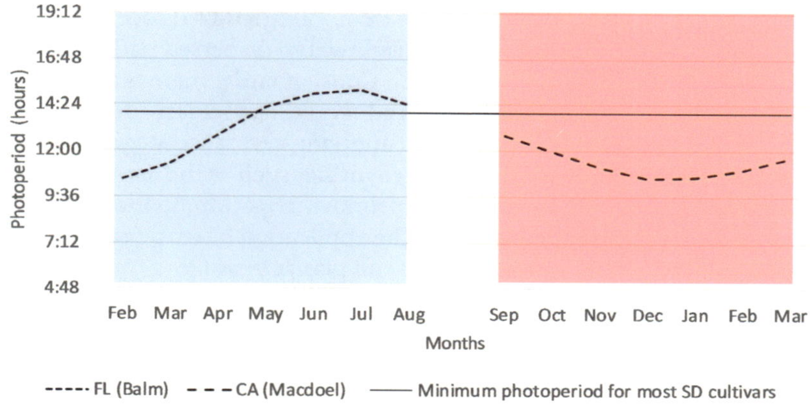

Figure 2.
Monthly photoperiod at MacDoel, California, USA during the strawberry nursery stage (blue) and at Balm, Florida, USA during the strawberry growing season (red).

and January, to later come back up to 22°C in late February and March, around the end of the strawberry season (**Figure 1**). Hence, as photoperiod is already less than 14 h at the time of planting and minimum temperatures are adequate for flower induction after mid-October, the main challenge for Florida growers is transplant establishment under high air temperatures of mid-September and early October (**Figure 1**).

3.2 Strawberry BR establishment

Because of the impaired root system of the traditional BR transplants, in addition to Florida's high air temperature at the time of planting, growers rely on sprinkler irrigation for transplant establishment to moderate air temperatures around the crown and promote root development. Traditionally, BR transplants require 8–10 h of high-impact sprinkler irrigation during the first 10–12 days after transplanting to be fully established. This technique reduces the air temperature around the crown and promotes root and shoot growth of the transplants. The physical phenomenon is based on the energy balance between the water applied and the rest of the production system. Water at the surface of the plant tissue and plastic mulch will evaporate, absorbing approximately 540 calories/mL, as long as the air vapor pressure is lower than the saturated vapor pressure.

Sprinkler heads are usually spaced 14.5 m × 14.5 m apart, averaging 48 sprinklers per ha. Each sprinkler head delivers an average of 15–19 L/min [26], resulting in a water depletion of roughly 3,883,410 L/ha, with close to 3% [27] reaching the planting whole. This amount of water is equivalent to two-thirds of the total water required during the season [28], without considering freeze protection. Overhead irrigation costs were estimated at $11,507/ha in 2012–2013, accounting for 16% of the total cost [29]. This system is only applicable under Florida conditions, as the sandy soils surrounding the Plant City area will allow for a rapid drainage of the irrigation water. The system has generated controversy for many years. The two primary water withdrawals in Florida are the general public and agricultural consumption. In the Plant City area, water resources are shared between agricultural and urban uses [27, 30]. Special regulations for water use in agriculture were implemented in 2010, when several freeze events took place and a high amount of water was used to protect the crop from freeze damage. This activity allegedly caused a drop in the Floridian aquifer level of 18 m. It appears that, because of these events, about 140 sinkholes and more than 750 dried wells occurred in the area [31]. Additionally, overhead water spreads water-dispersed pathogens and promotes weed germination in furrows [32]. Consequently, there is a need to reduce the amount of water used for strawberry production, particularly during transplant establishment. Current research focuses on applying several strategies to decrease irrigation volumes during strawberry transplanting, such as the use of containerized transplants to minimize the need for sprinkler irrigation, reducing irrigation volumes with low-volume sprinklers, and the application of crop protectants or anti-transpirants for lessening water needs and plant stress [26].

4. Alternative establishment methods

4.1 Strawberry plugs

SPs are a suitable alternative to BR transplants. The active root system and water retention capacity of the growing media allows for a quicker establishment of the transplants with minimal irrigation requirement, reduced diseases pressure and higher yield [30, 33–36]. The main limitation of SP implementation is their higher cost ($0.37–$0.38 per transplant) compared to BR transplants. The price difference is related to higher labor and shipping costs, since fewer transplants can be transported per shipping unit. The transition from BR to SP transplants represents an increment in production cost of $10,455/ha, assuming a plant density of 43,560 plants/ha [33].

Several authors had evaluated the performance of SP transplants in Florida reporting higher early yield, quicker transplant establishment rate, and higher fruit size [30, 33, 34, 36]. Hochmuth et al. [30] reported a 98% increment in earlier fruit weight for SP transplants compared to BR transplants without irrigation establishment. Although, total fruit yield was similar for both transplants. The differences in early yield between transplants signified an increment in profitability of the SP system of $2855/ha. Similarly, Giménez et al. [37] reported 24.5% higher early yield for SP compared to BR in soilless media. The increased early yield of SP is related to a quicker establishment rate and accumulation of chilling hours during nursery stage [38]. SP transplants have a similar production process as BR with the added cost of establishing the runners in the planting trays and maintenance under protected conditions until an active root system develops. SPs are grown from unrooted runners called tips. The tips are planted into plastic trays containing usually a peat-based media.

Producing short-day SP transplants in Florida could lower the costs of transplants and increase its application in the relatively warm climates. However, SP exposed to Florida growing conditions without adequate conditioning for flower induction results in similar total yield as BR but reduced early yield [33]. Torres-Quezada et al. [33] evaluated requirements for time in nursery and tray sizes for Florida-produced SP from 2012 to 2016. Strawberry mother plants from three cultivars 'Florida Radiance', 'Strawberry Festival', and 'Florida 127' were planted in soilless media under greenhouse conditions. After 4 months, runners tips were collected from the mother plants and established in either 30-, 40-, 50-, or 75-cell trays. Additionally, SPs were grown for either 4 or 6 weeks before planted at the field. SP transplants did not receive conditioning for flower induction and were established at the field with 20% of the total water required for BR transplants for establishment.

Overall, BR transplant resulted in 63% higher early yield than all SP treatments, although both transplant types resulted in the same total yield with an average of

29,300 kg/ha. Furthermore, SP transplants growth in 50-cell trays for 4 weeks was recommended as an adequate production system for Florida-produced SP. The difference in early yield was attributed to the high air temperatures of September (avg. 26.5°C) in Florida. These temperatures led to a delay in flower bud initiation for SP compared to BR. Furthermore, the high air temperatures probably promoted excessive vegetative growth of SP. Florida-produced SP had a higher dry biomass accumulation compared to the BR transplants, likely related to the active formation of runners and crowns. The increased vegetative growth could explain the increment in production later in the season, as flower buds are originated at the crown site, while BR had lower dry biomass accumulation probably related to pre-season induction and continuous flowering. Early yield differences between transplants are influenced by growing conditions before transplanting. However, SP with or without conditioning can be established with 80% less water than BR transplants, resulting in water savings of almost 820,800 gal per acre per season [33].

4.2 Intermittent irrigation and low-volume sprinklers

It is possible to modify irrigation scheduling for strawberry establishment to reduce the amount of water applied. Similar yield was found for BR transplants established with constant overhead irrigation, and interval of (min on/off) 5/15, 10/20, 5/10, and 15/15 [38]. Intermittent irrigation allows for water savings ranging from 50 to 75% of the traditional water used through high-impact sprinklers. Several authors concluded that foliage should not be allowed to wilt, and low humidity and wind speed greater than 16 km/h can accelerate leaf drying. Golden et al. [39] stated "Keen observations during the establishment period will determine intermittent irrigation cycles of transplants that can reduce water usage and fertilizer leaching without affecting early or seasonal fruit yield".

Similarly, low-volume sprinkler irrigation had been reported to be a suitable option for strawberry establishment. In 2011–2012, Santos et al. [27] evaluated intermittent irrigation with sprinklers delivering 5.7 L/min (10 min on and 10 min off), continuous irrigation with sprinklers delivering 5.7 L/min, and continuous irrigation with sprinklers delivering 17 L/min (control). 'Treasure' BR transplants with three to five leaves from a Canadian nursery were planted in early October 2011 in Florida. Data showed no significant differences among treatments for early yield and fruit number, regardless of the water volumes or intermittent scheduling (**Figures 3** and **4**). Low-volume sprinkler irrigation in combination with intermittent irrigation might allow water savings ranging from 16 to 33% compared to traditional overhead irrigation.

4.3 Crop protectants

Another alternative for strawberry establishment are crop protectants [26–28, 40]. Crop protectants provide a shield that reduces environmental stress on plants. Several naturally occurring materials are available in the market for growers for foliar application, such as kaolin clay, calcium carbonate, or aluminum silicate. Kaolin clay is natural degradable white mineral that, when applied to leaves, reflects infrared and ultraviolet radiation, thus reducing temperature rises in the tissue.

During the 2008–2009 and 2009–2010 strawberry seasons in Florida, seven transplant establishment treatments originated from the combination of duration of sprinkler irrigation and kaolin clay foliar application were evaluated. Kaolin clay treatments were applied with a handheld foliar sprayer using a rate of 28 kg/ha. Authors compared 10 days of sprinkler irrigation (control), to 8, 6, and 4 days of sprinkler irrigation with and without a kaolin clay application at next day on

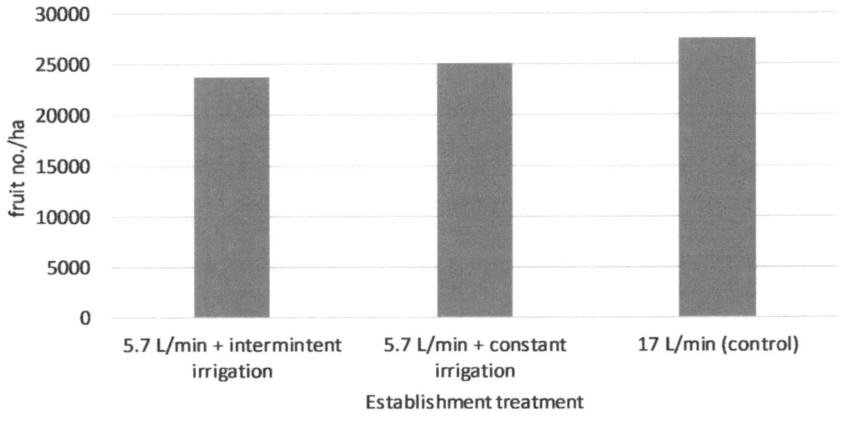

Figure 3.
Effect of irrigation volume and scheduling on strawberry early fruit number at balm, Florida, USA in the 2011–2012 strawberry season [27].

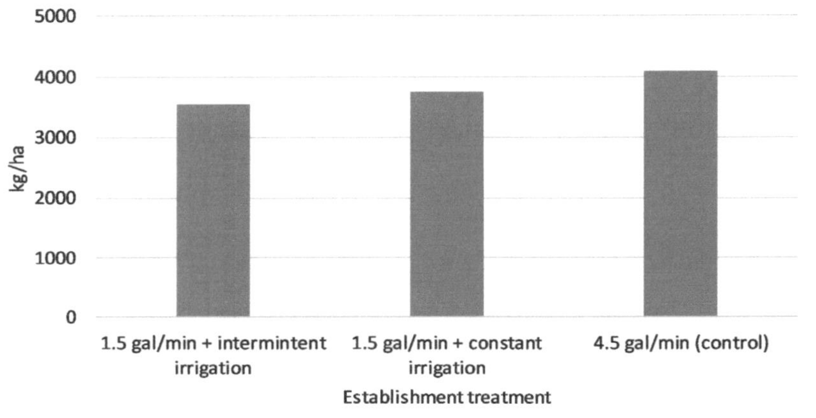

Figure 4.
Effect of irrigation volume and scheduling on strawberry early yield at balm, Florida, USA in the 2011–2012 strawberry season [27].

BR establishment. Data indicated that 6 days of sprinkler irrigation followed by a kaolin clay application at the 7 day resulted in similar early and total yield as 10 days of sprinkler irrigation [26]. Application of this establishment system represents potential water savings of 164,160 gal/acre.

Similarly, Hernández-Ochoa [28] evaluated 10 days of sprinkler irrigation (control) against 7 days of sprinkler irrigation with or without kaolin clay (11 kg/ha), aluminum silicate (11 kg/ha), or calcium carbonate (28 L/ha). Data indicated no difference among control and 7 days of sprinkler irrigation with either kaolin clay, aluminum silicate, or calcium carbonate. Furthermore, 7 days of sprinkler irrigation without a crop protectant application resulted in 22% lower early yield.

Given the promising results on different research stations, Santos et al. [27] evaluated the effect of reduced-volume irrigation programs for strawberry establishment and kaolin clay at larger scale in Plant City, Florida. A study was conducted in Hillsborough County, Florida, at six growers' farms covering 6.4 ha. Authors evaluated 7 days of sprinkler irrigation delivering 17 L/min of water plus kaolin clay in the 8th day at the rate of 28 kg/ha with an application volume of 568 L/ha of water. Additionally, 10 days of sprinkler irrigation delivering 17 L/min of water were used as a control. Experimental plots consisted of an average of 500 plants with six replications. Authors found no differences in plant establishment, leaf greenness, and plant diameter between treatments, with a 30% reduction of irrigation water for establishment. It was estimated that the cost of application of kaolin clay was $90/ha at the moment of the study. This expense was less than three times the cost of diesel fuel needed for the extra 3 days of overhead irrigation.

5. Conclusion

About 14.7 million m^3 of water are used for strawberry establishment in Florida between mid-September and early October. Several research initiatives had been conducted to find alternatives to reduced irrigation water for establishment. Strawberry growers could reduce their consumption of irrigation water for establishment to less than 20% of their current usage, by introducing SP or completely substituting BR for SP transplants in their system. However, the higher prices of SP seem to be a limitation for their implementation, reducing grower's interest into exploring the applications of SP transplants. Additional research is needed to optimize the production of Florida-produced SP. Newly released cultivars with tendencies toward day-neutrality ('Florida Beauty') could be a suitable option to increase early yield of SP with no preconditioning.

Alternately, growers could explore the possibility of introducing intermittent irrigation into their system, as research suggests potential water savings of nearly 33% without effecting early or total yield, with minimal modifications to their irrigation systems. Grower's adoption of low-volume sprinkler irrigation seems less likely, as it will involve a higher investment to modify the nozzles and number of sprinkler per acre. In addition, the traditional overhead irrigation currently used for plant establishment is also commonly used to protect the plants against potential cold snaps later in the season.

The less expensive option to reduce irrigation water for establishment is the application of crop protectants. There is a large body of research evaluating the effect of kaolin clay on strawberry establishment, with similar results across seasons and locations. Nevertheless, grower's adoption of this technology has been minimal. It is necessary to increase the efforts of on-farm demonstrations to promote the use of this technology. Additionally, interactions with planting dates and stress reducing amendments, such as silica application should be evaluated. An ideal scenario will combine alternatives to completely eliminate the use of overhead irrigation for establishment. However, there is still a great deal of work needed to increase grower's confidence in these technologies.

Author details

Emmanuel Torres-Quezada[1]*, Isabel Torres-Quezada[2] and Bielinski Marcelo Santos[3]

1 Horticultural Sciences Department, University of Florida, Gainesville, Florida, USA

2 Instituto Hispano-Luso de Investigaciones Agrarias, Universidad de Salamanca, Salamanca, Spain

3 Freedom Ag Research LLC, Riverview, Florida, USA

*Address all correspondence to: etorres1618@ufl.edu

References

[1] USDA-United States Department of Agriculture. Quick Stats. Strawberry, Florida [Internet]. 2020. Available from: https://quickstats.nass.usda.gov/results/41DD4CEA-DDB6-36EB-A688-4D08F8B68654 [Accessed: 01 March 2020]

[2] Darnell RL, Cantliffe DJ, Kirschbaum DS. The physiology of flowering in strawberry. In: Janick J, editor. Horticultural Reviews. Vol. 28. New York: Wiley; 2003. pp. 325-345. ISBN: 0-471-21542-2

[3] Hancock JF. Strawberries. In: Erez A, editor. Temperate Fruit Crops in Warm Climates. Dordrecht: Springer; 2000. DOI: 10.1007/978-94-017-3215-417

[4] Edger PP, Poorten TJ, Van Buren R, Hardigan MA, Colle M, Mckain MR, et al. Origin and evolution of the octoploid strawberry genome. Nature Genetics. 2019;**541**:547. DOI: 10.1038/s41588-019-0356-4

[5] Folta KM, Barbey CR. The strawberry genome: A complicated past and promising future. Horticultural Research. 2019. DOI: 10.1038/s41438-019-0181-z

[6] Tennessen JA, Govindarajulu R, Asdman T, Liston A. Evolutionary origins and dynamic of octoploid strawberry subgenomes revealed by dense targeted capture linkage maps. Genome Biology and Evolution. DOI: 10.1093/gbe/evu261

[7] Darrow G. The Strawberry. 1st ed. New York: Holt, Rinehart and Wiston; 1966

[8] Savini G, Neri D, Zucconi F, Sugiyama N. Strawberry growth and flowering, and architectural model. International Journal of Fruit Science. 2008;**29**:50. DOI: 10.1300/J492v05n01_04

[9] Kumar S, Dey P. Effects of different mulches and irrigation methods on root growth, nutrient update, water-use efficiency and yield of strawberry. Scientia Horticulturae. 2010;**318**:324. DOI: 10.1016/j.scienta.2010.10.023

[10] Galletta GJ, Bringhurst RS. Strawberry management. In: Galletta GJ, Himelrick DG, editors. Small Fruit Crop Management. Englewood, NJ: Prentice Hall; 1990. pp. 83-156. ISBN: 0131854550 9780131854550

[11] Sønsteby A, Solhaug KA, Heide OM. Functional growth analysis of 'sonata' strawberry plants grown under controlled temperature and daylength conditions. Scientia Horticulturae. 2016;**26**:33. DOI: 10.1016/j.scienta.2016.08.003

[12] Kesici M, Gulen H, Ergin S, Turhan E, Ipek A, Koksal N. Heat-stress tolerance of some strawberry (*Fragaria × ananassa*) cultivars. Notulae Botanicae Horti Agrobotanici Cluj-Napoca. 2013;**244**:249. DOI: 10.15835/nbha4119009

[13] Ganmore-Neumann R, Kafkafi U. The Effect of Root Temperature and NO_3^-/NH_4^+ Ratio on Strawberry Plants. I. Growth, Flowering, and Root Development. New York: Wiley; 1983. DOI: 10.2134/agronj1983.00021962007500060020x

[14] Udagawa Y, Ito T, Gomi K. Effects of root temperature on some physiological and ecological characteristics of strawberry plants 'Reiko' grown in nutrient solution. Japan Society of Horticultural Science. 1989;**624**:633. DOI: 10.2503/jjshs.58.627

[15] Gulen H, Eris A. Effect of heat stress on peroxidase activity and total protein content in strawberry plants. Plant Science. 2004;**739**:744. DOI: 10.1016/j.plantsci.2003.11.014

[16] Gulen H, Eris A. Some physiological changes in strawberry (*Fragaria × ananassa* 'Camarosa') plants under heat stress. The Journal of Horticultural Science and Biotechnology. 2003;**894**:898. DOI: 10.1080/14620316.2003.11511715

[17] Ikeda T, Suzuki N, Nakayama M, Kawakami Y. The effects of high temperature and water stress on fruit growth and anthocyanin content of pot-grown strawberry (Fragaria × ananassa Duch. cv. 'Sachinoka') plants. Environmental Control in Biology. 2011;**209**:2015. DOI: 10.2525/ecb.49.209

[18] Guan Z, Suh DH, Khachatryan H, Wu F. Import Growth and the Impact on the Florida Strawberry Industry. 2017. Available from: https://edis.ifas.ufl.edu/fe1022 [Accessed: 05 March 2020]

[19] Dittmar P, Boyd N, Stall W. Weed Management in Strawberry. 2016. Available from: https://edis.ifas.ufl.edu/wg037 [Accessed: 05 March 2020]

[20] Whitaker VM, Boyd NS, Peres NA, Desaeger J, Noling JW, Lahiri S. Chapter 16. Strawberry production. In: Freeman JH, Paret M, Dittmar PJ, editors. Vegetable Production Handbook of Florida, 2019-2020. IFAS Extension; 2020 Available from: http://edis.ifas.ufl.edu/pdffiles/cv/cv29200.pdf

[21] Hochmuth G, Albregts E. Fertilization of Strawberries in Florida. 2017. Available from: https://edis.ifas.ufl.edu/cv003. [Accessed: 05 March 2020]

[22] Agehara S, Santos BM, Whidden J. Nitrogen Fertilization of Strawberry Cultivars: Is Preplant Starter Fertilizer Needed? 2017. Available from: https://edis.ifas.ufl.edu/hs370 [Accessed: 05 March 2020]

[23] Wu F, Guan Z, Whitaker V. Florida Strawberry Growers Need more Early Yield to Improve Profitability. 2017. Available from: https://edis.ifas.ufl.edu/fe1032 [Accessed: 05 March 2020]

[24] Guan Z, Wu F, Whidden A. Top Challenges Facing the Florida Industry: Insights from a Comprehensive Industry Survey. 2018. Available from: https://edis.ifas.ufl.edu/fe972 [Accessed: 05 March 2020]

[25] Hancock JF. Strawberries. Wallingford, UK: CABI Publications; 1999. ISBN: 0851993397 9780851993393

[26] Santos BM, Salame-Donoso TP, Whidden AJ. Reducing sprinkler irrigation volumes for strawberry transplants establishment in Florida. HortTechnology. 2012;**224**:227. DOI: 10.21273/HORTTECH.22.2.224

[27] Santos BM, Stanly CD, Whidden AJ, Salame-Donoso TP, Whitaker VM, Hernández-Ochoa IM, et al. Improved sustainability through novel water management strategies for strawberry transplant establishment in Florida, United States. Agronomy. 2012;**312**:320. DOI: 10.3390/agronomy2040312

[28] Hernández-Ochoa IM, Santos BM. Comparison of foliar and root-dip crop protectants for strawberry transplant establishment. In: Proceedings of the Florida State Horticultural Society; 02-04 June 2013. Sarasota, Florida. 2013. pp. 142-144

[29] Guan Z, Wu F, Whidden A. Florida Strawberry Production Costs and Trends. 2017. Available from: https://edis.ifas.ufl.edu/fe1013 [Accessed: 05 March 2020]

[30] Hochmuth G, Cantliffe D, Chandler C, Stanley C, Bish E, Waldo E, et al. Fruiting responses economics of containerized and bare-root strawberry transplants established with different irrigation methods. HortTechnology. 2006;**205**:210. DOI: 10.21273/HORTTECH.16.2.0205

[31] Aurit MD, Peterson RO, Blanford JI. A GIS analysis of the relationship between sinkholes, dry-well complaints and groundwater pumping for frost-freeze protection of winter strawberry production in Florida. 2013. Available from: https://journals.plos.org/plosone/article?id=10.1371/journal.pone.0053832. [Accessed: 06 March 2020]

[32] Strand L. Integrated pest management for strawberries. University of California Statewide Integrated Pest Management Project. Agri. and Natural Resource Publ. 3351

[33] Torres-Quezada EA, Zotarelli L, Whitaker VM, Darnell RL, Morgan K, and Santos BM. Production techniques for strawberry plugs in west-central Florida. 2020. Available from: https://journals.ashs.org/horttech/view/journals/horttech/aop/article-10.21273-HORTTECH04529-19/article-10.21273-HORTTECH04529-19.xml [Accessed: 06 March 2020]

[34] Bish EB, Cantliffe, Hochmuth GJ, Chandler CK. Development of containerized strawberry transplants for Florida's winter production system. In: Proceedings of the III International Strawberry Symposium of the International Society of Horticultural Science, Vol. 461. 1997. p. 468. DOI: 10.17660/ActaHortic.1997.439.77

[35] Durner EF, Poling EB, Maas JL. Recent advances in strawberry plug transplant technology. HortTechnology. 2002;**545**:550. DOI: 10.21273/HORTTECH.12.4.545

[36] Kokalis-Burelle N. Effects of transplant type, plant growth-promoting rhizobacteria, and soil treatment on growth and yield of strawberry in Florida. Plant and Soil. 2003;**273**:280

[37] Giménez G, Andriolo JL, Janisch D, Cocco C, Dal PM. Cell size in trays for the production of strawberry plug transplants. Pesquisa Agropecuária Brasileira. 2009;**726**:729. DOI: 10.1590/S0100-204X2009000700012

[38] Bish EB, Cantliffe DJ. Temperature conditioning and container size affect early season fruit yield of strawberry plug plants in a winter, annual hill production system. HortScience. 2002;**762**:764

[39] Golden EA, Duval JR, Albregts EE, Howard CM. Intermittent sprinkler irrigation for establishment of bare root strawberry transplants. Available from: https://journals.flvc.org/edis/article/view/109149/104310 [Accessed: 06 March 2020]

[40] Torres-Quezada EA, Zotarelli L, Whitaker VM, Darnell RL, Morgan K, Santos BM. Planting dates and transplant establishment methods on early-yield strawberry in West-central Florida. HortTechnology. 2018;**615**:623. DOI: 10.21273/HORTTECH04079-18

Chapter 11

Managing and Sustaining the Coupled Water-Land-Food Systems in the Context of Global Change: How Qualitative System Dynamic Modelling Can Assist in Understanding and Designing High-Leverage Interventions

Julius H. Kotir

Abstract

The water-land-food system is essential for sustaining the basic human needs. While the demand for these resources is increasing rapidly, their sustainability has been hampered by a plethora of challenges, including rapid population growth, climate change, land-use change, and land degradation. To attain a sustainable supply and efficiently manage these resources, interactions between all resources and the factors constraining/sustaining them need to be understood. In this chapter, four systems archetypes based or grounded in the systems thinking framework and system dynamics approach were employed to explore and identify the key system drivers, factors, and processes that influence the behaviour and sustainability of water-land-food resources nexus in the Volta River Basin, West Africa. Development of the archetypes centered on a generic causal loop diagram constructed with stakeholders in previous studies capturing the linkages between the population, water system, environmental and socioeconomics. These system archetypes illustrate that the past and the current paradigm of water and land and agricultural production management is unsustainable. The results highlight key areas, which could be useful for the current and future sustainable management, even under uncertain system understanding or deficiencies in quantitative data.

Keywords: system dynamics, system archetypes, systems thinking, drivers of change, water resources management, agricultural production, Volta River basin

1. Introduction

Variability and global change are realities of the Earth system, and during the past few decades, there has been growing evidence that planetary-scale changes are occurring rapidly [1–4]. Indeed, change is one of the few reliable phenomena

IntechOpen

in coupled social-environmental systems [5]. The critical feature of these global changes is described as 'directional', because it is characterised by a constant pattern over time [6]. They occur in both biophysical and socio-economic systems and manifest across all levels – from local to global [7]. Global change processes have dramatic effects and consequences for social-ecological system on which human communities depend. However, how societies respond to these changes can equally affect many managed natural resource management systems. To build a clear understanding, Anastasopoulou [8] argued that it is imperative to recognise the "agents or drivers" of those changes, which are a fundamental part of human existence.

The fundamental agents of environmental change that are external to particular systems can be considered as drivers of that change (e.g., climate change and socioeconomic change, national or international policy [5, 9, 10]. Drivers of change represent either the past, current or future conditions that modify the environment [8, 9]. Although some changes are caused by natural processes, it is widely argued that human activities (e.g., agriculture and the burning of fossil fuels) are the underlying forces driving change [11]. During the past two centuries, anthropogenic actions have induced significant changes in many environmental systems [2]. According to ([12], p. 13), "as early as the fourth century BC, Plato persuasively described extensive and insightful human impacts on forests: Hills that were once covered by forests and produced abundant pasture now produce only food for bees." The Sahara Desert was also described as a landscape of lakes and forest 7000 years ago [13]. Several change phenomena are also caused by globalisation, described as the compression of space and time scales concerning the flows of information, people, goods and services [14]. These processes and activities give rise to the phenomenon of global change [15].

The influence of humans on the global environmental system is so profound and persistent that the Nobel Laureate Paul Crutzen observed that we are now in a geological age called the Anthropocene [2]. Indeed, it is widely recognised that sustainability is the theme of our times and represents the greatest challenge in the Anthropocene [16]. While the concept Anthropocene is manifested in the nature, scale, and magnitude of human activities in the world, its societal significance rests on how we can take advantages of the changes to inform future decision choices and actions [17]. Indeed, understanding the Anthropocene calls for systematic thinking concerning the future, as both drivers and the concomitant consequences of human activities intensify towards an unsustainable trajectory [2, 15, 17].

Against the backdrop of changing environmental and socio-economic conditions, decision-makers are confronted with the situation of whether to act reactively or proactively. Often, they consider these changes and challenges as simple problems. Occasionally, however, the change is large and complex, thereby limiting their ability to design sustainable solutions to address them. If this happens, decision-makers find us to be facing an enormous problem, which can lead to far-reaching consequences for life support systems. Thus, the issue of rapid change has raised concern among scientists that several of the social-ecological systems present today could collapse by the end of the 21st century [18]. The situation has, therefore, necessitated a focus on the identification of key drivers of change and the resulting system dynamics to consider if it is possible that existing societies will be able to avoid their own decline or demise [3, 19]. Consequently, there is an increase in socio-economic and environmental system analysis and modelling studies that seek to gain an understanding of the trends and drivers of change in natural resource systems in the context of a changing earth system. These generally aim to improve the theory and strategic management of problems inherent social-ecological systems. Thus, understanding the problem of global change and the associated drivers of change in social-ecological systems are an urgent and relevant focus of this study. Further, given the increasing multiplicity of drivers of change associated with global change, there is a pressing need to develop an improved understanding of the interactive effects of multiple drivers, factors, and processes to better understand their responses to a changing environment.

The issue of global change and the associated drivers have resulted in fundamental transformations of many water-land-food systems [15, 20], such as River Basin systems around the world, including the Volta River Basin (VRB), which provides the case study context for this study. The VRB is an important trans-boundary river system (or 'catchment') in West Africa. As one of the 60 river basins in Africa, it supports the production of food, fibre, hydropower, and other products that are vital to West Africa's economy and the livelihoods of 25 million people who depend on the availability of the water that flows through the river basin system. During the last four to five decades, demographic pressures, land-use change, high rainfall variability, climate change, and the increased competition for land and water have combined temporally and spatially to affect sustainable water resource management and agricultural development within the river basin [21, 22]. There is tension between the aspirations of socio-economic development and environmental sustainability. However, the management of any water resource system can be challenging and difficult because of the complexities arising from the functioning of hydrological cycles and biological systems [23]. This is exacerbated when multiple stakeholder 'perspectives, interest, values and concerns regarding the use of water for human-related purposes are involved [23–25]. It is important to mention that the complex problems and challenges in the VRM is not different from the situation in Lake Chad basin in West and Central Africa due to massive exploitation by Cameroon, Chad, Niger and Nigeria [26–29].

As is often the case in many social-ecological systems or environmental systems, the most common approach to addressing problems in water resource systems is to adopt a linear cause–effect methodologies, reductionist, analytical approach (founded on positivistic understanding of science), where the focus is on only one or a few factors or parts of the system, and to accept that those explanations can only be partial [1, 24, 25]. However, the problems in most social-ecological systems, such as water resources systems are systemic, which means that biophysical and social systems are tightly interconnected and interdependent and cannot be understood in isolation [24, 25, 30]. They cannot be comprehended within the fragmented methodology characteristic of academic discipline and government agencies. This is because many current sustainability problems and challenges are closely linked in ways that challenge conventional linear causality [31]. As [32, 33] emphasised, such an approach will not resolve any of our difficulties but will tend to shift them around in a complex web of social and environmental relations. In sum, the problems and degradation of most catchments caused by several drivers of change continue to persist because they are rarely viewed, understood and managed using the systems approach. Consequently, actions to achieve sustainable goals will have to be based on an integrated modelling approach and a collaborative decision-making process.

In this chapter, we used systems archetypes based on system dynamics within the systems thinking to explore and identify the key system drivers, factors, and processes that influence the mode of behaviour and sustainability of water-land-food resources nexus in the Volta River Basin (henceforth, VRB), West Africa. The main aim to analyse and diagnose the difficulties in the management of sustainable development issues within the basin in order to find effective pathways to address these difficulties. Following this introduction, we present a brief definition of drivers of change (Section 2). A brief introduction to systems thinking and system dynamics modelling, and its associated tools are presented in Section 3, followed by methods and application of systems thinking framework and tool in Section 4. Section 5 presents the results, with a focus on the manifestation of the various system archetypes within the basin. Finally, the conclusion summarises the key results.

2. Defining and understanding drivers of change

The first step in system dynamics is the identification of the key issues and variables in the system whose behaviour over time defines the problem [31, 34, 35]. Accordingly, it is important to define what this study means by drivers of change. Over the past decade or so, a significant amount of work has emerged over the issue of drivers of system change [36]. The definition of a driver is aptly captured in two well-known frameworks – the Drivers-Pressures-State-Impact-Response (DPSIR) framework [37]; and the Millennium Ecosystem Assessment (MA) framework [38, 39]. Within the DPSIR framework, drivers are the underlying sources of environmental change that are exogenous to the system or region (e.g., climate and socio-economic change, national and international policy) [39]. They represent either the past, present or future conditions that lead to changes in the environment [9]. However, Tzanopoulos [40] argued that the usage of the term pressures in the framework seems to connote an implicit value and places emphasis on the negative impacts of human activity on environmental systems. Another noted limitation of the DPSIR framework is the dearth of constancy concerning its application to address environmental problems [9, 41]. According to ([41], p. 13), the DPSIR framework appears as "a deterministic and linear 'causal' description of environmental problems, which certainly overlooks the complexity of the environmental and socio-economic systems."

Thus, the definition of a driver captured in the Millennium Ecosystem Assessment framework appears to be one of the broadest and most widely used. In the MA framework, "a driver is any factor that changes an aspect of an ecosystem" [38, 39]. Different types of drivers are also distinguished in the framework: 'direct', and 'indirect drivers' of change. A 'direct driver' unequivocally influences ecosystem processes. 'Direct drivers' are predominantly physical, chemical, and biological, such as climate change, land cover change, air and water pollution, irrigation, use of fertilisers, harvesting, and the introduction of invasive alien species. An 'indirect driver' on the other hand, operates more diffusely by changing one or more direct drivers. These are mainly demographic, economic, socio-political, scientific and technological, and cultural and religious factors. 'Drivers' within the DPSIR framework are comparable to the 'indirect drivers' in the MA framework, while 'pressures' correspond to the 'direct drivers' of the MA [9, 40]. 'Direct' and 'indirect drivers' can be respectively be considered as proximate causes and underlying driving forces, according to [42, 43]. Regarding scale, proximate causes are seen to operate directly at the local level, while, underlying driving forces may manifest directly at the local scale, or indirectly, from the national or even global scale [42]. The categorisation of drivers based on the scale at which they operate has also been espoused [44]. However, the distinction between 'direct' and 'indirect drivers' may be difficult to delineate in some cases. For example, demographic variables can, for example, be direct drivers, but also represent underlying drivers (population growth) [45].

In several other studies, the factors or drivers of change in most ecosystems have also been variously characterised as 'exogenous controls', 'slow' changing variables and 'fast' changing variables [6, 46–50] or 'slower-acting', long-term drivers of change and 'fast-acting', short term drivers of change [51]. Exogenous controls are external factors such as regional climate or biota and global market conditions that strongly influence the properties of a system scale [6]. Critical 'slow' changing variables or processes are factors, such as population growth; income growth, soil fertility, household capital wealth among others, tend to act rather slowly and gradually over a lengthy time, and evolve in a somewhat predictable manner with impacts in the long-time period [46, 51]. In contrast, fast-moving variables or drivers of change (e.g. droughts, floods, rainfall variability, soil water content, crop yield, household disposable income, disease and pest outbreaks etc.) are variables that change very rapidly and might have influence on the agricultural system in the short time period [51, 52]. Slow-moving variables within natural resources systems greatly influence fast-changing variables at the same spatial scale [6].

In this study, the MA definition of drivers of change is used as it offers a flexible definition and analysis of drivers [40]. Thus, all types of drivers: direct, indirect, exogenous, endogenous, fast and slow-moving drivers or variables from both biophysical and socio-economic domains are considered, since most coupled social-environmental systems are not only affected by one individual driver, but rather a combination of different types of drivers at multiple scales [6, 52, 53]. "Drivers" are sometimes referred to as "variables". Thus, the two terms are used interchangeably. The focus here is to investigate how these drivers change over time and influence the sustainability of the VRB, particularly water availability and sustainable agricultural development.

3. Systems thinking and system methodology

For more than 60 years or so, systems thinking or systems approach [31, 34, 54–56] with its concomitant concepts and tools such as feedback, stocks and flows, time delays, and nonlinearity has evolved as one of the most promising approaches to confront this complexity. The idea of complex systems thinking can be traced back to Ludwig von Bertalabffy's General System Theory (GST) [57], and Ervin Laszlo's notion of systems philosophy [58]. Systems thinking approach is based on the notion that sustainability problems need to be informed by a holistic consideration of the system processes (biophysical, social, and economic), their dynamic interaction, and how they adapt to diverse changes [1, 59]. It challenges us to view the world as a complex system, in which we understand that "you can't just do one thing and that everything is connected to everything else." ([31], p. 4).

A systems approach has arisen as natural resource managers have reflected upon the practical implications of being holistic in their analysis of complex environmental systems. In terms of its application and purpose, [60] aptly explained that a "systems approach is necessary to serve the decision-makers' needs to understand the working system, compare impacts among decision scenarios, analyse trade-offs among options, ask 'What if?' questions, avoid the creation or transfer of problems in pursuing solutions to the problem at hand, adapt strategies based on future monitoring of the system, and respond to unintended consequences." The application of the systems approach to water resources management problems has been recognised as one of the most significant developments around water resources management [24]. In the context of natural resource management such as water resources planning, a systems approach is concerned with pursuing what can be described as an integrated environmental modelling (IEM) agenda, which is inspired by contemporary environmental challenges, policy-decisions, and facilitated by multidisciplinary science and computer capabilities – thus allowing the environment and its relationship to social systems and activities (i.e., social and economic) to be analysed as a complex integral whole [60, 61].

The idea of systems thinking provides a plethora of tools and methods for gaining a deeper understanding of sustainable development problems. One such tool is system dynamics [31, 34, 54]. System dynamics operate in a whole-system fashion using feedback-based object-oriented simulation is applied to explain and gain an insight into the complex behaviour and relationships between the key environmental, economic, social and institutional drivers, factors, and processes that determine the current and future dynamics of the Volta River Basin (VRB) water resource system in West Africa. System dynamics is an approach grounded in control theory and the theory of nonlinear dynamics [31]. System dynamics is a perspective and a set of conceptual tools that enable us to understand the structure and dynamics of complex systems [31]. It deals with "the time-dependent behaviour of managed systems as a means of describing the system and understanding, through qualitative and quantitative models, how information feedback governs its behaviour, and designing robust information feedback structures and control policies through simulation and optimisation" ([62], p. 10). According to [63], system dynamics models (even in their conceptual forms) are valuable learning tools that can assist us to increase our understanding of systems, allows modellers and stakeholders to integrate diverse knowledge, and enhance important systems thinking.

The field of system dynamics has focused on refining the classification of generic structures. These generic "infrastructures" are commonly based on stocks and flows [31, 64], generic "system archetypes" based on causal loop diagrams [55, 65, 66]. Stocks are accumulations characterising the state of the system and generate the information upon which decisions and actions are based [31]. Stocks (or levels) corresponds to accumulations of something (concrete or abstract) that can be measured at one point in time, whereas flow (inflow, outflow or biflow) refers to the activities that cause material or information to change over time [31, 35, 67]. System archetypes based on causal loop diagrammes are one class of system tools that can be used to capture the "common stories" or pattern of behaviour in system thinking – dynamic phenomena that repeatedly occur in diverse settings [55, 66]. They are generic system structures consisting of a common dynamic mechanism from which both unintended behaviour over time and discrete events emerge [68]. They are powerful tools for diagnosing problems and identifying high-leverage interventions that will create fundamental change [66]. In addition, system archetypes are particularly helpful in identifying rapidly- and slowly-changing variables and stabilising and destabilising forces [69]. Consequently, they can be used as a diagnostic tool to explain problems that recur over time. Senge [55] proposed nine system archetypes: (1) balancing process and delay, (2) limits to growth, (3) shifting the burden, (4) eroding goals, (5) escalation, (6) success to the successful, (7) tragedy of the commons, (8) fixes that fail, and (9) growth and underinvestment. Each system archetype is accompanied by a well-established set of strategies for dealing with the problematic behaviour through effective interventions in the underlying structure of the system [68].

These archetypes are generally presented in the form of a causal loop diagram (CLD) also referred to as dynamic hypothesis. A CLD typically consists of variables connected by arrows denoting the causal influences among the variables [31] . Variables are usually connected by link polarities (i.e., combinations of positive and/or negative links), which describe the structure of the system, and not the behaviour of the variables [31]. A positive link indicates "that if the cause increases, the effect increases above what it would otherwise have been, and if the cause decreases, the effect decreases below what it would otherwise have been, whereas a negative link denotes that if the cause increases, the effect decreases below what it would otherwise have been, and if the cause decreases, the effect increases above what it would otherwise have been" ([31], p. 139) (see **Figure 1**). CLDs are generally formal, flexible, simple, and largely qualitative [55, 65, 70]. Further, a CLD is characterised

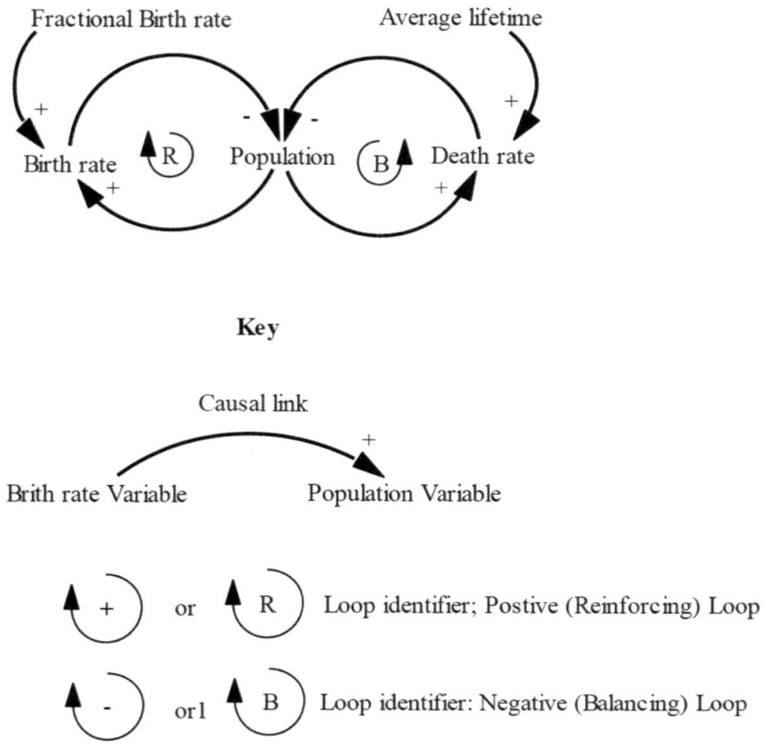

Figure 1.
Causal loop diagram notation (adapted from Sterman [31]).

by two fundamental feedback loops: reinforcing (positive) and balancing (negative) loops. Reinforcing (R) feedback loops are prevented from growing or declining uninterruptedly with balancing (B) loops, which create self-correcting processes that lead to stability and equilibrium and reaching a goal or objective [31, 35].

There is also the presence of delays, which relates to the time it takes diverse groups of stakeholders to make decisions (information delays), the time it takes to implement processes (material delay), or time required for various processes to occur [35]. CLDs are useful for mapping, inferring, and visualising what contributes to growth, decline, delay, or stability, and mostly used at the strategy level r [35]. Although the individual feedback loops are critical to enabling informed decision-making, from the management point of view, it is the system's governing archetypal behaviour that can help managers recognise patterns of behaviour that are already present in a system [71–73]. Thus, reinforcing and balancing feedback loops are principally the basic system archetypes [73]. In this chapter, system archetypes have been used to better understand the feedback structure and long-term behavioural patterns of interacting elements of biophysical and socio-economic issues in the VRB.

4. Methods: application of systems thinking framework and tool

4.1 Characteristics of the study area

The systems thinking approach and its concomitant tool (system archetypes) based on System dynamics was applied in the Volta River Basin, which is in West

Africa. It is the 9th largest in sub-Saharan Africa. It occupies an area of about 400,000Km^2 within the sub-humid to semi-arid West African Savannah zone (**Figure 2**). It extends approximately between latitude 50.30 N–140 30 N and between 20.00 E and 50.30 W. The widest stretch is roughly on longitude 50 30 W to 20 00 E; however, it becomes narrower as it enters the sea (the Atlantic Ocean) at the Gulf of Guinea [74, 75]. It is a trans-boundary river basin shared among six riparian West African countries: Burkina Faso, Ghana, and Togo, Benin, Cote d'Ivoire, and Mali, making it an ethnically and culturally diverse basin. The basin's population stood at 23.8 million in 2010; however, this is expected to reach 56.1 million by 2050 [22]. The spatial distribution of the population within the basin varies with an average population of about 58 persons/km^2; however, this average masks differences between riparian countries [21]. Subsistence or small-holder agriculture and livestock production is the mainstay of the basin economy. The main challenge is how to manage the natural resources of the basin to improve food security, reduce poverty and promote economic development, without further degradation of the natural ecosystems for present and future generations [21].

4.2 Construction of the system model

In this study, the development of the system model followed three steps as follow: a general definition of the system boundary, the identification of the problematic issues (drivers or critical variables), and modelling of the interactions between the key drivers and components (generic CLD). Models of system dynamics are delineated by closed boundaries (causally closed models) where endogenous components and factors (those originating from within) are assumed to form the system structure and predominantly dictate the behaviour of the system [35]. Defining a study boundary encompasses selecting a scale/boundary of analysis by drawing artificial boundaries

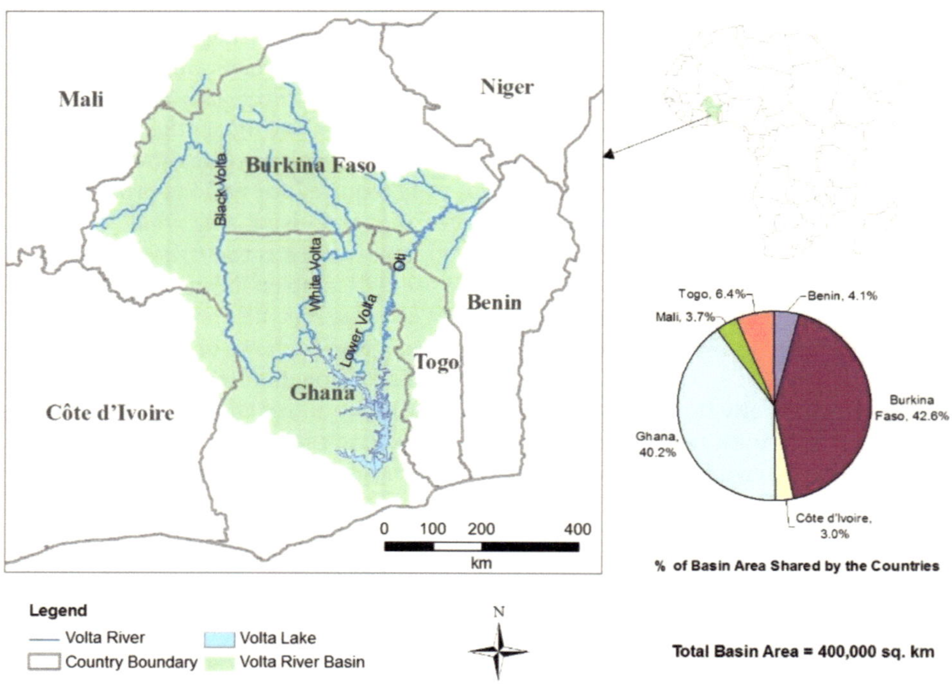

Figure 2.
The Volta River basin showing important political boundaries [76].

around it [77]. Also, the establishment of boundaries is necessary for a simpler, more tractable, and more feasible approach [78] to the phenomenon under investigation. The place or scale selected then becomes the focus of the study, with an understanding that processes at smaller and larger scales, in addition to historical and future trajectory, are crucial for gaining adequate insight into the sustainability of natural resources systems [77]. As [79] suggest, scaling or boundary issues can be partly be addressed appropriately "bounding" social-ecological systems. Thus, the geographical boundary of this study is restricted to the Volta River Basin of West Africa.

The second next stage of the analysis involved exploring and identifying the environmental and socio-economic drivers of change and processes, with a focus on understanding how such changes influence sustainable agriculture development within the Volta River Basin (VRB) [80]. To do this, a combination of comprehensive review of existing studies, semi-structured interviews and structured expert judgements technique (see [81–83]) was used to identify and characterise the key biophysical and socio-economic drivers and processes of change within the Volta River Basin, West Africa. Specifically, interviews were conducted with farmers, extension officers and scientists working in the areas of water, soil, environmental science, rural geography, agricultural science and economics, rural sociology and political science. Overall, these individuals identified 51 drivers of change as most critical to the sustainability of the basin (see **Figure 3**).

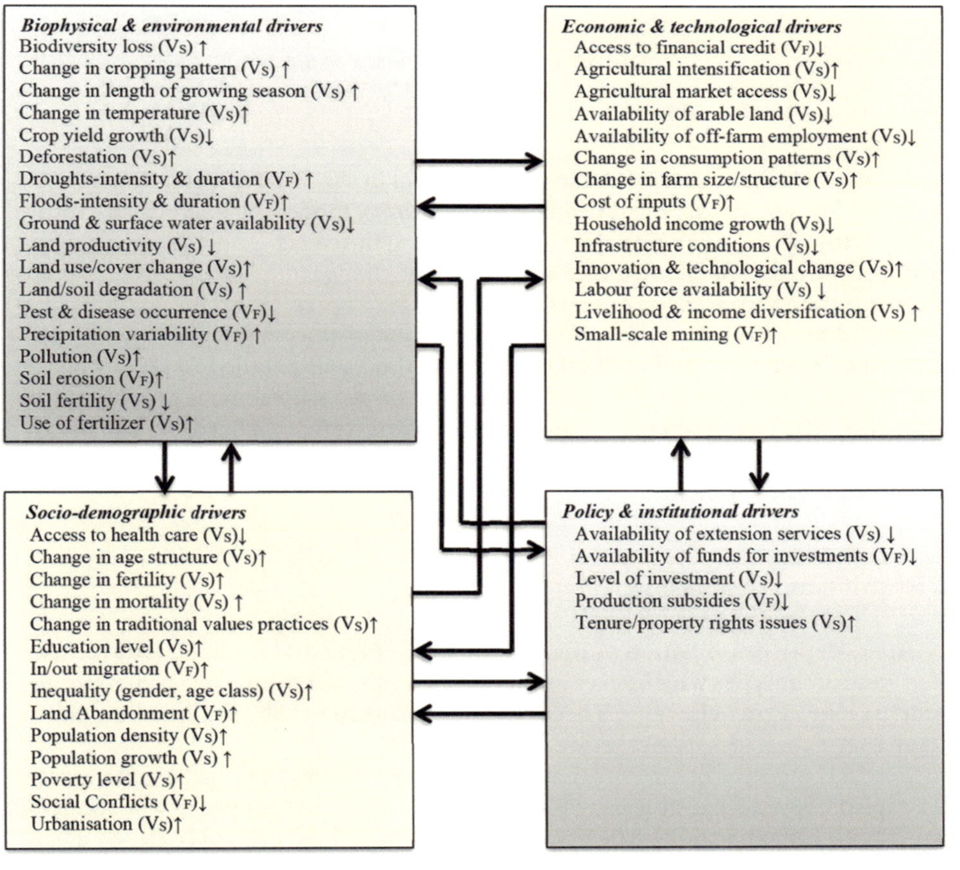

Figure 3.
A simplified model of drivers of change identified in the Volta River basin and their interactions. VS denotes "slow changing variables", while VF denotes "fast changing variables". ↑ indicates increasing trend in the driver, while ↓ indicates decreasing trend [80].

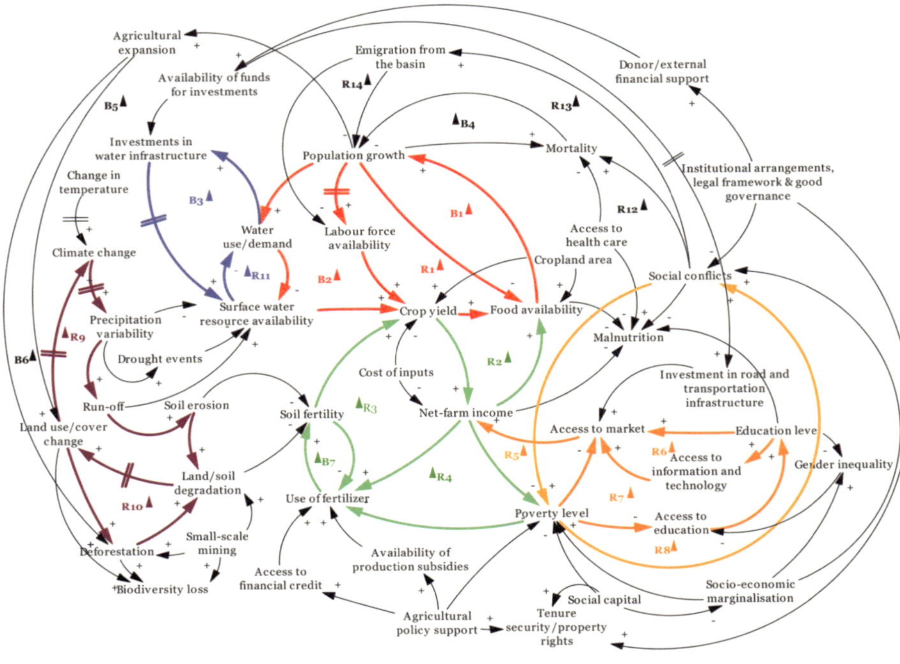

Figure 4.
Integrated conceptual model of the Volta River basin. ("+") indicate a positive link; ("–") indicates negative link. (R) Denotes a reinforcing (or positive) loop; (B) denotes a balancing (or negative) loop. \\ (delay marks) on the arrows denotes time delay perceived to be relevant to the dynamics of the system [84].

Third, and finally, a conceptual system model in the form of a causal loop diagram (CLD), was constructed through participatory modelling exercise to capture the structure and function of the VRB, indicating the cause–effect relationships and feedback loops between the important drivers of change and key variables based on the information from the driver identification (see **Figure 4**). In this chapter, CLD is referred to as the generic model. The description of the main drivers giving rise to problem symptoms and issues identification process is detailed in [80], while the methods underpinning the construction of the generic model is provided in [84]. Here, the main interest is to present five main system archetypes, which can be identified from the generic CLD to assist in sustainable natural resources and agricultural development.

5. Results and discussion

An in-depth examination of the generic CLD (**Figure 4**) revealed four forms of system archetypes which serve as diagnostic tools, describing or predicting the system's long-term behaviour. These are Limits to growth" Shifting the Burden", Fixes-that-Fail, and, and Tragedy of the Commons.

The first mode of behaviour that can be observed from the conceptual model is "Limits to Growth" hypothesis, which states that a reinforcing process of accelerating growth (or expansion) will always be counteracted (or pushed back) by a balancing process [85]. This archetype consists of a reinforcing and a balancing loop, as illustrated in **Figure 5a**. In this example, it appears that water shortage induced by climate variability and change (e.g., high rainfall variability, droughts) appear to be the limiting factors constraining agricultural production and water availability

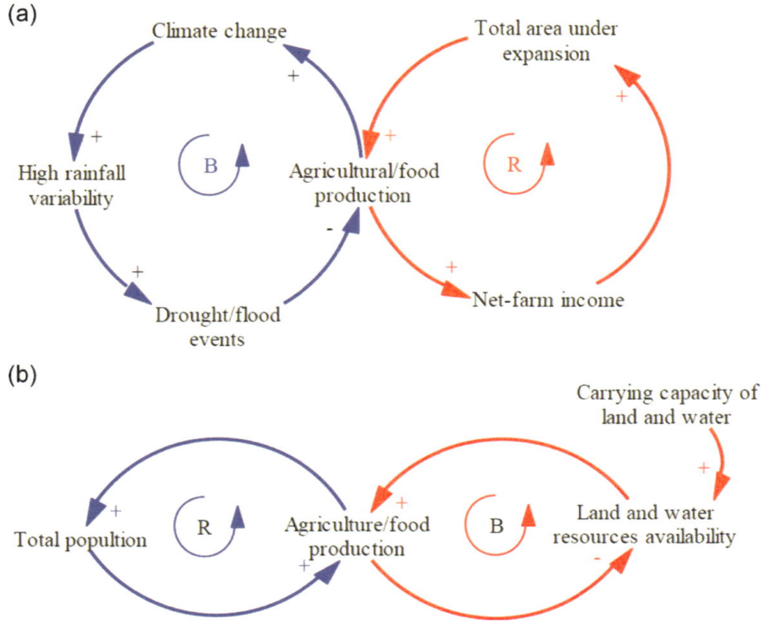

Figure 5.
Limits to growth archetypes in VRB for climate change and agricultural production (a) and population dynamics and agricultural production (b).

in the basin. The dominant management strategy and policy within the basin has so far, been focused on increasing agricultural production while neglecting other productive sectors (e.g., tourism). However, as depicted the resources (such as water and land) required to support sustainable agricultural production may reach their limits (i.e., carrying capacities) due to population growth and climate change. **Figure 5b** also illustrates how agricultural development and food production stimulated on by population growth is limited by the unavailability of water and land, once the system reached carrying capacity. Overall, these limitations may lead the system to the path of unsustainability or functional collapse, thereby exacerbating food and water insecurity. In its simplest form, "Limits to growth" could be seen as highly resilient, because the system's ability to shift to an alternate state is non-existent. However, few systems are this resilient. Thus, the management lesson learned from this archetype is that some element always pushes the system back, so that 'if we do not plan for limits, we are planning for failure [55, 71].

This is even more so, given recent analysis in the basin which predicted that water availability will be further decreased by elevated temperatures and increased evapotranspiration [86]. In order to anticipate future problems and eliminate them before they become a threat, the growth engines and potential limiting or constraining forces need to be identified and addressed. In this regard, supporting adaptation strategies and investment in water infrastructure efforts will help to alleviate the problem in the longer term. There is a need for a long-term approach, to foresee the best strategies for adaptation to climate change and manage risk in the variable environment of the basin [87, 88].

Available evidence indicates that farmers within the basin have traditionally pursued shifting cultivation in response to population growth and declining soil fertility. As population pressure increased, they opened new land by extending farming into forests, wetlands, hillsides, and pastures. In the short term, this strategy has increased food production but the implications of agricultural expansion as "quick fix" is gradually emerging as continued expansion is leading to other undesirable environmental consequences (e.g., land/soil degradation, deforestation) which is exacerbating the problem of low agricultural production and food insecurity. In the systems thinking realm, this behaviour demonstrates quick fixes "Fixes that Fail" mode of behaviour archetype (**Figure 6**). The theory of Fixes that Backfire archetype posits that short-sighted solutions that relieve the symptoms of a problem without addressing the root causes create a weak balancing loop that will entail unintended consequences [72]. The quick-fix solution triggers a stronger reinforcing loop, which causes the problem to re-erupt in the future in an aggravated form, often with challenging unintended consequences. Douxchamps et al. [88] provide a good illustration of how the archetype of "Fixes that Failed" manifested in the basin in their analysis of some policy failures within the basin. For instance, in attempt to control persistent erosions in the 1960s, agriculture water management strategies were promoted throughout the basin for cash crop production in large scale state projects relying on technology transfer as means of dissemination. However, after the first wave of droughts of the 1970s and the associated food shortages, the focus moved to staple crop production and promotion of soil and water conservation techniques through large scale projects. This was attributed to approaches that were too much top-down, with experts as exclusive actors, projects were too shorts with "silver bullet" solutions, there was a lack of consideration for farmers' preferences and traditions.

Consequently, when the second wave of droughts retuned in the 1980s, the smallholders were not better prepared and once again they were severely impacted by loss of yields and income. To avoid this problem in future, there is the need for decision-makers to think in terms of participatory approach and pay attention to indigenous knowledge [88, 89]. The analysis indicates that to move forward, policymakers and stakeholders should pay more attention to fundamental solutions rather than quick fixes that often create unintentional consequences [68]. This mode of behaviour also suggests that we need to identify high-leverage interventions that minimise investment while still resolving the fundamental problem.

Since the early 1980s, policymakers have persistently relied on donor and external financial support to address the issue of chronic poverty, water scarcity, and low agricultural production2050 [22]. As depicted in **Figure 7**, this is a classic case of 'Shifting the Burden' to the donors and external funders rather than finding innovative solutions to the problems. The Shifting the Burden archetype rest on the linear reductionist thinking, which characterises a situation where managers tend to implement an

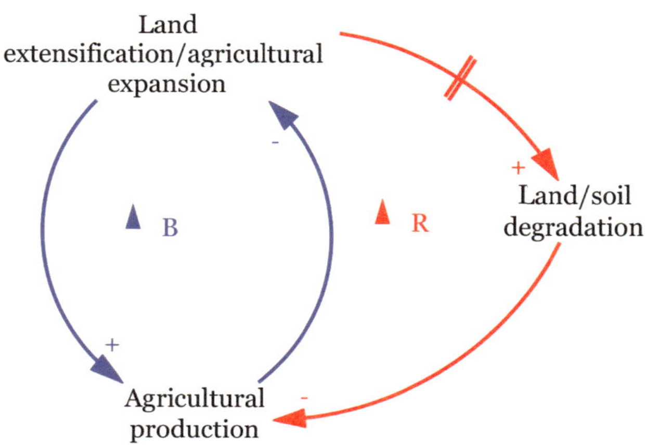

Figure 6.
"Fixes that Fail" archetype in relation to agricultural expansion and land expansion in the VRB.

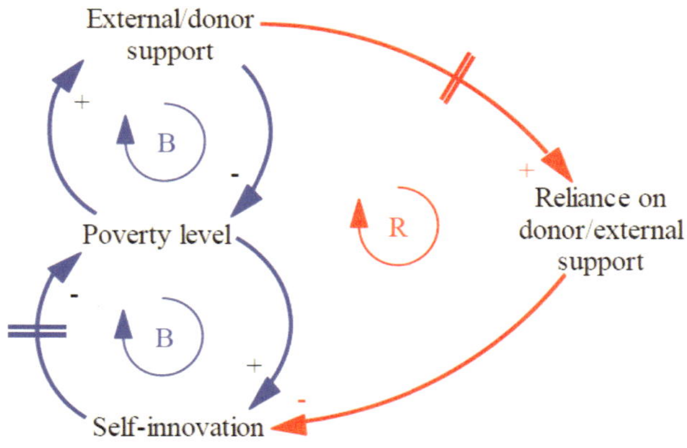

Figure 7.
"Shifting the Burden" archetype for poverty reduction in the VRB.

'easy fix' to a problem, rather than a finding a sustainable long-term solution. The Shifting the Burden archetypes indicates how a problem can exacerbate when we depend so much on donor, NGO or external support model of development instead of self-innovation or capacity development to address socio-economic problems. The situation does not look good given that currently, donor support within the basin is waning and issues of poverty, food and water insecurity, and low agricultural production are retuning, therefore, exacerbate the real problems. Further, this archetype demonstrates while it is undoubtedly true that donors have had a positive role in providing support for natural resources programmes, a narrowly focused policy can make the situation worse, especially if they generate policy resistance [90, 91]. Policy resistance results from the tendency for an intervention to be jeopardised by the system's response to the intervention itself [31, 64, 90].

The final system archetype identifiable from the overall conceptual model is Tragedy of the Commons". In the tragedy of the commons archetype, a reinforcing loop is created by the activity of system actors with the aim of the intention of increasing rewards for themselves. However, an unintended consequence is that the activity results in overuse of and damage to the environment, which reduces the magnitude of the outcome for all [65]. As stated earlier, the water resources in the Volta Basin contribute significantly to the economic development of the six riparian countries. This is the case particularly for Burkina Faso and Ghana, where more than 60% of the area of each country is located within the VRB [89]. Interestingly, but not surprisingly, rising demands on the resources have resulted in intense competition between the two countries. For example, while Ghana uses the water for industrial purposes, such as hydropower generation, Burkina Faso uses it for agricultural purposes.

In the Tragedy of the Commons archetype, the two competing countries (Ghana and Burkina Faso are represented (**Figure 8**). Each of these countries is involved in the use of the common resources, which in this case is the water resource available in the basin. As both countries activities go up, their net gains also go up. In other words, initially, the reinforcing loops R1 and R2 drive the system such that each country achieves some level of socio-economic development. Consequently, increasing their level of activities to the resources the reinforcing loops allows the countries to achieve more significant gains all the time. All the activities sum up to the total activity. Thus, an increase in the total amount of water used reduces the water available per user, thus making both countries more vulnerable to disruptions of the water supply. This occurs because the total activity is greater than the resource limits. The tragedy occurs, therefore when the resource is depleted,

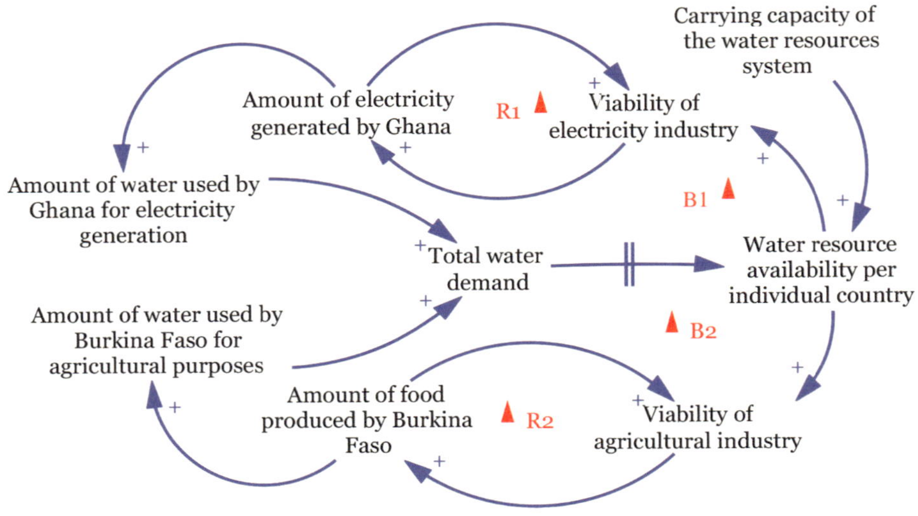

Figure 8.
Water resource usage "Tragedy of the Commons" archetype.

suggesting the need set up a joint management strategy. At this point, the balancing loops B1 and B2 dominate the system's dynamic behaviour. This archetype demonstrates how the development ambition of these countries could be hampered, which, in turn, could exacerbate poverty in the basin.

In this situation, there is a substantial risk of a further tragedy of the water commons unless the two countries work closely together in terms of using the available water resources. There is also the need for a mechanism, which promotes the coordinated development and management of water, land and related resources, without compromising the sustainability of vital eco-systems. There must also be an agreement to share and sustainably use the available resources.

6. Conclusion

In this chapter, generic system structures (system archetypes) based on system dynamics is used to integrate the relationships between the environmental, economic, social and institutional factors feedbacks driving the behaviour and viability of the Volta River Basin in West Africa, particularly as they relate to water resources management and agricultural production systems. Specifically, four common systems archetypes: Limits-to-Growth, Fixes-that-Fail, Shifting the Burden" and Tragedy of the Commons" are used to illustrate how system structure works. These system archetypes illustrate that the past and the current paradigm of water and land and agricultural production management is unsustainable. The analysis showed how decisions in one part of the system might impact decisions at other parts. For example, the limit to growth archetype illustrates the effect of climate change, population growth on water, and agricultural production and land availability. The "Shifting the Burden" and "Fixes that Fail" highlight the implication of using long-term rather than short term solutions to solve problems involving the interaction between water, food and agricultural systems. The "Tragedy of the Commons" mode of behaviour pointed how different development goals pursued by various countries in the basin (Ghana and Burkina Faso) have the potential to lead to depletion of the available water and land resources and economic returns for countries. It has also been shown that decision-makers need to be aware that synergies and trade-offs between sectors need to be considered in the management and allocation of water and land and food resources.

The chapter also provides a practical demonstration of how common patterns of dynamic behaviours may be used to support water resource management decision-making exemplified in the VRB, including planning for the systemic problems before they become a threat, limiting the reliance on donor support, avoiding an easy and quick fix to the underlying problems, promoting coordinated development and management of water. As with many system tools, the conceptual model developed in this study is the simplification of real problems in the basin. They are not comprehensive models of the very complex reality in the system. Nevertheless, they can serve as useful diagnostic tools for improving decision-makers' ability to analyse and foresee potential systemic problems and, communicating such issues with others and developing strategies to cope with them effectively.

Acknowledgements

This research was supported financially by The Commonwealth Scientific and Industrial Research Organisation (CSIRO), Australia through the Integrated Natural Resource Management (INRM) science program and School Research Grant (SRG) from the School of Earth and Environmental Sciences, University of Queensland, Australia. The author also appreciates the critical feedback from the anonymous editor and reviewers.

Author details

Julius H. Kotir[1,2]

1 School of Earth and Environmental Sciences, University of Queensland, Brisbane, QLD, Australia

2 CSIRO Agriculture and Food, Toowoomba, QLD, Australia

*Address all correspondence to: julius.kotir@csiro.au; jkotir22@gmail.com

References

[1] Liu J et al. Systems integration for global sustainability. Science. 2015;**347**(6225):1258832

[2] Steffen W et al. Planetary boundaries: Guiding human development on a changing planet. Science. 2015;**347**(6223):1259855

[3] Schimel D et al. Analysis, integration and modeling of the earth system (AIMES): Advancing the post-disciplinary understanding of coupled human–environment dynamics in the Anthropocene. Anthropocene. 2016;**12**:99-106

[4] Bradford JB et al. Anticipatory natural resource science and management for a changing future. Frontiers in Ecology and the Environment. 2018;**16**(5):295-303

[5] Diekmann A, Franzen A. Environmental concern: A global perspective. In: Mayerl J, Krause T, Wahl A, Wuketich M, editors. Einstellungen und Verhalten in der empirischen Sozialforschung. VS, Wiesbaden: Springer; 2019. pp. 253-272

[6] Chapin FS, Folke C, Kofinas GP. A framework for understanding change. In: Chapin FS, Kofinas PG, Folke C, editors. Principles of Ecosystem Stewardship Resilience-Based Natural Resource Management in a Changing World. New York: Springer Science+Business Media, LLC; 2009. pp. 3-28

[7] Petschel-Held G et al. Drivers of ecosystem change. In: Findings of the Condition and Trends Working Group of the Millennium Ecosystem Assessment, Hassan R, et al., editors. Cosystems and Human Well-being: Current State and Trends. Washington D.C: Island Press; 2005

[8] Anastasopoulou S, et al. Identufying and Assessing socio-economic and environmental drivers that affect ecosystems and their services, Report Project RUBICODE. 2009

[9] Rounsevell M, Dawson T, Harrison P. A conceptual framework to assess the effects of environmental change on ecosystem services. Biodiversity and Conservation. 2010;**19**(10):2823-2842

[10] Barnett J. Global environmental change I: Climate resilient peace? Progress in Human Geography. 2018;**43**(5):927-936

[11] Oldfield F et al. The anthropocene review: Its significance, implications and the rationale for a new transdisciplinary journal. The Anthropocene Review. 2014;**1**(1):3-7

[12] Vallejo R. Problems and perspectives of dryland restoration. In: Bautista S, Aronson J, Vallejo RV, editors. Land Restoration to Combat Desertification Innovative Approaches, Quality Control and Project Evaluation. Valencia, Spain: Fundación Centro de Estudios Ambientales del Mediterráneo – CEAM; 2009. pp. 13-22

[13] Brown O, Crawford A, Brown O, Crawford A. Climate Change and Security in Africa, Canada: Manitoba: IISD, 8; 2009

[14] Berkes F. Implementing ecosystem-based management: Evolution or revolution? Fish and Fisheries. 2012;**13**(4):465-476

[15] Momblanch A et al. Untangling the water-food-energy-environment nexus for global change adaptation in a complex Himalayan water resource system. Science of the Total Environment. 2019;**655**:35-47

[16] Wu J. Landscape sustainability science: Ecosystem services and

human well-being in changing landscapes. Landscape Ecology. 2013;**28**(6):999-1023

[17] Bai X et al. Plausible and desirable futures in the anthropocene: A new research agenda. Global Environmental Change. 2015;**39**:351-362

[18] Ostrom E. A general framework for analyzing sustainability of social-ecological systems. Science. 2009;**325**(5939):419

[19] Polhill JG et al. Modelling systemic change in coupled socio-environmental systems. Environmental Modelling and Software. 2016;**75**:318-332

[20] Zare F et al. Improved integrated water resource modelling by combining DPSIR and system dynamics conceptual modelling techniques. Journal of Environmental Management. 2019;**246**:27-41

[21] Kolavalli S, Williams TO. Socioeconomic trends and drivers of change. In: Williams TO, Smakhtin V, Biney AC, Mul LM, editors. The Volta River Basin: Water for food, economic growth and environment. New York: Routledge; 2016. pp. 33-50

[22] Williams TO et al. The Volta River basin: Water for food, economic growth and environment. In: Earthscan Series on Major River Basins of the World. Routledge; 2016

[23] Antunes P et al. Participation and evaluation for sustainable river basin governance. Ecological Economics. 2009;**68**(4):931-939

[24] Simonovic SP. Managing Water Resources: Methods and Tools for a Systems Approach. London: Earthscan James & James; 2009

[25] Pahl-Wostl C et al. From applying panaceas to mastering complexity: Toward adaptive water governance in river basins. Environmental Science and Policy. 2012;**23**:24-34

[26] Sylvestre F et al. The Lake CHAd deep DRILLing project (CHADRILL)–targeting~ 10 million years of environmental and climate change in Africa. Scientific Drilling. 2018;**24**:71-78

[27] Adeyeri O et al. Analysis of climate extreme indices over the Komadugu-Yobe basin, Lake Chad region: Past and future occurrences. Weather and Climate Extremes. 2019;**23**:100194

[28] Moritz M, Scholte P, Hamilton IM, Kari S. Open access, open systems: Pastoral resource management in the Chad Basin. In: Ludomir LR, McGovern, Thomas H, editors. Global Perspectives on Long Term Community Resource Management. Switzerland AG: Springer; 2019. pp. 165-187

[29] Mahmood R, Jia S, Zhu W. Analysis of climate variability, trends, and prediction in the most active parts of the Lake Chad basin, Africa. Scientific Reports. 2019;**9**(1):6317

[30] Gain AK, Giupponi C. A dynamic assessment of water scarcity risk in the lower Brahmaputra River basin: An integrated approach. Ecological Indicators. 2015;**48**:120-131

[31] Sterman JD. Business Dynamics: Systems Thinking and Modeling for a Complex World. Boston, Massachusetts, USA: Irwin/ McGraw-Hill; 2000

[32] Capra F. The Turning Point: Science, Society, and the Rising Culture. London: Flamingo; 1982

[33] Capra F. The Web of Life: A New Scientific Understanding of Living Systems. New York: Random House Inc; 1996

[34] Forrester JW. Industrial Dynamics. Vol. 2. Cambridge, MA: MIT Press; 1961

[35] Amadei B. A systems approach to modeling the water-energy-land-food nexus, System Dynamics Modeling and Dynamic Scenario Planning. Vol. II. New York: Momentum Press; 2019

[36] Walker BH et al. Drivers, "slow" variables, "fast" variables, shocks, and resilience. Ecology and Society. 2012;**17**(3):30

[37] Rapport D. Towards a comprehensive framework for environmental statistics: A stress-response approach. Statistics Canada 11-510, Ottawa, 1979; 1979

[38] MA. Ecosystems and Human Well-Being: A Framework for Assessment. Washington, DC: Island Press; 2003. p. 245

[39] MA. Ecosystem and Human Well-Being. Vol. 2. Washington DC: Island Press; 2005

[40] Tzanopoulos J et al. Scale sensitivity of drivers of environmental change across Europe. Global Environmental Change. 2013;**23**(1):167-178

[41] Maxim L, Spangenberg JH, O'Connor M. An analysis of risks for biodiversity under the DPSIR framework. Ecological Economics. 2009;**69**(1):12-23

[42] Geist HJ, Lambin EF. What drives tropical deforestation. LUCC Report Series. 2001;**4**:116

[43] Geist HJ, Lambin EF. Proximate causes and underlying driving forces of tropical deforestation. Bioscience. 2002;**52**(2):143-150

[44] Hazell P, Wood S. Drivers of change in global agriculture. Philosophical Transactions of the Royal Society, B: Biological Sciences. 2008;**363**(1491):495-515

[45] Kolb M, Mas J-F, Galicia L. Evaluating drivers of land-use change and transition potential models in a complex landscape in southern Mexico. International Journal of Geographical Information Science. 2013;**27**(9):1804-1827

[46] Carpenter SR, Turner MG. Hares and tortoises: Interactions of fast and slow variables in ecosystems. Ecosystems, 2000;**3**(6):495-497

[47] Gunderson LH, Pritchard L. Resilience and the Behavior of Large-Scale Systems. Vol. 60. Washington D.C: Island Press; 2002

[48] Bathiany S et al. Abrupt climate change in an oscillating world. Scientific Reports. 2018;**8**(1):5040

[49] Berrouet LM, Machado J, Villegas-Palacio C. Vulnerability of socio—Ecological systems: A conceptual framework. Ecological Indicators. 2018;**84**:632-647

[50] Bukowski L. Designing complex engineered systems for the risky environment. In: Reliable, Secure and Resilient Logistics Networks. Cham: Springer; 2019. pp. 93-150

[51] Msangi S, Rosegrant M. World agriculture in a dynamically changing environment: IFPRI's long-term outlook for food and agriculture. In: Conforti P, editor. Looking Ahead in World Food and Agriculture: Perspectives to 2050. Rome: FAO; 2011. pp. 57-93

[52] Cosens B. Introduction to the Special Feature Practicing Panarchy: Assessing legal flexibility, ecological resilience, and adaptive governance in regional water systems experiencing rapid environmental change. 2018

[53] Huber-Sannwald E et al. Navigating challenges and opportunities of land degradation and sustainable livelihood development in dryland social–ecological systems: A case study from Mexico. Philosophical Transactions of

the Royal Society, B: Biological Sciences. 2012;**367**(1606):3158-3177

[54] Forrester JW. Industrial dynamics: A major breakthrough for decision makers. Harvard Business Review. 1958;**36**(4):37-66

[55] Senge PM. The Fifth Discipline: The Art & Practice of the Learning Organization. Sydney, New South Wales, Australia: Random House; 1990

[56] Richmond B, Peterson S. An Introduction to Systems Thinking. High performance systems. Hanover: isee systems; 2001

[57] Von Bertalanffy L. General System Theory: Foundations, Development, Applications. Braziller: New York; 1969

[58] Laszlo E. Introduction to Systems Philosophy: Toward a New Paradigm of Contemporary Thought. New York: Gordon & Breach; 1972

[59] Levin S et al. Social-ecological systems as complex adaptive systems: Modeling and policy implications. Environment and Development Economics. 2013;**18**(02):111-132

[60] Laniak GF et al. Integrated environmental modeling: A vision and roadmap for the future. Environmental Modelling and Software. 2013;**39**:3-23

[61] Hamilton SH et al. Integrated assessment and modelling: Overview and synthesis of salient dimensions. Environmental Modelling and Software. 2015;**64**:215-229

[62] Coyle RG. System Dynamics Modeling. A Practical Approach. London: Chapman and Hall; 1996

[63] Kelly RA et al. Selecting among five common modelling approaches for integrated environmental assessment and management. Environmental Modelling and Software. 2013;**47**:159-181

[64] Forrester JW. A response to Ansoff and Slevin. Management Science. 1968;**14**(9):601-618

[65] Wolstenholme EF. Towards the definition and use of a core set of archetypal structures in system dynamics. System Dynamics Review. 2003;**19**(1):7-26

[66] Kim DH. Systems Archetypes I: Diagnosing Systemic Issues and Designing High-Leverage Interventions. Encino CA: Pegasus Communications; 2000

[67] Ford A. Modeling the Environment: An Introduction to System Dynamics Modeling of Environmental Systems. 2nd ed. Washington, DC: Island Press; 2010

[68] Brzezina N et al. Development of organic farming in Europe at the crossroads: Looking for the way forward through system archetypes lenses. Sustainability. 2017;**9**(5):821

[69] Bennett E et al. Scenarios for ecosystem services: Rationale and overview. In: Carpenter SR, editor. Ecosystems and Human Well-Being: Scenarios: Findings of the Scenarios. Vol. 2. Washington DC, USA: Millenium Ecosystem Assessment, Island Press; 2005

[70] Bennett E, Cumming G, Peterson G. A systems model approach to determining resilience surrogates for case studies. Ecosystems. 2005;**8**(8):945-957

[71] Senge PM. The Fifth Discipline: The Art and Practice of the Learning Organization. London: Random House Business Books; 2006

[72] Gohari A et al. Water transfer as a solution to water shortage: A fix that can backfire. Journal of Hydrology. 2013;**491**:23-39

[73] Mirchi A et al. Synthesis of system dynamics tools for holistic conceptualization of water resources problems. Water Resources Management. 2012;**26**(9):2421-2442

[74] Gordon C et al. West Africa–water resources vulnerability using a multidimensional approach: Case study of Volta Basin. In: Pielke RA, Adegoke J, Wright YC, editors. Climate Vulnerability: Understanding and Addressing Threats to Essential Resources. Vulnerability of Human Health to Climate. Vol. 1. USA: Elsevier Inc. Academic Press; 2013. pp. 283-309

[75] Barry B et al. The Volta River basin. In: Comprehensive Assessment of Water Management in Agriculture Comparative Study of River basin Development and Management. Colombo: International Water Management Institute (IWMI); 2005

[76] Gao Y, Margolies A. Transboundary water governance in the Volta River basin. 2009. Available from: https://wikis.uit.tufts.edu/confluence/display/aquapedia/Transboundary+Water+Governance+in+the+Volta+River+Basin [Accessed: 23-08-2015]

[77] Schröter D, Polsky C, Patt AG. Assessing vulnerabilities to the effects of global change: An eight step approach. Mitigation and Adaptation Strategies for Global Change. 2005;**10**(4):573-595

[78] Robinson J et al. Land-use and land-cover projections. In: Meyer W, Turner B, editors. Changes in Land Use and Land Cover: A Global Perspective. Cambridge, UK: Cambridge University Press; 1994

[79] Carpenter S et al. From metaphor to measurement: Resilience of what to what? Ecosystems. 2001;**4**(8):765-781

[80] Kotir JH et al. Drivers of change and sustainability in linked social–ecological systems: An analysis in the Volta river basin of Ghana, West Africa. Society and Natural Resources. 2017;**30**(10):1229-1245

[81] Perera AH, Drew A, Johnson JC, editors. Expert Knowledge and its Application in Landscape Ecology. New York: Springer; 2012

[82] Drescher M et al. Eliciting expert knowledge of forest succession using an innovative software tool. In: Perera HA, Drew A, Johnson JC, editors. Expert Knowledge and its Application in Landscape Ecology. New York, USA: Springer Science+Business Media, LLC; 2012. pp. 69-86

[83] Meyer MA, Booker JM. Eliciting and analyzing expert judgment: A practical guide. In: ASA-SIAM Series on Statistics and Applied Probability. London: American Statistical Association and the Society for Industrial and Applied Mathematics (ASA-SIAM); 2001

[84] Kotir JH et al. Systemic feedback modelling for sustainable water resources management and agricultural development: An application of participatory modelling approach in the Volta River basin. Environmental Modelling and Software. 2017;**88**:106-118

[85] Meadows DH et al. The Limits to Growth. New York: Universe Books Publishers; 1972

[86] Laube et al. GLOWA Volta Policy Brief. 2008. Available from: https://www.internationalrivers.org/sites/default/files/attached-files/glowa_volta_policy_brief_bui_dam_17_03_08.pdf. [Accessed: 02-08-2019]

[87] Yaro JA, Hesselberg J, editors. Adaptation to Climate Change and Variability in Rural West Africa. Switzerland: Springer International Publishing; 2016

[88] Douxchamps S, Ayantunde A, Barron J. Evolution of Agricultural Water Management in Rainfed Crop-Livestock Systems of the Volta Basin. Colombo, Sri Lanka: CGIAR Challenge Program for Water and Food (CPWF); 2012. 74p. (CPWF R4D Working Paper Series 04)

[89] Mul M et al. Water Resources Assessment of the Volta River Basin. Colombo, Sri Lanka: International Water Management Institute (IWMI; 2015

[90] Sterman JD. Sustaining sustainability: Creating a systems science in a fragmented academy and polarized world. In: Weinstein MP, Turner RE, editors. Sustainability Science. New York: Springer; 2012. DOI: 10.1007/978-1-4614-3188-6_2

[91] Newell B, Marsh DM, Sharma D. Enhancing the resilience of the Australian National Electricity Market: Taking a systems approach in policy development. Ecology and Society. 2011;**16**(2):15

Chapter 12

Need for a Collaborative Natural Resource Management Strategy for the Marine Environment—The Case of Plastics in the Mediterranean

Michel Soto Chalhoub

Abstract

Natural resource management issues are at the heart of sustainability and are seldom limited to a localized community. We address marine plastic pollution which not only infests local beaches, but is found in the present research to have high mobility, a serious impact on human health, and a damaging effect on ecosystems. Plastics have reached the deepest points of our oceans and while all oceans are affected, the Mediterranean Sea is particularly vulnerable to pollution because of its high biodiversity density, its enclosed geometry, and its bathymetry. We collected primary and secondary data and drew on separate studies performed by the author. We gauged public attitudes towards plastic waste management in Lebanon and found that the public is aware of the issue and supports the formation of a Mediterranean Rim consortium to address both remedial and preventive strategies. A regression analysis is introduced where a dependent variable represents the need for regional natural resource strategies. It was found to be positively and significantly correlated with the establishment of national policies, engineering innovation as a preventive strategy, and the adoption of local implementation. Our case study in Lebanon unveiled lack of public policies for solid waste management and marine plastic litter, causing implementation challenges. We recommend that the problem of plastic pollution be tackled with cross-border cooperation among neighboring countries around the Mediterranean.

Keywords: natural resource management, plastic pollution, Mediterranean Sea, regional environmental collaboration, policy development, private sector advocacy

1. Introduction

Environmental problems have a deep impact on public health, the economy, and society at large. Plastics top the list among other types of solid waste pollutants due to their properties and tenacity [1]. Plastic littering is a violation of several local and international agreements; it travels in sea water spreading its damaging effects on marine fauna and flora. Environmental valuation requires

IntechOpen

accounting for environmental damage and the resulting social costs. In many countries, the absence of environmental valuation combined with lack of policies exacerbates the problem. Weakness in public management, at both levels of legislation and implementation, are other salient factors of major concern. To compensate for weaknesses in local policies across nations and to combat negative littering practices, international agreements were created to impose prohibitions against plastic littering in the marine environment. The London Dumping Convention created in 1972 (MARPOL Convention, Annex V) and MARPOL Protocol of 1978 declared plastics in international waters as unlawful. The 1982 Law of the Sea Convention mandates preservation of the marine environment. Several other United Nations agreements ban dumping plastic substances in the ocean. Many states committed themselves legally to such agreements. The weakness, however, resides in implementation and enforcement [2–5]. In a country like Lebanon where data were collected in the present research, non-governmental organizations and ecological movements took the lead over public sector services to close this policy gap. International organizations and environmental activists argue that the establishment of dump sites and landfills on the shore, as it has been practiced in Lebanon in the last two decades, is a straight violation of the Barcelona Convention, a 1995 legislation designed to protect and preserve the marine environment in the Mediterranean [6].

Previous studies by the author gauged public attitudes towards marine plastic litter with an emphasis on the nexus between engineering and public policy. It was argued that engineering solutions on their own could be developed and may prove to be effective. However, such solutions cannot be implemented if they are not supported by public policy. The separate study by the author is briefly reviewed to emphasize the results of a linear regression model with a dependent variable, Y, which represented the need to develop regional strategies for natural resource management. The independent variables were defined as (1) the establishment of national policies specific to marine protection against pollution, (2) use of technology as remedial solutions, (3) use of engineering innovation as preventive solutions in the private sector, and (4) local enforcement. The third variable was based on the premise that radical innovative solutions would be required to transition into a plastic-free end-use. A statistically significant and positive correlation was found with the first, third, and fourth variables, while there was no statistical significance with the second variable. In the following sections, we illustrate the dire need for policies focused on solid waste management and in particular marine plastic litter. We then draw on policy examples from other countries and recommend local adaptation and adoption. Still, local policy development may be solely a small component of the problem offering only a patchwork of piecemeal solutions. Plastic pollution requires a broader and long-term outlook where teamwork, cooperation, and scientific knowledge-sharing in the Mediterranean region are a firm prerequisite.

2. Plastic pollution is a regional and global problem

Literature shows that coastal areas of developing countries which lack waste management policies and remedial infrastructure are of primary concern. However, the status of plastic pollution in the world's oceans poses a challenge to both industrialized and developing countries alike. Large plastic items released in the ocean do not degrade but rather degenerate into very small pieces—microplastics—which are particles smaller than 5 mm. These particles are mobile over hundreds of acres on the ocean surface and within lower layers. The spread of microplastics is caused by currents and oceanographic mixing processes. The Mediterranean is particularly vulnerable to polluting activities including plastic debris [7, 8].

In the last few decades, plastic accumulation reached remote offshore areas and formed trash gyres, islands, and vortexes [9]. Harmful effects of plastics on marine life include starvation, suffocation, and entanglement. Thousands of marine fauna and hundreds of species have been affected thus far. Floating plastics help transport non-indigenous marine species to intrude on other native colonies, causing a threat to marine biodiversity and the food chain. Floating plastic particles become vehicles to toxic pollutants that stick on their surface causing concentrated sources of environmental pollution in ocean gyres. With this visible recognition that drifting plastic debris cause adverse effects on ecosystems, innovative techniques are required [10]. A major challenge is to quantify plastics in the oceans because there is a lack of accurate information about sources, quantities, trajectories, accumulation, and final status.

3. Vulnerability of the Mediterranean

3.1 History and biodiversity

The Mediterranean Sea is considered to be the cradle of civilization. This pond is seriously affected by marine litter because its geometry forms a closed basin with limited mixing with other oceans. Due to their weather, beauty, and history, countries around the Mediterranean are densely populated with an active tourism industry. Lebanon's coast houses some of the most ancient cities including Tyre (2750 BC), Sidon (4000 BC), Beirut (3000 BC), and Byblos (5000 BC). Other countries on the Mediterranean rim have long-standing history, heritage, and ancient landmarks. Historic monuments on the coast are vulnerable to pollution, whether spills, solid, or plastic waste.

The Mediterranean is recognized for its natural diversity. It makes less than 1% of the world's ocean area and 0.3% of the world's total ocean water volume, and yet it is home to over 11% of marine species. This constitutes a high biodiversity density in terms of water volume and ocean area. NOAA's (2010) literature provides comparative data about oceans and seas including their geometric properties (**Table 1**).

This eco-diversity includes endemic species knowing that the Mediterranean's moderate temperature and salinity provide a favorable breeding medium for many endangered species. Online literature and blogs tweets provide ample documentation and pictures of marine animals entangled in plastics, or thwarted from motion, or starved from plastics filling their stomachs mistaken for nutrients. All such popularized evidence is conclusive about the harmful and deadly effects of microplastics on marine life. There is evidence that living organisms across the Lebanese coast are threatened directly by marine litter which made the Mediterranean Sea a global priority for conservation [11].

In recent years, the issue of plastic pollution escalated and became visible to most international organizations whereby this enclosed sea, which used to top the list of tourism attraction and maritime activity, was called in 2018 the Mediterranean Plastic Trap (**Figure 1**). Weak or no policies, dense human activity, and polluted rivers all contribute to the problem. A glaring issue pertains to rivers carrying debris of all sorts, including plastics, from land to sea. The Nile for example takes place in the top 10 polluting rivers according to various studies in literature. As will be seen in later sections, the counterclockwise prevailing current around the Mediterranean rim carries waste from coast to coast exhibiting a highly mobile pollution. The problem is a shared problem and therefore requires a shared solution.

Table 1: Volumes of the World's Oceans from ETOPO1

	Area* (km^2)	% Ocean Area	Volume (km^3)	% Ocean Volume	Avg. Depth (m)	Max Depth (m)
Arctic Ocean	15,558,000	4.3	18,750,000	1.4	1205	5567
Atlantic Ocean	85,133,000	23.5	310,410,900	23.3	3646	8486
Baltic Sea	*406,000*	*0.1*	*20,900*	*0.0*	*51*	*392*
Mediterranean	*2,967,000*	*0.8*	*4,390,000*	*0.3*	*1480*	*5139*
North Atlantic	*41,490,000*	*11.5*	*146,000,000*	*10.9*	*3519*	*8486*
South Atlantic	*40,270,000*	*11.1*	*160,000,000*	*12.0*	*3973*	*8240*
Indian Ocean	70,560,000	19.5	264,000,000	19.8	3741	7906
Pacific Ocean	161,760,000	44.7	660,000,000	49.4	4080	10,803
North Pacific	*77,010,000*	*21.3*	*331,000,000*	*24.8*	*4298*	*10,803**
South Pacific	*84,750,000*	*23.4*	*329,000,000*	*24.6*	*3882*	*10,753*
South China Sea	6,963,000	1.9	9,880,000	0.7	1419	7352
Southern Ocean*	21,960,000	6.1	71,800,000	5.4	3270	7075
Total:	**361,900,000**◊	**100.0**	**1,335,000,000**	**100.0**	**3688**	**10,803**
Error Estimates:	0.1%		1%			

* Boundaries between oceans vary depending upon agency, making comparisons with other published estimates difficult.
◊ Total surface area of Earth is 510,072,000 sq. km. The oceans cover ~70.9%.
* Southern Ocean area and volume calculated from ETOPO1 Bedrock version (includes Weddell and Ross seas without ice cover).
* Deepest ocean depth is in the Marianas Trench, measured at 10,911 meters. Maximum depths from ETOPO1 are not expected to exactly match known measured maximum depths as ETOPO1 represents average depths over ~4 sq. km areas.

Eakins, B.W. and G.F. Sharman, Volumes of the World's Oceans from ETOPO1, NOAA National Geophysical Data Center, Boulder, CO, 2010.

http://www.ngdc.noaa.gov/mgg/global/etopo1_ocean_volumes.html

Table 1.
World oceans and Mediterranean data (source: ETOPO1 and NOAA, 2018).

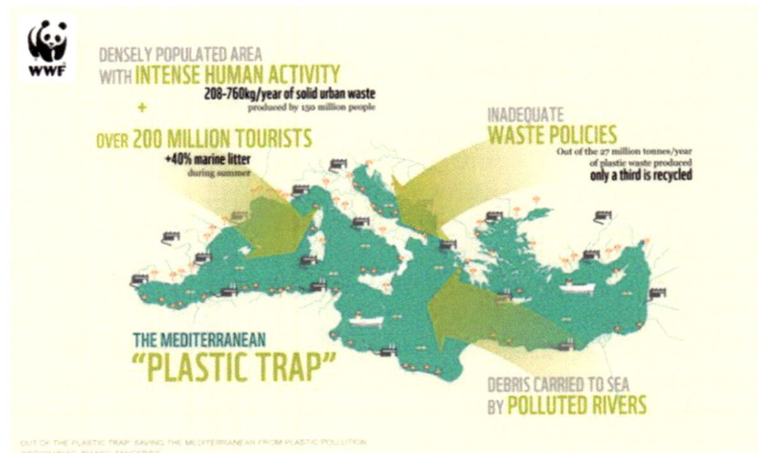

Figure 1.
Mediterranean map summarizing status. Source: [7].

3.2 Physical properties: waves and currents

Contrary to popular perceptions, the Mediterranean commands significant water depths up to 5000 meters, with a bottlenecked exchange of waters with the outside world through the Gibraltar Straight—a shallow orifice on seabed about 300 m below free water surface. The Mediterranean replenishes fresh water from rivers having estuaries around its basin, keeping its salinity at about 38 parts per thousand, while the Atlantic varies from 33 to 37; North Sea 34. Any form of intrusion on its natural status, pollution by spill or litter, accidental or not, may prove irreversible and catastrophic for such an enclosed basin (**Figure 2**).

The vulnerability of the Mediterranean to any polluting agent have been underlined by the author in previous publications including the quest and race for fossil fuel oil and gas extraction off the Lebanese coast. In recent years, extraction operations were launched in the region while Lebanon is considering the prospects of becoming an oil and natural gas producer in its waters. However, environmental

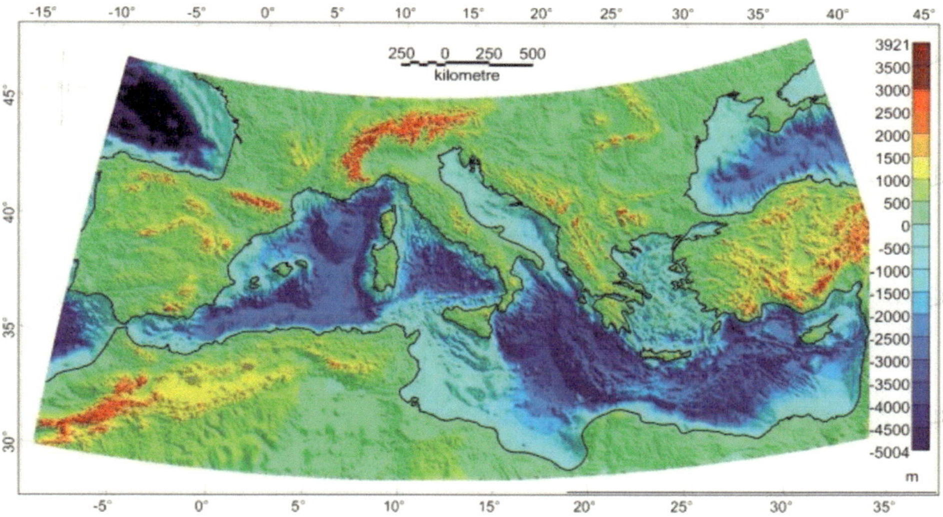

Figure 2.
The Mediterranean—water depth distribution.

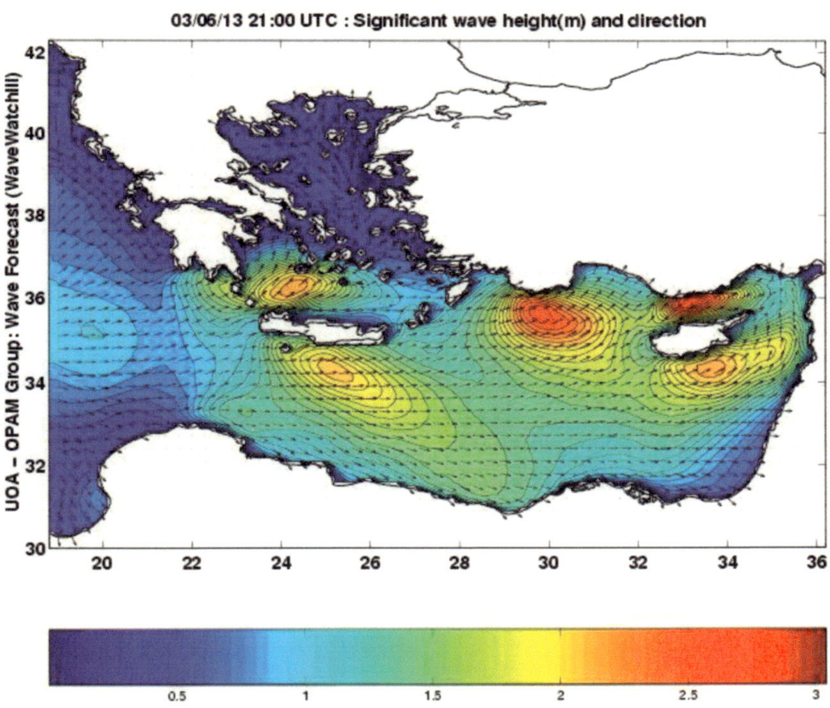

Figure 3.
The Mediterranean. Wave height, distribution, and surface current direction.

concerns are directly related to operational leaks, accidental spills, or deliberate damage to storage facilities due to potential conflicts. If such environmental concerns are properly accounted for in the social cost-benefit appraisal, a regional agreement would turn towards clean renewable energy and away from offshore fossil fuel production.

Hydrodynamic data about the Mediterranean is shown in **Figure 3**. A differentiation is in scope between the Mediterranean and open oceans in terms of mixing and suspended matter transport processes. Water current velocity in the Mediterranean averages 0.6 m/s while it exceeds 2.5 m/s in open oceans. Knowing that the energy generated by wave motion is proportional to the square or cubic power of the water particle velocity, depending on flow regime, ocean waves can generate 17–72 times the energy generated in a closed basin like the Mediterranean. Therefore, the absorptive and abrasive capacity of the Mediterranean in decomposing or breaking down waste is much lower than the one of open oceans [12].

The fact that the Mediterranean is surrounded with sovereign countries offers opportunities of cooperation among those nations to establish a program against plastic littering. According to the United Nations Convention of the Laws of the Seas, "... States of this area have a general obligation to cooperate when facing a disagreement..." (UNCLOS, Part IX, Art. 123). A preventive approach is recommended in the long term, but a swift remedial clean-up program is necessary through the establishment of a Mediterranean cooperative for that purpose [12].

4. Case of the Lebanese coast

4.1 Plastic is the predominant pollutant on Lebanon's shores

On Lebanese shores, in nearby seafloor and sea surface, plastic constitutes the litter component of highest proportion, making over 90% of total solid waste. This environmental problem has public health and economic consequences that need to be addressed with urgency.

During the July 2006 regional conflict, Lebanon suffered oil spills due to damage to its crude oil reservoirs in its southern territory. Such toxic matter travels on microplastics and exacerbates the danger of disrupting natural marine habitat. Local experience during municipal solid waste (MSW) crises shows that plastics may not constitute the largest proportion of MSW, but once it reaches the sea, it become by far the predominant component. This is due to the fact that organic MSW components disintegrate while plastics remain. UNEP/MAP (2015) studies on the Mediterranean showed that plastics make-up over 85% of floating litter, of which 45–95% lay on seafloor [1]. Categories of plastic litter in the Mediterranean were also identified and it was found that the largest percentage pertains to packaging plastic including bottles and drink containers, food boxes, bags, in addition to single-use disposable items including cotton sticks, lighters, and plastics dining utensils.

4.2 Lack of public policies related to plastic pollution: public awareness and fatigue

There have been some early efforts in establishing anti-plastic pollution policies in Lebanon, starting with policy proposals for solid waste in general [13]. Despite the passing of some laws, violations in implementation are originating from within local governments (municipalities) that undermine efforts expended by NGOs and environmental activists [14]. This problem is linked to Lebanon's solid waste crisis which has been recurring over the last decades [15]. The landfill at Costa Brava in Beirut, Lebanon, attests to a complex combination of blurred policies, self-interest, marginalization of public rights, and violation of fundamental concepts of public goods [16]. Following the 2015 solid waste crisis and the shutdown of the Naameh landfill in May of that year, Costa Brava was opened in 2016 as a temporary fix or alternative. Public opinion followed immediately protesting against this project. Activists established a physical presence on location and assisted local communities to petition to the UNEP. The project estimated at USD 60 million went against any rational environmental assessment, or lack thereof, and violated the Barcelona Convention [17].

The issue of plastic littering in Lebanon goes beyond a traditional awareness building campaign because the local population is already well-informed about plastics litter and its negative consequences. There is an overall lethargy in Lebanon about several environmental problems and lassitude among the Lebanese regarding their livelihood, health, and safety as a result of public sector mismanagement over several decades [18]. Problems of immediate concerns—economic slump, badly defined projects with mega budgets such as misplaced water dams, among other societal problems—all compete on the "attention span" of the Lebanese citizen [12, 19, 20]. We highlight these facts for two reasons. First, an advocacy campaign on plastics amidst an economic slump is challenging. Convincing a plastics producer to fundamentally change its product line requires engagement at a corporate strategy level. Second, awareness campaigns in local communities are also challenging as they require a message crafted well beyond the unaesthetic scene of a plastic-saturated shore (**Figure 4**). There is a need for product innovation or process development to combat plastic litter. Reluctance within the private sector to invest in innovative techniques and actionable solutions, and a fatigued local public that has gone through tough cycles of social unrest, have contributed to getting Lebanon in an unfavorable situation in relation to plastic littering among other problems [21].

4.3 Need for evidence-based advocacy and multidisciplinary collaboration

To combat plastic littering in Lebanon, both awareness-building and advocacy are recommended in parallel. The first may be performed with the general public, educational institutions, municipalities, and other entities. The second can be implemented with the private sector, including the major local plastic manufacturers. Cases from other countries provide evidence about the role of manufacturers [22]. Organizations such as The Lonely Whale has been encouraging companies to form teams and collaborate to scale down plastics volume across the entire supply chain; from raw material orders, to processing, manufacturing, and distribution. Member companies include so far some global manufacturing giants such as General

Figure 4.
Zouk Mosbeh beach cleanup, January 23, 2018, as garbage washed ashore in a storm. Source: J. Eid/AFP/Getty images, adopted by [21].

Motors, Hewlett Packard, Dell, Bureo, and Herman Miller. Similar possibilities could be explored for advocacy in Lebanon.

Plastic pollution gives rise to multi-faceted problems that require multidisciplinary collaboration. A deep understanding of the severity of the situation related to solid waste in general, and plastics in particular, requires a diligent approach that establishes a clear link between plastic pollution on one hand, and engineering, public policy, health, economic, and technical implication and potential solutions on the other hand. Advancing towards solutions must include prevention and remediation measures that should be planned for and implemented in tandem. Technical solutions must be backed by public policy design. Academic institutions, industries, and public sector entities are expected to work hand-in-hand to achieve tangible outcomes.

Recent studies showed that microplastics are eaten by fish, which are consumed by humans, causing unsafe food. This serious impact on marine life and infiltration in seafood has direct implications on public health. Numerous diseases have been reported to be on the rise in Lebanon. Various research projects at a global level established that plastics contain chemical and hazardous substances that cause a wide range of health problems including eye irritation, liver dysfunction, and cancer [23, 24]. Microplastics follow us to our kitchens and dining rooms as they were found in our food including table salt.

5. Plastics from land to sea Mediterranean subbasins and currents

Past studies of the Mediterranean subbasins showed a complex system of eddies, gyres, straights, and channels within a relatively small enclosed sea. Plastics were found in the deepest spots of oceans and are floating in the shape of islands as well, posing quantification challenges. Understanding Mediterranean bathymetry and dynamics is essential to capture how plastics are traveling from source to destination. Some of the early maps provide a simplified model of the subbasins and currents. An overall counterclockwise motion persists in the Mediterranean [25]. This motion is characterized by a south–north movement along the Lebanese coast. The 11 subbasins within the Mediterranean; numbered 1, 2a, 2b, 2c, 3 through 9, are shown in **Figure 5**.

A better understanding of traveling plastic trash can be developed from key concepts in fluid mechanics applied to subbasins. For instance, eddies transport debris in a circular or semi-circular motion and can be categorized into small eddies ranging up to 50 km; medium eddies from 50 to 150 km; large eddies between 150 and 250 km. The Mediterranean has the Gibraltar and Messina traits, the Otranto, Sardinia, and Sicily channels. Gyres in the Mediterranean run clockwise primarily due to the orientation of the Strait of Gibraltar, but they are elsewhere counterclockwise due to Coriolis effects.

Advances in satellite imaging technology offer a more sophisticated means to track sea water motion and facilitate the detection of existing and potential gyres of plastic waste islands. These technological advances further confirm the need for a concerted regional effort whereby several countries plan, operate, and cooperate on fighting plastic pollution in the Mediterranean. There is no evidence that the Mediterranean carries a permanent trash island but litter accumulation areas have been reported. Historical data collected in the Mediterranean Sea was used to compute the probability of debris particles to reach subbasins, in an attempt to identify possible retention areas. If retention areas are identified, the prediction of the potential location of floating trash islands becomes more manageable.

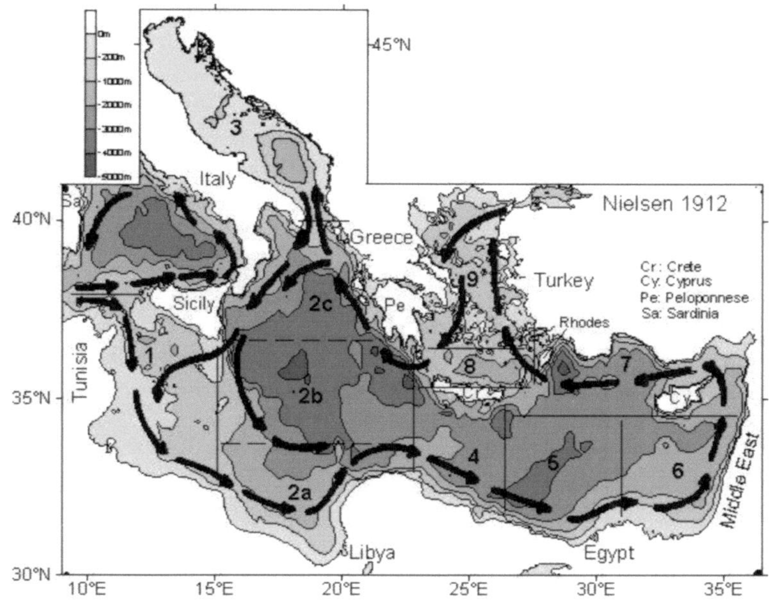

Figure 5.
Mediterranean subbasins 1: Channel of Sicily, 2a: Southern Ionian, 2b: Central Ionian, 2c: Northern Ionian; 3: Adriatic; 4: Southern Cretan; 5: Western Levantine (deeper than 3000 m: The Herodotus trough); 6: Southeastern Levantine; 7: Northern Levantine; 8: Northern Cretan; 9: Aegean. Source: ifremer.fr, February 25, 2019.

The evolution of litter based on climatological reconstructions shows a tendency of floating litter to collect in the southern portion with a long-term accumulation in the Southeastern Levantine Basin. Data analyzed by Zambianchi et al., show that drifters start from a dispersed status and end along coasts on the East Mediterranean including Lebanon as well as some North African countries for both summer and winter seasons [26].

6. Mathematical model, empirical analysis, and results

We formulated and performed a linear regression to gauge public attitudes in Lebanon by defining a dependent variable, Y, representing the need to develop regional strategies for natural resource management. The independent variables were defined as (1) the establishment of national policies specific to marine protection against pollution, (2) use of technology as remedial solutions, (3) use of engineering innovation as preventive solutions in the private sector, and (4) local enforcement. The selection of these variables was based on preliminary focus interviews and on evidence from the collection and analysis of secondary data. The variables were designed to gauge public attitudes towards regional collaboration to team up on protecting the environment. Focus interviews showed a predisposition of the community for regional collaboration because these issues affect human health beyond ecosystem protection or territorial claims. The outreach used a 1–5 Likert scale and included 750 recipients, of which 426 responded with 281 replies that covered the above variables.

Regression results showed a statistically significant and positive correlation with the first, third, and fourth variables at 5% significance level, there was no statistical significance with the second variable. In a previous analysis, we found positive correlation between the "willingness to contribute at a local community level" and remedial actions such as beach cleanup, but the present analysis addresses a regional strategy. Public attitudes show that it would be very important to start with local public policies that would be carried to regional cooperative summits during which a strategy for the whole Mediterranean would be drafted, refined and agreed upon.

In our previous analysis, we also found that respondents were skeptical about prospects of regional collaboration in the East Mediterranean whereby focus interviews at the time showed that 46% of interviewees expressed disappointment about the lack of regional collaboration in public policy design. Nevertheless, both analyses show agreement between the qualitative and quantitative results indicating that communities are eager to see policies established at a local level, and implemented regionally in collaboration with Mediterranean rim countries. Community inputs were positive about regional treaties but this prospect was described by many as wishful thinking as evidenced by many respondents in the process of qualitative data collection during focus interviews.

7. From remedial reactions to preventive strategies: innovation against plastic pollution

7.1 Remedial reactions are necessary but not sufficient

There is no doubt that remedies need to be implemented urgently such as beach cleanup, collection, sorting, recycling, and re-use. In almost all environmental problems, remedial actions evolve as a result of a damage that was already done, and therefore the author considers them as mere reactions. The case of plastic pollution and littering in a closed pond-like sea is no different. There is a large amount of research literature on plastic recycling with a call for the establishment of an industry cycle to put plastics in a "closed loop" from first-time manufacturing to re-processing to new products—but again, made of plastics in their present chemical formulation. In that context, a brief description of recyclability may shed light on the shortcomings of remedial reactions. In fact, not all plastics are easily recyclable, let alone requirements for energy and carbon footprint. Plastics come in different materials, and various levels of recyclability. All plastic containers carry at their bottom a triangular sign inscribing a number; a recycling code. The recycling code corresponds to the type of plastic used to manufacture the item. There are many types of plastics, but it is customary to summarize them in seven types that are known to carry these code numbers for recycling purposes.

Polyethylene terephthalate (PET or PETE)—PET is part of the polyester series and is typically used to manufacture bottles for water or soda. Sometimes they are used for clothing and for containers of traysthat can be heated in a microwave. PET is widely recycled as it lends itself to the process and is commonly reused.

Low-density polyethylene (LDPE) is a polymer used in many applications such as bags, gas pipes, water pipes, bottles, toys, and plastic wrap. It is not common to recycle LDPE using simple home-based programs. However, LDPE plastic bags and other containers can be reused and therefore are not classified as single-use items.

High-density polyethylene (HDPE) is a polymer used in many applications such as garbage bags, liquid soap and shampoo bottles, caps, lids, and common grocery bags. HDPE used for items other than bags can be recycled in most places. Bags can be reused or can be returned to grocery stores for collection and recycling.

Polyvinyl chloride (V or Vinyl or PVC) is used for a variety of applications but most commonly in construction, namely plumbing installations. Other applications include bathroom curtains, garden or service hoses, raincoats and waterproof boots. It is not common to recycle PVC collected from used or dismantled plumbing networks. However, PVC containers and bottles can be recycled and manufactured as exterior rainwater drainage pipes or road cones and vehicle barriers.

Polypropylene (PP) is used for outdoor furniture, medicine containers, food boxes, diapers, and rope.

Polystyrene (PS) is used to make disposable picnic items, compact disk cases and cassettes. PS could be used as foam—referred to as Styrofoam—for packaging, disposable plates, egg trays, delivery or take-out boxes. PS can be recycled but it consumes more energy than other plastics and is therefore uneconomical.[1]

Other plastics are marked "O" which is a group that includes various mixes of polymers. Examples of this group include (1) polylactic acid used to manufacture containers, (2) polycarbonates, used for eye glasses, DVDs, construction greenhouse panels, (3) acrylonitrile butadiene styrene or ABS, used for games, such as Legos and puzzle pieces, and (4) nylon, used for rope, wire, clothing, components in car tires.

7.2 Need for preventive strategies

In light of these facts, and given that most respondents seem to be well-versed in terms of the pros and cons of recycling, the statistical analysis showed that public attitudes clearly support the use of engineering innovation in fighting plastic pollution. Overall, there is a belief that the private sector—whether manufacturers or traders in plastic import and export—can play a fundamental role in the process. Relevant to the regression analysis, the third independent variable in the mathematical model reflects a potential engagement by major plastics manufacturers and traders. There is an urgent need to introduce innovative products such as bio-degradable substitutes to plastics, and innovative processes such as plastic-to-fuel operations. In that spirit, advocacy with local manufacturers, importers, and exporters of plastics from raw materials to finished products would set a track for preventive strategies and an anticipation of consumer behavior. Advances in product development such as bio-degradable plastic-like materials, and in manufacturing techniques as it has been the case in the USA, Japan, and Europe, must be explored for local adaptation and application in Lebanon. Engineering innovation is expected to play a major role in preventive strategies, along with the development of policies that are specific to plastic pollution.

7.3 Preventive strategies need to be regional

While research aimed at new product development support preventive strategies, other types of research grew in parallel to manage existing plastic waste, or remedial strategies. The subject of plastic pollution does not lack public attention, but it has been tackled in piecemeal solutions and in disparate geographic areas. The Regional Activity Centre for Sustainable Consumption and Production (SCP/RAC) developed a compilation of solutions that they termed as innovative and inspiring. The project was done as part of the EU-funded SwitchMed Programme.[2]

Out of dozens of attempts and campaigns in different countries, SCP/RAC selected the top 25 solutions that were hoped to be replicated in other geographies. Each of these solutions requires consideration as part of a potential roadmap for Lebanon. The subsequent phases of this program could elaborate a subset

---

[1] In the United States, several cities banned foamed PS.

[2] SwitchMed coordinates between the European Union, the United Nations Industrial Development Organization (UNIDO), the UN Environment and Action Plan for the Mediterranean and its Regional Activity Centre for Sustainable Consumption and Production (SCP/RAC), and the UN Environment located near Santa Barbara, California, USA.

of these solutions and include them in an organized advocacy campaign during implementation. The proposed solutions are classified under products or processes and are identified as being private business initiatives or public sector action. For example, the EcoOcean is a new product developed through funding from the EU; the EcoOcean material. This is a trademark of EcoCortec which introduced a bio-based polymer to make bags and wrapping from polyhydroxyalkanoate (PHA). According to the company, its composition includes 77% bio-based resins with sugar cane at its base. When in contact with the marine environment or a natural terrain, EcoOcean biodegrades by anaerobic digestion. Anaerobic digestion is a technique that was introduced in the United States in the 1960s and fully implemented in California in the 1980s [27]. The intended use of this product is not to dispose of it in the ocean. However, in case it reaches the ocean, full-scale experiments conducted by the company showed that it biodegrades within a few weeks or a few months, depending on water particle dynamics. This is a critical improvement over classical plastics that remain for hundreds of years. The experiments targeted microbial action breaking the bag down to microcosms. Testing included detailed studies through microscopic examination and molecular investigation to identify microbial communities and compare them with the effects of classical plastics. It was found that some of the sea animals were feeding on this biodegradable material. As for practical use, the material was tested against moisture, heat, and tensile stress and was found usable for daily choirs. However, it is the opinion of the author of the present roadmap report that such material requires a long-term follow-up to ascertain the nature of microbial communities that would develop. Countries like Lebanon that are not as endowed in research funding and facilities as the originating countries, could be an end-user that would adopt such techniques once fully proven against any potential side-effects.

Each proposed solution, when considered on its own, seems to contribute to combating litter in the Mediterranean. Those solutions could be considered for other locations as well. However, they fall short of having a coordinated program across countries for a mobile pollutant that travels in the waters similarly to air pollutants that have a negative externality. Given the facts at hand, there is a case for coordinated public policies backed by local advocacy campaigns.

8. Movements towards policy against plastics

We turn to a few examples in the State of California, which is considered as one of the most innovative states in pro-actively developing policies against plastic pollution. The approach is done in a combination of awareness-building, advocacy, legislation, and enforcement. Consider the sign in **Figure 6** posted by the US Forest Service in Los Padres National Forest that explain in a very few words how harsh it is to litter plastic bottles into the environment. This forest is renowned for its pristine status and ecosystem (**Figure** 7).

Additionally, the State of California currently charges the highest littering fines. Such fines are used to deter the resident or the visitor from littering (**Figure** 8).

There are many geographic similarities between California and several Mediterranean countries including Lebanon, Cyprus, Turkey, Greece, and Croatia to name a few. The old saying that in Lebanon you can drive to ski then drive back to the beach on the same day is applicable as you can go east, enjoy cooler weather and mountains covered with snow then drive back west to the shore. Lebanon and California are both active in terms of sports, outdoors, healthy cuisine, eating habits, and enjoying the beach by both locals and visitors. California residents boast about the nice weather all year round where the lifestyle is loaded with hiking,

Figure 6.
Sign posted by the US Forest Service in los padres National Forest.

Figure 7.
Los Padres National Forest.

Figure 8.
State of California posts the highest fines in the USA for littering.

picnics, beach volleyball, wind surfing, and beach camping. Both Lebanon and California have the same latitude or distance north of the equator.

In November 2016, California voters passed Proposition 67. *The proposition requested a ban on single-use plastic bags*. Thousands of volunteers who provided community service by collecting plastic trash during California's coastal cleanup day reported back that they saw a substantial decrease in plastic bag refuse. Further data collected in California showed that plastic bag litter dropped by 72% between 2010 and 2017. By November 2017, plastic bags made less than 1.5% of all litter, down from 10% in 2010. In 2017, volunteers found in Monterey County only 43 plastic bags (in number) during the clean-up campaign, compared with almost 2500 bags in 2010. In a 2010 ranking about most frequently littered items, plastic bags ranked third after cigarette butts and fast food packaging. By late 2017, they fell out of the top 10 most littered items (Phillips, 2017). The importance of natural resource management cannot be more emphasized and this is exemplified by having a dedicated position as a State Secretary for Natural Resources.

> *"For decades, plastic bags were one of the most common items collected during the annual California coastal cleanup, ... This year, as California continues to transition to reusable bags, we are seeing a substantial decline in plastic grocery bag litter on beaches, rivers and parkways." John Laird, California Secretary for Natural Resources*

Another example is worth mentioning at the local [city] government level—also termed "municipal level" in most countries. Over 100 cities across the State of California passed their own bag bans before the statewide policy was enacted. As decentralization is discussed in Lebanon, local governments, or municipalities, can take the initiative in establishing a local city code against plastic disposal, sorting, and even management at the source.

> *"When I took on the problem of plastic bag pollution four years ago, California retailers were distributing more than 19 billion single-use plastic bags every year," "Today, that number is zero. Once again California is leading the way, creating cleaner communities for all."*
>
> *Alex Padilla, California Secretary of State -.*

The policy evolved in certain cities such as San Francisco to combine curbside collection and recycling booths along with plastic bag bans. This policy combines remediation with prevention.

Since the passing of anti-littering legislation in California, 40 other countries have taken action through taxing single use plastic bags, or by banning them fully or partially. In 2016, the European Union announced that by end of 2019, the consumption of plastic bags in member states would not exceed 90 bags per person per year. France implemented a full ban on lightweight plastic bags at checkout counters. Research by the Earth Policy Institute showed that one trillion single-use plastic bags are used each year, and most of them ultimately make it to the ocean through waterways. Overall, over 8 million tons of plastic per year are thrown into oceans (Earth Policy Institute, 2018). However, such policies must be studied for a potential downside as well. Upon further consideration, for a cotton bag to have a more favorable environmental footprint than a plastic bag, it needs to be reused 130 times (KQED). Nevertheless, most Mediterranean countries are in need for local and regional policies as part of a marine anti-pollution grand strategy.

9. Conclusions

Plastic pollution in the marine environment grew into a global and regional concern threatening ecosystems and human health. Private sector entities including manufacturers and traders are expected to play an essential role in the design process of public policies and actively partake in their implementation. The Mediterranean is particularly vulnerable to plastic pollution due to its enclosed geometry, its disproportionate depth in comparison with its shallow strait, and its population density around its rim. Our linear regression analysis on public attitudes in Lebanon shows that the readiness of local communities to actively fight plastic pollution is positively and significantly correlated with an appeal to establish national public policies specific to plastic littering, and a request for advocacy with the private sector. There were concerns about sorting MSW at the household level given that contractors remix and dump them in open land. Respondents support regional collaborative treaties to protect the environment, but there is a perception that chances of success for such prospects are dim. Regional policies need to be explored further with the possibilities to form joint teams of experts, and develop innovative techniques across borders.

Radical change cannot happen without engineering innovation and advocacy with the private sector. Transitioning into a plastic-free end-use requires plastics manufacturers and traders to adopt novel techniques. There is an urgent need to introduce innovative products and processes such as plastic-to-fuel operations, as part of long-term preventive strategies. Future research is recommended to further develop public policies, both locally and regionally to handle this shared problem and its negative externalities.

Author details

Michel Soto Chalhoub
Department of Civil and Environmental Engineering, Notre Dame University, Zouk Mosbeh, Lebanon

*Address all correspondence to: mchalhoub@live.com

References

[1] United Nations Environment Programme (UNEP). Marine Litter Assessment in the Mediterranean—Mediterranean Action Plan (MAP). Greece: Athens; 2015

[2] Kindt JW. Marine Pollution and the Law of the Sea. Buffalo, NY: W. S. Hein; 1986

[3] Bowker M. Caught in a Plastic Trap. International Wildlife, May–June: 70; 1986

[4] Langley LS. Plastic Pollution Threatening Marine Wildlife. Charleston News and Courier, June 5: Dl col. 1. 1988

[5] U. N. General Assembly. Law of the Sea: Report of the Secretary-General, U.N. General Assembly, 45th Session, Agenda Item 43, Nov. 19, 1990 7 U.N. Doc. A/45/721; 1990

[6] Joyner CC, Frew S. Plastic pollution in the marine environment. Journal of Ocean Development and International Law. 1991;**22**(1):33-69. (published online, 2009, https://www.tandfonline.com/doi/ref/10.1080/00908329109545949?scroll=top).

[7] WWF—Worldwide Fund for Nature. The Mediterranean at Risk of becoming a Sea of Plastic. June 8, 2018; 2018

[8] Chalhoub MS. Solid Waste Management and Public Policy Challenges: Are Plastics Commanding the Lion's Share? Working Paper in Engineering Practice. Louaize, Lebanon; 2017

[9] Eriksen M, Lebreton LCM, Carson HS, Thiel M, Moore CJ, Borerro JC, et al. Plastic Pollution in the World's Oceans: More than 5 Trillion Plastic Pieces Weighing over 250,000 Tons Afloat at Sea. PLoS One. 2014;**9**(12):e111913. DOI: https://doi.org/10.1371/journal.pone.0111913

[10] MEDSEA—Med Sea Foundation. Clean-up Together to Clean Everyone's House. 2019. Available from: http://www.medseafoundation.org/index.php/en/news-int-eng/132-clean-up-together-to-clean-everyone-s-house

[11] IUCN—International Union for Conservation of Nature. Endangered Species in the Mediterranean – Data; 2017

[12] Chalhoub MS. Modeling Solid Waste Conveyance into the East Mediterranean: Uncertainties and Challenges in Engineering and Public Policy, Working Paper, Louaize, 2016.

[13] BBC. Lebanon is Drowning in its own Waste. 2018. Available from: http://www.bbc.com/future/story/20180328-lebanon-is-drowning-in-its-own-waste

[14] HRW—Human Rights Watch. Lebanon: No Action to Enforce New Waste Law. 2018. Available from: https://www.hrw.org/news/2018/10/18/lebanon-no-action-enforce-new-waste-law

[15] Chalhoub MS. Public policy and technology choices for municipal solid waste management a recent case in Lebanon. Journal of Environmental Science and Health, Taylor & Francis Online. 2018;**4**(1):1-18

[16] Daily Star. Cabinet Approves Plans to Expand Costa Brava Landfill. 2018. Available from: http://www.dailystar.com.lb/News/Lebanon-News/2018/Jan-12/433384-cabinet-approves-plan-to-expand-costa-brava-landfill.ashx

[17] EJA—Environmental Justice Atlas. Costa Brava Landfill: Lebanon. 2017. Available from: https://ejatlas.org/conflict/costa-brava-landfill-lebanon

[18] Reuters World News. Lebanon's Public Sector Plagued by Inefficiency,

Waste. 2018. Available from: https://www.reuters.com/article/us-lebanon-politics-waste/lebanons-public-sector-plagued-by-inefficiency-waste-idUSKBN1FP1SC

[19] Carnegie MEC—Carnegie Middle East center. Is Lebanon Heading towards Eonomic Bankruptcy? 2017. Available from: https://carnegie-mec.org/diwan/73280

[20] Beirut Today. Is Lebanon's Economy on the Brink of Collapse? Beirut Today. 2019. Available from: http://beirut-today.com/2019/01/16/lebanons-economy-brink-collapse/

[21] Haugbolle S. Lebanon is Facing and Economic and Environmental Disaster, Foreign Policy. 2019. Available from: https://foreignpolicy.com/2019/02/20/lebanon-is-facing-an-environmental-and-economic-disaster-hezbollah-hariri-aoun/

[22] Forbes. Fighting Plastic Pollution from the Top. Melissa Cristina Marquez, 27 December 2017. 2018. Available from: https://www.forbes.com/sites/melissacristinamarquez/2018/12/27/fighting-plastic-pollution-from-the-top/#365a7e297616

[23] Proshad R, Kormoker T, Saiful Islam M, Asadul Haque M, Rahman M, Rahman Mithu M. Toxic effects of plastic on Human health and environment: Consequences of health risk assessment in Bengladesh. International Journal of Health. 2018;**6**(1):1-5

[24] Ikezuki Y, Tsutsumi O, Takai Y, Kamei Y, Taketani Y. Determination of bisphenol concentrations in human biological fluids reveals significant early prenatal exposure. Humanities Report. 2002;**17**:2839-2841. DOI: 10.1093/humrep/17.11.2839

[25] Nielsen JN. Hydrography of the Mediterranean and adjacent waters. Report of the Danish Oceanographic Expedition 1908-1910 to the Mediterranean and Adjacent Waters. 1912;**1**:77-192

[26] Zambianchi E, Trani M, Falco P. Lagrangian transport of marine litter in the Mediterranean Sea. Frontiers in Environmental Science. 2017;**5**(5):1-15

[27] Chalhoub MS. Anaerobic Digesters Design for Sludge Treatment in the County of Los Angeles. Report No. 005-91-02-02, Parsons Eng. Lib. Pasadena, CA: Archives/Stacks; 1991

Chapter 13

Treatment of Solid Waste Containing Metals by Biological Methods

Marlenne Gómez-Ramírez and Sergio A. Tenorio-Sánchez

Abstract

Methods for the treatment of hazardous wastes are based on two main approaches: either hydrometallurgy or pyrometallurgy. Biological methods are considered viable environmental-friendly technologies and have been developed in the last years and have been associated with lower cost and energy requirements, in comparison with nonbiological processes. In these methods, it is important to find suitable microorganisms to degrade organic substances under favorable conditions to complete the treatment. The advantages of biotechnological treatment of hazardous wastes are biodegradation or detoxification of a wide variety of hazardous substances using natural microorganisms, as well as the availability of a wide range of biotechnological methods for the total destruction of these wastes without the production of secondary hazardous derivatives. However, to intensify the biological treatment, it is a necessary requirement to add nutrients and acceptors of electrons, including the control of the optimal conditions. Thus, biotechnology provides a solution for the ecological degradation of harmful heavy metals and toxic chemicals. The main purpose of this chapter is to present and discuss the biological methods used in the treatment of solid waste containing metals and the advantages and disadvantages of each method.

Keywords: solid waste, metals, biological methods, bio-treatment

1. Introduction

The fast-developing of industries, such as mining, smelting operations, farming, energy stations, processing in refineries, coal burning in power plants, petroleum combustion, nuclear power stations and high tension lines, plastics, textiles, microelectronics, wood preservation, paper processing plants, and agricultural and anthropogenic activities, generally use metal-containing compounds which, due to the inappropriate waste disposal practices, have contributed to the contamination of soil and water with organic compounds and heavy metals with permanent toxic effects on ecosystems and humans [1, 2]. To counteract the effects of such contaminants, several methods and techniques have been implemented, each having its advantages and disadvantages. Currently, there are various types of waste contaminated with metals, and various treatments are applied depending on the type of waste to be treated, among them are as follows:

A. *Domestic agricultural and industrial water*: the conventional techniques for removing dissolved heavy metals include chemical precipitation, carbon adsorption, ion exchange, evaporations and membrane processes, electrodialysis, and photocatalysis [3, 4].

B. *Contaminated soils*: remediation techniques such as excavation, soil leaching/acid extraction, and soil washing are inadequate, costly, and often involved the storage of contaminated effluents in designated areas. The use of plants in metal extraction (phytoremediation) has appeared as a safe and cost-effective alternative in the removal of heavy metals excess from soil and water [1].

C. *Municipal solid waste* (MSW): it is a complex material, which varies greatly in composition. In most of countries, solid wastes in land fill (open dump sites) are the most common means of disposal [5]. Lack of MSW management and disposal is leading to significant environmental problems. This includes soil, air water, and esthetic pollution. Such environmental problems are associated with human health disorder [6]. Composting is one of several methods for treating biosolids. Compost production is normally produced by two methods, an aerobic process and anaerobic pre-treatment of MSW followed by an aerobic curing step. There are many methods for removal of metal and toxic elements from soil and compost such as hydrothermal; subcritical water treatment; chemical leaching using inorganic mineral acids like sulfuric acid, hydrochloric acid, and nitric acid; or use of chelating reagents like nitrilotriacetic acid (NTA), ethylenediaminetetraacetic acid (EDTA), and diethylenetriaminepentaacetic acid (DTPA). Alkaline solutions like ammonium and sodium hydroxides are also sometimes used. However, these treatments have some common disadvantages such as high cost and generating potential toxic by-products [5, 7]. On the other hand, the compost and sewage sludge additions to agricultural and other soils, with background concentrations of heavy metals, raise the soil content and the availability of heavy metals for transfer into crop plants [8].

D. *Hazardous waste*: it includes waste batteries, electronic waste, waste X-ray films, fly ash, petroleum spent catalyst, and metal finishing industrial waste. Several technologies are used for the treatment of this kind of industrial waste; these are pyrometallurgy, hydrometallurgy, and bio-hydrometallurgy. Pyrometallurgical recovery consists of the thermal treatment of ores and metal containing wastes to bring about physical and chemical transformations. The hydrometallurgical recovery uses mainly the leaching process, by using aqueous solutions containing a lixiviant brought into contact with a material containing a valuable metal. The leached metals are concentrated and purified by using precipitation, cementation, solvent extraction, and ion exchange [9].

E. *Landfill mining*: in many regions of the world, landfills have long been seen as a final way to store waste at minimum cost. Landfill mining has been suggested as a strategy to address such problems and in principle means the excavation, processing, treatment, and/or recycling of deposited materials [10].

Given the increase in the generation of waste contaminated with metals, strategies have been sought in which microorganisms are small factories for the transformation and/or decontamination of the waste through different mechanisms of each microorganism, thereby reducing the metal load in the residue, changing the oxidation state of the metal by making it less toxic, or recovering it either soluble or insoluble for reuse. Some metal tolerant microorganisms have the potential to be used in biotechnological processes for the recovery of valuable metals [11]. The bacteria have developed various resistance mechanisms to tolerate the harmful effects of toxic metals and have been abundant on the planet earth, and microbes have been exposed to them since basically the beginning of life, nearly 4 billion years ago [12]. Among them are mainly those that involve (1) cellular components that capture ions, neutralizing their toxicity, (2) enzymes that modify the redox state of metals or metalloids, turning them into less toxic forms, and (3) expulsion of metals or metalloids from cytoplasm through membrane-located transporter proteins [13].

The sections covered in the chapter are as follows:

1. Introduction

2. Biological systems for the treatment and recovery of metals.

3. Microorganisms with potential for the treatment and recovery of metals.

4. Treatment of spent catalysts of the petrochemical industry by microbial route.

5. Conclusion

2. Biological systems for the treatment and recovery of metals

Biotreatment is a biological process in which live, dead microorganisms or metabolites produced by them are used such as enzymes, biopolymers, siderophores, organic acids, inorganic acids, and biosurfactants. To eliminate pollution caused by metals or other contaminants, defense mechanisms are activated to detoxify their environment causing a transformation of the contaminant into less toxic compounds or the internalization of the contaminant inside the microbial cells [14, 15].

To understand and know the type of mechanism that each microorganism will use depend on how they interact with the environment and the contaminants; some factors are (1) microbial specie, (2) microbe-metal interactions, (3) growth medium composition, (4) pH, (5) temperature, (6) contact time, (7) oxygen, (8) osmotic pressure, (9) culture age, (10) microbial tolerance, (11) population density, (12) chemical and metal composition of solid wastes, (13) pulp density of waste, (14) size of particle of solid waste, (15) oxidation state of metals, and (16) presence of other toxic compounds [16–21]. The isolation of microorganisms from contaminated environments has led to finding microorganisms adapted to them, which have also developed certain metabolic strategies to detoxify their environment and, which are used for the treatment of different types of waste. The solid wastes generated from agricultural, electronic scraps, medical activity, metal finishing industry, industrial effluents, auto catalysts, manufacturing and recycling of batteries, fly ash, mining tailing, spent catalyst by petrochemical and petroleum refining industry mostly contain Ag, As, Ba, Be, Cd, Co, Cu, Fe, Li, Mo, Mg, Zn, Cr, Hg, Ni, V, Pb, Se, Zn, Ti, and so on and precious metals such as Au, In, Ag, Pd, Pt, and so on [9, 16–18, 20, 22–27]. Due to high metal content, waste containing metals are considered as artificial source of minerals and valuable metals that can be recovered [9, 18, 22, 23]. During treatment of solid waste, generally a low pulp density is used with ranges between 0.01 and 10% (w/v) and rarely higher than 16–80% (w/v) [19, 21, 22, 24, 26, 27]. While in biohydrometallurgy of low-grade ores, pulp density is generally 10% or higher because the ores are mainly reduced sulfides ores, which do not contain alkaline matter or toxic compounds that could inhibit the microbial growth or production of metabolite of interest to metal removal [16, 17].

Adapted microorganisms are used to carry out these biotreatments, or they are adapted to the characteristics that the pollutant presents (high concentration and variety of metals); however, in works related to the recovery of contaminated sites, the use of metabolic activity of microorganisms such as bacteria and fungi,

Biological process	Process description
Bioadsorption	The union between the microbial biomass and the metal can occur at an extracellular level and is carried out by coordinated complexes. The microorganisms used as biosorbents retain heavy metals on the surface of the cell when they come into contact with the metals through ionic interactions between them and the cell wall. The microbial cell can be alive or dead, and energy expenditure by the microorganism is not required [35]
Bioabsorption	The intracellular accumulation of a metal occurs in two stages: process of adsorption of the metal and subsequently the transport of the metal into the cell by an active transport system. The bioaccumulation processes require the metabolic activity of the cells; they also involve a transmembrane transport system, which is responsible for letting the captured metal into the cell wall or membrane inside the cell, once it was incorporated, the metal can remain sequestered by specific genetically encoded proteins, so it is required to expose the cell to metal ions to induce their expression [36]
Bioleaching/mobilization	It uses the ability of a variety of microorganisms (bacteria and fungi) to mobilize and leach metals from a solid matrix based on three principles: (1) the production of organic and/or inorganic acids; (2) through oxide-reduction reactions; and (3) secretion of complexing agents (siderophores, lipopeptide biosurfactants). The microorganisms used are autotrophic, heterotrophic bacteria as well as fungi. These microorganisms are capable of producing organic and inorganic acids, and the processes can be carried out directly, using the microorganism and its by-products, or indirectly in which only the acid or metabolite produced by the microorganism is used [21, 37–44]
Membrane transporters expelling harmful species from the cell cytoplasm	*Ejecting systems of cations* (1) Cation diffusion facilitators (CDF) are proteins that are distributed in the three domains (Bacteria, Archaea, and Eukarya). They generally not only transport zinc but can also expel other cations such as Cd, Co, Ni, and Fe. (2) P-type ATPases constitute a superfamily of metal transporters that are energized by the hydrolysis of ATP. They are widely distributed in the three domains of life, and their substrates are ions such as H^+, Na^+, K^+, Mg^{2+}, Ca^{2+}, Cu^+, Ag^+, Zn^{2+}, and Cd^{2+}. This type of ATPases is located in the inner membrane and can transport ions into the cellular interior, commonly physiological ions such as Mg^{2+}, or function as expulsion systems, removing toxic metals to the periplasmic space. (3) RND proteins, these are involved in resistance, nodulation, and cell division processes in different bacterial species, have only been identified in bacteria. RND proteins that participate in the expulsion of metals are commonly associated with a pair of auxiliary polypeptides: a small outer membrane protein and a periplasmic protein that binds (or fuses) to the inner and outer membranes [11, 45, 46]. *Anion ejection systems* In this group, there is a system of expulsion of toxic inorganic ions that use transporters to expel arsenic and chromium oxyanions. This system can work in a dual way: driven by the hydrolysis of ATP or by a chemiosmotic process [11].

Table 1.
Biological mechanisms involved in the removal of metals.

isolated from environments exposed to metals has been proposed [28]. This condition allows to obtain microorganisms adapted and/or resistant to metals of interest, whose metabolic activity could favor the mobilization and/or immobilization of metals from a contaminating matrix; this is through the accumulation or adsorption of metals by biomass or the production of metabolites such as organic and mineral acids, chelating agents (siderophores and biosurfactants), and enzymes [15]. **Table 1** shows some of the mechanisms used by microorganisms for the removal of metals. In these processes, the *cell wall* plays the main role since it is the first one that comes into contact with the metal ions, and these are deposited on the surface or between the cell wall structures, which, depending on the type of cell, will contain functional groups such as carboxyls, phosphonates, amines, and hydroxyl groups, among others [29]. These metal ions will be attracted by the negatively charged sites of cellular components. The cell wall in Gram-positive bacteria has a thickness of 20–80 nm and is made up of peptidoglycan or murein and is located on the plasma membrane, in which there are a lot of teichoic acids, which are polymers of glycerol or ribitol linked to a phosphate group, which are attached to the peptidoglycan layer by covalent bonds with the acid of acetyl muramic acid (6-hydroxy-N-acetyl-muramic) [30, 31] also called lipoteichoic acids because they leave the cytoplasmic membrane and have a negative charge. Teichoic acids extend over the entire surface of the peptidoglycan, and given their negative charge, they give the cell wall of the bacterium its net negative charge, being the teichoic and lipoteichoic acids the ones that participate in the entrapment of metal ions on the surface of the cell wall. The Gram-negative cell is a bit more complex, in which the peptidoglycan layer (cell wall) has a thickness of 2–7 nm surrounded by an outer membrane of 7–8 nm, and the peptidoglycan is between the plasma membrane and the outer membrane, which is composed of phospholipids, lipopolysaccharides (LPS), enzymes, and other molecules such as lipoproteins. The polysaccharide chains constitute the O-antigens of the Gram-negative bacteria; the lipopolysaccharides (LPSs) are formed by lipid chains and carbohydrates; these LPSs are joined to the outer membrane by ionic and hydrophobic interactions; the groups of LPSs and phospholipids have a net negative charge, so that they are attributed to the cell surface charge of Gram-negative cells; and these are the primary sites of interaction with metal ions [30, 31]. Due to these characteristics, bacteria can be used as biosorbents; in addition to that, their small size and rapid growth ability under pre-established conditions (temperature, pH, nutrients, aeration, etc.) allow the recovery of various metals or specific metals depending on the conditions used and the type of microorganism. Some species like *Bacillus* [16, 22, 32], *Pseudomonas* [33], *Streptomyces* [34], and *Microbacterium* [24, 27] have already been tested for the recovery of some metals such as Cr (VI), Cu, Cd, Fe (III), Pb, Hg, Ni, Zn, Pd, Pt, Th, U, and V.

3. Microorganisms with potential for the treatment and recovery of metals

Currently, there are commercial systems of biorecovery of metals that use different biosorbent matrices, among which are AlgaSORB™, AMT-BIOCLAIM™, BIO-FIX®, B.V. SORBEX, BIO-FIX®, MetaGeneR, and RAHCO Bio-Beads; the first uses a biosorbent material based on algae *Chlorella vulgaris* with a thickness of 1–3 mm consisting of an immobilized biofilm on a silica-gel matrix and is the most popular of these sorbents; this biological ion-exchange resin was able to bind both metallic cations and metallic oxoanions and could be competitive to commercial ion-exchange resins. The second consists of a biosorbent material based on immobilized *Bacillus subtilis* cells on extruded beds of polyethyleneimine (PEI) and glutaraldehyde, removes metals ions from wastewater, and recovered precious metals [47, 48]. Several works have reported improvement of the adsorption capacity of biosorbents after immobilization of microorganisms on matrices, and some of them are *Aspergillus niger*, *Rhizopus nigricans*, *Trichoderma viride*, *Pseudomonas fluorescens*, *Microbacterium oxydans*, *Cupriavidus* sp., *Sphingobacterium*, *Bacillus* strain CR-7, *Bacillus subtilis*, *Candida albicans*, *Saccharomyces cerevisiae*, *Saccharomyces uvarum*, and *Saccharomyces lipolytica* [47, 48].

The siderophores are molecules produced by some microorganisms and have been used to reduce the level of metal contamination in the environment specifically from soil and water. The siderophores are low molecular weight (<10 kDa) iron chelating compounds synthesized by many bacteria of which can be mentioned *Pseudomonas, Azotobacter*, *Bacillus*, *Enterobacter*, *Serratia*, *Azospirillum*, and *Rhizobium* [43, 44, 49] and are extremely effective in solubilizing and increasing the mobility of a wide range of metals such as Cd, Cu, Ni, Pb, Zn, and the actinides Th(IV), U(IV), and Pu(IV) [44]. This ability of siderophores mainly depends on their ligand functionalities, by which means siderophores may have a strong affinity or selectivity for a particular metal other than Fe with regard to the stability constants of this metal-siderophore complex [43].

However, bioleaching processes are the most reported for the treatment of metal contaminated waste or for the recovery of metals. The genus of *Acidithiobacillus* is the most reported autotrophic sulfur-oxidizing bacterium for metal solubilization, particularly because it has been able to tolerate high concentrations of heavy metals. Obtaining the energy required for its metabolism is received through aerobic oxidation and the reduction of sulfur compounds, including sulfides, elemental sulfur, thiosulfates, and Fe^{2+}, producing H_2SO_4 [38, 42, 50, 51]. During bioleaching, several mechanisms are involved, including (1) acidolysis, (2) complexolysis, (3) redoxolysis, and (4) bioaccumulation. However, operating costs are higher for fungal leaching (by heterotrophs) than bacterial leaching (by autotrophs) due to the need for an organic carbon source for their growth and organic acid excretion [5].

In the bioleaching, once the acid is produced in a medium, it favors a decrease in pH and creates a highly protonated medium (H^+) in which a series of electrochemical reactions are carried out, where solid compounds are transformed into soluble and extractable forms and subsequently can be recovered [5, 41]. There are iron-oxidizing species within *Acidithiobacillus* genus, as *Acidithiobacillus ferrooxidans*, which obtain their energy by oxidation of Fe^{2+} to Fe^{3+} [38]. In addition to *Acidithiobacillus* genus, some fungi, as *Aspergillus niger* [39, 41] and *Penicillium simplicissimum* [40], have been studied for the production and secretion of organic acids such as oxalic, malic, gluconic, and citric acid. The production of these acids involves a large number of enzymatic reactions, for example, gluconic acid is produced extracellularly in two steps, and the glucose in the medium is oxidized in a glycolysis process mediated by glucose oxidase. The secretion of these acids by the cell also lowers the pH in the medium, protonating it, causing the solubilization of metals from a solid matrix to the liquid medium. Given the solubility characteristics of metals in these acidic media, leaching processes have been successfully applied since the 1980s in large-scale treatments for the recovery of metals such as Ni, Co, Zn, Mo, V, Cd, Al, Cu, V, Fe, and Mn, from solid waste using microorganisms listed in **Table 2** [5, 25, 26, 38, 39, 40, 41, 51].

Indirect bioleaching is mainly used in industrial applications since it is believed to be the most appropriate for increasing the efficiency of leaching processes, avoiding toxicity problems toward microbial cells by being in the presence of the solid waste. However, some authors mention that the presence of cells and metabolite produced increases the percentages of metal recovery compared to

Bacteria and archaea	Fungi
Acidithiobacillus albertensis	*Aspergillus flavus*
Acidithiobacillus caldus	*Aspergillus foetidus*
Acidithiobacillus ferrooxidans	*Aspergillus niger*
Acidithiobacillus thiooxidans	*Penicillium chrysogenum*
Ferrimicrobium acidiphilum	*Penicillium simplicissimum*
Ferroplasma acidiphilum	*Penicillium tricolor*
Leptospirillum sp.	
Leptospirillum ferriphilum	
Leptospirillum ferrooxidans	
Sulfolobus metallicus	
Sulfolobus yangmingensis	
Sulfobacillus acidophilus	
Sulfobacillus thermosulfidooxidans	

Table 2.
Microorganisms used in bioleaching treatments.

indirect bioleaching processes [52]. Currently, the bioleaching process is the only one reported for the recovery of metals from depleted catalysts, where treatment efficacy has been proven up to 90% using *Acidithiobacillus* and *Aspergillus*. The first bioleach process development that was commercialized for agitated tank bioleaching of sulfide concentrates was at the Fairview Gold Mine in South Africa in 1986 with a current capacity of 65–80 t/d. Another plants of refractory gold tank bioleaching operations are located in Brazil (1991); West Australia (1993); Obuasi, Ghana (1994); Tasmania, Australia (2000); Shandong, PR China (2001); Krasnoyarsk, Russia (2001); Kazakhstan (2005); Victoria, Australia (2005); Ghana (2006); PR China (2006); and Uzbekistan (2008), with different capacities of operation [51]. At present, there are patented processes that are used in the world, among which stand out BIOX®, BioCOP™, BROGIM®, GEOCOAT®, and BacTech® [51]. GeoBiotics originally developed the GEOCOAT® system for the treatment of refractory gold deposits and has since expanded the technology for the treatment of copper, nickel and cobalt. The process incorporates elements of two successful and commercially proven technologies: heap leaching and biooxidation, depending on temperature of operation, the heap is inoculated with mesophilic or thermophilic microorganism [53]. The GEOCOAT® technologies, together with a wide variety of additional expertise and patents, constitutes the GeoBiotics technology suite, including high-temperature bioleaching, toxins removal, HotHeap™, BIOPRO™, and other complementary processes focused around pretreatment, aeration, stacking, and instrumentation [54].

4. Treatment of spent catalysts of the petrochemical industry by microbial route

In the case of the treatment of spent catalysts, the coke that is impregnated in the pellets modifies the particle size, in addition to restricting and decreasing the contact surface between microorganisms and metals, so a pretreatment is necessary to eliminate oil residues and subsequently enter the waste into the bioleaching process; therefore, the continuous treatment is often transformed into a batch treatment (batch processes) causing the process to slow down and increase the cost of the treatment [55, 56].

The most reported biological processes for the treatment of catalysts involve bioleaching processes using *Acidithiobacillus thiooxidans* and *Acidithiobacillus ferrooxidans* as producers of inorganic acids in direct bioleaching systems [38, 50]. Using inorganic acids and a concentration of 10% v/v of spent catalyst, recovery of Ni and V can go up to 98–99% and other metals, such as Mo, Co, Al, and Fe, in a smaller proportions (60–80%) [56]. Using a mixed culture of Fe/S oxidizers with *A. ferrooxidans*, *A. thiooxidans,* and *L. ferrooxidans*, a recovery was achieved of 83–90% of Ni and V from the spent catalyst at 10% (w/v) of pulp density [42].

Aspergillus niger is a heterotrophic fungus reported in bioleaching processes mediated by organics acids as oxalic acid, reaching recovery percentages of 62.8% of Ni when was used spent catalyst at a concentration of 1% (w/v) [39]. In another study, that used the same microorganism, recovery was 45.8% of Ni in a concentration of 3% (w/v) of spent catalyst [41]. Although these microorganisms are the most reported in the literature for the treatment of spent catalysts, other microorganisms of the genus *Bacillus* are being evaluated for these bioleaching processes, and *Bacillus megaterium* was studied for leaching Re and Pt using the cyanide produced by this microorganism [57]. The ability of *Bacillus megaterium* MNSH1-9K-1 and *Bacillus subtilis* PRGSd-9K-4 for the removal of Ni and V was evaluated by using a mineral medium plus a spent catalyst at 16% (w/v) of pulp density, finding removals of Ni and V of 149.5 and 920.5 mg/kg, respectively [22]. Species of genus *Bacillus* have been reported to remove metals Ni, V, Al, Fe, As, and Mg at different extents, and cell morphology changes have been detected at the end of biological treatment as a higher quantity of spores for *Bacillus thuringiensis* MNSH2-AH-3, 2 μm cells in pairs for *Bacillus megaterium* MNSS-AH-4, and long chain-vegetative cells having inclusions into the cell surface in *Bacillus* sp. PRGSd-MS-2 [16]. The ability of *Microbacterium oxydans* MNSH2-PHGII-1 and *Microbacterium liquefaciens* MNSH2-PHGII-2 has recently been reported for the removal of Ni and V metals by using a rich medium added of 16% of spent catalyst (w/v) finding removal percentages for Ni 45.4 and 51% and for V 30.4 and 41.4% for each microorganism, respectively [24]. *Microbacterium liquefaciens* is able to remove Ni and V from spent catalyst at 80% (w/v) pulp density in a glass-column system under the following laboratory conditions: 80% (w/v) pulp density, inoculum at 20% (3×10^8 CFU/ml), air at 80 ml/min, incubated at 30°C during 14 days. Under this condition, it was able to remove 1007.4 mg/kg of Ni, while V was removed at an extent of 5360.5 mg/kg [27]. Suspensions containing bioemulsifier produced by *Microbacterium* sp. strains were shown to be able to remove cadmium and zinc from contaminated industrial residue and its ability varied according to carbon source [58]. About the biosorption capacity of cadmium by the biopolymers Microbactan and MC3B-22, both synthetized by marine bacteria *Microbacterium* sp. MC3B-10 and *Bacillus* sp., respectively, the maximum sorption capacity of Cd^{2+} was 97 mg/g for Microbactan and 141 mg/g for *B. firmus* EPS, both at pH 7 and 28°C. In addition, microbactan and *B. firmus* exopolymeric substances (EPSs) were nontoxic to *Artemia salina nauplii*, which is an aquatic model organism widely used in aquaculture activities [59].

5. Conclusion

Microorganisms can adapt to different environments. Biological treatments consider characteristics of interest of the microorganisms used, such as resistance to metals, at acidic and alkaline pH, at low and high temperatures, taking advantage of organic and inorganic sources as a carbon source and energy, and even the ability to secrete substances such as polymers, enzymes and/or proteins, acids or siderophores, and so on, which allow their use directly or indirectly using microbial by-products. However, more studies are required to optimize the processes and conditions for each microorganism and the type of residue to be treated.

Acknowledgements

The authors would like to acknowledge the National Polytechnic Institute, Mexico.

Conflict of interest

The authors declare no conflict of interest.

Author details

Marlenne Gómez-Ramírez[1*] and Sergio A. Tenorio-Sánchez[2]

1 Department of Biotechnology, Center for Research in Applied Science and Advanced Technology, National Polytechnic Institute, Santiago de Querétaro, Querétaro, México

2 Department of Microbiology, National School of Biological Sciences, National Polytechnic Institute, Ciudad de México, México

*Address all correspondence to: mgomezr@ipn.mx

References

[1] Ramírez V, Baez A, López P, Bustillos R, Villalobos MA, Carreño R, et al. Chromium hyper-tolerant *Bacillus* sp. MH778713 assists phytoremediation of heavy metals by mesquite trees (*Prosopis laevigata*). Frontiers in Microbiology. 2019;**10**:1-12. DOI: 10.3389/fmicb.2019.01833

[2] Tchounwou PB, Yedjou CG, Patlolla AK, Sutton DJ. Heavy metals toxicity and the environment. NIH-PA. 2012;**101**:133-164. DOI: 10.1007/978-3-7643-8340-4_6

[3] Barakat MA. New trends in removing heavy metals from industrial wastewater. Arabian Journal of Chemistry. 2011;**4**:361-377. DOI: 10.1016/j.arabjc.2010.07.019

[4] Rajasulochana P, Preethy V. Comparison on efficiency of various techniques in treatment of waste and sewage wáter—A comprehensive review. Resource-efficient Technologies. 2016;**2**(4):175-184. DOI: 10.1016/j.reffit.2016.09.004

[5] Abdullah JJ, El-Imam AA, Greetham D, Du C, Tucker GA. The application of fungi for bioleaching of municipal solid wastes for the production of environmental acceptable compost production. Journal of Environmental Science and Public Health. 2017;**1**(3):167-194. DOI: 10.26502/jesph.96120016

[6] Abdel-Shafy HI, Mansour MSM. Solid waste issue: Sources, composition, disposal, recycling, and valorization. Egyptian Journal of Petroleum. 2018;**27**:1275-1290. DOI: 10.1016/j.ejpe.2018.07.003

[7] Ferronato N, Torretta V. Waste mismanagement in developing countries: A review of global issues. International Journal of Environmental Research and Public Health. 2019;**16**:1060. DOI: 10.3390/ijerph16061060

[8] Smith SR. A critical review of the bioavailability and impacts of heavy metals in municipal solid waste composts compared to sewage sludge. Environment International. 2009;**35**:142-156. DOI: 10.1016/j.envint.2008.06.009

[9] Jadhav UU, Hocheng H. A review of recovery of metals from industrial waste. Journal of Achievements in Materials and Manufacturing Engineering. 2012;**54**(2):159-167

[10] Krook J, Svensson N, Eklund M. Landfill mining: A critical review of two decades of research. Waste Management. 2012;**32**:513-520. DOI: 10.1016/j.wasman.2011.10.015

[11] Cervantes C, Espino-Saldaña AE, Acevedo-Aguilar F, León-Rodríguez IL, Rivera-Cano ME, Avila-Rodríguez M, et al. Interacciones microbianas con metales pesados. Revista Latinoamericana de Microbiología. 2006;**48**(2):203-210

[12] Silver S, Phung LT. A bacterial view of the periodic table: Genes and proteins for toxic inorganic ions. Journal of Industrial Microbiology & Biotechnology. 2005;**32**:587-605. DOI: 10.1007/s10295-005-0019-6

[13] Javanbakht V, Alavi SA, Zilouei H. Mechanisms of heavy metal removal using microorganisms as biosorbent. Water Science and Technology. 2014;**69**(9):1775-1787. DOI: 10.2166/wst.2013.718

[14] Agrawal J, Sherameti I, Varma A. In: Sherameti I, Varma A, editors. Handbook of Detoxification of Heavy Metals. Berlin, Heidelberg: Springer-Verlag; 2011. pp. 1-35. DOI: 10.1007/978-3-642-21408-0

[15] Kocberber N, Dönmez G. Chromium (VI) bioaccumulation capacities of adapted mixed cultures isolated form industrial saline wastewaters. Bioresource Technology. 2007;**98**:2178-2183. DOI: 10.1016/j.biortech.2006.08.017

[16] Gómez-Ramírez M, Rojas-Avelizapa NG, Hernández-Gama R, Tenorio-Sánchez SA, López-Villegas EO. Potential use of *Bacillus* genera for metals removal from a spent catalysts. Journal of Environmental Science and Health, Part A. 2019;**54**(8):701-710. DOI: 10.1080/10934529.2019.1585720

[17] Gómez-Ramírez M, Tenorio-Sánchez SA. Parameters invoolved in biotreatment of solid waste containing metals. In: Rojas-Avelizapa NG, editor. Book of Biotechnology for Treatment of Wastes Containing Metals. River Publishers: Denmark; 2019. pp. 43-64

[18] Girma G. Microbial bioremediation of some heavy metals in soils: An updated review. Indian Journal of Science Research. 2015;**6**(1):147-161

[19] Gómez-Ramírez M, Zarco-Tovar K, Aburto J, De León RG, Rojas-Avelizapa NG. Microbial treatment of sulfur-contaminated industrial wastes. Journal of Environmental Science and Health, Part A. 2014;**49**:228-232. DOI: 10.1080/10934529.2013.838926

[20] Gómez-Ramírez M, Rivas-Castillo AM, Monroy-Oropeza SG, Escorcia-Gómez A, Rojas-Avelizapa NG. Effect of glucose concentration on Ni and V removal from a spent catalyst by *Bacillus* spp. strains isolated from mining sites. Acta Universitaria. 2018;**28**(3):1-8. DOI: 10.15174/au.2018.1475

[21] Pradhan D, Mishra D, Kim DJ, Chaudhury GR, Lee SW. Dissolution kinetics of spent petroleum catalyst using two different acidophiles. Hydrometallurgy. 2009;**99**:157-162. DOI: 10.1016/j.hydromet.2009.07.014

[22] Arenas-Isaac G, Gómez-Ramírez M, Montero-Álvarez L, Tobón-Avilés A, Fierros-Romero G, Rojas-Avelizapa NG. Novel microorganisms for the treatment of Ni and V of spent catalysts. Indian Journal of Biotechnology. 2017;**16**:370-379

[23] Fornalczyk A. Industrial catalysts as a source of valuable metals. Journal of Achievements in Materials and Manufacturing Engineering. 2012;**55**(2):864-869

[24] Gómez-Ramírez M, Montero-Álvarez LA, Tobón-Avilés A, Fierros-Romero G, Rojas-Avelizapa NG. *Microbacterium oxydans* and *Microbacterium liquefaciens*: A biological alternative for the treatment of Ni-V-containing wastes. Journal of Environmental Science and Health, Part A. 2015;**50**(6):602-610. DOI: 10.1080/10934529.2015.994953

[25] Gómez-Ramírez M, Rivas-Castillo A, Rodríguez-Pozos I, Avalos-Zuñiga RA, Rojas-Avelizapa NG. Feasibility study of mine tailing's tretament by *Acidithiobacillus thiooxidans* DSM26636. World Academy of Science, Engineering and Technology. 2018;**12**(12):468-471. DOI: 10.5281/zenodo.2363155

[26] Rivas-Castillo AM, Gómez-Ramírez M, Rodríguez-Pozos I, Rojas-Avelizapa NG. Bioleaching of metals contained in spent catalysts by *Acidithiobacillus thiooxidans* DSM 26636. World Academy of Science, Engineering and Technology. 2018;**12**(11):430-434. DOI: 10.5281/zenodo.2021685

[27] Rojas-Avelizapa NG, Gómez-Ramírez M, Alamilla-Martínez DG. Metal removal from spent catalyst using *Microbacterium liquefaciens* In solid culture. Advanced Materials Research. 2015;**1130**:564-567. DOI: 10.4028/www.scientific.net/AMR.1130.564

[28] Husaini A, Roslan HA, Hii KSY, Ang CH. Biodegradations of aliphatic hydrocarbon by indigenous fungi isolated form used motor oil contaminated sites. Journal of Microbiology and Biotechnology. 2008;**24**:2789-2797. DOI: 10.1007/s11274-008-9806-3

[29] Van der Wal A, Norde W, Zehnder AJB, Lyklema J. Determination of the total charge in the cell walls of gram-positive bacteria. Colloids and Surfaces B. 1997;**9**(1-2):81-100. DOI: 10.1016/S0927-7765(96)01340-9

[30] Abdi O, Kazemi M. A review study of biosorption of heavy metals and comparison between different biosorbents. Journal of Materials and Environmental Science. 2015;**6**(5):1386-1399

[31] Auer GK, Weibel DB. Bacterial cell mechanics. Biochemistry. 2017;**56**(29):3710-3724. DOI: 10.1021/acs.biochem.7b00346

[32] Rivas-Castillo AM, Guatemala-Cisneros ME, Gómez-Ramírez M, Rojas-Avelizapa NG. Metal removal and morphological changes of *B. megaterium* in the presence of a spent catalyst. Journal of Environmental Science and Health, Part A. 2019;**54**(6):533-540. DOI: 10.1080/10934529.2019.1571307

[33] Lin CC, Lai YT. Adsortion and recovery of lead (II) from aqueous solutions by immobilized *Pseudomonas aeruginosa* PU21 beads. Journal of Hazardous Materials. 2006;**137**(1):99-105. DOI: 10.1016/j.jhazmat.2006.02.071

[34] Bakran FM, Aly MM, Zabermawi NMO. Removal of some heavy metals from industrial wastewater by Actinomycetes isolated from contaminated soil. IOSR-JPBS. 2019;**14**(5):58-69. DOI: 10.9790/3008-1405035869

[35] Vijayaraghavan K, Yun Y-S. Bacterial biosorbents and biosorption. Biotechnology Advances. 2008;**26**(3):266-291. DOI: 10.1016/j.biotechadv.2008.02.002

[36] Mustapha MU, Halimoon N. Microorganisms and biosorption of heavy metals in the environment: A review paper. Journal of Microbial and Biochemical Technology. 2015;**7**(5):253-256. DOI: 10.4172/1948-5948.1000219

[37] Rojas-Avelizapa NG, Hipólito-Juárez IV, Gómez-Ramírez M. Biological treatment of coal combustion wastes by *Acidithiobacillus thiooxidans* DSM 26636. Mexican Journal of Biotechnology. 2018;**3**(3):54-67. DOI: 10.29267/mxjb.2018.3.3.54

[38] Gholami RM, Borghei SM, Mousavi SM. Bacterial leaching of a spent Mo-Co-Ni refinery catalyst using *Acidithiobacillus ferroxidans* and *Acidithiobacillus thiooxidans*. Hydrometallurgy. 2011;**106**:26-31. DOI: 10.1016/j.hydromet.2010.11.011

[39] Santhiya D, Ting Y-P. Use of adapted *Aspergillus niger* in the bioleaching of spent refinery processing catalyst. Journal of Biotechnology. 2006;**121**(1):62-74. DOI: 10.1016/j.jbiotec.2005.07.002

[40] Amiri F, Mousavi SM, Yaghmaei S. Enhancement of bioleaching of a spent Ni/Mo hydroprocessing catalyst by *Penicillium simplicissimum*. Separation and Purification Technology. 2011;**80**:566-576. DOI: 10.1016/j.seppur.2011.06.012

[41] Amiri F, Mousavi SM, Yaghmaei S, Barati M. Bioleaching kinetics of a spent refinery catalyst using *Aspergillus niger* at optimal conditions. Biochemical Engineering Journal. 2012;**67**:208-217. DOI: 10.1016/j.bej.2012.06.011

[42] Beolchini F, Fonti V, Ferella F, Vegliò F. Metal recovery from spent refinery catalysts by means of

biotechnological strategies. Journal of Hazardous Materials. 2010;**178**:529-534. DOI: 10.1016/j.jhazmat.2010.01.114

[43] Ahmed E, Holmströ SJM. Siderophores in environmental research: Roles and applications. Microbial Biotechnology. 2014;7:196-208

[44] Schalk IJ, Hannauer M, Braud A. New roles for bacterial siderophores in metal transport and tolerance. Environmental Microbiology. 2011;**13**(11):2844-2854. DOI: 10.1111/j.1462-2920.2011.02556.x

[45] Nies DH, Silver S. Ion efflux systems involved in bacterial metal resistance. Journal of Industrial Microbiology. 1995;**14**:186-199

[46] Nies DH. Efflux-mediated heavy metal resistance in prokaryotes. FEMS Microbiology Reviews. 2003;**27**:313-339. DOI: 10.1016/S0168-6445(03)00048-2

[47] Michalak I, Chojnacka K, Witek-Krowiak A. State of the art for the biosorption process-a review. Applied Biochemistry and Biotechnology. 2013;**170**:1389-1416. DOI: 10.1007/s12010-013-0269-0

[48] Fosso-Kankeu E, Mulaba-Bafubiandi AF. Review of challenges in the escalation of metalbiosorbing processes for wastewater treatment: Applied and commercialized technologies. African Journal of Biotechnology. 2014;**13**(17):1756-1771. DOI: 10.5897/AJB2013.13311

[49] Ali SS, Vidhale NN. Bacterial siderophore and their application: A review. International Journal of Current Microbiology and Applied Sciences. 2013;**2**(12):303-312

[50] Shahrabi-Farahani M, Yaghmaei S, Mousavi SM, Amiri F. Bioleaching of heavy metals from a petroleum spent catalyst using *Acidithiobacillus thiooxidans* in a slurry bubble column bioreactor. Separation and Purification Technology. 2014;**132**:41-49. DOI: 10.1016/j.seppur.2014.04.039

[51] Gericke M, Neale JW, van Staden PJ. A Mintek perspective of the past 25 years in minerals bioleaching. Journal—South African Institute of Mining and Metallurgy. 2009;**109**:567-585

[52] Mishra D, Kim D, Ralph DE, Ahn JG, Rhee YH. Bioleaching of spent hydro-processing catalyst using acidophilic bacteria and its kinetics aspect. Journal of Hazardous Materials. 2008;**152**:1082-1091. DOI: 10.1016/j.jhazmat.2007.07.083

[53] Harvey TJ, Merwe WBD, Afewu K. The application of the GeoBiotics GEOCOAT® biooxidation technology for the treatment of sphalerite at Kumba resources´ Rosh Pinah mine. Minerals Engineering. 2002;**15**:823-829

[54] Harvey TJ, Bath M. The GeoBiotics GEOCOAT® technology—Progress and challenges. In: Rawlings DE, Johnson BD, editors. Handbook of Biominig. Springer-Verlag: Berlin Heidelberg; 2007. pp. 97-112

[55] Asghari I, Mousavi SM. Effects of key parameters in recycling of metals from petroleum refinery waste catalysts in bioleaching process. Reviews in Environmental Science and Biotechnology. 2014;**13**:139-161. DOI: 10.1007/s11157-013-9329-8

[56] Kim D-J, Pradhan D, Ahn J-G, Lee S-W. Enhancement of metals dissolutions from spent refinery catalyst using adapted bacteria culture—Effects of pH and Fe (II). Hydrometallugy. 2010;**103**:136-143. DOI: 10.1016/j.hydromet.2010.03.010

[57] Motaghed M, Mousavi SM, Rastegar SO, Shojaosadati SA. Platinum

and rhenium extraction from a spent refinery catalyst using *Bacillus megaterium* as a cyanogenic bacterium: Statistical modeling and process optimization. Bioresource Technology. 2014;**171**:401-409. DOI: 10.1016/j.biortech.2014.08.032

[58] Aniszewski E, Peixoto RS, Mota FF, Leite SGF, Rosado AS. Bioemulsifier production by *Microbacterium sp.* strains isolated from mangrove and their application to remove cadmiun and zinc from hazardous industrial residue. Brazilian Journal of Microbiology. 2010;**41**:235-245

[59] Camacho-Chab JC, Castañeda-Chávez MR, Chan-Bacab MJ, Aguila-Ramírez RN, Galaviz-Villa I, Bartolo-Pérez P, et al. Biosorption of cadmium by non-toxic extracellular polymeric substances (EPS) synthesized by bacteria from marine intertidal biofilms. International Journal of Environmental Research and Public Health. 2018;**15**:314. DOI: 10.3390/ijerph15020314

Section 4

Exploitation and Conservation of Forest, Wild Plant and Wildlife Resources

Chapter 14

Protected Areas in Cameroon at the Mercy of the 2035 Emergent Project

Bienvenu Magloire Takem Mbi and Aloysious Kohtem Lebga

Abstract

Cameroon is investing efforts to protect the environment through the creation of protected areas (PAs) while at the same time longing to attain its development objectives of becoming an emergent country in 2035 through the exploitation of its natural potentials. Attaining both objectives is usually accompanied with conflicts between different ministerial departments. This paper consequently seeks to identify those PAs that overlap with other projects (mining, agro-industries, and forest exploitation) and calculate the surface area of the former that has been taken up by the later. Data were obtained from the Interactive Forestry Atlas of Cameroon Version 3.0 produced by the World Resources Institute (WRI) and its partners. Internet sites and existing reports on environmental and development issues in Cameroon among others served as important sources of information. Results demonstrate that an approximate area of more than 1 million hectares (ha) of PA land have been taken-up by the three economic development-oriented projects mentioned above. That is an estimated 1,173,479 ha, 3575 ha and 1814.44 ha of PA land that have been taken-up by mining sites, agro-industries, and forest exploitation, respectively. For both objectives to be attained, concerted efforts from all ministerial departments concerned is mandatory.

Keywords: protected area, vision 2035, mining sites, agro-industries, emergent project

1. Introduction

The government of Cameroon adopted in 2003 the poverty reduction strategy document which is generally considered as a milestone in the process of reforms embarked on by the government at the end of the year 2000. It is highlighted in this document that Cameroon is endowed with significant assets but also faces major challenges which are how to diversify its economy, consolidate growth, and improve the standard of living of its population [1]. Consequently, the central objective of these reforms, which the Government is pursuing with determination, is to significantly reduce poverty and attain a strong and sustainable economic growth [1]. To attain these objectives, a number of priority areas of focus in line with Cameroon's key development objectives were identified. Among them, one has priority 2 which is focused on "strengthening growth by diversifying the economy" and priority 4 whose main objective is "developing basic infrastructures and natural resources while protecting the environment" [1].

However, the overall growth rate was not up to the expected level necessary for drastic poverty reduction. Consequently, the Government decided to revise the economic growth and poverty reduction strategy. To prepare the revised growth and employment it was necessary to realize some major projects, notably: the formulation of an economic development vision by 2035 amongst others [2]. This vision 2035 reads as follows: "Cameroon: an emerging, democratic and united country despite its diversity" [1, 17]. Four major goals have been developed to help the government in attaining the vision. These are (i) reducing poverty to a socially acceptable level; (ii) becoming a medium-income country; (iii) acquiring the status of a newly industrialized country; and (iv) reinforcing national unity and consolidating the democratic process [2].

In order for Cameroon to attain the first three goals, the country has to accelerate its growth rate through the intensification of agro-pastoral and pisci-cultural activities as well as mineral extraction.

Concerning agriculture and to show the countries zeal to attain the objectives, president Paul Biya stated in his 2011 election campaign speech in Maroua that:

> *... I have the ambition to transform our country into a real breadbasket for Central Africa. ... at present, our agriculture accounts for 45,000 jobs and by implementing the measures and granting the new incentives envisaged, agriculture is expected to create 165,000 jobs by 2014 and 200,000 by 2016*[1].

On the 10th of February 2016, that is the eve of the 50th anniversary of the youths' day celebration in Cameroon, the president again reiterated the importance of agricultural to the Cameroonian youths by stating that:

> *The soil has never betrayed anyone. Do not be afraid to take the plunge and become the agricultural entrepreneurs that Cameroon needs. It is a noble and rewarding trade in the so called real economy. I therefore urge the elders to shoulder their responsibility: it is proper to urge the youths to work the land and it is unwise to dissuade them from doing so.* Paul Biya[2].

Regarding the mineral extraction sector, Cameroon is still endowed with important unexploited natural potentials and to accelerate its industrialization, it intends to intensify the exploration and then exploitation of these potentials. Priority will be on petrol, gas, bauxite, aluminum, iron, zinc, nickel, cobalt amongst others [3].

These poverty reduction and development objectives notwithstanding, Cameroon has equally engaged itself in some environmentally and protected areas related conventions. Cameroon signed and ratified the Convention on Biological Diversity (CBD) in 1992 and 1994 respectively. Even before the signing of the CBD, Cameroon already demonstrated its commitments to environmental protection by creating the Ministry of the Environment and Forestry in April 1992. Two years later, that is, in 1994, a forestry legislation was enacted so as to take into consideration the recommendations of the Rio Summit and its related conventions [4]. In 1996, a new law relating to the environment was promulgated [5].

---

1 Campaign speech made by President Paul Biya in Maroua on October 6, 2011 during the occasion of the 2011 presidential election.

2 This is an excerpt of President Paul Biya's message to the youth. This message was delivered over CRTV (Cameroon Radio and Television Corporation) on the 10th of February 2016 on the eve of the 50th anniversary of the youths' day celebration in Cameroon.

The enactment of these laws were supervised by the ministry of the environment and forestry, responsible for all forestry and environmentally related issues in Cameroon until December 2004, when it was split by a presidential decree into the ministry of forestry and wildlife and the ministry of the environment and the protection of nature[3]. In a decree re-organizing the government in December 2011, the latter ministry was renamed, ministry of the environment, protection of nature and sustainable development[4] certainly due to the intrinsic link that exist between the environment and development.

Cameroon is accordingly investing efforts to protect the environment (especially through the creation of protected areas) while at the same time longing to attain its development objectives of becoming an emergent country in 2035 through the exploitation of its natural potentials which are all harbored by the same environment. Attaining both objectives is usually accompanied with a number of conflicts/overlaps between different ministerial departments. It is for this reason that this paper seeks to identify those environmental protection schemes (protected areas) and economic-development geared projects (large scale agriculture, wood and mineral exploitation projects) that are in conflict with each other. Concretely, the paper intends to (i) identify those protected areas that overlap with other projects and (ii) calculate the surface area of these protected areas that have been taken up by these projects.

1.1 Worth and the place of protected areas in life's sake

The International Union for the Conservation of Nature-IUCN and the World Commission on protected areas have defined a PA as:

> *An area of land and/or sea especially dedicated to the protection and maintenance of biological diversity, and of natural and associated cultural resources, and managed through legal or other effective means* [6].

Also adopted at the global level, at least by the 188 countries currently party to the Convention, is the PA definition of the Convention on Biological Diversity-CBD.

> *A geographically defined area which is designated or regulated and managed to achieve specific conservation objectives* [7].

A PA may be a wetland, a tropical or deciduous forest, a cultivated landscape of value, an alpine region, a savanna, a marine area or any number of other types of natural or partially modified ecosystems or indeed any combination of types of ecosystems [8]. According to [9], PAs are a traditional means for pursuing wildlife management and have become increasingly central to conservation strategies. PAs are important tools for the conservation of biological diversity and are cornerstones of sustainable development strategies since they harbor great biological richness and are a major source of material and non-material wealth [10]. According to [11], PAs are the most common tool for *in situ* conservation of biodiversity globally. They are consequently, established in order to conserve forest of biodiversity value from damaging processes, such as deforestation. The evidence reviewed in the report of [12] indicates that there is less deforestation within formally protected areas than in

---

[3] Decree No 2004/320 of December 8, 2004 re-organizing the government of the Republic of Cameroon.

[4] Decree N° 2011/410 of December 9, 2011 organizing the Government of the Republic of Cameroon.

the areas surrounding them. They have thus proven themselves to be an effective tool for the conservation of biodiversity in situ [13].

Protected areas are also the basis for assessing how engaged and committed governments are in conserving biodiversity [14] and so lie at the heart of global commitments intended to preserve for the benefit of present and future generations a range of goods and services essential for life on earth [15]. The importance of PAs is reflected in their widely accepted role as an indicator for global targets and environmental assessments [16]. PAs occupy an important position in the strategic plan for biodiversity 2011–2020 and the Aichi targets which were adopted at the tenth conference of the parties (CoP10) [17]. Target 11 which is related to PAs stipulates that by 2020, at least 17% of terrestrial and inland water areas, and 10% of coastal and marine areas, especially areas of particular importance for biodiversity and ecosystem services, are conserved through effectively and equitably managed, ecologically representative and well-connected systems of PAs and other effective area-based conservation measures, and integrated into the wider landscapes and seascapes [17]. This certainly explains why the world's system of PAs has grown exponentially over the past 25 years, particularly in developing countries where biodiversity is greatest. There are currently over 130,000 protected areas worldwide, covering around 13.9% of the Earth's land surface and 5.9% of the territorial marine surface [18] as against 12.2% of the surface of the globe in 2008 [19] and 8.82% in 1997 [20].

Concurrently, the mission of PAs has expanded from biodiversity conservation to improving human welfare. The result is a shift in favor of PAs allowing local resource use. This implies that aside from their environmental benefits, they can also generate significant economic resources as they represent important stocks of natural, cultural and social capital, supporting the livelihood and wellbeing of many. For example a study conducted in 2003 found that 33 of the world's 105 largest cities obtain a significant proportion of their drinking water from PAs [10]. Providing this water through other means would likely be a costly endeavor and beyond the means of some cities. They can also create investment opportunities and employment. For example, in Guatemala, the Maya Biosphere Reserve generates an annual income of approximately US $47 million while creating employment for 7000 people [10]. Governments therefore recognized PAs as economic institutions which have a key role to play in the alleviation of poverty and the maintenance of the global community's critical life-support systems.

2. Material and data sources

The Republic of Cameroon is a nation with contrasting natural milieu and diversity. This has earned the country the common appellation of "Africa in miniature". Approximately, half of its surface area of 47,550,000 hectares (475,500km^2), is covered by the dense humid forests with the other portion covered with savanna and steppe vegetation. Specifically, these forests cover about 45.6% of the national territory [21]. Most of the forests form part of the Congo Basin forest which is the second largest area of dense tropical forest in the world, following the Amazon basin [22]. This country which extends from latitudes 2° to 13° north of the equator and longitudes 8° 25′ and 16°20′ east of the Greenwich Meridian is ranked second in terms of forest cover in Africa after the Democratic Republic of Congo (DRC). It is bordered by Nigeria to the west, Chad to the north, the Central African Republic to the east, Congo, Gabon and Equatorial Guinea to the south and the Atlantic Ocean to the south west.

In Cameroon, 9000 species of flora have been registered of which 156 are endemic. Equally, 297 species of mammals, (10 endemic), 849 species of birds

(11 endemic), 373 species of reptiles and amphibians (19 endemic) and 451 species of fish have been cataloged [23].

A number of protected areas have consequently been created with the intention to conserve these biological wealth. However, since the country basically depends on available natural resources for its growth, the attribution of exploitation permits for large scale agricultural development projects, mining and forestry exploitation has always been done without appropriate consultation between the various ministerial departments and appropriate field work so as to verify the land use and land cover of the area being allocated. Consequently, a number of these permits are attributed closed to protected areas and some even overlap with these PAs and other land use types. Identifying these PAs and evaluating the area taken up by these various exploitation permits is the major objective of this work.

In order to attain this objective, data was obtained from the database produced by a team composed of staff of the World Resources Institute (WRI), the Ministry of Forestry and Wildlife (MINFOF) of Cameroon, and other partners including the Centre Technique de Forêt Communale (CTFC), and GIZ-Pro-PFE. The WRI and MINFOF have collaborated since 2002 to build national capacity to monitor and manage forests focusing on modern techniques of information management. Together, this information is assembled in the interactive forest atlas of Cameroon, a complete cartographic database containing forest land use allocation and related activities in Cameroon. For the present chapter, Internet sites and the Interactive Forestry Atlas of Cameroon Version 3.0 produced by the above-mentioned structures in 2012 served as important sources of data. Existing reports on forestry and environmental issues in Cameroon notably the national biodiversity strategy action plan (NBSAP) and Cameroon's national reports to the CBD (especially the fifth national report published in 2014) amongst others served as important sources of information.

Data for protected areas, mining and agro-industrial sites as well as forest management units (FMU) were extracted from the WRI database. Since we intended to identify those protected areas that overlap with mining exploitation sites, these first two sets of data were extracted and overlaid on each other. As these data come from the same database, they could easily overlay due to fact that they have the same coordinate system, that is, WGS 84. The same operation was carried out for PAs and agro-industries, the former and FMU as well as with PAs that had multiple conflict zones.

The surface area for the overlapping zone was gotten by employing the Geoprocessing tool in ArcGIS 10.5. Specifically, the overlapping zone was clipped by using a clip operation in the same software and then the surface area taken-up in hectares was calculated with the use of the calculate geometry tool. These operations helped in the realization of the objectives of this work which were to identify those protected areas that overlap with other development geared projects and then calculate the surface area of these protected areas that have been taken-up.

3. Results

Statistics demonstrate that a total of 15 PAs covering about 2,626,870 hectares have conflicting boundaries with mining permit sites in Cameroon. The total surface area of these PAs that overlapped with mining permits[5] is estimated at 1,173,479 hectares which is approximately 45% of the total surface area that is in conflict with mining activities (**Table 1**).

[5] These permits could be exploitation, exploration and permits for research.

Name of PA	Official surface area (ha)	Area taken-up by mining activity (ha)	% of total surface area taken-up by mining activity
National Parks			
Bénoué	180,000	163,220	91
Bouba Ndjida	220,000	83,938	38
Bouba Bek	238,225	188,225	79
Campo Ma'an	264,064	160,004	60
Ebo	112,000	39,635	35
Kimbi-Fungom	95,380	15,235	16
Kom	67,843	57,235	84
Korup	125,900	12,026	10
Lobéké	217,854	80,273	37
Nki	309,362	182,104	59
Vallé de Mberé	77,760	2559	3
Sub-Total	**1,908,388**	**984,454**	**51.5**
Wildlife Reserves			
Dja	526,000	62,643	12
Ngoyla	156,672	107,373	68
Sub-Total	**682,672**	**170,016**	**25**
Wildlife sanctuaries			
Mengame	27,723	11,405	41
Tofala Hill	8087	7604	94
Sub-Total	**35,810**	**19,009**	**53**
Grand Total	**2,626,870**	**1,173,479**	**44**

Source: [24, 25].

Table 1.
Area and percentage area of PAs taken-up by mining activities.

Table 1 illustrates that 15 PAs divided into three categories have conflicting boundaries with mining permits. These are national parks (11), 2 wildlife reserves and sanctuaries each. While 51.5% of the surface area of national parks are conflict zones, 25% and 53% of wildlife reserves and wildlife sanctuaries in that order overlap with mining permits. The overlapping area of PAs and mining permit ranges from 94% for the Tofala Hill Wildlife Sanctuary, to 91% for the Bénoué National Park and 12% and 3% for the Dja Wildlife Reserve and the Vallé de Mberé National Park respectively.

The spatial distribution of both these PAs and mining sites as well as their zones of conflicts is presented on **Figure 1**.

Figure 1 demonstrates the distribution of PAs and mining sites that overlap with each other in Cameroon. It illustrates that protected areas in the East and South regions of the country are the most affected. A total of eight PAs in these regions have their boundaries overlapping with those for mining exploitation sites. While the South west and North Regions have two PAs each that have their limits overlying, the North West, Adamawa and Littoral each have one PA meeting with mining sites.

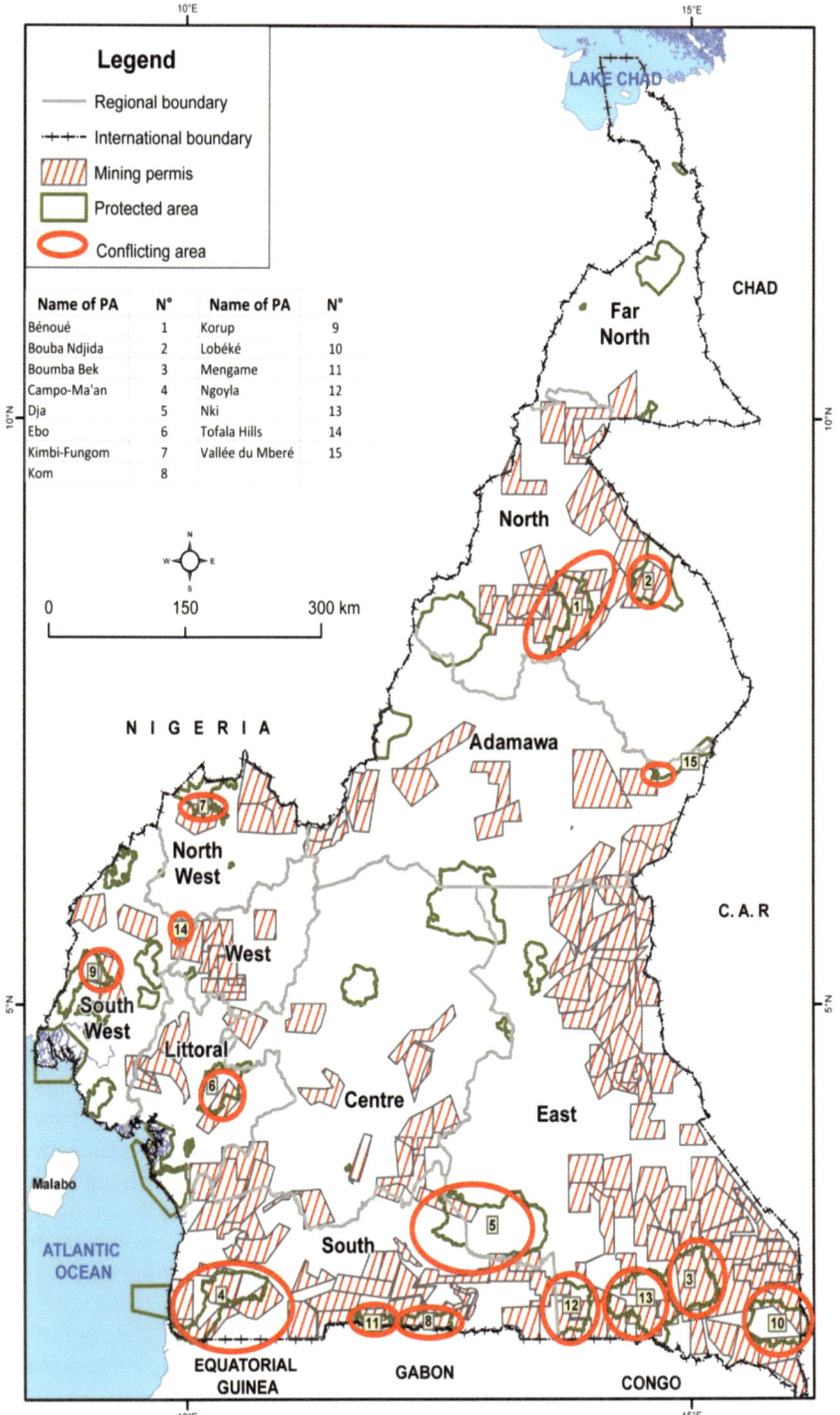

Figure 1.
Overlapping areas of PAs and mining permits.

Name of PA	Surface area (ha)	Conflicting area (ha)	% Of conflict area
Ndongere	237,311	74	0.031
Korup	125,900	137	0.001
Douala-Edea	262,935	3412	1.246
Rumphi Hills	46,655	170	0.003
Bayang_mbo	66,000	25	0.037
Lac Ossa	4572	61	1.334
Total	**743,373**	**3575,07**	**0.480**

Table 2.
Area of conflict between PAs and agro-industries.

Name of PA	Surface area (ha)	Conflicting area (ha)	% Of conflict area
Mengame	27,723	1097,38	4
Kom	67,843	6970	0.102
Ebo	112,000	435,13	0.388
Korup	125,900	212,67	0.168
Total	**333,466**	**1814,88**	**0.544**

Table 3.
PAs and FMUs with incompatible limits.

Concerning PAs that have conflicting boundaries with agro-industrial structures, statistics revealed the following (**Table 2**).

Table 2 demonstrates that six PAs have overlapping boundaries with agro-industries. These PAs have a surface area of 743,373 ha. Out of this area, 3575 ha, that is about 0.48% of this surface area has been taken-up by agro-industries. The most affected PAs are Lac Ossa and Douala-Edea with 1.334 and 1.246% of their surface areas, respectively, that conflict with agro-industries.

The major agro-industries operating in these areas are *Hévéa Cameroun* (HEVECAM) which is specialized in the cultivation of rubber, *Société Camerounaise de Palmeraies* (SOCAPALM) and SGSOC Heracles (Global Sustainable Oil Cameroon) for palm nut cultivation and *Plantation du Haut Penja* (PHP) for bananas. It is worth noting that these structures are both nationally and internationally owned.

Apart from the allocation of permits for mining and agro-industrial activities that have been ear-marked by the government of Cameroon as corner-stones for raising revenue and consequently economic growth and national development, forestry exploitation has for a long time served in this respect. Forestry Management Units-FMUs (known in French as UFAs), have accordingly been allocated for exploitation without taking into consideration the existing protected areas in the landscape. The boundaries of some of these FMUs therefore intersect with those of some PAs (**Table 3**).

Four PAs limits correspond with those of FMUs. Out of a surface area of 333,466 ha, 1814,88 ha, that is approximately 0.544% of the area overlaps with each other. The most affected of these PAs is the Mengame Wildlife sanctuary where about 109,738 ha (4%) of its surface area corresponds to that of a FMU.

The three economic oriented activities have taken up an area of more than 1 million hectares approximately, which is about 31.82% of the surface area of the PAs

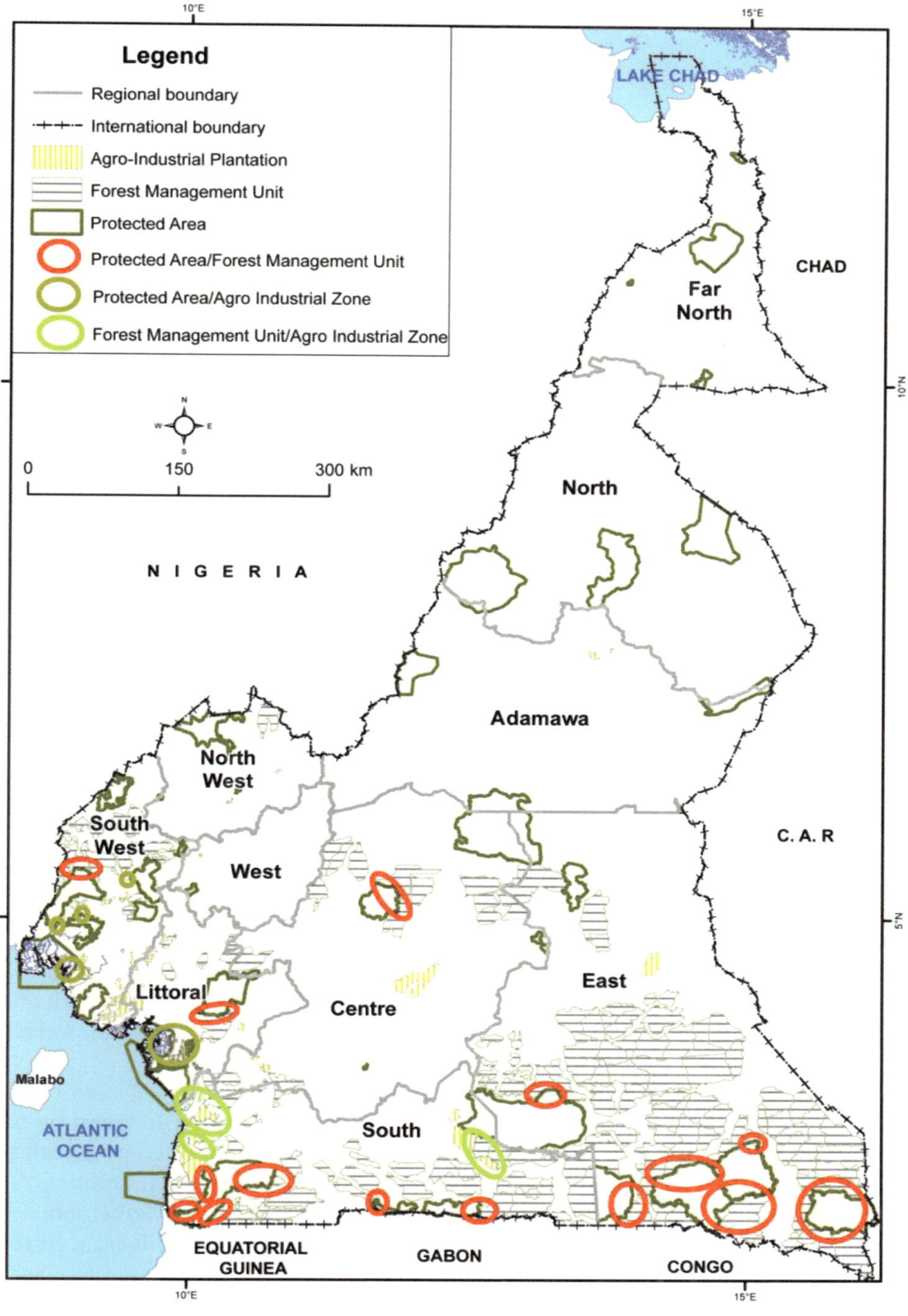

Figure 2.
Overlap of PAs, agro-industries and FMUs.

concerned. While mining exploitation activities have occupied close to 44.6% of the surface area of the PAs in question, agro-industries and FMUs, are overlaid on 0.480 and 0.544% of these PAs, respectively.

It should be noted that not only PAs overlapped with economic related activities. Results demonstrate that the economic related activities sometimes have conflicting

Name of PA	Area (ha)	Mining		Agro-industries		FMUs		Total area	Total %
		Area (ha)	% Of area	Area (ha)	% Of area	Area (ha)	% Of area		
Mengame	27,723	11,405	41	0	0	1097,38	4	12,502,38	45
Ebo	112,000	39,635	35	0	0	435,13	0.388	40,070,13	35.77
Korup	125,900	12,026	10	137	0,001	212,67	0.168	12,240,04	9.72

Table 4.
PAs with multiple exploitation boundary conflicts.

boundaries too. This overlapped of PAs with agro-industries and FMUs as well as agro-industries conflicting with FMUs is illustrated on **Figure 2**.

Figure 2 proves that conflict between PAs and FMUs is predominant in the South and East regions of the country while that between the former and agro-industries is dominantly in the South West region of the country.

Analysis further reveals that while some of the PAs have been affected by just one form of exploitation, that is either mining, agro-industrial or forestry exploitation, the following have been touched by one or two of the above-mentioned type of activities (**Table 4**).

Referring to the PAs with multiple exploitation boundary conflicts, Mengame Wildlife Sanctuary, Ebo and Korup National Parks have 45, 35.77, and 9.72% correspondingly of their area super-imposed on the three activities mentioned above.

4. Conclusion

This study has proved that Cameroon is putting efforts to respect the engagements it took at the international level by signing and ratifying the CBD in 1992 and 1994 in that order. It has done so by creating a number of protected areas. However, within the framework of its development agenda, the country has its 2035 vision which is to become an emergent country. For this vision to come to fruition, the country has embarked on the diversification of its income sources. It has consequently granted several mining; agro-industrial and forest exploitation permits to both international and national companies without taking into consideration the location of some protected areas that have been created.

Results illustrate that 15 PAs have their boundaries overlapping with mining sites. This gives an estimated 1,173,479 ha of PAs land that have been taken-up by mining exploitation permits in Cameroon. The results is corroborated by a preliminary research, by [26] which revealed that a total of at least 33 oil and mining permits have been granted inside of 16 different protected areas in Cameroon. According to [27], from 2011, a total of 494 mining permits were delivered. Among these are 90 exploration and 4 exploitation permits, 150 quarry exploitation permits, and 250 artisanal exploitation permits [28]. This is approximately 2 years after the growth and employment strategy paper which is the reference framework for the government's action over the period 2010–2020 and the Cameroon vision 2035 working documents were adopted.

It is a palpable proof that the government of Cameroon is matching words to action, as mining exploitation was recognized as a major asset to stimulate the national economy, though this is being done to the detriment of other environmentally protected land use schemes such as protected areas. The result of a study by [29] demonstrates that around 96 of the 147 protected areas evaluated in their work are affected by artisanal and small-scale mining in the world. According to [30], approximately 7% of mines for four key metals directly overlap with PAs and a further 27% lie within 10 km of a PA boundary. Given the rapidly growing demand for metals, there is an urgent need to limit or mitigate such conflicts. Though this present study was not able to determine the degree of destruction caused by mining exploitation on PAs, [28], concluded in one of its reports that "all these mining activities have caused a total deforestation of the exploitation sites." The overlapping as well as allocation of mining permits close to PAs leads to conflict with national conservation objectives and according to [26], this represents an important threat and loss of biodiversity in the protected areas especially in renowned PAs as the Korup, Bouba Ndjida, and the Dja Biosphere reserve. Also, Ref. [31] concluded in their research that extractive industries can be a major cause of forest loss, as observed in parts of Papua New Guinea, India's Madhya Pradesh and Guyana.

Further results show that six PAs have overlapping boundaries with agro-industries. About 3575 ha, of PAs land have been taken-up by agro-industries. The major agro-industries operating in these areas are *Hévéa Cameroun,* which is specialized in the cultivation of rubber, *Société Camerounaise de Palmeraies* and Global Sustainable Oil Cameroon for palm nut cultivation and *Plantation du Haut Penja* for bananas. The ministry of the environment, protection of nature, and sustainable development recognizes the role of these agro-industries in land grapping. In one of its reports in 2014, it concluded that "there is currently a growing demand for land for new plantations opened on thousands of hectares of oil palms, rubber, coffee, cocoa, tea, and cotton. Large agro-industrial plantations with new land include: HEVECAM a rubber plantation which extended its plantation by four new blocks totaling 18,889 ha and SGSOC which is setting up a new palm plantation in an area of approximately 60,000 ha" [28]. Agriculture in all its facets accounts for 19.7% of GDP [13].

As concerns PAs and forestry exploitation, it was revealed that four PAs' limits correspond with those of FMUs making 1814,88 ha that overlaps with each other. Cameroon's forestry sector represents about 15,000 and 170,000 direct and indirect employment respectively and represents the third revenue source of the country after agricultural and petrol exportation [13]. This easily explains why a number of FMUs have been allocated for exploitation. As a result of the allocation of mining, agro-industrial and forest exploitation permits coupled with other land use activities in and out of protected areas, the forest area fell from 22.5 million ha in 1975 to 19.5 million in 2005, a difference of almost 3 million ha, corresponding to an annual loss of 100,000 ha/year. This lost is certainly accompanied with that of the biodiversity that is harbored in the forest. In order for this trend to be reversed, concerted efforts from all ministerial departments concerned is necessary.

Author details

Bienvenu Magloire Takem Mbi* and Aloysious Kohtem Lebga
National Institute of Cartography, Department for Geographical Research, Yaoundé, Cameroon

*Address all correspondence to: takemmbi@yahoo.fr

References

[1] Republic of Cameroon: Poverty Reduction Strategy Paper [Report]. Yaounde, Cameroon; 2003

[2] Republic of Cameroon: Growth and Employment Strategy Paper: Reference Framework for Government Action Over the Period 2010-2020 [Report]. Yaounde, Cameroon; 2009

[3] Republic of Cameroon: Cameroon Vision 2035; Working Document [Report].Yaounde, Cameroon; 2009

[4] Republic of Cameroon: Law No 94/ 01 of 20 January 1994, to Lay Down Forestry, Wildlife and Fisheries Regulations. Yaounde, Cameroon; 1994

[5] Ministry of the Environment and Forestry: National Environment Management Plan. Volume 1 [Main Report]. Yaounde, Cameroon; 1996

[6] The International Union for the Conservation of Nature-IUCN: Guidelines for Protected Area Management Categories [Report]. Gland, Switzerland; 1994

[7] Secretariat of the Convention on Biological Diversity-SCBD. Handbook of the Convention on Biological Diversity Including Its Cartagena Protocol on Biosafety, 3rd ed. Montreal, Canada: Convention on Biological Diversity Secretariat; 2005. p. 1533

[8] Phillips A. Economic Values of Protected Areas: Guidelines for Protected Area Managers [Report]. Gland, Switzerland and Cambridge, United Kingdom; 1998

[9] Naughton-Treves L, Margaret B, H, Katrina B. The role of protected areas in conserving biodiversity and sustaining local livelihoods. Annual Review of Environment and Resources. 2005;**30**: 219-252

[10] Secretariat of the Convention on Biological Diversity-SCBD. Protected Areas in Today's World: Their Values and Benefits for the Welfare of the Planet [Technical Series no 36]. Montral, Canada; 2008

[11] Ferraro PJ. Protected areas and human well-being. In: Paper Presented at the on Economics and Conservation in the Tropics: A Strategic Dialogue; 2008

[12] Sánchez-Azofeifa GA, Quesada-Mateo C, Gonzalez-Quesada P, Dayanandan S, Bawa KS. Protected areas and conservation of biodiversity in the tropics. Conservation Biology. 1999; **13**(2):407-411

[13] Shadie P, Epps M. Securing Protected Areas in the Face of Global Change: Key Lessons Learned from Case Studies and Field Learning Sites in Protected Areas. Bangkok, Thailand: IUCN; 2008. p. 49

[14] Boitani L, Richard MC, Holly TD, Georgina MM, Jeff P, Hugh PP, et al. Change the international union for conservation of nature protected area categories to reflect biodiversity outcomes. PLoS Biology. 2008;**6**(3): 0436-0438

[15] Mulongoy KJ, Chape SP, editors. Protected Areas and Biodiversity: An Overview of Key Issues. Montreal, Canada: CBD Secretariat and Cambridge, United Kingdom: UNEP-WCMC; 2004. p. 56

[16] Chape S, Harrison J, Spalding M, Lysenko I. Measuring the extent and effectiveness of protected areas as an indicator for meeting global biodiversity targets. Philosophical Transactions of the Royal Society B. 2005;**2005**(360): 443-455

[17] Secretariat of the Convention on Biological Diversity-SCBD. Report of

the Tenth Meeting of the Conference of the Parties to the CBD [Report]. Nagoya, Japan; 2011

[18] Ervin J, Sekhran N, Dinu A, Gidda S, Vergeichik M, Mee J. Protected Areas for the 21st Century: Lessons from UNDP/GEF's Portfolio [Report]. New York: United Nations Development Programme and Montreal, Canada: Convention on Biological Diversity; 2010

[19] United Nations Environment Programme-World Conservation Monitoring Centre, UNEP-WCMC. State of the world's Protected Areas: An Annual Review of Global Conservation Progress [Report]. Cambridge, United Kingdom: UNEP-WCMC; 2008

[20] Zimmerer KS, Galt RE, Buck MV. Globalization and multi-spatial trends in the coverage of protected area conservation (1980–2000). Ambio. 2004;**33**:520-529

[21] Food and Agriculture Organisation-FAO. State of the World's Forest 2007. Rome, Italy: Food and Agriculture Organisation of the United Nations; 2007. Available from: http://www.fao.org/docrep/009/a0773e/a0773e00.HTM [Accessed: 3 January 2020]

[22] Central African Regional Programme for the Environment. The Forest of the Congo Basin [Internet]. 2006. Available from: http://carpe.umd.edu/documents,accessed [Accessed: 20 November 2019]

[23] Ministry of the Environment and Nature Protection. Convention on Biological Diversity [Third National Report]. Yaounde, Cameroon; 2005

[24] World Resources Institute. Atlas Forestier Interactif du Cameroun. Version 3.0 [Database]. 2012

[25] Ministry of Forestry and Wildlife-MINFOF. Secteur forestier et faunique du Cameroun. Faits et Chiffres [Report]. Yaounde, Cameroon ; 2018

[26] Schwartz B, Hoyle D, Nguiffo S. Emerging Trends in Land-Use Conflits in Cameroon: Overlapping Natural Resource Permits Threaten Protected Areas and Foreign Direct Investment [an Ad Hoc Working Paper]; 2012

[27] Ministry of Forestry and Wildlife, Mamfe. Takamanda National Park, Park Protection Report [Report]. Mamfe, Cameroon; 2013

[28] Ministry of the Environment, Nature protection and sustainable development. Cinquieme Rapport National du Cameroun a la Convention de la Diversité Biologique [Report]. Yaounde, Cameroon; 2014

[29] Villegas C, Weinberg R, Levin E, Hund K. Artisanal and Small-Scale Mining in Protected Areas and Critical Ecosystems Programme (ASM-PACE): A Global Solutions Study. WWF and Estelle Levin, Ltd Report [Report]; 2012

[30] Duran PA, Rauch J, Gaston K. Global spatial coincidence between protected areas and metal mining activities. Biological Conservation. 2013; **160**:272-278

[31] Hund K, Schure J, Van der Goes A. Extractive industries in forest landscapes: Options for synergy with REDD+ and development of standards in the Democratic Republic of Congo. Resources Policy. 2015;**54**:97-108

Chapter 15

Sustainable Management of Tropical Dry Forests: An Overview from Cameroonian Context and the Special Case of Mozogo-Gokoro National Park

Rodrigue Constant Sandjong Sani, Mama Ntoupka, Toua Vroumsia, Tchobsala and Adamou Ibrahima

Abstract

Climate change, desertification, and biodiversity are critical factors in the ongoing multilateral mobilization for sustainable management of natural resources. In order to investigate the administration of a national park, this chapter focuses firstly on the directions taken by the international normative arsenal in the Cameroonian context of forest governance and specifically the reminder of some regulatory texts concerning national parks. After addressing the issue of management of protected areas in the dry Far North of Cameroon, the second part examined the special case of the Mozogo-Gokoro National Park, located in this region, with reference to the results of a survey and administrative report consultations. The analysis reveals a gap between international and national legal instruments and their actual implementations. The park's status as a plant conservation model in Sudano-Sahelian zone is mostly attributable to empirical local practices adapted to the resilience of vegetation.

Keywords: Cameroon, efficiency, *in situ* conservation, international agreements, regulation

1. Introduction

In the dry Sahelian and Sudanian zones in Africa, the constantly growing population is permanently exerting pressures on nature, making unstable ecological systems [1–3]. Climate variability and the fragility of soils are added to constitute worrying risks for the stability of natural ecosystems [4–6]. In addition in these regions, climatic fluctuations at different time scales (seasonal, interannual, and decennial) strongly affect the dynamics of vegetation [7, 8]. Land degradation is also more pronounced there, with a negative impact on biodiversity and soil properties [4]. Human activities have a major effect on these changes [9]. Protected areas representing the main refuges of biological diversity must particularly face these various constraints, hence the recommendation of sustainable management standards starting from the international level.

The international community recommends, in dry areas as elsewhere on the planet, the sustainable management of natural ecosystems as a solution adapted to various threatening factors for the preservation of the environment [10–13]. It is a complex process, involving appropriate planning and integrating the multiplicity of constraints and actors [10, 11, 14, 15].

The definition commonly used at the international level is formulated as follows: "Sustainable forest management means the management and use of forests and woodlands in a way and at such intensity that they maintain their biological diversity, their productivity, their regenerative capacity, their vitality and their capacity to satisfy, now and for the future, the relevant ecological, economic and social functions at local, national and global levels, and that they do not cause damage to other ecosystems" [16, 17]. Sustainable management of dry tropical forests has also been defined as the planning and execution of actions to ensure the conservation and use of a forest according to defined objectives and the physical and socioeconomic context, for the satisfaction of needs of the present and future generations [11, 18]. It helps to conserve and enhance the value of the land, water, plant, and animal heritage, using technical means that are economically and socially appropriate and respectful of the environment. It also implies clearly defined and realistic objectives which can be modified according to biological, ecological, socioeconomic, and political constraints [10]. It contributes to achieving a compromise between what is desirable and what is possible to do as well as to the proper use of all the resources available through continuous and permanent actions. It is presented as an option for adaptation and mitigation of sensitive changes affecting ecosystems [10, 15, 19]. The theoretical realization of a management plan in dry area ecosystems is structured in three [18] or four stages [11, 20]: the knowing and description of the existing; defining objectives, tools, and means; negotiating and drafting a management plan; and the implementation of this plan, its monitoring, and control, which led to the definition of assessment and certification systems for sustainable management.

In other words, it is about developing a multidisciplinary and participative approach, which would allow multiple interventions in the optics of sustainable development. Cameroon, not being on the sidelines of this international advocacy, has set to work on the implementation of these texts through several programs focused on the conservation of natural resources and the fight against desertification. There is a need to ensure over time that this policy is effectively applied, as well as the texts and strategic actions put in place to increase efficiency in forest management. Some authors point out some obstacles in these processes, mainly in relation to governance [21, 22].

In the first part of this chapter on a presentation of the context of sustainable management of dry forests in Cameroon, the description of the normative and institutional frameworks, aspects of the regulations concerning national parks, and the situation of forest governance in the semiarid region of the Far North of Cameroon is discussed alternatively. The second part of the chapter focused mainly on the evaluation of the management efficiency of the Mozogo-Gokoro National Park (MGNP), located in this dry area of the country. Interactive initiatives involving especially scientific actors are recommended in this process [23]. It was thus a question of completing the preliminary work of Sandjong Sani et al. [24], by introducing new data highlighting the constraints, threats, and gaps in the management, and analysis of park evolution, confronting the opinions of various stakeholders and formulating explanatory hypotheses.

2. Context of sustainable forest management in Cameroon dry lands

2.1 Evolution of the normative and institutional frameworks

Profound changes have marked forest management in Cameroon since the colonial era, as specified in the National Forest Action Plan document [25]. Originally, the exploitation of degrading resources of natural ecosystems was almost systematic. It was done without rigorous management planning and division of the territory based on the use and allocation of land according to their different vocations. The forest classification took into account requirements such as the practice of hunting tourism, reforestation, and the protection of endangered areas or the enrichment of impoverished ones. In addition, irregularities had been noted, in particular the weakness of taking into account the socioeconomic and demographic evolution of the zones classified in the delimitation of protected areas, the exclusion of populations in forest management, and a forest administration deficient in skills and technical and financial means for monitoring and effective control of the forest heritage [25]. The consequences were the disappearance of materialized limits, the degradation of the spaces set aside, conflicts from either side of the national territory, and a mining or degrading exploitation of forest resources [26].

Having noted all these shortcomings and in the spirit of an incentive-based multilateral mobilization, the Cameroonian government has adopted, since 1994, new legislative and regulatory texts and programs including the consequent modifications [26]. The zoning of the national territory is systematized (but applied only in the southern part of the country), a diversity of actors are involved in management planning, and the participatory aim is clarified through the concepts of community forest and communal forest and the exercise of right of use in carrying out sustainable development plans. Despite these resolutely sustainability-oriented measures, other noted anomalies led to the establishment of a new important political vision for planning, closely linked to the entire forest and environment sector: the Forest and Environment Sector Program, abbreviated as FESP [26]. Other management initiatives specifically related to the Far North region have come in support, among others, the National Reforestation Program (NRP) and the National Action Plan to Combat Desertification (NAP-CD).

The FESP was set up by the Cameroonian government with the help of the international community, to contribute to the implementation of a new policy of sustainable and participatory management of the country's forest and wildlife resources. The primary objective of this program is to enable the establishment of a coherent framework for all interventions. It is a national sectorial development program established by the government but remains open to funding from all donors as well as contributions from civil society and nongovernmental organizations or NGOs [26]. The FESP set itself the following overall objective: the conservation, management, and exploitation of forest and wildlife resources respond to the local, national, regional, and global needs of present and future generations. Conjectured since its final design for a period of 10 years, it was finally in 2006 that the FESP was able to start with the lifting of the last constraint linked to the availability of external funding for the program. Assessment standards have also been developed.

The National Reforestation Program and the National Action Plan to Combat Desertification were launched in 2006. They were initiated following the observation by the FAO in 2005 of the state of degradation of savannas and the random nature of natural regeneration, especially in areas exploited for long periods and for the application of ratified international conventions [27]. Previously, the Poverty

Reduction Strategy Paper (PRSP) [28] had been adopted in 2003, based on the Millennium Development Goals (MDGs), and focusing one of its objectives on natural resource management and environmental protection.

Beyond this great strategic vitality of planning concerning the forestry sector, some problems are pointed out in the application of texts, especially relating to bad governance [29]. Pitfalls are noted in the traceability of resource extraction and sharing activities, regarding the rights of access of local people to resources and concerning the securing of rights acquired by law.

At the initiative of Ministry of Economy, Planning and Regional Development (MINEPAT), the Strategy Document for Growth and Employment (SDGE) 2010–2020 [30] was established with the planning for emergence of the country by 2035 [31]. Unfortunately, shortcomings were noted in its implementation, and a much better perspective was envisaged with the National Development Plan calibrated over 10 years (2020–2030). In this political vision of programming, the forest sector is well placed. Two main ministries are responsible for implementing the strategic axes concerning the forestry sector.

The Ministry of Forests and Wildlife (MINFOF) should integrate in the different annual or priority action plans the sustainable management, enhancement, promotion, and improvement of the tourist landscape of protected areas. In addition, the Ministry of the Environment, Nature Protection and Sustainable Development (MINEPDED) is also involved in forest management. It intervenes in the implementation and monitoring of the REDD$^+$ mechanism [32, 33]. A National Observatory on Climate Change (ONACC), created in 2009 and placed under its supervision, is responsible, among other things, for proposing to the government mitigation and/or adaptation measures to the harmful effects and risks linked to climate change and to facilitate the achievement of compensation for the climate services provided by forests through sustainable management, conservation, and restoration of ecosystems. The National Adaptation Plan on Climate Change (NAPCC) drawn up in 2015 and the National Biodiversity Strategy and Action Plan revised in 2012 (NBSAP II) are also part of the missions of this ministry [34]. The Ministry of Tourism and Leisure (MINTOUR) intervenes indirectly in the promotion and development of certain nature conservation sites, for ecotourism purposes.

Furthermore, in forest governance in Cameroon, the use of multilateral and bilateral cooperation is a reality. The government relies on an instrument for consultation and management of the forestry sector at the sub-regional level, such as the Central African Forest Commission (COMIFAC) and on other related structures like Network of Protected Areas of Central Africa (RAPAC), Observatory of Forests in Central Africa (OFAC), or the Partnership for Forests of the Congo Basin (PFBC). MINFOF benefits in its daily missions from the support of a considerable number of international and regional cooperation organizations and from the support of donors, such as the European Union (EU), International Union for the Conservation of Nature-Central and West Africa Program (IUCN-PACO), the World Bank, the World Wide Fund for Nature (WWF), German technical cooperation (GIZ), the Center for Development and Environment (CED), the Wildlife Conservation Society (WCS), the Global Environment Facility (GEF), the German Development Bank (KfW), etc. [22]. Thus, despite the threats of terrorism (in the Far North of the country) and the insecurity imposed by certain armed groups (in the northwest and southwest regions), Cameroon enjoys relative political stability, benefits from the responsiveness of its forest, and environmental administrations and the dynamism of its civil society. The country has long served as a laboratory for sustainable forest management initiatives in the Congo Basin [35].

2.2 Specific regulations for the sustainable management of national parks

A protected area is a geographically clear and defined space, recognized, dedicated, and managed by any effective means, legal or other, in order to promote the long-term conservation of nature, ecosystem services, and the cultural values that it abounds [12]. This rational management cannot be effective without the knowledge of ecological, cultural, socioeconomic, and even economic values of the protected area. The 13 successive stages distinguished by IUCN in developing effective management planning for a protected area are as follows [13, 36]:

- Pre-planning, that is to say, preparing the management plan by appointing a team dedicated to the task for a good organization.
- Data collection, identification of obstacles, and various consultations.
- Evaluation and analysis of the data collected in order to obtain information on resources.
- Identification of constraints, opportunities, and threats.
- The development of a management vision and objectives.
- The development of options to achieve this vision and these objectives, including zoning.
- The preparation of a draft management plan.
- Public consultation on the project.
- Evaluation of tenders, revision of the draft plan, production of a final version, analysis of tenders, and report on the results of the consultation process.
- Actions to have the management plan approved.
- The effective implementation of the plan.
- Monitoring and evaluation.
- The decision to revise and update the management plan and reflections on responsibilities.

In summary, a management plan is required in the conservative planning approach of protected areas. This is a necessity in drylands where serious threats to biodiversity exist.

Protected areas are classified into six categories by IUCN, according to their management objectives [12]. We cannot therefore in theory categorize a protected area without information on its management objectives. Category II represents national parks that are managed primarily for ecosystem conservation and recreation. Two others are added to the IUCN categories, created by UNESCO, which very often overlap: biosphere reserves and world heritage sites [37].

In the regulatory texts of Cameroon, in particular the 1994 forestry law [38] and subsequent implementing decrees [39, 40], national parks and other protected areas (wildlife reserves, areas of hunting interest, state-owned game-ranches, wildlife sanctuaries, buffer zones) are part of the state's permanent forest estate. In Cameroonian law, a national park is defined as a perimeter in one piece, whose conservation of fauna, flora, soil, subsoil, atmosphere, water, and, in general, the natural environment presents a special interest which is important to preserve against any effort of natural degradation and to withdraw from any intervention likely to alter its appearance, composition, and evolution [39]. The following activities are prohibited: hunting and fishing, except in the management process; agricultural, pastoral, and forestry activities; the wandering of domestic animals; overflight by an aircraft at an altitude below 200 m; the introduction of native or imported zoological or botanical species, except for scientific purposes or within the framework of management operations authorized by the ministry responsible for wildlife [39].

These Cameroonian texts define sustainable management as the implementation, on the basis of objectives and a plan agreed in advance, of a certain number of activities and investments, with a view to sustained production of forest products and services, without affecting the intrinsic value or compromising the future productivity of the forest and without causing undesirable effects on the physical and social environment. Any activity in protected areas is therefore subject to the development of a management plan.

The management plan is a document adopted by the minister in charge of forests, based on the results of a so-called management inventory. It includes the objectives assigned to the protected area, the infrastructure to be built, the operating methods and conservation conditions, the regeneration programs, the related forecast costs, as well as the plan revision periodicity. The governance of protected areas is state-based. However, it is possible to associate a public body playing an intermediary role like decentralized local authorities and to subcontract certain activities to private or community structures (local communities, associations, and NGOs) in the realization of management plans.

2.3 Status of national park management in the Far North Region

The Cameroonian government has so far established the Waza, Kalamaloué, and Mozogo-Gokoro National Parks in the semiarid Far North region as well as 17 forest reserves. Waza National Park is presented alone as the only *in situ* conservation site to have an ecological monitoring system relating to the management plan [22]. However, the protected areas of this region, mainly in savannah ecosystems, are of great importance for the conservation of the large mammalian fauna of Africa, with more than 40 different species of large and medium mammals, and more than 300 species of birds, some of which are endemic or endangered [41].

Regarding the management of forest cover in this region, the absence of zoning of the forests, like those of the southern part of the country, frequently leads to numerous conflicts of use between the activities of farmers and ranchers (clearing, pastures) and those of conservation and tourism stakeholders [22]. A study carried out in this environment by Gautier and Ntoupka [42] indicates a change in the perception of the community of users of tree resources, favorable to their protection. Peasants in this densely populated region have become aware, for the most part, of the exhaustion of plant resources. They are committed to preserving the tree capital they have or to reforest. This change in perceptions is not necessarily linked to a change in practices favorable to the reconquest of the trees. Aging, residual wooded parks, without recovery or good management, are still observed [42]. However, changes in perception and attitude are also observed among the actors of the administration and development agents [42]. The first set themselves up as technical advisers to the population instead of resource conservators; the second operate a new reflection on trees and land with the need to rehabilitate the traditional forest heritage [43, 44].

Despite these positive aspects, practices prohibited under the law are still observed in protected areas [27]. The implications of the changing legal arsenal of forest sector for protected areas in the region are sometimes ineffective and limited [27, 44]. To remedy this illegal appropriation, several management strategies with direct or indirect effects in these conservation areas are applied. They are carried out through the state (programs and projects under the supervision of MINEPDED, MINFOF, and MINEPAT), multinational structures (e.g., PRESIBALT or Program for the Rehabilitation and Reinforcement of Socio-ecological Resilience Systems in the Lake Chad Basin), donors and cooperation organizations (World Bank, EU, IUCN, GIZ, etc.), and NGOs such as ACODED (Concerted Action for Sustainable Development) and Actions for Biodiversity and Land Management (ABIOGeT). The State also invests in the enrichment of forests and the restoration of degraded ecosystems. The National Forestry Support Development Agency (ANAFOR) and the Regional Committee for Drought Control are government technical partners in these various projects. Several NGOs are also supporting the sustainable management of natural resources in the region through initiatives aimed at the development and the fight against poverty of local populations, often affected by displacement due to the conflict against "Boko Haram." In this case, we can cite the Support Service for Local Development Initiatives (SAILD) and the "RESILIANT" consortium (Inclusive Economic and Social Recovery and the Fight against Food and Nutritional Insecurity in the North and Far North Territories of Cameroon), bringing together several NGOs counting, among their intervention sites, the two main municipalities of influence of the MGNP (Koza and Mozogo).

It is deplorable to note that due to the context of insecurity, all the national parks of the Far North region are experiencing a drop in tourist numbers. There is evidence of significant economic losses felt at the state level but also by the local population. To deal with this unfortunate situation affecting the management of protected areas, obtaining a sufficient database of physical and human environments at all times is an essential step.

3. Special case of the management of Mozogo-Gokoro National Park

3.1 General information about the site

Mozogo Gokoro National Park is situated between 10°56′ and 10°57′ North latitude and between 13°54′ and 13°58′ East longitude. This IUCN Category II protected area is located in Mayo-Moskota sub-division of Mayo-Tsanaga Division in the Far North region of Cameroon. Covering an area of 1400 ha, this site was created as a forest and wildlife reserve by decree No. 165 of June 12, 1932, of the High Commissioner of the French Republic in Cameroon and erected as a National Park by decree No. 120 of December 5, 1968, of the Secretariat for the Development of the State of Cameroon [45]. It is headed by a conservator under the direct supervision of the divisional delegate.

It should be noted that this protected area was delimited without cadastral references, almost at the edge of the vegetation. These limits can therefore be moved by the population according to their interests. Moreover, the park does not have a buffer zone, as provided for by regulations. With a fairly dense population of the riverside area (more than 300 inhabitants/km^2), cultivated areas, pastures, and human constructions are observed up to the edge of the park. Together with Waza National Park, the site constitutes the 600,000 ha of the Ramsar site of the Waza-Logone floodplains, making 10% of the wetlands in the West African Sahel [22].

Under a Sudano-Sahelian climate, the vegetation is fairly dense and consists mainly of mosaics of dense to clear dry forests and gallery forests [45]. It shelters a moderately diversified fauna with species of artiodactyles, primates, carnivores, rodents, insectivores, and especially many reptiles [24]. However, the animal presence is insufficiently known, even if it is considered to be very rewarding and generally arouses particular interest among managers of protected areas.

3.2 Methodological approach

The population living near the MGNP was the main target of an ethnoecological survey. For the sake of confrontation, several other groups of influencing actors of management, direct or indirect, from the local, divisional, and regional levels were considered, notably the local forest administration, the decentralized administrations attached to the forest sector, the cooperation organizations, development projects, and NGOs. This investigation was carried out in two phases due to the insecurity and the unavailability of certain people to be interviewed.

Firstly, from December 2011 to January 2012, 45 representatives of the local population, mainly among the elderly with a seniority of at least 30 years in outlying areas of the park, were surveyed in households. For this group of actors, five people were interviewed in each of the seven peripheral localities (Mawa, Karazawa, Gabas, Gokoro, Nguetchewe, Yamgazawa, and Mozogo) and 10 more in Mozogo, the chief town of Mayo Moskota sub-division. According to data from the last general population census, Mozogo is home to around 4/5 of the population living around the park [46]. A number of 30 people sampled are generally considered to be a suitable minimum, when analyses are not directed towards the strict distinction of specific groups in a population [46]. Furthermore, three representatives of the local forestry administration (two former conservators and the one in office in 2012) were also interviewed during this phase.

In the second phase from February to March 2018, the survey concerned 35 people with seniority in the region (dated at least from the first phase of the study), and administrative reports from 2011 were also consulted. Thus, the continuation of the interviews made it possible to complete the group of local forest administration at six, with two eco-guards and the conservator in post in 2018. In addition, 7 representatives of the divisional and regional forest administration, 18 representatives of deconcentrated administrations and forest-related organizations in divisional and regional levels (environment, tourism, land use planning, and development), and finally 7 actors from NGOs, cooperation organizations, and development projects intervening at the regional level in the management of natural resources (GIZ, IUCN, SAILD, ACODED, PRESIBALT, and Support Project to Improve Livestock Productivity knowing by the French acronym PAPE) were interviewed during this period.

In short, besides the diversity of influencing actors and the representativeness of the localities and the seniority of residence, other criteria such as age and sex were taken into account in this sampling. In total, the overall sample consisted of 83 respondents, including 45 from the local population and 38 representatives of local, divisional, and regional administrations or organizations. Respondents were questioned on the basis of closed, semi-closed, or open questions, essentially relating to the perception of the space–time evolution of the park, its importance, and its management. The names of the species cited as vernacular names were determined during the survey and were subsequently carried out in the field or at the national herbarium (for plant names), even using the determination keys [47–50], with updating according to the nomenclature of Roskov et al. [51]. Photographs of plant and animal specimens were sometimes used for this identification. The help of resource persons, who have a good command of localities and local vernaculars, was often essential.

3.3 Constraints, threats, importance, and management gaps

The activities of the people surveyed among the local population, likely users of the park's resources, are diverse and varied (**Figure 1**). However, agriculture is the main activity of the populations living near the park (53.33% of surveyed). It is often associated with trade (11.11%); sedentary cattle breeding, especially goats and sheep (15.56%); or traditional medicine (6.67%). This evaluation of the various activities of the populations living near the park indicates the strong current pressure on the resources of the park, with population growth, through the search for agricultural land, pastures, and wood cuts. Authors such as Dupuy et al. [14] argue that this predisposition poses a serious threat to vegetation, in addition to drought, socio-political factors and scientific and technical difficulties.

Precisely, the results of the survey indicate, within the local population, strong anthropogenic pressure capable to affect negatively the vegetation of the park (**Figure 2(a)**). The main indicators of anthropogenic pressure cited by the farmers are wood cutting (51.11%), poaching (48.88%), bush fires (44.44%), and pastures

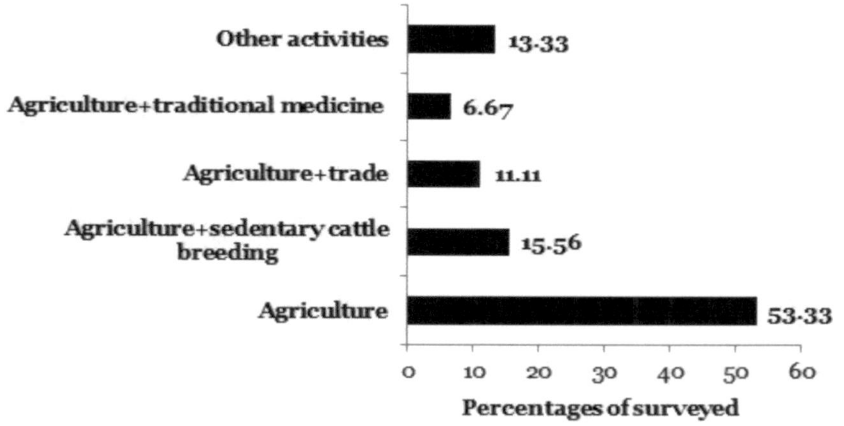

Figure 1.
Activities of respondents in the local population.

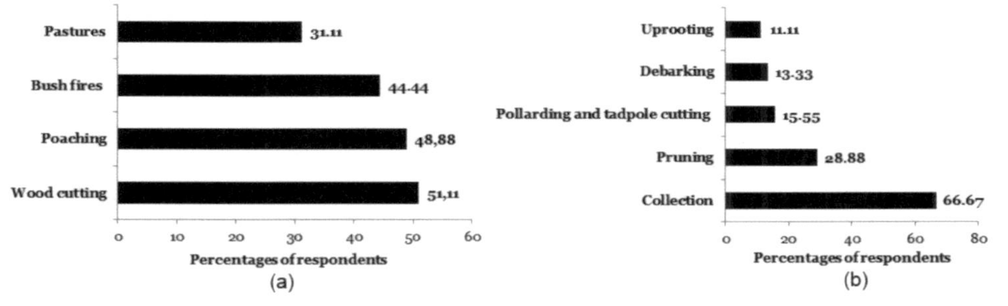

Figure 2.
Indicators of anthropogenic pressures in the park: (a) different forms of anthropogenic pressures, (b) wood resources harvesting methods.

(31.11%). Bush fires have been reported much more in the past and around the protected area. All villages are affected by illegal resource withdrawals. These samples are taken mainly in the dry season, due to the ease of access, linked to the existence of multiple tracks, in addition to the 20 km provided by the administration. For the more coveted wood resource, the harvesting mechanisms are not always compatible with regeneration and growth (**Figure 2(b)**). These are pollarding and tadpole cutting (15.55%), debarking (13.33%), and uprooting (11.11%). Other threats to the stability of the park and inadequacies in management are witnessed by several farmers, as **Figure 3** confirms.

A production role undoubtedly stems from the removal or expression of needs for diversified resources (firewood or service wood, non-timber forest products) by 78.12% of residents [24]. Regarding the appreciation of the management of the park, the regressive dynamics of woody trees is mainly a corollary of the excessive cutting of wood. The inventory of methods of harvesting wood resources is all the more important since Bellefontaine [52] encouraged those involved in the forest environment to seek management techniques favorable to the natural regeneration of woody species. The magnitude of human pressures in natural ecosystems has led Sist et al. [53] to conjecture forest management which will mainly take place in so-called "anthropogenic" forests.

When confronted with the opinions of other actors of influence (**Table 1**), the results showed a maximum agreement (from 73.33 to 100%), concerning the anthropic pressures which can negatively affect the vegetation. The illegal exploitation of the park's resources, particularly wood, is also observed by the vast majority of actors (71.42–100%). It emerged specifically from interviews with conservators and eco-guards that all the riparian regions are affected by illegal harvesting and that they are mainly carried out during the dry season, from October to June, at dawn, at twilight, or overnight. To be more precise, with regard to poaching, they add that gunshots are heard late at night; traces of heating fires and hiding spots are observed around the artificial ponds created. They also specify that bush fires are relatively absent, sometimes observed at the edge, and very quickly controlled.

Moreover, apart from the local population, the other actors of influence, especially non-forestry ones (57.15–77.67%), seem to attach less importance to the MGNP in the region, than, for example, to the Waza National Park inscribed on the world heritage of UNESCO. Most of those interviewed recognize the richness of

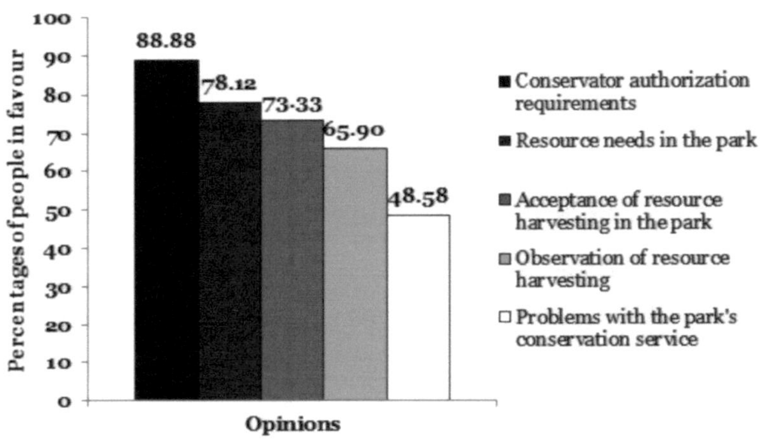

Figure 3.
Selected farmers' views on park management.

DOI: http://dx.doi.org/10.5772/intechopen.91982

Elements of confrontation	A*	B*	C*	D*	E*
Major area of competence or activity	Agriculture (53.33)	Forestry (100)	Forestry (100)	Variable (no area > 50%)	Variable (no area > 50%)
Main source of information on the site	Direct contact with the site (88.88)	Direct contact with the site (100)	Administrative documents, personal knowledge and experience (85.71)	Personal knowledge (66.66)	Personal knowledge (71.42)
Limit information**	70.18	100	28.57	16.66	17.33
Visit to the heart of the park**	73.33	100	33.33	16.66	28.57
Information on the evolution of biodiversity**	70.18	83.33	14.28	05.55	14.28
Agreement on the existence of anthropogenic pressures**	73.33	100	100	83.88	100
Main pressure expressed**	Wood harvesting (77.77)	Wood harvesting (100)	Wood harvesting (100)	Wood harvesting (83.33)	Wood harvesting (71.42)
Assessment of degree of importance of the park**	Very high (88.88)	Very high (100)	High (57.14)	Low (33.33)	Low (42.85)
Essential value identified	Forest products (88.88)	Rich biodiversity (100)	Rich biodiversity (100)	Rich biodiversity (61.11)	Rich biodiversity (85.71)

Elements of confrontation	A*	B*	C*	D*	E*
Main problems raised relating to park management	• Conservator approval requirements (88.88) • Wildlife presence devastating crops (48.58)	• Absence of a management plan (100) • Difficulties in water supply for wildlife (100) • High anthropogenic pressures (100) • Important land pressure for agriculture and animal husbandry (100) • Poor execution of certain projects (construction of ponds, watchtower, etc.) (100)	• Insufficient human, material, and financial resources (85.71) • Galloping demography (42.85) • Poor governance and corruption (28.57) • Absence of a national structure in charge of protected areas (14.28) • Poaching of the defense forces (14.28)	• No priority given to the MGNP considered as a protected area of lesser importance (88.88) • Absence of a consultation framework (33.33) • Degradation of public morals (11.11) • Insufficient skills in the implementation of decentralization projects (11.11)	• Fear of insecurity (85.71) • Large influx of refugees and displaced persons (57.14) • Insufficient roads passable in all seasons (14.28) • Climate change (14.28) • Lack of patriotism (14.28) • Little participatory management (14.28) • Non-respect of grazing areas (14.28)

A, local population; B, local forestry administration; C, divisional and regional forestry administration; D, deconcentrated attached administrations; E, cooperation organizations and NGOs.
The numbers indicate the % of individuals favorable to opinion.
**Parameters used for the calculation of $\chi 2$.*

Table 1.
Confrontation of the opinions of various influential actors in MGNP.

the park's biological resources but point out several problems that could hamper sustainable management, especially relating to the absence of a management plan. The analysis in **Table 1** makes it possible to confirm that knowledge of the park varies significantly depending on the type of influencing actor ($\chi 2 = 227.94$; $P < 0.0001$). This result tends to confirm the diverging interests of the diversity of actors, noted in the governance of protected areas by UICN [13] or by Saleh [54]. This difference in perception indicates that there are gaps in information about the park, which can be explained by the remoteness of the site on a daily basis, or by belonging to a professional body not related to the forestry sector. This is evidence of a lack of harmonization of sectorial policies and multi-scale governance impacting protected area management that Sist et al. [53] considered as factors hindering their conservation. In a similar study [55], a perception of the plant cover varying according to the distance from the W national park of Burkina Faso was also highlighted.

Furthermore, consultations of administrative reports reveal deficits in the implementation of reference standards in the management of national parks and non-participative governance predominantly state-owned. In agreement with the opinion obtained from the interviews of local forest administrators, several other difficulties emerge from these documents transmitted to the hierarchy with suggestions for solutions. We can cite, among others, staff often in insignificant numbers with limited skills, insufficient equipment and materials necessary for ecological monitoring and follow-up, poor collaboration with the police forces involved in the procedures of sanction, the absence of a buffer zone profitable to the population, the difficult water supply (almost permanent drying of one of the two artificial ponds since 2009 and the drinker with solar energy pumping is not functional), and the easy access to the park through several trails in addition to the 20 km of tracks arranged by the administration inside the park.

3.4 Analysis of evolution of the park

In the local population, the average age of those surveyed is 49.7 ± 8.4 years. It is sufficient for the perception of evolution of the park, given the seniority (at least 30 years old) of most respondents (64.33%). Many local residents (70.18%) claimed to know the boundaries of the park and are therefore able to assess changes in the area and structure of the vegetation. This assessment is one of the main criteria to becoming aware of the existence of a protected area and thus preventing its encroachment.

Figure 4 gives a view of the peasant's perception of the evolution of the area and the structure of the vegetation. Contingency tables were constructed from the values obtained for the application of the independence test. It confirms that the area of the park has changed over time ($\chi^2 = 13.28$, $P < 0.05$). The structural dynamics (density and size of trees) are globally perceived with confusion, that is to say, not statistically significant ($P > 0.05$) with regard to both its increase ($\chi^2 = 0.038$), its decrease ($\chi^2 = 0.010$), and its stability ($\chi^2 = 0.02$). By somewhat including the bordering area, Wafo [27] noted using remote sensing, a spatio-temporal variation of the elements of land use between 1986 and 2001, in particular an increase of burns, clear forest, altitude forest, and bare soil with little vegetation cover and a decrease of crop areas, herbaceous and fallow, and savannah with trees and shrubs. Using a different nomenclature, Sandjong Sani et al. [56] showed between 1982 and 2015, in the same site, the extension, although slow, of more open vegetation to the detriment of dense dry forests and gallery forests, in particular especially relating to anthropogenic disturbances. This spatiotemporal study has, through the analysis of interannual vegetation indices, demonstrated a regressive and extensive fluctuating evolution of the vegetation.

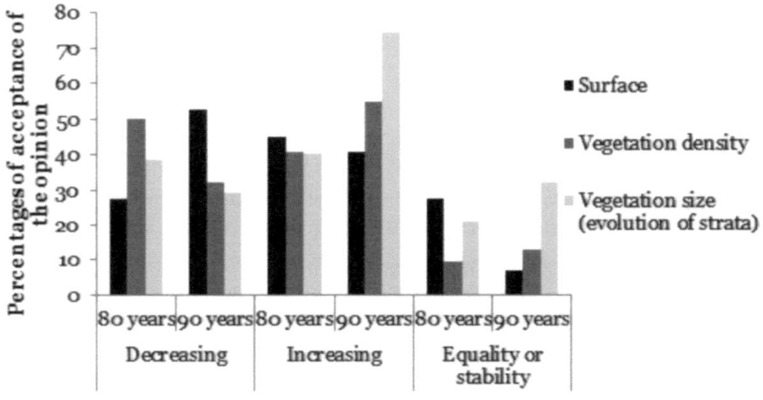

Figure 4.
Peasant assessment of the park surface and vegetation structure compared to the periods of the 1980s and 1990s.

The local population has an idea of the animal or plant species that are decreasing, increasing, or disappearing in the park and its surroundings. **Figure 5** gives an idea of this perception. An analysis of this table shows the regressive trend in animal (74.78%) and plant (74.65%) biodiversity in the park (dominance of the species cited as decreasing or disappearing). The animals mentioned fall into the following groups: mammals and reptiles, the majority of which have already been reported in the literature, with the exception of those considered missing in the park (lions, elephants, buffaloes, giraffes, hyenas, leopards, and red monkeys). The absence of certain disseminating animal species in the park may explain the disappearance or reduction of certain plants. Seventy percent of the plants listed belong to the woody group. This is an indicator which attests the sufficient knowledge and the importance of this resource for farmers. Some of these woody species were not inventoried in the parallel floristic study [45] or were cited as having disappeared from the park (**Table 2**).

With the analysis of the decline in animal and plant biodiversity, it is noted that the percentages of species cited in the responses, and only in the surrounding, are low due to the degradation of vegetation at these sites due to various anthropogenic practices. By comparing these opinions with the groups of different stakeholders interviewed, it appears that the local forest administration mainly (83.33–100%) has a clearer idea of the evolution of plant and wildlife populations, in line with the local population (70.18–88.88%).

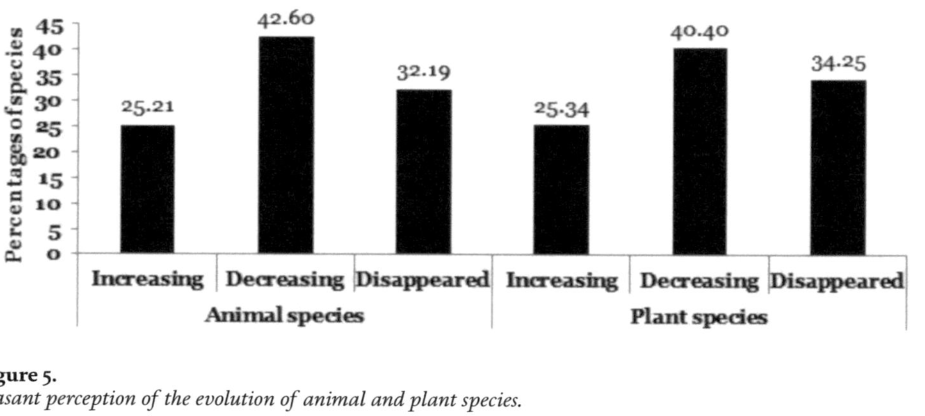

Figure 5.
Peasant perception of the evolution of animal and plant species.

No.	Vernacular names (Mafa)	Scientific names	Families
1	Gonokoud	*Annona senegalensis**	Annonaceae
2	Gangar	*Borassus aethiopum*	Arecaceae
3	Lakalak	*Daniellia oliveri**	Fabaceae
4	Pekelde	*Ficus abutilifolia**	Moraceae
5	Mindek	*Ficus dicranostyla**	Moraceae
6	Kouzlar	*Ficus sycomorus* subsp. *sycomorus*	Moraceae
7	Tondaz	*Haematostaphis barteri**	Anacardiaceae
8	Mbalmbal	*Maytenus senegalensis*	Celastraceae
9	Waf roua	*Parkia biglobosa*	Fabaceae
10	Foreu	*Senna siamea*	Fabaceae
11	Wandar	*Ziziphus mauritiana**	Rhamnaceae

**Species listed as disappeared from the park.*

Table 2.
Species cited by the riparian population not listed in the floristic inventory.

Wildlife extinction can be explained by migration, habitat degradation, or poaching [14]. Wafo [27] explains that the reduction in wildlife is due to the small size of the park and proximity to the local population. This loss of animal biodiversity can be justified by the fragmentation of vegetation around the park and its isolation. Climate constraints, competitive dynamism of species, and human pressures are also justifiable reasons. The impact of human activities, which may cause changes in plant succession and environmental degradation, is an explanatory hypothesis approved by several authors [55, 57].

Other analyses of plant evolution, Aubreville [58] and Letouzey [59] have previously stated that the vegetation has reconstituted itself and should not be considered as a primary forest relic. In the same way, Boutrais et al. [60] believed that with crop exclusion and lack of fire, shrubs from a likely degraded initial forest firstly proliferated in thicket formation, and woody strata removed the savannah and reconstituted a closed forest cover. These views are slightly different from Dewaulle [61], who described the park's vegetation as primitive, having been protected by beliefs or prohibitions. Yengué [62] states that MGNP is the only protected area in the Far North region that is in a good state of conservation. Moreover, it cannot be denied that the dynamics of this vegetation are linked to the presence of a more or less varied fauna.

Following recent parallel work [45, 56, 63], the park's great preservation and resilience to various pressure factors can be questioned. Natural accessibility constraints with the domination of the thorny species *Senegalia ataxacantha* in the flora, complacency in the application of rules of access restriction in local governance, and peasant practices and uses favorable to plant conservation are explanatory assumptions of such status. Despite many challenges in the management of MGNP, it appears that one of the main ways of conserving natural ecosystems in drylands remains protected areas, particularly national parks. It is therefore necessary to question the effectiveness of the normative systems of national park management in the Sudano-Sahelian zone, which are too rigorous and controlled mainly by state actors.

4. Conclusion

In summary, after recalling the regulatory framework for the sustainable management of natural ecosystems in the context of Cameroon, this chapter reveals the deficit of their effective implementation through investigations conducted in MGNP, following a participatory approach. Local stakeholders involved in the management process better understand the dynamics of vegetation, as well as the importance of the park, indicating the multiple resources available or the rich biodiversity. They also show an analysis of regressive floristic and wildlife changes in the park's evolution, mainly due to anthropogenic pressures (wood cuts, grazing, poaching, and bushfires). The lack of a sustainable management plan in accordance with the existing legislation was noted as a major shortcoming. In accordance with inclusive and multi-sectorial governance, the weakness noted can be corrected in the conception and implementation of a sustainable management plan for this park.

Acknowledgements

The authors thank all the people who contributed to the successful completion of the surveys and the writing of the final version.

Author details

Rodrigue Constant Sandjong Sani[1*], Mama Ntoupka[2], Toua Vroumsia[3], Tchobsala[1] and Adamou Ibrahima[3]

1 Faculty of Science, Department of Biological Sciences, University of Maroua, Maroua, Cameroon

2 Institute of Agricultural Research for Development (IRAD Forest), Foumban, Cameroon

3 Faculty of Science, Department of Biological Sciences, University of Ngaoundéré, Ngaoundéré, Cameroon

*Address all correspondence to: sanirocos@yahoo.fr

References

[1] Ntoupka M. Impact des perturbations anthropiques (pâturage, feu, et coupe de bois) sur la dynamique de la savane arborée en zone soudano-sahélienne du Nord du Cameroun. Thèse de Doctorat de l'université Paul Valery-Montpellier III. 1999

[2] Reynolds JF, Maestre FT, Kemp PR, Stafford-Smith DM, Lambin E. Natural and human dimensions of land degradation in drylands: Causes and consequences. In: Canadell JG, Pataki DE, Pitelka LF, editors. Terrestrial Ecosystems in a Changing World. Berlin Heidelberg (Germany): Springer; 2007. pp. 247-257

[3] Descroix L, Diedhiou A. Etat des sols et évolution dans un contexte de changements climatiques. In: Dia A, et Duponnois R, dir. La Grande Muraille Verte, Capitalisation des recherches et valorisation des savoirs locaux. Marseille: IRD Éditions; 2012. pp. 161-198. DOI: 10.4000/books.irdeditions.3247

[4] MEA (Millennium Ecosystem Assessment). Ecosystems and Human Well-being: Desertification Synthesis. Washington, DC: World Resources Institute; 2005. p. 26

[5] Davies J, Poulsen L, Schulte-Herbrüggen B, Mackinnon K, Crawhall N, Henwood WD, et al. Conserving Dryland Biodiversity. Nairobi: IUCN Drylands Initiative (Cambridge, UK: UNEP-WCMC; Bonn: UNCCD); 2012. p. 84

[6] Allen K, Dupuy JM, Gei MG, Hulshof C, Medvigy D, Pizano C, et al. Will seasonally dry tropical forests be sensitive or resistant to future changes in rainfall regimes? Environmental Research Letters. 2017;**12**:023001

[7] Seghieri J. Rythmes saisonniers d'une savane soudano-sahélienne en relation avec l'hydrodynamique du sol. Ecologie. 1996;**t.27**(2):67-78

[8] Philippon N, Martiny N, Camberlin P, Richard Y. Impact des précipitations sur l'activité photosynthétique de la végétation en Afrique semi-aride sub-saharienne. In: Journées de Climatologie—Nantes. Climat et société: Climat et végétation; 2008. pp. 77-90

[9] IPCC. Les changements climatiques et la biodiversité. In: Groupe d'Experts Intergouvernemental sur l'Evolution du Climat. Document technique V du GIEC. WMO, UNEP; 2002. 75 p

[10] Geny P, Waechter P, Yatchnovsky A. Environnement et développement durable, guide de la gestion des ressources naturelles. In: Roche F, editor. Paris; 1992. pp. 211-218

[11] Bellefontaine R, Gaston A, Petrucci Y. Aménagement des forêts tropicales sèches. Rome: FAO, Cahiers FAO Conservation 32; 1997. p. 321

[12] Dudley N. Lignes directrices pour l'application des catégories de gestion aux aires protégées. UICN: Gland, Suisse; 2008

[13] UICN-PAPACO. La planification des aires protégées: Études de cas portant sur l'élaboration et la mise en œuvre des plans de gestion d'aires protégées en Afrique du Centre et de l'Ouest Nouvelles des Aires Protégées en Afrique. Nouvelles des Aires Protégées en Afrique. 2012;**50**:1-9

[14] Dupuy B, Maître HF, Amsallem I. Techniques de gestion des écosystèmes forestiers tropicaux: état de l'art. Working paper FAO/FPIRS; 1999. p. 146

[15] Singh VS, Pandey DN, Prara Kasas NP. What determines the success of joint forest management?

Science-based lessons on sustainable governance of forests in India. Resources Conservation and Recycling. 2011;**56**:126-133. DOI: 10.1016/j.resconrec.2011.09.015

[16] Ministerial Conference on the Protection of Forests in Europe. General Guidelines for the Sustainable Management of Forests in Europe. Resolution H1, Helsinki, Finland: United Nations Economic Commission for Europe/Food and Agriculture Organization; 1993. p. 5

[17] Leroy M, Derroire G, Vendé J, Leménager T. La gestion durable des forêts tropicales. De l'analyse critique du concept à l'évaluation environnementale des dispositifs de gestion. France: Agence Française De Développement, Collection "À Savoir"; 2013. p. 236

[18] Eba'a AR. Principes et concepts essentiels en aménagement forestier. In: Foahom B, Jonkers WBJ, Nkwi PN, Schmidt P, Tchatat M, editors. Seminar Proceedings, Sustainable Management of African Rain Forest, Held in Kribi, November 1999, Cameroon, Part 1. The Tropenbos Foundation: Wageningen; 2001. pp. 3-11

[19] Zornoza R, Acosta JA, Bastida F, Domínguez SG, Toledo DM, Faz A. Identification of sensitive indicators to assess the interrelationship between soil quality, management practices and human health. The Soil. 2015;**1**:173-185. DOI: 10.5194/soil-1-173-2015

[20] Christensen NL, Bartuska AM, Brown JH, Carpenter SD, Antonio C, Francis R, et al. The report of the ecological Society of America Committee on the scientific basis for ecosystem management. Ecological Applications. 1996;**6**(3):665-691

[21] Nké NJ. Déforestation au Cameroun: causes conséquences et solutions. Alternatives Sud. 2008;**15**(155):156-175

[22] Doumenge C, Palla F, Scholte P, Hiol Hiol F, Larzillière A. Aires protégées d'Afrique centrale, État 2015. Cameroun: OFAC, Kinshasa, République Démocratique du Congo et Yaoundé; 2015. p. 256

[23] Borrini-Feyerabend G, Dudley N, Jaeger T, Lassen B, Pathak Broome N, Phillips A, Sandwith T. Gouvernance des aires protégées: de la compréhension à l'action. Collection des lignes directrices sur les meilleures pratiques pour les aires protégées N°20, Gland, Suisse: IUCN. 2014. p. 124

[24] Sandjong Sani RC, Ntoupka M, Ibrahima A, Vroumsia T. Essai d'analyses de la conception paysanne de l'évolution, de la gestion et de l'utilité du Parc National de Mozogo-Gokoro (Cameroun) en vue de son aménagement. International Journal Biological and Chemical Sciences. 2013;7(6):2434-2449. DOI: 10.4314/ijbcs.v7i6.24

[25] Republic of Cameroon. Plan d'Action Forestier National (PAFN), projet 13. Ministère de l'Environnement et des Forêts (MINEF). 1994. pp. 148-149

[26] Republic of Cameroon. Programme Sectoriel Forêt-Environment, Document de programme. Ministère de l'Environnement et des Forêts (MINEF); 2003. p. 95

[27] Wafo T. Les aires protégées de l'Extrême-Nord Cameroun, Entre politiques de conservation et pratiques locales. Thèse de Doctorat. France: Université d'Orléans, Pôle Universités Centre Val de Loire; 2008. p. 325

[28] Republic of Cameroon. Document de Stratégie de Réduction de la Pauvreté. République du Cameroon; 2003. p. 33

[29] Fraticelli M, Perdriault M, Pinsart C, Rafer J. La gouvernance des forêts au Cameroun. Editeurs: CED, CAFT, AGTER; 2013. p. 133

[30] Republic of Cameroon. Document de Stratégie pour la Croissance et l'Emploi 2010-2020. Ministère de l'Economie, du Plan et de l'Aménagement du Territoire (MINEPAT); 2009. p. 147

[31] Republic of Cameroon. Cameroun Vision 2035. Document de travail. Ministère de l'Economie, de la Planification et de l'Aménagement du Territoire (MINEPAT); 2009. p. 65

[32] Republic of Cameroon. Stratégie et Plan d'Action National pour la Biodiversité-Version II. Ministère de l'Environnement, de la Protection de la Nature et du Développement durable (MINEPDED); 2012. p. 169

[33] Republic of Cameroon. Plan National d'Adaptation aux Changements Climatiques du Cameroun. Ministère de l'environnement, de la protection de la Nature et du Développement Durable (MINEPDED); 2015. p. 154

[34] Republic of Cameroon. Readiness Preparation Proposal (R-PP) for REDD+. Forest Carbon Partnership Facility (FCPF), World Bank; 2012. p. 111

[35] De Wasseige C, Tadoum M, Eba'a Atyi R, Doumenge C, editors. The Forests of the Congo Basin—Forests and climate change. Belgium: Weyrich; 2015. p. 128

[36] Thomas L, Middleton J. Lignes directrices pour la planification de la gestion des aires protégées. Gland: Suisse, UICN; 2011. p. 67

[37] Ramade F. Le grand massacre. l'avenir des espèces vivantes. Hachette Littératures; 1998. p. 287

[38] Republic of Cameroon. Loi N°94/01 du 20 Janvier 1994 portant régime des forêts, de la faune et de la pêche au. Cameroun. République du Cameroun; 1994. p. 24

[39] Republic of Cameroon. Décret N°95/466/PM du 20 juillet 1995 fixant les modalités d'application du régime de la faune. République du Cameroun; 1995. p. 22

[40] Republic of Cameroon. Décret N°95/531/PM du 23 aout 1995 fixant les modalités d'application du régime des forêts. République du Cameroun; 1995. p. 39

[41] Dowsett RJ, Dowsett-Lemaire F. New species and amendments to the avifauna of Cameroon. Bulletin of the British Ornithologists' Club. 2000;**120**:179-185

[42] Gautier D, Ntoupka M. Une inflexion dans la dégradation des ressources arborées au Nord-Cameroun. Cahiers Agricultures. 2003;**12**(4):235-240

[43] Seignobos C, Iyebi-Mandjek O. Atlas de la Province Extrême-Nord Cameroun. Paris: IRD; 2000. p. 171

[44] Gautier D, Seignobos C. Histoire des actions de foresterie dans les projets de développement rural au Nord Cameroun. In: Actes du colloque, Savanes africaines: Des espaces en mutation, des acteurs face à de nouveaux défis, Garoua (Cameroun); N'Djamena (Tchad). PRASAC; Jamin JY, Seiny Boukar L, éditeurs scientifiques; 2003. pp. 1-8

[45] Sandjong Sani RC, Ntoupka M, Vroumsia T, Ibrahima A. Phytoecological valorization attributes of Mozogo-Gokoro National Park (Cameroon). Environmental Monitoring and Assessment. 2019;**191**(79):1-21. DOI: 10.1007/s10661-019-7186-9

[46] Baker SE, Edwards R, editors. How Many Qualitative Interviews is Enough? Expert Voices and Early Career Reflections on Sampling and Cases in Qualitative Research Southampton. GB National Centre for Research Methods (National Centre for

Research Methods Reviews). University of Southampton; 2012 Available from: http://blog.soton.ac.uk/dissertation/files/2013/09/how_many_interviews.p

[47] Malzy P. Quelques plantes du Nord Cameroun et leur utilisation. Journal d'Agriculture tropicale et de Botanique appliquée. 1954;**TI**(56):1-37

[48] Geerling C. Guide de terrain des ligneux sahéliens et soudano-guinéens. Nederland: Mededelingen Landbouwhogeschool Wageningen 82-3; 1982. p. 340

[49] Barreteau D, Le Bléis Y. Lexique Mafa, Langue de la famille tchadique parlée au Cameroun. Geuthner: ORSTOM; 1990. p. 473

[50] Arbres AM. Arbustes et Lianes des Zones Sèches d'Afrique de l'Ouest. 4ème éd. ed. Montpellier, France: CIRADMARGRAF—MNHN; 2009. p. 574

[51] Roskov Y, Abucay L, Orrell T, Nicolson D, Flann C, Bailly N, et al., editors. Species 2000 & ITIS Catalogue of Life, 2016 Annual Checklist. Available from: www.catalogueoflife.org/annual-checklist/2016. Naturalis, Leiden, The Netherlands: Species 2000; 2018

[52] Bellefontaine R. Régénération naturelle à faible coût dans le cadre de l'aménagement forestier en zones tropicales sèches en Afrique. VertigO—La Revue Electronique en Sciences de l'Environnement. 2005;**6**(2):1-15. DOI: 10.4000/vertigo.4335. Available from: http://vertigo.revues.org/4335

[53] Sist P, Pacheco P, Nasi R, Blaser J. Management of natural tropical forests in the past and present and projections for the future. In: Katila P, Galloway G, de Jong W, Pacheco P, Mery G, editors. Forests Under Pressure—Local Responses to Global Issues. Vienne: IUFRO (IUFRO World Series, 32); 2014. p. 497-511

[54] Saleh A. Un modèle et son revers : la cogestion des réserves de biosphère de Waza et de la Bénoué dans le Nord du Cameroun. Thèse de Doctorat en Géographie de l'Université du Maine; 2013

[55] Gansaonré RN. Dynamique du couvert végétal et implications socio-environnementales à la périphérie du parc W/Burkina Faso. VertigO—La revue électronique en sciences de l'environnement. 2018;**18**(1). DOI: 10.4000/vertigo.20249. Available from: http://journals.openedition.org/vertigo/20249

[56] Sandjong Sani RC, Ntoupka M, Ibrahima A, Toua V, Etouna J. Inducement of sustainable management planning of Mozogo-Gokoro National Park (Cameroon) by images processing. Journal of Biodiversity and Environmental Sciences. 2017;**11**(5):74-91

[57] Jiagho ER, Zapfack L, Banoho LPRK, Tsayem-Demaze M, Corbonnois J, Tchawa P. Diversité de la flore ligneuse à la périphérie du Parc national de Waza (Cameroun). VertigO—La revue électronique en sciences de l'environnement. 2016;**16**(1):1-19. DOI: 10.4000/vertigo.17249. Available from: http://journals.openedition.org/vertigo/17249

[58] Aubreville A. Flore forestière soudano-guinéenne, A.O.F., Cameroun, A.E.F. Paris: Société d'éditions géographiques Mar. colon; 1950. p. 523

[59] Letouzey R. Etude phytogéographique du Cameroun. Paris. Encycl. Biol. No 69: Paul Lechevalier; 1968. p. 511

[60] Boutrais J, Boulet J, Beauvilain A, Gubry P, Barreteau D, Die'j M, et al.,

editors. Le Nord du Cameroun des Hommes, une région. Paris. Collection Mémoires No 102: Éditions de l'Office de la Recherche Scientifique et Technique Outre-mer; 1984. p. 539

[61] Dewaulle J-C. Désertification de l'Afrique au Sud du Sahara. Bois et Forêts des Tropiques. 1973;**149**:3-20

[62] Yengué JL. L'évolution du couvert ligneux dans l'Extrême-Nord du Cameroun. Utilisation de la photographie aérienne et de l'imagerie satellitaire. Thèse de Doctorat en Géographie, Université Paris I—Panthéon-Sorbonne, version numérique; 2000

[63] Sandjong Sani RC, Ntoupka M, Vroumsia T, Ibrahima A. Caractérisation structurale de la végétation ligneuse du Parc National de Mozogo-Gokoro (Cameroun). Flora et Vegetatio Sudano-Sambesica. 2018;**21**:7-24. DOI: 10.21248/fvss.21.56

Chapter 16

Challenges of Conservation and Sustainable Management of African Rosewood (*Pterocarpus erinaceus*) in West Africa

Adjonou Kossi, Houetchegnon Towanou, Rabiou Habou, Segla Kossi Novinyo, Abotsi Komla Elikplim, Johnson Benziwa Nathalie, Alaba Pyoabalo, Ouinsavi Christine A.I. Nougbodé, Quashie Akossiwoa Marie-Luce, Kokutse Adzo Dzifa, Mahamane Ali and Kokou Kouami

Abstract

Pterocarpus erinaceus is an endemic and threatened plant species in arid and semiarid zones of West Africa and is highly exploited for timber, animal feeding, and various medicinal uses. The species is currently native to the Guinean forest-savannah mosaic ecoregion and reported from Senegal to Cameroon. The values of the main characteristics of the *P. erinaceus* forest stands (density, average diameter, average height and average stem height) vary significantly ($P < 10^{-3}$) from the Guinean zone to the Sahelian zone. It has high technological performance and can be classified as heavy and very hard wood with a density of the order of 0.80 ± 0.07 g/cm^3 and an average hardness of 12 ± 3.7 g/cm^3. The species is the subject of large-scale international traffic between West Africa and Asia, which is by far the greatest threat to the species. The various uses induce repeated mutilation and increase pressures on the species resulting in a significant reduction in its natural populations. In response to this situation, measures are proposed, including large-scale plant production strategies, the definition of minimum felling diameters, policy measures, etc., to meet the restoration needs of natural stands of *P. erinaceus* and the fight against climate change.

Keywords: *Pterocarpus erinaceus*, socioeconomic services, wood properties, uncontrolled logging, sustainable management, West Africa

1. Introduction

During the last decades, the deforestation is, for the developing countries, the second most worrying environmental issue after the climate changes [1–4].

IntechOpen

The exploitation rate of the tropical forests reached such an alarming level that its sustainability is questionable. Indeed, demand for timber and non-timber forest products has been increasing worldwide, and forests are endowed with multiple products and services which meet the needs of human populations [5, 6]. However, human actions such as deforestation, overexploitation of natural resources, agriculture, overgrazing and bush fires, coupled with the adverse effects of climate change are currently contributing to the loss of many indigenous plant species of great importance for populations' survival [7]. Among the most exploited species, *Pterocarpus erinaceus* Poir. is a spontaneous and endemic plant species in the Guineo-Sudanian and Sudano-Sahelian phytogeographic zones [8, 9].

P. erinaceus, known as African rosewood, is widely exploited as timber and service wood but also as one of the preferential fuelwood [10, 11] and is estimated to be the most heavily traded tropical hardwood in the world [12]. It has high performance and technological characteristics [13]. *P. erinaceus* is exploited not only for its timber which is traded internationally to Asian countries, mainly China, but also for a range of non-timber products including food for human consumption, fodder for animals, medicinal products, and raw materials for crafts such as tannins, dyes, sap, resin, etc. [9, 10, 14, 15]. For instance, the natural stands of *P. erinaceus* are very exploited, with heavy pressure on the species and habitats. Moreover, illegal and uncontrolled logging of the species, linked to international trade, became the main threat in the last years.

West Africa is experiencing overexploitation of *P. erinaceus* which is the world's leading rosewood-producing region. This region accounts for 80% by volume of all rosewood log export to China in 2016. West Africa is the largest producer of rosewood logs supplying 80% by volume of export to China in 2016. For instance, between January 2015 and December 2016, an annual average of 764,000 m^3 worth US$840 million of rosewood was imported into China from West African countries [12]. Countries heavily affected by overexploitation include Senegal (2010–2014), the Gambia (2011–2012), Benin (2012–2013), Guinea-Bissau (2012–2014), Côte d'Ivoire (2013–2014), Ghana (2013–2014), and Nigeria (2014–2015). The vicious exploitation is not about to slow down since China and Asia's middle class which has increasing demand for rosewood-made furniture is expected to increase at 16–20%. The consequences of uncontrolled exploitation of the species are changes in its population structure and composition, with potential detrimental effect on regeneration capacity, seed production (loss of seed trees), decrease in genetic diversity and risk of genetic erosion, and loss of socioeconomic services to livelihoods. Studies of [16, 17] have shown that poor harvesting and practices by the various stakeholders (farmers, drovers, and peasants) have a negative impact on the development and regeneration of the species.

The increased demand for rosewood from Asia is seriously threatening the region's natural ecosystems and its ability to adapt to climate change. But at the same time, the species is a huge opportunity for trade if the appropriate measures are taken. The objective of this chapter is to present a synthesis of the state of knowledge on natural stands of *P. erinaceus* in West Africa. Specifically, it is a question of presenting the information available on (i) the forms of use and uses of the organs of the species through different communities in West Africa, (ii) the structural parameters of the species and their variability according to ecological zones, (iii) the technological properties of the species and their variability according to the climatic gradient, and (iv) the strategies proposed for the protection, conservation and sustainable management of the species in order to meet the restoration needs of natural stands of *P. erinaceus* and the fight against climate change.

2. Species presentation and geographical distribution

2.1 Species presentation

Pterocarpus erinaceus is a small- to medium-size tree about 12–15m tall, or more, with straight bole, cylindrical up to 1 m in diameter, often low-branched, with open crown, rounded and ovoid to slight buttresses (**Figure 1A**). Its bark is scaly, cracked, blackish, and deeply fissured, with brown spots striped with red threads exuding a translucent reddish resin that hardens quickly on contact with air. Its densely pubescent twigs become glabrous and gray later [18–20].

P. erinaceus leaves are alternate, composed, alternate, once-compound, imparipinnate with hairy linear stipules (falling early) have a long spine 15–25 cm long, on which are inserted 4–5 pairs of leaflets alternate. The terminal leaflet is a little more developed than the smaller inferiors. These elliptical leaflets of 5–10 cm long and 3–6 cm wide have a rounded base or a short wedge-shaped base, a rounded or obtuse apex, usually emarginated (**Figure 1B**). They are papery and thick, with brownish hairs when young, but glabrescent as they age.

Light-yellow papilionaceous flowers (**Figure 2**), coming in loose or short panicles, appear on leafless trees at the end of the dry season, usually between December and February [21] before new leaves develop; but sometimes the inflorescences develop with the young leaves. They are asymmetrical, fragrant, 10–12 mm long, and pedicellate, with embossed petals and with a pubescent calyx with five short teeth [18–20]. They are also often visited by the bees that are probably responsible for the pollination.

The fruit, flat samara, is surrounded by a membranous circular wing more or less pleated, bearing on both sides many spiny hairs, rigid and entangled. It is

Figure 1.
Pterocarpus erinaceus. (A) Tree in its natural environment, (B) appearance of the leaves, and (C) appearance of the fruits.

Figure 2.
Flowering tree of P. erinaceus.

4–7 cm in diameter and straw yellow in color and persists for a long time on the tree. It contains one–two seeds of often very different sizes [22]. The young fruits are light green and turn light brown when dry (**Figure 1C**). The seeds are flat to slightly thick, about 10 × 5 mm, smooth, and red to dark brown. The seedling has an epigeal germination and leafy cotyledons [17].

2.2 Geographical distribution

The species is native to the Guinean forest-savannah mosaic ecoregion of West Africa (**Figure 3**), which lies between the Guinean rainforest and the Sudanian

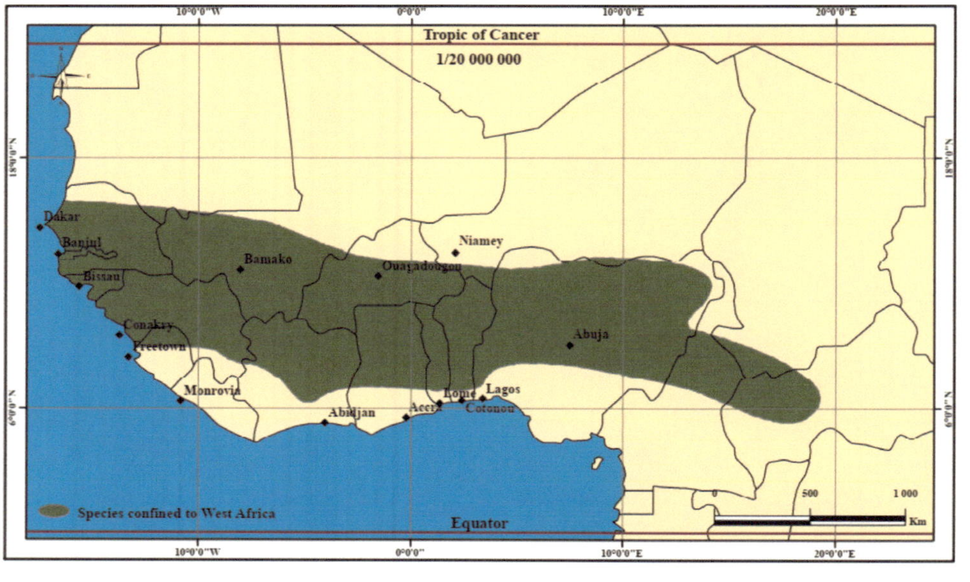

Figure 3.
Distribution de P. erinaceus in West Africa (Source: Ligneux du Sahel V.1.0, 2008).

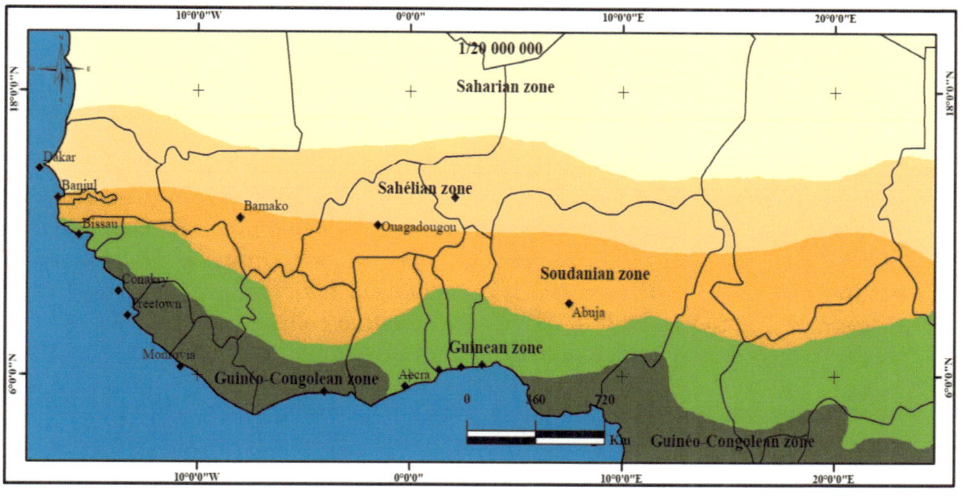

Figure 4.
Ecological zones of West Africa.

savannah [23]. It has been listed throughout the region, including Senegal, the Gambia, Guinea-Bissau, Guinea, Mali, Côte d'Ivoire, Burkina Faso, Ghana, Niger, Benin, Togo, Nigeria, and Cameroon (**Figure 3**). It is present up to the latitude of 14°N, but at this latitude the individuals are small and stunted. From this latitude, the species *P. lucens* dominates and is more abundant. To the south, the range of *P. erinaceus* extends to the moist forest limit in Côte d'Ivoire and the humid coastal savannas in Guinea, Togo, and Benin, where a gallery species, *P. santalinoides*, is common along rivers and temporary streams.

According to [24] classification, based on the total annual classes of rainfall, the species is distributed through three ecological zones, namely, Guinean zone, Sudanian zone, and Sahelian zone (**Figure 4**). *P. erinaceus* grows in dry open forests of semiarid and subhumid soils with an average annual rainfall of 600–1200 mm and a moderate or very long dry season that can last from 8 to 9 months. The average annual temperature in its range is 15–32°C, but the species tolerates high temperatures exceeding 40°C. The tree grows at low altitude (0–600 m) and also grows on shallow soils. Individuals tolerate drought and, once rooted, withstand different annual dry seasons.

3. Socioeconomic status and perceptions of *Pterocarpus erinaceus* in West Africa

Socioeconomic survey carried out in three countries (Burkina Faso, Niger, and Togo) allowed to collect data on uses and perceptions of *P. erinaceus* in West Africa [13]. Results indicate that *P. erinaceus* organs (leaves, barks, roots, sap) are used in the treatment of more than 33 diseases or pathologies in these countries. According to [25], *P. erinaceus* contains a high level of protein (19%) which makes it a very good agroforestry species [26]. The individuals in the farms, the fallows, and the classified forests are frequently pruned to feed the cattle. The leaves of the species are also sold in urban centers in Burkina Faso and Mali, as fodder.

In Burkina Faso, where the resource is relatively more abundant, 30 different local products from *P. erinaceus* wood have been identified including the balafon, the djembe, the mask, the statuettes, etc.:

- In Niger, *P. erinaceus* is the only green fodder during the lean season (April–June). The fodder collection is generally focused on young leaves and flowers. Under the current effect of climate change, stands of *P. erinaceus* are in sharp decline and are tending toward extinction in Niger, which marks the northern limit of its natural range.

- In Togo, it is essentially the exploitation and export of lumber in the form of squares, logs, boards, and other carpentry products that are more developed [27]. Logging is based on the selective collection of key timber and fuel wood in natural habitats [10]. *P. erinaceus* is broadly used as first-class timber wood (**Figure 5**) and fuelwood [10, 28]. These selective collections pose a serious threat to the country's plant genetic resources [29].

The socio-professional category of the populations and the availability of the resource strongly influence the uses of the species in West Africa. The species is highly sought after by craftsmen for making musical instruments such as "balafon" and "djembe" (**Figure 6A** and **B**) especially among para-Gourma people in Burkina Faso, Niger, and Togo.

In addition, the endogenous knowledge of sociocultural communities is quite often contrasted with *P. erinaceus*:

- In Burkina Faso, Nouné and Dioula communities use the parts of *P. erinaceus* especially in measles treatments, spider bites, low back pain, foot pimples, cough, etc. The Dioula communities use the plant for, among other things, cases of general tiredness, heart problems, dermatoses, dysentery, hemorrhoids, diarrhea to provoke menstruation in women, for magico-therapeutic treatments, etc. Diseases treated by Dioula communities are close to those treated by Fulani communities in Burkina Faso. Lele, Mossi, and Komono communities also show almost the same practices of using *P. erinaceus* organs in the treatment of diseases.

- In Niger, the Dandy are distinguished from other ethnic groups with a larger number of diseases treated with the species, including among others gastric

Figure 5.
P. erinaceus logs being loaded into vehicles for export.

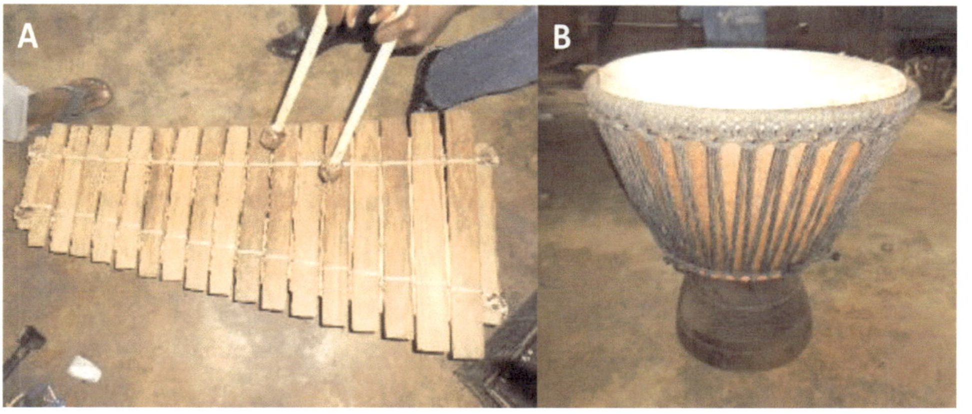

Figure 6.
Musical instruments manufactured from P. erinaceus for sale on the Bobo-Dioulasso market in Burkina Faso: (A) balafon and (B) djembe.

problems, anemia, fever, sexual weaknesses, etc. These uses are similar to those observed in Hausa (Tchanga) located in the same geographical area. In contrast, the organs of *P. erinaceus* are used very little in traditional medicine among the Zarmas, Tuaregs and Peulhs communities of Niger.

- In Togo, Para-Gourma, Kabyè, and Tem use the species in the treatment of more than 18 diseases, including impotence, anemia, menstrual periods in women, and dermatoses such as skin scurf, intestinal wounds, and white losses in women. In Kabyè and Tem communities, the organs of the species are also used to facilitate delivery in pregnant women, cure ringworm and scorpion bites, etc.

4. *Pterocarpus erinaceus* stands' patterns in West Africa

4.1 Trees' characteristic variability according to ecological gradient

The analysis of the main characteristics of the *P. erinaceus* forest stands in the three climate zones indicates that the average tree density ranges between 1.17 ± 0.75 trees/ha (Sahelian zone) and 74.9 ± 1.44 trees/ha (Guinean zone). In the Sudanian zone, it is 35.05 ± 41.2 trees/ha. The values of the densities vary significantly from one climate zone to another ($P < 10^{-3}$). For the trees average diameter, the values range between 22.07 ± 8.98 (Guinean zone) and 49.63 ± 19.44 cm (Sahelian) at the Sudanian zone. In this zone, the average diameter is 29.02 ± 15.44 cm. A significant difference was also noted for this parameter within the three zones ($P < 0.001$). Regarding the basal area, the values obtained range from 0.30 ± 0.10 (Sahelian zone) to 3.15 ± 1.30 m^2/ha (Guinean zone). In the Sudanian zone, it is 2.46 ± 2.88 m^2/ha in average. The difference among the three zones is statistically significant ($P < 0.001$) (**Table 1**).

The analysis of the total average height and the average stem height of *P. erinaceus* stands shows various values depending on whether it is in the Sahelian zone, in Sudanian zone, or Guinean zone. For the average total height, the stands of the Sudanian zone (9.51 ± 2.75 m) are significantly different ($P < 0.001$) from the other two zones (10.18 ± 2.27 m for the Sahelian zone and 10.09 ± 2.88 m for the

Structural parameters		Ecological zones			Probability
		Sahelian	Soudanian	Guinean	
Density (trees/ha)	Avg ± SE	1.17 ± 0.75	35.05 ± 41.2	74.9 ± 1.44	<0.001
Average diameter (cm)	Avg ± SE	49.63 ± 19.44	29.02 ± 15.44	22.07 ± 8.98	<0.001
Average height (m)	Avg ± SE	10.18 ± 2.27[a]	9.51 ± 2.75	10.09 ± 2.88[a]	<0.001
Average merchantable height (m)	Avg ± SE	4.08 ± 1.35	3.63 ± 1.49	2.58 ± 2.63	<0.001
Basal area (m^2/ha)	Avg ± SE	0.30 ± 0.10	2.46 ± 2.88	3.15 ± 1.30	<0.001
Height of Lorey (m)	Average	11.34	10.91	11.73	<0.001

NB: Avg, average; SE, standard error.
[a]No significant differences for these values.

Table 1.
Main forest characteristics of the three climatic zones.

Guinean zone). Regarding the merchantable height, it ranges between 4.08 ± 1.35 m (Sahelian zone) and 2.58 ± 2.63 m (Guinean zone). For this parameter, the difference observed among the three zones is statistically significant ($P < 0.001$; **Table 1**). For the height of Lorey, the values obtained for the three zones range between 10.91 m (Sahelian zone) and 11.73 m (Guinean zone) and indicate a significant difference ($P < 0.001$).

4.2 Demographic structures

4.2.1 Distribution of trees in diameter and height classes

The analysis of the demographic structure (distribution of trees in diameter classes and height classes (dbh ≥ 10 cm) of the *P. erinaceus* stands indicates a different situation depending on the climate zone considered (**Figure 7A** and **B**):

- In the Sahelian zone, the distribution of the *P. erinaceus* diameter classes reveals a predominance of the individuals with diameter classes ranging between 30 and 65 cm, that is, 55.09% of the entire stand. The young individuals with diameter class ranking between 10 and 30 cm and larger individuals with diameter ranging between 65 and 100 cm are very poorly represented, that is, 11.13, and 29.77%, respectively, of the stand (**Figure 7A1**).

- In the Sudanian zone, the distribution of diameter classes indicates a predominance of the individuals with diameter class ranging between 15 and 40 cm, that is, 74.4% of the stand. The young individuals with a diameter ranging between 10 and 15 cm and larger individuals with diameter ranging between 40 and 95 are poorly represented, that is, 17.11 and 8.4%, respectively, of the stand (**Figure 7A2**).

- The Guinean zone is characterized by a preponderance of individuals with diameter class ranging between 10 and 25 cm, that is, 69.10% of the stand. The individuals with diameter class higher than 25 cm are poorly represented, that is, 30.8% of the stand. All the structures in diameter are fit ($P > 0.05$) with the theoretical distribution of Weibull and shape parameters $c > 1$, characteristics of the stand with predominance of middle-aged individuals (**Figure 7A3**).

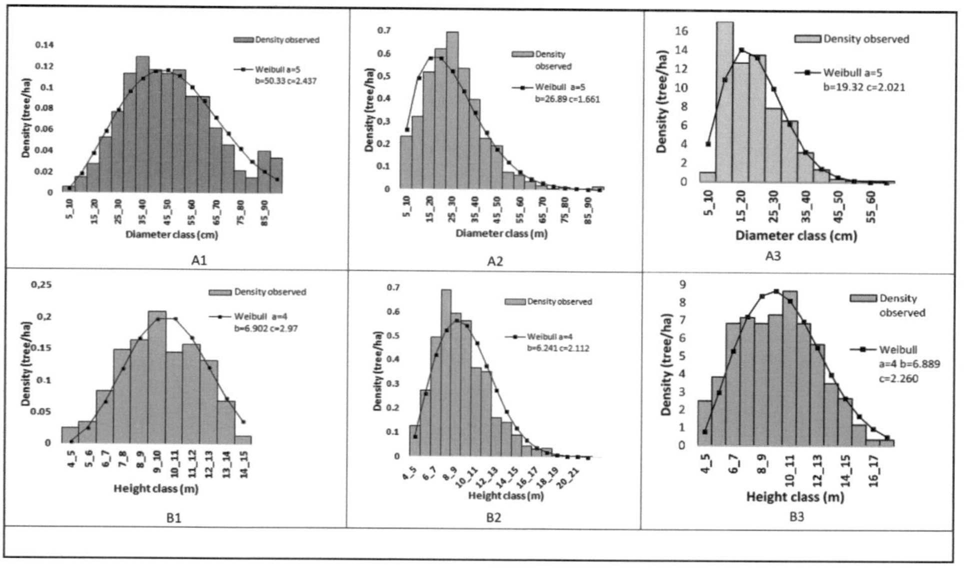

Figure 7.
Demographic structures of the stands of P. erinaceus in Guineo-Sudano-Sahelian zone: (A) diameter distribution and (B) height distribution.

The analysis of the structures shows a modal distribution of height classes for all the three climate zones. The individuals with heights ranging between 8 and 12 m are the most represented. These structures in height fit well with the theoretical distribution of Weibull ($P > 0.05$) with shape parameters c ranging between 2.1 and 2.9 (**Figure 7B1, B2**, and **B3**).

4.2.2 Natural regeneration capacity of P. erinaceus

P. erinaceus has a good regeneration capacity in seed, stump, and roots [16, 25]. Germination tests in Burkina Faso, Côte d'Ivoire, and Mali have shown that the species has a good germination capacity, with rates up to 95% if the seeds are shelled [17, 25, 30]. This should present good prospects for the production of seedlings for reforestation. Unfortunately, if the germination rate is very encouraging, this is not the case for the initial growth of seedlings. The main difficulties associated with the plantation of *P. erinaceus* are precisely the weak growth of young seedlings and their young flexible stem [17, 25]. This makes young seedlings vulnerable to wildfires, pests, trampling of animals, and adverse climatic conditions, preventing most of them from crossing the first years of life [9, 31].

In fact, the dynamics of natural regeneration of *P. erinaceus* show that the young plants come almost exclusively from underground stumps [9]. In natural conditions, the best regeneration technique for this species appears to be the regeneration of cut stems at 10 cm from the soil [17, 25].

5. *P. erinaceus* wood technology and ecological variability in West Africa

5.1 General characteristics of *P. erinaceus* wood

Studies carried out on *P. erinaceus* wood properties show that it could be classified in heavy and very hard wood with a density of 0.80 ± 0.07 g/cm^3 and an

Properties	Mean	Stand deviation	Minimum	Maximum	Coefficient of variation (%)
Basic density (g/cm^3)	0.80	0.06	0.61	0.92	8
Tangential shrinkage (%)	5.7	1	3.2	8.7	17.7
Radial shrinkage (%)	3.2	0.7	1.6	5.3	21.6
Anisotropy	1.8	0.2	1.2	2.2	12
FSP (%)	19.1	2.7	15.3	25	14
MOE (MPa)	14,500	1922	9717	19,127	13
MOR (MPa)	140	26.5	85.8	206.5	18.9
Compressive strength (MPa)	70	10	49	95	14.5
Monnin hardness	12	3.7	5.8	23.8	28.6

Table 2.
Main physical and mechanical characteristics of P. erinaceus wood.

average hardness of 12 ± 3.7 g/cm^3 (**Table 2**). In terms of dimensional stability, radial shrinkage and tangential shrinkage are yielding, respectively, 3.2 ± 0.7 and 5.7 ± 1.0%, making *P. erinaceus* wood a stable wood with shrinkage anisotropy of <2. This high stability of *P. erinaceus* wood can be attributed to the high content of extracts (15.50–19.46%) of *P. erinaceus* wood [32]. Various studies on tropical

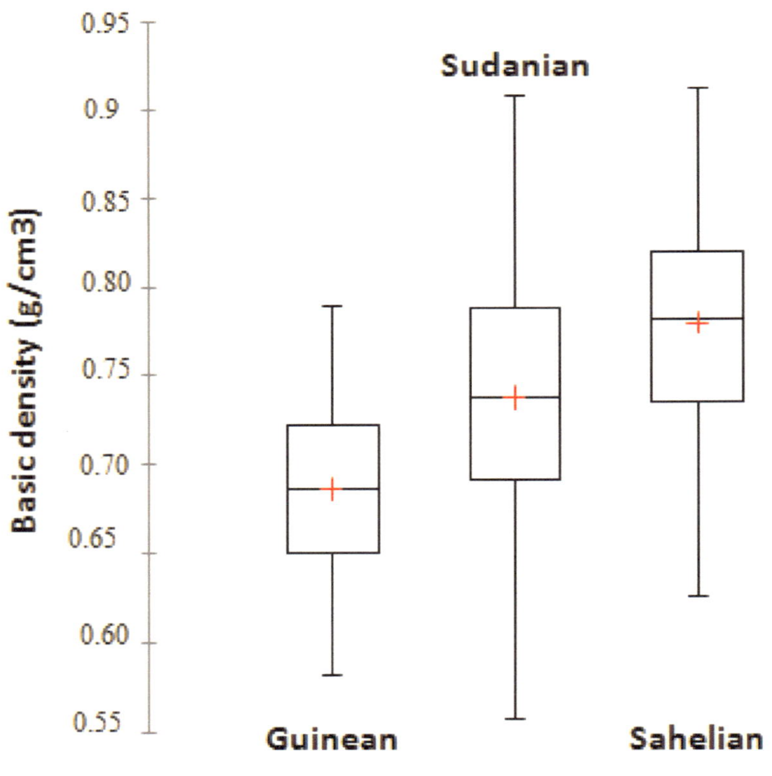

Figure 8.
Variation of basic density according to phytogeographic zones.

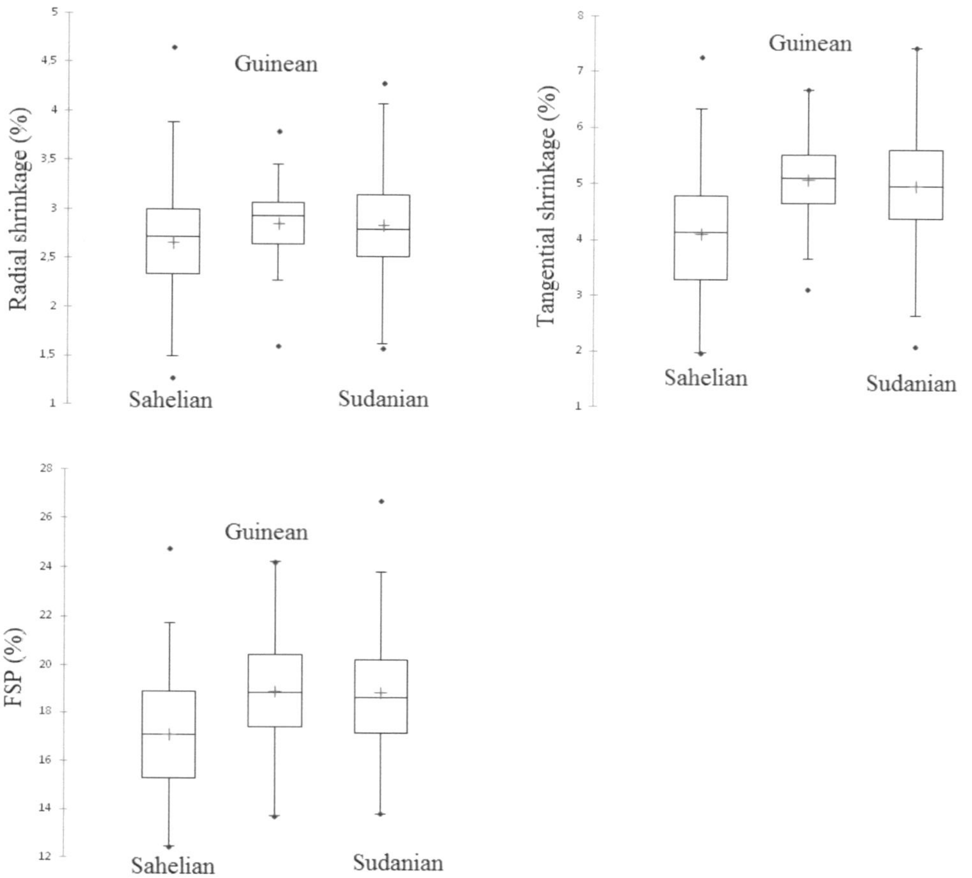

Figure 9.
Variation of radial and tangential shrinkage and FSP according to phytogeographic zones.

species such as *Pterocarpus soyauxii*, *Pterocarpus vernalis*, and *Swietenia macrophylla* confirm the close links between wood stability and extractable content [33]. Indeed, the presence of extracts enhances the stability of the wood by reducing the sensitivity to thermodynamic variations of the environment.

The average compressive and static bending fracture stresses are, respectively, 70 ± 10 and 140 ± 2.5 MPa, and the modulus of elasticity is in the order of $14{,}500 \pm 1922$ MPa [13]. The physical and mechanical characteristics of *P. erinaceus* wood confirm that certain uses of this wood in several African countries are quite appropriate, notably the manufacture of acoustic materials [13]. Empirically, the wood of *P. erinaceus* is known and sought, among other things, for making xylophone in West Africa and Sahel. Mostly wood used to produce xylophones are of high density (between 0.80 and 0.95 g/cm^3) and a high modulus of elasticity in the range of 14–20 GPa [34]. Moreover, [35, 36] have shown that the use of wood in such case requires a high insensitive to humidity variations.

5.2 Variability of properties of *P. erinaceus* wood

5.2.1 Variability of physical properties

Analysis of *P. erinaceus* wood density according to phytogeographic zones indicates significant variability ($P < 0.05$). This variability results in an increase in the

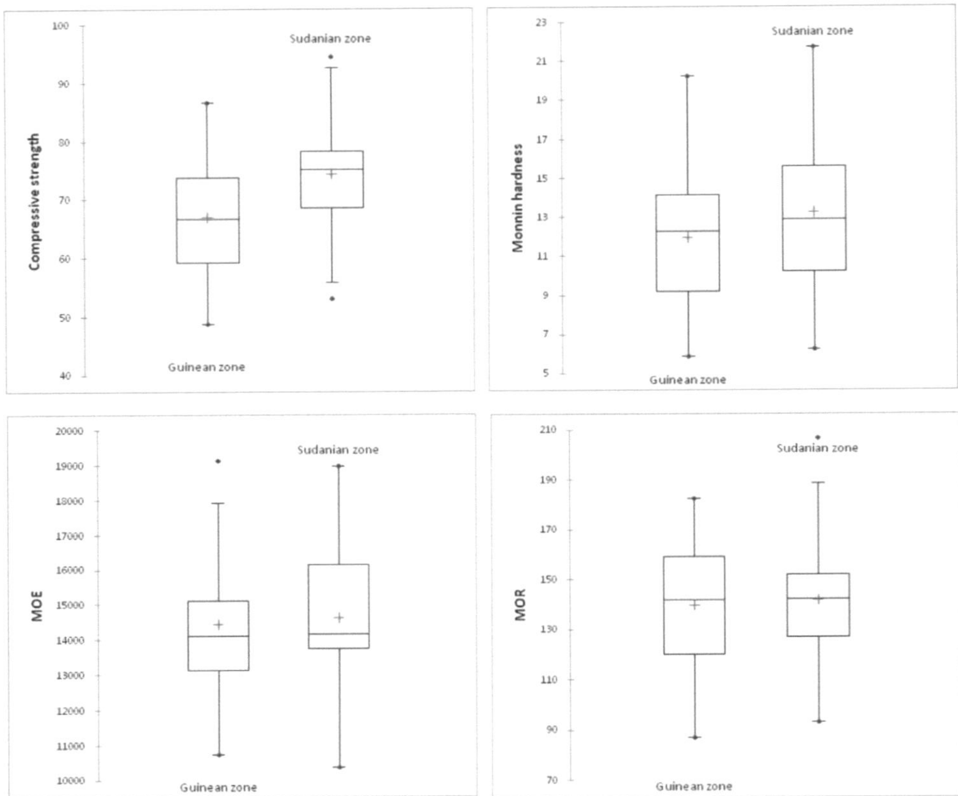

Figure 10.
Variation of mechanical properties according to phytogeographic zones.

density following the decreasing rainfall gradient in North–South [37]. The highest value of density is obtained in the Sahelian zone (0.78 ± 0.01 g/m^3) and the lowest in the Guinean zone (0.68 ± 0.01 g/m^3; **Figure 8**).

Like wood density, radial and tangential shrinkage and FSP vary significantly from one phytogeographic zone to another ($P < 0.05$). Indeed, the trees of *P. erinaceus* from the Sahelian zone present radial (2.7%) and tangential (4.1%) shrinkages significantly lower than those of the Sudanian and Guinean zones. The radial shrinkage gives an average of 2.8 and 2.95% for trees from the Guinean and Sudanian zones, respectively. As for shrinkages, the trees of the Sahelian zone have a FSP (17.1%) significantly lower than the other (**Figure 9**). In other words, the trees of *P. erinaceus* in the Sahelian zone have a more stable wood than the trees in the Guinean and Sudanian zones [37].

Regarding the influence of the radial position, only the FSP is negatively related to the cambial age [13]. This is consistent with the results of [36], which showed the influence of the level of extract, especially with benzene alcohol, on the PSF. For wood density, the work of [37] showed a very small decrease in density as a function of cambial age ($R^2 = 0.11$). This generally shows that the physical properties of *P. erinaceus* wood remain very little, if any, influenced by cambial age.

5.2.2 Variability of mechanical properties

The climatic variability of the mechanical properties was analyzed according to two phytogeographic zones (Guinean and Sudanian; data on the Sahelian zone are not available). The analysis of the average values of the mechanical properties according to the phytogeographic zones does not indicate a significant difference ($P > 0.05$) for the MOE, the hardness, and the static bending strength (MOR) (**Figure 10**). Indeed, the MOE indicates, respectively, 14,150 ± 1900 and 14,100 ± 2300 MPa for the Guinean and Sudanian zones. For Monnin hardness, the values indicate on average 13.09 ± 3.87 in the Sudanian zone and 12.08 ± 3.33 in the Guinean zone. As regards static bending fracture stresses, it gives an average of 137.5 ± 25.5 MPa in the Guinean zone and 145 ± 27.5 MPa in the Sudanian zone. Only the values of the compressive strength vary significantly from one zone to another ($P < 0.05$). It is 66.5 ± 9.4 MPa in the Guinean zone and 73.5 ± 10.3 MPa in the Sudanian zone.

In terms of the variability of properties according to the age, the analysis of the mechanical properties according to the number of rings counted from pith to bark showed that only the compressive and static bending strength were correlated with the cambial age [13]. The juvenile wood zone appears slightly more "resistant" in compressive strength and MOR than the adult wood zone. But this correlation remains weak, as shown by the coefficients of determination obtained (compressive strength: R^2 = 0.09, MOR: R^2 = 0.13). Age would therefore have very little influence on the mechanical properties of wood.

6. Restoration and conservation of *P. erinaceus stands in West Africa*

6.1 Large-scale plant production strategies of *P. erinaceus* for restoration programs of degraded forest ecosystems

The production strategies of *P. erinaceus*, like all plant species, are based on the use of classical cultural methods of sexual propagation (seedling germination) and vegetative propagation (horticultural cuttings, layering, etc.).

6.1.1 Sexual propagation

Several studies indicate that natural regeneration is often abundant and that the species may be somewhat invasive enough to be preserved for a few years from grazing, bush fires, vegetation, and pruning [17, 38]. For germination, all the seeds extracted from fruits can be used. It is essential to ensure the good health of these two organs and to avoid taking those who have suffered attacks (animals, insects, fungi, etc.), mechanical damage (breakage, injury, and holes), etc. Germination rates (70–90%) can be obtained with seeds extracted from fruit collected directly on the trees or collected on the ground. With healthy seeds from fruit hulling, sown without pretreatment on cotton soaked in distilled water, average germination rates were recorded at 84% for of 2 days of germination trials.

The substrate used during these trials was composed of vermiculite, vermiculite + earth (1v/1v) and vermiculite + compost (1v/1v), with cotton or paper as support (**Figure 11**). The seedlings of *P. erinaceus* are quite fragile at germination and are not able to support the weight and opacity of a compact substrate. There is no specific pretreatment to apply to seeds, but they can be soaked in water for 24 h before sowing to hasten their hydration and promote homogenous germination. The first germinations are observed 24 h after sowing [38, 39]. The advantage of the use of seedlings lies in the fact that they lead to variability in the monitored seedlings.

The influence of seed storage period on their germination capacity shows greatly variable germination capacities, with a maximum of 93.75% and a minimum of 10.71%, with general decrease in the germination rate between the fifth and the ninth month. The germination capacity varies according to the origin of the seeds.

Figure 11.
Nursery of P. erinaceus on vermiculite in seedling cells.

6.1.2 Vegetative propagation of P. erinaceus

6.1.2.1 Marcottage ability of Pterocarpus erinaceus

6.1.2.1.1 Rooting rate of marcots

Ref. [40] revealed that from 100 marcots monitored, 97 were stripped. The rooting rate observed is 55.67%. In the apical part, 18 marcots were unpacked with an average diameter of 11.33 ± 2.53 mm, and 9 of them rooted, which have a success rate of 50%. In the unattached middle part of 37 with an average diameter of 19.30 ± 4.01 mm, 16 have rooted which gives a rate of 56.75%. Among the 42 marcots of the proximal part whose average diameter is 21.87 ± 3.95 mm, 24 root coots have rooted with a success rate of 57.14%. In general, it was founded that the marcots made in the proximal part of the tree gave the highest success rate (**Table 3**; **Figure 12A, B,** and **C**).

Table 3 illustrates the relationship between the success rate and the diameter classes of marcotted stems. Indeed, the rods' diameter between 20 and 30 mm followed by rods with a diameter of between 10 and 20 mm has the highest success rate. Stems with a diameter of between 5 and 10 mm have only a success rate of 20%.

6.1.2.1.2 Ability of marcots' rooting

The success rate observed is about 55.6% [40]. The analysis of the success rate, i.e., the rate of rooting of the layers, showed that the layers of the proximal part located near the main stem of the tree are more suitable for layering with a rate of 57.14% followed by middle-aged layers with a rate of 56.7%, at the center of the branch; the lowest marcotting ability is observed at the level of the apical layer, i.e., at the end

Levels	Initial number	Average diameter (mm)	Rooted number	Success rate (%)
Apical	18	11.33 ± 2.53a	9	50.00
Median	37	19.30 ± 4.01b	21	56.75
Proximal	42	21.87 ± 3.95c	24	57.14

Table 3.
Rooting rate and number of rooted marcots.

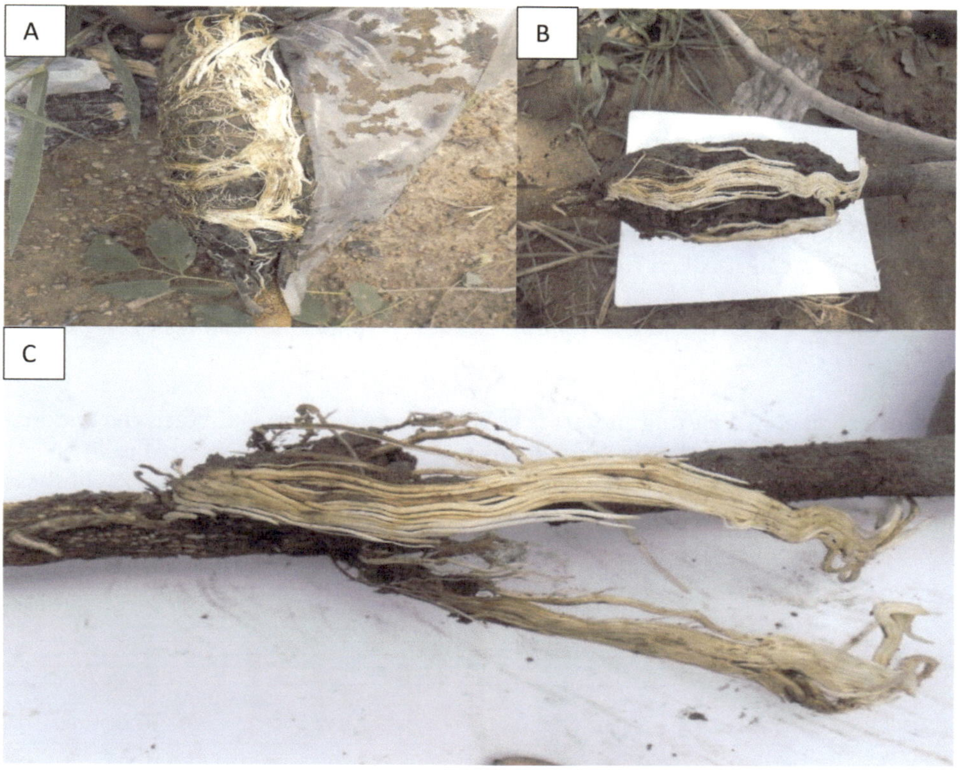

Figure 12.
Marcots ingrained legend: (A) marcot unpacked, (B) marcot with clod of soil, and (C) roots produced and rid of clods of earth.

of the branch toward the terminal buds with a rate of 50%. The evolution of this rate shows that the success of marcottage depends on the age of the marcotted branch part. Indeed, the level located near the main stem is the oldest and in addition has the highest average diameter capable of storing a large amount of sap developed in its liber and supporting rhizogenesis.

6.1.2.2 Budding ability of Pterocarpus erinaceus stem cuttings

Experimental trials were conducted to evaluate the effect of the indoleacetic acid (IAA) dose, cutting diameter and soaking time on the budding, and degeneration and rooting of *P. erinaceus* cuttings (Appendix 2). With this, two sets of experiments were carried out to assess the effect of IAA dose, diameter of cuttings and soaking duration on budding, and degeneration and cutting rooting of *P. erinaceus*. The first experimental tests were designed on the basis of three factors that are diameter of the cuttings with two levels ([0–1.5 cm] and [1.6–3]), the dose of IAA with six levels (0, 500, 750, 1000, 1500, and 2000 mg/l), and soaking duration in IAA with four levels (0, 10, 20, and 30 min).

A total number of 48 ($2 \times 6 \times 4$) treatments, repeated 11 times, were established. The data collected were related to the number of cuttings budged and number of cuttings that degenerated after diameter of shoots as well as number of leaves produced.

Based on these tests, it was pointed out that the budding started on the fourth day after establishment of the tests. The budding rate of the cuttings is 79.8% after 8 weeks. The budding rates are statistically similar whatever the diameter class

(78.89, 80.56, and 80.56%, respectively, for cuttings with diameter comprising [2–2.5 cm], [2.6–3 cm], and [3.1–3.5 cm]). In contrast, levels of IAA dose and soaking duration of cuttings have statistically significant ($P < 0.05$) effects on the budding (**Table 4**). The chances of budding of the cuttings soaked in IAA at doses 750, 1500, and 2000 mg/l are, respectively, 5.70, 2.55, and 3.71 times higher than the control tests (without application of IAA). All cuttings treated with IAA showed a budding rate much higher (>80%) than the one in control tests (62.22%, **Figure 10**). Similarly, budding rates after 8 weeks range from 79.26% for cuttings soaked for 10 s to 89.63% for cuttings soaked for 1 h (**Figure 13**).

6.1.2.3 Cutting diameter and IAA appropriate dose for successful rooting in P. erinaceus stem cuttings

The efficiency of cutting success is largely related to rooting. Indeed the budding alone does not explain the chances of survival of the young shoots because it is based on the reserves stored by the cuttings to occur. So after the depletion of these reserves in the absence of a root system that can take over to feed the young shoot, it dries up and dies. This explains the favorable budding and bud bursting response

Treatments	Odds ratio	STD	P > |z|
	IAA dose (mg/l)		
750	5.70	1.95	0.000
1500	2.55	0.72	0.001
2000	3.71	1.13	0.000
	Soaking duration (s)		
10	2.32	0.64	0.002
1200	4.86	1.59	0.000
3600	4.86	1.59	0.000

STD, standard error; P, budding probability at 5%.

Table 4.
Effect of diameter class, IAA dose, and soaking time on the budding of P. erinaceus after 8 weeks.

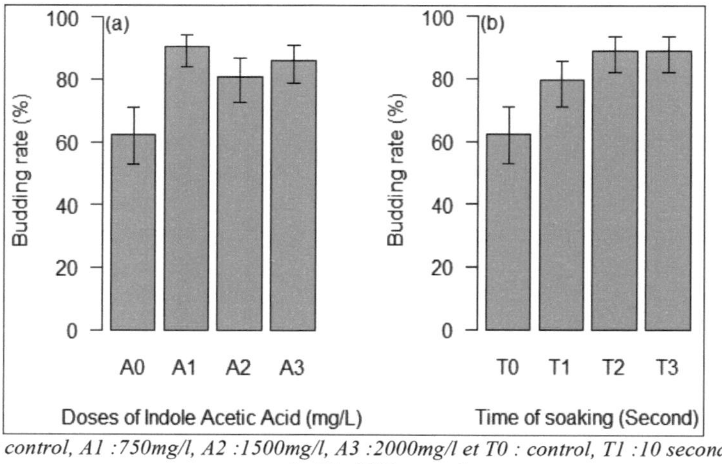

Legend : A0 : control, A1 :750mg/l, A2 :1500mg/l, A3 :2000mg/l et T0 : control, T1 :10 seconds, T2 :1200 seconds, T3 :3600 seconds

Figure 13.
Budding rates of the cuttings according to doses of IAA (a) and time of soaking (b) after 8 weeks.

observed in the three diameter classes. This result corroborates perfectly those of [38, 41] revealing that diameter has a marginal effect on bud development.

However, contrary to previous trials that concluded that stem cuttings of *P. erinaceus* cannot be rooted and degenerated after a while [38, 41], the results of the previous trial show that cuttings with diameters between 2 and 3 cm can root perfectly when soaked in IAA dose of 1500–2000 mg/l for 20 min to 1 h. In this experiment, cuttings with small diameter, non-soaked cuttings (control), and cuttings soaked in IAA for 10 s have not rooted. The cuttings that survived with leafy shoots until 24 weeks are those which made large amount of callus and rooted sufficiently as the callus formation is a necessarypreliminary for cutting rooting (**Figure 14**).

6.2 Minimum felling diameter of *P. erinaceus*

Ref. [42] determined *P. erinaceus* minimum felling diameter to ensure a sustainable management of its natural stands in West Africa. The methodological approach was based firstly on the calculation of the restoration rates and the rotation cycles and secondly on the distribution of the stand basal area in diameter classes. The results show that for the Guinean and Sudanian zones, the best restoration percentage ($P \geq 50\%$) is obtained for 35 m in diameter. Percentages equivalent to 356.5% are therefore obtained for the Guinean zone and 53.4% for the Sudanian zone for a rotation period estimated at 20 years (Appendix 3). In the Sahelian zone, the best restoration percentage ($P \geq 50\%$) is only obtained when testing the 65 cm diameter.

Figure 14.
Rooted cuttings of Pterocarpus erinaceus: a: cutting with callus; b&d: rooted cuttings without clod of soil; c: rooted cuttings with clod of soil.

For this diameter, a restoration rate is obtained at 111.9% for a rotation period estimated at 20 years (Appendix 3).

In addition, the distribution of the basal areas per trees diameter classes recorded in each of the three climate zones indicates a curve which is similar to a bell-shaped distribution. Therefore, for the Guinean and Sudanian zones, the maximum value of the basal area is obtained for the center with diameter class equal to 35 cm (**Figure 15**). As for the Sahelian zone, the maximum value of the basal area is obtained for the center of the diameter class equal to 65 cm.

In view of the foregoing results, two minimum felling diameters for Guineo-Sudano-Sahelian zone in West Africa are considered. This includes the diameter 35 cm for the Guinean and Sudanian zones (P = 356.5% for the Guinean zone and P = 53.4% for the Sahelian zone for a rotation of 20 years) and the diameter 65 cm for the Sahelian zone (P = 111.9% for a rotation period estimated at 20 years).

The analysis of the restoration percentages depending on the diameter classes and the time helps deducing that the *P. erinaceus* stands are restored in a relatively shorter time in Guinean zone. However, the Sahelian zone seems not to offer favorable conditions for the rapid restoration of this species stands (**Figure 13**). The high restoration rate of the species in the Guinean zone may be explained by the fact that the exploitation of the species there is frequently timber. This form of exploitation allows the selective cutting of the large-diameter trees and leaving behind the seedlings. Since the ecological conditions are favorable in this zone (high rainfall), there is a regeneration (usually in the form of stump sprouts), and seeds are produced. However, in the Sahelian zone, the pollarding for fodder is an important exploitation form of the species.

6.3 Conservation measures to preserve *P. erinaceus*

The intensity of the exploitation of the species sparked off concerns about its sustainability among a range of countries including Benin, Burkina Faso, Ghana, Senegal, and Togo. In order to curb the unrestrained exploitation of rosewood, countries (including Ghana and Togo) adopted harvesting and timber/log export

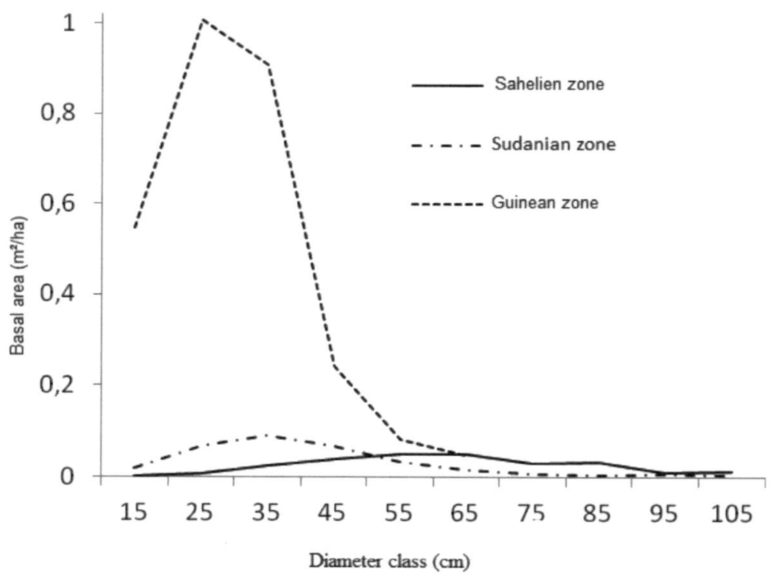

Figure 15.
Distribution of the basal area in terms of diameter classes across climatic zones.

bans. However, these regulations were routinely violated. Chinese custom data showed continuous rosewood export from producer countries under timber/log export ban for well over 2–3 years under after the bans were imposed.

Consequently, seeking stricter control of exploitation and trade of rosewood, Senegal and other range countries in West Africa listed the species on CITES Appendix III in 2016 and later up-listed it to Appendix II in 2017. In spite of the CITES Appendix listing, there are still incidences of illegal logging and trade in the exporting and importing countries. Due to incidence of illegal logging and irregularities in the issuance of CITES permit, Nigeria has recently (effective November 2018) been suspended from trading in *P. erinaceus* until it adequately addresses issues of forest law enforcement trade and governance.

Faced with these situations, some countries have placed a moratorium prohibiting its exploitation (the case of Togo where a moratorium has been put in place since June 2016). This decision of the Ministry of the Environment and Forest Resources of Togo was largely based on the results of our studies and warnings of the status of the species in the country. In 2016, the African Union organized a symposium on the illegal exploitation of the species in Guinea-Bissau. During this symposium, it was clearly pointed out that the abusive exploitation and the bush fires make the renewal of the natural stands of *P. erinaceus* difficult.

The increased rate of unsustainable exploitation and illegal logging of *P. erinaceus* is driven by noncompliance and ineffective enforcement of regulatory framework governing timber exploitation and trade. Rosewood exploitation and trade have continued despite the ban in the affected countries and/or strict trade regulatory control such as CITES. National regulatory frameworks and law enforcers' endeavors within national territories have proved helpless against regional and intercontinental trade dynamics. The situation does not only deprive local communities (where the species is endemic) of due economic benefits but also deprives the state of huge revenue such as taxes and fees that could have been used for national development. For example, in 2013, it was estimated that Ghana lost 70% of the revenue that should have accrued to the state due to illegal exploitation of rosewood [12]. The limited effectiveness of the domestic measures against rosewood exploitation and the recent irregularities in the issuance of CITES permit in Nigeria call for a stronger regional collaboration and robust and technologically advanced timber tracking system and wood identification methods that can help stem illegalities.

P. erinaceus is also one of the priority species that focused the attention of number of scientists. Then several authors have pointed out the increased rate of illegal felling and over export of the species in African countries such as Benin, the Gambia, Ghana, Guinea-Bissau, Nigeria, and Mozambique [43–46]. Faced with this persistent threat, the domestication of this species is important to ensure its sustainability. Several actions have been carried out in favor of the species to reduce the pressure on it and make it an opportunity for the region. Assessing the impact of felling/export ban and CITES designation on the exploitation and trade of the species in Ghana [12] has concluded on the necessary ex situ conservation measures such as seed banking, field gene banking, tissue culture, and plantation development to conserve this endangered plant species in order to avoid the possibility of commercial extinction.

7. Conclusion

The analysis of the state of knowledge on natural stands of *P. erinaceus* in West Africa has shown that different social and sociocultural categories know and use the products of the species. Approximately 46 uses have been identified by the different sociocultural and socio-professional groups. In addition to using the species as lumber, fuel wood, and fodder, *P. erinaceus* is widely used as a medicinal plant.

In terms of the forest characteristics of *P. erinaceus* stands, studies indicate a significant difference in density, average diameter, mean total height, and basal area between the three climatic zones. The Guinean and Sudanian zones seem to present more favorable environmental conditions for the development of *P. erinaceus* stands. Regarding the potential and strategies of natural regeneration, studies have shown that the species has a good capacity of natural regeneration by sowing, stump rejects, suckers, and marcots. This opens up prospects for the production of seedlings and planting trials with *P. erinaceus* for the restoration of degraded natural stands. The results also showed that *P. erinaceus* has a very high ecological plasticity allowing it to adapt in several different climates. This large ecological range of the species offers opportunities to set up conservation plots in reserved areas regardless of site conditions in West Africa.

Studies have shown a difference in the properties of *P. erinaceus* wood according to climatic zones. This difference is reflected in the superiority of the properties of trees from the Sahelian zone followed by those of the Sudanian zone. This result provides information to the West African forest services on the behavior of this species, which could be the subject of a plantation program. In addition, knowledge of the technological characteristics of *P. erinaceus* wood according to the conditions of the environment and the age contributes to the management of the forest resources to ensure a sustainable production of wood. Indeed, these characteristics are among the important criteria to be included in the selection. For a long time confined to the selection of the growth, survival of trees, the current strategy for the genetic improvement of forest species is to include wood quality criteria.

Finally, to promote the rapid restoration of *P. erinaceus* stands, two regionalized minimum felling diameters were proposed based on the results of the structural parameter evaluation and the reconstitution percentage calculations and rotation times. For the Guinean-Sudanian zones, the minimum felling diameter adopted was 35 cm for a restoration percentage of 366.6 (Guinean zone) and 53.4% (Sudanian zone) for a period of 20 years. In the Sahelian zone, the minimum felling diameter adopted was 65 cm for a rotation period of 20 years. These parameters are an essential tool to limit over-logging of forest tree species and to ensure their sustainable management. Various forest authorities will consequently have scientific tools to better protect forest resources through the enforcement of restrictive measures concerning the selective logging of valuable timber.

Acknowledgements

The authors are grateful to:

- The commission of the West African Economic and Monetary Union (UEMOA) for financing a part of this research within the framework of the Project “Support for Higher Education in the member countries of UEMOA (PAES)”

- The Economic Community of West African States (ECOWAS) for financing a part of this research within the ECOWAS research and innovation support program (PROGRAMME PARI)

- The “Sud Expert Plantes et Développement Durable (SEP2D)” program for financing a part of this research

- The "Agence Universitaire de la Francophonie (AUF)" for financing a part of this research

The study was also supported by the International Foundation for Science through a research grant provided to Dr. Kossi Novinyo Segla.

We are also grateful to BioWooEB Research Unit of the French Agricultural Research Centre for International Development (CIRAD) for its material and financial support.

Appendices: vegetative propagation protocol by air layering

A.1 Theoretical and methodological framework

P. erinaceus, which is particularly appreciated for its wood and the quality of the fodder it provides, is threatened in several localities in western Burkina Faso [20]. Natural seedlings are very infrequent, and their survival after one or two dry seasons as well as that of young plantations is very low. The study of its regeneration by economic means such as "vegetative propagation" could then promote the regeneration of the species and increase the possibilities of its exploitation and its valorization in Burkina Faso and Niger and in many other forest subregions [22].

Furthermore, the scientific and technical information necessary for good control of reproduction and vegetative propagation of this species is not yet available. In addition, in the field of low-cost vegetative propagation (PVFC), very few trials have been carried out in the world and especially in Africa [22].

Layering consists in inducing the appearance of roots on the stems of a woody species. This is done by contacting the stems with a suitable substrate (soil, sawdust, etc.). When the branch or stem of a woody species is placed directly against the ground to induce the root system, it is called layering. When the contact with the substrate is above ground, it is called air layering.

A.2 Experimental protocol

Beforehand a mixture of earth and sawdust was prepared. The mixture consists of 40% sawdust and 60% earth. For each marcot, two annular incisions spaced from each other by 5 cm in height and without damaging the wood are applied to the branch. This results in a vertical incision of the bark from one annular incision to another. The portion of the bark is removed, leaving bare wood (**Figure A1A**). The consequence is the interruption of the circulation of the sap developed from the upper part to the lower part of the incised stem. The bare part of the bark is wrapped with a transparent plastic sheet containing the mixture of earth and sawdust that serves as a support for the roots.

Then seal the ends together with the tape while taking care not to trap the air. This support covers up to 10 cm on either side of the incised part, that is to say, to create a sufficiently large substrate to allow the possible roots to grow normally (**Figure A1B**). The supply of water is provided by injection with the aid of a syringe. In general, watering was done weekly. If the marcot is dry, a quantity of 20 ml can be injected or twice a 10 ml syringe. After the injection of water, the holes induced by the needle of the syringe are immediately closed with tape to minimize the evaporation of water.

Figure A1.
Aerial carving of P. erinaceus. (A) Annealing of the stem and (B) soil wrapped by a plastic sheet.

B. Experimental design and data collection for vegetative propagation of *P. erinaceus* by stem cuttings

Pterocarpus erinaceus stems were harvested from healthy mature trees whose diameter at 1.30 m ranged from 15 to 35 cm, in the morning before periods of high temperatures to limit their dehydration. Cuttings were collected at approximately the same levels on young branches. Stem cuttings were 15 cm length and with 20 cm diameter. Two sets of experiments were carried out to assess the effect of indoleacetic acid dose, diameter of cuttings and soaking duration on budding, and degeneration and cutting rooting of *P. erinaceus*.

The first experimental tests were designed on the basis of three factors that are diameter of the cuttings with two levels ([0–1.5 cm] and [1.6–3 cm]), the dose of

Figure A2.
Experimental settlement in the nursery: Pterocarpus erinaceus cuttings.

IAA with six levels (0, 500, 750, 1000, 1500, and 2000 mg/l), and soaking duration in IAA with four levels (0, 10, 20, and 30 min). A total number of 48 (2 × 6 × 4) treatments, repeated 11 times, were established. The data collected were related to the number of cuttings budged and number of cuttings that degenerated after diameter of shoots as well as number of leaves produced.

As all cuttings with a diameter comprising between 0 and 1.5 cm having budded (including the control) degenerated within 20 days after budding while some of those with diameter >2 cm rooted, another experimental test was settled in a split plot design based on the previous three factors, changing the modalities as followed: cutting diameter with three levels ([2–2.5 cm], [2.6–3 cm], and [3.1–3.5 cm]), the dose of IAA with three levels (750, 1500, and 2000 mg/l), and soaking duration in IAA with three levels (10 s, 20 min, and 1 h). A total number of 27 (3 × 3 × 3) treatments, repeated three times, were established. The main factor was the cutting diameter.

The subsidiary factors were randomly distributed in the sub-blocks. There was one control in each sub-block exempt of IAA treatment. The experimental tests were conducted on 540 leafless stem cuttings and put in pots filled with forest soil substrate (**Figure A2**). The plots were manually watered one–two times per day. Data collected were related to the cutting budding, bud bursting, number of shoots, shoot diameter, and height. The number of budded cuttings and leafy shoots was noted weekly for 8 weeks. The number of rooted cuttings, diameter, and height of leafy shoots was noted until 24 weeks.

C. Minimum felling diameter of *P. erinaceus* in Guineo-Sudano-Sahelian zone

Diameter classes (cm)		15	25	35	45	55	65	75	85	95	105
Transition time (years)		10	30	50	70	90	110	130	150	170	190
Recovery percentage (%)	Guinean zone	0	37.3	356.5	1589.3	4648.7	4694.9	—	—	—	—
	Sudanian zone	0	6.9	53.4	206.7	534.9	1064.1	1765.5	2312.7	5073.6	5063.5
	Sahelian zone	0	0.3	3.1	14.6	41.9	111.9	235.6	626.6	1282.5	1316.3

Source: Segla et al. [38].

Author details

Adjonou Kossi[1]*, Houetchegnon Towanou[2], Rabiou Habou[3], Segla Kossi Novinyo[1], Abotsi Komla Elikplim[1], Johnson Benziwa Nathalie[1], Alaba Pyoabalo[1], Ouinsavi Christine A.I. Nougbodé[2], Quashie Akossiwoa Marie-Luce[1], Kokutse Adzo Dzifa[1], Mahamane Ali[3] and Kokou Kouami[1]

1 Faculty of Sciences, University of Lomé (Togo), Lomé, Togo

2 Faculty of Sciences and Technology, University of Parakou, Parakou, Benin

3 Faculty of Agronomic Sciences, University of Diffa, Diffa, Niger

*Address all correspondence to: kossiadjonou@hotmail.com

References

[1] Angelsen A, Kaimowitz D. Rethinking the causes of deforestation: Lessons from economic models (English). The World Bank Research Observer. 1999;**14**(1):73-98

[2] World Bank. Sustainable development in a dynamic world: transforming institutions, growth, and quality of life. World Development Report 2003. New York, Washington, DC: Oxford University Press; 2002. p. 272

[3] Arcand J-L, Guillaumont P, Guillaumont JS. Deforestation and the real exchange rate. Journal of Development Economics. 2008;**86**(2): 242-262

[4] Damette O, Delacote P. On the economic factors of deforestation: what can we learn from quantile analysis?. Working Papers 1110. Chaire Economie du Climat; 2011

[5] Lamien N. Fructification du Karité (*Vitellaria paradoxa* C. F. Gaertn.): Facteurs de déperdition, Amélioration et prévision des rendements à Boundoukuy, Ouest Burkina-Faso. Thèse de doctorat. Université de Ouagadougou; 2006. p. 114

[6] Ouôba P. Flore et végétation de la forêt classée de Niangoloko, Sud-Est du Burkina-Faso. Thèse de doctorat. Université de Ouagadougou; 2005. p. 139

[7] Assogbadjo AE, Glèlè KR, François HA, Akomian FA, Gbèlidji FV, Tina KJT, et al. Ethnic differences in use value and use patterns of the threatened multipurpose scrambling shrub (*Caesalpinia bonduc* L.) in Benin. Journal of Medicinal Plant Research. 2011;**5**(9):1549-1557

[8] Sylla SN, Samba RT, Neyra M, Ndoye I, Giraud E, Willems A, et al. Phenotypic and genotypic diversity of rhizobia nodulating *Pterocarpus erinaceus* and *P. lucens* in Senegal. Systematic and Applied Microbiology. 2002;**25**:572-583

[9] Ouédraogo A, Adjima T, Hahn-Hadjali K, Guinko S. Diagnostic de l'état de dégradation des peuplements de quatre espèces ligneuses en zone soudanienne du Burkina Faso. Sécheresse. 2006;**17**(4):485-491

[10] Kokou K, Nuto Y, Atsri H. Impact of charcoal production on woody plant species in West Africa: A case study in Togo. Scientific Research and Essays. 2009;**4**(9):881-893

[11] Fontodji JK, Atsri H, Adjonou K, Radji AR, Kokutse AD, Nuto Y, et al. Impact of charcoal production on biodiversity in Togo (West Africa). In: López-Pujol J, editor. The Importance of Biological Interactions in the Study of Biodiversity. Rijeka, Croatia; 2011. pp. 215-230. ISBN 978-953-307-751-2

[12] Dumenu WK. Assessing the impact of felling/export ban and CITES designation on exploitation of African rosewood (*Pterocarpus erinaceus*). Biological Conservation. 2019; **236**(2019):124-133

[13] Sègla KN, Adjonou K, Radji AR, Kokutse AD, Kokou K, Habou R, et al. Importance socio-économique de *Pterocarpus erinaceus* Poir. au Togo. European Scientific Journal. 2015; **11**(23):119-217

[14] Petit S, Mallet B. L'émondage d'arbres fourragers: détail d'une pratique pastorale. Bois et Forêts des Tropiques. 2001;**270**(4):35-45

[15] Karou D, Dicko MH, Sanon S, Simpore J, Traore AS. Antimalarial activity of *Sida acuta* Burm f. (Malvaceae) and *Pterocarpus erinaceus* Poir. (Fabaceae). Journal of Ethnopharmacology. 2003;**89**:291-294

[16] Adjonou K, Ali N, Kokutse AD, Segla KN. Etude de la dynamique des peuplements naturels de *Pterocarpus ericaceus* Poir. (Fabaceae) surexploités au Togo. Bois et Forêts des Tropiques. 2010;**306**(4):45-55

[17] Duvall CS. *Pterocarpus erinaceus* Poir. In: Louppe D, Oteng-Amoako AA, Brink M. (éd.). Prota 7 (1): Timbers/ Bois d'oeuvre 1. Wageningen, Pays-Bas, Prota. 2008

[18] Mydell HV. Arbres et Arbustes du Sahel. Leurs propriétés et Leurs Utilisations. Eschborn; 1983

[19] Arbonier M. Arbres, Arbustes et Lianes des zones séches d'Afriques de l'Ouest, deuxième édition. Paris, France: CIRAD, MNHN, UICN; 2002. 573 P

[20] Touré Y. Etude des potentialités agroforestières, de la multiplication et des usages de *Pterocarpus erinaceus* Poir. en zone soudanienne du Burkina Faso. Burkina-Faso: Mémoire d'Ingénieur, Université Polytechnique de Bobo-Doualasso; 2001. p. 120

[21] ICRAF. Annual Report 1997. Nairobi; 1998. p. 135

[22] Ouédraogo H. Structure démographique et modes de régénération de *P. erinaceus* Poir. et autres espèces prioritaires utilisées dans l'artisanat à l'Ouest du Burkina faso. Université Polytechnique de Bobo-Dioulasso (IDR), Mém. Ing., 2007. p. 77

[23] CITES. CoP17 Inf. 79. Analysis of the demand-driven trade in Hongmu timber species: Impacts of unsustainable and illegality in source regions. In: Seventeenth Meeting of the Conference of Parties. Johannesburg, South Africa; 2016

[24] Hountodji YCH. Dynamique environnementale en zones sahélienne et soudanienne de l'Afrique de l'Ouest: Analyse des modifications et évaluation de la dégradation du couvert végétal. Thèse de Doctorat. Belgique: Université de Liège; 2008. p. 153

[25] Cuny P, Sanogo S, Sommer N. Arbres du Domaine Soudanien. Leurs Usages et Leur Multiplication. Sikasso: Mali, Ier, Berne, Suisse, Intercoopération; 1997, 122 p

[26] Ali N. *Pterocarpus erinaceus* (Fabaceae) dans la Région Centrale du Togo: usages et impacts de l'exploitation sur la distribution spatiale et caractéristiques structurales. Togo: Mémoire de technicien supérieur agricole de l'Infa de Tové; 2009. p. 43

[27] Segla KN, Adjonou K, Rabiou H, Radji AR, Kokutse AD, Bationo A, et al. Spatial distribution of *Pterocarpus erinaceus* Poir. (Fabaceae) natural stands in the Sudanian and Sudano-Guinean zones of West Africa: Gradient distribution and productivity variation across the five ecological zones of Togo. Annual Research & Review in Biology. 2015;**6**(2):89-102. DOI: 10.9734/ARRB/ 2015/14771

[28] Ouro Djer, E, Djagba T, Sewa AA, Ouro-Landjo S, Albada A. Situation des ressources génétiques forestières du Togo. Atelier sous-régional FAO/IPGRI/ ICRAF sur la conservation, la gestion, l'utilisation durable et la mise en valeur des ressources génétiques forestières de la zone sahélienne, note thématique sur les ressources génétiques forestières, document FGR/13F, Département des forêts. Rome, Italie: FAO; 2001. p. 25

[29] Adjonou K. Structure et indicateurs biologiques de gestion durable des reliques de forets sèches du Togo [Thèse de doctorat]. Togo: Université de Lomé; 2011. p. 119

[30] Louppe D, Ouattara N. Croissance en plantation de quelques espèces ligneuses locales. Korhogo (Côte d'Ivoire). Korhogo, Côte d'Ivoire, Idefor; 1993. p. 12

[31] Nacoulma BMI. Dynamique et stratégie de conservation de la végétation et de la phytodiversité du complexe écologique du Parc National du W du Burkina Faso [Thèse de doctorat]. Ouagadougou, Burkina Faso: 2012. p. 151

[32] Traore B. Influence de la structure anatomique et des métabolites secondaires sur les propriétés physiques et la qualité acoustique du bois de Vène provenant du mali [Thèse de doctorat]. Université Laval; 2009. pp. 206

[33] Bremaud I, Minato K, Langbour P, Thibaut B. Physico-mechanical indicators of interspecific variability in vibration damping of wood. Annales des Sciences Forestières. 2010;**67**:707

[34] Holz D. Acoustically important properties of xylophone-bar materials: Can tropical woods be replaced by European species? Acta Acustica. 1996; **82**:878-884

[35] Yano H. The changes in the acoustic properties of Western red cedar due to methanol extraction. Holzforschung. 1994;**48**(6):491-495

[36] Brémaud I, Minato K, Thibaut B. Mechanical damping of wood as related to species classification: A preliminary survey. In: 6th International Conference on Plant Biomechanics, Cayenne; 16-21 November 2009. 2009

[37] Segla KN, Adjonou K, Rabiou H, Moussa MB, Radji AR, Kokutse AD, et al. Stand structures and minimum felling diameter of the *Pterocarpus erinaceus* Poir in arid and semi-arid habitats of West Africa. South African Journal of Botany. 2016;**103**:17-24

[38] Kokou K, Adjonou K, Segla KS, Rabiou H, Bationo AB. et al. *Pterocarpus erinaceus* (Poir) en Afrique de l'Ouest: Usages, structure des peuplements, qualités de bois, normes d'exploitation et sylviculture au Burkina Faso, Niger et Togo. Fiches Techniques. 2015. N° P-ZI-IAD-002 N° DON: 2100155007376; p. 28

[39] Bamba N, Ouattara ND, Konan D, Bakayoko A, Tra Bi FH. Effets de cinq prétraitements Sur la germination du vène (*Pterocarpus erinaceus* Poir., Fabaceae) dans la Réserve du Haut Bandama (Côte d'Ivoire). European Scientific Journal. 2018;**14**:438

[40] Rabiou H, Diouf A, Bationo AB, Segla KN, Adjonou K, Kokutse AD, et al. Vegetative propagation by aerial layering of *Pterocarpus erinaceus*: In the Sudanian zone. International Journal of Recent Advances in Multidisciplinary Research. 2017;**4**(10):2902-2908

[41] Bodjrènou RT, Houètchégnon T, Kéita NT, Ouinsavi C. Effets de l'acide naphtalène acétique, du type de substrat et de la grosseur des boutures Sur le bouturage de tige de *Pterocarpus erinaceus* Poir. (Fabaceae). European Scientific Journal. 2018;**14**(27):297-316

[42] Segla NK, Rabiou H, Adjonou K, Mamoudou BM, Saley K, Radji RA, et al. Population structure and minimum felling diameter of *Pterocarpus erinaceus* Poir in arid and semi-arid climate zones of West Africa. South African Journal of Botany. 2015;**103**:17-24 ISSN: 0254-6299

[43] Treanor NB. China's Hongmu consumption boom: Analysis of the Chinese rosewood trade and links to illegal activity in Tropical Forested Countries. Forest Trends Series-Forest trade and finance. Forest Trends Series and UKAid. 2015

[44] Dumenu WK, Bandoh WN. Exploitation of African rosewood (*Pterocarpus erinaceus*) in Ghana: A situation analysis. Ghana Journal of Forestry. 2016;**32**:1-15

[45] Jafaru MY. General news of 29 Mar 2017. MP alarmed at increased rate of illegal felling of rosewood. 2017. Retrieved from: https://www.graphic.

com.gh/news/generalnews/mp-alarmed-at-increased-rate-of-illegal-felling-of-rosewood.html

[46] Futukpor A. Online news of August 9, 2018. Felling of rosewood increases. 2018. Retrieved from: http://www.ghananewsagency.org/social/felling-of-rosewoodincreases-136896

Chapter 17

The Utilization and Conservation of Indigenous Wild Plant Resources in the Limpopo Province, South Africa

Sebua S. Semenya and Matjutla J. Mokgoebo

Abstract

The knowledge pertaining to uses of indigenous wild plants and their conservation methods by the rural communities of the Limpopo Province (South Africa) is not fully reconnoitered. The available data highlighting these aspects are scattered in general ethnobotanical literatures. The current study therefore sought to collate, analyze, and describe such information. Search engines and local libraries were used to document information. A total of 50 useful wild plant species belonging to 32 botanical families, mainly the Fabaceae (28%, n = 9) and Cucurbitaceae (13%, n = 4), were harvested by rural communities inhabiting the Limpopo Province. These species were mainly exploited wholly for medicinal (62%, n = 31) and food (20%, n = 10) purposes. Leaves, bark, fruits, and roots, respectively, were the most commonly used plant parts. Overall, the traditional conservation approaches employed by the indigenous people to ensure continual supply of these organs for different livelihoods encompass traditional beliefs and taboos, sustainable harvesting practices as well as domestication of plants. However, not all these approaches promote effective conservation and sustainable utilization of wild plant resources.

Keywords: indigenous plants, Limpopo province, management, traditional conservation methods, useful wild plants

1. Introduction

Throughout history, plant resources have supported human being, providing goods such as food in the form of fruits and vegetables, materials for a variety of utensils, fodder, construction timber, fuel wood, and medicinal plants [1–5]. In addition, plants have also provided man with a range of cultural services, including spiritual services, inspiration, and esthetic values [6]. Therefore, sustainable plants harvesting and uses are fundamental for human survival, especially since gathering activity continue to increase in importance, in response to a growing demand for the wild plants products [7].

Globally, loss of habitat by deforestation and unsustainable harvesting methods, among other factors, threatens the survival of the plant resources in the wilderness [8–11]. This situation is dire in various African countries wherein the majority of people depend heavily on plants to meet their livelihoods [12]. Consequently, the wild plant resources are rapidly diminishing, indicating a need to adopt the management techniques that promote a sustainable harvesting practice to ensure the continual supply of plant products to meet various human livelihoods.

In Africa as is the case in other continents of the world [13–16], natural plant resource utilization and management has been in the traditions of local communities, expressed variously in the beliefs as well as practices employed in their conservation [17]. These practices includes among others, removal of few roots from plants, harvesting of a bark that is the size of the palm of one's hand, taboos and social controls promoting sustainable harvesting of plants [18]. Studies conducted in countries such as Kenya [19], Ghana [20], Lesotho [21], Zimbabwe [22], Nigeria [3], Tanzania [23], Uganda [24], Benin and Gabon [25], Rwanda [26], and Ethiopia [27] indicated that these practices are very common among the indigenous communities and have evolved through the historical interaction of people and their environment.

However, in South Africa, data on indigenous wild plant resource utilization and associated management/conservation practices are scattered in general ethnobotanical literatures [28–32]. This makes it difficult for policy makers and conservationists to realize the potential of traditional conservation and innovation techniques in wild indigenous plant resource conservation. The current study therefore sought to collate and describe uses of the indigenous wild plants by rural communities in the Limpopo Province (South Africa), and implemented practices contributing to the conservation as well as the management of these plants.

2. Materials and methods

Overall, the data set used in this study was created by selecting articles that focused on the utilization and conservation of indigenous wild plant resources in the Limpopo Province, South Africa. The search for these articles was obtained from the main online scientific sites including Science Direct, SciFinder, Pubmed, Google Scholar, Medline, and SCOPUS. Searches were also undertaken in the library, University of Venda, University of Limpopo, and the search engines like ProQuest, Open-thesis, OATD, and EThOS [33]. The species name, botanical families, plant authority, and synonyms were verified using books, journal articles, and Internet sources such as the International Plant Name Index (www.ipni.org).

The articles selected met the pre-determined criteria, namely, inclusion and exclusion. The inclusion criteria encompass: (1) the articles reporting on the studies conducted in the Limpopo Province that highlighted or focused on the use and conservation of indigenous wild plant resources, (2) the identity of the utilized species including use part/s and traditional value/application/s and associated conservation strategy implemented, (3) the articles published between 1950 and May 2019, and (4) the articles that are written in English. The exclusion criteria include articles published as abstract, letters, and data that could not be extracted or overlapped with data from other articles. Of 410 collected articles published in the period between 1950 and May 2019, 52 met the exclusion criteria, thus did not form part of this book chapter. The conservation status of the plants was determined via the South African National Red Data List of Plants [34]. Generally, data were independently evaluated for completeness and reliability. Descriptive statistics such as frequencies and percentages were used in the analysis.

3. Results and discussion

3.1 Diversity of useful wild indigenous plant resources

The present study documented a total of 50 useful plant species belonging to 32 botanical families, mainly the Fabaceae (28%, n = 9) and Cucurbitaceae (13%, n = 4), that are harvested by rural communities inhabiting the Limpopo Province of South Africa (**Table 1**). These families are repeatedly recorded in various ethnobotanical studies conducted in South Africa [45, 46] and elsewhere [46–48], as being highly represented with a greater number of plants exploited by indigenous people to meet their livelihoods. Cucurbitaceae and Fabaceae are not only widespread in communal lands of the Limpopo Province but they also comprise many plants commonly known as foods and natural medicine. Therefore, their predominance in this study came as no surprise. According to de Albuquerque [49], indigenous people highly value and experiments on plants that are more accessible or locally abundant. However, plant species from the rest of the botanical families were rarely harvested for their products, perhaps due to their less adaptation in a wide range of altitudes across the aforementioned province. As such, they are less susceptible targets of the local people to experiment with.

3.2 Plant utilization categories

The consumption of wild plants is an ancient African tradition which serves multiple purposes. In the present study, analysis of ethnobotanical uses categories indicated that more taxa were exploited exclusively for medicinal (n = 32) and food (n = 10) purposes. Some of the commonly harvested medicinal plants documented include *Elaeodendron transvaalense* (Burtt Davy) R.H.Archer (HIV/AIDS), *Hypoxis hemerocallidea* Fisch., C.A.Mey. and Avé-Lall. (Gonorrhea and HIV/AIDS), *Leonotis leonurus* (L.) R.Br. (asthma and chest pain), and *Lippia javanica* (Burm.f.) Spreng. (asthma, rhinitis sinusitis, and tuberculosis), used as therapies for the mentioned ailments (**Table 1**). Therapeutic applications of these species are well supported by scientific studies [36, 50, 51], thus partly explaining their utilization by people of the Limpopo Province. Plant-based medicines such as *Alepidea amatymbica* Eckl. and Zeyh, *Brackenridgea zanguebarica* Oliv., *Celtis africana* Burm.f., *Encephalartos transvenosus* Stapf and Burtt Davy, *Mundulea sericea* (Willd.) A. Chev, *Rauvolfia caffra* Sond., and *Sclerochiton ilicifolius* A. Meeuse were considered as having mysterious and magical powers used to expel evil, fight opponents, and as luck charms (**Table 1**). For the food plant category, all the species were reported to be either eaten as leafy vegetable with porridge (*Momordica balsamina* L., *Momordica boivinii* Baill, and *Vigna unguiculata* L.) or exploited for their edible fruits (*Berchemia discolor* (Klotzsch) Hemsl, *Dovyalis caffra* (Hook. F. and Harv.) Hook. F, *Grewia bicolor* Juss., *Pappea capensis* Eckl. and Zeyh, *Vangueria infausta* Burch, and *Ximenia caffra* Sond.). The consumption of these plants by indigenous people in the Limpopo Province is primarily attributed to multiple factors including food scarcity, nutri-medicinal value, and local cultural practices.

Other categories that had explicit use were for provision of livelihoods such as firewood (n = 2; *Vachellia karroo* Hayne and *Vachellia rehmanniana* Schinz), water storage (n = 1; *Breonadia salicina* (Vahl) Hepper and J.R.I. Wood.). *Vachellia karroo* and *V. rehmanniana* are preferred as firewood species due to both their local availability and long burning period, which provide lasting heat and light [41].

The remaining plants, namely, *Anthocleista grandiflora* Gilg (used to cover maize grains to encourage germination when malt is prepared, and female bodies during rituals, and as medicine for high blood pressure), *Boscia albitrunca* Gilg and

Botanical family and species name	Used part	Traditional value	Conservation status (red data list)	Traditional plant conservation practices
Acanthaceae *Sclerochiton ilicifolius* A. Meeuse	Root	Used to guard against evil spirits and fight enemies	Least concern	Only harvested by people who are trained in harvesting rituals, and are not collected from areas where people frequent, as it is believed this will diminish the effectiveness of the plant [35]
Alliaceae *Tulbaghia violacea* Harv. var. violacea	Bulb	Nasal congestion and tuberculosis (TB)	Least concern	Harvesting involves their cutting with a knife from the base leaving roots in ground intact [36]
Apiaceae *Alepidea amatymbica* Eckl. and Zeyh	Rhizome	Used to guard against evil spirits and fight enemies	Endangered A2d	Only harvested by people who are trained in harvesting rituals, and are not collected from areas where people frequent, as it is believed this will diminish the effectiveness of the plant [35]
Apocynaceae *Rauvolfia caffra* Sond.	Whole plant	Believed to attract rain	Least concern	Prohibited from being harvested [37]
Asteraceae *Kleinia longiflora* DC	Twig	Chest pain, painful eyes, pneumonia and sore throat	Least concern	Harvested by hand via breaking of the required amounts in the wild [36]
Asphodelaceae *Aloe falcata* Baker	Leaf	Chest pain and fatigue	Least concern	Harvesting involved removal of few leaves with a knife far from to the base [36]
Aloe marlothii A. Berger subsp. *Marlothii*	Leaf	Chest pain, sore throat and pneumonia	Least concern	Harvesting involved removal of few leaves with a knife far from to the base [36]
Amaryllidaceae *Gethyllis namaquensis* (Schonland) Oberm.	Bulb	Chlamydia and diabetes mellitus	Least concern	Cultivated in home gardens [38]
Anacardiaceae *Sclerocarya birrea* (A. Rich.) Hochst.	Bark	Female infertility	Least concern	Cultivated in home gardens [38]
	Leaf	Fodder		Protected within dryland agricultural farming system [39]. Fruits can only be harvested when they have fallen to the ground. Failure to adhere is believed to cause fever or snakes would appear in homesteads [40]
	Fruit	Traditional beer		
	Whole plant	Rituals ceremonies are performed on the tree as a way of appeasing the ancestors		

Botanical family and species name	Used part	Traditional value	Conservation status (red data list)	Traditional plant conservation practices
Cannabaceae *Celtis africana* Burm.f.	Stem	Used to make magical sticks which are driven into the ground to protect against witchcraft	Least concern	Tree cannot be planted in the homestead. Taboos associated with the tree are enforced through beliefs such that violators or the community will experience illnesses [40]
Capparaceae *Boscia albitrunca* Gilg and Gilg-Ben.	Root	HIV/AIDS	Least concern	Cultivated in home gardens [38]
	Fruit	Eaten as food		Protected within dryland agricultural farming system [39]
Celastraceae *Elaeodendron transvaalense* (Burtt Davy) R. H.Archer	Root	HIV/AIDS	Near threatened A4ad	Cultivated in home gardens [38]
Gymnosporia senegalensis (Lam.) Loes	Root	Blood disorders	Least concern	Only small quantity of lateral roots are harvested [41]
Cucurbitaceae *Citrullus lanatus* (Thunb.) Matsum. and Nakai	Fruit	Headache	Least concern	Hand-picked and some fruits with seeds are left behind to allow natural regrowth during favorable season [36]
Cucumis zeyheri Sond.	Fruit	Lack of appetite and TB	Least concern	Hand-picked and some fruits with seeds are left behind to allow natural regrowth during favorable season [36]
Momordica balsamina L.	Leaf	Edible vegetable eaten with porridge	Least concern	Only the tender leaves are selected allowing the leaves to reach maturity [40]
Momordica boivinii Baill.	Leaf	Edible vegetable eaten during times of drought	Least concern	Only the tender leaves are selected allowing the leaves to reach maturity. Leaves must not be harvested or touched by menstruating women; otherwise, it is believed that the vegetable will shrink in size [40]
Dioscoreaceae *Dioscorea sylvatica* Eckl.	Tuber	Gonorrhea	Vulnerable A2cd	Cultivated in home gardens [38]
Fabaceae *Vachellia karroo* Hayne	Stem	Firewood	Least concern	Harvesting and felling of species from the graveyard are forbidden, because graveyards are believed to be the home of the ancestors [41]
Vachellia rehmanniana Schinz.	Stem	Firewood		

Botanical family and species name	Used part	Traditional value	Conservation status (red data list)	Traditional plant conservation practices
Cassia abbreviata Oliv. subsp. beareana (Holmes) Brenan	Bark	Chest pain, fatigue, and sore throat	Least concern	Stripped only on the eastern side leaving other sides untouched [36]
Colophospermum. mopane Kirk ex Benth.	Stem and leaf	Firewood and fodder	Least concern	Protected within dryland agricultural farming system [39]
Dichrostachys cinerea (L.) Wight and Arn.	Stem	Construction of huts and livestock enclosures	Least concern	The harvesting is restricted to matured branching stems. Felling of immature species is prohibited [42]
	Whole plant	Firewood		Collection is confined to the dead wood. A fine is imposed on people who cut live wood [41]
Erythrina lysistemon Hutch	Bark	Chest pain, sore throat, and TB	Least concern	Stripped only on the eastern side leaving other sides untouched [36]
Mundulea sericea (Willd.) A. Chev	Root	Protect against witchcraft	Least concern	The tree is prohibited from being used as firewood in homesteads where cattle are present [40]
Peltophorum africanum Sond.	Bark	Post-partum	Least concern	Cultivated in home gardens [38]
Vigna unguiculata L.	Leaf	Eaten as vegetable	Not evaluated	Hand-picked [43]
Gentianaceae	Bark	High blood pressure	Not evaluated	There are taboos preventing this species from being cut down, used as firewood or taken back to the homestead [40]
Anthocleista grandiflora Gilg	Leaf	Used to cover maize grains to encourage germination when malt is prepared		
		Used to cover female bodies during rituals		
Hyacinthaceae *Drimia elata* Jacq	Bulb	Female infertility, impotence, gonorrhea, HIV/AIDS, and hypertension	Data deficient — taxonomically problematic	Cultivated in home gardens [38]
Drimia sanguinea (Schinz) Jessop	Bulb	Chest pain, pneumonia, and TB	Near threatened A2d	Harvesting involved cutting with a knife from the base leaving roots in the ground intact [36]
Hyacinthaceae *Eucomis pallidiflora* Baker. subsp. pole-evansii (N. E.Br.) Reyneke	Bulb	Aphonia, chlamydia, fatigue, impotence, sore throat, and TB	Near threatened B2ab (v)	Harvesting involved cutting with a knife from the base leaving roots in the ground intact [36]
Hypoxidaceae *Hypoxis hemerocallidea*	Tuber	Gonorrhea and HIV/AIDS	Least concern	Cultivated in home gardens [38]. Harvesting involves cutting with a knife from

Botanical family and species name	Used part	Traditional value	Conservation status (red data list)	Traditional plant conservation practices
Fisch., C.A.Mey. and Avé-Lall				the base leaving roots in the ground intact [36]
Flacourtiaceae *Dovyalis caffra* (Hook. F. and Harv.) Hook. F	Fruit	Eaten as food	Least concern	Protected within dryland agricultural farming system [39]
Kirkiaceae *Kirkia wilmsii* Engl	Tuber	Used to treat hypertension	Least concern	Only the older tubers are being harvested [35]
Lauraceae *Cryptocarya transvaalensis* Burtt Davy	Bark	Asthma, pneumonia, sore throat, and TB	Least concern	Stripped only on the eastern side leaving other sides untouched [36]
Lamiaceae *Leonotis leonurus* (L.) R.Br.	Leaf	Asthma and chest pain	Least concern	Acquired by handpicking without breaking the twigs in homegardens [36]
Malvaceae *Adansonia digitata* L.	Fruit	Eaten as food	Least concern	Protected within dryland agricultural farming system [39]
Grewia bicolor Juss	Fruit	Eaten as food	Least concern	Protected within dryland agricultural farming system [39]
Moraceae *Ficus burkei* (Miq.) Miq.	Fruit	Headache	Least concern	Hand-picked, throwing of stones at the tree to detach fruits, knocking them down with long sticks and collecting them from the grounds [36]
Rhamnaceae *Berchemia discolor* (Klotzsch) Hemsl	Fruit	Eaten as food	Least concern	Protected within dryland agricultural farming system [39]
Rubiaceae *Vangueria infausta* Burch	Fruit	Eaten as food	Least concern	Only collected from the ground [42]
Breonadia salicina (Vahl) Hepper and J.R.I. Wood	Whole plant	Tree used to store water	Least concern	Tree is prohibited from entering homesteads, and a failure to adhere to the taboo results in sterility among household members. The species is also prohibited from being used for firewood, hedge fencing, building work, or wood carving [40]
Rutaceae *Zanthoxylum capense* Harv.	Root	HIV/AIDS	Least concern	Cultivated in home gardens [38]

Botanical family and species name	Used part	Traditional value	Conservation status (red data list)	Traditional plant conservation practices
Zanthoxylum humile (E.A. Bruce) P.G. Waterman	Root	HIV/AIDS	Least concern	Cultivated in home gardens [38]
Ochnaceae	Bark	Protect people against witchcraft; protect the whole homestead from evil people and for discouraging opponents in sporting events such as soccer	Critically endangered A2ad; B1ab (ii, v)	After the collection of plant materials for medicinal or magical purposes, it is prohibited to take them to the house or be touched by women because they may hamper menstruation [44]
Brackenridgea zanguebarica Oliv.		Used as catalyst for other medicines to enhance its potency		Tree is prohibited from entering homesteads, and a failure to adhere to the taboo results in sterility among household members. The species is also prohibited from being used for firewood, hedge fencing, building work, or wood carving [40]
Olacaceae	Fruit	Eaten as food	Least concern	Only collected from the ground [42]
Ximenia caffra Sond.				
Poaceae	Culm	Broom and fodder	Least concern	The harvesting of the species is restricted to the culms. The base is not harvested to give the species a chance to regrow in the next season [42]
Sporobolus pyramidalis P. Beauv				
Sapindaceae *Pappea capensis* Eckl. and Zeyh	Fruit	Eaten as food	Least concern	Cutting of green branches and twigs for harvesting is highly prohibited [41]
Verbenaceae	Leaf	Asthma, rhinitis sinusitis, and TB	Least concern	Acquired by handpicking without breaking the twigs in homegardens [36]
Lippia javanica (Burm.f.) Spreng.				
Zamiaceae	Bark	Used to guard against evil spirits and fight enemies	Least concern	Only harvested by people who are trained in harvesting rituals, and are not collected from areas where people frequent, as it is believed this will diminish the effectiveness of the plant [35]
Encephalartos transvenosus Stapf and Burtt Davy				

Table 1.
Diversity of useful wild plant resources and traditional conservation strategies in the Limpopo province, South Africa.

Gilg-Ben (eaten as food and HIV/AIDS medicine), *Colophospermum mopane* Kirk ex Benth (firewood and fodder), *Dichrostachys cinerea* (L.) Wight and Arn. (construction of huts and livestock enclosures, and firewood), and *Sclerocarya birrea* (A. Rich.) Hochst (used to treat female infertility, fodder, valued for rituals ceremonies as a way of appeasing the ancestors and for making traditional beer) fell under the multiple-use category and were cherished for the mentioned livelihoods. Plants belonging to this category are more likely to be overharvested due to their multiple cultural values [52, 53].

Overall, all the above-stated use groups is a reflection of a close relationship between the local people and their natural environment, which has led to the development of a rich knowledge based on plants, plant-use, and related practices [54]. Comparisons of our finding regarding the most dominant plant use category concur to that noted by other researchers in South Africa [55, 56], and other African countries such as Ethiopia [57], Lesotho [58], and Botswana [59]. Contrary findings were noted in Kenya [47], Brazil [60], and India [61]. This may be the result of cultural differences in knowledge of the plant resource uses. Nonetheless, it should be stated that a larger number of wild plants used as medicines and foods for human was expected in this review, first due to the fact that traditional medicine is highly rooted in many cultures of the Limpopo Province [38, 62, 63], and second because rural people in this province grew-up eating wild edible plants and their majority *live below the poverty* line [64]. Thus, it is acceptable to postulate that the use of plant resources for food and medicinal purposes by indigenous people of the Limpopo Province will increase tremendously in the foreseeable future. This is because the indigenous communities have enticements to utilize and conserve wild plants when their livelihoods depend on gathering of their products.

3.3 Plant habit and used plant part/s

The growth form analysis of 50 documented useful plant resources revealed that trees (62%, n = 31), herbs (30%, n = 15), and shrubs (13%, n = 4), respectively, were harvested for their products in the present study. These are the common plant habits exploited by indigenous people in South Africa [55, 65] and other African countries [57, 66] to meet their various needs. It should be stated that the supremacy of trees in the present study is attributed to multifaceted factors including cultural beliefs attached to them (i.e., provision of rain) and their utilization in local ritual ceremonies and a wide range of products (i.e., medicines, foods, fodders, fruits, and firewood, among other provisions) they provide to local communities. Equally, herbaceous taxa were considerably represented mainly due to numerous values they provide (**Table 1**). However, the shrubby species, namely, *Aloe falcata* Baker, *Kleinia longiflora* DC, *Leonotis leonurus* (L.) R.Br. and *Lippia javanica* (Burm.f.) Spreng were only harvested for therapeutic purposes, which probably explain their lower preference by local communities of the Limpopo Province. Generally, sustainable harvesting of products from the afore-stated growth forms should be promoted in the Limpopo Province for the sake of both conservations of the plants and livelihoods of local people.

The actual impact of wild plant harvesting depends on the specific growth form or type of resource that is removed [67]. Different plant exudates from herbs, shrubs, and trees recorded in the current study were obtained by local communities to meet their livelihoods, with fruits, followed by leaves, bark, and roots, respectively, being the most preferred. Other plant parts were used to a lesser extent (**Figure 1**). The widespread use of leaves and fruits by indigenous people to meet their different needs is well documented in ethnobotanical literatures [68–70]. Their high uses in this study are mainly attributed to their economic value (i.e., source of cash generated from the sale of fresh fruits) and use as food supplements by many rural communities in the Limpopo Province. Other factors that contributed to high exploitation of fruits are their local abundance in many free access

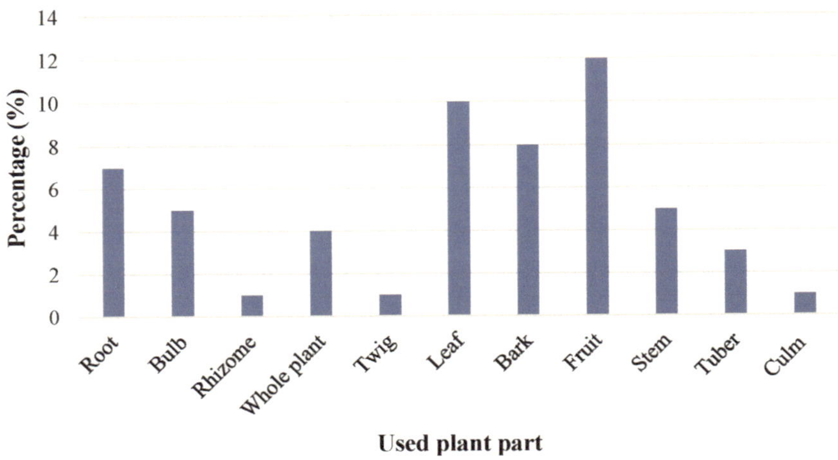

Figure 1.
Plant parts harvested to meet livelihoods.

communal lands of this province and the fact that they are consumed raw without any processing.

Leaves were the second most commonly used plant part and were mainly exploited as medicines and vegetable (**Table 1**). Consumption of leaves for these livelihoods is locally believed to be ascribed to their efficacy as remedies and rich *nutrients*. From a conservation standpoint, the high harvesting of leaves is less destructive to the survival of plants [71, 72]. The opposite of this can be said for bark and roots. High usage of these organs exclusively as medicines in this study is directly linked to the traditional beliefs that they store more healing power than any other plant part [44, 73]. This belief, however, has a great potential to encourage their extensive harvesting, which in turn will make the targeted plant species vulnerable to overexploitation. The rest of morphological plant parts did not appear to be of great value to the indigenous people of the Limpopo Province (**Figure 1**).

3.4 Conservation status of plant species

The present study revealed that all 50 plant resources documented are listed on the South African National Red Data List of Plants, with the majority (82%, n = 41) appearing as Least Concern. This finding has a positive conservation implication mainly because more widespread and abundant species in the wild are included in this category [36]. Therefore, it is acceptable to state that most useful taxa in the Limpopo Province might be still fairly abundant within the wilderness.

However, 12% (n = 6) of Red Data listed plants recorded in this study are of conservation concern with the following status: Critically Endangered (*Brackenridgea zanguebarica* Oliv.), Endangered (*Alepidea amatymbica* Eckl. and Zeyh.), Near Threatened (*Drimia sanguinea* (Schinz) Jessop, *Eucomis pallidiflora* Baker. subsp. pole-evansii (N.E.Br.) Reyneke and *Elaeodendron transvaalense* (Burtt Davy) R.H. Archer) and Vulnerable (*Dioscorea sylvatica* Eckl.). The rest as either Not Evaluated (4%, n = 2) or have Data Deficient (2%, n = 1) status. It is worth stating that most of the abovementioned species are constantly reported by plant resource harvesters in the Limpopo Province as very difficult to find in their natural habitats, with prime rationale being excessive exploitation for commercial purposes [35, 74]. Another factor put forward by indigenous people of the Limpopo Province that jeopardize these plants is gathering by outsiders and other local people who are not trained on both the traditional harvesting of useful wild plants and approaches to conservation.

3.5 Traditional plant conservation strategies

Interestingly, this study also revealed that the indigenous people of the Limpopo Province, who depend on the recorded wild plant resources for survival, have evolved ways of managing them (**Table 1**). Generally, traditional leaders (i.e., chiefs and headmen) are the ones managing the utilization of these resources via traditional rules and regulations, and this is common practice in other provinces of South Africa [75] and other African countries [76]. On the contrary, Kepe [77] found that in areas that are held as common property by all villagers in Mkambati area of the Eastern Cape Province (South Africa), people do not have to ask for permission to collect wild plant resources. In the present study, anyone who breaks the traditional management strategies were fined a certain amount of money and restricted to harvest wild plant resources for a specified period of time. Overall, the traditional approaches used in this study to conserve plant diversity encompass the following;

3.5.1 Traditional beliefs and taboos

These techniques are used to guide the social behavior of the community members in the harvesting of wild plant resources [78, 79]. For instance, organs from plant species with medicinal value particularly those that are used for magical purposes such as *A. amatymbica* (rhizome), *E. transvenosus* (bark), and *S. ilicifolius* (root) are only collected by people who are trained in harvesting rituals and are not obtained from areas where people frequent, as it is believed this will diminish the efficacy of the medication [35]. Generally, from a conservation standpoint, the effectiveness of traditional practices associated with all the abovementioned magical plants are overshadowed by the fact that they have other values (i.e., non-medicinal magical values), which are not regulated by the traditional beliefs systems. We concur with Mowo et al. [80] who stated that despite the strengths, some traditional practices have weaknesses that may limit their use in management plans that favor sustainability.

Similarly, *C. africana* which is used to make medicine to protect against witchcraft is not allowed to be planted in the homestead, and failure to adhere to this is believed to results in to the violators or the community members being infected with illnesses [40]. Although this taboo might create fear among the community members and thus instill the value of respect for the species which will ultimately serve to limit its harvesting, this can only be effective if *C. africana* is wholly used for magical purposes. Unfortunately, studies conducted in the Limpopo Province indicated *C. africana* is a multipurpose tree, that is in addition of being valued for magic purposes, it is also highly harvested as drug for nose, ear, and tooth infections [63], for vegetable and craftwork [45].

The same can be said for *B. zanguebarica*; traditionally, after the collection of materials for medicinal or magical purposes from this tree, it is prohibited to take them to the house or be touched by women because they may hamper menstruation [44]. However, the over-exploitation of *B. zanguebarica* within its natural area of occurrence [81], and its frequent availability in *muthi* shops (shops selling medicinal plants) owned by females across the Limpopo province [35, 41] is a clear indication that most local people, especially commercial harvesters do not follow the traditional taboos that are relevant in promoting the plants' conservation.

Therefore, the use of traditional beliefs as an instrument of conserving *B. zanguebarica* would not be possible without the harvesters' compliance.

Another plant species valued as medicine for magic, *M. sericea*, is prohibited from being used as firewood in homesteads where cattle are present [40]. This however can only aid in the conservation of *M. sericea* in deep rural areas of the Limpopo Province wherein the use of firewood and cattle nurturing is prevalent in many households, but with no additional uses attached to it for other livelihoods. The prohibition of *R. caffra* from being harvested due to the traditional beliefs that it attracts rain, as a conservation strategy [37], will not have great impact due to the fact that local rural communities also rely on the species for the provision of wood for craftwork and medicine [45].

Restricted harvesting and felling of *V. karroo* and *V. rehmanniana* from the graveyards, due to the belief that these areas are ancestral home [41], can only aid in the conservation of these trees found in the graveyards and provided that local community strictly adhere to such belief. Overall, the effectiveness of traditional beliefs and taboos for the conservation of plant resources as instituted by traditional leaders in the Limpopo Province is hindered by numerous factors such as non-compliance by community members, traditional leaders being inexperienced in implementing and enforcing regulations, as well as very young leaders who do not command respect [41]. This is in contrast with the finding of Gwali et al. [24] who stated that in rural areas of Uganda, the enforcement of traditional beliefs and taboos is very difficult due to high economic and social depression resulting from the long and protracted period of political and social instability. Thus, it can be said that certain taboos and traditional bye-laws may not be adequate conservation approaches for wild plant resources in many rural communities of Africa including the Limpopo Province. Comprehensive studies focusing on traditional belief systems used in the management of wild plant resources across this province would shed light on those that promote the effective conservation.

3.5.2 Sustainable harvesting practices

Findings from this study also revealed that indigenous people of the Limpopo Province have developed the sustainable harvesting strategies of diverse parts from the recorded wild plant resources. Harvesting of bulb from *D. sanguinea* (Schinz) Jessop., *E. pallidiflora* Baker. subsp. pole-evansii (N.E.Br.) Reyneke, and *Tulbaghia violacea* Harv. var. *violacea* basically involve their cutting with a knife from the base leaving roots in the ground intact. This practice will encourage the reproduction and regeneration of the harvested species, therefore ensuring the continual supply of the product from the same taxa. Similarly, selective collection of only older tubers from *Kirkia wilmsii* Engl. [35] and small quantity of *Gymnosporia senegalensis* (Lam.) Loes lateral roots [41] will not have detrimental effect on the survival of this tree.

Generally, the traditional techniques used to obtain leaves in this study seemed to be sustainable. For instance, their harvesting from species such as *Aloe marlothii* A. Berger subsp. *marlothii* and *A. falcata* Baker involved the removal of few leaves with a knife far from the base. This harvesting technique encourages re-growth of leaves post collection [82]. Similarly, collection of *L. leonurus* by handpicking without breaking and cutting the twigs/branches minimize damages to the trunk, thus leaving the tree less susceptible to disease infestation. The same can be said with the harvesting of *K. longiflora* twigs, which were obtained by hand via breaking of the required amounts in the wild. Explicit harvesting of tender leaves from *M. balsamina*, *M. boivinii*, and *V. unguiculata* for consumption as vegetable allows the leaves to reach maturity [40]. This in turn allows the species to reach maturity stage and regrow in the subsequent season [42].

The methods of obtaining fruits from species such as *Citrullus lanatus* (Thunb.) Matsum. and Nakai, *Cucumis zeyheri* Sond., and *Pappea capensis* Eckl. and Zeyh includes hand-picking without breaking the twigs. This method is also common among indigenous people of Africa [83–85]. In addition to being hand-picked, *Ficus burkei* (Miq.) Miq. fruits were also harvested by throwing stones at the trees to detach them and subsequently collecting from the grounds [36]. Fruits from *Vangueria infausta* Burch. and *Ximenia caffra* Sond. are only allowed to be obtained from the ground following abscission [42]. Although this harvesting method is sustainable, collection of a greater number of fruits from the ground has the potential to inhibit natural seeds dispersal, which will ultimately affect the population expansion. This is because fruits play an important role in the seed dispersal of many of the abovementioned plants.

Bark is harvested from trees such as *Cassia abbreviata* Oliv. subsp. beareana (Holmes) Brenan, *Cryptocarya transvaalensis* Burtt Davy, *Dichrostachys cinerea* (L.) Wight and Arn., and *Erythrina lysistemon Hutch.,* only on the eastern side leaving other sides untouched (**Table 1**). An assessment of the recovery rate of bark growth post-exploitation using this method showed a good healing wound, thus suggesting that the impact of its harvesting does not affect the existence of the species [86]. A possible explanation for this is that tree receives adequate sunlight on the eastern site, which plays a crucial role in the healing process.

3.5.3 Domestication

Two systems of wild plant cultivation practiced by indigenous people of the Limpopo Province include (a) propagation in the home gardens and (b) an agroforestry system where by naturally growing plants are maintained and protected within dryland agricultural farming system. Species domesticated in the home gardens encompassed *B. albitrunca*, *D. sylvatica*, *Drimia elata* Jacq., *E. transvaalense*, *Gethyllis namaquensis* (Schonland) Oberm, *H. hemerocallidea*, *Lippia javanica* (Burm.f.) Spreng, *Peltophorum africanum* Sond., *S. birrea*, *Zanthoxylum capense* Harv., and *Zanthoxylum humile* (E.A.Bruce) P.G.Waterman. Cultivation of these plants is generally attributed to their increasing scarcity in the wilderness. This initiative, nevertheless, has the potential to lessen harvesting pressure of the aforementioned species occurring in the wilderness and ensure instant supply of their required part/s. Furthermore, it will aid in the conservation of threatened therapeutic species such as *D. sylvatica* and *E. transvaalense*. However, this can have conservation impacts only if the users harvest the plants exclusively from their home gardens. Wiersum et al. [87] found that medicinal plant domestication by indigenous people is less based on preserving biodiversity, but more on maximizing harvest to certify individual needs and to generate income.

Native wild trees such as *Adansonia digitata* L., *B. discolor*, *C. mopane*, *D. caffra*, and *G. bicolor* that grew naturally in the local agricultural farming system were managed and conserved in order to obtain sustainable multiple supply of desired products and services from them (**Table 1**). This is a common practice among rural communities in other provinces of South Africa [88], other African countries [89, 90], and elsewhere [91]. Generally, adaptation of agroforestry practices of conserving *A. digitata*, *B. discolor*, *C. mopane*, *D. caffra*, and *G. bicolor* by cultural communities in the Limpopo Province will not only contribute towards the provision of food and cultural materials but will also enhance local environmental resilience. The role of traditional agroforestry practices in this regard cannot be overemphasized [92–95]. To realize the effective role played by these practices in the conservation of wild indigenous plant resources, we recommend that indigenous communities of the Limpopo Province should prioritize the tree species, which provide multiple useful products and ecosystem services.

4. Conclusions

The present study should be viewed as an initial attempt to comprehend the utilization of wild plant resources and their traditional conservation strategies in the Limpopo Province of South Africa. Overall, this study indicated that rural people are endowed with extensive knowledge on native wild plant uses and associated innovative techniques of conserving them as evidenced in **Table 1**. However, not all the practices associated with the latter promote effective conservation and sustainable use of wild plant resources. As such, those that promote the protection of plants should be promoted and integrated in the local management plans of flora. This is will go a long way in complementing the contemporary conservation approaches (i.e., legislative measures) of wild plant resources, and ultimately ensure the continual availability of these resources for poor rural households of the Limpopo Province and other areas of South Africa.

Acknowledgements

We are grateful to the Universities of Limpopo and Venda for funding this study.

Conflict of interest

The authors declare no conflict of interest.

Author details

Sebua S. Semenya[1]* and Matjutla J. Mokgoebo[2]

1 Technology Transfer Office, Research Administration and Development Department, University of Limpopo, Sovenga, South Africa

2 Department of Geography and Geo-Information Sciences, University of Venda, Thohoyandou, South Africa

*Address all correspondence to: sebua.semenya@ul.ac.za; sebuasemenya@gmail.com

References

[1] Cunningham AB. African Medicinal Plants: Setting Priorities at the Interface between Conservation and Primary Healthcare. People and Plants Working Paper. No. 1. Paris: UNESCO; 1993

[2] Shackleton SE, Campbell B, Lotz-Sisitka H, Shackleton C. Links between the local trade in natural products, livelihoods and poverty alleviation in a semi-arid region of South Africa. World Development. 2008;**36**:505-526

[3] Bdullahi J, Usman I, Samaila G, Zuni A. Importance of indigenous knowledge in biodiversity conservation: A case study of communities surrounding Kpashimi forest reserve, Niger state, Nigeria. Journal of Environmental Science, Toxicology and Food Technology. 2013;**5**:10-17

[4] Turner NJ. The Earth's Blanket. Traditional Teachings for Sustainable Living. Vancouver: Douglas & McIntyre; 2008

[5] Simelane ZP. Indigenous Knowledge on Tree Conservation in Swaziland [Doctoral dissertation]. Johannesburg: University of the Witwatersrand; 2009

[6] Xu J, Ma ET, Tashi D, Fu Y, Lu Z, Melick D. Integrating sacred knowledge for conservation: Cultures and landscapes in Southwest China. Ecology and Society. 2005;**10**(2):1

[7] Shackleton CM, Shackleton SE, Cousins B. The role of land-based strategies in rural livelihoods: The contribution of arable production, animal husbandry and natural resource harvesting in communal areas in South Africa. Development Southern Africa. 2001;**18**(5):581-604

[8] Rai LK, Prasad P, Sharma E. Conservation threats to some important medicinal plants of the Sikkim Himalaya. Biological Conservation. 2000;**93**(1):27-33

[9] Kiringe JW. Ecological and anthropological threats to ethno-medicinal plant resources and their utilization in Maasai communal ranches in the Amboseli region of Kenya. Ethnobotany Research and Applications. 2005;**3**:231-242

[10] Uprety Y, Poudel RC, Shrestha KK, Rajbhandary S, Tiwari NN, Shrestha UB, et al. Diversity of use and local knowledge of wild edible plant resources in Nepal. Journal of Ethnobiology and Ethnomedicine. 2012; **8**(1):16

[11] Khoury CK, Amariles D, Soto JS, Diaz MV, Sotelo S, Sosa CC, et al. Comprehensiveness of conservation of useful wild plants: An operational indicator for biodiversity and sustainable development targets. Ecological Indicators. 2019;**98**:420-429

[12] Nanyingi MO, Mbaria JM, Lanyasunya AL, Wagate CG, Koros KB, Kaburia HF, et al. Ethnopharmacological survey of Samburu district, Kenya. Journal of Ethnobiology and Ethnomedicine. 2008; **4**(1):14

[13] Hongmao L, Zaifu X, Youkai X, Jinxiu W. Practice of conserving plant diversity through traditional beliefs: A case study in Xishuangbanna, Southwest China. Biodiversity and Conservation. 2002;**11**(4):705-713

[14] Ahirwar RK, Singh GK. Biodiversity conservation of traditional knowledge and natural resources management of Madhya Pradesh. International Journal of Scientific Research. 2015;**4**(2): 1579-1580

[15] Camacho LD, Gevaña DT, Carandang AP, Camacho SC. Indigenous knowledge and practices for the sustainable management of Ifugao forests in cordillera, Philippines.

International Journal of Biodiversity Science, Ecosystem Services & Management. 2016;**12**(1–2):5-13

[16] Naithani M, Kumar M. Ethnomedicinal plants: Efforts on their cultivation and conservation in Pabau block, Pauri Garhwal. SM Tropical Medicine Journal. 2017;**2**(1):1013

[17] Ayaa DD, Waswa F. Role of indigenous knowledge systems in the conservation of the bio-physical environment among the Teso community in Busia County-Kenya. African Journal of. Environmental Science and Technology. 2016;**10**(12):467-475

[18] Monica KC, Mark K, Paul O. Traditional controls of harvesting and conserving medicinal plants in Keiyo south Sub-County, Kenya. International Journal of Humanities and Social Science. 2016;**6**(11):54-63

[19] Muya LG. Use, Conservation and Management of Plants for Indigenous Herbal Medicine in Kenya: The Case of Kitui District [Doctoral dissertation]. Waterloo: University of Waterloo; 1994

[20] Abbiw D, Agbovie T, Akuetteh B, Amponsah K, Dennis F, Ekpe P, et al. Conservation and sustainable use of medicinal plants in Ghana, Conservation Report. 2002. Available from: http://www.unep-wcmc.org/species/plants/Ghana

[21] Mokuku T, Mokuku C. The role of indigenous knowledge in biodiversity conservation in the Lesotho highlands: Exploring indigenous epistemology. Southern African Journal of Environmental Education. 2004;**21**:37-49

[22] Maroyi A. Local plant use and traditional conservation practices in Nhema communal area, Zimbabwe. International Journal of African Renaissance Studies-Multi-, Inter- and Transdisciplinarity. 2012;**7**(1):109-128

[23] Msuya TS, Kideghesho JR. The role of traditional management practices in enhancing sustainable use and conservation of medicinal plants in west Usambara Mountains, Tanzania. Tropical Conservation. 2009;**2**(1): 88-105

[24] Gwali S, Okullo JB, Eilu G, Nakabonge G, Nyeko P, Vuzi P. Traditional management and conservation of shea trees (Vitellaria paradoxa subspecies nilotica) in Uganda. Environment, Development and Sustainability. 2012;**14**(3):347-363

[25] Quiroz D, van Andel T. Evidence of a link between taboos and sacrifices and resource scarcity of ritual plants. Journal of Ethnobiology and Ethnomedicine. 2015;**11**(1):5

[26] Irakiza R, Vedaste M, Elias B, Nyirambangutse B, Serge NJ, Marc N. Assessment of traditional ecological knowledge and beliefs in the utilisation of important plant species: The case of Buhanga sacred forest, Rwanda. Koedoe. 2016;**58**(1):1-1

[27] Gandile AU, Tessema SM, Nake FM. Biodiversity conservation using the indigenous knowledge system: The priority agenda in the case of Zeyse, Zergula and Ganta communities in Gamo Gofa zone (southern Ethiopia). International Journal of Biodiversity and Conservation. 2017;**9**(6):167-182

[28] Prins EE. Prohibitions and pollution at a medicinal plant nursery: Customary implications associated with ethnobotanical reserves in conservative areas of KwaZulu-Natal. Southern African Humanities. 1996;**8**(12):81-93

[29] Twine W, Moshe D, Netshiluvhi T, Siphugu V. Consumption and direct-use values of savanna bio-resources used by rural households in Mametja, a semi-arid area of Limpopo province, South Africa. South African Journal of Science. 2003;**99**(9):467-473

[30] Cocks ML. Wild Plant Resources and Cultural Practices in Rural and Urban Households in South Africa: Implications for Bio-Cultural Diversity Conservation [Phd thesis]. Wageningen: Wageningen Universitty; 2006

[31] Van Wyk AS, Prinsloo G. Medicinal plant harvesting, sustainability and cultivation in South Africa. Biological Conservation. 2018;**227**:335-342

[32] Mbongwa NS. The Perceptions, Attitudes and Knowledge of Traditional Healers and Traders about Using Cultivated Plants in South Africa [Doctoral dissertation]. Johannesburg: University of Witwatersrand; 2018

[33] Semenya SS, Maroyi A. Data on medicinal plants used to treat respiratory infections and related symptoms in South Africa. Data in Brief. 2018;**21**:419-423

[34] South African National Biodiversity Institute. 2019. The Red List of South African Plants Version 2017.1. Available from: http://redlist.sanbi.org/

[35] Moeng ET, Potgieter MJ. The trade of medicinal plants by muthi shops and street vendors in the Limpopo province, South Africa. Journal of Medicinal Plants Research. 2011;**5**(4):558-564

[36] Semenya SS, Maroyi A. Source, harvesting, conservation status, threats and management of indigenous plant used for respiratory infections and related symptoms in the Limpopo province, South Africa. Biodiversitas. 2019;**20**(3):789-810

[37] Mphephu TS. Sustainable Natural Resource Utilisation: A Case Study of Ethnobotanically Important Plant Taxa in the Thulamela Local Municipality, Limpopo Province [Doctoral dissertation]. Johannesburg: University of Johannesburg; 2017

[38] Semenya SS, Potgieter MJ. Medicinal plants cultivated in Bapedi traditional healers' homegardens, Limpopo province, South Africa. African Journal of Traditional, Complementary, and Alternative Medicines. 2014;**11**(5):126-132

[39] Tshisikhawe MP, Malunga G. Ethnobotanical profile of indigenous tree species protected within Dryland agricultural farming system. Journal of Agriculture and Allied Sciences. 2017;**2**: 15-21

[40] Constant NL, Tshisikhawe MP. Hierarchies of knowledge: Ethnobotanical knowledge, practices and beliefs of the Vhavenda in South Africa for biodiversity conservation. Journal of Ethnobiology and Ethnomedicine. 2018;**14**(1):56

[41] Rasethe MT, Semenya SS, Potgieter MJ, Maroyi A. The utilization and management of plant resources in rural areas of the Limpopo province, South Africa. Journal of Ethnobiology and Ethnomedicine. 2013;**9**(1):27

[42] Rankoana S. Sustainable use and management of indigenous plant resources: A case of mantheding community in Limpopo province, South Africa. Sustainability. 2016; **8**(3):221

[43] Monnig HO. The Pedi. J. L. van Schaik (Pty) Ltd. Pretoria. 1967

[44] Tshisikhawe MP. An Ecological Evaluation of the Sustainability of Bark Harvesting of Medicinal Plant Species in the Venda Region, Limpopo Province, South Africa [Doctoral dissertation]. Pretoria: University of Pretoria; 2012

[45] Magwede K, Van Wyk BE, Van Wyk AE. An inventory of Vhavenḓa useful plants. South African Journal of Botany. 2019;**122**:57-89

[46] Mogale MM, Raimondo DC, VanWyk BE. The ethnobotany of central Sekhukhuneland, South Africa.

South African Journal of Botany. 2019; **122**:90-119

[47] Bussmann RW. Ethnobotany of the Samburu of Mt. Nyiru, South Turkana, Kenya. Journal of Ethnobiology and Ethnomedicine. 2006;**2**(1):35

[48] Gemedo-Dalle T, Maass BL, Isselstein J. Plant biodiversity and ethnobotany of Borana pastoralists in southern Oromia, Ethiopia. Economic Botany. 2005;**59**(1):43-65

[49] de Albuquerque UP. Re-examining hypotheses concerning the use and knowledge of medicinal plants: A study in the Caatinga vegetation of NE Brazil. Journal of Ethnobiology and Ethnomedicine. 2006;**2**(1):30

[50] Nsuala BN, Enslin G, Viljoen A. "Wild cannabis": A review of the traditional use and phytochemistry of Leonotis leonurus. Journal of Ethnopharmacology. 2015;**174**:520-539

[51] Maroyi A. Lippia javanica (Burm. f.) Spreng.: Traditional and commercial uses and phytochemical and pharmacological significance in the African and Indian subcontinent. Evidence-based Complementary and Alternative Medicine. 2017;**2017**

[52] Shanley P, Luz L. The impacts of forest degradation on medicinal plant use and implications for health care in eastern Amazonia. Bioscience. 2003; **53**(6):573-584

[53] Semenya SS, Potgieter MJ, Erasmus LJC. Bapedi phytomedicine and their use in the treatment of sexually transmitted infections in Limpopo province, South Africa. African Journal of Pharmacy and Pharmacology. 2013;**7**(6):250-262

[54] Carvalho AM, Frazao-Moreira A. Importance of local knowledge in plant resources management and conservation in two protected areas from Trás-os-Montes, Portugal. Journal of Ethnobiology and Ethnomedicine. 2011;**7**(1):36

[55] Maroyi A. Diversity of use and local knowledge of wild and cultivated plants in the eastern cape province, South Africa. Journal of Ethnobiology and Ethnomedicine. 2017;**13**(1):43

[56] Nortjie JM, Wyk BE. Useful plants of Namaqualand, South Africa: A checklist and analysis. South African Journal of Botany. 2019;**122**:120-135

[57] Senbeta F, Gole TW, Denich M, Kellbessa E. Diversity of useful plants in the coffee forests of Ethiopia. Ethnobotany Research and Applications. 2013;**11**:049-069

[58] Letsela T, Witkowski ET, Balkwill K. Plant resources used for subsistence in Tshehlanyane and Bokong in Lesotho. Economic Botany. 2003;**57**(4):619

[59] Neelo J, Kashe K, Masamba W. Ethnobotanical survey of wood plants in Shorobe and Xobe villages, northwest region of Botswana. Ethnobotany Research and Applications. 2015;**14**:367-379

[60] de Lucena RFP, do Nascimento VT, de Lima Araújo E, de Albuquerque UP. Local uses of native plants in an area of Caatinga vegetation (Pernambuco, NE Brazil). Ethnobotany Research and Applications. 2008;**6**:3-14

[61] Kumar S, Das G, Shin HS, Kumar P, Patra JK. Diversity of plant species in the steel city of Odisha, India: Ethnobotany and implications for conservation of urban bio-resources. Brazilian Archives of Biology and Technology. 2018;**61**:1-19

[62] Liengme CA. Plants used by the Tsonga people of Gazankulu. Bothalia. 1981;**13**(3–4):501-518

[63] Mabogo DE. The Ethnobotany of the VhaVenda [Doctoral dissertation]. Pretoria: University of Pretoria; 2003

[64] Pauw KA. A profile of the Limpopo province: Demographics, poverty, inequality, and unemployment. Provide Project. Limpopo Province: Government Printers; 2005

[65] De Beer JJ, Van Wyk BE. An ethnobotanical survey of the agter–Hantam, northern Cape province, South Africa. South African Journal of Botany. 2011;**77**(3):741-754

[66] Hoare AL. The Use of Non-timber Forest Products in the Congo Basin: Constraints and Opportunities. London: Rainforest Foundation; 2007

[67] Ndangalasi HJ, Bitariho R, Dovie DB. Harvesting of non-timber forest products and implications for conservation in two montane forests of East Africa. Biological Conservation. 2007;**134**(2):242-250

[68] Addis G, Urga K, Dikasso D. Ethnobotanical study of edible wild plants in some selected districts of Ethiopia. Human Ecology. 2005;**33**(1): 83-118

[69] De Vynck JC, Van Wyk BE, Cowling RM. Indigenous edible plant use by contemporary Khoe-san descendants of South Africa's cape south coast. South African Journal of Botany. 2016;**102**:60-69

[70] Amente DA. Ethnobotanical survey of wild edible plants and their contribution for food security used by Gumuz people in Kamash Woreda; Benishangul Gumuz regional state; Ethiopia. Journal of Food and Nutrition Sciences. 2017;**5**:217-224

[71] Wynn SG, Fougere B. Veterinary Herbal Medicine. Amsterdam, Netherlands: Elsevier Health Sciences; 2006

[72] Khumalo SG, Fröde A, Sola P. Guidelines for the Sustainable Harvesting of Traditional Medicinal Plants in Zimbabwe. Harare, Zimbabwe: Ministry of Environment and Tourism; 2019

[73] Semenya SS, Maroyi A. Plants used by Bapedi traditional healers to treat asthma and related symptoms in Limpopo province, South Africa. Evidence-Based Complementary and Alternative Medicine. 2018;**33**:2183705. DOI: 10.1155/2018/2183705

[74] Semenya SS, Potgieter MJ, Erasmus LJ. Indigenous plant species used by Bapedi healers to treat sexually transmitted infections: Their distribution, harvesting, conservation and threats. South African Journal of Botany. 2013;**87**:66-75

[75] Petersen L, Reid AM, Moll EJ, Hockings MT. Perspectives of wild medicine harvesters from Cape Town, South Africa. South African Journal of Science. 2017;**113**(9–10):1-8

[76] Kangalawe RY, Noe C, Tungaraza FS, Naimani G, Mlele M. Understanding of traditional knowledge and indigenous institutions on sustainable land management in Kilimanjaro region, Tanzania. Journal of Soil Science. 2014;**4**(13):469

[77] Kepe T. Medicinal plants and rural livelihoods in Pondoland, South Africa: Towards an understanding of resource value. International Journal of Biodiversity Science and Management. 2007;**3**(3):170-183

[78] Cunningham AB. Integrating local plant resources and habitat management. Biodiversity and Conservation. 1994;**3**(2):104-115

[79] Ndawonde BG. Medicinal Plant Sales: A Case Study in Northern Zululand [Doctoral dissertation]. KwaDlangezwa: University of Zulnland; 2006

[80] Mowo JG, Adimassu Z, Catacutan D, Tanui J, Masuki K,

Lyamchai C. The importance of local traditional institutions in the management of natural resources in the highlands of East Africa. Human Organization. 2013:154-163

[81] Tshisikhawe MP, Van Rooyen MW, Gaugris JY. Is the present Brackenridgea nature reserve large enough to ensure the survival of Brackenridgea zanguebarica Oliv.? Koedoe. 2013;**55**(1)

[82] Marumo M, Naicker-Manick P, Tshitwamulomoni L, Samahlubi S. Resource Assessment for *Aloe ferox* in South Africa. Republic of South Africa. Technical Report. Pretoria: Department of Environmental Affairs; 2014

[83] Ham C, Akinnifesi FK, Franzel S, Jordaan DD, Hansmann C, Ajayi OC, et al. Opportunities for Commercialization and Enterprise Development of Indigenous Fruits in Southern Africa. Indigenous Fruit Trees in the Tropics: Domestication, Utilization and Commercialization. World Agroforestry Centre: Nairobi. Wallingford, UK: CAB International Publishing; 2007. pp. 254-272

[84] Masarirambi MT, Mavuso V, Songwe VD, Nkambule TP, Mhazo N. Indigenous post-harvest handling and processing of traditional vegetables in Swaziland: A review. African Journal of Agricultural Research. 2010;**5**(24): 33-41

[85] Legwaila GM, Mojeremane W, Madisa ME, Mmolotsi RM, Rampart M. Potential of traditional food plants in rural household food security in Botswana. Journal of Horticulture and Forestry. 2011;**3**(6):171-177

[86] Magoro MD, Masoga MA, Mearns MA. Traditional health practitioners' practices and the sustainability of extinction-prone traditional medicinal plants. International Journal of African Renaissance Studies. 2010;**5**(2):229-241

[87] Wiersum KF, Dold AP, Husselman M, Cocks M. Cultivation of medicinal plants as a tool for biodiversity conservation and poverty alleviation in the Amatola region, South Africa. Frontis. 2006:43-57

[88] Mukolwe MO. The potential of agroforestry in the conservation of high value indigenous trees: A case study of Umzimvubu District, Eastern Cape. Genetic Resources and Crop Evolution. Pietermaritzburg: University of Natal; 1999

[89] Kindt R. Methodology for Tree Species Diversification Planning for African Agroecosystems [Doctoral dissertation]. Ghent, Belgium: Ghent University; 2002

[90] Bayala J, Kalinganire A, Tchoundjeu Z, Sinclair F, Garrity D. Conservation Agriculture with Trees in the West African Sahel–A Review. ICRAF Occasional Paper. Nairobi: World Agroforestry Centre; 2011

[91] Mulukh DD, Mhaiske VM, Narkhede SS, Patil VK, Rane AD. Farmers' Preferences for Indigenous Trees Suitable for agroforestry Technologies in Ratnagiri District of Maharashtra state. Journal of Advanced Agricultural Research and Technology. 2018;**2**(1):33-39

[92] Fifanou VG, Ousmane C, Gauthier B, Brice S. Traditional agroforestry systems and biodiversity conservation in Benin (West Africa). Agroforestry Systems. 2011;**82**(1):1-3

[93] Sistla SA, Roddy AB, Williams NE, Kramer DB, Stevens K, Allison SD. Agroforestry practices promote biodiversity and natural resource diversity in Atlantic Nicaragua. PLoS One. 2016;**11**(9):e0162529

[94] Pietersen S, López-Acosta J, Gomez-Díaz J, Lascurain-Rangel M. Floristic diversity and cultural

importance in agroforestry systems on small-scale farmer's livelihoods in Central Veracruz, México. Sustainability. 2018;**10**(1):279

[95] Viswanath S, Lubina PA, Subbanna S, Sandhya MC. Traditional agroforestry systems and practices: A review. Journal of Advanced Agricultural Technologies. 2018;**2**(1): 18-29

Chapter 18

Brazilian Amazon Plants: An Overview of Chemical Composition and Biological Activity

Reinaldo Martins Cunha Junior, Pâmella Buenos Aires Domingues, Rafael de Oliveira Ambrósio, Caio Augusto Freitas Martins, Jéssica Genoveva Boline Passarelli Capaz Pinto da Silva and Fabio Alessandro Pieri

Abstract

Currently, the number of diseases has been increasing and reaching the population directly, and the deliberate use of drugs is creating resistance of pathogens in several drugs, a fact evidenced by the increased ineffectiveness of drugs and the persistence of infections in the body. Given this, it is necessary to search for new alternative drugs that can effectively promote effective therapy. It is possible to highlight, in Brazil, the diversity of the Amazonian flora, which has several species with considerable potential as a source of new molecules with identified biological activity. Thus, a literature review was conducted in order to describe the applications of some Amazonian extracts and their chemical characteristics and biological activity. The Amazon rain forest has considerable diversity of plant species with biological properties that may be useful to public health. Further research is needed to identify new compounds with health benefits.

Keywords: Amazonian extracts, biological activity, chemical composition, alternative treatment

1. Introduction

The Amazon rain forest is known to have an extensive territory, including several Brazilian states and some other American countries, full of a considerable diversity of fauna and flora forming a rich ecosystem. Thus, due to the diversity of plants and the side effects of the drugs currently used, such as the increasing antimicrobial resistance, it is necessary to obtain new alternatives to enable the effective treatment and/or prevention of diseases [1].

Brazilian biodiversity is recognized as one of the most representative of the earth's biosphere and plays an important role in its maintenance and in human health by providing basic products and ecosystem services. In addition, Brazilian

Amazon provides a lot of products including food (such as livestock, fruits, and vegetables), wood, and even drugs [2].

Given this, the aim of this chapter is to conduct a review, presenting some Amazonian species included in Brazilian Amazon biodiversity, as well as the biological activity of their extracts.

2. *Astrocaryum vulgare Mart* (tucumã)

The Amazon has innumerable native species of fruit plants that have economic, technological, and nutritional potential, which has been arousing the interest of scientific studies in many fields, such as food science, pharmaceutical, cosmetic, flavoring, and essences. Allied to these virtues is the tucumã (*Astrocaryum vulgare* Mart.), species belonging to the family of Arecaceae, popularly known by the name of tucumanzeiro. Fruits and seeds are used in human and animal food and leaves and stems in the construction of houses by the people in the interior of the Amazon. This species commonly found in the Amazon region can reach 10 to 15 m in height and 15 to 20 cm in diameter of trunk. It has the characteristic of presenting flowers and fruits almost all year round. The normally ellipsoid orange fruits, when ripe, are 3 to 5 cm long and have a characteristic odor [3].

2.1 Chemical composition

The sticky and fibrous pulp is very rich in vitamin A, 90 times more than the avocado and 3 times higher than the carrot, also having high vitamin B (thiamine) and high vitamin C content, compared with the citrus fruits. Tucumã also has high energy value (247 calories per 100 grams) and presents relevant content of glycids (19.1%), lipids (16.6%), and proteins (3.5%) [3].

2.2 Biological activity

In addition to good nutritional values, tests were performed on hydroalcoholic, methanolic, and ethanolic extracts in the epicarp of the fruit, and according to Mathias [4], the tucumã presents better antioxidant activity of hydroalcoholic extracts. Thus, the antimicrobial activity of plant extracts was evaluated by determining the minimum inhibitory concentration [5]. However, despite numerous other benefits presented in traditional acknowledgment, the tucumã extracts did not show antimicrobial activity against any of the strains (*Bacillus*, *Enterobacter*, *Enterococcus*, *Escherichia*, *Salmonella*, *Shigella*, *Streptococcus*, *Listeria*, *Staphylococcus*, *Geobacillus*) [4, 5].

In a recent study by Bernardes et al. [6], tucumã presented high medicinal potential due to its composition rich in carotenoids, flavonoids, fibers, and polyunsaturated fatty acids, indicating its use on lipid metabolism and the prevention of disorders from the cardiovascular system. In this study, hyperlipidemia was induced by intraperitoneal injection of Poloxamer 407 in rats resulting in an elevated blood lipid level (hyperlipidemia). Tucumã was not active in reducing these increasing lipids; however, it acts on modulation of purinergic enzymes that could present the ability to keep vascular homeostasis, reducing platelet aggregation and consequent arterothrombosis, which could be converted in reducing of hyperlipidemia and cardiovascular diseases.

According to Azevedo [7] the antimicrobial activity of hexanic and methanolic extracts of tucumã pulp were tested against standard strains of the bacteria *Staphylococcus aureus* (ATCC6538), *Escherichia coli* (ATCC 35218), and *Pseudomonas aeruginosa* (ATCC 9027) and against the yeast *Candida albicans* (ATCC 12031) by microplate dilution technique [8]. No antimicrobial activity of the hexanic and methanolic extracts of the tucumã pulp against *Staphylococcus aureus*, *Escherichia coli*, and *Pseudomonas aeruginosa* was observed confirming previous studies, without antibacterial activity [4, 5]. Also, no antimicrobial activity of the hexanic and methanolic extracts of the tucumã pulp was obtained against *Candida albicans* [7].

Tucumã is a fruit rich in bioactive compounds still little explored by the scientific community. Lectins are proteins capable of selective and reversible binding to various carbohydrate types without altering the chemical structure of any glycosyl linker residue. Tucumã mesocarp extract was obtained in 1:3 saline phosphate buffer (PBS) and was studied to verify its lectinic activity on crude extract and its fractions, by a hemagglutination assay which was performed against rabbit, human, and sheep blood. The results pointed to positive lectinic activity only by crude extracts, suggesting that the different fraction could act synergistically in crude extract, but fractioning technique used could have separated the synergistic active principles, making the obtained fractions inactive [9].

One study [10] measured the interference of oils extracted from tucumã in the composition of the dental biofilm and the progress of enamel demineralization and dental caries that is a multifactorial disease that is still prevalent worldwide. With relevant action of microorganisms in biofilm formation on the tooth surface, reducing of dental plaque formation bacteria could be reverted in decreasing of caries. The relationship between biofilm microorganisms and dietary elements (carbohydrates) may influence the etiology of this disease. The study performed an in situ work with volunteers that were kept with dental enamel blocks fixed on their palates, treated with solutions. One group used a sucrose solution (20%) and other groups with sucrose solution added with natural oils including tucumã (20%). Mineral loss of enamel blocks was assessed by Knoop surface microhardness and optical coherence tomography. There was a reduction of the count of cariogenic bacteria *Streptococcus mutans*, total *Streptococcus*, and *Lactobacillus casei* in the tucumã oil group compared with the sucrose control group, and also the mineral loss was lower ($p < 0.05$). These findings present tucumã oil as a potential source of compounds for the manufacture of anticaries drugs in the future [10].

Neuropsychiatric diseases carry with them a complicated pathophysiology, some of which have recently been associated with excess of free radicals compared with each cell's intrinsic protective system (oxidative stress) and mitochondrial dysfunction, resulting in an exacerbated inflammatory response. Due to the complexity of the pathophysiology of neuropsychiatric diseases, research with natural products with bioactive and pharmacological characteristics is necessary, such as the use of nanotechnology to improve the bioavailability of these compounds and with the potential to delay, prevent, and treat such pathologies. In one study [11], tucumã oil nanoemulsions were prepared to help protect their bioactive compounds and improve their biodistribution. The stability of the formulations was tested for 90 days under different storage conditions. The SH-SY5Y and B2 neuronal strains were used to evaluate the safety profile of free tucumã oil and its nanoemulsion, in addition to its power to activate cell proliferation. Based on the results initially observed, tucumã oil nanoemulsion was tested against inflammatory activity in BV-2 cells activated by lipopolysaccharides. The best conservation condition of nanoemulsion was under refrigeration. Regarding cytotoxicity evaluations in BV-2 and SH-SY5Y cells, no significant damage was observed. Regarding the anti-neuroinflammatory effect evaluations of tucumã nanoemulsion, it was observed that although nanoformulation did not maintain cell proliferation levels equal to the negative control, there was a reduction in cell reactivity, oxidative profile normalization, and cell cycle regulation. Thus, it can be suggested that tucumã oil has a potential anti-inflammatory effect and that through its nanostructuring this effect can be optimized and may perhaps overcome the blood–brain barrier and modulate possible chronic inflammatory stimuli that correlate with neuropsychiatric or neurodegenerative disease [11].

3. *Caryocar* sp.

The genus *Caryocar* belongs to the Caryocaraceae family and has species that are popularly known as pequi, piqui, or pequiá. The most studied species of the genus are *Caryocar brasiliense*, *Caryocar villosum*, and *Caryocar coriaceum* [12].

This genus is easily found in Central and South America. According to some authors, the fruit may be called by different names according to the region in which it is found, such as the following: the fruits of *C. brasiliense* that are more commonly found in the Midwest of Brazil and Minas Gerais are called pequi; *C. coriaceum* fruits common in the Northeast of Brazil are called piqui; and *C. villosum* fruits from the Amazon region are called piquiá [13].

Caryocar spp. are a drupaceous fruit, globose, and green in color, with one to four segments [13]. The ripe fruit of pequi is a shell composed of a thin brownish-green exocarp and an outer mesocarp composed of a white, inedible mass. Within the fruit is a nucleus that has an inner mesocarp or inner flesh, the generally edible fruit component, light yellow in color, abundant, oil-rich flesh, and an almond within the spinous endocarp [12, 13].

3.1 Chemical composition

The fruit of pequi is rich in several important components, such as monounsaturated fatty acids (MUFA), bioactive compounds, fibers, minerals [13], and carotenoids [12]. The amount of each may vary according to the species analyzed, the environmental conditions in which it is inserted, the part of the fruit, as well as the type of analysis that was used [13].

The pulp of *Caryocar* spp. has a substantial amount of MUFA, and dietary fiber and minerals are found, of which calcium, magnesium, and potassium stand out. Fruit peel is abundant in dietary fiber, including soluble fiber and phenolic compounds, but in oil high levels of oleic acid are found [12].

Carotenoids are natural pigments of various fruits of Brazil. The presence of this pigment in *Caryocar* spp. occurs with values comparable to those of papaya and guava, which are considered fruits rich in carotenoids. The carotenoids found in the pulp were β-carotene, lycopene, ζ-carotene, cryptoflavin, β-cryptoxanthin, anteraxanthin, zeaxanthin, mutatoxanthin, violaxanthin, lutein, and neoxanthin [13]. However, as stated earlier, the amount present in each species varies due to several factors. In the review of Nascimento Silva and Naves [12], this difference varying between 155 and 270 μg/g of carotenoids in *C. brasiliense* species was found, whereas from *C. villosum* it was between 17 and 69 μg/g.

In the study by Chisté et al. [14], the pulp of *C. villosum* was chemically characterized, and the most representative components were total lipids (25.5% wet basis), gallic acid, ellagic rhamnose, and ellagic acid as the main phenolic compounds and all-trans-antheraxanthin and all-trans-zeaxanthin as the main carotenoids.

Carotenoid profile analysis in pequi pulp has been a challenge for researchers. For best results, various procedures for carotenoid extraction with different solvents, temperatures, time periods, and equipment were performed. In addition to the pulp and species extraction methodology, the ripening stage of the fruit also interferes with the composition, since carotenoid synthesis intensifies during the ripening period. Storage conditions need to be evaluated, as light-protected packaging minimizes compost loss [12].

The extraction of bioactive compounds from plant materials is strongly influenced by the solubility of each specific structure in the solvent used. Knowing this, Chisté et al. [14] evaluated *C. villosum* extracts using different solvents with different polarities, which was ethanol/water (1:1, v/v), ethanol/ethyl acetate (EAC) (1:1, v/v), and ethyl acetate. The extracts produced solid mass ranging from 10.8 to 46.4%, depending on the solvent. The ethyl acetate and ethanol/ethyl acetate extracts showed the highest total lipid content and the highest solid mass yield. The ethanol/water extract presented the highest values of total phenolic compounds (9.2 mg garlic acid equivalent (GAE)/g of lyophilized extract), total flavonoids (3.8 mg catequin equivalent (CE)/g of freeze-dried extract), and total tannins (7.6 mg tannic acid equivalent (TAE)/g of lyophilized extract), followed by the other extracts, ethanol/ethyl acetate and ethyl acetate extracts, that had the lower content of these compounds. This result can be explained considering that the main phenolic acids (gallic acid, ellagic acid and derivatives) found in *C. villosum* pulp have high affinity for high-polarity solvents. In fact, water or ethanol and mixtures between them are widely used for the quantitative extraction of phenolic compounds from different plant sources.

Regarding the total carotenoid content, the ethanol extract presented the highest value (0.1 mg/g), while the ethanol/water mixture presented the lowest value (0.01 mg/g). Since the composition of carotenoids from *C. villosum* pulp has been reported to be primarily hydroxyl groups (xanthophylls), it is more polar than carotenes generally found in large quantities in fruits of the Amazon. This fact explains why the use of high-polarity solvents (such as water and ethanol/water) has low efficiency in carotenoid extraction [14].

In *C. brasiliense* pulp, larger total phenolic compounds were found than in almond. In almond oil of this same species, the values of gallic acid (GAE) were higher, up to 392 mg of GAE/100 g of oil [13].

According to the literature, the total phenolic content of pulp fluctuates even in the same species. Studies with *Caryocar* spp. reported that the total phenolic content ranges from 178 to 334 mg/100 g gallic acid equivalents (GAE), 209 mg/100 g GAE for *C. brasiliense*, and 59 mg/100 g GAE for *C. villosum*. Although the total phenolic content of *C. brasiliense* pulp is the lowest among other species of the genus, it is still higher than Cerrado Biome fruits, such as jenipapo with an average of 48 mg/100 g, and fruits such as banana with 56 mg/100 g or mango with 78 mg/100 g [12].

3.2 Biological activities

In addition to the nutritional benefits, pequi has important biological activities. These include healing, anti-inflammatory, and antimicrobial activities and protection against genome damage and oxidative damage. These benefits are mainly attributed to the presence of MUFA and phytochemical compounds [13].

Gallic acid and ellagic acid are the phenolic compounds most present in *C. villosum* pulp. These compounds suppressed tumors, inhibiting cell proliferation-related gene expression and angiogenesis in 1,2-dimethylhydrazine (DMH)-induced tumors, transgenic prostate adenocarcinoma, and mice-bearing prostate xenografts. In addition to these activities, some epidemiological studies have reported that ingestion of polyphenol-rich sources reduces the risk of developing chronic diseases such as cardiovascular disease, type 2 diabetes, cancer, and neurodegeneration [12].

Carotenoids and phenolic compounds obtained from *C. coriaceum* pulp have important antioxidant action. Active flavonoids have the ability to neutralize pathogens and eliminate reactive oxygen species (ROS) either directly or indirectly, activating pathways that enable ROS degradation [15].

Doxorubicin (DOX), from the anthracycline group, is a drug given to treat cancer. However, it has side effects, such as cardiotoxicity exerted through the production of free radicals. In the study of Moura et al. [16], ethanolic extract of pequi bark (PSEE) was administered daily to DOX-treated rats; this led to increased activity of the enzyme glutathione reductase (GDH-Rd). This enzyme is responsible for maintaining the cellular protection system intact through a biochemical cascade. The presence of elevated GDH-Rd in the heart tissue of PSEE-treated rats showed higher antioxidant activity than those who did not undergo the treatment.

In addition to these effects, there are reports of the leishmanicidal effect of the fruit. Therefore, the search for alternative treatments, including the use of natural products with less toxicity than conventional treatments, has become more frequent [17].

In leishmaniasis disease, an inflammation must occur to control the parasitic load, being triggered by the interaction of the parasite with the host immune cells. However, an exacerbated response can cause tissue damage, similar to those seen in leishmaniasis. Thus, an antioxidant action of *C. coriaceum* controls the inflammatory response for effective disease control [15].

The study by Tomiotto-Pellissier [17] aimed to verify the leishmanicidal action of *C. coriaceum* leaf extracts obtained from extraction by EAC and methanol (MET). The extracts were able to induce the parasite mitochondria membrane depolarization in the promastigote phase; such membrane is crucial for parasite survival, since *Leishmania* spp. have a single mitochondria, which is the main site for generating cellular ATP through oxidative phosphorylation, making it a promising antiparasitic target. Mitochondrial respiratory chain dysfunction can produce an enormous amount of ROS within the organelles. Both EAC and MET promoted the increase of ROS in the promastigote phases. In addition, the cascade triggered by loss of mitochondrial integrity followed by increased ROS production can lead to parasite death through an apoptosis-like mechanism. The results showed that although both extracts had similar results, the treatment with EAC was a more efficient activity against promastigote forms than MET. The presence of catechins and steroids only in the EAC extract, and the greater amount of flavonoids than MET, could explain the more pronounced results found in the treatment with EAC. In addition, the effects could be given by the synergistic action of the compounds present in the extracts.

Its antimicrobial effect has been tested by Alves et al. [15]. The ethanolic extracts of peel and pulp of *C. coriaceum* had activity against six pathogenic strains, three of the genus *Malassezia* sp., and three from *Microsporum canis*. The minimum fungicidal concentration (MFC) and the minimum inhibitory concentration (MIC) were 39.1 μg/mL (MFC) and 9.8 μg/mL to 19.5 μg/mL (MIC) against *Malassezia strains* and 4.9 to 9.8 μg/mL (MFC) and 4.9 μg/mL (MIC) against *M. canis*. Besides that, the authors evaluated the antioxidant activity the extracts compared with a standard (rutin), obtaining higher activity of the extracts, with highlight to the pulp extract that had activity 3.6 times higher than rutin.

4. *Hymenaea* sp. (Jatobá)

Jatobá (*Hymenaea* sp.) belongs to the family Fabaceae and subfamily Caesalpiniodeae and has been highlighted for a long time by folk medicine. The word jatobá has its origin from the Tupi language of Brazilian Indians, meaning "hard fruit tree," and this species is used for various purposes, such as medicinal, food, ornamental, and timber use [18]. Its distribution occurs in Central America to South America, mainly in the Amazon basin, and this genus comprises about 25 described species in America [19].

The use of this plant for medicinal purposes is not restricted to the use of its leaf or fruit extracts. The structures used are the most diverse as stem bark, leaves, and roots and are prepared, for example, by infusion, cooking, maceration and syrup for phytotherapeutic extraction, and isolation of the active compounds. Such extracts can be used for anti-inflammatory, healing, soothing, influenza, cough, pneumonia, gastritis, ulcer, burning urethra, stroke, anemia, and more, showing how this plant is extremely important for culture and traditional popular medicine in Brazil [18].

4.1 Chemical composition

The species *Hymenaea stigonocarpa* was studied by Cardoso et al. [20] to analyze the nutritional content of pulp of fruits. The results pointed to low pulp yield (17.1%) and moisture (8.8 g/100 g) and a rich presence of dietary fiber (44.3 g/100 g), energy (193.0 kcal/100 g), and protein (5.6 mg/100 g). Vitamin E and folates were present in higher levels than other common fruits (53.5 and 495.5 μg/100 g, respectively). Carotenoids and vitamin C were present in low concentrations (0.4 mg and 8.9 mg/100 g, respectively). The authors concluded that the fruit of this species known as "jatobá of cerrado" is a source of vitamin C, a good source of folates, and an excellent source of dietary fiber.

In the work of Veras et al. [19], leaves of *H. cangaceira* were hydrodistilled to obtain a yellow essential oil. Within this oil 15 compounds were detected, which were 85.38% of the total composition of the oil. The analysis of the composition of this oil presents a high percentage of sesquiterpenes (79.04%), besides having as main components ß-caryophyllene (23.38 ± 0.51%), germacrene D (14.66 ± 0.14%), α-guaiene (9.75 ± 0.07%), β-elemene (7.05 ± 0.02%), α-copaene (6.34 ± 0.15%), and α-humulene (4.65 ± 0.12%) [19].

Aguiar et al. [21] evaluated chemical composition of ripe and unripe peels of *H. courbaril*, founding sesquiterpenes as main compounds of both samples (86.1 and 93.3%, respectively). In ripe peels majority of the compounds were α-copaene (11.1%), spathulenol (10.1%), β-selinene (8.2%), γ-muurolene (7.9%), and caryophyllene oxide (6.9%); unripe samples provided an oil with germacrene D (31.9%), β-caryophyllene (27.1%), bicyclogermacrene (6.5%), α-humulene (4.2%), and α-copaene (4.2%) as the major compounds.

The crude ethanolic extract and ethyl acetate fraction obtained from stem barks of a tree of *H. martiana* was analyzed for the identification of flavonoid content. The results showed 11 peaks in the chromatograms that were identified as taxifolin, eucryphin, astilbin and three diastereoisomers, engeletin and two diastereoisomers, quercitrin, and 2,6,3′,4′-tetrahydroxy-2-benzylcoumaran-3-one. The ethyl acetate fraction presented 3.8 times higher concentration of astilbin than the crude extract [22].

4.2 Biological activities

Veras et al. [19] stated that the biological effects of the compounds described above (*H. cangaceira*) are as follows:·caryophyllene has anti-inflammatory, antibacterial, antifungal, antirheumatic, antioxidant, antitumor, analgesic, and antiviral activities. Germacrene has been described with antitumor, analgesic, anti-inflammatory, and antioxidant activities, as well as α-amylase and acetylcholinesterase inhibitory activity. Guaiene has reports as a cyclooxygenase inhibitor, 5-lipoxygenase, and acetylcholinesterase and has antioxidant and anti-inflammatory activities. Elemene is described as potent antimicrobial, antioxidant, and anesthetic. Copaene has antimicrobial, antileishmanial, antigenotoxic, and antioxidant activities. Humulene is referred as an anti-inflammatory, analgesic, and antiallergic agent [19].

In a research conducted by the Federal Rural University of Pernambuco, the effectiveness of the essential oil of jatobá leaf (*H. cangaceira*) against *Staphylococcus aureus* ATCC 43300 (MRSA), *S. aureus* ATCC 29213 (MSSA), *Pseudomonas aeruginosa* ATCC 27853, *Klebsiella pneumoniae* ATCC 700603, *Candida tropicalis* ATCC 750, and *C. krusei* ATCC 6258 was observed. The result of inhibition of both fungi and bacteria was positive for the oil of jatobá in different concentrations, and it must highlight the high activity against Gram-negative bacteria with MICs ranging between 4 and 16 μg/mL, result similar to cefepime, the control drug used [19]. The same authors also present in this work other important bioactivities, such as high antioxidant and analgesic activities and absence of toxicity on rats and erythrocytes.

In other work from the Federal University of Sergipe, *H. martiana* leaf extract was tested in inhibition of isolates of *Salmonella* spp., *Escherichia coli*, and *Staphylococcus aureus* and reduces its counts in raw milk. The minimum bactericidal concentrations (MBC) against bacteria were 125.3 μg/mL against *S. aureus* (ATCC 25923), 781.2 μg/mL against *E. coli* (ATCC 35218), and 1556.5 μg/mL against *S. enterica* subsp. *enterov* serovar Choleraesuis ATCC® 10708. The authors inoculated these bacteria on milk samples at different concentrations and used the extract in MBC concentrations to try to avoid bacterial growing on milk. However the results were not as expected, since there was growing of bacteria in concentrations of 10^4 and 10^6 UFC/mL. Only in lower concentration of bacteria on milk does inhibition on growing of bacteria occur. The author suggests that the biological compounds present in milk may have reacted with the bioactive compounds of the extract, reducing their antibacterial activity [23].

Aguiar et al. [21] evaluated the activity of essential oil of ripe and unripe fruits of *H. courbaril*, as larvicide against *A. aegypti* larvae. The oil from ripe fruits was a strong larvicide against the larvae, presenting death of 50% of larvae with almost half of the concentration necessary for unripe fruit oil to obtain the same result (LC50 14.8 + 0.4 and 28.4 + 0.3 μg/mL). The authors assigned this difference to the higher concentration of oxygenated sequiterpenes in first oil, mainly spathulenol.

5. *Mammea americana* (apricot)

Mammea americana, popularly known as apricot, wild apricot, or apricot from São Domingos, is a fruit originating from the West Indies and northern South America, currently found mainly in the Amazon and some few other regions [24].

According to a study by Mourão and Beltrati [25], in which they characterized the morphology and anatomy of the fruit, it was possible to typify the apricot as a berry, whose "bark" consists of the epicarp and mesocarp that together represent 13.3% of the fruit's weight. The endocarp represents 70.7%, and the remainder of the fruit is represented by the large seeds, which account for 16% of the fruit weight [26].

The first commercial orchards were established in the mid-1980s, with seedlings that originated from seeds. Due to this fact, there was a large proportion of male plants and several phenotypic variations in the chemical and physical characteristics of the fruits. As an example, from a sample of 50 fruits originating from

10 different mother plants, it was possible to identify an average fruit weight of 852.8 g, with minimum and maximum limits of 502.3 g and 1443.0 g. Thus, it is possible to verify that the fruit weight is derived from the genetic origin trait, although it suffers a lot of influence from the environment [26].

The apricot tree can be disseminated through a sexual or asexual route. However, being a species that presents male plants and hermaphrodite plants, the orientation is that their diffusion is effected by vegetative processes. Thus, the most widely used method is grafting. Its spread by grafting ensures early production and enables the orchard to have only hermaphrodite plants [27].

It is grown in igapós and flooded river banks in the Amazon region, mainly in the state of Pará. It's a medium-sized tree that can reach 20 m in height; the apricot easily propagates through seeds, which germinate between 12 and 18 days. The plant can start flowering from 6/8 years [28].

5.1 Chemical composition

Through the study by Nascimento [29], it was possible to identify the composition of apricot, which has a vitamin content of 27.26 ± 1.03 mg of ascorbic acid/100 g in the apricot pulp. It was also possible to characterize the carotenoid content in apricot pulp which was 161.34 ± 0.40 bs and dehydrated product 103.53 ± 0.65 bs (μg/100 g β-carotene). By analyzing the results of quantifying antioxidant activity from the substitution calculations in the equation of the Trolox curve line, according to the ABTS method, a value of 31.96 ± 0.76 μM Trolox/g bs was obtained from fresh apricot. The analyses that dealt with the quantification of antioxidant activity from the consumption calculations of the DPPH radical obtained a value of 192.51 ± 0.13 fruit/g DPPH bs in the apricot sample in natura.

5.2 Biological activity

Regarding its biological activity, it is possible to identify, through studies found in the literature, extracts of *Mammea americana* generating results in the medical field.

According to studies by Toma et al. [30] that analyze the action of apricot extracts as antiulcerants in mice, the extracts showed antiulcerogenic effects with significant reduction in the damage of gastric lesions through the model of anti-inflammatory-induced injury. In NSAID/cholinomimetic-induced model, ethanolic and dichloromethane extracts of apricot showed antiulcerogenic effects with significant reduction in the damage of these gastric lesions by 36 (8.3 ± 2.0 mm) and 42% (7.5 ± 1.4 mm), respectively, as compared to the control group (13.0 ± 0.9 mm), increased the pH values, and promoted reduction of acid production.

According to the studies by Braga et al. [31], the antioxidant activity and the quantification of bioactive compounds (total carotenoids, CT; total polyphenols, PT; and total flavonols, FT) and the physical and centesimal characterization of the compounds of apricot fruits (*Mammea americana*) were evaluated. Antioxidant activity was measured by two different methods, oxygen radical absorbance capacity (ORAC) and the Trolox equivalent antioxidant capacity (TEAC). By ORAC, the results showed antioxidant activity with results of 30.97 ± 2.30 μmol equivalent Trolox/100 g, within the results showed of acerola (*Malpighia emarginata*) according the authors. In the TEAC test, the result was 11.82 ± 1.40 μmol equivalent Trolox/100 g, inside the range of acai also. For these two methods, the antioxidant activity of apricot was lower than other fruits like murici (*Byrsonima crassifolia*) and ingá (*Inga* spp.) For the bioactive compounds present in apricot in this work, 2.61 ± 0.73 mg equivalent catechin/100 g of FT, 25.41 ± 2.30 mg equivalent gallic acid/100 g of PT, and 7.55 ± 0.78 mg equivalent β-carotene/100 g CT were found.

From these results, the high content of carotenoids must be highlighted, which indicate that apricot is a promising source of pro-vitamin A.

According to a study found in the literature, it was possible to identify high trypanocidal activity in extracts of *Mammea americana*. In this way, compounds were obtained from *M. americana* fruit peels, and their action against the parasite was tested. The compounds were tested in vitro against epimastigotes (intracellular phase, without locomotion organelles, with little cytoplasm and large nucleus) and trypomastigotes (extracellular phase, circulating in the blood) of *Trypanosoma cruzi*, the etiological agent of Chagas disease. The most potent compounds were mammea A/BA, A/BB, A/AA, A/BD, and B/BA (designation based on chemical characteristics), with MC100 (minimum concentration at which all of the epimastigotes or trypomastigotes died after a 48-hour incubation) values ranging between 15 and 90 g/ml. Several active coumarins were also tested against normal human lymphocytes in vitro, which showed that mammea A/AA and A/BA did not show toxicity. Thus, through this study, it was possible to identify that these mammea-type coumarins have trypanocidal action and if they deepen the study of the compound, it may become possible to identify an important source of compounds with trypanocidal action [32].

6. *Platonia insignis* Mart (Bacuri)

Platonia insignis Mart consists of a species in the Clusiaceae family, being popularly named as bacuri. It has a fruit of appreciated flavor and is very famous in the Amazon region. The generic name, *Platonia,* is a tribute to the philosopher Plato (in Portuguese, Platão), and insignis means remarkable in reference to the size of the fruit [33]. The bacuri belongs to the subfamily Clusioideae and the genus Platonia and encompasses about 1000 species, present in tropical, subtropical, and temperate regions of the world. Approximately 90 species correspond to plants, involving trees, shrubs, lianas, and herbs of economic interest for the production of edible fruits, fine woods, and chemical derivatives of pharmaceutical and industrial interest [34–37].

Ethnobotanical utility concerns the use of oil extracted from its seeds, such as in the production of soap and as anti-inflammatory. The seeds are used to make bacuri oil, which is popularly used in the treatment of skin diseases and as a wound healer in animals. It is noteworthy that the investigation of *P. insignis* extracts and compounds is based on popular use. However, pharmacological studies conducted with the plant point to it as promising source for elaboration of phytomedicines with healing, anti-inflammatory, anticonvulsant, antimicrobial, cytotoxic, and antioxidant activities and to be used in treatment of several diseases such as cancer, Alzheimer, and Parkinson [38].

6.1 Chemical composition

Rocha [39] evaluated the chemical composition of *Platonia insignia* leaves and classified the chemical constitution as positive, moderately positive, strongly positive, or negative, as can be seen in **Table 1**.

6.2 Biological activity

Phenolic compounds present in the extract, such as catechins and flavononols, are widely distributed in the plant kingdom and associated with various biological activities, such as the fact that flavonoids have activity on capillary, anti-inflammatory, antiviral, antitumor, and hormonal permeabilities [40, 41]. Among the phenolic

Coumarins	Presence of substances
Phenols	Strongly positive
Condensed tannins	Strongly positive
Catechins	Strongly positive
Steroids	Strongly positive
Alkaloids	Strongly positive
Flavanonols	Moderately positive
Saponins	Moderately positive
Coumarins	Negative
Hydrolyzable tannins	Negative
Anthocyanidins and anthocyanidins	Negative
Flavones, flavonols, and xanthones	Negative
Chalcones and aurones	Negative
Leucoanthocyanidins	Negative
Flavonones	Negative
Triterpenoids	Negative

Note: Results expressed as average of the qualitative and semiquantitative evaluation tests of chemical constituents performed in triplicate in the hydroalcoholic extract, by Rocha [39]. Strongly positive; moderately positive; positive; negative. Source: in [39], adapted.

Table 1.
Qualitative and semiquantitative evaluation of the chemical constituents in the hydroethanol extract of Platonia insignis *Mart leaves.*

compounds, flavonoids were found in large quantities in bacuri extract, which exhibit several biological properties, such as anti-inflammatory, hormonal, and antioxidant action [42].

In addition, saponins can be found in tissues susceptible to bacteria, fungi or insects, due to their relationship with the plant defense system. This substances have hemolytic activity, formed with hypocholesteromic antifungal action and with the ability to change the permeability of membranes [41, 43, 44].

Alkaloids, in turn, are known for their antimalarial, antimicrobial, and cytotoxic activities [45]. Moreover, according to [46] review, *P. insignis* has antiepileptic and vasorelaxant activity.

Finally, there are compounds in bacuri, such as kaempferol and quercetin glycosides, that express significance in the regulation of hyperglycemia, due to the strong stimulation of glucose and oleic acid absorption [47].

7. Conclusion

Given the information previously constructed, it is possible to infer, therefore, that the Amazon rain forest has a considerable diversity of plants, which have several biological activities that may be of great concern for public health application. This is a little example of the power of biodiversity present in the Brazilian Amazon and of the natural resources with biopotential for treatment of a large number of diseases, being a promising source of new drugs that could be alternatives for the traditional drugs used nowadays that present side effects, such as toxicity to the patient and emergence of bacterial resistance to antibiotics, among others. Thus, many new studies are needed to identify compounds with desirable health activities, and the Amazon, by their potential biodiversity, seems to be the best place to look.

Acknowledgments

The authors thank the support of the National Council for Scientific and Technological Development (CNPq), the Coordination for the Improvement of Higher Education Personnel (CAPES), and the Minas Gerais State Research Support Foundation (FAPEMIG).

Author details

Reinaldo Martins Cunha Junior, Pâmella Buenos Aires Domingues, Rafael de Oliveira Ambrósio, Caio Augusto Freitas Martins, Jéssica Genoveva Boline Passarelli Capaz Pinto da Silva and Fabio Alessandro Pieri*
Life Sciences Institute, Campus Governador Valadares, Federal University of Juiz de Fora, Governador Valadares, MG, Brazil

*Address all correspondence to: fabio.pieri@ufjf.edu.br

References

[1] Borellli DL. Aziz Ab'Sáber: Problemas da Amazônia brasileira. Estudos Avançados. 2005;**19**(53):7-35

[2] Alho CJR. Importância da biodiversidade para a saúde humana: Uma perspectiva ecológica. Estudos Avançados. 2012;**74**:151-166. DOI: 10.1590/S0103-40142012000100011

[3] da Amazônia P. Tucumã [Internet]. Available from: http://www.amazoniadeaaz.com.br/sem-categoria/o-que-e-tucuma/ [Accessed: 05 November 2019]

[4] Mathias CS. Estudo químico e atividades biológicas dos frutos de tucumã (*Astrocaryum aculeatum Meyer*) [dissertation]. Manaus: Universidade Federal do Amazonas; 2014

[5] Pinto TJA, Kaneko TM, Ohara MT. Controle Biológico de Qualidade de Produtos Farmacêuticos, Correlatos e Cosméticos. 2nd ed. São Paulo: Atheneu Editora; 2003. p. 325

[6] Bernardes VM. Efeito do tucumã (*Astrocaryum aculeatum*) no metabolismo de nucleotídeos e nucleosídeo de adenina em plaquetas de ratos com hiperlipidemia induzida [thesis]. Santa Maria-RS: Universidade Federal de Santa Maria; 2018

[7] Azevedo SCM. Estudo do potencial biotecnológico da polpa de tucumã (*Astrocaryum aculeatum*) *in* natura e da conservação das suas propriedades nutricionais em embalagens a vácuo [dissertation]. Manaus: Universidade do Estado do Amazonas; 2016

[8] CLSI. Performance Standards for Antimicrobial Susceptibility Testing; Twenty-Fourth Informational Supplement. Wayne, PA: Clinical and Laboratory Standards Institute; 2014. 34:1. p. 226

[9] Aragão AB, Thomaz SMOBB. Purificação e avaliação da atividade lectínica do extrato de tucumã (*Astrocaryum vulgare Mart*.) nativo da região Amazônica. Journal of Basic and Applied Pharmaceutical Sciencies. 2015;**36**(S1):20

[10] Emmi DT. Influência dos óleos do tucumã (*Astrocaryum vulgare*) e da pupunha (*Bactris gasipae*) na composição do biofilme dental e dinâmica do processo de cárie em esmalte: um estudo *in* situ [thesis]. São Paulo: Universidade de São Paulo; 2013

[11] Ramos AP. Nanoemulsão do óleo do tucumã (*Astrocaryum vulgare mart*.) como agente neuroprotetor *in* vitro [thesis]. Santa Maria-RS: Universidade Franciscana; 2019

[12] Nascimento-Silva NRRD, Naves MMV. Potential of whole Pequi (*Caryocar spp*.) fruit-pulp, almond, oil, and Shell-as a medicinal food. Journal of Medicinal Food. 2019;**2**:952-962. DOI: 10.1089/jmf.2018.0149

[13] Torres LRO, Santana FC, Shinagawa FB, Mancini-Filho J. Bioactive compounds and functional potential of Pequi (*Caryocar spp*.), a native brazilian fruit: A review. Grasas y Aceites. 2018;**69**:E257. DOI: 10.3989/gya.1222172

[14] Chisté RC, De Toledo Benassi M, Mercadante AZ. Efficiency of different solvents on the extraction of bioactive compounds from the amazonian fruit *Caryocar villosum* and the effect on its antioxidant and colour properties. Phytochemical Analysis. 2013;**25**: 364-372. DOI: 10.1002/pca.2489

[15] Alves DR, Morais SM, Tomiotto-Pellissier F, Miranda-Sapla MM, Vasconcelos FR, Silva ING, et al. Flavonoid composition and biological activities of ethanol extracts of *Caryocar coriaceum* Wittm., a native plant from

Caatinga biome. Evidence-based Complementary and Alternative Medicine. 2017;**2017**:1-7. DOI: 10.1155/2017/6834218

[16] Moura LR, Viegas AA, Almeida LM, Neves REJ, Lima CS, Moura VMBD. Effect of Pequi shell ethanolic extract on glutathione reductase activity in rats exposed to doxorubicin cardiotoxicity. Revista Brasileira de Medicina Veterinária. 2018;**40**:e89018. DOI: 10.29374/2527-2179.bjvm89019

[17] Tomiotto-Pellissier F, Alves DR, Miranda-Sapla MM, de Morais SM, Assolini JP, da Silva Bortoleti BT, et al. *Caryocar coriaceum* extracts exert leishmanicidal effect acting in promastigote forms by apoptosis-like mechanism and intracellular amastigotes by Nrf2/HO-1/ferritin dependent response and iron depletion: Leishmanicidal effect of *Caryocar coriaceum* leaf exracts. Biomedicine & Pharmacotherapy. 2018;**98**:662-672. DOI: 10.1016/j.biopha.2017.12.083

[18] Silva MR, Lamarca EV. Registros etnobotânicos e potenciais medicinais e econômicos do jatobá (*Hymenaea courbaril*). Revista Ibirapuera. 2018;**15**:8-12

[19] Veras BO, Oliveira MBM, Oliveira FGS, Santos YQ, Oliveira JRS, Lima VLM, et al. Chemical composition and evaluation of the antinociceptive, antioxidant and antimicrobial effects of essential oil from Hymenaea cangaceira (Pinto, Mansano & Azevedo) native to Brazil: A natural medicine. Journal of Ethnopharmacology. 2019;**247**:112265. DOI: 10.1016/j.jep.2019.112265

[20] Cardoso LM, Bedetti SF, Ribeiro SMR, Esteves EA, Pinheiro-Sant'ana HM. 'Jatobá do cerrado' (*Hymenaea stigonocarpa*): Chemical composition, carotenoids and vitamins in an exotic fruit from the Brazilian Savannah. Fruits. 2013;**68**:95-107. DOI: 10.1051/fruits/2013056

[21] Aguiar JCD, Santiago GMP, Lavor PL, Veras HNH, Ferreira YSF, Lima MAA, et al. Chemical constituents and Larvicidal activity of Hymenaea courbaril fruit Peel. Natural Product Communications. 2010;**5**(12):1977-1980. DOI: 10.1177/1934578X1000501231

[22] Pacheco AGM, Branco A, Câmara CA, Silva TMS, Silva TMG, Oliveira AP, et al. Identification of flavonoids in Hymenaea martiana Hayne (Fabaceae) by HPLC-DAD-MSn analysis. Natural Product Research. 2019;**8**:1-6. DOI: 10.1080/14786419.2019.1672062

[23] Santana TC. Uso do extrato de folhas do Jatobá (*Hymenaea martiana Hayne*) na redução das contagens de *Salmonella spp*., *Escherichia coli* e *Staphylococcus aureus* em leite cru [dissertation]. São Cristóvão: Universidade Federal de Sergipe; 2015

[24] Cavalcante PB. Frutas comestíveis da Amazônia. 5th ed. Belém: Edições CEJUP/Museu Paraense Emílio Goeldi; 1991. p. 279

[25] Mourão KSM, Beltrati CM. Morphology and anatomy of developing fruits and seeds of *Mammea americana L.* (*Clusiaceae*). Revista Brasileira de Biologia. 2000;**60**:701-711. DOI: 10.1590/S0034-71082000000400023

[26] Carvalho JEU, Muller CH. Biometria e rendimento percentual de polpa de frutas nativas da Amazônia. Comunicado Técnico 139. Belém-PA: Embrapa Amazônia Oriental; 2005. p. 4

[27] VIillachica H, Carvalho JEU, Müller CH, Diaz SC, Almanza M. Frutales y hortalizas promissorios de la Amazonia. Lima: TCA-SPT; 1996. p. 367

[28] Brasil. Alimentos regionais brasileiros. 2nd ed. Brasília–DF: Ministério da saúde; 2015. p. 481

[29] Nascimento CS. Obtenção de Abricó (*Mammea americana L.*) desidratado

utilizando Secagem por Refractance Window [dissertation]. Belém: Universidade Federal Do Pará; 2015

[30] Toma W, Hiruma-Lima CA, Guerrero RO, Brito AR. Preliminary studies of *Mammea americana* L. (Guttiferae) bark/latex extract point to an effective antiulcer effect on gastric ulcer models in mice. Phytomedicine. 2005;**12**:345-350. DOI: 10.1016/j.phymed.2003.06.009

[31] Braga ACC, Silva AE, Pelais ACA, Bichara CMG, Pompeu DR. Atividade Atioxidante e Quantificação de Compostos Bioativos Dos Frutos De Abricó (*Mammea Americana*). Alimentação e Nutrição. 2010;**21**:31-36

[32] Reyes-Chilpa R, Estrada-Muñiz E, Vega-Avila E, Abe F, Kinjo J, Hernández-Ortega S. Trypanocidal constituents in plants: 7. Mammea-type coumarins. Memórias do Instituto Oswaldo Cruz. 2008;***103***:431-436. DOI: 10.1590/s0074-02762008000500004

[33] Yamaguchi KKL, Lamarão CV, Lima ES, Veiga-Junior VF. Química e Farmacologia do Bacuri (*Platonia insignis*). Scientia Amazonia. 2014;**3**:39-46

[34] Brummit RK. Vascular Plant Families and Genera. Kew: Royal Botanic Gardens; 1992. p. 804

[35] Barroso GM, Peixoto AL, Ichaso SLF, Guimarães EF. Sistemática de angiospermas no Brasil. Vol 1. 2nd ed. Viçosa, MG: Editora UFV; 2002. p. 309

[36] Joly AB. Botânica: Introdução à taxonomia vegetal. 11th ed. São Paulo: Editora Nacional; 1993. 777p

[37] Yaacob O, Tindall HD. Mangoste encultivation. Rome: Plant eProduction and Protection Paper; 1995. p. 100

[38] Santos Júnior RQ, Soares LC, Maia-Filho ALM, Araujo KS, Santos IMSP, Costa-Junior JS, et al. Estudo histológico da cicatrização de feridas cutâneas utilizando a banha de bacuri (*Platonia insignis Mart.*). ConScientiae Saúde. 2010;**9**:575-581

[39] Rocha ES. Produção de bioprodutos com atividade antimicrobiana a partir do extrato das folhas de *Platonia insignis* Mart. (Bacuri) [Thesis]. Tocantins: Universidade Federal do Tocantins; 2017

[40] Castelo KFA. Estudo químico dos extratos ativos de bacuri (*Platonia insignis*) [dissertation]. Manaus: Universidade Federal do Amazonas; 2018

[41] Simões CMO, Shenkel EP, Mello JCP, Mentz LA, Petrovick PR. Farmacognosia: Da planta ao medicamento. 5th ed. Porto Alegre-Florianópolis: Editora da UFSC; 2004. p. 1102

[42] Dovichi SS, Lajolo FM. Flavonoids and their relationship to diseases of the central nervous system. Nutrire: Revista da Sociedade Brasileira de Alimentação e Nutrição. 2011;**36**:123-135

[43] Wina E, Muetzel S, Becker C. The impact of Saponins or Saponin-containing plant materials on ruminant production - a review. Journal of Agricultural and Food Chemistry. 2005;**53**(21):8092-8105. DOI: 10.1021/jf048053d

[44] Araújo LLN, Fari MJM, Safadi GMVV. Prospecção fitoquímica da espécie *Justicia pectoralis* Jacq. var. stenophylla leonard pertencente à família Acanthaceae. Revista Eletrônica de Ciências Humanas, Saúde e Tecnologia. 2014;**3**(2):4-14

[45] Oloyede KG, Oke MJ, Raji Y, Olugbade T. Antioxidant and anticonvulsant alkaloids in *Crinum ornatum* bulb extract. World Journal of Chemistry. 2012;5:26-31

[46] Silva APSCL, Araújo LC, Melo BC, Silva-Filho JCCL, Oliveira MCP, Oliveira GLS, et al. *Platonia insignis* Mart with pharmacological applications to the central nervous system: A review. Boletim Informativo Geum. 2016;**7**:24-31

[47] Ho GT, Kase ET, Wangensteen H, Barsett H. Effect of phenolic compounds from elderflowers on glucose-and fatty acid uptake in human myotubes and HepG2-cells. Molecules. 2017;**22**:90. DOI: 10.3390/molecules22010090

Chapter 19

The Contribution of Research in Combating Wildlife Poaching in Tanzania: Review of Existing Literature

Jafari R. Kideghesho

Abstract

Conservation challenges such as human population growth, land use changes, human-wildlife conflicts, poaching, encroachment, wildlife diseases and pollution, among others, have grown in recent decades. Their solutions and policy responses require scientific approaches based on informed decisions. This chapter seeks to inform the contribution of research in addressing wildlife poaching in Tanzania, one of the serious management challenges facing the wildlife sector in the country. It reviews a number of publications to establish contribution of numerous scientific studies on wildlife poaching conducted in Tanzania. The review identifies different ways in which research can contribute in combating the problem—including establishing status and trends of poaching, understanding the drivers and effects of poaching, inspiring interventions at different levels and recommending the appropriate policy actions and strategies.

Keywords: wildlife, poaching, research, publications, Tanzania

1. Introduction

In the recent decades, wildlife poaching, driven by the demand for bushmeat and trophies, has been increasingly featured as one of the major global crimes [1–3]. The crime, ranking the third after human trafficking and drugs [4, 5], has some far-reaching repercussions ecologically, economically and politically. The large and charismatic wildlife species have been the main targets of poaching, leading to a dramatic decline of their numbers. For instance, in 1930 the number of elephants in Africa ranged from 5 to 10 million [6]. The number plummeted to 1.3 million in 1979, and in 1989 only 600,000 remained [7, 8]. The number dropped further to about 350,000 in 2016 [9, 10]. The population of black rhino, which was widely distributed in Africa, declined from almost 100,000 in the 1960s to less than 3% in the 1990s [11, 12]. These species are ecologically important as keystone and umbrella species due to their ecological role in ecosystems [13–15]. Extinction of keystone species and, subsequently, ecological cascade effects in ecosystems are one of the ecological repercussions of wildlife poaching [16–19]. The ecological cascade effect involves a series of secondary extinctions triggered by the primary extinction of a keystone species in an ecosystem.

The detrimental impacts of poaching on household and national economies are apparent. This is due to a role played by wildlife species, especially large mammals, as principal resources in tourism. In Africa, availability and diversity of wildlife species are the main factors which influence tourists' willingness and decision to visit a particular destination and pay for available services and products. Large and charismatic species such as elephants, rhinos, buffaloes, lions and leopards offer unique experience and opportunity for hunting and game viewing. Poaching of these species deprives the households, communities and governments substantial benefits generated through tourism. The annual analysis of the global economic impact of Travel and Tourism in 2017 indicated that, in Tanzania, where almost 80% of tourism is wildlife-based, tourism contributed 17% of the GDP and 25% of the foreign currency. It created 1,092,500 jobs in 2017 and was projected to rise by 6.6% in 2018. Revenues reached USD 2.43 billion in 2018, up from USD 2.19 billion in 2017 [20].

In order for conservation, as a land use, to excel and win popular support from people and the government, it must be able to compete effectively with alternative land uses by generating adequate benefits to households, communities and the government [3, 21]. It is unlikely for this to happen when significant numbers of the charismatic species capable of attracting revenues through tourism are exterminated by poachers. Failure to do so waters down the commitment to conservation and rationale to forgo economic activities which are ecologically destructive [3, 21–26]. For instance, in Tanzania, in the face of human population growth, there has been a growing pressure from local communities and politicians urging the government to open protected lands for agriculture and livestock grazing. Land use conflicts between conservation authorities and local communities have also increased. In addressing this long-term concern, on 15 January 2019, H.E. the President of the United Republic of Tanzania directed the conservation authorities to identify the protected areas which were devoid of wildlife and allocate them to landless peasants and pastoralists. Expounding his directive, the President stated bluntly:

> *"I am not happy to see cattle keepers rejected everywhere. If there is a wildlife reserve which is not being utilized, we shall change the law, take part of it and distribute to pastoralists as well as farmers [27]."*

The President's Directive was implemented on 23 September 2019, when the government deregistered 12 game controlled areas and 14 forest reserves covering 707,659 and 46,715 acres, respectively, in order to redistribute to farmers and pastoralists (The Citizen, 24 September 2019).

Wildlife poaching is also linked to global insecurity and erosion of government credibility. The revenues generated from poaching are believed to finance civil wars and terrorist activities in Africa, thus affecting conservation programmes and making some destinations risky places for tourists [28–33]. Poaching lowers credibility and reputation of the governments in international forums. The countries with high gravity of poaching have been implicated with poor governance, corruption and lack of accountability [34, 35].

This review identifies different ways in which research can contribute in combating the problem—including establishing status and trends of poaching, understanding the drivers and effects of poaching, inspiring interventions at different levels and recommending the appropriate policy actions and strategies.

2. Wildlife poaching in Tanzania

Tanzania's wildlife sector is faced with numerous challenges, wildlife poaching ranking at the top, among others. Poaching is pursued to cater for subsistence and commercial needs. Household poverty and a need to meet the dietary requirements are the main drivers for subsistence poaching [35–38]. Commercial poaching is mainly motivated by high market demand and, consequently, high economic returns accruing to criminals [4, 5]. Both subsistence and commercial poaching are linked to a dramatic decline of population and local extinction of wildlife species in different parts of Tanzania [35, 36].

Tanzania had registered two major poaching episodes in her history. The first episode occurred between the 1970s and 1980s following global economic meltdown which weakened the law enforcement capacity [3, 35]. The populations of two keystone species, elephant and rhino, were reduced to less than 30 and 10%, respectively [39, 40]. In 1991, the elephant population was less than 58,000 individuals compared to 203,000 in 1977, while rhino population dropped from 3795 in 1981 to 275 in 1992 [40].

The second major poaching episode emerged between 2009 and 2016. Though its span was shorter, it had colossal impact on wildlife species, particularly elephant. In a period of 3 years, the country's population plummeted to 109,000 in 2009 from 143,000 in 2006 [34, 41]. Further declines were noted in 2013 and 2015, when the numbers recorded were 50,500 [41] and 43,500 [34], respectively. The major drivers of poaching were the increased demand for ivory in Asian countries and widespread corruption in different sectors within and outside the country.

3. The role of research in combating poaching

Basically, scientific studies seek to find answers to numerous questions and guide decision-making process. They provide an opportunity for knowledge and experience sharing on best practices, challenges and strategies to address the problems. Furthermore, they bring changes on understanding and inspire the necessary reforms along with forming the basis for future studies about the subject. Scientific studies on poaching in Tanzania have sought to understand the magnitude, drivers, trends and effects of poaching, behaviors and characteristics of poachers, seasons, poaching hotspots, strategies employed in poaching and genetic makeup of species, among others.

3.1 Understanding the drivers and effects of poaching

Numerous studies in Tanzania have established the magnitude, drivers or factors influencing poaching and the resultant effects. These studies acknowledge the gravity of poaching as a major challenge facing conservation with far-reaching economic, security, ecological and social repercussions [3, 35–37, 42]. The drivers of poaching identified include poverty, inadequate conservation budget, cultural reasons, immorality and corruption, high opportunity cost of conservation and political instability associated with refugee influx from neighboring countries (**Table 1**). The effects established, among others, include financial losses, loss of biodiversity, insecurity and loss of national credibility (**Table 1**; **Figure 1**).

Understanding the drivers of poaching is crucial if practical solutions of the challenge are to be sought. For instance, addressing poverty and provision of alternative livelihood strategies may be an appropriate intervention against food and income poverty among the communities living around the protected areas [10, 35, 36, 42–44]. Similarly, adequate budget allocation to wildlife sector can improve law enforcement and reduce poaching [35, 46], while implementing good governance policies and curbing corruption can equally lower the levels of poaching [35]. Furthermore, knowing the magnitude and effects of poaching rings a

	Drivers of poaching	Source
1.	Household poverty – limited livelihoods options	[10, 35, 36, 42–44]
2.	Poor economic policies	[3, 35]
3.	High economic returns from wildlife products	[3, 21, 35, 45]
4.	Limited budget – inadequate resources for anti-poaching patrols	[35, 46]
5.	Political interference, insufficient support from other institutions and low employees morale	[35]
6.	Cultural reasons	[47]
7.	Corruption and poor governance	[10, 34, 35, 42]
8.	Population growth	[35, 44, 45, 48, 49]
9.	Increased demand for wildlife products within and outside the country	[3, 10, 35]
10.	Failure of wildlife conservation to compete effectively with alternative economic activities	[21, 35]
11.	Political instability/refugees influx	[37, 42, 50]
	Effects of poaching	**Source**
1)	Impact on tourism and economic losses	[3, 35, 51, 52]
2)	Inadequate budget for conservation	[3, 35]
3)	Credibility of the country eroded	[3, 35]
4)	Increased political conflicts; refugees and terrorism	[3, 35]
5)	Loss of habitats; wildlife populations decline and local extinction	[3, 35, 37, 53–57]
6)	Reduced incentive for conservation and a need to adopt land uses which are incompatible with conservation	[3, 35]
7)	Violent behavior against the wildlife rangers and staff	[35]

Table 1.
Drivers/causes of poaching as identified in different studies.

warning bell for conservation authorities to act promptly by adopting appropriate interventions to address the challenge.

3.2 Identifying groups of poachers to be targeted and effective strategies against them

Knowledge on characteristics of poachers (e.g. in terms of age, gender, wealth, residence, ethnicity, poaching strategies and behaviors) helps to identify a specific group of poachers which should be targeted for anti-poaching operations and the most appropriate strategy to deal with such group. For instance, if bushmeat trade is more common among the male-headed households living in proximity to the protected area, efforts to address the challenge should target these households [58]. Studies seeking to uncover strategies employed by poachers to surmount anti-poaching efforts and avoid arrest by rangers can provide an entry point for devising the best ways to counteract poaching strategies and improving planning for anti-poaching programmes [59]. Understanding the drivers and factors affecting poaching can help in changing the behaviors of criminals. For example, if the drivers are associated with poverty or lack of alternative sources of income, provision of alternative economic options can reduce pressures on wildlife. If poaching is linked to particular ethnic or affiliations, mitigation strategies should target these specific

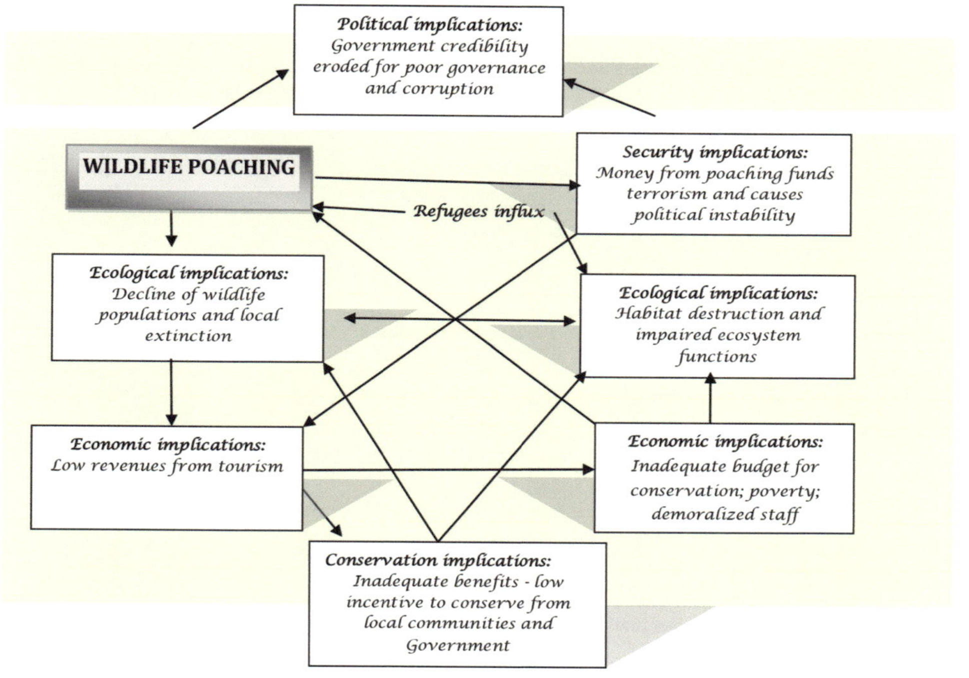

Figure 1.
The schematic presentation of the political, security, ecological and economic implications of wildlife poaching [3, 35].

groups. For instance, in Western Serengeti, where bushmeat poaching is endemic, it is estimated that approximately 40% of the crime is committed by people of Ikoma tribe [44, 60]. By using this fact, the conservation authorities can take advantage of traditional practices and systems of this particular tribe to address the challenge of poaching [61, 62].

3.3 Establishing the priority geographical sites for intervention

Studies seeking to understand the areas of high risks of poaching (poaching hotspots) and seasons are useful in informing the sites where the conservation managers should focus for intervention in terms of allocating human and financial resources to achieve maximum anti-poaching results. Examples of studies of this nature were conducted in Selous [46, 63] and Western Serengeti [44]. Wasser et al. [64, 65] used DNA to track the origin of large seizures of elephant ivory since the 1989 trade ban. The results revealed that most of the ivory originated from a relatively small area in the Selous and Niassa protected areas along the Tanzania and Mozambique border. This evidence was important for the planning of law enforcement operations to curtail further elephant losses and disrupt the organized transnational crime [64].

3.4 Recommending policy actions and strategies

The objective of wildlife research is to provide solutions for problems and challenges facing the sector. Research findings are the bases for informing policy actions and recommending appropriate strategies to address the existing and potential conservation challenges. A number of research articles reviewed in this chapter have recommended some policy actions for combating poaching (**Table 2**).

	Policy action/strategy	Source
1.	Strengthen law enforcement and patrols (increase number of rangers and equipment, increase penalties) and intelligence-led operations within and outside the protected areas.	[42, 57, 66–68]
2.	Increased budget for conservation	[35]
3.	Appropriate and timely compensation for wildlife staff	[35]
4.	Community involvement, incentive schemes	[22, 42, 67, 69]
5.	Application of technologies (forensic, poaching detection technologies, SMART etc.)	[49, 70, 71]
6.	Enhanced sustainable livelihood opportunities and delivery of alternative sources to reduce dependency on vulnerable habitats and wildlife (Distractions)	[44, 49, 68, 72–74]
7.	Employment opportunities to local communities	[67]
8.	Promote political stability within and outside the country	[35, 37, 50]
9.	Intensify war against corruption	[35]
10.	Address the challenge of political interests overriding professionalism	[35]
11.	Reduce demand for wildlife products	[35, 75]
12.	Improve conservation education programmes	[44, 49, 67]
13.	Address the problem of household poverty and unemployment	[21, 22, 35, 72, 73]
12.	Encourage presence of researchers in areas with minimal protective status and low government surveillance	[76]
11.	Addressing root causes of poaching through strategies that go beyond coercive measures	[77]

Table 2.
Policy actions and strategies recommended for addressing poaching problem from various research articles.

Besides coming up with recommendations, wildlife research can also play an important role in evaluating the efficiency and effectiveness of the existing conservation policies and strategies [78–82]. Research may also inform the best ways of implementing the specific policy actions for combating poaching.

3.5 Building justification for local and international intervention

In order to combat poaching effectively, it is imperative that the problem is critically analyzed to establish its magnitude, trends and effects. This calls for adequate data and information, which are obtained through a planned and executed research targeting a number of indicators for poaching (number of poachers arrested, type and number of weapons confiscated, species and number of animals killed, number of carcasses, number of staff injured or killed and poaching hotspots).

The research findings about the magnitude, status, trends and impacts of wildlife poaching in the country have been crucial in shaping the policy decisions towards the appropriate course of action. They have inspired considerable support and interventions in combating the challenge from the general public, conservationists, media, influential personalities and international community. The interventions prompted by these findings are discussed briefly hereunder.

3.5.1 Local intervention

Tanzania has made several interventions in stepping up efforts to address a challenge of poaching. One of such interventions is collaboration with other countries through ratification and implementation of a number of regional and international conventions, protocols and agreements. Examples of these protocols include the Convention on International Trade in Endangered Species of Wild Fauna and Flora (CITES) of 1979, Protocol Concerning Protected Areas and Wild Fauna and Flora in the Eastern African Region (1985), Lusaka Agreement on Co-operative Enforcement Operations Directed at Illegal Trade in Wild Fauna and Flora (1994); and SADC Protocol on Wildlife Conservation and Law Enforcement (1999). Besides, on different occasions, Tanzania was compelled to launch nationwide anti-poaching operations to reverse the poaching trends and safeguard the populations of its wildlife species (**Table 3**).

Other interventions adopted recently have included formulation of National Elephant Action Plan, a National Ivory Action Plan and National Strategy for Combating Poaching and Illegal Wildlife Trade [83]. The Conservation and Management Plans have also been developed to guide the conservation of species which are facing a high risk of poaching and other threats. Examples of species with such Plans are elephant and rhino [84, 85] (**Figure 2**).

Following poaching crisis and subsequently launching of *Operation Uhai* in 1990, Tanzania adopted community-based conservation as a new conservation approach to complement the centralized (also known as 'fences and fines') approach. This resulted from a perceived failure of the latter to conserve wildlife [82]. It was also clear that, though it was proven to be effective, 'Operation Uhai' was an expensive undertaking which could hardly be sustained as a long-term strategy. Community-based conservation was premised on the assumption that long-term conservation success depends on the involvement of local communities

	Operation	Period	Results
1)	*Operation Uhai ('Operation life'):* The six-month *Operation Uhai* to curb poaching and to rupt ivory trade.	1989–90	Over 2,000 people were arrested and 10,000 firearms were confiscated.
2)	*Operation "SpiderNet":* Coordinated efforts of law enforcement and intelligence agencies, including National and Transnational Serious Crimes Investigation Unit (NTSCIU) and Tanzania National Parks Authority (TANAPA), to combat ivory poaching and arms smuggling in Katavi.	2014–15	Hundreds of firearms were confiscated; dozens of arrests were made with special emphasis on villages within the Katumba Refugee Camp which was implicated with giving shelter to Hutu rebels with ties to the Rwandan genocide
3)	*Operation Kipepeo (Butterfly):* in Selous Ecosystem to curb elephant poaching	2009	Some criminals were arrested and firearms confiscated
4)	*Operation "Tokomeza Ujangili" (Eradicate Poaching):* The goal of operation was to curb poaching in protected areas, identify and arrest suspected poachers and organized groups, and seize property of poaching suspects.	2013	952 suspects were arrested and 104 pieces of ivory were seized. However, the operation was canceled after alleged human rights abuses conducted by Tanzanian authorities, which included rape, torture, murder, and illegal seizures of property (including livestock).
5)	*Tanzania's National and Transnational Serious Crimes Investigation Unit (NTSCIU):* Operations Against Major Wildlife Traffickers	2016–18	Major criminal syndicates, high-profile poachers and wildlife traffickers were arrested
6)	*Operation Costa:* (in collaboration with other East African nations of Burundi, Ethiopia, Kenya, Rwanda, Tanzania, and Uganda) to stem illegal wildlife trade with a focus on ivory.	2009	Over 100 people were arrested and roughly 1,500 kg of elephant ivory were seized along with hundreds of other wildlife products

Table 3.
Some of the major operations conducted in Tanzania to curb wildlife poaching.

Figure 2.
Tanzania elephant and rhino management plans.

in management and guaranteeing them tangible benefits [22, 25, 79, 80, 82]. Essentially, the idea behind the approach is to motivate local communities to align their behaviors with conservation goals by refraining from activities which are illegal and destructive to wildlife including poaching.

However, Community Based Conservation approach has not been a panacea to a poaching challenge. Multiple strategies are being pursued along with further transformation of the natural resources sector. The complexity of wildlife crime has increased following technological advancement and access and use of more sophisticated firearms among the poachers [3, 35]. The government has, thus, adopted a paramilitary model in managing its natural resources in view of increasing efficiency and effectiveness in combating the challenge.

3.5.2 International interventions

Intervention in combating poaching by the international community has often involved financial and technical support along with imposing sanctions to pressurize the individual countries to comply with international commitments in fighting wildlife crime. The following are examples of interventions from the international community:

a. In March 2013, the CITES Standing Committee singled out Tanzania along with the seven other countries—Kenya, Uganda, Malaysia, Vietnam, the Philippines, China and Thailand as the 'Gang of eight' due to worst record in illegal ivory trade [3, 86]. This followed a widespread elephant poaching that occurred in the 2010s. The Committee directed each of the offending countries to submit a detailed National Elephant Action Plan to curb the illegal ivory trade or face a ban on all legitimate wildlife trade.

b. In 2014 the World Heritage Committee inscribed the Selous Game Reserve on the List of World Heritage in Danger [87]. The Committee called on the international community, including ivory transit and destination countries, to support Tanzania in the fight against this criminal activity. Tanzania was further required to submit an Emergency Response Action Plan for Selous Game Reserve to the Committee.

c. During the 2014 London Conference on illegal wildlife trade, the London Declaration was adopted in which 46 countries including Tanzania and 11 international organizations resolved to adopt a number of measures to reverse the trend of wildlife crime. These measures included ending the market for illegal wildlife products, putting in place effective legal frameworks and deterrents, strengthening enforcement and guaranteeing sustainable livelihood options, nurturing poverty reduction strategies and building on and strengthening the wider global efforts to combat the crime [88]. The declaration took on board the scientific facts on the magnitude of the crime and the potential effects which it could bring to national security and sustainable development.

d. In 2016, UNDP launched a large-scale project which sought to support the Government of Tanzania in implementing the National Strategy to Combat Poaching and Illegal Wildlife Trade by strengthening legislation and capacity to tackle poaching and wildlife trafficking at the national level [89]. The Project also seeks to enhance the collaboration to fight illegal wildlife trade between Tanzania and neighboring countries, which is in alignment with the objectives of the overall Global Wildlife Programme, launched in 2015 by the Global Environment Facility (GEF).

3.5.3 Influential personalities

Research findings, particularly on population numbers and trends, have also played a significant part in inspiring actions from important personalities. For example, in July 2013, the US President, Barack Obama, issued an Executive Order 13648 outlining measures to combat wildlife trafficking. The Order pledged financial and technical support to governments to address the challenge [90]. The royal family in the UK has also been in the forefront in supporting efforts to address poaching and illegal wildlife trade through funding and conducting numerous campaigns. For example, in February 2014, Prince William, the Duke of Cambridge, and his father, Prince Charles, the Duke of Wales, released a video clip urging global efforts to end poaching and illegal wildlife trade:

> *"We have come together, as father and son, to lend our voices to the growing global effort to combat the illegal wildlife trade - A trade that has reached such unprecedented levels of killing and related violence that it now poses a grave threat not only to the survival of some of the world's most treasured species, but also to economic and political stability in many areas around the world. [91]"*

Many other personalities expressed concerns over wildlife crime and urged actions from different stakeholders. These included UN Secretary General, Ban Ki Moon, Heads of States and other people.

4. Conclusions

Wildlife poaching remains one of the top threats to wildlife and humankind despite efforts devoted to conservation work. Poaching has serious ecological, political, social, security and economic ramifications. It is responsible for a dramatic decline of wildlife populations and species extinction, habitat loss, household poverty and economic loss to government. Furthermore, poaching erodes credibility of governments when high poaching levels is attributed to poor governance, corruption and lack of accountability. In recent years, the crime has emerged as one of the main security issues due to its role in funding civil wars and terrorist activities.

Research has the potential to contribute effectively to wildlife conservation through combating poaching. It provides a better understanding of the relationships between the drivers of poaching and individual poacher motivation and, therefore, provides an entry point towards developing the effective policy actions and strategies. The studies which establish the magnitude, trends and effects are important in inspiring interventions at different levels, while understanding the poaching hotspots and vulnerable species targeted by poachers can help in allocating time and resources for anti-poaching operations. Knowledge on types, behaviors and characteristics of poachers is important in devising the policy responses which can suit each type.

Despite the relevance and potential of different scientific studies in guiding decision-making and providing practical solutions against poaching, the evidence on how much do wildlife managers and authorities make use of the findings generated in addressing the challenge is scant. Further studies are, therefore, imperative to address this knowledge gap. This will ensure that time and financial resources used in research are not wasted and that the findings are used effectively to solve conservation problems rather than being left to gather dust in the shelves.

Author details

Jafari R. Kideghesho
College of African Wildlife Management, Mweka (CAWM), Moshi, Tanzania

*Address all correspondence to: kideghesho@yahoo.com; jkideghesho@mwekawildlife.ac.tz

References

[1] TRAFFIC. Illegal Hunting and Trade of Wildlife in Savanna Africa May Cause Conservation Crisis. ScienceDaily; 2012

[2] Ripple WJ, Newsome TM, Wolf C, Dirzo R, et al. Collapse of the world's largest herbivores. Science Advances. 2015;**1**(4):e1400103

[3] Kideghesho JR. Elephant poaching crisis in Tanzania: A need to reverse the trend and the way forward. Tropical Conservation Science. 2016;**9**(1):369-388

[4] Convention on International Trade for Endangered Species of Flora and Fauna (CITES). Wildlife crime ranks among trafficking in drugs, arms and humans. 2013. Available from: http://cites.org/eng/news/sg/2013/20130926_wildlife_crime.php [Accessed: July 15, 2015]

[5] United Nations Office on Drugs and Crime (UNODC). Wildlife crime worth USD 8-10 billion annually, ranking it alongside human trafficking, arms and drug dealing in terms of profits. UNODC chief. 2015. Available from: https://www.unodc.org/unodc/en/frontpage/2014/May/wildlife-crime-worth-8-10-billion-annually.html [Accessed: July 10, 2015]

[6] Worldwide Fund for Nature (WWF). African Elephants. 2019. Available from: http://wwf.panda.org/knowledge_hub/endangered_species/elephants/african_elephants/ [Accessed: September 20, 2019]

[7] Barbier E, Burgess J, Swanson T, Pearce D. Elephants, Economics and Ivory. London: Earthscan Publications; 1990

[8] Bulte EH, van Kooten GC. Economics of antipoaching enforcement and the ivory trade ban. American Journal of Agricultural Economics. 1999;**81**(2):453-466

[9] Steyn P. African Elephant Numbers Plummet 30 Percent, Landmark Survey Finds. National Geographic. 2016. Available from: https://www.nationalgeographic.com/news/2016/08/wildlife-african-elephants-population-decrease-great-elephant-census/

[10] Hauenstein S, Kshatriya M, Blanc J, Dormann CF, Beale CM. African elephant poaching rates correlate with local poverty, national corruption and global ivory price. Nature Communications. 2019;**10**:2242

[11] Dublin H, Wilson A. The Fight for Survival: Four Decades of Conserving Africa's Rhinos. Conservation Advisory Services, Le Muids, Switzerland: Desktop Publishing; 1998

[12] Leader-Williams N. Regulation and protection: Successes and failures in rhinoceros conservation. In: Oldfield S, editor. The Trade in Wildlife: Regulation for Conservation. London: Earthscan; 2003

[13] Roberge JM, Angelstam P. Usefulness of the umbrella species concept as a conservation tool. Conservation Biology. 2004;**18**:76-85

[14] Mouquet N, Gravel D, Massol F, Calcagno V. Extending the concept of keystone species to communities and ecosystems. Ecology Letters. 2013;**16**:1-8

[15] Cromsigt JPGM, te Beest M. Restoration of a megaherbivore: Landscape level impacts of white rhinoceros in Kruger National Park, South Africa. Journal of Ecology. 2014;**102**(3):566-575

[16] Ripple WJ, Abernethy K, Betts MG, Chapron G et al. 2016j. Bushmeat hunting and extinction risk to the world's mammals. Royal Society Open Science. 2016;3(10): 160498

[17] Poulsen JR, Rosen C, Meier A, Mills E, Nuñez CL, Koerner SE, et al. Ecological consequences of forest elephant declines for afrotropical forests. Conservation Biology. 2018;**32**:559-567

[18] Diplock N, Johnston K, Mellon A, Mitchell L, Moore M, Schneider D, et al. Large mammal declines and the incipient loss of mammal-bird mutualisms in an African savanna ecosystem. PLoS One. 2018, 2018;**13**(8):e0202536. DOI: 10.1371/journal.pone.0202536

[19] Daskin JH, Pringle RM. Warfare and wildlife declines in Africa's protected areas. Nature. 2018;**553**(7688):328-332

[20] Tanzania Invest.com. Available from: https://www.tanzaniainvest.com/tourism/tanzania-tourism-revenues-and-arrivals-up-in-2018 and follow us on www.twitter.com/tanzaniainvest [Accessed: September 24, 2019]

[21] Knapp EJ. Why poaching pays? A summary of risks and benefits illegal hunters face in Western Serengeti, Tanzania. Tropical Conservation Science. 2012;**5**(4):434-445

[22] Emerton L, Mfunda I. Making wildlife economically viable for communities living around the Western Serengeti, Tanzania. In: Evaluating Eden Series Discussion Paper, No. 1. London: International Institute for Environment and Development; 1999

[23] Holmern T, Røskaft E, Mbaruka J, Mkama SY, Muya J. Uneconomical game cropping in a community-based conservation project outside the Serengeti National Park, Tanzania. Oryx. 2002;**36**(4):364-372

[24] Kideghesho JR, Røskaft E, Kaltenborn BP. Factors influencing conservation attitudes of local people in Western Serengeti corridor, Tanzania. Biodiversity and Conservation. 2007;**16**(7):2213-2230

[25] Kideghesho JR, Tarimo L. Recent research on CWM in Tanzania—Successes, benefits, and challenges. A Paper Presented at the Tanzania Natural Resources Forum Roundtable Meeting on Wildlife for Communities in Tanzania: Taking Stock of Governance of Wildlife by Communities; 2-3 November 2011; Giraffe Hotel, Dar es Salaam; 2011

[26] Wambura G. Prospects of the Authorized Associations Consortium (AAC). A Paper Presented at the Tanzania Natural Resources Forum Roundtable Meeting on Wildlife for Communities in Tanzania: Taking Stock of Governance of Wildlife by Communities; 2-3 November 2011; Giraffe Hotel, Dar es Salaam; 2011. Available from: https://www.ucl.ac.uk › pima › docs › reference › 16_cwm_roundtable [Accessed: August 12, 2019]

[27] The Guardian. Magufuli: Give people idle wildlife reserves, forests. The Guardian 16; 2019

[28] Kalron N. Africa's White Gold of Jihad: Al-Shabaab and Conflict Ivory. Elephant League. 2012. Available from: http://elephantleague.org/project/africas-white-gold-of-jihad-al-shabaab-and-conflict-ivory/ [Accessed: July 09, 2015]

[29] Marais A, Fennessy S, Fennessy J. Giraffe conservation status—Country profile: Democratic Republic of Congo. Giraffa. 2012, 2012;**6**(2):13-16

[30] Tumanjong E. Foreign Poachers Target Cameroon Elephants: Expert. The World Post. 2012. Available from: http://www. huffingtonpost.com/huff-wires/20121204/af-cameroon-elephant-poaching/ [Accessed: July 12, 2015]

[31] Somaville K. Ivory, Insurgency and Crime in Central Africa: The Sudans Connection. 2014. Available from: http://africajournalismtheworld.com/tag/janjaweed-ivory/ [Accessed: July 10, 2018]

[32] Nellemann C, Henriksen R, Raxter P, Ash N, Mrema E, editors. The Environmental Crime Crisis—Threats to Sustainable Development from Illegal Exploitation and Trade in Wildlife and Forest Resources. A UNEP Rapid Response Assessment. United Nations Environment Programme and GRID-Arendal, Nairobiand Arendal. 2014. Available from: http://www.unep.org/unea/docs/RRAcrimecrisis.pdf

[33] Vira V, Ewing T. Ivory's Curse-the Militarization and Professionalization of Poaching in Africa. Washington D. C: Born Free USA; 2014

[34] Environmental Investigation Agency (EIA). Vanishing point: criminality, corruption and the devastation of Tanzania's elephants. Environmental Investigation Agency, Washington DC. 2014. Available from: http://eiainternational.org/wp-content/uploads/EIA-Vanishing-Point-lo-res1.pdf [Accessed: July 10, 2018]

[35] Kideghesho JR. Reversing the trend of wildlife crime in Tanzania: Challenges and opportunities. Biodiversity and Conservation. 2016;**25**:427-449

[36] Loibooki M, Hofer H, Campbell KLI, East M. Bushmeat hunting by communities adjacent to Serengeti National Park: The importance of livestock ownership and alternative sources of protein and income. Environmental Conservation. 2002;**29**:391-398

[37] Jambiya G, Milledge S, Mtango N. Night Time Spinach: Conservation and Livelihood Implications of Wild Meat Use in Refugee Situations in North-Western Tanzania. TRAFFIC East/Southern Africa. 2007

[38] Martin A, Caro T, Borgerhoff MM. Bushmeat consumption in western Tanzania: A comparative analysis from the same ecosystem. Tropical Conservation Science. 2012;**5**(3):352-364

[39] IUCN. Updated African Elephant Database Reveals Declining Elephant Populations. Available from: www.elephantdatabase.org [Accessed: July 12, 2019]

[40] Sas-Rolf. M't. Does CITES Work? Four Case Studies. IEA Environment Briefing No. The Institute of Economic Affairs, London; 2000

[41] Convention on International Trade for Endangered Species of Flora and Fauna (CITES). CITES Cop15, Doc. 68 annexe 6a; 2010

[42] Lotter W, Clark K. Community involvement and joint operations aid effective anti-poaching in Tanzania. Parks. 2014;**20**(1):19-28

[43] Hariohay KM, Fyumagwa RD, Kideghesho JR, Røskaft E. Awareness and attitudes of local people toward wildlife conservation in the Rungwa game Reserve in Central Tanzania. Human Dimensions of Wildlife. 2018;**23**(6):503-514

[44] Samwel DN. Local people knowledge on bushmeat hunting in the Serengeti ecosystem: A case study of Topi (*Damaliscus lunatus*) [MSc dissertation]. Trondheim: Norwegian University of Science and Technology; 2017

[45] Campbell KLI, Hofer H. People and wildlife: spatial dynamics and zones of interaction. In: ARE S, Arcese P, editors. Serengeti II: Dynamics, Management and Conservation of an Ecosystem. Chicago: Chicago University Press; 1995. pp. 534-570

[46] Kyando MT, Ikanda D, Roskaft E. Hotspot elephant-poaching areas in the eastern Selous game reserve, Tanzania. African Journal of Ecology. 2017;**55**(3):365-371

[47] Kaltenborn BP, Nyahongo JW, Kideghesho JR. The role of hunting in the Serengeti. In: Proceedings of the 2nd Annual Scientific Conference of the Tanzania Wildlife Research Institute (TAWIRI); 1-3 December 2002; Arusha, Tanzania; 2003. pp. 32-40

[48] Metzger KL, Sinclair ARE, Hilborn R, Grant J, Hopcraft C, Mduma SAR. Evaluating the protection of wildlife in parks: The case of African buffalo in Serengeti. Biodiversity and Conservation. 2010;**19**:3431-3444

[49] Bitanyi S, Nesje M, Kusiluka LJM, Chenyambuga SW, Kaltenborn BP. Awareness and perceptions of local people about wildlife hunting in western Serengeti communities. Tropical Conservation Science. 2012;**5**(2):208-222

[50] Kideghesho JR, Msuya TS. Managing the wildlife protected areas in the face of global economic recession, HIV/AIDS pandemic, political instability and climate change: Experience of Tanzania. In: Sladonja B, editor. Protected Areas Management. London: IntechOpen Science/Open minds; 2012. pp. 65-91. ISBN: 980-953-307-448-6

[51] Naidoo R, Fisher B, Manica A, Balmford A. Estimating economic losses to tourism in Africa from the illegal killing of elephants. Nature Communications. 2016;**27**:13379

[52] World Tourism Organization (UNWTO). Towards Measuring the Economic Value of Wildlife Watching Tourism in Africa - Briefing Paper UNWTO. 2014

[53] Rusch GS, Stokke S, Røskaft E, Mwakalebe G, Wiik W, Arnemo JM, et al. Human-wildlife interactions in western Serengeti, Tanzania. Effects of land management on migratory routes and mammal population densities. Norwegian Institute for Nature Research Report; 2005

[54] Setsaas TH, Holmern T, Mwakalebe G, Stokke S, Røskaft E. How does human exploitation affect impala populations in protected and partially protected areas?—A case study from the Serengeti ecosystem, Tanzania. Biological Conservation. 2007;**136**:563-570

[55] Marealle WN, Fossøy F, Holmern T, Stokke BG, Røskaft E. Does illegal hunting skew Serengeti wildlife sex ratios? Wildlife Biology. 2010;**16**:419-429

[56] Strauss MKL, Kilewo M, Rentsch D, Packer C. Food supply and poaching limit giraffe abundance in the Serengeti. Population Ecology. 2015;**57**:505-516

[57] Walelign SZ, Nielsen MR, Jacobsen JB. Price elasticity of bushmeat demand in the greater serengeti ecosystem: Insights for managing the bushmeat trade. Frontiers in Ecology and Evolution. 2019. DOI: 10.3389/fevo.2019.00162

[58] Manyama FF, Nielsen MR, Roskaft E, Nyahongo JW. The importance of bushmeat in household income as a function of distance from protected areas in the Western Serengeti Ecosystem, Tanzania. 2019. DOI: 10.5539/enrr.v9n3p49

[59] Rija AA, Kideghesho JR. Poacher's strategies to surmount anti-poaching efforts in Serengeti, Tanzania. In: Martin EH, Hadfield LA, Melubo K, Jensen RR, Durrant J0, Hardin PJ, et al. editors. Protected Areas in Northern Tanzania. In Press

[60] Mfunda IM, Røskaft E. Bushmeat hunting in Serengeti, Tanzania: An important economic activity to local people. International Journal of Biodiversity and Conservation. 2010;**2**:263-272

[61] Kideghesho JR. Co-existence between the traditional societies

and wildlife in western Serengeti, Tanzania: Its relevancy in the contemporary wildlife conservation efforts. Conservation and Biodiversity. 2008;**17**(8):861-1881

[62] Kideghesho JR. The potentials of traditional African cultural practices in mitigating overexploitation of wildlife species and habitat loss: Experience of Tanzania. International Journal of Biodiversity Science and Management. 2009;**5**(2):83-94

[63] Zafra-Calvo N, Lobo JM, Prada C, Nielsen MR, Burgess ND. Predictors of elephant poaching in a wildlife crime hotspot: The Ruvuma landscape of southern Tanzania and northern Mozambique. Journal for Nature Conservation. 2018;**41**:79-87

[64] Wasser SK, Clark WJ, Drori O, Kisamo ES, Mailand C, Mutayoba B. Combating the illegal trade in African elephant ivory with DNA forensics. Conservation Biology. 2008;**22**(4):1071

[65] Wasser SK, Brown L, Mailand C, Mondol S, Clark W, Laurie C. Genetic assignment of large seizures of elephant ivory reveals Africa's major poaching hotspots. Science. 2015;**349**(6243). DOI: 10.1126/science.aaa2457

[66] Duffy R, St Freya J. Poverty, poaching and trafficking: What are the links? Evidence on demand. Climate, Environment, Infrastructure and Livelihoods. London; 2013

[67] Hariohay KM, Fyumagwa RD, Kideghesho JR, Ranke PS, Røskaft E. Drivers of conservation crimes in the Rungwa-Kizigo-Muhesi game reserves, Central Tanzania. Global Ecology and Conservation. 2019. DOI: 10.1016/j.gecco.2019.e00522

[68] Nielsen MR, Jacobsen JB, Thorsen BJ. Factors determining the choice of hunting and trading bushmeat in the Kilombero Valley, Tanzania: Choice of hunting and trading bushmeat. Conservation Biology. 2014;**28**:382-391

[69] Archabald K, Naughton-Treves L. Tourism revenue sharing around National Parks in Western Uganda: Early efforts to identify and reward local communities. Environmental Conservation. 2001;**28**:135-149

[70] Mgimba M. Prevention of wildlife trafficking and poaching in Tanzania by using forensic science technological approach. Journal of Forensic Science and Criminal Investigation. 2017;**2**(1):JFSCI.MS.ID.555577

[71] Banzi JF. A sensor based anti-poaching system in Tanzania national parks. International Journal of Scientific and Research Publications. 2014;**4**(4):1-7

[72] Knapp EJ, Peace N, Bechtel L. Poachers and poverty: Assessing objective and subjective measures of poverty among illegal hunters outside Ruaha National Park, Tanzania. Conservation and Society. 2017;**15**:24-32

[73] Wilfred P, MacColl AD. Income sources and their relation to wildlife poaching in Ugalla ecosystem, Western Tanzania. African Journal of Environmental Science and Technology. 2010;**4**(12):886-896

[74] Rentsch D, Damon A. Prices, poaching, and protein alternatives: An analysis of bushmeat consumption around Serengeti National Park, Tanzania. Ecological Economics. 2013;**91**:1-9

[75] Holden MH. Increase anti-poaching law-enforcement or reduce demand for wildlife products? A framework to guide strategic conservation investments. Conservation Letters. 2018;**2018**:e12618

[76] Piel AK, Lenoel A, Johnson C, Stewart FA. Deterring poaching in western Tanzania: The presence of wildlife researchers. Global Ecology and Conservation. 2015;**3**:188-199

[77] Mabele MB. Beyond forceful measures: Tanzania's 'war on poaching' needs diversified strategies more than militarised tactics. Review of African Political Economy. 2017;**44**(153):487-498

[78] Adams WA, Hulme D. If community conservation is the answer in Africa, what is the question? Oryx. 2001;**35**(3):193-200

[79] Kicheleri RP, Treue T, Kajembe GC, Mombo FM, Nielsen MR. Power struggles in the management of wildlife resources: The case of Burunge wildlife management area, Tanzania. In: Kideghesho JR, Rija AA, editors. Wildlife Management: Failures, Successes and Prospects. London: IntechOpen; 2019. pp. 81-102

[80] Mariki SB. Successes, threats, and factors influencing the performance of a community-based wildlife management approach: The case of Wami Mbiki WMA, Tanzania. In: Kideghesho JR, Rija AA, editors. Wildlife Management: Failures, Successes and Prospects. London: IntechOpen; 2019. pp. 103-123

[81] Nelson F, Agrawal A. Patronage or participation? Community-based natural resource management reform in sub-Saharan Africa. Development and Change. 2008;**39**(4):557-585

[82] Songorwa AN. Community-based wildlife management (CWM) in Tanzania: Are the communities interested? World Development. 1999;**27**(12):2061-2079

[83] United Republic of Tanzania. National Strategy for Combating Poaching and Illegal Wildlife Trade. Dodoma, Tanzania; 2014

[84] Tanzania Wildlife Research Institute. Tanzania Elephant Management Plan 2010-2015. Arusha, Tanzania; 2010

[85] United Republic of Tanzania. Conservation and Management Plan for Black Rhino in Tanzania 2019-2023. Dodoma, Tanzania; 2019

[86] Otieno J. CITES Threatens Sanctions on 'Gang of Eight' Over Poaching, Illegal Ivory Trade. Available from: http://www.theeastafrican.co.ke/news/East-Africa-joins-the-infamous-Gang-of-Eight-over-poaching/ [Accessed: August 09, 2015]

[87] IUCN. Illegal Trade Puts More World Heritage Sites in Danger. 2014. Available from: https://www.iucn.org/content/illegal-trade-puts-more-world-heritage-sites-danger

[88] UK Department for Environment, Food and Rural Affairs. 2015. London Conference on the Illegal Wildlife Trade 12-13 February 2014 Declaration. Department for Environment, Food and Rural Affairs, Department for International Development, Foreign and Commonwealth Office and Home Office. 2014. Available from: https://www.gov.uk/government/uploads/system/uploads/attachment_data/file/281289/london-wildlife-conference-declaration-140213.pdf [Accessed: July 12, 2015]

[89] UNDP. 2018. Combating Poaching and Wildlife Trade. Available from: http://www.tz.undp.org/content/tanzania/en/home/projects/combating-poaching.html

[90] Leader J. Obama's Executive Order To Combat Wildlife Trafficking Lauded By Conservation Groups. 2013.

Available from: https://www.huffpost.com/entry/obama-executive-order-wildlife-trafficking_n_3536536 [Accessed: August 16, 2019]

[91] https://www.eonline.com/news/508752/prince-william-and-prince-charles-make-plea-to-stop-illegal-wildlife-trade-watch-now). 2014 [Accessed: July 12, 2015]